Sunset

Recipe Annual

1998 EDITION

Lemony, silken-textured Meyer Custard-Cream Pie (page 58)

By the Editors of Sunset Magazine
and Sunset Books

Sunset Books Inc. ■ **Menlo Park, California**

SUNSET BOOKS

Director, Sales & Marketing
Richard A. Smeby

Editorial Director
Bob Doyle

Production Director
Lory Day

Art Director
Vasken Guiragossian

STAFF FOR THIS BOOK
Managing Editor
Cornelia Fogle

Indexer
Rebecca La Brum

Production Coordinator
Patricia A. Williams

SUNSET PUBLISHING CORPORATION

President/Chief Executive Officer
Stephen J. Seabolt

VP, Chief Financial Officer
James E. Mitchell

VP, Publisher
Anthony P. Glaves

VP, Consumer Marketing Director
Robert I. Gursha

VP, Manufacturing Director
Lorinda Reichert

VP, Editor-in-Chief, Sunset Magazine
Rosalie Muller Wright

Managing Editor
Carol Hoffman

Senior Editor, Food & Entertaining
Jerry Anne Di Vecchio

Designer, Food & Entertaining
Dennis W. Leong

Southwest Eggs Benedict (page 277)

A Taste of the West

Welcome to the 1998 edition of the *Sunset Recipe Annual*, our 11th collection of all the past year's food articles and recipes from *Sunset Magazine*.

Throughout the year, we salute the bounty of the West. Among this year's articles, you'll discover the Northwest's summer food treasures, Hawaiian-style bouillabaisse, a ranch Thanksgiving, and Southwestern holiday specialties from New Mexico. Join us in savoring the delights of the West's best apples, fresh oysters, juicy apricots, and perfectly ripe tomatoes.

You'll find ideas for entertaining and plenty of low-fat recipes, including a collection of Southwestern dishes in January and three international menus in July. Several new monthly columns join our favorites. And, of course, you'll find nutritional information listed for each recipe.

Here's to another year of great cooking and eating!

Cover:
Fish with Mango Salsa (page 144). Cover design: Vasken Guiragossian. Photographer: Geoffrey Nilsen.

Back cover photographers:
(Top to bottom) Richard Jung, Paul Franz-Moore, E. J. Armstrong.

First printing November 1997
Copyright © 1997 Sunset Books Inc., Menlo Park, CA 94025. First edition. All rights reserved, including the right of reproduction in whole or in part in any form.

ISBN 0-376-02015-6 (hardcover)
ISBN 0-376-02016-4 (softcover)
ISSN 0896-2170
Printed in the United States

♻ printed on recycled paper

Material in this book originally appeared in the 1997 issues of *Sunset Magazine*. All of the recipes were developed and tested in the Sunset test kitchens. If you have comments or suggestions, please let us hear from you. Write us at Sunset Books, Cookbook Editorial, 80 Willow Road, Menlo Park, CA 94025.

Contents

A Letter from Sunset

DEAR READER,

What a productive year this has been!

On the personal side, our busy food writers' families have grown by three sons and one grandson. We couldn't be more delighted.

On the professional side, plans for a new test kitchen are set to go. This is your last view of the one that has served us so well for almost three decades, providing a proving ground for hundreds of *Sunset* recipes. Despite the changes in floor plan, we'll be keeping many of the old kitchen's key features: multiple work stations in a single spacious room; home-style (not restaurant) equipment, to ensure that our recipes work for you at home; gas and electric ovens of various makes; range tops that vary from standard types to a big, handsome professional-style model designed for home use. We'll have microwave ovens of varying wattages, and small appliances and cooking utensils of many brands, made from a variety of materials.

So what's new? Among other things—hookups for our computers, facilities for in-kitchen film projects, and, of course, the very latest in equipment.

As we wait for the rebuilding to begin, we've put together a *Recipe Annual* that, like its predecessors, brings you every food story and recipe from the past year's *Sunset Magazine*. As you leaf through the book, you'll notice an evolution in design: our new editor, Rosalie Muller Wright, has made it a priority to create a magazine that is more inviting to read, with recipes that are easier to use.

There are other changes, too. Our roster of regular features is growing. Each month begins with *Food Guide*, my exploration of Western food trends—including great recipes, favorite tools and ingredients, and notes on all sorts of things, from cookbooks to clever cooking methods. New this year is a full-page monthly *Wine Guide*, a

NITA WINTER

Growing families keep Sunset's food team in touch with the challenge of preparing both everyday and party meals. At left: Betsy Reynolds Bateson with Matthew (1½) and, in front, Amanda (almost 5). In the back row: Andrew Baker and Linda Lau Anusasananan with daughter Lisa, 17 (Chalida, 19, was on a camping trip at photo time). In the baby row: Jerry Di Vecchio with grandson Henry Barton Gripenstraw (5 months); Elaine Johnson with twin sons Jasper and Rowan (7 months); Christine Weber Hale with son Christopher (7 months). Elijio Hernandez (in the shadow) holds daughter Victoria (3); Barbara E. Goldman is with granddaughter Zoë Pollak (5½).

provocative and spirited commentary by respected wine journalist Karen MacNeil. *Kitchen Cabinet* continues its 68-year run of reader-contributed favorites. Linda Lau Anusasananan selects, tests, and edits the recipes for this column; she also writes the occasional feature *Why?*, addressing common cooking questions and problems.

The Quick Cook, by Christine Weber Hale (recently joined by Andrew Baker), discusses techniques, products, ingredients, and menu ideas that let you put good meals on the table faster. *The Low-Fat Cook*, by Elaine Johnson and an occasional guest editor, presents a variety of lean, tempting dishes. Our commitment to cooking quick, light, and healthy also shows up this year in two major articles: January's "Flavors of the Southwest" and July's "International Low-Fat." All the recipes in these features come from readers—proof that you, too, favor this kind of cooking.

If you know *Sunset*, you know that food is only one of our four basic departments; travel, home, and gardening get equal billing. As you might expect, many food stories are joint efforts—we might discuss dining out on vacation, for example, or suggest ways to cook home-grown foods. This year, we've included articles on restaurants in Phoenix, Seattle, Portland, and other cities, as well as features on apple Edens of the West (September), Northwest farmers' markets (August), and growing and cooking heirloom beans (March) and tomatoes (September).

Besides our readers, other lively people enrich this *Recipe Annual*, among them cheese makers Ig Vella and John Rumiano (March), author Georgeanne Brennan (April), and apricot grower Stephen Brenkwitz (June). In November, we share a traditional Thanksgiving with the wine-making Wente clan, and a lavish but low-fat meal with cooking teacher Kristene Fortier. And a whole raft of folks from New Mexico provide great menus for December.

As always, we give you new ideas, from a Hawaiian-style bouillabaisse (page 96) to ice creams flavored with dessert wines (page 127). But the basics are still here: pot pies (page 64), the perfect grilled steak (page 112), irresistible desserts (pages 266–270). My pick for our most exciting recipe of the year? April's low-fat Classic Creamy Cheesecake (page 76) is just about perfect! It tastes marvelous, and it really lets you say good-bye to guilt.

So enjoy all the pleasures this *Recipe Annual* has to offer. And be prepared for next year, too: *Sunset Magazine* celebrates its centennial in 1998, and we have some splendid surprises planned for you.

Cheers!

Jerry Di Vecchio
Senior Editor, Food and Entertaining

TO USE OUR NUTRITIONAL INFORMATION

The most current data from the USDA is used for our recipes: calorie count; fat calories; grams of protein, total and saturated fat, and carbohydrates; and milligrams of sodium and cholesterol.

This analysis is usually given for a single serving, based on the largest number of servings listed. Or it's for a specific amount, such as per tablespoon (for sauces); or by unit, as per cookie.

Optional ingredients are not included, nor are those for which no specific amount is stated (salt added to taste, for example). If an ingredient is listed with an alternative, calculations are based on the first choice listed. Likewise, if a range is given for the amount of an ingredient (such as ½ to 1 cup milk), values are figured on the first, lower amount.

Recipes using broth are calculated on the sodium content of salt-free broth, homemade or canned. If you use canned salted chicken broth, the sodium content will be higher.

Vivid Southwest flavors highlight recipes featured in our Quick, Light & Healthy section, beginning on page 13.

PENINA

January

foodguide

by **JERRY ANNE DI VECCHIO**

PAUL FRANZ-MOORE

a **TASTE** *of the* **WEST**

A fresh look at duck

Like beauty, fat on a duck is only skin deep. It doesn't streak through the muscle as in beef. So when you skin a duck, which is easy, you end up with meat that competes with chicken for leanness. And as an alternative to the ubiquitous chicken breast, duck breast is not only a relief, it's also juicier and more flavorful.

However, that duck skin doesn't have to go to waste. Roast it separately.

The breast of Pekin duck, the bird typically sold whole at the market (and used in the Chinese dish Peking duck), is worth the effort to get. Usually it's available by special order at a poultry or meat market or the meat counter at a supermarket (allow one or two days). Boned Pekin breasts run $7 to $12 a pound. Another choice, Muscovy duck breasts, are stronger-tasting and sometimes more expensive, but the meat becomes much milder with this recipe's salt-sugar cure.

Duck Breast with Escarole and Toast

Prep and cook time: About 1 hour

Notes: If using boned Muscovy duck breasts (which are typically packaged as individual halves), you need 1½ to 1¾ pounds total. Use butter or olive oil instead of duck fat if you don't cook the skin. About 80 percent of the fat in duck skin cooks out, so the crisp cracklings are less rich than you might think—but no accurate nutritional information exists.

Makes: 4 servings

2 boned **Pekin duck breasts** (about 2 lb. total)

2 tablespoons **salt**

1 tablespoon **sugar**

great product

The wood *molinillo* (beater), whirling hot chocolate to foamy perfection, has mostly given way to the blender, even in Mexico. But hot chocolate there is still made with wedges of dark, cinnamon-spiced chocolate, usually called Mexican-style sweet chocolate. Two brands produced in Mexico are readily found here: Ibarra and Abuelita. An 18- to 19-ounce package of the round chocolate bars, scored to snap apart, costs $2.60 to $3.60.

For a cup of the beverage, drop two or three chocolate wedges into a blender with 1 cup steaming-hot milk and whirl until chocolate melts. But don't stop there. Coarsely grind the chocolate bars in a blender or food processor to …
• *Sprinkle* onto cappuccinos and caffe lattes and over ice cream.
• *Make dessert tacos:* Spread a flour tortilla with butter, peanut butter, or cream cheese and sprinkle generously with ground chocolate. Fold tortilla over filling and broil until crisp on each side. Brush top with butter and sprinkle with more chocolate.
• *Make a dessert sauce:* Warm 1 part ground chocolate with 2 parts sour cream, stirring until chocolate melts; don't boil. Delicious hot or cold on orange slices or as a dip for biscotti.

BOOKS *on* FOOD

The culinary spirits of many houses

G rowing up in Los Angeles, Regina Cordova learned from a tender age the culinary and cultural distinctions among foods connected to her Mexican and New Mexican heritage. In *Celebración: Recipes & Traditions Celebrating Latino Family Life* (Main Street Books/Doubleday, New York, 1996; $18.95), she takes the next step, documenting the flavors of the Latino community.

Cordova, with Emma Carrasco, gathered and tested recipes from more than 200 cooks, and the book gives individual voice to the culinary treasures of 16 Latin-American countries as well as the southwestern United States. The cookbook is a project of the National Council of La Raza (a Latino service organization).

In five chapters and 214 pages, the customs and the essence of the table in South and Central America, Mexico, and the American Southwest are richly revealed with anecdotal remarks from the cooks who share their recipes for Empanadillas de Masa de Yuca (cheese-filled yucca turnovers), Ropa Vieja (shredded flank steak with sauce), and syrup-glazed Buñuelos (sweet fritters). The ingredients for these dishes are easily found in Latino groceries and supermarkets, but should an item elude you, the book lists sources.

---

2 heads **escarole** (about 1½ lb. total)

8 diagonally cut **French bread** slices about ½ inch thick (about 10 oz. total)

¼ cup **chicken broth**

Prepared wasabi (green horseradish)

Pickled ginger

1. Pull skin from duck, cutting where needed to release.

2. Lay skin flat in a 9- or 10-inch-wide pan. Bake in a 350° oven until browned, about 30 minutes; turn skin over several times. Drain on paper towels. Pour fat from pan into a container; reserve. Wipe pan clean; set aside. Reduce oven temperature to 300°.

3. As skin bakes, mix salt and sugar and rub all over duck breasts. Put meat in a

bowl and let stand 15 to 20 minutes, then rinse well and pat dry. Discard liquid that forms.

4. Rinse and drain escarole, trim out core, and coarsely chop leaves.

5. Lightly brush one side of each bread slice with 2 teaspoons reserved duck fat. Set bread, fat side up, in a single layer in a 10- by 15-inch pan. Bake in the 300° oven until pale gold and crisp, 20 to 25 minutes. Keep warm.

6. Put 2 teaspoons reserved duck fat in a 10- to 12-inch ovenproof frying pan over high heat. When hot, add breasts and brown on each side, about 6 minutes total. Put duck and pan in the 300° oven. Bake until breasts are just pink in the center (130° to 140°; cut to test), about 5 minutes. Remove from oven. Keeping breasts warm, let stand at least 10 minutes for juices to settle.

7. Meanwhile, finely dice duck skin,

return it to its pan, and put in the oven. Bake until sizzling, about 15 minutes. Keep warm.

8. When breasts have rested at least 5 minutes, put 1 teaspoon duck fat and the chicken broth in a 5- to 6-quart pan over high heat. Add escarole and stir until barely wilted, about 2 minutes.

9. Using a slotted spoon, transfer escarole to 4 warmed dinner plates.

10. Slice duck breasts across the grain and lay equal portions on plates. Sprinkle with duck skin. Accompany with toast, wasabi, and pickled ginger.

Per serving without skin: 531 cal., 36% (189 cal.) from fat; 37 g protein; 21 g fat (6.6 g sat.); 47 g carbo (5.7 g fiber); 898 mg sodium; 167 mg chol.

Per serving without skin and toast: 183 cal., 11% (20 cal.) from fat; 31 g protein; 2.2 g fat (0.5 g sat.); 10 g carbo (3.7 g fiber); 466 mg sodium; 150 mg chol.

PAUL FRANZ-MOORE

Norwegian Chicken Meatballs

Prep and cook time: About 15 minutes
Makes: 4 servings

1	pound **ground chicken**
4½	teaspoons **cornstarch**
1	**large egg**
2¼	cups **chicken broth**
¼	teaspoon **salt**
½	teaspoon grated **lemon** peel
	About 2 tablespoons chopped **fresh dill** or 1½ teaspoons dried dill weed
¼	pound **gjetost cheese**, cut into ¼-inch dice
4	to 6 cups hot cooked **egg noodles** or rice

1. With a fork, stir chicken to mix well with 1½ teaspoons cornstarch, egg, ¼ cup broth, salt, grated lemon peel, and 1 tablespoon fresh dill (or 1 teaspoon dried).

2. Bring 2 cups broth to simmering in a 10- to 12-inch frying pan. As broth heats, drop level tablespoon portions of chicken into the liquid, keeping pieces slightly apart. Cover and simmer until meat is white in center (cut to test), 3 to 4 minutes.

3. With a slotted spoon, transfer chicken to a bowl. Mix remaining 1 tablespoon cornstarch with 2 tablespoons water until smooth, and whisk into broth. Turn heat to high, add cheese, and whisk until it melts.

4. Return chicken to sauce, mix gently, and heat for about 1 minute. Pour over noodles in a bowl and sprinkle with remaining dill.

Per serving: 568 cal., 36% (207 cal.) from fat; 34 g protein; 23 g fat (9.3 g sat.); 56 g carbo (3.5 g fiber); 484 mg sodium; 202 mg chol.

COOK'S *discovery*

Brown cheese

It's not new, and it's often overlooked—except by its devotees. Gjetost (*yea*-toast), which comes from Norway, is sold either in little red boxes labeled Ski Queen or cut and wrapped with plastic. Norwegians often call it "brown cheese" and can't start the day without paper-thin slices of it on paper-thin crisp bread. My mother used to call gjetost the "Fels Naptha cheese" because it looks like a bar of the so-named soap.

Gjetost isn't made like most cheeses. Cow's and goat's milk, along with whey, are boiled until reduced to an amber color. When warm and fresh-made, the cheese tastes like sweet caramel with a tangy nip. I just happened to be in a Norwegian gjetost factory when a batch was finished: my companions—food writers—viewed my addiction to this cheese as odd, but once they tasted the warm stuff, my status improved. What's really odd is how mellow and delicious this sweet cheese is in meat sauces.

---

quick **TIPS**

Peeled red peppers

A jar of this, a can of that. How old-fashioned this sounds. But much depends upon what's inside. Jars of peeled mild red peppers have slipped quietly but plentifully onto market shelves in the last few years, and they've become a staple in my home.

For a quick salad, pour the **canned red peppers** and juice onto a platter and drizzle with **olive oil** and **balsamic vinegar**. To add freshness, sprinkle the salad with **fresh basil** or cilantro **leaves**, then top with drained **canned anchovies.**

For a lean soup with a luxurious, velvety texture, try *Red Pepper Bisque.* Pour 1 jar (12 oz.) **canned red peppers** with juice into a 2- to 3-quart pan. Add 1 can (14½ oz., or 1¾ cups) **chicken broth**, 1 chopped **onion** (½ lb.), and 1 peeled and thinly sliced **russet potato** (about ½ lb.). Boil gently, covered, until potato begins to fall apart, about 20 minutes. Purée soup in a blender or food processor, reheat if necessary, then ladle into bowls. Add **plain nonfat yogurt** and **salt** to taste. Makes 4 servings.

Per serving: 111 cal., 6.5% (7.2 cal.) from fat; 3 g protein; 0.8 g fat (0.3 g sat.); 22 g carbo (1.8 g fiber); 232 mg sodium; 1.6 mg chol. ◆

NORMAN A. PLATE

You owe yourself a great Chardonnay

Most Chardonnays are reminiscent of white shirts from Sears. They're serviceable, unobjectionable, and convenient. Too bad most of them also lack personality.

This is not necessarily the fault of winemakers. Although Chardonnay grapes are a snap to make into decent wine, they're very difficult to make into truly great wine.

And what does a great Chardonnay have that an "ungreat" one doesn't? Integration, expressiveness, complexity, and connectedness. These four attributes, in concert, are the hallmarks of a great wine; they give it its personality.

Integration is a state of total harmony among the components of a wine. An integrated wine reveals itself as a sphere in the mouth—so harmonious that you cannot easily sense any one component. By comparison, a poorly integrated wine presents itself like a triangle. You can taste the "points" of alcohol, oak, and tannin. Just think of all those oaky, oafish Chardonnays.

Expressiveness is the quality a wine possesses when its aromas and flavors are clearly projected. While some wines seem feeble, muddled, or diffused, others beam out their character with clarity and focus. Imagine the picture projected by a black-and-white television without an antenna compared to one in high-definition color. Far too many Chardonnays, alas, are fuzzy TV.

Complexity is not a thing like, say, "creaminess," but is instead a phenomenon. Complex wines pull you into them and compel you to keep smelling and sipping because each time you do, you find something new in the wine.

Sadly, too many Chardonnays are one-trick ponies. Taste them once and you've got it.

Connectedness is perhaps the most elusive of these qualities and the most difficult to ascertain. It is the sense you derive from the wine's aroma and flavor that the wine could not have come from just anywhere, but is rather the embodiment of a single piece of earth. Connectedness, the bond between a wine and the plot of land it was born in, gives a wine true personality.

Wine without connectedness may be of good quality, but like a Holiday Inn in Tuscany, there is a limit to how deep one's aesthetic appreciation of it can be.

Unfortunately, too many Chardonnays in the world taste like they came from one giant mythic vat. They are wines from anywhere and everywhere.

None of this means we should stop drinking Chardonnay, but it does mean we should occasionally savor a great one. Historically speaking, the hugely expensive Chardonnays from France's Burgundy region have been considered the world's best. Today, however, California also offers exquisite examples. Here are some of the greatest:

- **Stony Hill Chardonnay 1994, $21.** As pure and clear as the sound of church bells. (Sold direct from the winery; 707/963-2636.)
- **Shafer "Red Shoulder Ranch" Chardonnay 1994, $23.** Lavish honeysuckle flavors.
- **Rombauer Carneros Chardonnay 1995, $24.** Delicious and effortless to drink.
- **Chalone Estate Chardonnay 1994, $27.** Graceful, intense, and complex.
- **Peter Michael "Mon Plaisir" Chardonnay 1994, $36.** Hauntingly elegant and rich.
- **Kistler "Kistler Vineyard" Chardonnay 1993, $40.** Lip-smacking and lush. ◆

WINE DICTIONARY: *acidity*

Acids are those natural components in wine that give some wines a zesty, refreshing quality. Acids also help wine to age. Wines with the proper amount of acidity relative to the alcohol are vibrant and lively in the mouth. Wines with little acidity relative to the alcohol are the opposite: flat and blowsy. Wines with an extremely high level of acidity often taste sharp and biting.

by LINDA LAU ANUSASANANAN

The finer points of microwave cooking

Zap—turkey leftovers are steaming for lunch. Zap—your vegetables are rewarmed just before you sit down to the big dinner. Cooking or heating in a microwave oven is fast, neat, cool, and easy enough for children to manage. As a result, microwave ovens have become so much a part of our lives that many homes have more than one, and the ovens are put to use every day—if only to reheat coffee. And, come the holidays, it's hard to imagine entertaining without one.

Calling this microwave-generating tool an oven has long been the source of much confusion. Instead of heating from the outside in, it heats internally. Household electricity converted to high-frequency microwaves excites the moisture and fat molecules in food, and the resulting vibrations create friction that produces heat within the food itself. Therefore, how you cook and what you can cook is quite different in the microwave oven than in a conventional oven.

WHY DO POTATOES COOKED IN A MICROWAVE OVEN TURN GLUEY WHEN MASHED?

The starch in potatoes is held in structures called buds, or granules. When whole, unpeeled potatoes cook in a microwave oven, the water inside them heats rapidly, and when it gets hot enough, the steam that can't escape breaks open the starch buds, releasing their gluey starch.

To avoid this problem, cut peeled potatoes into small cubes and add a little water to cook them, covered, in the microwave oven. The smaller pieces cook faster and more evenly, and the steam escapes without damaging the starch buds.

After cooking potatoes this way, handle them as you would regular boiled potatoes.

WHY DO BROCCOLI FLORETS GET BROWN SPOTS WHEN ZAPPED?

If the broccoli is cooked without any liquid, as you can in the microwave oven, the vegetable takes in oxygen that turns some of its green color brown. If broccoli cooks in water or steam, the moisture drives off the oxygen, and the vegetable stays green. The solution: cook broccoli in a little water in a covered container in the microwave oven.

WHY DOES IT SOMETIMES TAKE LONGER FOR FOOD TO COOK IN A MICROWAVE OVEN?

The rate at which a microwave oven heats food has to do with how much food it is heating. It heats small amounts quickly; increase the volume of food and you increase the amount of time required. If the food is doubled, the time required to heat it may be doubled.

For example, whether you cook one or six artichokes in a pot of simmering water, the cooking time is the same. But if you cook six artichokes in the microwave oven, they may take up to six times as long as a single artichoke.

Big pieces of food—or casseroles for four to six servings—heat differently in the microwave than in a conventional oven. The waves tend to be absorbed before they completely penetrate, so foods are heated unevenly internally. You need to let the food stand briefly after microwaving to give the heat time to equalize. If you microwave longer and skip the standing time, the outside edges of foods (or sometimes the center) will overcook—even scorch—and the internal temperature willstill be uneven. In situations like these, a regular oven often works better and faster.

WHY CAN I USE PAPER AND PLASTIC IN THE MICROWAVE OVEN?

The long microwaves simply pass through paper and plastic containers and wrap without heating them. However, once the food is hot, it will transfer heat. If the plastic is designed for microwave use or for cooking, there is no problem. But if the plastic is heat-sensitive, as produce bags and some wrapping materials are, it can melt onto or into the hot food. Avoid these products when you need to get the food really hot.

WHY DO MANUFACTURERS SUGGEST INVERTING A CERAMIC PLATE UNDER A POPCORN BAG IN A 500-WATT (OR LESS) MICROWAVE OVEN?

When the water in the popcorn gets hot, the heat transfers to the plate. The plate holds the heat next to the popcorn and makes more of the kernels pop. ◆

EMERGENCY DESSERT SAUCES

For the easiest dessert for a party or a family dinner, dress up ice cream with one of these quick sauces that are hot by the time the ice cream is ready to scoop.

MOCHA VELVET. Put 4 ounces chopped **semisweet chocolate,** 2 tablespoons **coffee liqueur,** and 1 tablespoon **rum** in a 2- to 4-cup glass measuring cup (the handle makes it easy to grab). Heat in a microwave oven on full power (100 percent) for 30 seconds; stir. Then heat at 10-second intervals, stirring between, until chocolate is melted. Ladle over vanilla, chocolate, coffee, or peppermint **ice cream.** Makes ½ cup.

BITTER ORANGE SAUCE. Put ⅓ cup **orange marmalade,** ¼ cup **whipping cream,** and 1 tablespoon **orange-flavor liqueur** in a 4-cup glass measure. Heat in a microwave oven on full power (100 percent) for 1½ minutes; stir. Then heat for about 2 minutes, until sauce is reduced to ½ cup. Pour over vanilla, chocolate, eggnog, or strawberry **ice cream.**

Quick Light & Healthy

Flavors *of the* Southwest

Soups and stews, tortilla classics, salsas and sauces—
here's everything for a new year of good eating

In our fantasy life, the maid does the shopping, Alice Waters cooks dinner, and the royalties from our workout video cover the mortgage. In reality, life is a little different: We want to eat well, but we have little time. And if we don't cook, no one does. Which brings us to our second annual Quick, Light & Healthy special section.

This year's recipes come from *Sunset* readers who know how to keep the fun in cooking while making delicious food achievable. Use ingredients that are readily available, and not too many of them, they say. Keep it simple. And if you're looking for a healthful, low-fat meal with a lot of punch, try the vivid flavors of the Southwest.

No recipe derives more than 30 percent of its calories from fat, and nearly all of the recipes can be made in 30 minutes or less. (To measure time, we started the clock once the ingredients and equipment were assembled.)

We've added easy menu suggestions to ensure a carefree, healthful new year—until Alice and the royalty checks show up.

Charge up Tortilla Soup (page 14) with chili-coated tortillas cut into lightning bolts and baked crisp.

by **ELAINE JOHNSON** *and* **CHRISTINE WEBER HALE**
FOOD PHOTOGRAPHS *by* **PENINA**   **FOOD STYLING** *by* **POUKÉ**

Soups & Stews

Richard Alexei of San Francisco is a chef and food writer turned personal trainer.

"These days I rarely go out to eat," he says, finding that the food he likes best is best made at home. "I like to eat just as well as I did before, but healthier. One thing I emphasize is not just reducing fat, but using a lot of very healthy ingredients—vegetables such as squashes, whole grains, and high-fiber foods like beans."

For his black bean soup, Alexei starts with the traditional seasonings of red chilies and cumin and adds squash for sweetness, along with smoky chipotles. He likes to serve the soup with extra-fresh corn tortillas from one of the Latino markets in the Mission district near his home.

A good diet and good-for-you recipes come up frequently in conversation as Alexei works out with clients, and he's compiling his ideas for a cookbook.

MICHAEL JOHNSON

If time permits, Richard Alexei makes black bean soup with fresh squash.

Black Bean and Pumpkin Soup

Prep and cook time: About 30 minutes

Notes: Try substituting 2 cups of puréed cooked kabocha squash for the pumpkin. For a spicier soup, use 2 chipotles.

Makes: 5 servings

- 2 tablespoons **ground New Mexico** or California **chilies**
- 1 teaspoon **cumin seed**
- 1 can (14½ oz.) **diced tomatoes (no salt added)**
- 1 cup coarsely chopped **onion**
- 2 cloves **garlic**
- 1 or 2 **canned chipotle chilies,** drained
- 1 tablespoon **salad oil**
- 2 cans (15 oz. each) **reduced-sodium black beans**
- 2 cups **reduced-sodium chicken broth**
- 1 can (16 oz.) **pumpkin**
- **Fresh cilantro** sprigs
- **Lime** wedges
- **Reduced-fat sour cream**

1. In a 5- to 6-quart pan over medium-high heat, stir New Mexico chilies and cumin just until they start to smoke, 1 to 2 minutes. Scrape into a blender and add tomatoes with their juice, onion, garlic, chipotles, and oil; whirl until smooth.

2. Pour chili mixture into pan. Bring to a simmer over medium-high heat, partially cover, and stir occasionally until slightly thickened, about 5 minutes. Stir in beans with their liquid, broth, and pumpkin. Bring to a simmer over high heat, then reduce heat and simmer, covered, for 10 minutes to blend flavors.

3. Whirl about 2 cups of the soup in blender until smooth, then return to pan. Garnish soup with cilantro sprigs and offer lime wedges and sour cream to season to taste.

Per serving: 197 cal., 17% (33 cal.) from fat; 10 g protein; 3.7 g fat (0.6 g sat.); 39 g carbo (11 g fiber); 576 mg sodium; 0 mg chol.

When Cathy Harrison of Vallecito, California, makes this soup, she often prepares her own flavored low-fat tortilla "chips" to use instead of soft tortilla strips in the soup and as garnish. She simply sprays corn tortillas with water, sprinkles them with chili powder, salt, and pepper, cuts them into ¼-inch-wide strips (you can also create other shapes, as shown on page 13), and bakes them in a 350° oven until crisp, about 14 minutes.

Tortilla Soup

Prep and cook time: About 30 minutes

Makes: 4 servings

- 1½ cups sliced **red onions**
- 1 clove **garlic,** minced
- 1 teaspoon **olive oil**
- ¼ cup **ground California** or New Mexico **chilies**
- 1 teaspoon **ground cumin**
- 6 cups **chicken** or vegetable **broth**
- 1½ cups **frozen corn kernels**
- 1 can (14½ oz.) **sliced regular** or Mexican-style stewed **tomatoes**
- 5 **corn tortillas** (6½ in.)
- ½ cup shredded **jack cheese**
- **Fresh cilantro** sprigs

1. In a 4- to 5-quart pan over medium-high heat, frequently stir onions, garlic, and oil until onions are limp, about 6 minutes; if necessary to prevent sticking, add 1 to 2 tablespoons water.

2. Add chilies and cumin; stir 30 seconds, then mix in broth, corn, and tomatoes. Cover and bring to a boil over high heat; reduce heat and simmer 5 to 10 minutes to blend flavors.

3. Stack tortillas, cut in half, stack again, and slice crosswise into ¼-inch-wide strips. Place strips in soup bowls. Ladle soup on top, sprinkle with cheese, and garnish with cilantro.

Per serving: 305 cal., 30% (90 cal.) from fat; 14 g protein; 10 g fat (4.1 g sat.); 46 g carbo (6.5 g fiber); 583 mg sodium; 21 mg chol.

This stew from Stella Perea of Corrales, New Mexico, is typical of native New Mexican dishes. Perea, who grew up in New Mexico, owns Perea's restaurant, where she serves items such as blue-corn enchiladas and vegetarian tamales. This recipe was handed down from her grandmother. Perea uses lean pork or round steak—we substituted smoked pork because we like its flavor and, since it's cooked, it saves time. She serves the quick chili stew as a meal on its own with her homemade tortillas or adds pinto beans and Spanish rice as accompaniments.

Green Chili Stew

Prep and cook time: About 30 minutes
Makes: 4 servings

- 3 **thin-skinned potatoes** (about 1½ lb. total), scrubbed
- 2 **tomatoes** (about ½ lb. total)
- 3½ cups **reduced-sodium chicken broth**
- 1 can (7 oz.) **diced green chilies**
- 2 cloves **garlic**, minced
- 1 pound **boneless smoked extra-lean pork chops**
- 1 teaspoon **salad oil**

  Hot sauce

1. Cut potatoes into ½-inch pieces. Core and chop tomatoes. In a 5- to 6-quart pan, combine potatoes, tomatoes, broth, chilies, and garlic. Bring to a boil over high heat; cover, reduce heat, and simmer until potatoes are tender when pierced, 12 to 15 minutes.

2. While potatoes simmer, trim off and discard excess fat from pork. Cut pork crosswise into ¼-inch-wide strips, then cut strips in half. To a 10- to 12-inch nonstick frying pan, add oil and pork; cook over medium-high heat, stirring often, until pork is lightly browned, about 7 minutes. Remove from heat; set aside.

3. When potatoes are tender, stir in pork; simmer just long enough to warm meat through, about 2 minutes. Add 1 or 2 drops of hot sauce, if desired.

Per serving: 370 cal., 29% (108 cal.) from fat; 24 g protein; 12 g fat (2.8 g sat.); 40 g carbo (3.6 g fiber); 2,393 mg sodium; 60 mg chol.

Having grown up in a family of healthful eaters, Lisa Bohon-Hock of Sacramento has always been interested in good nutrition. Her mother used to make this recipe with beef neck bones, but Bohon-Hock substitutes chicken breasts to keep fat at a mini-

Prepared red chili sauce, canned hominy, and boneless, skinless chicken breasts are shortcuts in a surprisingly authentic-tasting pozole.

mum. She always serves the pozole with a vegetable (squash is a winter favorite) and tortillas, quesadillas, or bread.

Quick Chicken Pozole

Prep and cook time: About 25 minutes
Makes: 3 or 4 servings

- 3 cloves **garlic**, minced
- 1 **onion** (about 6 oz.), chopped
- 1 teaspoon **salad oil**
- 1¼ pounds **boneless, skinless chicken breasts**
- 1 can (10 oz.) **red chili sauce**
- ½ teaspoon **dried oregano**
- 2 cups **reduced-sodium chicken broth**
- 2 cans (about 15 oz. each) **white** or yellow **hominy** (or one can of each color), rinsed and drained

  Shredded **iceberg lettuce**

  Lime wedges

1. In a 3- to 4-quart pan, combine the garlic, onion, and salad oil. Cook, stirring often, over medium-high heat until the onion is lightly browned, about 5 minutes.

2. While the onion cooks, cut the chicken into bite-size pieces. When the onion has browned, add the chicken pieces, red chili sauce, oregano, and chicken broth. Bring to a boil, reduce heat, and simmer until chicken is no longer pink in center of thickest part (cut to test), 7 to 8 minutes.

3. Add hominy, reheat to simmering, and serve. Offer lettuce and lime wedges to add to taste.

Per serving: 362 cal., 14% (49 cal.) from fat; 37 g protein; 5.4 g fat (0.9 g sat.); 36 g carbo (7 g fiber); 1,172 mg sodium; 82 mg chol.

A hot oven—not oil—turns vegetarian chimichangas crisp and golden.

Tortilla Classics

Meals in Patti Atterberry's Lodi, California, home must be two things: healthful and fast enough to fit into her 80-hour workweek. On the health front, she satisfies her yen for Mexican food with crisp, vegetable-filled chimichangas that are baked, not fried. As for fast, Atterberry says, "I named them after my friend Paulette, who claims she can't cook. They're so easy even she can do them."

Paulette's Baked Chimichangas

Prep and cook time: About 30 minutes
Makes: 6 servings

1 can (29 oz.) **pinto beans**, rinsed and drained

1 can (4 oz.) **sliced ripe olives**, drained

1 can (7 oz.) **diced green chilies**

1 cup **prepared coleslaw mix with carrots**

1 cup shredded **sharp cheddar cheese**

1¾ cups **tomato salsa**

6 **nonfat** or reduced-fat **flour tortillas** (10 in.)

Reduced-fat sour cream

Sliced **green onions**

1. In a bowl, combine beans, olives, chilies, coleslaw mix, cheese, and 1 cup of the salsa.

2. Wrap tortillas in a cloth towel and microwave on high (100 percent) until hot and pliable, about 1½ minutes. Lay tortillas flat. Spread each with ⅙ of bean mixture in a band near edge. Fold over sides and roll up tightly to enclose.

3. Place bundles seam side down on a lightly oiled 12- by 15-inch baking sheet. Bake in a 425° oven until crisp and brown, about 15 minutes. Top each chimichanga with additional salsa, sour cream, and green onions.

Per chimichanga: 345 cal., 25% (85 cal.) from fat; 15 g protein; 9.4 g fat (4.3 g sat.); 49 g carbo (6.8 g fiber); 1,316 mg sodium; 20 mg chol.

Amy Michaels of Seattle developed this recipe to use canned chipotle chilies she had bought during a family visit to Santa Fe. Although Michaels's husband loves traditional tacos, the nutrition-conscious couple particularly enjoy this version, which uses fresh kale from their garden in addition to ground turkey flavored with garlic, chili powder, cumin, and tomato. Michaels serves the tacos with a chopped cabbage salad and black beans.

Turkey-Chipotle Soft Tacos

Prep and cook time: About 30 minutes
Makes: 4 servings

- 1 pound **ground turkey**
- 2 cloves **garlic**, minced
- 1 **onion** (about 10 oz.), chopped
- 1 tablespoon **chili powder**
- 2 teaspoons **ground cumin**
- ¼ pound **kale** or Swiss chard
- 2 **canned chipotle chilies**, drained
- 1 can (15 oz.) **tomato sauce (no salt added)**
- 8 **nonfat flour tortillas** (6½ to 7 in.), warmed

1. In a 12-inch nonstick frying pan, combine turkey, garlic, onion, chili powder, and cumin. Cook over medium-high heat, stirring often, until meat is lightly browned, 7 to 8 minutes.
2. While meat browns, chop kale and chipotles. When meat is ready, add kale, chipotles, and tomato sauce to pan and stir. Cover tightly and simmer, stirring occasionally, until kale is wilted, about 10 minutes.
3. Transfer mixture to a serving bowl; spoon into tortillas to eat.

Per serving: 419 cal., 21% (90 cal.) from fat; 28 g protein; 10 g fat (2.3 g sat.); 55 g carbo (6.9 g fiber); 722 mg sodium; 83 mg chol.

Cheryl Wong of Marina, California, takes a near-instant route to achieve the flavors of chili verde. Instead of slowly simmering the chicken in a sauce, she dresses shredded cabbage with purchased green-chili salsa, adds the quickly cooked chicken, then wraps the works in flour tortillas (on cover).

Chicken Chili Verde Tacos

Prep and cook time: About 25 minutes
Makes: 4 servings

- 3 cups **prepared shredded cabbage**
- 1 cup lightly packed **fresh cilantro**
- 1 cup **green-chili salsa**
- 1 pound **boneless, skinless chicken breasts**
- 1 teaspoon **salad oil**

- 1 **onion** (½ lb.), slivered lengthwise
- 3 cloves **garlic**, minced
- 1 teaspoon **ground cumin**
- ½ teaspoon **dried oregano**
- 8 **reduced-fat** or regular **flour tortillas** (7 to 8 in.)

1. Combine cabbage, cilantro, and salsa in a serving dish; set aside.
2. Cut chicken crosswise into ½-inch-wide strips. In a 10- to 12-inch nonstick frying pan over medium-high heat, stir oil, onion, and garlic for 2 minutes. Increase heat to high, add chicken, and stir often until meat is no longer pink in center, 4 to 6 minutes. Add cumin and oregano; stir for 15 seconds. Spoon into a serving dish.
3. Wrap tortillas in a cloth towel and cook in a microwave oven on full power (100 percent) until hot, about 1½ minutes. At the table, spoon the cabbage and chicken mixtures into the tortillas.

Per serving: 356 cal., 17% (62 cal.) from fat; 32 g protein; 6.9 g fat (0.5 g sat.); 39 g carbo (4.6 g fiber); 858 mg sodium; 66 mg chol.

Lawrence Raimon of Santee, California, learned how to cook at an early age by watching cooking shows on television. Raimon and his wife collect spices from around the world (they currently have close to 150), which he likes to experiment with in the kitchen. These savory salmon fajitas (pictured below) reflect his cooking style—fresh, healthful, and quick.

Larry's Salmon Fajitas

Prep and cook time: About 25 minutes
Makes: 3 servings

- 1¼ pounds **salmon fillets,** boned, skinned, and cut into 1-inch cubes
- 1 **onion** (about 6 oz.), thinly sliced
- 2 tablespoons **lemon juice**
- 1 teaspoon **ground cumin**
- 1 teaspoon minced **fresh ginger**
- 1½ teaspoons **hot sauce**
- ⅛ teaspoon **hot chili flakes**
- 4 large leaves (about 3 oz. total) **romaine lettuce**
- 3 **tomatoes** (about 1 lb. total)
- 6 **nonfat flour tortillas** (6 ½ to 7 in.), warmed

  Nonfat sour cream

1. In a bowl, combine salmon, onion, lemon juice, cumin, ginger, hot sauce, and chili flakes; mix well. Cover; chill 10 minutes. Meanwhile, shred lettuce and core and chop tomatoes; cover and chill separately until serving time.
2. Heat a 12-inch nonstick frying pan over medium-high heat. When hot, add salmon mixture. Cook, stirring often, until fish is just opaque but still moist-looking in center, about 6 minutes.
3. Serve immediately. To eat, wrap salmon mixture in tortillas; add lettuce, tomatoes, and sour cream to taste.

Per serving: 514 cal., 30% (153 cal.) from fat; 45 g protein; 17 g fat (2.5 g sat.); 45 g carbo (4.9 g fiber); 439 mg sodium; 104 mg chol.

Cook and roll spicy marinated salmon in warm tortillas for a new take on fajitas.

Salads & Sides

Anne Williams Callison of Denver says her favorite souvenirs are of the edible variety. Whenever she visits San Francisco, she takes a culinary drive along the coast, making a stop at Dominic's, a roadside stand in Watsonville. There she picks up sweet dried tomatoes for her flavorful couscous. Callison particularly enjoys the couscous with grilled chicken or beef rubbed with chilies.

Toasted Pine Nut Couscous

Prep and cook time: About 20 minutes

Notes: Buy small dried-tomato pieces, or snip halves with scissors.

Makes: 4 servings

- ¼ cup **pine nuts**
- 2¼ cups **reduced-sodium chicken broth** or water
- ½ cup small pieces **dried tomatoes** (not oil-packed)
- 1 clove **garlic,** minced
- ½ teaspoon **ground cumin**
- 1⅔ cups (10 oz.) **couscous**
- 2 tablespoons minced **parsley**
  Salt

1. In a 2- to 3-quart pan over medium-high heat, stir pine nuts until golden, about 2 minutes; remove from pan.

2. In the same pan, bring the broth, tomatoes, garlic, and cumin to a boil over high heat. Stir in the couscous, cover, remove from heat, and let stand 5 minutes. Add the pine nuts and parsley, and fluff with a fork. If desired, season to taste with salt.

Per serving: 357 cal., 13% (46 cal.) from fat; 14 g protein; 5.1 g fat (0.8 g sat.); 63 g carbo (5.4 g fiber); 334 mg sodium; 0 mg chol.

Some people set their sights on the Publishers Clearing House Sweepstakes or a state lottery. Roxanne Chan of Albany, California, has found a more lucrative way to use her free time: she creates recipes to publish and enter in cooking contests.

About the cooking contests, Chan explains, "Even though I enjoy creating recipes for the sake of coming up with a good idea, it's fun to win a contest." And in the past dozen years, she's won 350 of them. So far, the big-cash jackpots have eluded her. But she's scored a new car, a kitchenful of appliances, and numerous international trips.

Chan has also scored binderfuls of clippings from her publications. Southwestern Quinoa Salad is her 51st recipe to appear in *Sunset* over 16 years. We've come to count on Chan's healthful and delicious ideas for using grains and fresh produce, and on her creative eye for combining a variety of textures and colors.

For this light, refreshing salad, Chan built on the South American origin of quinoa by adding other foods native to the Americas—beans, corn, and peppers—plus Southwestern seasonings.

Southwestern Quinoa Salad

Prep and cook time: About 30 minutes

Notes: Look for quinoa next to other grains in your supermarket. Use fresh-squeezed lime juice.

Makes: 6 servings

- 1¼ cups **quinoa,** rinsed well and drained
- ⅓ cup **lime juice**
- 1 tablespoon **olive oil**
- ½ teaspoon **ground cumin**
- 1 can (15 oz.) **reduced-sodium black beans,** rinsed and drained
- 1 cup **frozen corn kernels,** thawed, or drained canned corn
- 1 cup chopped **jicama**
- ¾ cup chopped **canned roasted red peppers** (not oil-packed)
- ¼ cup chopped **fresh cilantro**
- 2 tablespoons minced **red onion**
- 2 tablespoons minced **fresh jalapeño chili**
  Salt
  Butter lettuce leaves

1. In a 2- to 3-quart pan over high heat, bring quinoa and 2½ cups water to a boil. Reduce heat and simmer, covered,

Roxanne Chan's culinary creativity has made her a recipe-contest champ.

until water is absorbed, 10 to 15 minutes. Rinse to cool; drain well.

2. Meanwhile, in a bowl combine lime juice, oil, cumin, beans, corn, jicama, roasted peppers, cilantro, onion, and chili. Mix in quinoa, then season to taste with salt. Spoon over lettuce leaves.

Per serving: 237 cal., 17% (41 cal.) from fat; 8.7 g protein; 4.6 g fat (0.5 g sat.); 44 g carbo (9.2 g fiber); 190 mg sodium; 0 mg chol.

Sarojni Mehta-Lissak of Long Beach, California, comes from a family of passionate home cooks. "My dad is from India, and I was raised with Indian food. His whole side of the family loves cooking." From an early age, Mehta-Lissak also took an interest, watching her parents at the stove. By the time she was in high school, she was checking out cookbooks instead of novels from the library.

She married into a family that's equally enthusiastic about food. Her husband is a vegetarian, and they experiment with many ethnic dishes and flavorings, such as achiote, which she encountered in the Yucatán peninsula.

The same sense of adventure extends to Mehta-Lissak's low-fat cooking. Generous levels of seasonings, not oil, give her dishes their character.

A trip to a Mexican restaurant inspired this aromatic rice dish. She enjoys it with tacos or tostadas and a green salad livened up with jicama, cilantro, red onions, and red bell peppers.

At dinnertime Mehta-Lissak gets a hand from her daughter, Sumi, who at age 2 is already following in her mother's footsteps. "She loves being in the kitchen. She helps peel carrots to go in the rice—I put my hand over hers on the grater."

Cilantro Rice

Prep and cook time: About 30 minutes
Makes: 4 or 5 servings

  1 cup **fresh cilantro**
  2 cloves **garlic**
  1 **fresh jalapeño chili,** stemmed
2½ cups **vegetable broth**
  2 teaspoons **olive oil**
1½ cups **long-grain white rice**
  1 teaspoon **onion powder**
½ teaspoon **ground cumin**
⅓ cup grated **carrot**
    Salt
    Fresh cilantro sprigs

Sarojni Mehta-Lissak's young daughter is already an active kitchen participant.

1. In a blender, whirl 1 cup cilantro, garlic, chili, and 1 cup broth until smooth.

2. In a 3- to 4-quart pan over medium heat, stir oil, rice, onion powder, and cumin until rice is pale golden, 5 to 8 minutes. Stir in cilantro mixture, remaining broth, and carrot. Cover, bring to a boil over high heat, then reduce heat and simmer until liquid is absorbed, about 18 minutes.

3. If desired, season to taste with salt. Garnish with cilantro sprigs.

Per serving: 238 cal., 8.4% (20 cal.) from fat; 5.3 g protein; 2.2 g fat (0.3 g sat.); 48 g carbo (1 g fiber); 132 mg sodium; 0 mg chol.

Tina Williams of Pasadena is constantly thinking about new ways to cook food. Her pondering has paid off with this refreshing pasta salad—perfect for potlucks and picnics because it holds well. She sometimes serves the salad as a hot entrée, simply omitting the cooling step for the cooked pasta. Williams, who is interested in healthful cooking that tastes delicious, adds bold seasonings when cutting back on fat and salt.

Mexican Pasta Salad

Prep and cook time: About 30 minutes
Notes: Start heating water for pasta in a covered pan before assembling the rest of the ingredients.
Makes: 4 to 6 servings

  8 ounces **dried fusilli** or rotelle **pasta**
  6 **green onions,** ends trimmed
  3 **Roma tomatoes** (about ½ lb. total)
  2 **fresh jalapeño chilies**
  1 **red bell pepper** (about ½ lb.)
  1 cup minced **fresh cilantro**
  1 can (8½ oz.) **reduced-sodium kidney beans,** rinsed and drained
¼ cup **red wine vinegar**
  1 tablespoon **salad oil**
  2 tablespoons grated **parmesan cheese**
    Salt

1. Cook pasta, uncovered, in 3 to 4 quarts boiling water until tender to bite, about 12 minutes. Drain, then rinse

with cold water until cool; drain well.

2. While pasta cooks, chop the green onions and Roma tomatoes. Stem, seed, and mince jalapeños. Stem, seed, and cut the bell pepper into thin, short slivers.

3. In a large bowl, combine the pasta, onions, tomatoes, jalapeños, bell pepper, cilantro, and beans. Add the vinegar, oil, and cheese; mix well. Transfer to a serving platter. If desired, add salt to taste.

Per serving: 222 cal., 15% (34 cal.) from fat; 8.7 g protein; 3.8 g fat (0.7 g sat.); 39 g carbo (4.2 g fiber); 92 mg sodium; 1.3 mg chol.

Tina Brown of Chino, California, shares a potato dish that's a long-time favorite in her family: spicy hash browns made with only 2 teaspoons of oil. Try them for breakfast or dinner with poached eggs and toast or tortillas.

South-of-the-Border Potatoes

Prep and cook time: About 30 minutes
Notes: If you have only a 10-inch nonstick pan, simmer all of the potatoes, then finish the recipe in 2 batches.
Makes: 4 servings

  4 cups chopped peeled **thin-skinned potatoes**
  2 teaspoons **olive oil**
  1 teaspoon **chili powder**
  1 teaspoon **ground coriander**
  1 teaspoon **ground cumin**
  1 teaspoon **garlic powder**
  1 cup diced **Roma tomatoes**
    About ¼ cup chopped **fresh cilantro**
¼ cup sliced **green onions**
    Salt
    Tomato salsa
    Nonfat sour cream

1. Place the potatoes and 1½ cups water in a 12-inch nonstick frying pan. Cover tightly with a lid or foil and bring to a boil over high heat. Simmer over medium heat until the potatoes are tender when pierced, 5 to 7 minutes. Drain the potatoes in a colander and wipe pan clean.

2. To pan, add oil, chili powder, coriander, cumin, and garlic powder; stir over medium-high heat for 30 seconds. Add potatoes, stir to coat, then mix in tomatoes, ¼ cup cilantro, and green onions. Over high heat, occasionally turn mixture with a wide spatula until browned, 5 to 6 minutes. Season to taste with salt and sprinkle with a little more cilantro. Offer salsa and sour cream to add to taste.

Per serving: 159 cal., 16% (26 cal.) from fat; 3.7 g protein; 2.9 g fat (0.3 g sat.); 31 g carbo (3.5 g fiber); 24 mg sodium; 0 mg chol.

Marilou Robinson of Portland loves Mexican food and says, "You can skip a lot of sour cream and cheese if you add enough cilantro and peppers." This zesty, no-fat slaw—great for barbecues, picnics, and potlucks—has plenty of each. If there's any left over, Robinson heats it in the microwave just until hot but still tender-crisp and serves it as a vegetable side dish.

Confetti Coleslaw

Prep time: About 15 minutes
Makes: 6 servings

- 1 pound **prepared shredded cabbage**
- 1 cup peeled and shredded **jicama**
- 1 **red bell pepper** (about 6 oz.), stemmed, seeded, and cut into thin strips
- ¾ cup **prepared shredded carrots**
- ½ cup lightly packed **fresh cilantro**
- 1 **onion** (about 4 oz.), cut in half
- ⅓ cup **cider vinegar**
- ¼ cup **catsup**
- 2 tablespoons **prepared mustard**
- 2 tablespoons **sugar**
  Salt and **pepper**
  Fresh cilantro sprigs

1. In a large bowl, mix together cabbage, jicama, bell pepper, and carrots.
2. In a blender or food processor, combine ½ cup cilantro, onion, vinegar, catsup, mustard, and sugar. Whirl until smooth. Add to cabbage mixture and mix well. Season with salt and pepper to taste and garnish with cilantro sprigs.

Per serving: 78 cal., 5.8% (4.5 cal.) from fat; 2.2 g protein; 0.5 g fat (0.1 g sat.); 18 g carbo (3.6 g fiber); 205 mg sodium; 0 mg chol.

Tangy-sweet Confetti Coleslaw pairs well with Southwest dishes like Spicy Swordfish.

Salsas & Sauces

James French of Boise developed this easy way to perk up prepared salsa: simply mix in some fresh tomatoes, green onions, and lime juice. It's the perfect foil for mild swordfish. The sauce is also tasty over other fish and with chicken, pork, and beef.

Spicy Swordfish

Prep and cook time: About 15 minutes
Makes: 4 servings

- 4 **swordfish steaks,** ¾ to 1 inch thick (1½ lb. total)
- 1 **tomato** (about 6 oz.)
- 1 **green onion**
- 1 cup **chunky tomato salsa**
- 1 tablespoon **lime juice**
- ¼ teaspoon **hot sauce** (optional)

1. Rinse swordfish and pat dry. Arrange steaks on broiler pan rack and broil 4 to 6 inches from heat until fish is just opaque in center of the thickest part but still moist-looking (cut to test), 11 to 15 minutes. Turn once.
2. While fish cooks, core and dice tomato and slice onion. Mix tomato, onion, salsa, lime juice, and hot sauce.
3. Arrange fish on a platter or on individual plates and top with salsa.

Per serving: 214 cal., 26% (56 cal.) from fat; 30 g protein; 6.2 g fat (1.7 g sat.); 6.3 g carbo (0.6 g fiber); 782 mg sodium; 59 mg chol.

Dana Luedtke's description of herself could apply to a lot of us— she loves good food, loves Southwestern flavors, and is always watching her weight. Happily, this Portland resident also enjoys experimenting in the kitchen and has come up with a number of common-sense tips for flavorful low-fat, nutritious dishes.

"I use a minimum of oil and substitute yogurt for many other ingredients," she says. Her favorite ingredients are naturally lean. "I've really taken to cilantro and love roasted bell peppers and chilies." In this recipe, Luedtke makes a creamy sauce from yogurt, mildly spicy

1 pound **dried linguine**

¾ pound **red bell peppers**

1 teaspoon **salad oil**

1 pound **boneless, skinless chicken breasts**

2 cups **plain nonfat yogurt**

2 teaspoons **cornstarch**

2 bottles (8 oz. each) **mild red taco sauce**

¼ cup chopped **fresh cilantro**

1. Cook pasta, uncovered, in 3 to 4 quarts boiling water until barely tender to bite, 5 to 7 minutes.

2. Meanwhile, stem and seed bell peppers and cut lengthwise into ¼-inch slices. In a 10- to 12-inch nonstick frying pan over medium-high heat, frequently stir peppers and oil until peppers are limp and browned, 12 to 14 minutes; reduce heat if peppers start to darken too much.

3. Cut chicken into ¼- by 2-inch strips. When pasta is barely tender to bite, add chicken to pasta water and cook until meat is no longer pink in center (cut to test), 2 to 3 more minutes. Drain mixture and return to pan.

4. Blend yogurt with cornstarch. Add mixture and taco sauce to peppers; stir often over medium heat until bubbling, 3 to 5 minutes.

5. Add the pepper-yogurt sauce and chopped cilantro to the pasta and chicken; mix to coat.

Per serving: 461 cal., 6.1% (28 cal.) from fat; 32 g protein; 3.1 g fat (0.6 g sat.); 74 g carbo (2.6 g fiber); 700 mg sodium; 45 mg chol.

Ralph Pujolar of San Francisco has been reading *Sunset* for more than 65 years. Though his wife does most of the cooking, he loves getting into the kitchen every now and then to "fiddle." Steamed rice (white or brown) and a crisp green salad are his favorite accompaniments for this dish.

Salsa Pork

Prep and cook time: About 25 minutes

Notes: Start cooking the rice first, then prepare the sauce and chops.

Makes: 6 servings

1½ cups **medium** or hot **tomato salsa**

1 can (20 oz.) **unsweetened crushed pineapple**

6 **boneless center-cut pork loin chops,** about 1 inch thick (about 2 lb. total)

6 cups hot cooked **rice**

1. Combine salsa and pineapple in a 12- to 14-inch frying pan. Bring to a boil over high heat and stir often until reduced to 2½ cups, about 10 minutes.

2. While sauce cooks, trim and discard outer fat from pork chops. Broil chops 4 to 6 inches from heat until lightly browned and no longer pink in thickest part (cut to test), about 9 minutes, turning once.

3. Arrange chops on a platter; top with sauce. Serve with rice.

Per serving: 574 cal., 16% (89 cal.) from fat; 41 g protein; 9.9 g fat (3.6 g sat.); 76 g carbo (1.4 g fiber); 354 mg sodium; 94 mg chol.

taco sauce, and cilantro, and adds chicken and pan-roasted bell peppers.

Salsa Chicken with Linguine

Prep and cook time: About 30 minutes

Notes: Start heating water for the pasta in a covered pan before assembling the rest of the ingredients.

Makes: 6 servings

15 minutes, then into the oven

Arriving home from work late one evening with less than an hour to pull dinner together, Wendy Nankeville of San Francisco created this dish with odds and ends from her refrigerator and pantry. She loves "ad-lib" cooking and often throws together impromptu meals with fresh and healthful finds from the city's farmers' market. Nankeville pairs her casserole with a red leaf lettuce and yellow bell pepper salad tossed with a balsamic vinaigrette.

Vegetarian Tamale Casserole

Prep and cook time: About 45 minutes

Makes: 4 servings

10 **corn tortillas** (6½ or 7 in.)

2 cups **canned diced tomatoes with juice (no salt added)**

1 tablespoon **chili powder**

¼ teaspoon **ground cumin**

1 cup **frozen corn kernels,** thawed

¼ cup (about 2 oz.) stemmed, seeded, and chopped **fresh jalapeño chilies**

1 cup chopped **red bell pepper**

¾ cup sliced **green onions**

1 can (15 oz.) **reduced-sodium black beans,** rinsed and drained

2 tablespoons minced **fresh cilantro**

1 cup shredded **reduced-fat cheddar cheese**

1. In a lightly oiled shallow 3½- to 4-quart casserole, arrange 4 tortillas so they cover the bottom. Stack remaining tortillas and cut into ¾-inch-wide strips; set aside. Mix tomatoes and juice with chili powder and cumin. Pour over whole tortillas. Top tomatoes with corn, then jalapeños, bell pepper, ½ cup onions, beans, and cilantro. Cover with ½ cup water.

2. Arrange tortilla strips evenly over filling, then sprinkle with cheese. Cover casserole with foil. Bake in a 400° oven until hot, about 20 minutes. Uncover casserole and bake until cheese is completely melted, about 5 more minutes. Sprinkle with remaining green onions just before serving.

Per serving: 371 cal., 21% (78 cal.) from fat; 20 g protein; 8.7 g fat (3.9 g sat.); 62 g carbo (12 g fiber); 554 mg sodium; 20 mg chol.

Crushed tortilla chips and a sprinkle of cheese make a crispy crust for chicken.

Jane Ingraham of Tucson serves her tortilla chip–coated chicken breasts with an extremely easy and flavorful cooked salsa that takes only a few minutes but gives you the satisfaction of making a sauce yourself.

Crusty Mexican Chicken

Prep and cook time: About 25 minutes

Notes: Regular tortilla chips produce a slightly crispier coating and add about 3 grams of fat per serving.

Makes: 4 servings

- 1 tablespoon **lime juice**
- 1 tablespoon **honey**
- ⅔ cup (about 2 oz.) crushed **no-fat-added** or regular **tortilla chips**
- 4 **boneless, skinless chicken breast halves** (1¼ lb. total), fat trimmed
- 1 can (14½ oz.) **diced tomatoes (no salt added)**
- ¼ cup **fresh cilantro**
- 1 teaspoon **garlic powder**
- ½ teaspoon **dried oregano**
- ½ cup shredded **jack cheese**
  Fresh cilantro sprigs
  Lime wedges

1. In a bowl, combine lime juice and honey. Place tortilla chips in a bag. Dip chicken pieces 1 at a time in juice mixture, then drop into chips and shake to coat. Place in a 9-inch-square baking dish. Bake in a 475° oven until no longer pink in center of thickest part (cut to test), about 15 minutes.

2. Meanwhile, in a blender or food processor, whirl tomatoes and their juice, ¼ cup cilantro, garlic powder, and oregano until smooth. Pour into a 2- to 3-quart pan and bring to a boil over high heat. Boil, partly covered to prevent spattering, until reduced to 1¼ cups, 4 to 5 minutes.

3. Sprinkle chicken with cheese and bake just until cheese melts, 1 to 2 minutes more.

4. Spoon tomato sauce equally onto 4 dinner plates; place a chicken piece on each and garnish with cilantro sprigs. Offer lime wedges to season to taste.

Per serving: 305 cal., 21% (63 cal.) from fat; 39 g protein; 7 g fat (3 g sat.); 21 g carbo (1.6 g fiber); 183 mg sodium; 97 mg chol.

Mickey Strang of McKinleyville, California, has been a frequent *Sunset* contributor since 1946. Healthful cooking is not a fad to her. "Once you pass 60, how you've eaten shows up more and more in how good you feel," she says. "My husband and I eat fairly low-fat; I think that's one reason we're as spry and energetic as we are."

Four-pepper Baked Chicken

Prep and cook time: About 45 minutes

Makes: 4 servings

- 1 **each red, green,** and **yellow bell pepper** (1¼ lb. total)
- 8 **boneless, skinless chicken thighs** (1¼ lb.), fat trimmed
- 1 can (7 oz.) **whole green chilies,** cut lengthwise into 8 equal pieces
- 1 cup **reduced-fat sour cream**
- 1 teaspoon **cornstarch**
- 3 to 4 cups hot cooked **rice**
  Salt and **pepper**

1. Preheat oven to 475°. Stem and seed bell peppers and thinly slice lengthwise. Place in a 9- by 13-inch baking dish and bake until tinged brown, about 15 minutes.

2. Meanwhile, trim fat from chicken, fold together the halves of each thigh to make a neat bundle, then wrap each with a chili piece.

3. Place chicken bundles on top of bell peppers; bake for 15 minutes. Smoothly blend sour cream with cornstarch and spoon over bundles. Continue to bake until chicken is no longer pink in center (cut to test), about 8 minutes.

4. Broil chicken 3 inches from heat until sour cream is speckled brown, about 2 minutes. Lift chicken and vegetables to a platter or to 4 individual plates; pour pan juices into a small pitcher. Serve chicken with hot cooked rice and pan juices. Season to taste with salt and pepper.

Per serving: 514 cal., 25% (126 cal.) from fat; 37 g protein; 14 g fat (5.6 g sat.); 58 g carbo (2.9 g fiber); 462 mg sodium; 138 mg chol. ◆

A muffin with crunch

Crunchy sesame seed and aromatic Asian sesame oil give exceptionally rich, toasted flavor to these sweet muffins. And if you use black sesame seed, it contrasts boldly with the orange carrot bits.

Sesame-Carrot Muffins

Prep and cook time: 50 to 55 minutes
Notes: Look for black sesame seed and Asian sesame oil made from toasted seed in well-stocked supermarkets or Asian grocery stores.
Makes: 12 muffins

- 2 tablespoons *each* **white** (regular) and **black sesame seed,** or all of 1 kind
- 1½ cups **whole-wheat flour**
- ½ teaspoon **baking powder**
- ½ teaspoon **baking soda**
- ½ teaspoon ground **cinnamon**
- ¾ cup **sugar**
- 2 large **eggs**
- 3 tablespoons **Asian sesame oil**
- 1½ cups shredded **carrots**

1. Shake sesame seed in a 7- to 8-inch frying pan over medium-high heat until white seed is lightly browned and black seed begins to pop, about 5 minutes.
2. In a small bowl, mix 3 tablespoons sesame seed with flour, baking powder, baking soda, and cinnamon.
3. In a large bowl, beat to blend sugar, eggs, oil, and ¼ cup water. Stir in dry ingredients and carrots just until evenly moistened.
4. Divide batter among 12 paper-lined muffin cups (2½ in. wide). Sprinkle tops evenly with remaining sesame seed.
5. Bake muffins in a 350° oven until browned and tops spring back when lightly pressed, about 35 minutes.
6. Remove from pan; serve warm, or cool on racks.

Per muffin: 165 cal., 33% (54 cal.) from fat; 3.8 g protein; 6 g fat (1 g sat.); 26 g carbo.; 68 mg sodium; 35 mg chol. ◆

by CHRISTINE WEBER HALE

The French have a word for it: verjus

You could also call it tart grape juice—or the latest answer to balsamic vinegar

San Francisco chef Gary Danko, winner of the 1995 James Beard award for best California chef, waxes enthusiastic about fruity-tart *verjus,* the unfermented juice of unripe wine grapes.

"It's delicate enough to make a salad dressing that you want to pair with wine. You can use verjus to deglaze a roasting pan for a sauce, in a marinade or baste for meats, even in a spritzer. Because of the lack of big acid in verjus, dressings and sauces need a lot less fat to tame them."

This happy by-product of winemaking has been popular in Europe for centuries. When growers thin their grapes (to concentrate the flavor of the remaining grapes), the thinnings are pressed to make verjus (pronounced ver-*joo*). Now two California producers are bringing verjus to the kitchens of Western chefs and home cooks.

The product from Fusion Foods, called Napa Valley Verjus, is the most widely available. If a specialty foods store in your area doesn't carry it, order by mail; call (707) 963-0206. A 750-ml. bottle costs $9.95, a 375-ml. bottle $6.95, plus shipping. Navarro Vineyards sells verjus by mail only—a 750-ml. bottle costs $7.50, a 375-ml. bottle $4.75, plus shipping; call (800) 537-9463. Other wineries occasionally sell verjus at their tasting rooms.

Once opened, verjus keeps one to two weeks in the refrigerator. For longer storage, just freeze it in ice cube trays, then transfer the cubes to an airtight container.

Salmon Poached in Verjus

Prep and cook time: About 15 minutes
Makes: 2 servings

- 1 cup **verjus**
- ¼ cup finely chopped **shallots**
- 2 **salmon steaks,** each 1¼ inch thick (1 lb. total)
- 1 tablespoon **butter**

1. Place the verjus and the chopped shallots in an 8- to 10-inch frying pan over high heat. Add the salmon steaks. Cover and bring to a simmer. Reduce the heat and simmer until the fish is no longer translucent in the center, 4 to 5 minutes.
2. Lift the fish onto 2 dinner plates and keep warm. Strain the juices and return to the pan. Boil juices over high heat until they have been reduced to ⅓ cup, 5 to 7 minutes, then whisk in the butter. Pour over the fish.

Per serving: 429 cal., 38% (162 cal.) from fat; 40 g protein; 18 g fat (5.5 g sat.); 23 g carbo (0.2 g fiber); 159 mg sodium; 125 mg chol. ◆

simply VERJUS

Gary Danko shares these quick suggestions for enjoying verjus.

- *Verjus vinaigrette.* Combine ½ cup **verjus,** 1 tablespoon **extra-virgin olive oil,** 2 teaspoons minced **shallot,** ¼ teaspoon minced **garlic,** and **salt** and **pepper** to taste. Serve over mixed salad greens.
- *Verjus fruit salad.* Splash verjus over your favorite combination of fruit (use about 3 tablespoons of **verjus** per 2½ cups of **fruit,** such as bananas, apples, grapes, and kiwi fruit).
- *Verjus spritzer.* Place 2 **orange** slices in a large ice-filled glass. Pour 1 cup **unflavored sparkling water** and ¼ cup **verjus** on top; stir to blend.

by ELAINE JOHNSON

JOHN SAMORA

Zip Killeen, manager of Tee Pee Mexican Food, sits behind the renowned Mary-Lou (foreground), as well as impossible-looking baked chile rellenos.

Stalking the lost tortilla

A Phoenician faces midlife—and gains a few pounds—by searching for the authentic Mexican restaurants of her youth

I craved comfort food—I turned 40 this year. Recently, these two disparate facts sent me on a mission: to revisit the old, family-owned Mexican restaurants I had haunted as a svelte 20-something, back in the days when metropolitan Phoenix wasn't crowded with theme restaurants, and my squinting eyes didn't automatically search out the "lite" and "heart-smart" items on a menu. Call it denial, call it a midlife crisis: I had to find out if I could still handle the lost tortilla of my youth.

CAROLINA'S MEXICAN FOOD
My first stop during a week's worth of pilgrimages was Carolina's, a neighborhood eatery in south-central Phoenix. Much to my relief, the low-slung building—from its concrete floor to its worn seating—had changed little since my last visit. Okay—the menu above the front counter now advertises chicken (the invasion of the lite!) as a meat choice for the house tacos, enchiladas, and *burros* (burritos), but guacamole is still about as close as you get to salad.

Throwing cholesterol counts to the wind, I ordered the Oaxaca Special—a chorizo, bean, potato, and cheese burro—and vowed to feel famished enough someday to devour a foot-long chorizo-and-bean burro. I left cradling a bag of still-warm tortillas, with visions of quesadillas to buoy my spirits.

GARCIA'S LAS AVENIDAS
Garcia's Las Avenidas in west Phoenix is just three blocks from the site of the small take-out stand and two picnic tables that Olivia Garcia opened in 1956. From that humble beginning, Olivia and her late husband, Julio, created a franchise of Mexican restaurants. But there were neither neighbors nor family in the world of corporate chains, so in the '80s the Garcias sold their interest in the franchise and opened a new restaurant back in the old neighborhood.

Some of my college-era favorites are still on the menu: *pollo fundido* (chicken wrapped in a tortilla and deep-fried, with cream cheese and cheddar melted on top), *gorditas* (small quesadillas served with ranch-style beans), and *machaca* (spicy shredded beef) and eggs, a popular post-all-nighter eye-opener. Here, too, homemade menudo is on the menu, but only on weekends. (It's said to be a surefire hangover cure, which is why, theoretically, one should not have to eat it during the week.)

EL MOLINO
The last time I had eaten lunch at El Molino in southeast Phoenix, I had been the victim of a surprise bridal shower. I vaguely recalled the green corn tamales, the wonderful cheese enchiladas, and an embarrassing array of gift-wrapped boxes filled with fringed bedroom attire.

In the ensuing decade since my nuptials, Richard Carbajal Jr., grandson of Rosa Carbajal, who still runs El Molino in Phoenix, opened his own El Molino in Scottsdale. The recipes are the same, but in deference to contemporary din-

by **NORA BURBA TRULSSON**

ing trends in Scottsdale, Richard cut out the lard. In deference to my health (and in fear of possibly finding a tattered bit of fringe in the oleanders surrounding the old El Molino patio), I chose to lunch at the newer Scottsdale locale. The award-winning green corn tamales are still great, as are the green chili burros and rolled beef taquitos.

LOS OLIVOS MEXICAN PATIO

Also in Scottsdale, the Los Olivos Mexican Patio, a landmark building and restaurant, dates back to the days when the town had a vibrant barrio and commercial olive groves. The Corral family built the original adobe core of the building in the late 1920s; through the years they operated it as everything from a pool hall to a chapel.

Today, Los Olivos sits next to the Scottsdale Center for the Arts and is a favorite of generations of Scottsdale natives. I've always liked its free-form, Mayan-inspired remodel—and the great live music on the now-enclosed patio. Happily, *huevos rancheros* still makes the list of specials, as do buttery mushroom-and-cheese enchiladas.

Phoenix's Best Mex

Carolina's Mexican Food. Tuesdays through Saturdays for breakfast, lunch, and early dinner; Sundays for breakfast and lunch. 1202 E. Mohave St., Phoenix; (602) 252-1503.

Garcia's Las Avenidas. Daily for lunch and dinner. 2212 N. 35th Ave., Phoenix; 272-5584.

El Molino. Mondays through Saturdays for late breakfast, lunch, and dinner. 7033 E. Indian School Rd., Scottsdale; 946-4494.

Los Olivos Mexican Patio. Daily for lunch and dinner. 7328 E. Second St., Scottsdale; 946-2256.

Rosita's Place. Daily for breakfast, lunch, and dinner. 2310 E. McDowell Rd., Phoenix; 244-9779.

Tee Pee Mexican Food. Daily for lunch and dinner. 4144 E. Indian School, Phoenix; 956-0178.

Carolina Valenzuela hoists a #14 combo at her Phoenix restaurant.

ROSITA'S PLACE

The way I remember Rosita's Place, a portrait of John F. Kennedy hung above the back bar, and the old screen banged loudly each time a patron walked through the door. When I returned to the restaurant's newest location, in central Phoenix, the screen door and JFK had been replaced by more upscale trappings, but owner-chef Micela Medina's hearty soups still dominated the menu. There's *cosido* (chunks of beef and vegetables in a savory broth), *cazuela* (a machaca stew), shrimp *sopa* (soup), and, of course, menudo. Rosita's is also one of the few places in town where you can find *chicharrónes* (deep-fried pork skins) in a jalapeño sauce on the regular menu.

TEE PEE MEXICAN FOOD

My final stop was Tee Pee Mexican Food (the Tee Pee Tap Room to us old-timers), an east Phoenix hangout since the 1960s. The red vinyl booths, rock walls, and knotty-pine paneling haven't changed a bit since those days when my friends and I solved the world's problems over steaming plates of Sonoran-style tacos and fluffy chile rellenos.

This visit, I finally got around to ordering a Mary-Lou, which is essentially a quesadilla filled with green chilies. Somehow Mary-Lous have made their way onto the menus of virtually every Mexican restaurant in Phoenix. The Tee Pee's Mary-Lou, I've been told by authorities on this arcane subject, is the original, named after a patron who frequented the restaurant in the 1960s.

Doggie bag in hand, I left wondering how many quesadillas the mysterious Mary-Lou ordered in her lifetime. Maybe she invented the Mary-Lou to solve *her* midlife crisis. All I know is, after a week of eating in the carbo-*queso* hangouts of my youth, I am sated—and cured. ◆

NORMAN A. PLATE

Succulent oven-braised lamb shanks with vegetables are served on a bed of rice.

Sunset's Kitchen Cabinet

"When my husband and I were first courting, we found we had a lot in common, including a favorite restaurant meal at Paul's in Berkeley, which had closed before we met. Fortunately, I had learned to make the dish myself. Love blossomed, and in 20 years we never tire of Turkish Lamb," writes Pam Peeters. Rice or couscous makes a nice accompaniment.

Turkish Lamb Shanks

Pam Peeters
Sunol, California

Prep and cook time: About 2 hours

Makes: 4 servings

- 4 **lamb shanks** (about 1 lb. each), bones cracked
- 4 **onions** (about ½ lb. each), quartered
- 1 **bell pepper** (about ½ lb.), stemmed, seeded, and sliced
- 1 can (14½ oz.) **stewed tomatoes**
- 1½ cups **chicken broth**
- ½ teaspoon **pepper**
- ½ teaspoon **dried thyme**
  Hot cooked **rice** or couscous
  Salt

1. Place shanks in a 12- by 17-inch roasting pan. Bake, uncovered, in a 450° oven for 15 minutes. Add onions; continue roasting until shanks are browned, about 30 minutes longer.

2. Remove pan from oven; reduce heat to 400°. Add to pan the bell pepper, tomatoes with their juice, broth, pepper, and thyme. Cover tightly; continue baking until meat pulls easily from bone, about 1½ hours longer. Skim fat from pan juices; discard fat. Divide shanks, vegetables, and juices equally among 4 shallow bowls containing hot cooked rice. Add salt to taste.

Per serving: 447 cal., 24% (108 cal.) from fat; 56 g protein; 12 g fat (4.1 g sat.); 30 g carbo (6.8 g fiber); 459 mg sodium; 160 mg chol.

Bumpy Chicken

Richard Scales
Bellevue, Washington

His wife's love for capers spurred Richard Scales to experiment in the kitchen. The results are moist chicken breasts baked under a blanket of whole capers, finely chopped mushrooms, and onion.

Prep and cook time: About 40 minutes

Makes: 4 servings

- 2 cups (6 oz.) finely chopped **mushrooms**
- 1 **onion** (about 6 oz.), chopped
- 3 large cloves **garlic,** minced
- 4 **boneless, skinless chicken breast halves** (about 6 oz. each)
- 2 tablespoons **Dijon mustard**
- 2 tablespoons **capers,** drained
- 1 teaspoon **balsamic vinegar**
- ¼ teaspoon **hot sauce**
- 2 tablespoons **reduced-fat** or regular **mayonnaise**
  Parsley sprigs
  Salt

1. In a 10- to 12-inch nonstick frying pan, stir mushrooms, onion, and garlic over medium-high heat until mushrooms begin to brown, 8 to 10 minutes.

2. Meanwhile, rinse chicken and pat dry. Place breasts in a 9- by 13-inch baking dish and bake, uncovered, in a 375° oven for 10 minutes.

3. When the mushroom mixture is done, remove it from the heat. Stir in the mustard, capers, vinegar, hot sauce, and mayonnaise.

4. Spread the mushroom mixture over the chicken and continue baking until chicken is no longer pink in center of the thickest part (cut to test), 15 to 20 minutes longer. Transfer to plates and garnish with parsley sprigs. Add salt to taste.

Per serving: 246 cal., 16% (40 cal.) from fat; 41 g protein; 4.4 g fat (1.1 g sat.); 7.2 g carbo (1.3 g fiber); 452 mg sodium; 101 mg chol.

by LINDA LAU ANUSASANANAN

Cabbage and Radicchio Stir-fry

Patti Devlin
Lafayette, California

Every two weeks, Patti Devlin takes her four young children to the Berkeley Bowl, a market filled with fresh and often unusual foods of the world. The family makes all kinds of culinary discoveries, which Devlin frequently takes home to cook. One trip resulted in this sophisticated combination of sweet napa cabbage, bitter radicchio, and nutty sesame oil. The stir-fry might not suit all kids' tastes, but the Devlin children like its fresh flavor.

Prep and cook time: About 10 minutes
Makes: 4 to 6 servings

- 1 head (about 1¼ lb.) **napa cabbage**
- 1 head (about 10 oz.) **radicchio** or red cabbage
- 1 teaspoon **salad oil**
- 2 cloves **garlic**, minced
- 1 tablespoon minced **fresh ginger**
- 1 teaspoon **fennel seed**
- 2 tablespoons **soy sauce**
- ¼ cup chopped **fresh cilantro**
- 1 tablespoon **Asian (toasted) sesame oil**
- 1 tablespoon **black sesame seed** (optional)

1. Remove core from napa cabbage; discard core. Cut the cabbage crosswise into thin shreds to make about 2 quarts. Cut the radicchio in half through core; remove and discard core. Cut the radicchio into thin shreds to make about 1 quart.

2. Place a wok or 5- to 6-quart pan over high heat. When the pan is hot, add salad oil, the garlic and ginger, and the fennel seed; stir 30 seconds. Add the napa cabbage, the radicchio, and the soy sauce; cover pan and cook for 1 minute. Remove pan lid, and stir-fry until vegetables wilt, about 2 minutes longer. Stir in half of the chopped cilantro and all of the sesame oil.

3. Transfer vegetables to a serving dish; sprinkle with remaining cilantro and sesame seed before serving.

Per serving: 58 cal., 52% (30 cal.) from fat; 2 g protein; 3.3 g fat (0.5 g sat.); 6.3 g carbo (1.7 g fiber); 356 mg sodium; 0 mg chol.

Banana Almond Cake

Jan McHargue
Benicia, California

A bag of ripe bananas inspired Jan McHargue to create this coffee cake. You can enjoy the banana cake with its spicy brown sugar–almond topping and filling for brunch, with coffee, or for dessert.

Prep and cook time: About 1 hour and 10 minutes
Makes: 12 servings

- ½ cup (¼ lb.) **butter** or margarine
- ½ cup firmly packed **brown sugar**
- 1½ teaspoons **ground cinnamon**
- ¼ teaspoon **ground nutmeg**
- ½ cup **sliced almonds**
- ¾ cup **granulated sugar**
- 3 **large eggs**
- 2 teaspoons grated **orange** peel
- 1¼ cups mashed ripe **banana**
- 2½ cups **all-purpose flour**
- ½ cup **whole-wheat flour**
- 1½ teaspoons **baking powder**
- 1 teaspoon **baking soda**
- ½ teaspoon **salt**
- ⅔ cup **buttermilk**

1. Melt ¼ cup of the butter. Pour 2 tablespoons of the melted butter into an 8-cup bundt pan; brush the butter over pan sides and bottom. Mix together the brown sugar, cinnamon, nutmeg, and almonds. Sprinkle bottom of pan with half the brown sugar mixture; combine the remaining mixture with the remaining melted butter; set aside.

2. In a large bowl, beat remaining ¼ cup butter with granulated sugar until blended. Beat in eggs, 1 at a time, until blended. Beat in orange peel and banana.

3. Mix all-purpose and whole-wheat flours, baking powder, soda, and salt. Add to banana mixture along with the buttermilk; stir until well blended.

4. Pour half the batter into prepared pan. Spoon remaining brown sugar mixture evenly over top; cover with remaining batter.

5. Bake in a 350° oven until a long wood skewer inserted into the thickest part of the cake comes out clean, about 50 minutes. Cool the cake on a rack about 5 minutes, then invert cake onto a serving plate. Serve the cake warm or cool.

Per serving: 333 cal., 32% (108 cal.) from fat; 6.5 g protein; 12 g fat (5.5 g sat.); 52 g carbo (1.9 g fiber); 371 mg sodium; 74 mg chol. ◆

A ribbon of streusel runs through the center and glazes the top of a banana cake.

Chef Jean-Marc Fullsack serves a confetti of vegetables and pasta over white bean–pesto sauce (see page 40).

February

foodguide

by **JERRY ANNE DI VECCHIO**

SUZANNE SMITH

How you make chile rellenos can start arguments.

Here and in Mexico, I've come across chilies stuffed with cheese, meat, fish, shellfish, vegetables, and many less familiar ingredients. Sometimes the chilies are dipped in batter and fried, sometimes they are grilled, sometimes they are baked with a topping, sometimes they are layered with a filling. And the chili itself isn't always the same. Sometimes it's hot; most times it's not.

In fact, most anything goes—which troubles culinary traditionalists who favor specific combinations or a certain structure. To cooks like me, such flexibility is extremely appealing.

And I rejoice in how comforting, cozy, and cordial this simple version of chile rellenos is for a weeknight supper. When you cut through the tender-crisp topping into the mild chilies, they ooze with melted jalapeño cheese. With a crisp salad, more warm tortillas, and a gutsy Zinfandel, you forget about any arguments.

---

a **TASTE** *of the* **WEST**

The big cheese of chile rellenos

Chile Rellenos Casserole

Prep and cook time: 30 to 35 minutes
Makes: 5 to 6 servings

- 4 **corn tortillas** (6 to 7 in.)
- 1 tablespoon **salad oil**
- ½ cup finely chopped **onion**
- ¾ pound **jalapeño-flavor jack cheese**
- 2 cans (7 oz. each) **whole green chilies,** drained
- ½ cup chopped **fresh cilantro**
- 4 **large eggs**
- 2 tablespoons **all-purpose flour**

1. Stack tortillas and cut into about ½-inch squares.

tools →

My father, a putterer who could fix anything, was forever acquiring some oddly elegant tool—new or secondhand—designed to perform a special function, even if he used it only once. His search for these gizmos continued long after I had my own home, and occasionally an item would find its way into my kitchen. One of my favorites came from a junkyard: a big wood mallet, a bit weathered and stained, that Dad returned to life with a little sanding and a new handle.

Technically, it's the tool of cabinetmakers, carpenters, and tinners, who like wood because it causes less bruising than metal. This is also why I like wood. Its impact is gentler than metal's, making it ideal for pounding boneless pieces of meat and poultry (covered with sheets of plastic wrap to keep both mallet and meat clean). Pounded meats cook more quickly and are more tender, as Christine Weber Hale details in this month's Quick Cook, page 45.

I also like the way my mallet reduces chunks of dry bread to crumbs or pulverizes sheets of caramel or brittle candy—once those foods are neatly contained in a heavy plastic food bag.

Most food mallets have metal surfaces or are all metal, often with those vicious jagged teeth that beat meat to mush, imprint my wood countertops, tear holes in plastic, and have to be washed well. Another type, a thick metal disk with a stem, is literally a pain to use. With every pound, the hit transfers right into your arm.

If you want a wood mallet, you'll have to shop a hardware or building supply store. My old one, almost 4 inches wide, is rare today. Most wood mallets are 2½ to 3 inches wide and generally cost $10 or less. Don't delay shopping if you want one. Cheaper rubber mallets are rapidly replacing the wood ones—and although technically as effective, they smell.

2. In an 11- to 12-inch frying pan, combine 1 teaspoon oil and the onion. Stir often over medium-high heat until onion is limp, about 3 minutes. Add tortillas and remaining oil, turn heat to high, and stir until small bits start to brown, 8 to 10 minutes.

3. Scatter tortilla mixture in an 8- by 12-inch oval or rectangular casserole (at least 2 in. deep).

4. Shred 2 cups cheese; sprinkle 1 cup over the tortilla mixture. Cut remaining cheese into sticks about ¼ inch thick.

5. Drain chilies and stuff equally with cheese sticks. Lay chilies in a single layer in casserole. Sprinkle with cilantro.

6. Separate eggs. Whip whites with a mixer on high speed until they hold soft but distinct peaks; set aside.

7. Mix egg yolks (use unwashed beaters) with flour, then beat on high speed until paler in color, about 2 minutes. Beat half of the whites into the yolks, then fold in remaining whites and pour mixture over chilies, scraping bowl. Top egg mixture with shredded cheese.

8. Bake in a 375° oven until topping is golden brown and feels firm when lightly touched, about 15 minutes. Cutting through chilies, scoop from casserole to serve.

Per serving: 358 cal., 60% (216 cal.) from fat; 20 g protein; 24 g fat (11 g sat.); 17 g carbo (1.9 g fiber); 854 mg sodium; 202 mg chol.

Exposing leeks

Leeks, unlike dry onions, don't neatly seal their layered interior with a skin. As they grow, dust and grit (from the sandy soil they like best) usually sift down through the tough green leaves to lodge in the tender, pale green parts.

To make use of a leek's tender part, trim off the root end, pull off the coarse outer layers, trim off the coarse green leaves, and then cut the leek in half lengthwise. Grasping a half to preserve its shape, hold the top end under cool running water and flip it to separate the layers and rinse out any soil. To cook the leek halves as a single piece, tie their midsections together with cotton string. Otherwise, chop and use.

To cook leeks whole, trim off the root, pull off the coarse outer layers, and trim down to the white section. Usually, soil doesn't get into the white part of the leek, but if it does, you can see it, and you need to trim further.

As a cooked vegetable, leeks are mild and delectable. I like to steam them on a rack over boiling water in a covered pan until they're tender when pierced, 5 to 10 minutes. Season them with butter, extra-virgin olive oil, parmesan or blue cheese, or pesto—any flavor that complements onions.

foodguide

SUZANNE SMITH

SEASONAL *note*

A classic duo

When friends and family from the East visited as I was growing up, my mother liked to show off Western differences by serving grapefruit and avocado salad. To these outlanders, the salad was as novel as avocados were exotic.

Avocados eventually lost their exoticness, and as food fashions changed, the salad got a little rusty and faded into the background.

Of late, however, I've noticed grapefruit and avocado salad popping up on menus of restaurants most chic. What's new? The dressing has lightened up. Once it was predictably oily and full of poppy seed. Now it's merely refreshing and, in my opinion, much more suitable. With grapefruit at its peak and avocados plentiful again, why not lead off dinner with this attractive classic?

Grapefruit and Avocado Salad

Prep time: About 15 minutes
Makes: 4 servings

  2 **ruby grapefruit** (about 2 lb. total)
  1 firm, ripe **avocado** (about ¾ lb.)
  2 heads **Belgian endive** (6 to 8 oz. total), rinsed and drained
  6 tablespoons **lime juice**
  1 tablespoon **honey**
  4 teaspoons chopped **salted roasted pistachios**
     Salt

1. With a sharp knife, cut peel and outer membrane from grapefruit. To release fruit segments, hold grapefruit over a bowl and cut between membrane and fruit. Squeeze membrane juice into bowl. Discard peel and membrane.

2. Cut avocado in half, pry out and discard pit, then pull skin from avocado and discard. Moisten avocado halves with a little of the grapefruit juice and set aside.

3. Trim discolored stem ends from endive. Finely sliver endive vertically and lay slivers on 4 salad plates.

4. Cut avocado halves vertically into slices. Arrange equal portions of avocado and grapefruit segments with endive on each plate.

5. To grapefruit juice, add lime juice and honey. Whisk to blend. Drizzle salads with this dressing, then sprinkle with pistachios and add salt to taste.

Per serving: 179 cal., 55% (99 cal.) from fat; 2.7 g protein; 11 g fat (1.7 g sat.); 21 g carbo (3 g fiber); 34 mg sodium; 0 mg chol.

FOOD *news*

Sizing up filo

A little over two years ago in this column, I complained about filo dough. I was disgruntled because all the filo I'd ever bought came in 1-pound packages of very large sheets that had to be cut or folded to fit any pan I owned. And unless I was making baklava for 30, I had to plan carefully before opening the package in order to preserve the quality of the unused dough for future use—especially if the dough had been frozen.

Well, the folks at the Fillo Factory (yes, there are a lot of ways to spell filo) have come up with a ridiculously simple solution: they now package filo in ½-pound boxes that contain about 22 sheets of dough cut to a very usable 9-by 13-inch size. You can always overlap sheets if you want a bigger piece.

As I write, supermarket distribution for this product is in the works. But all you have to do to get fresh filo is pick up the phone and order for same-day shipping. The toll-free number is (800) 653-4556; ½ pound of filo costs $1.50, plus shipping. Your favorite pastries with crisp crusts are now easier than ever, and I'm happy.

BOOKS *on* FOOD

Mexico's tasty tidbits

Chilies roasting, succulent pork sizzling, parched corn masa toasting, the burst of lime as the fruit is squeezed—all are part of an aromatic cloud that floats day and night from the stands and stalls of street vendors in Mexico. Tempting morsels built from these ingredients are the subject of Reed Hearon's newest book, *Bocaditos: The Little Dishes of Mexico* (Chronicle Books, San Francisco, 1997; $15.95). In it, he explores many colorful types of *bocaditos*, "little bites." His roster of appetizers includes *botanas*, "plugs" or "stoppers" for appetites; *antojitos*, "little whims" that are often miniature versions of foods such as enchiladas and tamales; and *mariscos*, "seafood dishes." They aren't fussy. The look and tastes are bold and earthy, as if they came right from the hands of a vendor.

Hearon, who is well known as a chef and as creator of the San Francisco restaurants LuLu, Rose Pistola, and Café Marimba, immerses himself in the fabric of cuisines that inspire him. And in *Bocaditos*, he puts techniques such as dry roasting on a *comal* (a griddle of sorts), and ingredients such as the many chilies, into an easy-to-comprehend, contemporary form—without losing the spirit and flavor of authenticity.

This 120-page paperback includes about four dozen specific dishes (many are pictured in color) supplemented by building-block recipes—including *pipián verde* (pumpkin-seed sauce) and *picadillo* (a spicy meat filling)—that add potential for extensive variations. ◆

by KAREN MacNEIL

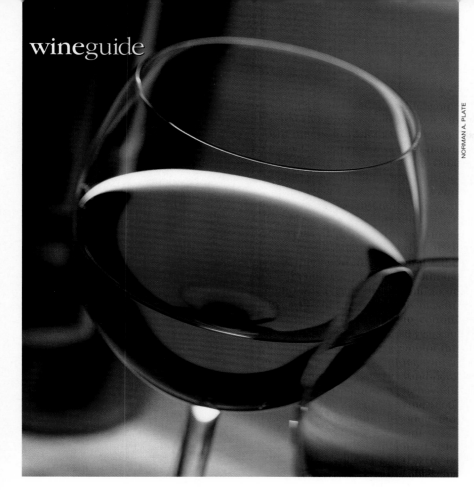

NORMAN A. PLATE

It's easy to love Zins

If Zinfandel were a guy, about half the women in America would want to marry him. Consider the facts: Zinfandel is big and muscular, generous and trustworthy. You can curl up with it and read trashy novels. Or you can bring it to a sophisticated restaurant. Zinfandel doesn't make you do all the work in the relationship. And (unlike some wines we know) it isn't on an ego trip. Best of all, Zinfandel has this way of making you fall in love with it.

Zinfandel is California's most widely planted (geographically speaking) red grape, and the wines made from it have always had a cult following. In the last year, however, the number of Zinfandel fans has skyrocketed, thanks to the multitude of extraordinary Zins that have come onto the market. Unlike, say, finding a great Merlot, finding a great Zinfandel is a piece of cake. As for price, it doesn't hurt that most Zinfandels are a steal.

The Zinfandel grape can be (and is) made into everything from white wine to sweet port in California. But what Zinfandel drinkers rave about is true Zinfandel—a massively mouth-filling dry *red* wine crammed with jammy, almost chewy blackberry, spice, and boysenberry flavors. True Zinfandel begs for that great American classic: a thick, juicy steak.

White Zinfandel, by contrast, is a fairly feeble, sweet wine generally produced in huge amounts from grapes grown in lesser vineyards. First made in 1972 by the Sutter Home Winery, white Zinfandel (which is actually light pink) is created by quickly removing the grapes' red skins before much color is imparted to the wine.

Zinfandel has a long history in California, though its precise origin remains a mystery and no one knows quite how it got here. Curiously, almost no other wine region in the world has plantings of the grape and, as a result, Zinfandel is often thought of as an indigenous North American variety. It is not, however, a native grape. Zinfandel belongs—as do Cabernet Sauvignon, Merlot, and Pinot Noir—to the classic European species *vinifera.*

Zinfandel vineyards are among the oldest in California. These prized vineyards produce wines of such rich concentration that to distinguish them vintners often use the term "old vines" on the label. Although the phrase has no legal definition, it's generally used to designate wines from vineyards that have been in continuous production for at least 40 years and often as long as 100 years. One of the oldest vineyards in California, in fact, is Amador County's "Grand-père" Vineyard, which is thought to have been planted with Zinfandel in the 1860s.

Here are some terrific Zinfandels to fall in love with.

- **Green & Red "Chiles Mill" Zinfandel 1994, $16.** Boysenberries and sweet brambles; lush, long, and soft.
- **Limerick Lane "Collins Vineyard" Zinfandel 1994, $16.** Like diving into a pool of boysenberries.
- **A. Rafanelli Zinfandel 1994, $15.50.** Gorgeously deep and spicy. Primordial.
- **Ridge Lytton Springs Zinfandel 1994, $20.** Stellar; among the most elegant of all Zinfandels.
- **Rosenblum "Napa" Zinfandel 1994, $14.** Dazzlingly bright cherry fruit.

Finally, if you find a '95 rather than a '94 of one of the above Zinfandels, don't hesitate to buy. ◆

WINE DICTIONARY: *aftertaste*

Also known as a wine's "finish," aftertaste is the flavor that lingers in the mouth after a wine has been swallowed. The best wines have a long aftertaste that is reminiscent of the flavor of the wine itself. Poor wines may have almost no aftertaste (thankfully) or else a strange, discordant aftertaste that may be related to faulty winemaking. — *K. M.*

SOME LIKE IT

hot!

The names hook you first. Ring of Fire. Devil Drops. Dan T's Inferno. Then you see the visuals: vampires, demons, scenes of pain. Yes, inside these bottles lurks a monster, a fiery beast with the power to scorch your tongue off. If the thought of hot sauces makes you run to the store, not the faucet, join the club. These liquid infernos are crowding grocery aisles, spawning Web sites on the Internet, and fueling the growth of stores like Hot Hot Hot in Pasadena, a self-described

by **ELAINE JOHNSON**
photographs by **GEOFFREY NILSEN**

head shop for heat seekers. A top seller at Hot Hot Hot and other stores is Dave's Gourmet Insanity Sauce, an off-the-scale sauce made with the same extract used in pepper spray. Which prompts the question: Is it lunacy that attracts us to hot sauces?

Perhaps not lunacy, but at least a little thrill-seeking and a chance to prove just how hot you can take it.

Veterans of the hot sauce world such as Tabasco and Pickapeppa have been grocery store staples for generations, enjoyed for their moderate heat and predictability. What's new are the boutique players, which are entering the market by the hundreds. Sheer zaniness seems to drive their sales—zany ingredients like sweet potatoes and bananas, zany packaging, zany personnel, and zany heat levels.

Hot sauces from the new "microbreweries" sport some of the most creative packaging in the food industry. "Our sauces arouse more than tastebuds!" is the motto of PepperTown USA in Van Nuys, California, maker of Bad Girls in Heat, Fifi's Nasty Little Secret, and Kitten's Big Banana, all with pinup-style graphics.

Having a crazy character at the company helm doesn't hurt sales, either. Dave Hirschkop, a fresh-faced 29-year-old San Francisco resident and "spicemeister" of Dave's Gourmet, may be the most legendary hot sauce guru. He shows up at trade shows in a straitjacket. Hirschkop was the first to create a hot sauce from a concentrate of capsaicin, the most common of the compounds that give chilies their bite. The idea was born five years ago, when he was running a burrito restaurant.

"Basically, I have a sick mind. We were open till late, and drunks would come in and be really obnoxious. I thought, how can I get rid of them? I started thinking about what makes chilies hot, and came up with this really hot sauce that I would put in their order. For most people, the amount on a tip of a pencil is enough to season a whole pot of food."

Personalities aside, the business of hot sauces still boils down to the chilies. Hot sauce microbreweries have convinced buyers that hotter is better

(though there's no industrywide heat measurement for hot sauces) and that a sauce made from habanero chilies is the best. "When habaneros first became mainstream, we had one or two habanero sauces. Now we have 80 or 90," says Tim Eidson, co-owner of Mo Hotta Mo Betta, a mail-order company specializing in hot and spicy foods.

Even the big kids on the block are responding. Having produced its Tabasco sauce (from chilies of the same name) since 1868, the McIlhenny Company

Chili crazy: the hot stuff sends Dave Hirschkop of Dave's Gourmet Insanity Sauce for his straitjacket.

recently introduced a habanero sauce, as well as a green jalapeño sauce.

WHAT MAKES *it* HURT *so* GOOD?

The heat of a chili (and a hot sauce made from it) depends on three factors. First, there's the genetic component. Habaneros are at the top of the charts for intrinsic heat, jalapeños quite a bit lower. But even within a variety, not all chilies are created equal: the 'Red Savina', a habanero from Ventura County, California, carries *The Guinness Book of World Records* distinction of hottest spice in the world. Frank Garcia, who named the 'Red Savina' after his mother, proudly notes that his chili is almost twice as hot as standard habaneros.

A plant's environment and growing conditions also affect heat. "Any stress can make chilies hotter: too much wind, too little heat, too little water," says Paul Bosland, professor of horticulture at New Mexico State University and a director of the nonprofit Chile Institute, an organization devoted to the study of capsicums.

The last part of the equation is our sensory perception. Different chilies have distinct flavor profiles that play their own heat tricks. Habaneros and their close cousins, Scotch bonnets, taste very fruity. "They burn in the back of the throat, and linger," says Bosland. "Tabascos glow all over the inner mouth. It's a sharp, quickly dissipating burn." Jalapeños have a green bell pepper flavor, while cayennes are sweet like red bell peppers; the heat from these and related chilies such as serrano and pasilla "hits you in the front of the mouth, tip of the tongue, and lips," says Bosland.

Why is one person's pain another's pleasure?

"There are two theories," he explains. "The first is that you're desensitizing your receptors for pain. You eat chilies and a molecular compound signals nerves to tell the brain you have pain. Eventually you use up the compound and you can't signal the brain. The other theory is Pavlovian: In the past, you've eaten chilies and your body produced endorphins to block the pain. Now when you eat chilies, your body remembers and makes endorphins in anticipation of the pain."

COOLING *the* FIRE

Even confirmed hot sauce aficionados know times when the rush of pleasure becomes a rush of pain. Theories abound on the best antidote for the sting. Some swear by a guzzle of beer, others argue in favor of a mouthful of bread or spoonful of sugar. We've had the best luck nibbling on lime wedges and eating yogurt or ice cream.

Cooling the fire is fine when pain strikes hard, but what people enjoy about hot sauces is the flirt with danger, the wild ride on a sensory roller coaster that leaves you gasping, glowing, and begging for more.

Our favorite global *scorchers*

Because intensity varies so much from one hot sauce to another, we've assigned heat levels to our favorite hot sauces, as well as to our recipes (see page 38):

🌶 Timid   🌶🌶🌶 Yikes!

🌶🌶 Feisty   🌶🌶🌶🌶 SOS!

We've grouped these sauces in five categories: three regional types (including sauces made in the style of a region but produced elsewhere), scorchers, and wild cards. Choosing our favorites was tough. After polling the experts, we narrowed the list to these top picks. Gotta-try-'em choices are starred.

LOUISIANA

These sauces are a fermented mash of cayennes or other chilies, vinegar, and salt. Most have a strong vinegar flavor.

🌶 *Iguana Red Pepper Sauce.* Tangy-sweet with a complex carrot base.

🌶🌶 *Spitfire Red Hot Pepper Sauce.* Tart with a hint of garlic, Scotch bonnet chili flavor.

🌶🌶🌶 *Tabasco Habanero.* Hotter, more complex, less tart than the original.

🌶 *Vampfire Hot Sauce.* Lemony, salty, good chili flavor.

CARIBBEAN

Sauces in this style are big on fruit or mustard and generally contain habaneros or Scotch bonnet chilies.

🌶 *Bad Girls in Heat.* Sweet, spicy, fruity with papaya, pumpkin, parsnip.

🌶 *Dat'l Do-It Devil Drops.* Tart, with carroty sweetness.

🌶 *Inner Beauty Real Hot Sauce.* Complex mustard-curry flavor, slightly sweet.

🌶 *Jump Up and Kiss Me Hot Sauce with Passion.* Fruity curry flavor.

🌶🌶 *Lottie's True Bajan Premium Hot Pepper Sauce.* Mustardy, tart, hint of papaya.

🌶🌶 *Matouk's Hot Sauce.* Tart papaya flavor.

LATIN AMERICA *and* SOUTHWESTERN U.S.

Latin American hot sauces are almost pure chili, though some from Belize have a carrot base. Our Southwestern sauces have a more Mexican style—a little cumin and chilies such as jalapeño (including smoky chipotles) and chili pequín.

🌶🌶 *Búfalo Chipotle.* Very smoky and rich.

🌶 *Cholula Hot Sauce.* Great chili pequín flavor.

🌶🌶🌶 *El Yucateco (red).* A habanero sauce that has a tomato base.

🌶🌶 *Firehouse Global Warming Tamarind Chipotle Sauce.* A fruity tamarind flavor with garlic, and a lightly smoky taste.

🌶🌶🌶 *Marie Sharp's Habanero Pepper Sauce.* True, fruity habanero flavor with a carrot base.

🌶🌶 *Ring of Fire Habañero Hot Sauce.* Extremely complex, fresh chili-tomato flavors.

SCORCHERS

Save these capsaicin extract sauces for cooking.

🌶🌶🌶🌶 *Dave's Gourmet Insanity Sauce.* Killer hot, slight chemical taste.

🌶🌶🌶🌶 *Endorphin Rush Beyond Hot Sauce.* Killer hot, slight chemical taste.

WILD CARDS

As the category suggests, these sauces are all over the map.

🌶🌶🌶 *Brother Bru-Bru's African Hot Sauce.* Generous amounts of garlic and vinegar with heat that sneaks up on you.

🌶 *Huy Fong Tuong Ot Sriracha Hot Chili Sauce.* Garlicky red chili flavor, Vietnamese-style.

🌶 *Poo Khao Thong Sriracha Chilli Sauce Strong.* Sweet and garlicky, Thai.

🌶🌶 *Pure Hell.* Fruity pineapple flavor with a kick.

Hot style: the best hot sauces combine spicy names and graphics with complex flavors.

New-wave chef's salad: toss in cactus strips, tomatillos, hominy, and a smoky citrus dressing.

Cryin' Cactus Salad

Prep and cook time: About 35 minutes

Notes: For heat level 1, omit fruit-based habanero chili hot sauce; for level 2, add 3 tablespoons; for level 3, add ⅓ cup. Tested with Búfalo Chipotle and Matouk's Hot Sauce.

Makes: 6 servings

- 4 quarts **romaine lettuce** pieces
- 1 jar (15 oz.) **nopalitos**, rinsed until no longer slippery, and drained
- 1 can (15 oz.) **yellow hominy**, drained
- 1 jar (7 oz.) **roasted red peppers**, cut into ½-inch strips
- 4 **tomatillos** (½ lb. total), husked and thinly sliced
- ½ cup **orange juice**
- ¼ cup **reduced-fat mayonnaise**
- ¼ cup **chipotle chili hot sauce**
  Fruit-based habanero or Scotch bonnet **chili hot sauce** such as papaya (up to ⅓ cup, optional)
- ½ pound **chorizo** (optional)
- 2 tablespoons minced **fresh cilantro**

1. Place romaine lettuce in a large, shallow bowl. Arrange nopalitos, hominy, red peppers, and tomatillos on top. Set aside.

2. In a blender, whirl orange juice, reduced-fat mayonnaise, and chipotle and habanero hot sauces until smooth. Set aside.

3. Squeeze chorizo from casings into a 10- to 12-inch frying pan over medium-high heat; discard casings. Break into chunks with a spoon and stir often until brown and crisp, 10 to 12 minutes. Drain on paper towels.

4. Scatter chorizo over salad. Stir cilantro into chili dressing. At the table, add dressing to salad and mix to coat.

Per serving: 149 cal., 20% (30 cal.) from fat; 4.1 g protein; 3.3 g fat (0.5 g sat.); 25 g carbo (5.6 g fiber); 1,355 mg sodium; 0 mg chol.

Hoppin' Habanero-Lime Chicken Fajitas

Prep and cook time: About 50 minutes

Notes: For heat level 1, mix tomatoes with ¼ teaspoon habanero chili hot sauce; for level 2, use ¾ teaspoon; for level 3, use 1½ teaspoons. Tested with Tabasco Habanero and Marie Sharp's Habanero Pepper Sauce.

Makes: 8 fajitas

- ¼ cup **lime juice**
- 3 tablespoons **tequila**
- 1 tablespoon **olive oil**
- ½ teaspoon **ground cumin**
- ½ teaspoon **dried oregano**
- About 6 tablespoons **habanero chili hot sauce**
- 2 cloves **garlic**, minced
- 1½ pounds **boneless, skinless chicken breast halves**
- 3 **onions** (1 lb. total), quartered lengthwise and peeled
- 1 cup chopped **tomatoes**
- 8 **flour tortillas** (8-in. size)
- 1 can (about 1 lb.) **black beans**, heated and drained
- 1 cup **low-fat sour cream**
  Lime wedges

1. In a 1-gallon zip-lock plastic bag, combine lime juice, tequila, oil, cumin, oregano, 6 tablespoons hot sauce, and garlic. Add chicken and onions, seal, and chill at least 15 minutes or up to 2 hours, turning occasionally.

2. Combine tomatoes and ¼ teaspoon to 1½ teaspoons hot sauce; set aside.

3. Oil a barbecue grill over a solid bed of hot coals or gas grill on high heat (you can hold your hand at grill level only 2 to 3 seconds). Lift onions from marinade and place on grill. Close lid on gas grill. Cook onions for 3 minutes, turn, cook a couple more minutes, then turn over and baste with marinade.

4. Lift chicken from marinade and place on grill; close gas grill. Turn and baste chicken and onions occasionally until onions are soft and browned and meat is no longer pink in thickest part (cut to test), about 8 minutes. Transfer chicken and onions to a board and keep warm.

5. Heat tortillas on grill, turning once, until softened and lightly speckled brown, 30 to 60 seconds.

6. Slice chicken crosswise. Place portions of chicken, onions, and beans in tortillas. Top with tomatoes, sour cream, and a squeeze of lime. Fold up bottom of tortillas, then fold in sides.

Per fajita: 326 cal., 19% (63 cal.) from fat; 27 g protein; 7 g fat (2.4 g sat.); 38 g carbo (5 g fiber); 582 mg sodium; 59 mg chol.

Bite-Back Ribs

Prep and cook time: About 50 minutes

Notes: For heat level 1, add 1 tablespoon habanero chili hot sauce; for level 2, add 2 tablespoons; for level 3, add 3 tablespoons. Tested with Huy Fong Tuong Ot Sriracha Hot Chili Sauce and Vampfire Hot Sauce, and with El Yucateco (red) habanero sauce.

Makes: 4 servings

3 pounds **pork loin back ribs** (baby back ribs), fat trimmed

¼ cup **catsup**

¼ cup **hoisin sauce**

2 tablespoons **lemon juice**

2 tablespoons **sugar**

2 cloves **garlic**, minced

¼ cup **sriracha** or Louisiana **hot sauce**

1 to 3 tablespoons **habanero chili hot sauce**

¼ teaspoon **ground cinnamon**

¼ teaspoon **ground allspice**

1. Line an 11- by 17-inch roasting pan with foil. Arrange pork ribs in pan in a single layer and bake in a 450° oven until browned, about 20 minutes. Turn ribs over and bake until other side is browned, about 10 minutes. Discard fat from pan.

2. Meanwhile, combine catsup, hoisin, lemon juice, sugar, garlic, sriracha hot sauce, habanero hot sauce, cinnamon, and allspice.

3. Baste ribs with half of sauce. Cook for 10 minutes, turn over, baste with rest of sauce, and bake until well-browned, 10 to 15 minutes more.

Per serving: 702 cal., 63% (441 cal.) from fat; 40 g protein; 49 g fat (18 g sat.); 21 g carbo (0.3 g fiber); 1,152 mg sodium; 194 mg chol. ◆

TEN QUICK WAYS *to* HEAT UP *your* DAY

1. For a fire-and-ice sorbet, blend a jalapeño, fruity habanero, or Scotch bonnet hot sauce into strawberry or lemon sorbet.
2. Shake jalapeño or chipotle hot sauce over eggs and hash browns for a real eye-opener.
3. Make deviled eggs with an Asian sriracha or African hot sauce.
4. Dunk cooked shrimp into a sauce of sour cream and Louisiana or fruity Caribbean hot sauce.
5. Cook rice with a generous shake of chipotle hot sauce to add smokiness.
6. Serve crab cakes or steamed artichokes with mayonnaise spiked with Louisiana hot sauce.
7. Brush chicken with a thick, mustard- or fruit-based hot sauce just before removing from grill or broiler.
8. Heat up your favorite guacamole with a little jalapeño hot sauce.
9. Fire up braised greens with a generous shake of a Louisiana hot sauce.
10. Live dangerously, and spike bloody Marys with a drop (or less) of capsaicin extract sauce.

Hot stops for hot sauces

To find the broadest range of sauces, as well as obscure brands, shop at stores that specialize in hot and spicy foods (many have tasting bars) or purchase by mail or over the Internet.

Fire Alley. About 150 hot sauces. Store (13207 Ventura Blvd., Studio City, CA), mail order (888/347-3255), and electronic sales (http://www.firealley.com).

Hot & Spicy Foods Company. Changing selection of 200 to 300 hot sauces. Mail order (800/647-7429) and electronic sales (http://www.hotspicyfoods.com).

Hot Hot Hot. About 225 hot sauces. Store (56 S. De Lacey Ave., Pasadena), mail order (800/959-7742), and electronic sales (http://www.hothothot.com).

Hot Licks. More than 150 hot sauces available. Store (865 W. Harbor Dr., San Diego) and mail order (619/235-4000).

House of Fire. About 175 hot sauces. Store (1108 Spruce St., Boulder, CO) and mail order (800/717-5787).

Mango 'n Chili. About 150 hot sauces. Store (9301A N. Division, Spokane), mail order (800/468-5292), and electronic sales (http://www.soar.com/~business/m/mango).

Mo Hotta Mo Betta. About 200 hot sauces. Mail order (800/462-3220) and electronic sales (http://www.mohotta.com/).

¡Ouchywawa! About 340 hot sauces. Store (2510B Main St., Santa Monica) and mail order (800/929-2927).

Peppers of Key West. Over 400 hot sauces. Mail order (800/597-2823).

Salsas, Etc. More than 220 hot sauces. Store (126 Great Mall Dr., Milpitas, CA), mail order (800/407-2572), and electronic sales (http://www.salsasetc.com/).

Some Like It Hot! More than 100 hot sauces. Mail order (800/806-4468) and electronic sales (http://www.3pco.net/slih/).

RICHARD JUNG

Serve a confetti of vegetables and pasta over white bean–pesto sauce.

Cooking with Jean-Marc Fullsack

An artistic low-fat chef practices what he preaches when he fixes meals for his family

What does a classically trained French chef who works with the guru of ultra-low-fat choose to cook on his own time?

"If people told me 10 years ago that I'd like brown rice, I'd have said they were insane," laughs Jean-Marc Fullsack. Today, his work with Dean Ornish

by **ELAINE JOHNSON**

is all about good flavor—and healthful foods such as brown rice. (Ornish's program combines an extremely low-fat, low-cholesterol diet with exercise and reduction of stress.)

At home, the San Francisco Bay Area resident follows the same healthful principles when he prepares meals for his family.

"I translate classical techniques to nonfat. For example, instead of meat sauces, I use really fine vegetable sauces," says Fullsack, who accompanies Ornish around the country teaching low-fat cooking and lifestyle techniques to heart patients, hospital staffs, and professional chefs—including the chef at the White House. Fullsack's ideas have been incorporated into several Ornish books, including his most recent: *Everyday Cooking with Dr. Dean Ornish* (HarperCollins, New York, 1996; $15, paperback).

Fullsack notes that many people—even those without heart problems—are beginning to adopt a low-fat lifestyle. "I've lost 15 pounds since working with Dean and feel much healthier. If I'm in a situation where I have to eat old-fashioned sauces, I feel full so quickly. I'd have trouble going back to my old diet."

The food Fullsack cooks for his family has to be fast to prepare, as well as healthful and good-tasting. One favorite recipe is based on a French pesto soup, but he uses white beans instead of oil to thicken the pesto. The soup becomes a sauce for whole-grain pasta (his choices often include pasta made from brown rice, quinoa, or spelt) with colorful vegetables.

Pasta with Provençal Basil Sauce

Prep and cook time: About 50 minutes

Notes: Buy brown-rice pasta at a health food store. Cut vegetables 5 to 6 inches long and the width of spaghetti with the julienne blade on an Asian shredder or mandoline. Or make long vegetable shreds with the wide tooth of a grater.

Makes: 4 servings

1 cup julienned or shredded **carrot**

¾ cup julienned or shredded **green zucchini** skin (optional)

¾ cup julienned or shredded **yellow zucchini** skin or more green zucchini skin (optional)

1½ cups **vegetable broth**

½ cup diced **onion**

¼ cup diced **celery**

¼ cup diced **turnip**

¼ cup diced peeled **russet potato**

1 can (15 oz.) **small white beans**

1 cup tightly packed **fresh basil** leaves

4 cloves **garlic**

12 ounces **brown-rice spaghetti** or whole-wheat spaghetti

Salt (optional)

2 cups **broccoli florets**

¾ cup diced **tomato**

Pepper

Lemon wedges (optional)

1. Cut carrot, and the green and yellow zucchini skin, as described in Notes on page 122. (Save remaining zucchini for other uses.) Set aside.

2. In a 3- to 4-quart pan over high heat, bring broth, onion, celery, turnip, and potato to boiling. Reduce heat, cover, and simmer until potato is tender to bite, about 6 minutes. Add half the beans and their liquid; return to simmering, then cook, covered, for 5 to 10 minutes to blend flavors. Keep warm and set aside.

3. In a blender or food processor, whirl remaining beans and liquid, basil, and garlic until smooth. Set aside.

4. Cook pasta, uncovered, in 4 quarts boiling water and 1 tablespoon salt until almost tender to bite, about 5 minutes; after 3 minutes, add broccoli. Stir in the julienned vegetables and boil until just tender to bite, about 1 minute. Drain, rinse with hot water, remove broccoli, and keep foods warm.

5. Stir basil mixture into broth mixture. Spoon into 4 wide, rimmed dinner plates. Mound pasta in the center. Scatter tomato and broccoli around plate rims. Offer pepper and lemon wedges.

Per serving: 449 cal., 5.1% (23 cal.) from fat; 23 g protein; 2.6 g fat (0.3 g sat.); 97 g carbo (21 g fiber); 459 mg sodium; 0 mg chol. ◆

PHILIP SALAVERRY

Toasted pecans, blue cheese, and ripe red- or green-skinned pears flavor spaghetti.

A quick seasonal pasta with pears

Blue cheese and pecans add to the surprise

Pears and blue cheese, a classic after-dinner combination in Europe, are equally satisfying in this pasta entrée, which we first tried at Ristorante Ecco in San Francisco. For the best flavor and texture, choose pears ripe enough to yield to gentle pressure near the stem.

Pear and Gorgonzola Pasta

Prep and cook time: About 20 minutes

Notes: Blue cheeses such as gorgonzola and cambozola have a rich, nutty flavor; Danish blue tastes sharper.

Makes: 4 servings

12 ounces dried **spaghetti**

2 soft-ripe Bartlett, red Bartlett, or d'Anjou **pears** (½ lb. each)

1 tablespoon **lemon juice**

1 cup (5 oz.) crumbled **gorgonzola** or other blue-veined cheese

½ cup chopped **Italian parsley**

½ cup **chicken broth**

½ teaspoon **cornstarch**

⅔ cup toasted **pecans**

Salt and **pepper**

1. Half-fill a 5- to 6-quart pan with water, and bring to a boil over high heat. Add spaghetti and boil, uncovered, until barely tender to bite, 7 to 9 minutes. Drain; return to pan.

2. Meanwhile, cut each pear lengthwise into eighths; core pieces, and slice them crosswise ¼ inch thick. In a bowl, gently mix the pears, lemon juice, gorgonzola, and parsley; set aside.

3. In a 1- to 2-quart pan over high heat, stir broth and cornstarch until boiling. Gently mix into drained spaghetti along with pear mixture. Transfer to a serving dish. Scatter pecans on top, and season to taste with salt and pepper.

Per serving: 628 cal., 37% (234 cal.) from fat; 21 g protein; 26 g fat (8.8 g sat.); 83 g carbo.; 509 mg sodium; 31 mg chol. ◆

by **ELAINE JOHNSON**

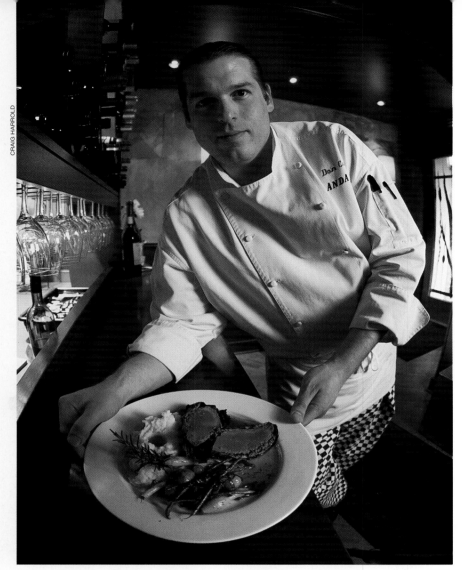

Andaluca's chef, Don Curtiss, holds a plate of his seared lamb loin in vine leaves.

Emerald City gems

Seattle has become one of the best tasting cities in the West.
A dozen adventurous restaurants explain why

Always a good place to eat, Seattle appears poised for greatness. Chefs are taking advantage of the region's culinary bounty as never before. Veteran restaurateurs are shaking loose from predictable formulas. And new cooking talent is injecting welcome notes of energy and creativity.

ANDALUCA

Cross the Pacific Northwest with the Mediterranean and it tastes like Andaluca, a newcomer whose deeply satisfying menu pays tribute to tapas, with a twist. Some of the plates are simple: roasted baby artichokes, bright with lemon, crisp with herbed crumbs, and gently sharp with parmesan. Others are gutsy: chicken wings spiked with toasted cumin, coriander, and harissa. All the food is beautiful, none more so than the chic little tower composed of layers of avocado, fresh Dungeness crab, and salsa, with a plume of frisée moistened with a champagne vinaigrette. Fittingly, the handsome dining room surrounds guests with luxe murals, fanciful curved booths, and a styl-

ish bar—just the sort of place you'd expect to sip a martini swirled with gold dust and gilded with a pedigreed olive. Sexy by night, Andaluca also makes a diverting lunch destination, particularly on Saturdays.
Where: 407 Olive Way.
Cost: Lunch entrées $8.50–$12, dinner entrées $12.50–$24.
Contact: (206) 382-6999.

ANTHONY'S PIER 66

Until recently, Seattle's major fish houses sailed on reputations that spoke more to impressive views than memorable meals. The arrival last summer of Anthony's Pier 66 overlooking Elliot Bay altered that course. Here's a big, conscientious chain restaurant that owns its own fish supplier and (in season) bothers to pick and deliver the fruit that makes its way into dessert—all in the same day. In a rush? Dive into the street-level Anthony's Fish Bar, offering fast food with finesse (the grilled-fish tacos are winners). Or try the Bell Street Diner, with its roomy booths, panoramic views, and gently priced comforts such as clam chowder, salmon pot pie, expertly fried seafood combinations, and wonderfully homey fruit crisps and cobblers. One flight up, a formal dining room caters to the expense-account crowd with platters tiered with three different tuna preparations (seared, raw, and marinated), a fanciful "dessert barge," and the city's finest crab cakes.
Where: 2201 Alaskan Way.
Cost: Dinner entrées $15–$25. Bell Street Diner lunch and dinner entrées $6–$14.
Contact: 448-6688.

CAMPAGNE

If you want to find out where a restaurant critic really loves to eat, ask him where he's willing to spend his own money. My response invariably leads diners to Pike Place Market and Campagne. No Seattle restaurant offers smoother or more professional and welcoming service. Tamara Murphy, the chef, oversees the lovely Provence-inspired menu that honors tradition with luscious *pâtés* and *soupe de pois-*

by TOM SIETSEMA

son but also ventures into whimsy with dishes such as lamb tartare drizzled with truffle oil and jazzed up with herb chips. Whether it's pomegranate-glazed squab accessorized with pumpkin gnocchi, or monkfish made glamorous with chanterelles, this is food that suits many moods. Around the corner and one flight down, on Post Alley, sits the younger, breezier Café Campagne, a charming tip-of-the-beret to French bistro fare—perfect omelets, steak frites, and baked cassoulet—complemented by lovely wines by the glass.
Where: 86 Pine St. and 1600 Post Alley.
Cost: Lunch entrées $7–$12, dinner entrées $18–$27. Café Campagne dinner entrées $9–$15.
Contact: (206) 728-2800 and 728-2233.

FLYING FISH

Fronted with floor-to-ceiling glass garage doors and bathed in soothing tropical hues, Flying Fish suggests Miami's South Beach, right down to the beautiful, see-and-be-seen clientele that flocks nightly to this white-hot watering hole. Working from an open kitchen in the rear of the room, chef Christine Keff turns out a long and imaginative menu that roams the globe for inspiration but most frequently drops anchor in Asian and Mediterranean ports. Pretty, upended spring rolls come stuffed with smoked rock shrimp. The signature crab cake includes a jolt of lemon grass. And if escolar or halibut cheeks are in the market, you're apt to find them in an innovative dish here.
Where: 2234 First Ave.
Cost: Dinner entrées $9–$19.
Contact: (206) 728-8595.

THE HERBFARM

With just three seatings a week, room for only 32 diners, and a reservations system that requires most of its guests to book a table during two call-in days a year, the Herbfarm requires perseverance to experience. But if any restaurant is worth the investment of time and money, this one is it.

The blissful setting appears to be out of a storybook. The restaurant is surrounded by manicured herb and vegetable gardens; when weather permits, dinner begins with an outdoor tour. In-

side, where candles and classical guitar music set a relaxing tone, chef Jerry Traunfeld works and talks from an open kitchen, spinning magic from the provender of the Pacific Northwest. In a nod to the seasons, his poetic nine-course dinner menus might showcase white truffles from Oregon, fresh sea urchin from the Washington coast, handcrafted cheeses, and wild nettles. No two meals are ever the same, though each gets a festive kickoff with a flute of sparkling wine, excited with fresh herbs, and ends sweetly with a tray of exquisite homemade confections.
Where: 32804 Issaquah–Fall City Rd. in Fall City.
Cost: Nine-course menu with five wines $129 to $150 per person.
Contact: (206) 784-2222.

IL TERRAZZO CARMINE

From the warm welcome to the bracing espresso, no other local dining room captures the feel of a genuine ristorante as authentically as the long-running Il Terrazzo Carmine. Airy and spacious, the restaurant's tiered dining room, with its eggshell-colored walls and attractive country-Italian touches, plays host to power brokers by day, romantics by night. Dive into dinner with a plate of antipasti or a half-portion of one of the kitchen's stellar pastas. Follow that with a rosy piece of beef, thick veal chop, or carefully cooked piece of fish—all treated to fresh, seasonal vegetable escorts—and end on a high note with a trembling flan. Amid an army of pale imitations, this place sets the standard for Italian dining.
Where: 411 First Ave. S.
Cost: Lunch entrées $9–$12.50, dinner entrées $9.50–$28.
Contact: 467-7797.

LAMPREIA

In a city that opts for casual fun over formality and self-importance, Lampreia stands out for both its meticulous attention to detail and its unabashed joy in such luxuries as foie gras, caviar, lobster, and whatever seasonal treasures might come its way. Chef-owner Scott Carsberg's veal chops are tender and flavorful—all the better for their elegant potato sauce and the haunting aroma of white-truffle oil that wafts

Laura Dewell's Pirosmani on Seattle's Queen Anne Hill resides in the gracious confines of a turn-of-the-century home.

across the table. Silken foie gras might be tiled with truffle shavings and paired with apples, plums, or peaches, depending on the time of year. And if anyone's making great cheeses, diving for the sweetest scallops, or foraging for wild white strawberries, you can count on finding them in this understated, golden-glowing dining room.
Where: 2400 First Ave.
Cost: Dinner entrées $17.50–$25.
Contact: 443-3301.

PALACE KITCHEN

Tom Douglas is to the Seattle restaurant scene what Mount Rainier is to the city's horizon. With Dahlia Lounge and Etta's Seafood already to his credit, he recently expanded his empire to include Palace Kitchen, a Gothic-leaning dining room whose focal points are a bustling horseshoe-shaped bar and the

vast stage set of an open kitchen, the latter bathed in red light. Wacky jewel-toned chandeliers drop from the ceiling. Curtains in gold and royal blue frame the soaring windows. Even the coat hooks look to be lifted from a castle. You can easily fashion a meal with selections from the long and eclectic list of appetizers: crisp-fried anchovies sporting a semolina crust, empanadas plump with curried goat and sweet potatoes, tiny ravioli filled with bits of Swiss chard and roast pork. Or order something from the grill. But save room for dessert (an elegant strudel for traditionalists, hot chocolate with doughnuts for wistful baby boomers). Don't worry if you can't find a table; the best people-watching involves a perch at the bar.
Where: 2030 Fifth Ave.
Cost: Dinner entrées $12–$18.
Contact: 448-2001.

PIROSMANI

Pirosmani is not a name that rolls easily off the tongue. And you'd be forgiven for being skeptical of a place that celebrates the food of a former Soviet Republic. But this restaurant, named for the revered Georgian artist Niko Pirosmani, serves some of the most original food in the Pacific Northwest. One taste of chef Laura Dewell's soulful cooking, which is a marriage of Georgian and Mediterranean dishes, and you, too, will be seduced. On the Georgian side, there might be roasted duck breast gilded with a walnut sauce that whispers of fenugreek and cinnamon. The more Mediterranean-inspired dishes run from fresh fish scented with garlic, thyme, and cloves to an extraordinary vegetarian tasting plate.
Where: 2220 Queen Anne Ave. N.
Cost: Dinner entrées $13–$22.
Contact: (206) 285-3360.

ROVER'S

The city's most refined contemporary French food can be explored at Rover's, in a comfortable and unpretentious setting that could pass for a country inn. Follow the lead of regulars and request one of chef-owner Thierry Rautureau's multicourse tasting menus. Luxury ingredients are used with abandon, presentations are labor intensive,

and the wine list offers the possibility of extraordinary drinking. Visiting celebrities often show up here, and the billionaires from Microsoft practically make this their home away from home.
Where: 2808 E. Madison St.
Cost: Dinner entrées $24–$39.
Contact: 325-7442.

SHIRO'S SUSHI

Umami is a Japanese word used to describe food at the peak of perfection. It is just that notion that draws legions of sushi lovers to spare, understated Shiro's. "Rice is the most important part" of sushi making, maestro Shiro Kashiba tells his guests. His grains are firm, plump, and moist, their flavor a delicate balance of rice-wine vinegar, salt, and sugar. A discerning shopper, Kashiba combs the city's best markets—twice a day—looking for exceptional fish and other seafood, keeping an eye open for delicacies such as silver perch, local squid, salmon roe, and ocean smelt—whatever's in season. Regulars don't bother looking at a menu, preferring to leave their orders to the master. Sushi isn't Shiro's only lure—the noodle soups and tempura are excellent—but it does provide heavy competition for the sushi bar's 11 seats and ringside show of umami.
Where: 2401 Second Ave., at Battery St.
Cost: Lunch entrées $6.95–$15, dinner entrées $16–$19.50.
Contact: 443-9844.

WILD GINGER

Jeem Han Lock of the wildly popular Wild Ginger isn't a household name, but anyone passionate about the cooking of China and Southeast Asia should get acquainted with this talented chef, who oversees a kitchen crew of 28 that is responsible for some of the most tantalizing food in the city: perfumed soups of great depth and subtlety, brochettes of exotically spiced fish or meat, crackling-crisp duck rubbed with star anise and cinnamon, and curries of exceptional flavor and balance. Habitués dine here on Monday evenings, when live jazz fuels the scene.
Where: 1400 Western Ave.
Cost: Lunch entrées $7–$13, dinner entrées $8–$23.
Contact: 623-4450. ◆

Oxtails as appetizer

Flavor makes up for the skimpy amount of meat on an oxtail (actually, beef tail)—and Bruce Cost of Bok Choy in Palo Alto brings out its best, Chinese-style. Set aside manners and sup the good juices from the bones.

Braised Oxtails

Prep and cook time: About 3 hours and 20 minutes
Makes: 4 appetizer servings

- 1 **oxtail** (about 2½ lb.), cut at joints
- ¼ cup **rice wine** (Shaoxing or sake)
- 4 **star anise**
- 8 thin slices (each about the size of a quarter) **fresh ginger**
- 3 cloves **garlic,** crushed
- 2 tablespoons **soy sauce**
- 1 tablespoon **dark soy sauce** (or 2½ teaspoons soy sauce plus ½ teaspoon dark molasses)
- 3 tablespoons firmly packed **brown sugar**
- 1 pound **daikon,** peeled and cut into 1-inch chunks
- 1 cup **fresh cilantro** leaves
  Salt

1. In a 5- to 6-quart pan, bring 1½ quarts water to a boil. Meanwhile, trim surface fat from oxtail. Rinse meat and add to pan. When boil resumes, skim off foam; add wine, anise, ginger, and garlic. Cover and simmer 1 hour.
2. Add regular soy, dark soy, and sugar; cover and simmer 1½ hours. Add daikon; cover and simmer until meat is very tender when pierced, 30 to 45 minutes.
3. With a slotted spoon, put meat and daikon in a bowl; keep warm. Discard the fat from pan juices. Boil juices, uncovered, over high heat until reduced to about ¾ cup, 10 to 15 minutes, then pour into bowl. Add cilantro; mix. Add salt to taste.

Per serving: 217 cal., 36% (79 cal.) from fat; 19 g protein; 8.8 g fat; 17 g carbo (2.2 g fiber); 890 mg sodium; (sat. fat and chol. unavailable). ◆

by **LINDA LAU ANUSASANANAN**

You can have pork with orange-cranberry sauce, couscous, and broccoli on your table in less than 30 minutes.

NORMAN A. PLATE

When time is short, think thin

Every minute counts if you don't get home until 6 on a weeknight and still need to prepare dinner for your family. That's why we're launching a new monthly feature, The Quick Cook. Our aim is to provide you with easy, delicious recipes—plus tips and shortcuts—to help you serve a dinner you'll be proud of, in 30 minutes or less.

WHAT'S *for* DINNER?

*Pork with
Orange-Cranberry Sauce*

*Steamed Broccoli
with Lemon and Parmesan*

Fluffy Couscous

*Cinnamon Ice Cream
with Caramel Sauce*

One shortcut is a basic cooking principle we sometimes forget: thinner cuts of meat cook faster. In fact, you'll cut the cooking time for steaks, pork or lamb chops, boneless chicken breasts, and turkey breast slices or cutlets to less than five minutes if you first pound them until they're very thin. Even with the time it takes to pound the meat, you'll save 10 to 15 minutes, depending on the cut.

"Thinning" meat is easy. Just trim off and discard any excess fat, then place the meat between two pieces of plastic wrap. With a heavy, flat-sided mallet or a clean hammer (see page 31 for one such tool), firmly pound all over until the meat is ¼ to ⅓ inch thick. Just don't pound hard enough to tear the meat.

But first, start two pans of water heating for the broccoli and the couscous, then zip through the pork recipe. Right

before dinner's ready, pull a quart of vanilla ice cream from the freezer to soften; come dessert time, stir in 1 teaspoon ground cinnamon and serve with purchased caramel sauce.

Pork with Orange-Cranberry Sauce. "Thin" 4 **boneless center-cut pork chops** (1½ lb. total) as directed at left. Melt 2 teaspoons **butter** or margarine and 2 teaspoons **olive oil** in a 10- to 12-inch nonstick frying pan over medium-high heat. When butter sizzles, add pork (if all the meat won't fit, cook in batches). Cook, turning once, until both sides are well browned and center is no longer pink (cut to test), 4 to 5 minutes total. Remove meat, transfer to a platter, and keep warm. Mix ¾ cup **beef broth,** ¼ cup **dried cranberries,** 2 tablespoons thawed **frozen orange juice concentrate,** 2 teaspoons **Dijon mustard,** and 1 teaspoon **cornstarch** until smooth. Add to pan and bring to a boil over high heat, stirring constantly; boil until slightly thickened, about 1 minute, then pour over pork. Serves 4.

Per serving: 423 cal., 55% (234 cal.) from fat; 35 g protein; 26 g fat (9 g sat.); 9.4 g carbo (0.5 g fiber); 195 mg sodium; 119 mg chol.

MORE THIN, SPEEDY ENTRÉES

• Pound boneless lamb loin chops as directed. Sauté; remove from pan. To pan, add a smoothly blended mixture of ¾ cup beef broth, ¼ cup dry red wine, 2 tablespoons *each* balsamic vinegar and honey, and 1 teaspoon cornstarch. Boil until slightly thickened; pour over meat. Drizzle sesame oil and sprinkle minced fresh mint leaves on top.

• Pound boneless beef steaks as directed. Sauté; remove from pan. To pan, add a smoothly blended mixture of ¾ cup beef broth, ¼ cup dry sherry, 2 tablespoons soy sauce, 1 tablespoon minced fresh ginger, and 1 teaspoon cornstarch. Boil until slightly thickened; pour over meat. Drizzle sesame oil and sprinkle chopped green onion on top.

• Pound boneless, skinless chicken breasts as directed. Sauté; drizzle with a mixture of Mexican crema (or sour cream), lime juice, minced fresh cilantro, and canned chopped green chilies. ◆

NORMAN A. PLATE (2)

A cilantro- and lime-spiced cream sauce dresses pan-browned swordfish.

Sunset's Kitchen Cabinet

Stephen Sumner loves fish. In this straightforward presentation, he sauces one of his favorites, swordfish, with cilantro and fresh lime juice.

Swordfish with Cilantro-Lime Cream
Stephen Sumner, San Diego

Prep and cook time: About 20 minutes

Makes: 3 servings

About 1 pound **swordfish steaks** (¾ in. thick)

2 to 3 tablespoons **Italian-style bread crumbs**

2 tablespoons **butter** or margarine

2 tablespoons minced **green onion**

2 tablespoons minced **fresh cilantro**, plus a few sprigs

2 tablespoons **lime juice**

3 tablespoons **whipping cream**

Lime wedges

1. Rinse swordfish steaks and pat dry. Dust with bread crumbs.

2. Melt butter in a 10- to 12-inch non-stick frying pan over medium-high heat; add swordfish and cook until browned on bottom, about 4 minutes. Turn fish over and cook until browned on other side and opaque but still moist in center (cut to test), 4 to 5 more minutes. Transfer fish to a warm platter; keep warm.

3. Add onion to pan and stir just to wilt, about 30 seconds. Add cilantro, lime juice, and cream, stirring until it boils vigorously, 1 to 2 minutes. Divide fish among 3 dinner plates. Pour sauce equally over fish. Garnish each plate with a lime wedge and cilantro sprigs.

Per serving: 297 cal., 55% (162 cal.) from fat; 28 g protein; 18 g fat (9.2 g sat.); 5.2 g carbo (0.3 g fiber); 338 mg sodium; 90 mg chol.

Lemon Walnut Date Bread
John T. Perchorowicz, Tucson

"Got lemons, make lemon bread" is John Perchorowicz's motto. His fondness for tart foods and date-nut bread, plus an abundance of lemons, motivated him to create this tangy syrup-soaked bread with the texture of fruitcake. If you don't have a food processor, finely chop the lemon and dates by hand, then mix in the remaining ingredients until well blended.

Prep and cook time: About 1¼ hours, plus at least 2 hours for absorption of syrup, and overnight chilling

Makes: 1 loaf (about 2 lb.), 18 to 24 servings

1 **lemon** (about 5 oz.)

1 cup chopped pitted **dates**

1¼ cups **sugar**

2 tablespoons **butter** or margarine, at room temperature

1 **large egg**

1¾ cups **all-purpose flour**

1 teaspoon **baking soda**

1 teaspoon **salt**

1 cup chopped **walnuts**

½ cup **lemon juice**

1. Coarsely chop lemon, including peel and rind; discard seeds. Place lemon and dates in a food processor; whirl until evenly chopped. Add ¾ cup sugar, the butter, and egg; whirl until blended and the lemon and dates are finely chopped.

2. In a bowl, mix flour, baking soda, and salt. Add to date mixture; whirl until blended. Stir in walnuts. Spread batter into a buttered and floured 4- by 8-inch glass loaf pan. Bake in a 325° oven until a toothpick inserted in center of thickest part comes out clean, about 1 hour.

3. Meanwhile, in a 1- to 1½-quart pan, combine remaining ½ cup sugar and lemon juice. Stir over medium heat until sugar dissolves, about 2 minutes.

4. When bread is done, use a long, thin skewer to make holes about ½ inch apart all over surface. Pour hot syrup evenly over hot bread in pan. Let stand at room temperature until bread absorbs all syrup, about 2 hours. Turn out of pan onto plate. Cover airtight; chill overnight or up to 3 days. Thinly slice to serve. Chill leftover bread airtight.

Per serving: 142 cal., 29% (41 cal.) from fat; 2.2 g protein; 4.5 g fat (1 g sat.); 25 g carbo (0.9 g fiber); 160 mg sodium; 12 mg chol.

by LINDA LAU ANUSASANANAN

Red Pepper–Tomato Soup
Laura Sabo, Portland

Inspired by a Valentine's Day recipe contest and her love of roasted red peppers and tomatoes, Laura Sabo created this delicious soup with heart-shaped croutons. Because contest entries were to be based on a romantic movie, she originally dubbed the soup "Sweetness in Seattle."

Prep and cook time: About 40 minutes

Makes: 4 cups, 2 or 3 servings

- 2 or 3 slices **French bread,** each about ½ inch thick
- 1 tablespoon **olive oil**
- ¾ teaspoon **dried basil**
- ¼ cup (about 1½ oz.) chopped **shallots**
- 1 can (14½ oz.) **reduced-sodium chicken** or vegetable **broth**
- 1 cup **canned peeled roasted red peppers,** rinsed and drained
- 1 can (16 oz.) **tomatoes**

  Salt and **pepper**

  Sugar
- 2 tablespoons **sour cream** or whipping cream (optional)

1. With a heart-shaped cookie cutter or a knife, cut heart shapes (3 inches wide or smaller) out of bread. Lay cutouts on a baking sheet and brush tops with about 2 teaspoons oil. Sprinkle evenly with ¼ teaspoon basil. Bake in a 350° oven until golden and crisp, about 15 minutes for a 3-inch-wide heart.

2. Meanwhile, in a 2- to 3-quart pan, cook shallots, stirring often, in remaining 1 teaspoon oil over medium-

high heat until shallots are translucent, about 3 minutes. Add broth, red peppers, tomatoes and their juice, and remaining ½ teaspoon basil. Bring to a boil over high heat; cover and simmer over low heat 5 to 10 minutes.

3. With a slotted spoon, ladle peppers, tomatoes, and shallots into a blender or food processor; whirl until smooth. Return purée to pan; stir into liquid. Add salt, pepper, and sugar to taste. Ladle soup into bowls. Spoon dollops of sour cream decoratively over soup; swirl the tip of a knife through sour cream. Immediately before serving, set heart-shaped croutons on top.

Per serving: 148 cal., 32% (48 cal.) from fat; 4.2 g protein; 5.3 g fat (0.8 g sat.); 20 g carbo (1.7 g fiber); 757 mg sodium; 0 mg chol.

Turkey Tamale Pie
Joan Stanley, Lafayette, California

To reduce fat in this old family standby, Joan Stanley replaced the ground beef with turkey. At first her husband found the turkey too pale for his taste, she says, but when she cooked it with chili powder, it resembled his familiar favorite.

Prep and cook time: About 50 minutes

Makes: 6 servings

- 1 tablespoon **salad oil**
- ¾ pound **ground lean turkey**
- 1 cup thinly sliced **green onions**
- 2 tablespoons **chili powder**
- 1 teaspoon **ground cumin**
- 1 jar (14 oz.) **spaghetti sauce**
- 1 can (15 oz.) **black beans** or kidney beans, rinsed and drained
- 1 **large egg**
- ¼ cup **milk**
- 1 can (4 oz.) **diced green chilies**
- 1 package (8½ oz.) **cornbread mix**
- ½ cup shredded **reduced-fat jack cheese** (optional)

1. Place oil in a 10- to 12-inch frying pan over medium-high heat. Crumble turkey into pan. Add onions. Cook and stir until onions are limp, about 3 minutes. Add chili powder and cumin and stir 2 to 3 minutes. Add ¾ cup water, spaghetti sauce, and beans. Bring to a boil. Reduce heat and simmer, uncovered, 10 to 12 minutes, stirring occasionally.

2. Meanwhile, in a bowl, lightly beat together egg and milk. Stir in chilies and cornbread mix.

3. Pour hot turkey mixture into a shallow 2½- to 3-quart baking dish. Sprinkle cheese over turkey mixture. Spread cornbread batter evenly over cheese. Bake, uncovered, in a 375° oven until cornbread topping is golden brown, 25 to 30 minutes. Scoop out servings with a spoon.

Per serving: 430 cal., 33% (144 cal.) from fat; 19 g protein; 16 g fat (3.9 g sat.); 52 g carbo (5.3 g fiber); 967 mg sodium; 78 mg chol.

Kashmir Tea
Farah Ahmed, Sunnyvale, California

On grand occasions, hosts in Pakistan often serve a fragrant spiced tea made with milk. There it is brewed with pink tea, but here in her new home, Farah Ahmed finds that good-quality black tea provides a similar taste. Dress up the tea with cream and nuts, or serve it plain.

Prep and cook time: About 20 minutes

Makes: 4 servings

- 2 **cardamom pods**
- 2 whole **cloves**
- 1 **cinnamon stick** (about 3 in. long)
- 1 quart **low-fat milk**
- 4 teaspoons **Darjeeling** or orange pekoe **tea leaves**

  About 1 tablespoon **sugar**
- ¼ cup **lightly whipped cream** (optional)
- 2 teaspoons **chopped unsalted roasted pistachios** (optional)

1. Slightly crush cardamom pods; remove and discard outer white hulls. Put black cardamom seeds and cloves into a 1½- to 2-quart pan. With a wood spoon, press spices to lightly crush. Add cinnamon stick, milk, and tea. Cook over medium heat, stirring often, just until milk comes to a boil, about 14 minutes. Remove from heat and cool slightly.

2. Pour tea mixture through a fine wire strainer into tea cups. Add sugar to taste. Garnish each cup with a dollop of whipped cream and ½ teaspoon of chopped pistachios.

Per serving: 137 cal., 31% (42 cal.) from fat; 8.1 g protein; 4.7 g fat (2.9 g sat.); 16 g carbo (0 g fiber); 129 mg sodium; 20 mg chol. ◆

An herb-topped crouton heart floats on roasted red pepper and tomato soup.

Prized for their mild flavor and floral aroma, Meyer lemons shine in this silken-textured pie and other desserts (see page 58).

March

foodguide

by **JERRY ANNE DI VECCHIO**

For size and style, a rack of lamb stands alone. It's petite, it cooks fast, and it commands attention when ready to carve. All said, rack of lamb is perfect as the entrée for two or three, especially if the occasion is a tad festive.

Whole shallots, sweetly cooked, go especially well with the meat. And now that they are cultivated on a large scale in Walla Walla, Washington, shallots are a better buy than once upon a time. I find them delicious as a vegetable or for seasoning.

To enrich the dish even more, cook a few morel mushrooms with the shallots. Dried morels are always available, but this time of year fresh morels might be, too, if weather conditions permit. Both require careful cleaning to get rid of the dirt and grit that love to lodge in their spongy-looking caps.

Racks vary in size, so order by weight and you'll get six to eight ribs.

E. J. ARMSTRONG

a **TASTE** *of the* **WEST**

Designer roast, off the rack

Lamb Rack with Shallots

Prep and cook time: 50 to 60 minutes

Notes: If omitting morels, replace their soaking liquid with 1 cup chicken or beef broth.

Makes: 2 or 3 servings

About ⅔ cup (1 oz.) **dried morel mushrooms** (optional)

1½ pounds **shallots** (¾ to 1 in. wide)

1 **rack of lamb** (about 2 lb., rib ends trimmed and backbone removed or cracked)

5 tablespoons **balsamic vinegar**

½ cup **madeira** or dry sherry

1 tablespoon **butter** or olive oil

About ¼ pound **watercress**, rinsed and crisped

Salt and **pepper**

tools

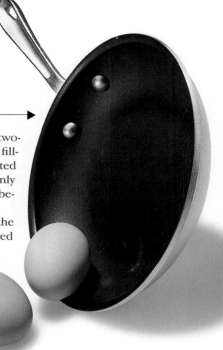

A 7-inch-wide (from rim to rim, more or less) curve-side frying pan is perfect for a one- or two-egg omelet. In this pan, the top of the egg mixture will still be moist enough to embrace a filling by the time the bottom firms. The same egg mixture cooked in the frying pan most touted for omelets—it's about 8 inches wide and looks only slightly larger—is so thin it cooks evenly and looks more like a crêpe. That extra inch is best for three-egg omelets, which I find beyond most appetites—and certainly mine—these days.

The omelet pan I own, from earlier times, doesn't have a nonstick lining like most of the newer 7-inch ones in the marketplace. But in my pan, eggs never stick because it's reserved for omelets. Should a bit of filling adhere, I scour it free with salt and a dry cloth. A nonstick finish omits these concerns, and the pan can serve more than one function.

Although many commercial-grade cookware manufacturers make a 7-inch omelet/frying pan, those models can be surprisingly hard to find. If they're in short supply at your cookware store, ask to order one, or seek one out in a cookware catalog. The pan shown, made by All-Clad, retails for $45 to $50 but is often specially priced at about $25.

SEASONAL *note*

Spuds with duds

For the past six years, Neil and Susan Hall and Allan and Barbara Fredrickson of Mount Vernon, Washington, have staged a cooperative "spud fest" in March.

About 100 attend, and the invitations read: "We'll provide baked potatoes and toppings. Please bring a salad or dessert, and your own beverage."

Why potatoes? They're plentiful, inexpensive, easy to like, easy to cook, and much easier to manage than the traditional St. Patrick's combo of potatoes with corned beef and cabbage.

The Halls and Fredricksons need a minimum of 150 baked potatoes. A local baker delivers them, fresh baked, in insulated chests, where they stay hot until piled into cloth-lined baskets as needed. Toppings are mostly purchased, ready-to-serve items such as sour cream, plain yogurt, pesto, chopped green onions, flavored vinegars, assorted cheeses (shredded, grated, or crumbled), heated pasta sauces, and cooked meats.

If you want to stage your own spud fest, try grouping the toppings in combinations like these:
- Pickled ginger, tiny cooked shrimp, chives, and seasoned rice vinegar.
- Oil-packed dried tomatoes, cold cooked green beans, grated parmesan cheese, and pepper.
- Cooked corn kernels, cheddar cheese, fresh cilantro, and prepared salsa.
- Sautéed mushrooms, marinara sauce, Italian sausage chunks, and grated parmesan cheese.
- Cooked chicken, bean sprouts, green onions, and Asian peanut sauce.

---

1. Put morels in a bowl and add 2 cups boiling water.

2. Peel shallots.

3. Trim and discard most of the surface fat from lamb.

4. Place an 11- or 12-inch ovenproof nonstick frying pan over medium-high heat. When pan is hot, put lamb rack, fat side down, in pan and cook until brown, 3 to 4 minutes; tip rack back and forth as needed to color evenly. Remove pan from heat (to reduce spattering) and add 2 tablespoons balsamic vinegar and 2 tablespoons madeira. Return to heat and shake pan until most of the liquid evaporates. Remove from heat again and put lamb, bones down, in a 9- by 13-inch pan. Set frying pan aside.

5. With your hand, gently squeeze the morels in water to release grit. Then lift out the mushrooms and squeeze dry. Holding morels under cool running water, again gently massage and squeeze them to release any grit that remains.

6. Put morels in frying pan. Pouring carefully, without disturbing grit in bowl, measure 1 cup soaking water and add to pan. Discard remaining water. Add shallots, remaining vinegar and madeira, and butter to frying pan. Cover and place on high heat until boiling, then uncover and boil gently until liquid is reduced by about a third, about 7 minutes.

7. Place one oven rack in the lowest position and another in the center of a 450° oven. Set frying pan with shallot mixture on lowest rack and bake until liquid is thick and bubbling, 18 to 22 minutes, shaking occasionally. Keep warm if ready before lamb.

8. Meanwhile, insert a meat thermometer into center of narrow end of lamb. Five minutes after the shallots have gone into the oven, put lamb on middle rack and roast until thermometer registers 135° for medium-rare, 12 to 15 minutes (large end will be rare; cook about 5 minutes longer for medium to medium-rare). Remove lamb and let stand at least 5 minutes.

9. Place lamb on a platter and add shallot mixture. Accompany with watercress. Cut meat apart between ribs. Season to taste with salt and pepper.

Per serving: 500 cal., 36% (180 cal.) from fat; 35 g protein; 20 g fat (8.5 g sat.); 44 g carbo (2.5 g fiber); 180 mg sodium; 101 mg chol.

All-season apricots

This apricot sorbet is like a beam of summer sunshine breaking through a winter sky. And if such radiance isn't enough to attract your attention and lift your spirits, then its convenience should. The apricots are ever-ready—canned and dried. Cook the dried ones in the canned fruit syrup, purée both kinds of apricots together, freeze, and enjoy.

Apricot Sorbet

Prep and cook time: About 25 minutes

Notes: If using a frozen-cylinder ice cream maker, first chill purée quickly by setting pan in ice water and stirring often until cold, 5 to 10 minutes. For additional embellishment, top servings with a little grated semisweet chocolate.

E. J. ARMSTRONG

Makes: About 4 cups, 6 servings

- 2 **cans** (15 to 16 oz. size) **pitted apricot halves in heavy syrup**
- 1 cup **dried apricots**
- 1 **lemon**

1. Drain apricot syrup into a 1½- to 2-quart pan. Add dried apricots. Grate peel and ream juice from lemon. Add peel and juice to pan. Bring mixture to a boil. Cover and simmer until fruit is plumped, about 10 minutes.

2. If desired, reserve 6 of the nicest-looking dried apricot halves for garnish. Combine remaining cooked fruit with syrup and the canned fruit in a blender or a food processor; smoothly purée.

3. Pour mixture into an automatic ice cream maker and freeze until dasher is hard to turn, about 15 minutes. (Or pour into a 9- by 13-inch metal pan and freeze until firm, about 2½ hours. Break into chunks and whirl in food processor until smooth. Serve at once, or cover and return to freezer until ready to serve, up to 2 weeks.)

4. Scoop apricot sorbet into dishes and top with reserved cooked apricots.

Per serving: 171 cal., 1.1% (1.8 cal.) from fat; 1.6 g protein; 0.2 g fat (0 g sat.); 44 g carbo (1.7 g fiber); 7.9 mg sodium; 0 mg chol.

Dairy delights

Mascarpone, Italy's velvety cream cheese, is one of those products that don't travel well. Imported mascarpone always tastes a bit stale and soured to me. And up until now, the mascarpones made in this country have fallen far, far short of the original.

This has changed. Two companies in the West are now making this soft cheese, and it's finding its way into specialty supermarkets, particularly natural-food stores. Each mascarpone is produced in its own style, as are those made in Italy.

Bella Gento mascarpone from Olympia Cheese Company in Olympia, Washington, is golden and very thick, with a delicate tang.

California Mozzarella Fresca in Benicia, California, produces a paler, slightly fluffier, subtly flavored mascarpone. (The company also makes a very fine fresh mozzarella cheese, not to be confused with the stringy kind of mozzarella on pizzas.)

Both mascarpones are sold in 8-ounce containers with suggested retail prices of $3.59 to $3.99. California Mozzarella Fresca also has 1-pound containers for about $6.70. (An 8-ounce unit of the fresh mozzarella cheese costs about $3.10; a pound, about $5.90.)

What do you do with mascarpone? Use it as you would cream cheese or whipped cream to flavor and fill pastries or to cook with. Mascarpone also whips—quickly; watch and take care not to overdo, or you'll end up with butter.

These dairy products are quite perishable, so be sure to check their shelf dates and, for the very best flavor, use shortly after opening.

The San Francisco food beat

It felt like déjà vu as I leafed through my preview copy of *The San Francisco Chronicle Cookbook,* edited by Michael Bauer and Fran Irwin (Chronicle Books, San Francisco, 1997; $18.95). The names, the places, the dishes, the foods—all were so familiar. And right they should be. This 432-page paperback includes dishes from some of Northern California's finest chefs and cooks, many of whom are dear friends of mine.

Through the years, the *Chronicle's* food pages have staunchly, imaginatively reinforced San Francisco's position as a dining and food mecca with international flair and reputation.

The 350 recipes culled from well-packed files give a taste of this diversity, with Jane Benet's (the late food editor of the *Chronicle*) Chilled Cucumber Soup, Oliveto's (a north Oakland restaurant) Tongue of Fire Beans with Parmesan and Anchovy Vinaigrette, chef Carlo Middione's Spaghetti alla Puttanesca, author Marion Cunningham's Raised Waffles, and author Flo Braker's Zesty Lemon Bars. ◆

NORMAN A. PLATE

For the wild among us

I would rather drink Sauvignon Blanc than Chardonnay any day. This was not always the case, however. After all, a passion for Sauvignon Blanc doesn't come easily or instantly. Like sushi, Sauvignon Blanc is a rite of passage. In the beginning, you're not sure you like it. The next few experiences are a little more intriguing. After a year or so, you're smitten.

What is it about the wine that's so seductive? It's hard to say, because Sauvignon Blanc is clearly the bad girl of white wines. The very word sauvignon comes from the French *sauvage*, meaning wild, unruly, unleashed. It isn't tame. It isn't polite. It doesn't wear matching earrings.

In other words, compared with the nice, round, amiable Chardonnay, Sauvignon Blanc is a rebellious minx of a wine. Its flavors and aromas—wild herbs, wet hay, gooseberries, gun smoke, and sometimes fresh figs—are never shy and can be downright sassy.

Moreover, some of the best Sauvignon Blancs have one more aroma, a difficult-to-describe sharpness that, for lack of a more genteel term, is sometimes referred to as "cat piss." It is generally considered one of Sauvignon Blanc's more unusual attributes.

In the end, though, one of Sauvignon Blanc's most compelling traits is the way it feels in the mouth. It's snappy, kinetic, alive. It's lean and taut, not round and plump; it's Jamie Lee Curtis, not Marilyn Monroe. This is because Sauvignon Blancs have a lot of perceptible acidity that you can feel going right up through the middle of the wine. Not surprisingly, it's this vibrant acidity that makes Sauvignon Blanc one of the best all-around whites for pairing with food.

At this point, some wine drinkers might be thinking, "That's not what the Sauvignon Blanc I buy is like … ."

Quite possibly not. Many California winemakers feel that Sauvignon Blanc is too extreme or assertive for American tastes. As a result, they use various winemaking techniques to intentionally mollify the wine's flavors and texture. By this specious logic, Sauvignon Blanc supposedly tastes better when it doesn't taste like itself. I hate these denuded wines.

Sauvignon Blanc grows all over the world, from Texas Hill Country to Israel's Golan Heights. However, the grape makes truly excellent wine in only a few places: the small districts known as Sancerre and Pouilly-Fumé in France's Loire Valley, Bordeaux, New Zealand, South Africa, and occasionally California, Washington State, and northern Italy.

Sancerre and Pouilly-Fumé tend to be the smokiest and most sophisticated Sauvignons; those from New Zealand, the most elegant and racy; and South Africa's Sauvignons are the most outrageously wild. In all three regions, 100 percent Sauvignon Blancs are made.

In Bordeaux, by contrast, Sauvignon Blanc is almost always blended with Sémillon, another white grape. Part of the purpose, once again, is to tone down Sauvignon although, as in a good marriage, these two grapes seem to pair well without completely masking each other's personality.

In California, Sauvignon Blanc is made both ways—as a 100 percent varietal and blended with Sémillon. Somewhat confusingly, some California Sauvignons (as well as those in Washington) are called Fumé Blanc instead of Sauvignon Blanc. Some vintners simply think the name Fumé Blanc sounds sexier. In fact, whether a wine is called Fumé Blanc or Sauvignon Blanc, it's made from Sauvignon Blanc grapes.

There are scores of exciting, delicious Sauvignon Blancs out there, including many from small producers. Moreover, California Sauvignons are generally easy to find because many wine drinkers are still afraid to venture past Chardonnay. If you come across any of the Sauvignon Blancs below, snatch up a few bottles immediately!

• **Chalk Hill Sauvignon Blanc 1994, $14** (Chalk Hill, California). A creamy bullet of smoke, flint, and bay leaves.
• **Château Carbonnieux 1993, $25** (Graves, Bordeaux, France). Graceful yet full of pizzazz. Waiting for seafood.
• **Cloudy Bay Sauvignon Blanc 1994, $15** (Marlborough, New Zealand). Racy, dramatic, and sophisticated. The rage in New York and London.
• **Comte Lafond Sancerre 1995, $22** (Loire Valley, France). Icicle-sharp gooseberry, grapefruit, and mineral flavors.
• **deLorimier "Spectrum" 1994, $12** (Alexander Valley, California). A superzesty Sauvignon-Sémillon blend, full of smoke, gunflint, and green tea.
• **Grgich Hills Cellar Fumé Blanc 1994, $14** (Napa Valley, California). Like being in a lime tornado. ◆

WINE DICTIONARY: *grassy*

A descriptive term for flavors and aromas reminiscent of wild grasses, meadows, and fields of just-cut hay, often overlaid with a "green," or vegetable, note. Grassiness can be positive or negative depending on its degree and on the subjective preferences of the taster. The varietal most often described as grassy is Sauvignon Blanc. — *K. M.*

A passion for beans

Elizabeth Berry nurtures her specialty beans as if they were members of the family. She's aided in her obsession by chef-friends who love to cook with them

"Now hold out your hands and close your eyes," says Elizabeth Berry, as excited as a kid on Christmas. She shows me a tiny, hand-sewn cotton pouch with two bumps: two beans, each as fat as a thumb and smooth as satin.

"I swear they're the beans of *Jack and the Beanstalk,*" exclaims Berry about her latest acquisition. "This guy sent them to me from Germany. He says the pods grow 12 inches long. But he only sent two! I'm going to grow them *very* carefully."

Many farmers grow ordinary beans like pintos or kidneys. A handful grow more unusual beans, as Berry does. But no one else makes plain old beans seem darn near magical.

She's been called the Bean Queen, and at her farm in Abiquiu, New Mexico, Berry's obsession threatens to take over her house. Beans fill the living room, kitchen, and bedroom in paper sacks, dishpans, bowls, envelopes, and zip-lock plastic bags. There are purple-and-black beans, chartreuse beans, yellow, white, and even indigo beans.

"When I grew my first beans nine years ago, I thought, 'A bean's a bean,'" says Berry. "But I gave them to a chef to try. He said they were the best he'd ever had, so I started growing more."

Soon Berry was searching for the best-tasting, most beautiful heirloom beans, varieties that might become extinct if no one creates a market for them. Two years ago she grew 650 varieties culled from the collection at Seed Savers Exchange in Iowa. Now people send her beans from all over the world.

She introduces 20 to 25 varieties at an annual chefs' tasting, where Santa Fe chefs such as Mark Miller of Coyote Cafe and Katharine Kagel of Cafe Pasqual's vote for their favorites. The next year, Berry grows the four most popular beans for seed, and as soon as she has 100 pounds (enough for 1 acre), she passes them on to another farmer to grow in bulk.

"I would grow beans just for their beauty. This way, I find a home for them," Berry explains. "It's fun to swap beans and all that, but I have a bigger vision. I want every supermarket in the country to have them. Each year I expand. It's just a matter of time, and good luck with weather."

This spring Berry will move operations from Abiquiu to her ranch in the Rio Chama wilderness (in northern New Mexico) to devote herself full-time to bean research and development.

Beneath dun-colored mesas where beans have been part of the culture for millenia, Berry plans for her *Jack and*

Elizabeth Berry's efforts to save heirloom beans from extinction have earned her the name Bean Queen.

by ELAINE JOHNSON

the Beanstalk beans. "I'm going to trellis them 20 feet high on my purple Inca corn. That will be spectacular!"

WHERE TO FIND HEIRLOOMS
Natural-food and grocery stores sell an increasing selection of specialty beans. You can also try the following mail-order sources. Bean names vary among producers. Prices do not include shipping charges.

Coyote Cafe General Store, 132 W. Water St., Santa Fe, 87501; (800) 866-4695. About 14 varieties, including all at left; $3.95 per ½ pound.

Gallina Canyon Ranch, Box 2334, Twin Falls, ID 83303. About 25 varieties, including all at left. For a list and order form, send self-addressed, stamped envelope and check for $1 made out to Elizabeth Berry. $4 per pound.

Phipps Country Store & Farm, Box 349, Pescadero, CA 94060; (415) 879-0787. About 100 varieties, including all at left. 69 cents to $3.99 per pound.

Zürsun, 754 Canyon Park Ave., Twin Falls, ID 83301; (800) 424-8881. About 24 varieties, including Appaloosa, Cannellini, Flageolet, and Scarlet Runner. $3 per pound.

White and Black Soup

Prep and cook time: 1¼ hours, plus at least 2 hours for soaking beans

Notes: This recipe has been adapted from *Cafe Pasqual's Cookbook,* by Katharine Kagel (Chronicle Books, San Francisco, 1993; $18.95).

Makes: 8 cups, 4 servings

2 cups (14 oz.) **dried white beans** such as Flageolet, Cannellini, or White Aztec

½ pound diced **smoked bacon** (preferably applewood-smoked)

¼ cup minced **fresh serrano chilies**

A gallery of beans

These heirloom beans are favorites of Elizabeth Berry and Santa Fe chefs. Characteristics of each differ somewhat among growers.

Black Valentine. Small jet-black bean with mealy texture and neutral flavor.

Cannellini. White with creamy texture; delicate sweet, nutty flavor. Larger variety may be called Italian Butterbean Cannellini, the smaller one, Eastern Cannellini.

Flageolet (also called Green Flageolet). Very slender, white to pale green bean. Mild taste; buttery, melting texture.

Flor de Mayo (also called Flor de Junio). Small red bean with medium-firm but creamy texture and subtly sweet flavor.

New Mexico Appaloosa. Mottled black and white or red and white. Smooth, creamy texture; mild, earthy flavor.

Scarlet Runner. Inch-long purple bean with black markings. Meaty, starchy texture and sweet chestnut flavor.

White Aztec (also called Pueblo). Thumb-size, plump white bean with a flavor and texture reminiscent of potatoes.

DEBORAH DENKER

½ cup minced **onion**

1 cup **brandy**

1 teaspoon **salt** (optional)

½ teaspoon **pepper**

About 1 cup **cooked black beans,** heated

Finely chopped **fresh cilantro**

1. Soak beans (see page 57).

2. In a 6- to 8-quart pan, bring 7 cups water and beans to a boil. Reduce heat; simmer, covered, 45 minutes.

3. Meanwhile, in a 10- to 12-inch frying pan over medium-high heat, stir bacon often until browned, about 5 minutes. Lift bacon from pan; drain on towels.

4. Discard all but 3 tablespoons fat from pan. Add chilies and onion; stir often until onion is brown, about 5 minutes. Stir in brandy.

5. Add mixture to beans, plus bacon, salt, and pepper. Simmer, covered, until beans are tender, about 30 minutes.

6. Ladle soup into bowls. Spoon beans on top of soup. Garnish with cilantro.

Per serving: 596 cal., 26% (153 cal.) from fat; 32 g protein; 17 g fat (5.4 g sat.); 73 g carbo (11 g fiber); 320 mg sodium; 20 mg chol.

Citrus and Bean Salad

Prep and cook time: About 1½ hours, plus at least 2 hours for soaking beans

Notes: Katharine Kagel of Cafe Pasqual's created this recipe.

Makes: 7 cups, 8 servings

2 cups (14 oz.) **dried beans** such as Red Appaloosa, Flor de Mayo, or Scarlet Runner

2 cups finely chopped **red onions,** plus ½ cup thinly sliced red onion

2 tablespoons minced **garlic**

About 1 teaspoon **salt**

1 cup minced **parsley**

¼ cup **olive oil**

¼ cup **lemon juice**

2 tablespoons fresh-ground **pepper**

1 tablespoon long, fine shreds **orange** peel

1 tablespoon long, fine shreds **lemon** peel

1 teaspoon long, fine shreds **lime** peel

3 **oranges** (1½ lb. total), peel and membrane removed, cut into round slices

---

1. Soak beans as directed on page 57.

2. In a 6- to 8-quart pan, bring 2 quarts water, beans, 1½ cups chopped onions, and garlic to a boil over high heat. Reduce heat and simmer, covered, for 40 minutes. Add 1 teaspoon salt and simmer until beans are just tender to bite, 30 to 40 minutes longer.

3. Drain beans and let cool in a bowl. Gently mix in remaining ½ cup chopped onion, parsley, oil, lemon juice, and pepper. Garnish with onion slices, and orange, lemon, and lime peels. Spoon over orange slices. Add salt to taste.

Per serving: 289 cal., 24% (68 cal.) from fat; 13 g protein; 7.6 g fat (1 g sat.); 45 g carbo (8.2 g fiber); 292 mg sodium; 0 mg chol.

Smoky Black Beans with Grilled Lamb

Prep and cook time: About 1½ hours, plus at least 2 hours for soaking beans

Notes: This recipe comes from Mark Kiffin, corporate executive chef of Coyote Cafe.

Makes: 4 servings

1 cup **dried black beans** such as Black Appaloosa or Black Valentine

2½ cups chopped **onions**

1 cup lightly packed **fresh cilantro**

1 **fresh serrano chili,** stemmed

2 cloves **garlic**

1 teaspoon **ground cumin**

½ teaspoon **dried oregano**

2 cups **beef** or lamb **broth**

¼ pound diced **smoked bacon** (preferably applewood-smoked)

½ cup **dry red wine**

1 pound **tomatoes** (about 3)

1 tablespoon minced **fresh marjoram** leaves (or 1 teaspoon dried marjoram), plus marjoram sprigs

1 teaspoon **balsamic vinegar**

Salt and **pepper**

4 **lamb loin chops** (about 1¼ in. thick each, 1½ lb. total), fat trimmed

1. Soak beans as directed on page 57.

2. In a 4- to 5-quart pan over high heat, bring 2 cups water, 1 cup chopped onion, cilantro, chili, garlic, ½ teaspoon cumin, and oregano to a boil. Reduce heat and simmer, covered, for 10 minutes. Whirl in a blender until smooth.

3. In pan combine onion mixture, broth, and soaked beans. Bring to a boil over high heat, then reduce heat and simmer, covered, for 45 minutes.

4. Meanwhile, in a 3- to 4-quart pan over medium heat, frequently stir bacon and 1½ cups onion until onion is deep golden, about 20 minutes. Stir in wine and set aside.

5. On a rack in a 12- by 15-inch broiler pan, broil tomatoes 2 inches from heat, turning until blackened all over, about 15 minutes. Coarsely chop; set aside.

6. Add bacon mixture, tomatoes, minced marjoram, and vinegar to beans. Simmer, uncovered, stirring often, until beans are tender to bite and enough liquid evaporates to make a thick stew, 30 to 40 minutes. Add salt and pepper to taste.

7. While beans simmer, sprinkle lamb all over with salt, pepper, and remaining cumin. Broil 2 inches below heat, turning once, until done to your liking, about 8 minutes for medium-rare.

8. Spoon bean mixture into 4 wide soup bowls. Top each with a lamb chop, and garnish with marjoram sprigs.

Per serving: 543 cal., 40% (216 cal.) from fat; 37 g protein; 24 g fat (8.5 g sat.); 46 g carbo (9.7 g fiber); 303 mg sodium; 80 mg chol.

Herbed Filet Mignon, Bean, and Arugula Salad

Prep and cook time: About 1 hour and 20 minutes, plus at least 2 hours for soaking beans

Notes: Katharine Kagel of Cafe Pasqual's collaborated with David Mendoza on this recipe.

Makes: 4 servings

1½ cups (¾ lb.) **dried white beans** such as White Aztec, Cannellini, or Flageolet

1 pound **filet mignon steaks** (about 1¾ in. thick), fat trimmed

½ cup **extra-virgin olive oil**

3 tablespoons minced **fresh sage** leaves

2 tablespoons minced **fresh thyme** leaves

2 tablespoons minced **fresh oregano** leaves

About 1 teaspoon **salt** (optional)

About ½ teaspoon **pepper**

1 tablespoon minced **garlic**

2 tablespoons **lemon juice**

1 quart lightly packed **arugula**

½ cup (1 oz.) wide shavings **parmesan cheese** (optional)

Lemon wedges

1. Soak beans as directed at right.

2. Brown meat in 1 teaspoon oil in a 10- to 12-inch frying pan over medium-high heat, turning as needed, about 20 seconds per side. Discard oil.

3. Lift meat to a 9-inch baking pan. Bake in a 350° oven until a thermometer inserted into side of a steak reaches 128°, 20 to 25 minutes. Let meat cool, then chill airtight until cold, about 1 hour.

4. Combine sage, thyme, and oregano; set aside 3 tablespoons of the mixture. Thinly slice meat across the grain and place in the 9-inch pan. Mix with 2 tablespoons oil, then sprinkle evenly with remaining herbs, salt, and pepper. Chill airtight at least 30 minutes or up to 4 hours.

5. While meat cooks and cools, bring beans and 2 quarts water to a boil over high heat in a 5- to 6-quart pan. Reduce heat and simmer, covered, for 40 minutes. Add 1 teaspoon salt and ½ teaspoon pepper. Simmer until beans are just tender to bite, 30 to 40 minutes. Drain; transfer to a bowl.

6. In a 6- to 8-inch frying pan over medium heat, stir remaining oil and the garlic until garlic is pale golden, about 2 minutes. Stir in reserved herb mixture. Combine with beans. Add lemon juice. If making ahead, chill airtight up to 4 hours.

7. Bring meat (and beans, if chilled) to room temperature. Arrange arugula in a wide bowl. Spoon beans and then beef on top. Garnish with parmesan and serve with lemon wedges to squeeze over salad.

Per serving: 711 cal., 46% (324 cal.) from fat; 46 g protein; 36 g fat (7.3 g sat.); 55 g carbo (9.9 g fiber); 98 mg sodium; 72 mg chol. ◆

White Aztec beans, filet mignon, fresh herbs, and shaved parmesan top a bed of arugula.

Bean basics

- **How to soak.** Sort beans for debris, then rinse. For every 2 cups dried beans, bring beans and 2 quarts water to a boil over high heat in a 5- to 6-quart pan. Cover, boil for 2 minutes, and remove from heat. Beans are ready to cook after soaking for 2 hours, but are more digestible after 4 hours. To use, drain and rinse.

    If cooked without soaking, beans will require more liquid and more time than our recipes note.

- **Adding salt and acidic foods.** If stirred in too early, ingredients such as tomatoes, wine, and citrus juices can toughen beans and slow down cooking. Wait to add them until 15 to 30 minutes before the end of the cooking time.

- **How much to cook.** One pound of dried beans (about 2¼ cups) yields 5 to 6 cups cooked.

- **How long to cook.** Different beans vary in the time they need to get tender, and in their natural creaminess versus starchiness. Also, you may want them firm for some uses, softer for others. Most beans lose their shape as they get soft, so watch them carefully toward the end of the cooking time to get the texture you want.

This silken-textured pie has luscious flavor but does use a lot of lemons. You can mail-order if you don't grow them and can't find them at the market.

The sweeter side of Meyer lemons

Prized for their floral aroma and mild flavor, they really shine at dessert

"Meyer lemons are the angels of the citrus world," exclaims Donia Bijan, chef-owner of L'Amie Donia restaurant in Palo Alto. "I could eat one—skin, seeds, and all—like an apple. They're so sweet, and yet they have a nice tartness that gives a kick to everything."

Lindsey Shere, pastry chef for Chez Panisse restaurant in Berkeley, adds, "The peel has a really wonderful, very flowery taste. They're especially well suited to desserts because of their complex flavor."

This current darling of chefs—thought to be a cross between a lemon and an orange—is growing in favor with home cooks and gardeners, too. Commercial growers around San Diego and in California's San Joaquin Valley are increasing production, and specialty produce purveyors are more will-ing to carry the thin-skinned, some-what perishable lemon. (Chilled, it keeps a few weeks.)

California Citrus Specialties (209/781-0886) sells Meyers by mail—3 pounds for $9.95, plus shipping. Call soon; the season ends in March.

Designed specifically for Meyers, our recipes use the juice and peel in gen-erous quantities for extraordinarily lemony, floral results.

Meyer Custard-Cream Pie

Prep and cook time: About 40 minutes, plus 2 hours for chilling
Makes: 8 servings

10 (about 2⅓ lb.) **Meyer lemons**
⅓ cup **cornstarch**
1 cup **sugar**
3 **large eggs**
1 cup **whipping cream**
    Baked, cooled 9-inch **pastry shell** (if purchasing, use a deep-dish crust)

1. Grate 2 teaspoons peel from lemons. With a zester or Asian shredder, make a few long, slender strands of peel from Meyer or regular lemons; set aside. Ream 1⅓ cups juice from the lemons.

2. In the top of a double boiler, mix cornstarch and sugar. Stir in juice and grated peel. Fill bottom of double boiler with 1 inch water. Place pans over high heat and bring water to a simmer; adjust heat to maintain sim-mer. Stir until mixture is thick and shiny, 8 to 9 minutes. In a bowl, whisk eggs to blend. Whisk in about ½ cup lemon mixture, then return all to pan. Stir until mixture is very thick and reaches 160° on an instant-read ther-mometer, about 5 minutes.

3. Remove top pan. Place in a bowl of ice and stir often until mixture is cool to touch, about 6 minutes.

4. In a bowl, beat cream with a mixer until stiff. Fold in lemon mixture, then spread evenly in pastry shell. Scatter reserved strands of peel on top. Chill, uncovered, until slightly firm to touch, about 2 hours. Serve, or wrap airtight and chill up to 1 day.

Per serving: 361 cal., 47% (171 cal.) from fat; 4.6 g protein; 19 g fat (8.3 g sat.); 45 g carbo (0.4 g fiber); 157 mg sodium; 113 mg chol.

by **ELAINE JOHNSON**

Meyer Lemon Sherbet

Prep and cook time: About 1 hour, plus 2 hours for freezing if a firmer texture is desired

Makes: 5½ cups, 10 servings

  8 (about 2 lb.) **Meyer lemons**
  1 envelope **unflavored gelatin**
  1 cup **sugar**
  ¾ cup **milk**

1. Grate 1 tablespoon peel and ream 1 cup juice from lemons; set aside.

2. Combine gelatin and ¼ cup cold water; set aside until gelatin is softened, about 5 minutes.

3. In a 2- to 3-quart pan over high heat, bring sugar and 1 cup water to a boil. Reduce heat and simmer until sugar is dissolved, about 1 minute.

4. Stir in gelatin, lemon peel and juice, and milk (mixture may look curdled). Place pan in a bowl of ice water and stir often until cold, 8 to 10 minutes.

5. Freeze mixture in an ice cream maker according to manufacturer's directions. (Or pour mixture into a metal 9- by 13-inch pan, cover airtight, and freeze until hard, about 3 hours. Then break into chunks with a spoon and whirl in a food processor until smooth.)

6. Serve sherbet, or freeze until firm enough to scoop, about 2 hours.

Per serving: 97 cal., 5.6% (5.4 cal.) from fat; 1.3 g protein; 0.6 g fat (0.4 g sat.); 23 g carbo (0 g fiber); 11 mg sodium; 2.6 mg chol.

Meyer Lemon Soufflés

Prep and cook time: About 55 minutes

Notes: The trick to making a perfect soufflé is to not overbeat the egg whites. If making ahead, let yolk mixture (step 3) and sauce (step 7) stand at room temperature up to 1 hour. Fifty minutes before serving, finish and bake soufflés; reheat sauce at the last minute.

Makes: 6 servings

  8 (about 2 lb.) **Meyer lemons**
      About 4 tablespoons **butter** or margarine
  ¼ cup **all-purpose flour**
  1 cup **half-and-half**
      About 1 cup **granulated sugar**
  6 **large eggs,** separated
  ¼ teaspoon **cream of tartar**

For a dramatic dessert, spoon a hole in the center of a warm lemon soufflé and pour in a tart-sweet lemon sauce.

E. J. ARMSTRONG

  2 teaspoons **cornstarch**
  1½ teaspoons **powdered sugar**

1. Grate 2½ teaspoons peel and ream ⅓ cup plus ½ cup juice from lemons; set aside.

2. Lightly butter 6 ramekins, 1¼- to 1½-cup size. Evenly space in a 10- by 15-inch rimmed baking pan.

3. Melt 4 tablespoons butter in a 2- to 3-quart pan over medium-high heat. Whisk in flour, then half-and-half and ⅓ cup granulated sugar. Whisk constantly until mixture comes to a boil; boil 30 seconds. Remove from heat. Whisk in ⅓ cup lemon juice, yolks, and 2 teaspoons lemon peel.

4. In the bowl of a mixer, beat egg whites until foamy. Add cream of tartar and beat until soft peaks form. Beat in ⅓ cup granulated sugar, 1 tablespoon at a time, just until whites hold straight, glossy peaks when beaters are lifted.

5. Stir about 1 cup egg whites into yolk mixture, then gently fold yolk mixture into whites until no streaks remain. Spoon mixture evenly into ramekins (they'll be full).

6. For a creamy texture, bake in a 375° oven until softly set (when gently shaken, soufflés should ripple in center only), 12 to 13 minutes. For a drier texture, bake 20 minutes.

7. Meanwhile, in a 1- to 2-quart pan, combine cornstarch and 6 tablespoons granulated sugar. Stir in remaining ½ cup lemon juice. Stir over medium-high heat until bubbling, 3 to 5 minutes. Stir in remaining ½ teaspoon lemon peel.

8. Sift powdered sugar over soufflés. At the table, spoon a hole in the center of each soufflé and pour in sauce.

Per serving: 369 cal., 46% (171 cal.) from fat; 8.2 g protein; 19 g fat (10 g sat.); 44 g carbo (0.1 g fiber); 171 mg sodium; 251 mg chol. ◆

CHEFS' TIPS *for* **USING MEYERS**

When substituting Meyer lemons for standard Eurekas, Donia Bijan says she is more heavy-handed. "If a recipe asks for the zest of two Eureka lemons, I might use five [Meyers]." Lindsey Shere, on the other hand, doesn't increase Meyer quantities in recipes calling for standard lemons; if necessary, she augments the tartness with a little Eureka lemon juice.

Shere makes allowances for Meyers getting increasingly sweeter and more orange as the season progresses from December to March.

In general, both chefs like Meyer lemons in delicate desserts such as sorbets and ice creams, custards, Bavarians, and tarts. The zest also does wonders for cookie doughs and poached fruit. Shere also loves the lemons candied.

PAUL FRANZ-MOORE

Inside its dark shroud, jack cheese ages until it's golden, mellow, and dry.

"Poor man's parmesan" is rediscovered

Born with the Gold Rush, transmuted by accident, dry jack comes into its own once again for eating and cooking

Row upon row of 8-pound wheels of dry jack cheese, the color of earth, fill the wood racks in the cool pungent air of the Vella Cheese Company's curing and aging room in Sonoma, California. To owner Ig Vella, this aromatic inventory is restored treasure.

Farther north, John Rumiano eyes a stash of drying jack with the same respect. His brother, Baird, makes the cheese in Crescent City, near the Oregon border. Then he sends the wheels down to John, in Willows, to be aged in the hand-poured concrete cellars built by their grandfather, Richard—who dubbed dry jack "poor man's parmesan."

Once there were as many as 60 companies that produced dry jack cheese. But during the Great Depression, and later when lower-priced imported cheeses had the competitive edge, dry jack struggled to survive. Today, only the Rumianos (in business since 1920) and the Vellas (operating since 1931) continue to supply the tenacious cult of dry jack fanciers who have refused to let this aged jack fade away.

Why?

It's the cheese.

Almost 150 years ago, during California Gold Rush days, a Scotsman in Monterey County, David Jacks, developed the cheese. Its distinctive, delicate flavor, pale moonglow hue, and creamy smooth texture were unique. Known as Monterey Jack cheese, for its birthplace and creator, it was soon the darling of the domestic fresh cheese market.

And it stood apart from the hard grating cheeses from Europe.

But when World War I slammed the door on those imports, the West's Italian immigrants were desperate for a substitute for their indispensable *parmigiano* and *romano*.

Fate stepped in. San Francisco wholesaler D. F. De Bernardi came across an overlooked cache of jack cheese that he had salted down and stored months before. Much to his surprise, the soft jack had dried as it aged, developing a dark gold color and fine mellow flavor with sweet nuttiness. It was also hard enough to grate well. With marketing savvy, De Bernardi coated the hard cheese wheels with oil, pepper, and lampblack (which has since been replaced by cocoa), as the Italians did, and presented it to a clamoring clientele, who loved this new dry jack.

Now, the clamor sounds again. Sales are on the upswing and production is increasing. "People have rediscovered it. It is sort of trendy," says Ig Vella.

Perhaps the championship cheese awards that Vella's Special Select Dry Monterey won at the U.S. Cheese Championships in 1995 and 1996 helped bring dry jack back into the spotlight. Or perhaps it's the growing interest in cheeses in general. Or perhaps it's value. As the prices of imports have soared, dry jack cheese, which costs about half as much, is looking good.

Dan Berman, owner and chef of Mixx Restaurant in Santa Rosa, California, offers more reasons for its growing popularity: "It's a real flexible cheese—grates easily, melts well, and ages nicely. People feel good eating local products."

At Lisa Hemenway's Restaurant, also in Santa Rosa, owner Hemenway shaves dry jack onto salad greens mixed with toasted pine nuts, pear slices, and Dijon mustard and balsamic vinegar dressing.

And wine professionals point out that dry jack is wine-friendly. Says wine writer Dan Berger, "Dry jack is a rare example of a mature cheese that matches the oxidicity of old Cabernets. Texturally, it gives a different sensual experience than chunks of parmesan."

Pascal Olhats, chef-owner of Pascal's Restaurant in Newport Beach, California, prefers dry jack cheese with a French white burgundy. "Together they both stand out," he says.

How do cheesemakers use dry jack? Baird Rumiano likes it "plain, shaved in thin slices, with a glass of good red wine." Vella recommends it "on all pastas, on eggplant, ratatouille, and Caesar salad … it depends on the day and phase of the moon."

COOKING WITH JACK

The dark coating on dry jack cheese is edible, but if you don't like its taste, just cut it off.

by **LINDA LAU ANUSASANANAN**

Jack facts

I t takes about 100 pounds of cow's milk to make an 8-pound wheel of dry jack cheese. The fresh cheese is hand-shaped in cloth bags, cured in brine, rubbed with the dark coating, then aged from six months to two years. The cheese shrinks at least 25 percent.

Many cheese shops and supermarkets throughout the West sell dry jack cut from wheels or in plastic-wrapped wedges. If you aren't able to locate a source, order directly from the following companies.

Rumiano Cheese Company, Box 863, Willows, CA 95988 (916/934-5438); or Box 305, Crescent City, CA 95531 (707/465-1535). Willow Maid dry jack is aged at least six months. It comes plain or smoked. The plain dry jack costs $3.95 per pound for cut pieces, $3.70 per pound for a whole wheel (about 8 lb.). Smoked dry jack sells for $5.95 per pound for cut pieces, $5.25 per pound for a whole wheel. Prices do not include shipping.

Vella Cheese Company, 315 Second St. E., Sonoma, CA

95476; (800) 848-0505. Bear Flag dry jack is aged for 7 to 10 months, Special Select Dry Monterey is aged for more than a year, and Golden Bear is aged for at least two years. Prices range from $32 to $36 for a half-wheel (3½ to 4 lb.) to $55 to $60 for a whole wheel (7 to 8 lb.). Prices include shipping.

Storing a hunk of dry jack. If you purchase a wheel of jack, put it on a wood rack in a cool place (50° to 55°) until you're ready to cut. Properly stored, it keeps up to a year. If the surface dries or mold develops, rub clean with a cloth and salad oil.

When cutting portions, you may need to tap the knife with a mallet to drive it through. Always leave the balance of the cheese in as large a piece as possible. Wrap cut cheese airtight, enclose in a paper bag, and refrigerate up to six months. Rub off the first signs of mold with salted water, or trim off and discard.

You can also grate the cheese and store in airtight containers in the refrigerator up to two weeks, or in the freezer up to a year.

Fried Almond-crusted Jack

Prep and cook time: About 25 minutes
Notes: Mary Ellen Oertel, chef at the Swiss Hotel in Sonoma, serves these nut-crusted slices as a first course, but with a green salad, they make a main dish for lunch or dinner.
Makes: 6 to 8 servings

Break through almond crust to release melting dry jack cheese.

1   **baguette** (8 oz.)

1   **wedge** (about ¾ lb.) **dry jack cheese**

    About ¾ cup **all-purpose flour**

1   **large egg,** beaten to blend

¾ cup finely **chopped almonds**

1   tablespoon **salad oil**

1   tablespoon **olive oil**

1. Cut baguette into ½-inch-thick slices and lay in a single layer in a 10- by 15-inch pan. Bake in a 350° oven until golden, about 15 minutes.

2. Meanwhile, with a knife or vegetable peeler, cut off and discard dark coating on cheese. Set cheese wedge on a flat side and cut 6 to 8 triangles of equal thickness.

3. Place flour, egg, and almonds on separate plates. Coat each cheese slice with flour, then egg, then almonds. Lay slices in a single layer.

4. Set an 11- to 12-inch frying pan over medium heat. When the pan is hot, add salad oil and olive oil. Lay the cheese slices in pan without crowding, and brown the slices on each side, 10 to 12 minutes total. With a wide spatula, transfer browned cheese to warm plate. Spoon cheese onto toast slices and eat.

Per serving: 390 cal., 55% (216 cal.) from fat; 17 g protein; 24 g fat (8.9 g sat.); 26 g carbo (2.4 g fiber); 410 mg sodium; 72 mg chol.

Soft Polenta with Dry Jack

Prep and cook time: About 30 minutes
Notes: When chef Drew Rosen made creamy polenta at the former Eastside Oyster Bar and Grill in Sonoma, he mellowed it further with dry jack. Look for semolina flour in natural-food markets.
Makes: 6 servings

1   cup **polenta**

⅓ cup **semolina flour** (or more polenta)

4½ cups **chicken broth**

1½ cups **whipping cream** or milk

1   tablespoon **butter** or margarine

3   to 4 ounces **dry jack cheese,** shaved, or 1 to 1⅓ cups grated dry jack cheese

    Salt and **pepper**

1. In a 5- to 6-quart pan, mix polenta and flour. Stir in broth and cream, mixing well. Bring to a boil over high heat, stirring often with a whisk or spoon to prevent lumps and sticking. Reduce heat; simmer uncovered, stirring often, until polenta feels creamy and smooth to taste, 15 to 20 minutes.

2. Stir butter and half the cheese into polenta; ladle into bowls. Sprinkle remaining cheese over polenta and add salt and pepper to taste.

Per serving: 467 cal., 50% (234 cal.) from fat; 12 g protein; 26 g fat (16 g sat.); 46 g carbo (5 g fiber); 195 mg sodium; 89 mg chol. ◆

Rich-flavored green, lemonnaise, and dried-tomato sauces let you dunk and feel virtuous at the same time.

SUZANNE SMITH

2 tablespoons **lemon juice**

2 teaspoons **extra-virgin olive oil**

½ teaspoon **dry mustard**

Salt and **fresh-ground pepper**

1. Fill a 6- to 8-quart pan halfway with water. Add vinegar and peppercorns; bring to a boil over high heat.

2. Meanwhile, slice about 1 inch off tops of artichokes; discard tips. Trim stems flush with bottoms. Pull off and discard small leaves from bottoms. With scissors, cut thorny tips from remaining outer leaves.

3. Add artichokes to water and simmer, covered, until bottoms pierce easily, 30 to 35 minutes; drain.

4. While artichokes cook, make lemonnaise. In a blender or food processor (a blender produces the best results), whirl tofu, lemon juice, oil, and mustard until smooth. Season with salt and pepper. (If making ahead, chill airtight up to 1 day; stir before using.)

5. Serve artichokes with sauce for dipping.

Per serving: 124 cal., 29% (36 cal.) from fat; 9.3 g protein; 4 g fat (0.6 g sat.); 16 g carbo (7.1 g fiber); 170 mg sodium; 0 mg chol.

VARYING YOUR DUNK SAUCE

For variations on lemonnaise (step 4 above), add ingredients to the basic recipe and whirl in a blender or food processor until smooth.

• *Aioli.* Add 1 clove minced **garlic.**

• *Caper-anchovy sauce.* Add 2 teaspoons drained **capers** and 1½ teaspoons **anchovy paste.**

• *Chili-cilantro sauce.* Instead of lemon juice, use 4 teaspoons **lime juice.** Add ½ to 1 stemmed **fresh serrano chili** and ⅓ cup packed **fresh cilantro.**

• *Dried-tomato sauce.* Add ¼ cup **dried tomato halves** (not oil-packed).

• *Green sauce.* Add 1 cup *each* lightly packed **spinach leaves** and **parsley,** and ½ cup chopped **green onions.**

• *Madeira sauce.* Add 2 tablespoons *each* **madeira** and minced **chives.**

• *Orange-coriander sauce.* Use only 1 tablespoon **lemon juice.** Add 4 teaspoons **orange juice** and ½ teaspoon *each* **ground coriander** and grated **orange peel.**

• *Tamari-sesame sauce.* Substitute **Asian (toasted) sesame oil** for olive oil. Add 1½ teaspoons **tamari.** ◆

Gilding the artichoke

Better, lighter dunks for enjoying the edible thorn

Dipped in mayonnaise, drizzled with olive oil, dunked in melted butter—we know plenty of naughty ways to savor that edible thistle, the artichoke. On its own, the artichoke is innocent of fat, and a large specimen contains a mere 60 calories. Yet naked artichokes are by no means festive. So how do you give the illusion of richness while honoring the artichoke's virtuous profile?

Jane Rubey, a cooking instructor and dietitian from Orinda, California, has created a deceptively creamy, pleasingly tangy sauce she calls "lemonnaise."

What's her secret? Silken tofu. It has none of the chalky texture or strong flavor of other kinds of tofu. In fact, not one of our tasters could pick it out in our lemonnaise sampling.

You can whirl up the sauce in just a couple of minutes, and it takes well to many variations. Add just one or two ingredients and it becomes an entirely different sauce. We list eight options.

Artichokes with Lemonnaise

Prep and cook time: About 45 minutes, including 2 minutes to prepare sauce

Makes: 4 servings

3 tablespoons **distilled white vinegar**

1 teaspoon **black peppercorns**

4 **artichokes** (each about 4 in. wide; 3 lb. total)

½ cup drained **extra firm,** firm, or soft **silken tofu**

Can you have too much pasta?

If you were to check my kitchen cupboards, you'd find at least five kinds of pasta. It's one of my favorite foods, and an essential pantry item for anyone interested in quick cooking.

Today's pastas range from plain to fancy (some tiny works of art cost a small fortune). But though boutique pastas can be delicious, you don't need a gourmet variety for a great meal. I make my favorite pasta dish with spaghetti—the kind that sells for less than $1 per pound. Although the ingredient combination may seem unusual, the flavor is amazing.

NORMAN A. PLATE

It takes only 20 minutes to prepare this zesty entrée.

What's for dinner?

Spaghetti with Clams, Tuna, and Bacon

Sliced tomato and cucumber salad

Warm sourdough bread

Fresh strawberries and almond biscotti

Spaghetti with Clams, Tuna, and Bacon

Prep and cook time: About 20 minutes

Makes: 4 servings

⅓ pound **bacon,** chopped

5 cloves **garlic,** minced

1 pound **dried spaghetti**

½ cup **chicken broth**

1 can (6½ oz.) **chopped clams**

1 can (2¼ oz.) **sliced black olives,** drained

1 can (6 oz.) **water-packed albacore tuna,** drained and flaked

Lemon wedges

Minced **parsley**

1. In a covered pan over high heat, begin heating enough water to cook spaghetti. Meanwhile, cook bacon in a 10- to 12-inch frying pan over medium-high heat, stirring often. Add garlic after 5 minutes; cook until bacon has browned, 8 to 10 minutes. Drain all but 2 tablespoons of fat from the pan.

2. When water is boiling, add spaghetti; cook, uncovered, until tender to bite, about 10 minutes. Meanwhile, to pan with bacon, add broth, clams with their juice, and olives. Bring bacon mixture to a boil over high heat; cover and keep warm.

3. Drain pasta well; toss with bacon mixture and tuna. Arrange on a serving platter or individual plates. Garnish with lemon and parsley.

Per serving: 645 cal., 21% (135 cal.) from fat; 35 g protein; 15 g fat (4.3 g sat.); 88 g carbo (3.3 g fiber); 542 mg sodium; 47 mg chol.

As the pasta business has grown, so has the number of sauces. Many prepared sauces are of good quality, and they're certainly fast and convenient. But I find it incredibly satisfying to make my own simple tomato sauce. It takes just 20 minutes—only slightly longer than heating a prepared sauce. I start with canned tomatoes and dress them up with whatever I have on hand. The re-sults taste surprisingly fresh. Here's my favorite combination—delicious over anything from capellini to ravioli, and great in lasagna.

20-minute Pasta Sauce. In a 5- to 6-quart pan, combine 1 chopped **onion,** 6 minced cloves **garlic,** and 1 tablespoon **olive oil.** Stir often over medium-high heat until onion is soft, about 5 minutes. While onion cooks, mince ¼ cup **fresh basil** leaves. Add to onion along with 1 can (28 oz.) **pear-shaped tomatoes** with their juice, ½ cup **dry red wine,** and ½ teaspoon **hot chili flakes.** Boil until reduced to 3 cups, about 10 minutes, stirring often and breaking tomatoes into small pieces. Use hot. Makes 3 cups sauce; 4 servings.

Per serving: 116 cal., 31% (36 cal.) from fat; 2.8 g protein; 4 g fat (0.6 g sat.); 15 g carbo (2.6 g fiber); 327 mg sodium; 0 mg chol.

MORE QUICK PASTA IDEAS

•Toss your choice of cooked pasta with the 20-minute Pasta Sauce above, crumbled cooked Italian turkey sausage, and slivered mustard greens.

•Combine cooked penne or linguine with chunks of creamy blue cheese, toasted walnuts, and enough chicken or beef broth to moisten. ◆

A decorative crust tops a filling of beef flank steak, stir-fry vegetables, green onions, and rice. Oyster sauce, garlic, and chilies add bold flavor.

Pot pies: the new generation

They're more flavorful—and as popular as ever

If you think that homemade pot pies and a busy schedule are incompatible, check out these savory updated versions. With help from some shortcut ingredients, your pie can be ready for the oven in just 40 minutes.

Handy stir-fry vegetables, flank steak, and rice create one flavorful filling. For another, chicken and potatoes combine with canned black beans, corn, tomatoes, and chilies. For ease and speed, use purchased refrigerated pie crusts.

Stir-fry Beef Pot Pie

Prep and cook time: About 1 hour and 40 minutes, including 1 hour baking

Notes: You can substitute 1 pound mixed frozen vegetables for fresh.

Makes: 1 pie, 6 servings

- 1 cup **medium-grain white rice**
- 1¼ cups **beef broth**
- ⅓ cup **oyster sauce**
- 2 tablespoons **cornstarch**
- 4 cloves **garlic,** minced
- ½ to 1 teaspoon **hot chili flakes**
- 1 pound **beef flank steak**
- 2 teaspoons **olive o   lad oil**
- 1 pound (about 5 c   fresh stir-fry vegetable mi   e (found in produce section)
- 1 cup **green onion   (1-in. size)
- 1 **unbaked refrige   crust** (½ of a 15-oz. pa   room temperature

1. In a 2- to 3-quart p   e with 1⅔ cups water. Brir   over high heat; cover, r   and simmer 15 minutes.   heat; let stand, covered, 15   er.

2. Meanwhile, mix   with oyster sauce, cornstar   chili flakes; set aside. Thin   cross grain into ⅛-inch-thic   il to a 10- to 12-inch no   pan over high heat; whe   eat. Cook, stirring consta   at is no longer pink, abo   Add remaining broth,   able mixture, and onion   red, just until vegetables   een, about 3 minutes. St   roth into meat mixture; b

3. In a bowl, combi   eat-vegetable mixture;   10-inch pie dish, 9-inch   1½-quart baking dish.

4. Unfold pie crust   ack-age directions. On   red board, roll into a 12   pie dish, or 1 inch la   of another shape. Pla   and vegetable mixture;   der and flush with pan r   mly against rim. Cut sha   and decorate top, or ma   de-corative slits in crust

5. Bake in a 350°   g is hot in center, abou   foil over crust if it begins   Let cool about 10 min   om dish or cut into wed

Per serving: 484 cal., 37   at; 22 g protein; 20 g fat (7   o (2.6 g fiber); 911 mg so

Southw
Chicken

Prep and cook time: nd 40 minutes, includir   g

by **BETSY REYNOLDS BATESON**

version, use ¾ pound potatoes instead, and substitute 4 cups broccoli florets for the chicken.

Makes: 1 pie, 6 servings

- 1 cup **chicken broth**
- 4 **boneless, skinless chicken breast halves,** cut into about ¾-inch chunks
- ½ pound **thin-skinned potatoes,** diced
- 3 tablespoons **cornstarch**
- 1 can (14½ oz.) **stewed Mexican-style tomatoes**
- 1 can (15 oz.) **black beans,** rinsed and drained
- 1 can (8¾ oz.) **corn kernels,** drained
- 1 can (4 oz.) **diced green chilies**
- ½ cup chopped **fresh cilantro**
- 1 **unbaked refrigerated pie crust** (½ of a 15-oz. package), at room temperature

1. In a 10- to 12-inch nonstick frying pan over high heat, combine ½ cup broth, chicken, and potatoes. Cover and cook, stirring occasionally, until chicken is no longer pink when cut in thickest portion and potatoes are just barely tender when pierced, about 5 minutes.

2. Stir together remaining broth and cornstarch.

3. When chicken is done, stir in cornstarch mixture and bring to a boil. Remove from heat. Stir in tomatoes with juice, black beans, corn, chilies, and cilantro. Pour into a 10-inch pie dish, 9-inch square pan, or 1½-quart baking dish.

4. Unfold 1 pastry round according to package directions. On a lightly floured board, roll into a 12-inch round for pie dish, or 1 inch larger than dish of another shape. Place over filling; fold edges under and flush with pan rim, and flute firmly against rim. Cut shapes from crust and decorate top, or make a couple of decorative slits in crust.

5. Bake pie in a 350° oven until filling is hot in center, about 1 hour. Lay foil over crust if it begins to overbrown. Let pie cool about 10 minutes, then spoon from dish.

Per serving: 384 cal., 28% (108 cal.) from fat; 25 g protein; 12 g fat (4.4 g sat.); 45 g carbo (4.3 g fiber); 801 mg sodium; 55 mg chol. ◆

A new hero

This hearty sandwich sheds meat and cuts fat, not flavor

Walk into almost any sandwich shop these days and you'll find that vegetarian options are among the most requested items. Even the hero sandwich, traditionally a nutritional nightmare loaded with high-fat luncheon meats, has been given a face-lift, as many of us make an effort to watch our diet and eat more vegetables. And judging by their popularity, these variations are just as satisfying as their meat-filled counterparts.

That certainly is true of this hearty version, which features layers of marinated artichoke hearts, arugula, roasted red peppers, cucumber, and two kinds of cheese on the crustiest sourdough rolls you can find. But don't stop here—use this recipe as a guide to create your own signature hero. Try substituting chopped niçoise olives for artichokes, or thinly sliced jicama for cucumber. In spring, add blanched pencil-thin asparagus spears. In summer, use vine-ripened sliced red and yellow tomatoes, basil leaves, and fresh mozzarella instead of red peppers, arugula, and gouda. Let your taste buds and the market be your guide.

Artichokes, arugula, and cheese are some ingredients in a flexible combo.

Vegetarian Hero Sandwich

Prep time: About 30 minutes
Makes: 4 sandwiches

- 4 crusty oblong **sourdough rolls,** each about 3 ounces
- 1 jar (6 oz.) **marinated halved artichoke hearts**
- ½ cup **reduced-fat garlic and herb–flavor Rondelé** or Boursin **cheese**
- 2 cups (about 2 oz.) **arugula** or spinach **leaves,** rinsed and crisped
- 1 cup **prepared roasted red peppers,** drained and cut into thin strips
- ¼ pound thinly sliced **smoked gouda cheese**
- Thinly sliced **red onion**
- 1 **cucumber** (½ lb.), peeled and thinly sliced

1. Halve each sourdough roll horizontally, leaving one long side attached. Scoop out some of the soft bread in the top half of the roll, leaving crust intact.

2. Drain artichokes, reserving 4 tablespoons marinade. Trim off and discard any tough leaves or tips. Cut in half lengthwise and set aside. Brush reserved marinade over scooped-out portion of each roll.

3. Spread the Rondelé equally over the bottom half of each roll. Top the cheese with equal portions of arugula, red pepper strips, artichokes, gouda, onion, and cucumber. Bring the top portion of the roll over the vegetables to close the sandwich.

Per sandwich: 455 cal., 36% (162 cal.) from fat; 20 g protein; 18 g fat (8.5 g sat.); 54 g carbo (4.6 g fiber); 1,343 mg sodium; 50 mg chol. ◆

by **CHRISTINE WEBER HALE**

A spicy mixture of black-eyed peas, corn, and avocado serves as dip or salad.

Sunset's Kitchen Cabinet

As chef for Soirée Catering in Santa Ana, California, Leslee Mendel Coy constantly invents new recipes. She first developed this double-duty dish for a cooking contest. Although it didn't capture first prize, it's a winner with her clients. Start with a spicy base of black-eyed peas, tomatoes, corn, and avocado. Scoop it up with tortilla chips for an appetizer, or add cabbage and it becomes coleslaw.

Cowboy Salsa
Leslee Mendel Coy
Lake Forest, California

Prep and cook time: About 30 minutes
Makes: 10 to 12 appetizer or 6 salad servings

- 2 tablespoons **red wine vinegar**
- 1½ to 2 teaspoons **hot sauce**
- 1½ teaspoons **salad oil**
- 1 clove **garlic,** minced
- ⅛ teaspoon **pepper**
- 1 firm-ripe **avocado** (about 10 oz.)
- 1 can (15 oz.) **black-eyed peas**
- 1 can (11 oz.) **corn kernels**
- ⅔ cup thinly sliced **green onions**
- ⅔ cup chopped **fresh cilantro**
- ½ pound **Roma tomatoes,** coarsely chopped
- **Salt**
- 1 bag (6 oz.) **tortilla chips** or 2 cups finely shredded cabbage

1. In a large bowl, mix vinegar, hot sauce, oil, garlic, and pepper. Peel, pit, and cut avocado into ½-inch cubes. Add to vinegar mixture and mix gently to coat.

2. Drain and rinse peas and corn. Add peas, corn, onions, cilantro, and tomatoes to avocado; mix gently to coat. Add salt to taste. Serve pea mixture with chips as an appetizer, or add cabbage and mix to make a salad.

Per appetizer serving: 159 cal., 42% (66 cal.) from fat; 3.9 g protein; 7.3 g fat (1.3 g sat.); 22 g carbo (2 g fiber); 272 mg sodium; 0 mg chol.

Thai Chicken Curry with Coconut Milk
Rachel Foster
Glendale, Arizona

When Rachel Foster lived in downtown Phoenix, she regularly ordered Thai curry at a favorite restaurant. One day the clerk at the small market next door gave her a recipe for the curry. Foster put the recipe to use when she moved out of town. She still gets a weekly dose of her favorite Thai dish, but she cooks it herself.

Prep and cook time: About 20 minutes
Makes: 2 or 3 servings

- ½ pound **green beans,** ends trimmed
- 2 **boneless, skinless chicken breast halves** (10 to 12 oz. total)
- 1 tablespoon **salad oil**
- 1 to 1½ tablespoons **prepared Thai red curry paste** (or 1 tablespoon minced fresh ginger, 1 teaspoon curry powder, 1 teaspoon chili powder, and ¼ to ½ teaspoon cayenne)
- 1 can (14 oz.) **reduced-fat coconut milk**
- 1 teaspoon **sugar**
- 1 can (8 oz.) sliced **bamboo shoots,** rinsed and drained
- **Fish sauce** or salt

1. Slice beans diagonally into 1½-inch lengths. Cut chicken into 1-inch cubes. Place a 10- to 12-inch frying pan over high heat. When pan is hot, add oil and beans; stir-fry 2 minutes.

2. Add chicken and cook, stirring occasionally, until lightly browned, about 4 minutes. Add curry paste, coconut milk, and sugar. Reduce heat to low and stir until curry paste is well blended. Add bamboo shoots; continue cooking until hot, 3 to 4 minutes. Add fish sauce to taste.

Per serving: 325 cal., 30% (99 cal.) from fat; 24 g protein; 11 g fat (5.6 g sat.); 18 g carbo (3 g fiber); 124 mg sodium; 55 mg chol.

Fresh Peas and Pasta
Bill Hunt
Burlingame, California

"My wife was repelled by over-cooked vegetables as a child and now refuses to eat them. But she can be seduced into eating them raw on oc-

by LINDA LAU ANUSASANANAN

casion," writes Bill Hunt. When fresh peas came into the market, he made this salad for the two of them. Her opinion? "Not bad"—a high compliment in her vocabulary, says Hunt.

Prep and cook time: About 25 minutes

Makes: 2 servings

- ½ cup **dried tiny pasta shells**
- 1 pound **fresh English peas,** shelled
- 3 tablespoons **reduced-fat** or regular **mayonnaise**
- 3 tablespoons finely chopped **sweet onion**
- 2 to 3 teaspoons **horseradish**
- 1 clove **garlic,** minced
  Salt and **pepper**
- 2 large **butter lettuce** leaves, rinsed and crisped

1. Cook pasta, uncovered, in 1 to 1½ quarts boiling water until barely tender to bite, 6 to 7 minutes. Put shelled peas in colander. Pour hot pasta and its cooking water over peas; drain. Let pasta and peas stand a few minutes, then rinse with cold water; drain well.

2. Mix mayonnaise, onion, horseradish, and garlic. Stir in peas and pasta. Add salt and pepper to taste. Place lettuce leaves on serving dishes. Spoon salad onto lettuce.

Per serving: 231 cal., 21% (48 cal.) from fat; 8.4 g protein; 5.3 g fat (0.9 g sat.); 38 g carbo (4.6 g fiber); 194 mg sodium; 0 mg chol.

Orange Salsa Pork Chops
Don Cook
Cathedral City, California

Don Cook combines well-liked foods—pork chops, salsa, and Mexican spices—to make one great dish. The salsa and orange juice thicken into a spicy, fruity sauce as the chops simmer. Serve with hot cooked rice.

Prep and cook time: About 50 minutes

Makes: 4 servings

- 4 **pork center-cut loin chops** (each about ¾ inch thick, about 6 oz.)
- 1 teaspoon **salad oil**
- 1 cup **orange juice**
- ½ cup **tomato salsa**
- 2 tablespoons firmly packed **brown sugar**
- ¼ teaspoon **ground cumin**

- ¼ teaspoon **ground ginger**
  Salt
  Fresh cilantro sprigs
  Orange slices

1. Trim excess fat from pork. Place a 10- to 12-inch nonstick frying pan over medium-high heat. When pan is hot, add oil and chops. Cook until browned on both sides, about 5 minutes total.

2. Add orange juice, salsa, sugar, cumin, and ginger. Bring to a boil, then reduce heat to low; cover and simmer until pork is tender when pierced, 40 to 45 minutes. Skim off fat; discard. Transfer pork to a serving dish and keep warm. Boil sauce, uncovered, over high heat until reduced to about 1 cup, about 4 minutes. Add salt to taste. Garnish with cilantro and orange slices.

Per serving: 230 cal., 27% (61 cal.) from fat; 25 g protein; 6.8 g fat (2.1 g sat.); 15 g carbo (0.1 g fiber); 397 mg sodium; 70 mg chol.

Irish Brown Bread
Cristina Faulkner
La Mirada, California

When Cristina Faulkner visited County Armagh, Ireland, the home of her husband's ancestors, she discovered this simple crusty brown bread. Faulkner replaced the buttermilk in the original recipe with yogurt. It's such a quick and easy bread to make, her son started baking it when he was 7.

Prep and cook time: About 50 minutes

Makes: 1 loaf (about 1¾ lb.)

- 1 cup **all-purpose flour**
- 2 tablespoons **sugar**
- 1 teaspoon **baking powder**
- 1 teaspoon **baking soda**
- ½ teaspoon **salt**
- 1½ tablespoons cold **butter** or margarine
- 2 cups **whole-wheat flour**
- ¼ cup **regular** or quick-cooking **rolled oats**
- 1½ cups **plain nonfat yogurt**
  Milk

1. In a bowl, mix all-purpose flour, sugar, baking powder, baking soda, and salt. With a pastry blender or 2 knives, cut in butter until mixture forms fine crumbs. Stir in whole-wheat flour and oats.

2. Add yogurt; stir gently. If mixture is too dry to hold together, stir in milk, 1 teaspoon at a time, just until dough holds together; it should not be sticky.

3. Turn dough onto a lightly floured board and knead gently 5 times to make a ball. Set on a lightly greased baking sheet. Pat into a 7-inch circle. With a floured knife, cut a large X on top of loaf.

4. Bake in a 375° oven until well browned, about 40 minutes. Cool on a rack. Serve warm or cool.

Per 1-oz. serving: 64 cal., 13% (8.1 cal.) from fat; 2.4 g protein; 0.9 g fat (0.4 g sat.); 12 g carbo (1.3 g fiber); 118 mg sodium; 2 mg chol.◆

Break off chunks of crusty brown bread to serve with soups or salads.

Light as a cloud, luscious with berries: low-fat cheesecake allows you to indulge without guilt (see page 74).

April

foodguide

by **JERRY ANNE DI VECCHIO**

JONELLE WEAVER

a TASTE *of the* WEST

A fine kettle of fish

Although I admire the beauty of my fish soup, I make and serve it for more practical reasons.

With salad, bread, and a dessert, this soup handsomely fills any bill of fare. The potatoes and mild fennel absorb the subtle richness released by a modest amount of shellfish and fish into the broth, wine, and cream base. Hardworking. Good value.

And yet, I wouldn't hesitate to serve this soup to Alice, the mad Hatter, the Red Queen, my son-in-law, or my boss, because the luxurious ingredients make it socially correct.

Fish Soup with Potatoes and Fennel

Prep and cook time: About 50 minutes

Notes: For the most dramatic presentation, use 12 whole shrimp (with heads). They're readily found in Asian fish markets and frequently available in other fish markets. To preserve the shape of whole shrimp, devein and cook them in their shells. To devein, insert a thin wood skewer perpendicularly through the back of the shell, sliding it under the vein, then gently pull the skewer up from beneath to lift the vein out. Repeat in several places as needed.

Makes: 6 servings

    4 cups **chicken broth**

    1 cup **Sauvignon Blanc** or other dry white wine

    ½ cup **whipping cream**

    1 teaspoon **fennel seed**

    ¾ teaspoon **fresh** or dried **thyme** leaves

    1½ pounds **Yukon Gold** or other thin-skinned **potatoes**

    2 heads **fennel** (3½ to 4 in. wide)

    ½ pound **mussels in shells**

CURTIS ANDERSON

The wood butter mold, maple leaves incised in its top, was already old when it traveled in a Conestoga wagon from Indiana to the Kansas homestead with my great-grandparents in the 1870s. But I wasn't much more than a toddler when Aunt Nora, the last of the family to live on that land, let me pack fresh-churned butter into the mold, then push it out onto a blue plate. How pretty those leaves looked before we cut into them. And how fresh the butter tasted when we smeared it onto slabs of bread—still warm from the woodstove oven.

My love for decorated butter has lingered, and my search for wood butter molds is ongoing. Old molds are most often found at country, Americana, or cookware antiques stores; collectors' magazines can lead you to specialized merchants. In specialty cookware stores, I've found individual butter-pat molds for about $6. Larger carved molds start at about $25.

As an art medium, butter is forgivingly pliable. If it gets too squishy, unpack it, chill it, and start again. Before filling a mold, pour steaming water over the interior to freshen it. Then briefly immerse the mold in ice water until cool. (Wood molds left in water too long will warp—and old ones may split.)

Some molds are hinged, others have a plunger to push the butter out. To fill molds, first fit hinged ones together. Then turn hinged or plunger molds upside down. Working quickly, press chilled butter chunks (most margarines are too soft to mold well) into every crevice of the mold, forcing out air pockets; use your fingers or the back of a spoon. Fill mold to capacity and scrape surface smooth. Once butter is packed, gently release it: use a knife tip to ease hinged sections apart, then lift tops straight up (twisting mars design); or press butter from a plunger mold, then ease top straight up. Results not perfect? Touch up or start over. Serve, or chill until firm, then wrap airtight.

½ to ¾ pound **shrimp** (16 to 20 per lb.)

1 pound **Chilean seabass**

1. In a 6- to 8-quart pan, combine broth, wine, cream, fennel seed, and thyme.

2. Peel potatoes and thinly slice into pan. Cover pan and turn heat to high.

3. Trim tops from fennel and save the feathery greens. Trim off root ends, bruised areas, and coarse fibers from sides of fennel. Rinse and thinly slice fennel and add to soup. When mixture boils, reduce heat and simmer until potatoes are very tender when pierced, about 20 minutes.

4. Meanwhile, rinse feathery fennel greens and chop.

5. Scrub mussels and pull off beards.

6. Shell, devein, and rinse shrimp.

7. Cut seabass into 1-inch chunks.

8. When potatoes are tender, add mussels. Cover and simmer 3 minutes. Add shrimp and seabass and simmer until mussels open, 3 to 5 minutes more. Ladle into bowls and sprinkle with reserved fennel greens.

Per serving: 291 cal., 30% (87 cal.) from fat; 27 g protein; 9.7 g fat (4.9 g sat.); 23 g carbo (2.4 g fiber); 285 mg sodium; 106 mg chol.

SEASONAL *note*

Greens with an attitude

My Italian father-in-law grew artichokes, peas, and broccoli to sell. But my mother-in-law grew broccoli rabe for their table, where I learned to love it.

The broccolis are related, but broccoli rabe (also called rapini) has more punch—a bitter bite typical of members of the chicory and mustard families. It's also a skinnier, leafier, leggier broccoli with tiny green flower buds at the stalk tips. And it's surprisingly available but easily overlooked—or confused with Chinese broccoli (gai laan), which is distinguished by small clusters of white flowers and rangier stalks.

Once, while I was visiting the Apulia region of Italy, broccoli rabe and ear-shaped orechiette pasta began almost every lunch and dinner for days. The greens were stir-fried in a little olive oil, seasoned with a few hot chili flakes, then mixed with the boiled pasta. Plain? Yes. But so satisfying, I actually made myself a batch as soon as I got home.

Stir-fried broccoli rabe. Rinse about 1 pound **broccoli rabe** and discard tough stem ends and yellowed leaves. Halve stems lengthwise if they're more than ⅜ inch thick. Then cut pieces into 3- to 4-inch lengths. Pour 1 to 2 tablespoons **olive oil** into an 11- to 12-inch frying pan over high heat. Add broccoli rabe, ¼ to ½ teaspoon **hot chili flakes,** and 3 to 4 tablespoons water. Stir-fry until greens are just tender to bite, 5 to 6 minutes. Serve as a vegetable or mix with 4 cups hot cooked **pasta** such as orechiette or large seashells. Season with **salt** to taste. Makes 3 or 4 servings.

Per serving: 246 cal., 16% (39 cal.) from fat; 9.1 g protein; 4.3 g fat (0.6 g sat.); 43 g carbo (2.2 g fiber); 20 mg sodium; 0 mg chol.

JONELLE WEAVER

BOOKS on FOOD

Easy Basics for a new century

In Portland not many months back, the owner of a store that specializes in cookbooks proposed that *Sunset* reissue its 15-year-old *Easy Basics for Good Cooking.* She described it as one of the most useful books available for the beginning cook and equally valuable for the culinarily adept.

Well, I have something better to offer: *Sunset's New Easy Basics Cookbook, Step by Step: The Fundamentals of Good Cooking* (Sunset Books, Menlo Park, CA, April 1997; $24.95). This 192-page book represents the effort of many—including food writers whose names you've seen through the years on our masthead. It was my pleasure to act as editor for the project.

Like the original book, this has a hard, spiral-bound cover. And the basics are still here, from cream puffs to flaky pastry, homemade broth to sauces, as well as easily referenced directions for roasting poultry and meat and cooking vegetables—updated with the most current information available.

The 170 new color photographs emphasize step-by-step directions. And the 283 recipes are for today's tastes and tools. Stir-frying has become a basic technique, each recipe has nutritional information, low-fat concerns are considered, the recipes reflect today's market, and illustrated guides help you with the new greens and mushrooms.

A recipe that is essential for every tart I make is this no-fail press-in dough. Like all the recipes in the book, this one gives standard and metric measurements—ready for the future.

Short Paste for Tarts

Prep and cook time: 40 to 50 minutes

Notes: Spread baked pastry with 1½ to 2 cups filling such as sweetened whipped cream or lemon curd, and cover with a layer of fresh berries, such as strawberries, then dust with powdered sugar.

Makes: One 11-inch tart, 8 servings

2 cups (250 g) **all-purpose flour**

¼ cup (50 g) **sugar**

¾ cup (6 oz., 170 g) **butter** or margarine, cut into chunks

2 **large egg** yolks or 1 large egg

1. In a bowl, combine flour and sugar. Add butter and, with your fingers, rub into flour mixture until well blended.

2. With a fork, stir in egg yolks until dough holds together. (Or whirl flour, sugar, and butter in a food processor until mixture resembles fine crumbs; add yolks and whirl until dough holds together.)

3. With your hands, press dough firmly into a smooth ball, kneading a bit to help bind the dough. (At this point, you may wrap the dough airtight and refrigerate up to 1 week; let come to room temperature before using.)

4. Press pastry into an 11-inch (28 cm) tart pan with a removable rim, pushing dough firmly into bottom and sides to make an even layer; the edge should be flush with pan rim. Bake in a 300° F (150° C) oven, uncovered, until lightly browned, 30 to 40 minutes. Let cool in pan. Fill tart and remove rim to serve.

Per unfilled serving: 305 cal., 56% (171 cal.) from fat; 4.1 g protein; 19 g fat (11 g sat.); 30 g carbo (0.8 g fiber); 178 mg sodium; 100 mg chol.

AT *the* MARKET

A word on fresh hams

To most of us, ham is the cured back leg of a pig. The *other* ham is the same cut, but the meat is fresh, and it's called fresh ham or fresh pork leg.

A whole leg is massive—20 to 25 pounds, so it's usually cut into the boneless roasts you see in meat counters. The tenderest section, the top of the round, comes from the inside top of the back leg. Trimmed of fat and skin, it typically weighs 3 to 5 pounds. The roast is tapered on one end, so it needs to be tied to cook evenly. Often fresh ham cuts are bound by a netted casing, which I find a nuisance because it gets imbedded in the cooked meat. I snip the casing off the raw meat, then retie the roast—or ask the butcher to do this for me.

To roast a 3- to 5-pound fat-trimmed, tied **fresh ham (pork leg) top round** (including the eye-of-the-round muscle), set it on a rack in a 9- by 13-inch pan. Rub meat with **olive oil,** then season well with **salt, pepper,** and **dried rubbed sage.** Roast in a 350° oven until a thermometer inserted into center registers 150° to 155°, about 1 hour and 50 minutes. Let roast stand at least 20 minutes, then cut into slices.

Per 3-ounce cooked serving: 179 cal., 40% (72 cal.) from fat; 25 g protein; 8 g fat (2.8 g sat.); 0 g carbo (0 g fiber); 54 mg sodium; 80 mg chol. ◆

Going to extremes: Pinot Noir

by **KAREN MacNEIL**

A really good wine is compelling, in large part, because it has a distinct personality. By "personality" I do not mean an identifiable character trait or two. After all, almost every wine has a couple of qualities that can be used to describe it: cherryish and wild, silky and smoky, or gaunt and tasting like burnt bacon—whatever.

No, personality is something more, though not easily described. A wine with personality has a soul, a spirit. A wine with personality is determined to express itself. Alas, such wines are not in the majority.

My own search for wines with personality usually brings me to the doorstep of Pinot Noir. Like countless other wine lovers, I have had my most exalted wine experiences with Pinot Noir.

And, it should be added, some of my most dismal. But that, too, is part of Pinot Noir's plan, its seduction strategy. The wine never lets you rest. The great ones are so delicious that you'll go through a dozen weasels hoping to capture the rapture again. Whoever nicknamed Pinot Noir "the heartbreak grape" knew what she was talking about.

So what is it that makes great Pinot Noir so special, so charismatic, so full of personality?

First, great wines made from Pinot Noir are indisputably sensual. For centuries, wine experts have described them in the most erotic of ways, comparing them, among other things, to falling in love.

Pinot Noir's sensuality is based on its smell, its taste, and its beguiling texture—the way it rests or dances or explodes against the taste buds. Unlike many types of wine, Pinot's physicality is trenchant. Great ones send shivers up your spine.

Part of the reason for this hedonism has to do with tannin—or more precisely, a lack thereof. Tannin is that component in a grape's skin and seeds that gives wine a structural backbone, makes it powerful, and, in the wine's youth anyway, can make it taste "tight" and ungenerous. Compared with Cabernet Sauvignon or Merlot, for example, Pinot Noir has very little tannin. And therein lies its natural suppleness.

Remarkably, Pinot Noir is also an intellectual's wine. In fact, the wine plays mind games better than any other varietal. You taste it, you think you've got a handle on it, and the next minute, 20 other smells and flavors show up in the glass. By the time you've finished the glass, you're convinced that there is still something else—something hopelessly impossible to describe—lurking just beyond knowing.

Pinot Noir is not easy to grow and, in fact, only makes good-to-great wine in a few places on earth. These regions are usually a little cool, overcast, and what viticulturists call "marginal." In other words, Pinot Noir, like an artist, needs to live life on the edge.

And what are those places? Above all, the Burgundy region of France, and then: Oregon and certain parts of California (notably Carneros, the Russian River Valley, the Santa Maria–Santa Ynez valleys of Southern California, and a few spots on the northern end of the Central Coast). And that's it. A handful of Pinots are made elsewhere on the globe, but these are mostly iconoclastic experimentations.

And now the bad news: French Burgundies are stratospheric in price. Because of their rarity and popularity, many of the very good wines hover around $60 a bottle; the "name" wines can cost several hundred dollars a bottle. These are clearly not everynight dinner wines.

More bad news: There are no bargain Pinot Noirs. The concept is an oxymoron. Pinot Noir is like caviar—if it's dirt cheap, you don't want it in your mouth.

For reasonably affordable Pinots, we must look to Oregon and California. And here, the news is exciting. Year after year, the top Pinots of Oregon and California get deeper, more delicious, and more refined. The best of them are riveting in their complexity and nuance.

There's just one thing: You have to be a person with personality to fall in love with them.

Au Bon Climat Pinot Noir "Isabelle" 1994, $50 (California). As the price suggests, this supercharged Pinot is not shy. Gripping and gutsy.

Byron Pinot Noir Reserve 1993, $23 (Santa Barbara County). Rugged, smoky, masculine. The Clint Eastwood of Pinots.

Eyrie Pinot Noir Reserve 1992, $26 (Willamette Valley, Oregon). One of the most delicate, graceful, and elegant Pinots made.

Saintsbury Pinot Noir 1995, $18 (Carneros). A very berried Pinot Noir; as delicious as a sorbet in summer.

Williams & Selyem Pinot Noir 1995, $29 (Russian River Valley). The most mind-bogglingly complex Pinot made in California.

Yamhill Valley Pinot Noir 1994, $20 (Willamette Valley, Oregon). Like hurling yourself into a blackberry patch. ◆

WINE DICTIONARY: *earthy*

A descriptive term for a wine whose aroma or flavor is reminiscent of the earth. The term refers to flavors that remind one of soil or things that grow in it (moss, truffles, etc.). Sometimes extrapolated to include the pleasant, sensual aromas of the human body. — *K. M.*

RICK MARIANI

Classic Creamy Cheesecake
(254 cal. per slice, 15% from fat)

good-bye guilt!!!

Cheesecake Cloud with Berries
(278 cal. per slice, 12% from fat)

A low-fat cheesecake for every taste, whether you crave pure chocolate or berries and cream

n a perfect world, indulging in desserts would leave no evidence. And even in a big slice of cheesecake, calories and fat wouldn't count. • Well, the world still isn't flawless, but cheesecake has moved a bite closer to "perfection" without losing those rich, creamy qualities we crave. • The reason is simple—more dairy options with a healthier attitude are at your fingertips. The old nonfat and low-fat standards have been joined by a growing number of new products. And fresh nonfat yogurt cheese is still one of the best-kept secrets in the kitchen. You have to make your own, but, fortunately, it takes almost no effort (see details, page 76). • So now you can make guilt-free cheesecakes in any style you yearn for—velvety and dense, fluffy and fragile, plain or flavored, traditional or new wave. Take your pick. They're all here.

by **LINDA LAU ANUSASANANAN** *with* **ELAINE JOHNSON**
photographs by **RICHARD JUNG**

Cheesecake Cloud with Berries

Prep and cook time: About 1½ hours, plus at least 3 hours to chill

Notes: Drain about 3 quarts nonfat yogurt to make the cheese for this cheesecake. The texture is most delicate if you drain the yogurt for the minimum time and firmer if cheese is well drained.

Makes: 8 to 10 servings

- ⅔ cup **graham cracker crumbs**
- 1½ tablespoons melted **butter** or margarine
- 3 **large eggs,** separated
- 1 **large egg** white
- ¼ teaspoon **cream of tartar**
- 1¼ cups **sugar**
- 2 tablespoons **cornstarch**
- 4 cups **nonfat yogurt cheese** (below)
- 1½ teaspoons grated **lemon** peel
- 2 teaspoons **vanilla**
- 2 tablespoons **currant jelly**
- 1 cup **raspberries,** rinsed and drained dry

1. Combine crumbs and melted butter. Pat evenly over bottom of an 8-inch cheesecake pan (at least 3½ in. deep) with removable rim.

2. Bake in a 325° oven until crust is slightly browner, about 15 minutes.

3. Meanwhile, with a mixer on high speed, beat the 4 egg whites and cream of tartar in a large bowl until foamy. Gradually add ½ cup sugar, about 1 tablespoon at a time, beating until the whites hold stiff, shiny peaks.

4. In another large bowl, stir remaining sugar with cornstarch, then add egg yolks, cheese, lemon peel, and vanilla. Beat (with unwashed beaters) until well blended.

5. Fold beaten whites into cheese mixture. Scrape the batter into hot or cool crust.

6. Bake in a 325° oven until center barely jiggles when cake is gently shaken, 50 to 60 minutes. Run a thin-bladed knife between cake and pan rim. Refrigerate cake, uncovered, until cool, at least 3 hours. (If making ahead, cover when cool and chill up to 1 day.)

7. Melt jelly (in a microwave oven or in a small pan over medium heat), stirring often. Cool, stirring occasionally, until jelly becomes a thick syrup, about 5 minutes.

8. Remove pan rim. Mound berries on cake and drizzle with jelly. To neatly cut this fluffy dessert, hold a long strand of string (such as dental floss) taut, slide it under the berries to the center of the cake, and push the string down to the pan. Slide out string and repeat to cut wedges. (If using a knife, wipe blade clean between cuts.) Slide a pie server under each wedge and lift out gently.

Per serving: 278 cal., 12% (34 cal.) from fat; 12 g protein; 3.8 g fat (1.5 g sat.); 46 g carbo (0.7 g fiber); 177 mg sodium; 68 mg chol.

Classic Creamy Cheesecake

Prep and cook time: About 1 hour, plus at least 2½ hours to chill

Notes: Drain about 4 quarts nonfat yogurt to make 5 cups cheese.

Makes: 12 servings

- 1 cup **graham cracker crumbs**
- 2 tablespoons melted **butter** or margarine
- 4 **large eggs**
- 1¼ cups **sugar**
- 5 cups **nonfat yogurt cheese** (see instructions at left)

Nonfat yogurt cheese: zero fat, big flavor

Drained yogurt can get as thick as cream cheese. And if you use nonfat yogurt, this cream cheese equivalent has no fat.

It takes at least 24 hours for yogurt to drain enough to use in baking, but the cheese is thicker and creamier if drained longer. The volume of cheese you get varies, as some brands of yogurt drain more than others. Also, some seeping may occur in the cheesecake if it stands a day or more. This is normal; just blot up the moisture.

Nonfat Yogurt Cheese

Prep and cook time: About 5 minutes, plus 24 hours to 4 days for draining

Notes: Do not use yogurt with gelatin; it will not drain. Improvise a drainer or buy one; sources follow. Discard cheese with mold or soured aroma.

Makes: 1⅓ cups (about ¾ lb.) to 1¾ cups (about 1 lb.) cheese

1. Set a strainer or colander over a deep pan or bowl, supporting it so base of strainer is at least 2 inches above pan bottom.

2. Line strainer with 2 layers of cheesecloth or a clean muslin or linen towel. Dump 1 quart (2 lb.) **plain nonfat yogurt** into cloth. Enclose strainer and pan with plastic wrap to keep airtight.

3. Chill at least 24 hours or up to 4 days, pouring off whey as it accumulates. Shorter draining produces a moister cheese and more volume. Longer draining produces a thicker cheese and less volume.

4. Scrape yogurt cheese from cloth

Keep cheese above liquid as it drains.

and use, or store airtight up to 9 days from when draining began. Drain off any whey that accumulates.

Per cup: 212 cal., 0% (0 cal.) from fat; 24 g protein; 0 g fat; 23 g carbo (0 g fiber); 212 mg sodium; 0 mg chol.

YOGURT CHEESE MAKERS

Drainers and funnels designed to make yogurt cheese are available in cookware and hardware stores. Most make only a cup or so of cheese at a time. Prices for units range from $8.50 for a set of two funnels to $20 for a self-contained unit. Mail-order sources are listed here.

Chef's Catalog, 3215 Commercial Ave., Northbrook, IL 60002; (800) 338-3232.

Sur La Table, Catalog Division, 410 Terry Ave. N., Seattle, WA 98109; (800) 243-0852. Retail stores in San Francisco, Berkeley, Seattle, and Kirkland, Washington.

TV Chefs, Box 84848, Seattle, WA 98124; (800) 288-7834. Sells a quart-size yogurt strainer; ask for item number LGYS132.

NORMAN A. PLATE

Ricotta Cheesecake with Ginger and Kiwi
(266 cal. per slice, 17% from fat)

1 tablespoon **vanilla**

Whole or sliced **strawberries** (optional)

1. Combine crumbs and melted butter. Pat evenly over bottom and about ½ inch up the side of a removable-rim 9-inch cheesecake or cake pan (at least 1¾ in. deep).

2. Bake in a 350° oven until crust is slightly browner, 10 to 12 minutes.

3. Meanwhile, in a large bowl, use a fork to blend eggs, 1 cup sugar, 3 cups cheese, and vanilla until well mixed. Scrape mixture into hot or cool crust.

4. Bake in a 350° oven just until center jiggles only slightly when cake is gently shaken, 40 to 45 minutes.

5. Meanwhile, stir remaining cheese with remaining sugar until smooth. Spoon onto cake and gently spread to cover top.

6. Return to oven and bake to firm topping slightly, about 10 minutes. Run a thin-bladed knife between cake and pan rim. Refrigerate cake, uncovered, until cool, at least 2 hours.

7. Serve, or if making ahead, wrap airtight and chill up to 1 day. Remove pan rim and garnish cake with berries; cut into wedges.

Per serving: 254 cal., 15% (38 cal.) from fat; 13 g protein; 4.2 g fat (1.7 g sat.); 38 g carbo (0.3 g fiber); 189 mg sodium; 76 mg chol.

Ricotta Cheesecake with Ginger and Kiwi

Prep and cook time: About 1 hour, plus at least 2½ hours to chill

Notes: Drain at least 3 cups nonfat yogurt to make 1 cup yogurt cheese, or use nonfat cream cheese instead.

Makes: 10 servings

⅔ cup (about 3 oz.) **gingersnap cookie** crumbs

½ cup minced **crystallized ginger**

2 tablespoons melted **butter** or margarine

1 carton (15 oz.; 1⅔ cups) **low-fat ricotta cheese**

4 **large egg** whites

2 tablespoons **lemon juice**

1 cup **nonfat yogurt cheese** (see page 76) or 1 package (8 oz.) nonfat cream cheese

1 cup **sugar**

1 tablespoon grated **lemon** peel

1 teaspoon **vanilla**

3 **kiwi fruit** (about ¼ lb. each)

1. Combine crumbs, ¼ cup ginger, and melted butter. Pat crumb mixture evenly over bottom of a removable-rim 8-inch cheesecake or cake pan (at least 1¾ in. deep).

2. Bake in a 350° oven until crust is slightly browner, 10 to 12 minutes.

3. Meanwhile, in a blender or food processor, whirl ricotta cheese, egg whites, and lemon juice until very smooth.

4. In a bowl, mix yogurt cheese, sugar, lemon peel, and vanilla. Add ricotta mixture and stir until well blended (the mixture is thin). Pour into hot or cool crust.

5. Bake in a 350° oven until center barely jiggles when cake is gently shaken, 50 to 55 minutes. Run a thin-bladed knife between cake and pan rim. Refrigerate cake, uncovered, until cool, at least 2½ hours. (If making ahead, wrap airtight when cool and chill up to 2 days.)

6. Remove pan rim. Peel kiwi fruit and slice crosswise. Arrange fruit in a ring in overlapping slices on cake; sprinkle with remaining ginger. Cut cake into wedges.

Per serving: 266 cal., 17% (45 cal.) from fat; 8 g protein; 5 g fat (2.6 g sat.); 47 g carbo (1 g fiber); 170 mg sodium; 16 mg chol.

Chocolate Chip Cheesecake (283 cal. per slice, 17% from fat)

Very Low-fat Apricot Cheesecake

The skinny on dairy

When fat is removed from milk, cheese, or yogurt, the milk solid and milk sugar content increase proportionally, significantly raising the calcium (and protein and carbohydrate) levels. These dramatic differences may influence your choice of ingredients.

PER 1 CUP	CAL. (FAT CAL.)	% FAT	CALCIUM G
SWEETENED CONDENSED MILK			
nonfat	880 (0)	0	800
low fat	960 (108)	11	800
whole	982 (243)	25	869
COTTAGE CHEESE			
nonfat	161 (0)	0	201
2% fat	203 (40)	20	154
regular	216 (86)	40	126
CREAM CHEESE			
nonfat	200 (0)	0	640
light	560 (360)	64	320
regular	792 (711)	90	181
RICOTTA CHEESE			
nonfat	240 (0)	0	1,278
low fat	240 (90)	38	399
part skim	339 (171)	50	669
whole milk	428 (288)	67	509
SOUR CREAM			
nonfat	280 (0)	0	320
low fat	280 (144)	51	320
regular	492 (432)	88	267
YOGURT CHEESE			
nonfat	212 (0)	0	743
low fat	265 (72)	27	637
whole	442 (279)	63	514

Chocolate Chip Cheesecake

Prep and cook time: 50 to 55 minutes, plus at least 2½ hours to chill

Notes: Beverly Farr of Goleta, California, created this recipe.

Makes: 10 servings

- ⅔ cup (about 3 oz.) **reduced-fat chocolate wafer cookie** crumbs
- 1½ tablespoons melted **butter** or margarine
- 3 packages (8 oz. each) **nonfat cream cheese**
- 1 can (14 oz.) **nonfat sweetened condensed milk**
- 3 **large egg** whites
- 2 teaspoons **vanilla**
- ½ cup **miniature chocolate chips**

1. Combine crumbs and melted butter. Pat evenly over bottom and about ¾ inch up the side of a removable-rim 8-inch cheesecake or cake pan (at least 1¾ in. deep).

2. In a food processor or bowl, whirl or beat cream cheese, milk, egg whites, and vanilla until very smooth. Stir in ¼ cup chocolate chips.

3. Scrape batter into prepared pan. Evenly sprinkle batter with remaining chocolate chips.

4. Bake in a 350° oven until cake jiggles only slightly in the center when gently shaken, about 30 minutes.

5. Run a thin-bladed knife between cake and pan rim. Refrigerate cake, uncovered, until cool, at least 2½ hours. Serve, or if making ahead, wrap airtight when cool and chill up to 2 days. Remove pan rim and cut cake into wedges.

Per serving: 283 cal., 17% (48 cal.) from fat; 14 g protein; 5.3 g fat (2.6 g sat.); 44 g carbo (0 g fiber); 461 mg sodium; 15 mg chol.

Very Low-fat Apricot Cheesecake

Prep and cook time: 50 to 60 minutes, plus at least 2½ hours to chill

Notes: Drain at least 3 cups nonfat yogurt to get 1 cup yogurt cheese for this recipe by Scott Davis of Oakland, California.

Makes: 10 servings

- 1¾ cups **dried apricots**
- ⅔ cup **graham cracker crumbs**
- 1½ tablespoons melted **butter** or margarine
- 3 tablespoons **apricot-flavor liqueur** or brandy
- 3 packages (8 oz. each) **nonfat cream cheese**
- ¾ cup plus 1 tablespoon **sugar**
- 1 **large egg**
- 2 **large egg** whites
- 1 cup **nonfat yogurt cheese** (see page 76) or reduced-fat sour cream
- ⅓ cup **apricot jam**

(287 cal. per slice, 9.1% from fat)

Chocolate-Orange Cheesecake *(209 cal. per slice, 25% from fat)*

1. Set aside 8 apricot halves. In a 1- to 2-quart pan, bring remaining apricots and ½ cup water to a boil, then cover and simmer just until fruit is plumped, about 10 minutes.

2. Meanwhile, combine crumbs and melted butter. Pat evenly over bottom and ¾ inch up side of an 8-inch cheesecake pan with removable rim.

3. In a food processor, smoothly purée cooked apricots and any liquid. Add liqueur, cream cheese, ¾ cup sugar, egg, and egg whites. Whirl until smooth (or combine ingredients in a bowl and beat with a mixer until smooth).

4. Scrape mixture into prepared pan. Bake in a 350° oven until cake jiggles only slightly in the center when gently shaken, about 25 minutes.

5. Mix yogurt cheese with remaining 1 tablespoon sugar. Spoon onto cake and gently spread to cover top. Bake just until topping is heated, about 5 minutes.

6. Run a thin-bladed knife between cake and pan rim. Refrigerate cake, uncovered, until cool, about 2 hours. Remove pan rim.

7. Melt jam (in a microwave oven or in a small pan over medium heat), stirring often. Rub jam through a fine strainer into a bowl; discard residue. Spoon about ¾ of the jam evenly over cold cheesecake, then spread gently to coat evenly.

8. Cut each reserved dried apricot half in half and arrange pieces on cake. Spoon remaining jam onto apricot pieces to coat evenly. Chill until jam is set, about 10 minutes. Serve, or if making ahead, cover with a bowl or a foil tent and chill up to 2 days. Cut cake into wedges.

Per serving: 287 cal., 9.1% (26 cal.) from fat; 15 g protein; 2.9 g fat (1.2 g sat.); 51 g carbo (2.1 g fiber); 435 mg sodium; 33 mg chol.

Chocolate-Orange Cheesecake

Prep and cook time: About 1 hour and 15 minutes, plus at least 2½ hours to chill

Notes: This cake tastes unbelievably rich, creamy, and fudgy. Garnish with mint leaves and orange slices.

Makes: 12 servings

- ⅔ cup (about 3 oz.) **reduced-fat chocolate wafer cookie** crumbs
- 1½ tablespoons melted **butter** or margarine
- 1 carton (1 lb.; about 1¾ cups) **small-curd low-fat cottage cheese**
- 1 package (8 oz.) **nonfat cream cheese**
- 2 **large eggs**
- 2 **large egg** whites
- 1 cup **sugar**
- ¾ cup **alkaline-treated cocoa**
- ¼ cup **orange-flavor liqueur** or orange juice
- 2 teaspoons grated **orange** peel
- ⅓ cup chopped **semisweet chocolate**

1. Combine crumbs and melted butter. Pat evenly over bottom and about ½ inch up side of a removable-rim 9-inch cheesecake or cake pan (at least 1¾ in. deep).

2. Bake in a 350° oven until crust is slightly toasted, 10 to 12 minutes.

3. Meanwhile, in a blender or food processor, whirl cottage cheese, cream cheese, eggs, and egg whites until very smooth.

4. In a large bowl, mix sugar and cocoa. Add cheese mixture, liqueur, and orange peel.

5. Heat chocolate in a microwave-safe bowl in a microwave oven at full power in 5-second intervals until soft. Stir until smooth, then scrape into cheese mixture. Beat with a mixer until smoothly blended. Pour into hot or cool crust.

6. Bake in a 350° oven until center barely jiggles when cake is gently shaken, 40 to 45 minutes. Run a thin-bladed knife between cake and pan rim. Refrigerate cake, uncovered, until cool, at least 2½ hours. Serve, or if making ahead, wrap airtight when cool and chill up to 2 days.

7. Remove pan rim and cut cake into wedges.

Per serving: 209 cal., 25% (52 cal.) from fat; 10 g protein; 5.8 g fat (2.9 g sat.); 32 g carbo (0 g fiber); 356 mg sodium; 43 mg chol. ◆

Sangria
(foreground),
strawberry
lemonade, and pastis
with almond syrup
complement appetizers
before dinner.

The cordial art of aperitifs

Food and garden writer Georgeanne Brennan
explores a French tradition in her new cookbook

As Georgeanne Brennan speaks of tender young lettuce with morning dew still clinging to its leaves, and freshly picked pencil-thin asparagus destined for a savory bread pudding, her eyes begin to sparkle. She seems for a moment to have slipped away to another place, and it's a good bet it's the French countryside.

That's where she acquired her passionate appreciation of food and gardening, and of a varied selection of fresh, high-quality meats, seafood, and, above all, produce. Her admiration for the *potager*—the traditional French kitchen garden that yields seasonal vegetables, fruits, herbs, and cutting flowers—inspired a desire to see potager-style cooking catch on in this country.

In 1982 Brennan founded Le Marché Seeds with partner Charlotte Glenn Kimball. The company imported seeds of European and Asian vegetables then considered rarities. Thanks to Le Marché and similar companies, a wide range of greens—among them radicchio, heirloom lettuces, frisée, and mizuna—is available in the U.S. today.

Brennan played a major role in the development of the farmers' market and organic gardening movements in this country, and in 1984 began writing newspaper columns about food and gardening. Cookbooks soon followed, among them *Potager: Fresh Garden Cooking in the French Style; The Vegetarian Table: France;* and *Down to Earth: Great Recipes for Root Vegetables.*

Her latest book, *Aperitif: Recipes for Simple Pleasures in the French Style* (Chronicle Books, San Francisco, 1997; $24.95), focuses on a tradition little known in this country. The aperitif "is both a beverage and a social activity ... firmly embedded in the French way of life," according to Brennan.

"At home, sitting around the kitchen table or gathered in the living room, outside beneath the shade of spreading trees, on terraces or balconies, family and friends come together to share an aperitif and conversation before the lunch or dinner hour," she writes. And unlike the American cocktail hour, the aperitif tradition involves the entire family, including children.

Brennan weaves personal experiences into her explanations of this gracious French tradition. In one chapter she spotlights *vins maison*—wines infused with fruits, herbs, or spices and fortified with a strong neutral spirit—including some fascinating recipes, such as Vin de Noix (infused with green walnuts) and Guignolet (a cherry-flavor wine made with the leaves, not the fruit). Most of these wines need to steep at least several months, so they're perfect projects to start now for holiday gifts.

by CHRISTINE WEBER HALE

In another chapter, "The Classics," she focuses on traditional aperitifs: sherry, pastis, Dubonnet, vermouth, Lillet, and Campari; another concentrates on nonalcoholic fruit drinks suitable for children and designated drivers. The final chapter is devoted entirely to food to serve with aperitifs. The dishes range from Toasted Almonds to the more complex Spicy Black Bean Wontons, Rosemary-Walnut Biscotti, and Wild Mushroom and Goat Cheese Galettes. The following recipes provide a hint of the book's flavors.

Sangria

Prep time: About 5 minutes

Makes: 4 to 6 servings

- 1 bottle (750 ml.) **dry red wine,** such as Zinfandel, Merlot, Pinot Noir, or burgundy, chilled
- 2 **oranges,** cut crosswise into slices
- 2 **lemons,** cut crosswise into slices
- 1 bottle (12 oz.) **sparkling mineral water,** chilled

Combine wine, fruit, and water in a punch bowl or pitcher and serve.

Per serving: 118 cal., 2.3% (2.7 cal.) from fat; 1.4 g protein; 0.3 g fat (0 g sat.); 14 g carbo (1 g fiber); 8.4 mg sodium; 0 mg chol.

La Mauresque (Pastis with Almond Syrup)

Prep time: Less than 5 minutes

Makes: 1 serving

- 2 tablespoons (1 oz.) **pastis** (anise-flavor liqueur)
- 1 tablespoon **almond syrup** (orgeat)
- 1 or 2 **ice cubes** (optional)

Pour pastis into a tall glass. Add almond syrup, 5 ounces cold water, and ice.

Per serving: 117 cal., 0% (0 cal.) from fat; 0 g protein; 0 g fat; 18 g carbo (0 g fiber); 0 mg sodium; 0 mg chol.

Strawberry Lemonade

Prep and cook time: About 20 minutes, plus 2 hours to chill

Makes: 4 servings (8 oz. each)

- 3 or 4 **lemons**
- About ¾ cup **sugar**

- ½ teaspoon **salt**
- 1 cup **strawberries,** hulled
- **Ice cubes** (optional)
- Thin **lemon** slices (optional)

1. Cut the lemons in half and ream juice from them. Pour the juice through a fine-mesh strainer into a measuring cup and discard the seeds and pulp. You should have ½ cup. Cover and refrigerate.

2. Place 4 cups water, ¾ cup sugar, salt, and strawberries in a pan and bring to a boil over medium-high heat. Stir often with a spoon and, using the back of it, crush the berries. Continue to boil, stirring often, until the sugar has dissolved, about 2 minutes. Let cool, cover, and refrigerate until well chilled.

3. Pour the chilled syrup through a fine-mesh strainer into a pitcher; discard the pulp. Add the lemon juice to syrup and stir well. Taste, and adjust to desired sweetness.

4. Pour lemonade into glasses. Serve with ice cubes and garnish with thin lemon slices.

Per serving: 164 cal., 0.5% (0.9 cal.) from fat; 0.3 g protein; 0.1 g fat (0 g sat.); 43 g carbo (1 g fiber); 274 mg sodium; 0 mg chol.

Cracked Green Olives with Fennel

Prep time: About 10 minutes

Makes: 1 cup; 4 servings

- 1 jar or can (about 10 oz.) **green olives with pits**
- 1 teaspoon **fennel seed**
- 1 piece **orange** peel, about 3 inches long and ⅛ inch wide
- ¼ cup **fresh tarragon**
- ¼ teaspoon **salt**
- ¼ cup **extra-virgin olive oil**

1. Drain the olives and discard the brine. Using the back of a spoon, press each of the olives just hard enough to crack it open. Do not remove the olives' pits.

2. Put the olives in a small bowl and add fennel seed, peel, tarragon, salt, and oil. Turn the olives to coat them. Cover the bowl and let the olives marinate in the refrigerator for a week before serving. Stored in the refri-

gerator, they will keep for a month or longer.

Per serving: 197 cal., 100% (197 cal.) from fat; 1.2 g protein; 21.9 g fat (2.9 g sat.); 1.8 g carbo (1.6 g fiber); 1,599 mg sodium; 0 mg chol.

Dates and Parmesan

Prep time: About 5 minutes

Notes: Brennan prefers the large, rich, and intensely sweet Medjool dates.

Makes: 4 servings

- 8 **dried dates**
- 2 ounces **parmesan cheese,** cut into very thin slices

Serve the dates and the cheese together on a single serving plate, or serve 2 dates and 1 or 2 slices of cheese on each of 4 individual plates.

Per serving: 114 cal., 30% (34 cal.) from fat; 5.5 g protein; 3.8 g fat (2.3 g sat.); 16 g carbo (1.1 g fiber); 228 mg sodium; 9.6 mg chol.

Anchovy Puffs

Prep and cook time: About 55 minutes

Makes: 120 puffs; 30 servings

- 2 cans (2 oz. each) **anchovy fillets in olive oil**
- 6 cloves **garlic,** peeled
- 1 sheet **frozen puff pastry** (½ of a 17¼ oz. package), thawed
- ¼ cup minced **fresh thyme** leaves

1. Remove the anchovy fillets from the oil, reserving the oil. Cut fillets into small pieces. Set aside. In a small bowl, combine the oil with the garlic cloves. Using the back of a fork or a mortar and pestle, mash garlic and oil to make a paste.

2. If necessary, roll thawed pastry sheet into a 10- by 12-inch rectangle. With a pastry brush, spread pastry sheet with the oil-and-garlic paste. Then cut pastry into 120 pieces, each 1 inch square. Top each square with a piece or two of anchovy and a pinch of thyme. Place pastry squares on an ungreased baking sheet.

3. Bake in a 325° oven until the pastry is golden brown and has risen almost an inch, about 25 minutes. Serve hot or at room temperature.

Per serving: 59 cal., 64% (38 cal.) from fat; 1.5 g protein; 4.2 g fat (0.6 g sat.); 4 g carbo (0.1 g fiber); 131 mg sodium; 1.7 mg chol. ◆

by CHRISTINE WEBER HALE

NORMAN A. PLATE

Where's the beef? Try lamb

It's tempting to fall back on tried-and-true quickies—like broiled hamburgers—when time is tight.

But ground beef isn't your only quick-burger alternative. Ground lamb cooks as quickly as beef, and it has its own unique character that teams well with a different spectrum of seasonings, including a refreshing touch of mint in the Greek fashion.

Ground lean lamb is available in most supermarkets. Its fat content varies, but it's usually similar to that of ground beef chuck. If the ground lamb is already shaped into patties, just break them up, season, and re-form.

Like any ground meat, ground lamb has a short storage life. So for freshest flavor, cook within 24 hours of purchase. Or, for future quick meals, season, shape, and freeze up to three months.

For moist, juicy results, broil lamb just until it is barely pink in the center. Otherwise the meat will be dry.

What's for dinner?

Greek Pocket Bread Sandwiches with Lamb

Sliced Tomatoes

Lettuce Leaves

Baby Carrots

Lemon Sorbet with Anise-flavor Liqueur

Greek Pocket Bread Sandwiches with Lamb

Prep and cook time: About 15 minutes

Notes: To slice cucumbers quickly, use a food processor.

Makes: 4 servings

1½ pounds **ground lean lamb**

2 cloves **garlic**, minced

1 tablespoon minced **fresh** or ¾ teaspoon dried **oregano** leaves

About ½ teaspoon **salt**

½ teaspoon **pepper**

2 **cucumbers** (each ¾ lb.)

½ cup **plain low-fat yogurt**

3 tablespoons minced **fresh mint** leaves

2 tablespoons **lemon juice**

4 **pocket breads** (about 6 in.), cut in half crosswise

1. In a bowl, mix lamb with garlic, oregano, ½ teaspoon salt, and pepper. Shape mixture into 8 equal oblong patties, each about ¼ inch thick.

2. Place patties on a rack in a broiler pan. Broil 4 to 6 inches from heat until meat is browned on each side and just barely pink in center (cut to test), 7 to 10 minutes total.

3. While lamb patties cook, peel cucumbers and thinly slice. Mix slices with yogurt, mint, and lemon juice to make a cucumber salad.

4. On each of 4 plates, place 2 lamb patties, ¼ of the cucumber salad, and 2 pocket bread halves. Tuck meat into bread, adding cucumber salad and salt to taste.

Per serving: 471 cal., 27% (126 cal.) from fat; 42 g protein; 14 g fat (5.2 g sat.); 41 g carbo (1.8 g fiber); 729 mg sodium; 118 mg chol.

MORE FAST IDEAS FOR GROUND LAMB

• Stir-fry to brown meat and sliced mushrooms, then cook briefly with sugar snap peas and sliced water chestnuts and season stir-fry with an Asian-sauce mix.

• Mix meat with crumbled blue or feta cheese and shape into burgers. Grill or broil, then serve on spinach leaves mounded on toasted, crusty bread.

• Season meat with chili powder or hot sauce, shape into balls, and pan-brown or oven-fry. Serve with prepared tomato pasta sauce over linguine. Or wrap in warm tortillas to make tacos, seasoning with salsa.

• Use browned meat to make lasagna or to top pizza.

• Use ground lamb in place of part of the ground beef in your favorite meat loaf recipe. ◆

Party potatoes

Your guests love mashed potatoes, but the pressure of whipping them up at the last minute is a drag. The solution? Turn mashed potatoes into a handsome, make-ahead casserole. These potatoes are dressy enough to give even the simplest menu—steak from the grill and a green salad—entertaining airs.

Spinach Pesto Potato Casserole

Prep and cook time: About 50 minutes

Notes: Mash boiled, steamed, or baked potatoes—hot or cold. If making ahead, cover and chill casserole up to 1 day; bake 55 minutes before adding nuts.

Makes: 10 to 12 servings

- 2 cups packed **washed spinach leaves**
- 1½ cups firmly packed **parsley**
- 2 cloves **garlic**
- ¼ cup **olive** or salad **oil**
- 1 teaspoon grated **lemon** peel
- 1 package (8 oz.) **cream cheese**
- 2 **large eggs**
  About 8 cups unseasoned mashed **potatoes**
- ⅓ cup **pine nuts**

1. In a food processor or blender, smoothly purée spinach, parsley, garlic, oil, and lemon peel.

2. With a mixer, beat cream cheese until fluffy, adding 1 egg at a time. Add potatoes and mix well.

3. Spread potato mixture in a shallow 3- to 3½-quart casserole. With the tip of a knife, impress shallow stripes or a lattice in potatoes, and spoon spinach mixture into these depressions.

4. Cover casserole tightly. Bake in a 375° oven until hot in center, about 35 minutes. Uncover and sprinkle nuts onto potatoes; bake 10 minutes more.

Per serving: 273 cal., 46% (126 cal.) from fat; 7.8 g protein; 14 g fat (5.4 g sat.); 31 g carbo (4.7 g fiber); 102 mg sodium; 56 mg chol. ◆

by CHRISTINE WEBER HALE

A better bagel

Sure, you can buy them. But this baking experience is worth some time in the kitchen this weekend

Bagels have moved in. They are naturally low in fat, high in complex carbohydrates, satisfyingly chewy, and flavorful unadorned. In short, they make great snacks.

Making your own bagels is an adventure. Boiling before baking gives them that characteristic density.

Bagels also take well to lots of added flavorings. These—studded with chunks of asiago cheese—were inspired by the popular version served at the Bagel Works in Palo Alto.

Asiago Bagels

Prep and cook time: About 3 hours

Makes: 12 bagels

- 2 packages **active dry yeast**
- 3 tablespoons **sugar**
- 1½ teaspoons **salt**
  About 6 cups **all-purpose flour**
- ¼ pound **asiago** or parmesan **cheese**
- 1 **large egg** yolk

1. Combine yeast and 2 cups warm (110°) water in a large bowl; let stand 5 minutes. Stir in sugar, salt, and 5½ cups flour until moistened.

2. Spread ½ cup flour on a board and scrape dough onto it. Knead dough until very smooth and elastic, 10 to 15 minutes; add more flour as required to prevent sticking.

3. Place dough in a lightly oiled bowl, cover with plastic wrap, and let rise in a warm place until almost doubled, about 40 minutes.

4. When dough is almost risen, bring 3 quarts water to boiling in a covered 4- to 5-quart pan over high heat.

5. Meanwhile, knead dough on a lightly floured board to expel air, then divide

Asiago cheese chunks give crusty top to chewy, golden bagels.

into 12 equal pieces. To shape bagels, knead each piece into a smooth ball. Holding the ball with both hands, poke your thumbs through the center to form a hole. With 1 thumb in the hole, work around the bagel to make it smooth and evenly thick.

6. Set bagels on lightly floured 12- by 15-inch baking sheets; let stand, covered with plastic wrap, just until they are slightly puffy, about 10 minutes.

7. With your hand, gently slip bagels into boiling water, adding 4 at a time to pan. Adjust heat to maintain a gentle boil and turn bagels often until they feel firm but are still slightly spongy, 3 to 5 minutes. Chill remaining bagels until you are ready to boil them.

8. With a slotted spoon, transfer bagels to a towel; drain briefly, then place bagels slightly apart on 2 lightly oiled 12- by 15-inch baking sheets.

9. In a food processor or with a knife, coarsely chop cheese.

10. Beat egg yolk to blend with 1 tablespoon water and brush mixture over bagels. Then pat cheese onto bagels, pressing gently to make the cheese stick.

11. Bake bagels in a 375° oven until browned, 30 to 35 minutes. Cool on racks. Serve warm or cool.

Per bagel: 289 cal., 12% (34 cal.) from fat; 9.8 g protein; 3.8 g fat (2.3 g sat.); 51 g carbo (2 g fiber); 385 mg sodium; 24 mg chol. ◆

by CHRISTINE WEBER HALE

A feathery-light meringue and fresh fruit create a luscious, practically nonfat dessert.

Sunset's Kitchen Cabinet

These light, sweet meringue clouds with fresh fruit filling are named after the Russian ballerina Anna Pavlova. The dessert originated in Australia and New Zealand, where numerous variations make it as common as apple pie is in the United States. Jane Shapton adapted this classic from a recipe her parents brought back from a recent trip.

Mini-Pavlovas

Jane Shapton, Portland

Prep and cook time: About 1½ hours

Makes: 6 servings

- 1 cup **superfine granulated sugar**
- 2 tablespoons **cornstarch**
- 4 **large egg** whites (about ½ cup)
- ¼ teaspoon **cream of tartar**
- 1 teaspoon **distilled white vinegar**
- 1 teaspoon **vanilla**
- 4 cups bite-size pieces mixed **fresh fruit,** such as strawberries, kiwi fruit, raspberries, mango, papaya, or melon
- ½ cup **orange-flavor liqueur,** or fresh orange juice and sugar to taste

  Softly **whipped cream** (optional)

  Fresh mint sprigs or unsprayed edible flowers

1. Line baking sheets with cooking parchment or buttered and floured foil. Draw six 3-inch-diameter circles on the parchment at least 3 inches apart.

2. Mix ⅓ cup sugar with the cornstarch; set aside.

3. With an electric mixer, beat egg whites and cream of tartar on high speed until soft peaks form. Gradually add remaining sugar, 1 tablespoon at a time, beating well after each addition. Then gradually beat in cornstarch-sugar mixture until whites are stiff and glossy. Beat in vinegar and vanilla until blended. Mound mixture evenly on circles. With the back of a large spoon, make a bowl-like indentation in the center of each mound.

4. Bake in a 300° oven until golden and dry to touch, 50 to 60 minutes. Cool completely on pan. If making ahead, store airtight up to 1 day. With a wide spatula, carefully transfer each meringue to a plate.

5. Mix fruit with liqueur; spoon mixture into the cavity of each meringue. Add whipped cream to taste. Garnish with mint.

Per serving: 260 cal., 1.4% (3.6 cal.) from fat; 3.1 g protein; 0.4 g fat (0 g sat.); 55 g carbo (2.9 g fiber); 39 mg sodium; 0 mg chol.

Asparagus Pesto Fettuccine

Paulette Le Blanc, Santa Barbara

A friend shared this pesto variation with Paulette Le Blanc. It's made from tender asparagus stems puréed with garlic and basil.

Prep and cook time: About 25 minutes

Makes: 4 servings

- 2 pounds **asparagus**
- 3 tablespoons **lemon juice**
- 2 tablespoons **extra-virgin olive oil**
- 3 to 4 cloves **garlic**
- ¼ cup coarsely chopped **fresh basil** leaves

  About 1 pound **fresh fettuccine** or linguine

  Salt and **pepper**

  Grated **parmesan cheese**

1. In a 5- to 6-quart pan, bring about 3 quarts water to a boil over high heat. Snap off and discard tough ends of asparagus. Add asparagus to boiling water. Cook, uncovered, until just barely tender to bite, 4 to 5 minutes. With tongs, lift out asparagus and drain; cool slightly.

2. In a blender or food processor, combine lemon juice, oil, garlic, and basil. Return water in pan to a boil. Add fettuccine. Cook, uncovered, until barely tender to bite, about 3 minutes.

3. Meanwhile, diagonally trim off top 3 to 4 inches of asparagus spears. Place asparagus tips in a colander. Coarsely chop stems and add to blender along

NORMAN A. PLATE

with 6 tablespoons hot water from pasta pan. Whirl until smooth.

4. Drain pasta into colander containing asparagus tips. Transfer tips and pasta to serving bowl. Pour asparagus purée over pasta and mix. Add salt, pepper, and cheese to taste.

Per serving: 434 cal., 21% (90 cal.) from fat; 19 g protein; 10 g fat (1.5 g sat.); 71 g carbo (4.4 g fiber); 36 mg sodium; 83 mg chol.

No-knead French Rolls
Jolene Catlin, West Valley City, Utah

"Some people believe you need to knead the dough a lot. I don't. Once it is mixed, that's all you have to do. The rising is the important part," says Jolene Catlin of this versatile no-knead yeast dough.

Prep and cook time: About 1½ hours
Makes: 16 rolls

1 package **active dry yeast**

1 tablespoon **sugar**

2 tablespoons melted **butter** or margarine

1 teaspoon **salt**

4 cups **all-purpose flour**

1. In a large bowl, combine yeast, 1½ cups warm water (110° to 115°), sugar, butter, and salt; let stand about 5 minutes. Stir in flour until well blended. Cover bowl with plastic wrap and let rise in a warm place until almost doubled, 45 minutes to 1 hour.

2. Punch dough down. On a floured board, cut dough into 16 equal portions. Roll each piece into a ball; place 2 to 3 inches apart on greased baking sheets. Cover lightly and let rise until almost doubled, 10 to 20 minutes.

3. Uncover and bake in a 400° oven until golden brown, 15 to 18 minutes. Serve warm or cool. If making ahead, store airtight at room temperature up to next day. Reheat, uncovered, in a 350° oven until warm, about 5 minutes.

Per roll: 137 cal., 15% (21 cal.) from fat; 3.4 g protein; 2.3 g fat (1.1 g sat.); 25 g carbo (1 g fiber); 153 mg sodium; 3.9 mg chol.

Italian Tossed Salad
C'Ann Fragione, San Francisco

"Hands are good when it comes to making salads," says C'Ann Fragione, who was taught by a true Sicilian cook, her father. She thinks it's important to coat the leaves with oil before adding the vinegar, and to "taste, taste, taste" as you dress the salad at the table.

Prep time: About 15 minutes
Makes: 8 to 10 servings

2 quarts (about ½ lb.) torn bite-size pieces **escarole** leaves

1 quart (about ¼ lb.) **dandelion** leaves, tough stems removed

1 **red onion** (about 6 oz.), thinly sliced

½ cup **canned lupini beans** or garbanzos, drained

½ cup thinly sliced **prepared peeled roasted red peppers**

½ cup **canned pepperoncini chilies**, stemmed, seeded, and sliced

½ cup **canned red cherry peppers**, stemmed, seeded, and sliced (keep small ones whole)

⅓ cup minced **fresh basil** leaves

⅓ cup minced **parsley**

2 cloves **garlic**, minced

About 1 tablespoon **extra-virgin olive oil**

About 1 tablespoon **balsamic vinegar**

Salt and **pepper**

½ cup **large ripe green olives**, drained

¼ cup **salt-cured black olives**

1. In a large shallow salad bowl, combine escarole, dandelion leaves, onion, lupini beans, roasted red peppers, pepperoncini chilies, red cherry peppers, basil, parsley, and garlic.

2. Mix gently with just enough oil to coat greens; add vinegar, salt, and pepper to taste. Garnish with green and black olives.

Per serving: 69 cal., 51% (35 cal.) from fat; 1.7 g protein; 3.9 g fat (0.5 g sat.); 7.3 g carbo (2 g fiber); 475 mg sodium; 0 mg chol.

Fish with Tomatoes and Chili
Michael W. Huff, Beaverton, Oregon

When he lived in Tennessee, Michael Huff served a hot, spicy tomato sauce with the local freshwater largemouth bass. In Oregon, he finds other white-fleshed fish work just as well.

Prep and cook time: About 25 minutes
Makes: 6 servings

1½ to 2 pounds firm white-fleshed **fish fillets** such as Chilean seabass, halibut, or rockfish

1 tablespoon **olive oil**

1 **onion** (about 6 oz.), chopped

2 cloves **garlic**, minced

3 to 4 tablespoons minced **fresh jalapeño chili**

1 can (14½ oz.) **diced tomatoes**

1 tablespoon **lemon juice**

1½ teaspoons **cornstarch**

2 tablespoons chopped **fresh cilantro**

Salt and **pepper**

1. Rinse fish and pat dry; cut into serving-size pieces. Rub fish with 2 teaspoons oil. Place fish pieces slightly apart in a single layer in a 10- by 15-inch baking pan. Bake in a 425° oven, uncovered, until fish is barely opaque in thickest part (cut to test), 10 to 15 minutes.

2. In a 10- to 12-inch frying pan, combine remaining oil, onion, garlic, and chili. Stir often over medium-high heat, until onion is lightly browned, about 5 minutes. Meanwhile, drain tomatoes, reserving juice. Mix reserved tomato juice, lemon juice, and cornstarch. Add tomatoes and juice mixture to onion; stir until mixture boils and thickens.

3. With a slotted spatula, transfer fish to plates. Spoon sauce over fish; sprinkle with cilantro. Add salt and pepper to taste.

Per serving: 161 cal., 26% (42 cal.) from fat; 22 g protein; 4.7 g fat (0.9 g sat.); 6.9 g carbo (1.1 g fiber); 191 mg sodium; 47 mg chol. ◆

Serve butterflied garlic shrimp with a vegetable that also cooks quickly on the grill, such as zucchini (see page 104).

May

foodguide

by **JERRY ANNE DI VECCHIO**

DANIEL CLARK

a **TASTE** *of the* **WEST**

Ranch-style chicken

Being quite nimble as a child, I often had the task of catching the chicken for Sunday dinner at one of our relatives' farms. As the chicken lost its head, I would turn my back for a sad, rarely silent moment. Plucking feathers, though, usually revived my spirits and my appetite.

One grandmother always stewed the whole bird with homemade egg noodles. An aunt, considered a fancy cook,

coated the chicken pieces with peppery paprika-seasoned flour and fried them crisp in home-rendered lard (she lived to be 96). In the Midwest in those days, chicken couldn't get much better.

Things were different in California. On a neighboring artichoke ranch, a wonderful cook named Ida would simmer her chicken with artichokes and mushrooms. It was my favorite dish.

In some ways, Ida was more ruthless

with the artichokes than the chicken. She tore off the coarse leaves, hacked off the thorns, peeled the stems, and yanked out the fuzzy chokes. In fact, she threw away more than she cooked—but I learned a lesson. Shorn to edibility, the artichoke releases its sweetness, as it does in this simple but memorable dish.

And even though I've switched to the market for ingredients, I still play tough with artichokes.

great product

In an Indian restaurant, I simply cannot resist the crackling-crisp pappadum wafers often tucked into the bread basket. Pappadums (also spelled pappadams, poppadums, and papadums—take your pick) are just one of India's many flat breads, and although they go well with curries and other traditional dishes, I love them for everyday snacking, as appetizers, and to accompany salads.

All the pappadums you buy here—in Indian food markets and in many supermarkets—come from India. They're made of cooked pastes of lentils or other legumes, or rice, rolled thin, and dried. Sometimes they are flavored with chilies or garlic. Pappadums are typically fried or toasted over a flame (tricky, unless you practice). Widely distributed Patak's pappadums (4 oz., about a dozen 4-inch wafers), also have microwave directions. But I like pappadums best when toasted under the broiler, in seconds. ***Toasted pappadums:*** Lay **pappadum** wafers slightly apart on a baking sheet. Broil 4 to 6 inches from heat until wafers begin to buckle, 20 to 25 seconds; watch closely—they scorch easily. Turn wafers over and broil until surface is blistered, 8 to 12 seconds. Transfer toasted wafers to a rack. Serve, or store airtight as soon as they are cool, up to 1 week.

Per wafer: 27 cal., 6.7% (1.8 cal.) from fat; 2 g protein; 0.2 g fat (0 g sat.); 4.7 g carbo (1 g fiber); 260 mg sodium; 0 mg chol.

Braised Chicken and Artichokes

Prep and cook time: About 50 minutes

Notes: Serve with mashed potatoes, soft polenta, or risotto.

Makes: 4 servings

- 8 **skinned chicken thighs** (1½ to 1¾ lb. total)
- 1 **onion** (4 to 5 oz.)
- ½ pound **mushrooms** (1- to 1½-in.-wide caps)
- 1½ cups **chicken broth**
- 1 tablespoon **balsamic vinegar**
- 2 tablespoons **tomato paste**
- ½ teaspoon **dried thyme**
- 4 **artichokes** (about 3½ in. wide)
- 2 tablespoons **vinegar** (any kind)
- ½ cup chopped **parsley**

  Salt and **pepper**

1. Trim and discard fat from thighs.

2. Chop onion. Rinse mushrooms and trim discolored stem ends.

3. Put chicken in an 11- to 12-inch nonstick frying pan over high heat. Lightly brown pieces, turning as needed, 3 to 5 minutes. Remove chicken from pan and set aside.

4. Add onion, mushrooms, and ½ cup broth to pan. Stir to free browned bits, cover, and cook 5 minutes, then uncover and stir often until mushrooms are lightly browned, about 5 minutes more. Remove from heat and stir in vinegar, tomato paste, thyme, and remaining broth. Then return chicken and juices to the pan.

5. Meanwhile, with a sharp knife, cut off and discard top ⅓ of each artichoke and trim discolored ends of stems. Break off and discard leaves down to the tender, pale green inner ones. Cut artichokes in quarters vertically. With knife, cut fuzzy chokes from artichoke hearts and pull out the tiny leaves with thorny tips. Immerse artichoke quarters in about 2 quarts water mixed with the 2 tablespoons vinegar (so artichokes will darken less). Swish artichokes to rinse, then drain.

6. Lay artichokes on top of chicken, cover pan, and bring to a boil over high heat. Reduce heat and simmer until chicken and artichokes are tender when pierced, about 15 minutes.

7. Sprinkle parsley over chicken mixture, then spoon onto plates and season to taste with salt and pepper.

Per serving: 249 cal., 22% (54 cal.) from fat; 31 g protein; 6 g fat (1.6 g sat.); 20 g carbo (7.8 g fiber); 325 mg sodium; 105 mg chol.

BOOK *notes*

Verdant thoughts

The *Children's Kitchen Garden: A Book of Gardening, Cooking, & Learning,* by Georgeanne and daughter Ethel Brennan (Ten Speed Press, Berkeley, May 1997; $16.95), is a friendly, 144-page book that grew out of a project at the East Bay French-American School. In the school garden, created by students and faculty, the rewards of growing food provide incentive to learn how to use environmentally sound techniques.

Although this book is designed for adults working with children from 5 to 12 years old, the information is so straightforward and basic, it's a timeless reference.

Fresh from the Farmers' Market: Year-Round Recipes for the Pick of the Crop, by Janet Fletcher, approaches fresh produce from the buyer's perspective. This handsome, 208-page book (Chronicle Books, San Francisco, May 1997; $19.95) extols the pleasures and benefits of farmers' markets. Organized by season, each section includes shopping guides and recipes that focus on the prime produce of the period. Her recipes will delight anyone who rejoices in good, fresh food.

foodguide

SEASONAL *note*

The tender crab

Eating any crab besides Dungeness might be considered un-Western. But the prospect of savoring soft-shell crab blows away my tenuous parochial loyalties.

Soft-shells are fascinating critters. As blue crabs, they flourish from New Jersey through the south into Louisiana and Texas. From late spring into fall, a blue crab molts as many as seven times annually during its three-year life span. Each time, it literally bursts out of the old shell, leaving behind every inedible fragment as well as its viscera. The new shell is so soft, and the crab so clean, you can eat the entire thing (although the gills are usually removed because they are slightly bitter). The crab may be a soft-shell for as long as a week.

Because shells harden more rapidly in water and the crab is killed by cold, soft-shells are packed with straw or moss in boxes for rapid transit at 40° to 50°. If they die, they don't deteriorate as rapidly as hard-shell crabs do. If, after a day or so, any dead ones still smell fresh and sweet, they are fine for cooking. Soft-shells are available fresh in many fish markets, but individually frozen ones are easier to find.

At Santa Monica's Typhoon restaurant, soft-shells are served with a vinegar and garlic sauce. They're great.

Sautéed soft-shell crabs with Asian mignonette. Allow 1 **soft-shell crab** (2½- to 3-oz. size) for an appetizer, 2 for an entrée. Gently lift (but don't detach) each side of the back shell of the crab and pull off and discard the soft gills; lay shell back in place. Rinse crab and pat dry. Coat crab with **all-purpose flour** and shake off excess.

To cook up to 6 crabs, melt 2 tablespoons **butter** or margarine in an 11- to 12-inch nonstick frying pan over medium-high heat. Add crabs and brown well, turning once or twice, about 7 minutes total. Lift from pan and drain briefly on paper towels.

Serve crabs hot and drizzle to taste with this sauce: combine 2 tablespoons **rice vinegar,** 2 tablespoons **lime juice,** 1 teaspoon minced **fresh ginger,** 1 teaspoon minced **parsley,** ½ teaspoon minced **garlic,** and ¼ teaspoon **salt.** Makes ¼ cup.

Per crab: 74 cal., 65% (48 cal.) from fat; 6.7 g protein; 5.3 g fat (2.9 g sat.); 0.7 g carbo (0 g fiber); 385 mg sodium; 72 mg chol.

DANIEL CLARK

BACK *to* BASICS

The cake with a thousand faces

At the Fancy Food Show in San Francisco a few months ago, I trudged through the North and South halls of the huge Moscone Convention Center until I was exhausted and almost stupefied by the endless conveniences offered. There must be a baking mix for every occasion.

So why bother to bake from scratch? Believe it or not, sometimes it's easier. Certainly, this versatile, tender, one-layer cake is for me—I always have the basics: butter, flour, sugar, baking powder, and a couple of eggs. And it's oven-ready in 10 minutes or less.

If I bake the cake plain, I can finish it with frosting, ice cream, or sauce.

Or, for additional nuances, I can flavor the batter with vanilla, a liqueur, orange or lemon peel, or a spice.

But the best part is that I can top the batter with fruit. The fruit makes a beautiful pattern as it sinks in during baking, and the cake is never soggy.

With each variation, I have a brand-new dessert. Now that's convenience.

Blackberry Cake

Prep and cook time: About 10 minutes to mix, 1 hour to bake

Notes: Use any juicy berry (except strawberries) or pitted cherries. Or cover the surface of the batter with a layer of fruit slices—plum, apricot, nectarine, peach, apple, or pear.

Makes: 8 servings

> About ½ cup (¼ lb.) **butter** or margarine, cut into chunks
>
> About 1 cup **all-purpose flour**
>
> About 1 cup plus 1 tablespoon **granulated sugar**

1 teaspoon **baking powder**

2 **large eggs**

1 cup **fresh** or frozen unsugared **blackberries**

1 tablespoon **powdered sugar**

1. Butter and dust with flour a 9-inch cake pan with removable rim.

2. In a bowl, combine 1 cup granulated sugar and ½ cup butter. Slowly beat with a mixer to blend, then beat on high speed until well mixed, about 3 minutes.

3. Add 1 cup flour, baking powder, and eggs. Stir to combine, then beat on high speed until the stiff batter is well blended, about 2 minutes.

4. Scrape batter into cake pan and spread top smooth.

5. Scatter berries evenly over batter. Sprinkle fruit with 1 tablespoon granulated sugar.

6. Bake on the center rack of a 350° oven just until cake begins to pull from pan rim, 55 to 60 minutes. Run a thin-bladed knife between cake and pan rim. Let cool at least 10 minutes or, if making ahead, wrap cake airtight when cool and let stand at room temperature up to 1 day.

7. Remove pan rim, dust cake with powdered sugar, and cut into wedges.

Per serving: 301 cal., 39% (117 cal.) from fat; 3.5 g protein; 13 g fat (7.9 g sat.); 43 g carbo (1.3 g fiber); 199 mg sodium; 85 mg chol. ◆

RICK MARIANI

The many faces of Riesling

Riesling has always reminded me of Judy Garland. There is Judy as young Dorothy in *The Wizard of Oz*—kind, innocent, pretty. Then there's Judy Garland, the mature woman—intense, gripping, fragile, and complex in the same split second. Rieslings, depending on where they are grown, can have either personality.

But before we talk about Riesling in any depth, we should tackle the issue of why the wine is not hugely popular in the United States. After all, for most of wine's history, wine experts and collectors have considered Riesling to be the greatest white grape in the world. In fact, records from the 19th century show that fine Rieslings were often the most expensive wines at auction.

How, then, did so prominent a wine fall off its pedestal? Well, in many parts of the world, it didn't. Not surprisingly, the Germans, Austrians, and Alsatians, who make the best Rieslings on the planet, all continue to believe in the grape's supremacy. Many British wine professionals do too.

But Riesling is rarely the first choice of American consumers. One theory has it that we like Teutonic precision in mechanical things (cars, appliances), but when it comes to wine, food, and romance, give us France.

I think there's something else at work as well. We are a culture for whom bigger is better, more (not less) is best. Riesling, the most gossamer of grapes, doesn't easily dovetail with our collective style.

Great Riesling is about clarity and transparency, not about body and power. Rarely found in other grape varieties, clarity and transparency are among the most difficult qualities to describe. But here goes.

Clarity is the sense that the wine's flavors are as clear and explicit as the sound of church bells. In contrast to Riesling, many white varieties have more opaque flavors that are rich, thick, and creamy.

Transparency is the sense that the wine's flavors are utterly naked and pure. Transparency is one of the hardest flavor concepts to grasp, which may be why it usually comes to one while drinking an especially stellar Riesling.

All of this, however, is dependent on one critical factor: a cool climate, where grapes mature ever so slowly.

The most famous cool climates for Riesling are in Germany, Austria, and the Alsace region of France. In these places, Riesling can be dazzling, with intense mineral and peach flavors and breathtaking clarity and transparency. Similarly, the cool vineyards of upper New York state, Washington, Ontario, British Columbia, and New Zealand can produce fabulously racy Rieslings.

In California's generous sun, Riesling is more gentle, less intense. More like Dorothy than a mature Judy Garland. California Riesling is therefore often considered the perfect picnic wine, and I also think it's the best wine in the world to sip while you're cooking.

Any discussion of Riesling is incomplete without speaking about sweetness. One myth is that Riesling is nearly always sweet. Not true. Many are bonedry, and others have just a smidgen of natural sweetness that is too low to be perceived by human taste buds.

Still others are a touch sweet. A good analogy would be a cup of coffee that has had a teaspoon of sugar added to it. In the United States, Rieslings like this are called "semi-dry."

Finally, there are nectarlike sweet Rieslings that are my favorite dessert wines, beating out even the vaunted Sauternes of France. Rieslings labeled "late harvest," "botrytis," "beerenauslese," "trockenbeerenauslese," and "eiswein" should not be missed.

Rieslings are so varied it's fun to put together a small tasting of samples from around the world—perhaps as a prelude to a dinner party.

Bründlmayer Zöbinger Heiligenstein Riesling "Alte Reben" 1995, $37 (Kamptal, Austria). A rare luxury.

H. A. Strub, Niersteiner Brückchen, Riesling Kabinett 1995, $14 (Rheinhessen, Germany). Bold and minerally with pronounced acidity.

Hogue Dry Johannisberg Riesling 1995, $6.50 (Columbia Valley, Washington). Light and delicate—waiting for fresh seafood.

Kuentz-Bas, Riesling "Cuvée Tradition" 1994, $12 (Alsace, France). Minerally and vigorous; lemon zest meets a mountain stream.

Navarro Cluster Select Late-Harvest White Riesling 1994, $19.50 half-bottle (Anderson Valley, California). Possibly the most opulent, elegant dessert wine in the United States. A honeyed-apricot silkiness. Available only from the winery; (707) 895-3686.

Trefethen Dry Riesling 1996, $12 (Napa Valley, California). Trefethen is one of the oldest and best producers of Riesling in the Napa Valley. ◆

WINE DICTIONARY:
late harvest

Late-harvest wines are made from grapes that have been picked late, after the normal harvest. Because these grapes contain a greater amount of natural grape sugar, dessert wines are usually made from them. Most of the world's great dessert wines, including French Sauternes and German trockenbeerenausleses, are made from late-harvest grapes. — *K. M.*

Bill's Trout

Latimer's father has been fishing in the Sierra since the '20s. This is how he cooks up a mess of trout. And it's still how Latimer likes them best.

Prep and cook time: About 20 minutes (5 at home, 15 in camp)

Notes: Clean fish soon after they're caught, keep cool, and cook within 24 hours. If cooked right away, the fish tend to curl in the pan, so gently flatten with a pancake turner to brown them evenly. Serve with stir-fried or grilled vegetables. Try leeks, fennel, zucchini, carrots, or bell peppers.

Makes: 4 servings

½ cup **cornmeal**

½ cup **all-purpose flour**

Salt and **pepper**

5 or 6 slices **bacon** (about ¼ lb.) to make 2 to 4 tablespoons bacon drippings (or use same amount of salad oil)

4 fresh-caught **trout** (up to 1 lb. each) or similar freshwater fish

1. At home: Put cornmeal, flour, salt, and pepper in a 1-gallon zip-lock plastic food bag. Pack bacon drippings in a small, widemouthed Nalgene jar (see page 94). Transport in an insulated chest.

2. In camp: Gut fish. If desired, or for fit in pan, cut off heads and tails. Rinse fish well.

3. Put fish in the plastic bag with the

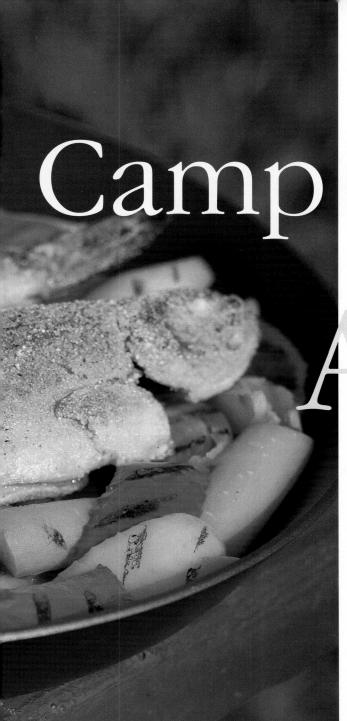

Camp cookin'

Recipes for fresh trout and Thai breakfast sausage, helpful planning tips, and the science of s'mores

A t the end of a long day of hiking, fishing, or chasing the kids around camp, the last thing you want is a big production at dinner. On the other hand, beans and wienies aren't exactly a cheery prospect, either.

But you can eat well, without an excessive amount of work, if you plan ahead and follow these recipes by Berkeley resident Carole Latimer, author of the backpacker's bible, *Wilderness Cuisine.* As the owner of Call of the Wild, she's been leading women's trips around the West (and cooking on them, too) since 1978. Latimer loves to cook almost as much as she loves to camp, but over the years she has learned to be practical. And when we tested her recipes on our Coleman two-burner camp stove, the results were delicious.

by **BARBARA GOLDMAN**

photographs by **NOEL BARNHURST**

cornmeal mixture and shake to coat.

4. Put bacon drippings in a nonstick 10- to 12-inch frying pan over medium heat. When hot, add fish to pan without crowding. Brown well and cook just until thickest part flakes easily when prodded to the bone, about 5 minutes per side, depending on size. If desired, serve bacon with fish.

Per serving fish: 435 cal., 41% (180 cal.) from fat; 48 g protein; 20 g fat (4.2 g sat.); 13 g carbo (0.7 g fiber); 148 mg sodium; 134 mg chol.

Menu-planning tips

Make a chart. To avoid the camp cook's most common mistake—bringing too much food—list the number of meals you'll be preparing, *then* make a shopping list.

Prepare ahead. A refrigerated or frozen one-pot meal reheated at camp makes a great first-night dinner. For recipes that require cooking in camp, mix dry ingredients at home.

Bring "bailout" foods. These include instant noodle soups (miso is good when you're cold or wet). Fresh pesto and tomato sauces can be frozen, which also helps keep your cooler cool.

(lesser amount for mildest flavor), fish sauce, egg, cornstarch, and sugar. Divide into 16 equal portions and shape into 16 patties, each ½ inch thick.

2. Pour oil into a 10- to 12-inch nonstick frying pan over medium-high heat. When hot, add a few patties, without crowding. Cook until brown on each side and no longer pink in center (cut to test), about 7 minutes total. Remove as cooked and drain on paper towels; add more patties to pan.

3. When patties are cool, freeze in a single layer in a metal pan until hard, then seal airtight in plastic freezer bags. Transport in an insulated chest.

4. In camp: Place frozen patties in a 9- to 10-inch nonstick frying pan over low heat, cover, and cook until warm, 3 to 5 minutes; turn at least once.

Per patty: 73 cal., 53% (39 cal.) from fat; 5.9 g protein; 4.3 g fat (0.9 g sat.); 2.4 g carbo (0.3 g fiber); 107 mg sodium; 34 mg chol.

Early California Stew

Make this stew at home a day or two ahead and refrigerate, or make well ahead and freeze. Reheat in camp and serve with tortillas, crusty bread, or basmati rice.

Prep and cook time: About 2¼ hours at home, plus reheating in camp

Notes: Heat varies in chipotle chilies; taste as you add. Fresh green Anaheim chilies (also called California or New Mexico) can be used instead of poblanos.

Makes: About 12 cups; 6 servings

3 **fresh poblano chilies** (also called pasilla chilies), about ½ lb. total

1 tablespoon **olive oil**

1½ pounds fat-trimmed **boneless beef chuck,** cut into ½-inch cubes

2 teaspoons **ground cumin**

2 teaspoons **dried oregano**

1 **onion** (8 oz.), chopped

2 cloves **garlic,** minced

2 teaspoons **red wine vinegar**

1 can (about 14½ oz.) **chopped tomatoes**

¼ to ½ ounce (⅛ to ¼ cup) **dried chipotle chilies**

1 **turnip** (¾ lb.), peeled

2 **carrots** (½ lb. total)

2 cans (15 oz. each) **pinto beans**

2 cans (15 oz. each) **white hominy**

Salt

1. At home: Stem, seed, devein, and coarsely chop poblano chilies.

2. In a 5- to 6-quart nonstick pan over medium-high heat, combine poblano chilies and 1½ teaspoons olive oil. Stir often until chilies are limp, about 5

Thai Turkey Sausage

Cook up a big batch of patties at home and freeze. Heat them in camp for a great breakfast with eggs or hash-browns (Latimer uses sweet potatoes), tangerine juice, and papaya wedges.

Prep and cook time: About 30 minutes at home, plus reheating in camp

Notes: It's easiest to mince lemon grass in a food processor or mini-chopper. For best texture, mince the remaining ingredients with a knife.

Makes: 16 patties; 8 servings

1 pound **ground turkey**

¼ pound **green beans,** ends and strings removed, minced

8 **green onions,** ends trimmed, minced

1 stalk (5 to 8 in.) **fresh lemon grass,** tough outer layers, stem end, and coarse leaves removed, minced

3 tablespoons minced **fresh cilantro**

2 to 3 teaspoons **fresh serrano chilies** (2 or 3), stemmed, seeded, and finely minced

2 tablespoons **Asian fish sauce** (*nuoc mam* or *nam pla*)

1 **large egg**

2 tablespoons **cornstarch**

¼ teaspoon **sugar**

About 2 tablespoons **olive oil**

1. At home: Mix turkey well with beans, onions, lemon grass, cilantro, chilies

10 camp-kitchen essentials

1 *Nonstick frying pan.* Ever try cooking scrambled eggs in a cast-iron pan? 'Nuff said.

2 *3-quart aluminum pot.* If you are planning to use it for pasta, get one with a nesting strainer.

3 *Can opener.* You'd be surprised how often this gets left behind.

4 *Oven mitt.* Towels burn; damp ones don't protect your hands. A fireproof barbecue mitt is best.

5 *Headlamp.* It leaves both hands free when you're cooking after dark.

6 *Nalgene containers.* You'll find these leakproof bottles and jars (above) at most outdoor supply stores.

7 *Plastic bags.* From zip-locks to

30-gallon trash bags. You can use them for food storage or, in a pinch, as rain ponchos.

8 *Plastic insulated cups.* They're better for drinking hot liquids than metal Sierra cups. Use 16-ouncers for measuring.

9 *Biodegradable soap.* For washing (use your aluminum pot as a sink).

10 *Cotton gardening gloves.* To protect hands around camp when cutting firewood, etc.

minutes. Pour chilies into a bowl.

3. To pan, add remaining oil, meat, cumin, and oregano. Stir occasionally until meat is browned, about 5 minutes. Add onion, garlic, and vinegar. Stir often until onion is limp, about 3 minutes.

4. To pan, add tomatoes with their juice and 1 cup water. Cover and simmer over low heat until meat is tender when pierced, about 1¼ hours.

5. Soak chipotles with 1 cup hot water until pliable, about 20 minutes. Stem, seed, devein, and mince chipotles.

6. Cut turnip and carrots into ½-inch-thick sticks no more than 3 inches long. Drain and rinse beans and hominy.

7. To pan, add turnip, carrots, beans, hominy, and poblano chilies; stir, then add chipotle chilies to taste. Cover and simmer until vegetables are tender when pierced, about 20 minutes. Season to taste with salt.

8. Uncover stew and let cool. Seal in plastic freezer bags. Chill up to 2 days, or freeze up to 2 months. Transport in an insulated chest.

9. In camp: In a covered nonstick pan over low heat, warm chilled (thawed) stew, stirring occasionally. Add a little water to thin slightly, if desired.

Per serving: 458 cal., 19% (87 cal.) from fat; 35 g protein; 9.7 g fat (2.4 g sat.); 58 g carbo (13 g fiber); 1,124 mg sodium; 68 mg chol.

Carole Latimer

One of Latimer's best tricks is to dry dishes inside a folded nylon screen.

Wilderness Cuisine, by Carole Latimer (Wilderness Press, Berkeley, 1991; $12.95), is available in bookstores. Or you can call (800) 443-7227 to order. For information about Call of the Wild, call (510) 849-9292 or check out the Web site at http://www.callwild.com.

Chicken Piccata

This meal is quick and easy, and takes very little home prep. The pasta provides the carbohydrates that hikers crave. Latimer serves it with a simple green salad and a good baguette.

Prep and cook time: About 25 minutes (10 at home, 15 in camp)

Makes: 4 servings

1¼	pounds **boneless, skinless chicken breast halves**
½	teaspoon **paprika**
2	tablespoons **lemon juice**
1	cup **dry white wine**
1	cup **reduced-sodium chicken broth** or water
3	tablespoons drained **capers**
2	tablespoons **cornstarch**
10	ounces **dried fettuccine,** linguine, or spaghetti
1½	teaspoons **olive oil**
1½	teaspoons **butter** or margarine
	Salt and **pepper**

1. At home: Slice chicken breast halves across grain into ½-inch-thick strips and mix with paprika. Seal in a plastic freezer bag and chill up to 1 day or freeze up to 1 month.

2. Mix lemon juice with wine, chicken broth, capers, and cornstarch. Pour sauce into a small unbreakable container and seal. Chill up to 3 days.

3. Transport chicken and sauce in an insulated chest.

4. In camp: Cook pasta, uncovered, in about 4 quarts boiling water until tender to bite, about 7 minutes.

5. Meanwhile, combine oil and butter in a 9- to 10-inch nonstick frying pan over high heat. When hot, add about half the chilled (thawed) chicken strips and stir-fry until pieces are slightly browned and still faintly pink in the center (cut to test), 2 to 3 minutes. With a slotted spoon, transfer cooked chicken to a bowl. Repeat to cook remaining chicken, then return cooked chicken to pan.

6. Shake sauce to mix and pour it into the pan with the chicken. Stir until sauce boils rapidly.

7. Drain pasta and serve topped with chicken and sauce. Season to taste with salt and pepper.

Per serving: 513 cal., 11% (54 cal.) from fat; 42 g protein; 6 g fat (1.7 g sat.); 58 g carbo (1.7 g fiber); 542 mg sodium; 86 mg chol. ◆

THE SCIENCE OF
S'mores

Graham crackers, chocolate, a toasted marshmallow. What more can be said about a s'more?

Plenty, if you're asking Reginald Mitchell, an associate professor of mechanical engineering at Stanford University. His specialty is combustion sciences, so he knows a good deal about marshmallows—when they're near a campfire, that is. Turns out toasting a marshmallow is actually a six-step process:

1. Swelling. As the marshmallow heats, the moisture in it expands, causing the marshmallow to swell.

2. Escape. As the moisture expands, it blows tiny holes through the marshmallow and escapes as steam.

3. Sugar rush. Depleted of moisture, the marshmallow is now a sucrose char. Oxygen in the air rushes to its surface—it's ready to burn.

4. Flame on. Oxygen diffuses from the air to the marshmallow's outer surface. At the surface, carbon reacts with the oxygen, producing a blue flame. This is called burning in the diffusion limited mode.

5. Oxidation. Simultaneously, carbon atoms grab oxygen atoms, producing carbon monoxide, then carbon dioxide.

6. Oxyinterruptus. Pulling the marshmallow from the fire and blowing it out interrupts the oxidation process. This creates soot, evidence of incomplete combustion.

Seconds, anyone? — *Ben Marks*

Bouillabaisse, Hawaii-style

Oahu chef Alan Wong makes the most of Pacific seafood—
the heart of this extraordinary stew

The moment the bowl was placed before me, I knew that chef and restaurateur Alan Wong's answer to the great French fish stew called bouillabaisse was a winner. Appropriately, Hawaii-grown fish and clams, and Maine lobster reared in Kona, were floating in the herb-scented saffron broth. The pungency of garlic and the unexpected sweetness of basil blended into an aromatic siren. A long, slender crouton was anchored at attention by the mashed potatoes mounded in the center of the bowl.

One spoonful and I was hooked. Each bite unveiled a fresh nuance. The creamy potatoes, laced with crab, held a hint of garlic provided by the aioli. The aioli also added to the complex flavors of the delicate broth and various fish. The crunchy baguette crouton had a touch of garlic, too.

Wong, who developed a passion for bouillabaisse while working with French chefs in New York City, takes an approach that's far less daunting than the traditional one. Instead of working from a staggering list of ingredients, he breaks the dish down into five individual recipes, each of which stands on its own and has steps that can be completed ahead. These separate elements unite quickly to become bouillabaisse.

Translating this French classic to the Pacific is hardly a leap of faith. In Tahiti, the French have created Gallic versions of many local recipes. Your translation will likely differ from Wong's—which he serves in the Oahu restaurant that bears his name—depending on your fish options. But some Hawaiian fish are distributed on the Mainland, and other fish work well, too. As Wong has demonstrated, each variation adds to the literature of bouillabaisse.

Oahu Bouillabaisse

Prep and cook time: About 2½ hours total, but if all the parts that can be prepared ahead are ready, final cooking and serving take 40 to 45 minutes

Notes: Hours to days ahead, make herb broth and aioli—both go into the potatoes. And you need the broth to poach the seafood. Cook the fish after the potatoes are mashed and while the croutons are toasting.

Makes: 6 servings

> **Smashed potatoes**
> (recipe follows)
>
> **Herb-poached seafood**
> (recipe follows)
>
> ⅔ cup diced **red bell pepper**
>
> ⅓ cup thinly sliced **chives**
> or green onions
>
> **Garlic croutons** (recipe follows)
>
> **Spicy aioli** (recipe follows)
>
> **Salt** and **pepper**

1. Mound hot potatoes equally in warm, wide soup bowls.

2. Arrange equal portions of herb-poached seafood around potatoes, then ladle the seafood hot broth over the seafood. Sprinkle servings with red bell pepper and chives.

3. Push 1 crouton upright into each potato mound, or lay on dish rim. Accompany the bouillabaisse with remaining croutons and the spicy aioli; add salt and pepper to taste.

Per serving: 910 cal., 39% (351 cal.) from fat; 64 g protein; 39 g fat (6 g sat.); 70 g carbo (6.3 g fiber); 1,168 mg sodium; 220 mg chol.

by **LINDA LAU ANUSASANANAN**   *photographs by* **KEVIN CANDLAND**

Dip into this lavish fish soup at any spot to come up with a delectable play of flavors. Savory mashed potatoes are at the heart.

Herb Broth

Prep and cook time: 35 to 40 minutes

Notes: Make broth up to 3 days in advance (you can freeze to store longer). It's the base for the bouillabaisse but makes a fine soup on its own.

Makes: 6½ cups, 5 or 6 servings

- 1 teaspoon **olive oil**
- ¾ cup chopped **celery**
- 1 cup chopped **onion**
- 1 cup chopped **fresh fennel**
- 1 cup chopped **red bell pepper**
- ½ teaspoon **madras curry powder**
- 2 tablespoons **brandy**
- 2 tablespoons **Pernod** (optional)
- 4 cups **chicken** or fish **broth**
- 1 bottle (8 oz.) **clam juice**
- ¼ cup **dry white wine**
- 1 tablespoon **canned tomato paste**
- ¹⁄₁₆ teaspoon **powdered saffron** (optional)

  Salt and **pepper**

1. In a 5- to 6-quart pan, combine oil, celery, onion, fennel, and bell pepper. Stir often over medium-high heat until onion is limp, 8 to 10 minutes. Add curry powder and stir until mixture is quite fragrant, 2 to 3 minutes.

2. Add brandy, Pernod, broth, clam juice, wine, tomato paste, and saffron. Bring to a boil. Cover and simmer until vegetables are very tender when pierced, about 15 minutes. Whirl mixture, a portion at a time, in a blender until smooth. If desired, pour broth through a fine strainer into a bowl, rubbing with a spatula; discard any residue. If needed, add water to make 6½ cups. Add salt and pepper to taste.

3. Use in bouillabaisse or ladle hot broth into bowls.

Per serving: 69 cal., 25% (17 cal.) from fat; 3 g protein; 1.9 g fat (0.6 g sat.); 6.1 g carbo (1.3 g fiber); 210 mg sodium; 2.5 mg chol.

Spicy Aioli

Prep time: About 5 minutes

Notes: Make up to 2 days ahead. Cover and chill to store.

Makes: ⅔ cup

- ⅔ cup **mayonnaise**
- 2 cloves **garlic,** pressed
- 1 tablespoon **lemon juice**
- 1 teaspoon **Dijon mustard**
- ½ teaspoon **cayenne**

Mix mayonnaise with garlic, lemon juice, mustard, and cayenne.

Per tablespoon: 108 cal., 100% (108 cal.) from fat; 0.2 g protein; 12 g fat (1.7 g sat.); 0.7 g carbo (0 g fiber); 96 mg sodium; 8.7 mg chol.

Smashed Potatoes

Prep and cook time: 35 to 40 minutes

Notes: If making ahead, cover potatoes tightly and keep warm in a 250° oven up to 30 minutes; stir in crab just before serving.

Makes: 6 cups, 6 servings

How much garlic? It's a matter of choice when you add this aromatic aioli to bouillabaisse.

- 3 pounds **russet potatoes**
- ¼ cup **spicy aioli** (recipe precedes)

    About ⅓ cup **herb broth** (recipe precedes) or chicken broth

- ⅓ pound **shelled cooked crab** (optional)

    Salt and **pepper**

1. In a 5- to 6-quart pan, bring 2½ quarts water to a boil.

2. Meanwhile, peel potatoes and cut into 1½-inch chunks. Add potatoes to boiling water, cover, and simmer until tender when pierced, about 20 minutes; drain.

3. Mash potatoes, adding aioli and enough broth to make potatoes creamy.

4. Stir in crab. Add salt and pepper to taste. Use in bouillabaisse or serve.

Per serving: 241 cal., 31% (75 cal.) from fat; 4.2 g protein; 8.3 g fat (1.2 g sat.); 38 g carbo (3.5 g fiber); 91 mg sodium; 5.9 mg chol.

Herb-poached Seafood

Prep and cook time: 30 to 40 minutes

Notes: Have lobster tails split lengthwise at the market, or use a heavy cleaver to cut through from the softer underside. Or replace lobster with additional shrimp. A dramatic option is whole shrimp (heads on), available in many Asian fish markets. To keep whole shrimp intact, don't shell. To devein, push a thin skewer perpendicularly through back shell under vein, then pull skewer up to lift out vein. Repeat as needed, then rinse shrimp.

Fish, shrimp, and scallops can be cleaned, cut, and chilled up to 4 hours ahead. Chill clams and mussels covered with a damp cloth (not airtight). Scrub shortly before cooking.

Makes: 6 servings

- ½ cup chopped **fresh basil** leaves
- 2 tablespoons chopped **fresh cilantro**
- 2 tablespoons chopped **parsley**
- 2 tablespoons minced **shallots**
- 1 teaspoon minced **garlic**
- ¾ pound **boned** and **skinned opakapaka** or rockfish, cut into 1½-inch chunks
- ¾ pound **sea** (large) **scallops,** rinsed and cut in half
- 18 **shrimp** (about 1 lb., 16 to 20 per lb.), peeled and deveined

- 6 cups **herb broth** (recipe precedes) or chicken broth
- 24 **clams** or mussels (pull off beards) in shells, suitable for steaming, scrubbed
- 3 **Maine,** spiny, or rock **lobster tails** (about ½ lb. each), split in half lengthwise, or 6 to 12 shrimp (16 to 20 per lb.)

1. Mix basil, cilantro, parsley, shallots, and garlic with fish, scallops, and shrimp. Set aside.

2. Bring broth to a boil in a 5- to 6-quart pan over high heat. Add clams and lobster. Cover and simmer until clams open and lobster is barely opaque in thickest part (cut to test), 5 to 10 minutes. As clams open, lift them from the simmering broth with a slotted spoon and keep warm.

3. After 10 minutes, add seasoned fish, scallops, and shrimp to simmering broth. Bring to a boil over high heat, then tightly cover pan and remove from heat. Let stand until shrimp, scallops, and fish are barely opaque in thickest part (cut to test), 3 to 5 minutes. Use in bouillabaisse or, with a slotted spoon, divide seafood equally among wide, shallow bowls. Over high heat, bring broth to boiling, then ladle into bowls.

Per serving: 349 cal., 14% (48 cal.) from fat; 56 g protein; 5.3 g fat (1.2 g sat.); 11 g carbo (1.6 g fiber); 700 mg sodium; 200 mg chol.

Garlic Croutons

Prep and cook time: 30 to 35 minutes

Notes: If making ahead, store airtight up to 1 day.

Makes: About 18 pieces

- 1 **baguette** (8 oz.)
- 2 tablespoons **olive oil**
- 1 clove **garlic,** pressed

1. Slice baguette ¼ inch thick on a sharp diagonal to make pieces 3 to 6 inches long. Reserve end pieces for another use. Arrange slices in a single layer on a baking sheet.

2. Mix oil and garlic. Brush oil mixture over bread slices.

3. Bake in a 350° oven until croutons are crisp and golden, 18 to 25 minutes. Serve warm or cool.

Per piece: 46 cal., 37% (17 cal.) from fat; 1 g protein; 1.9 g fat (0.3 g sat.); 6.2 g carbo (0.3 g fiber); 72 mg sodium; 0 mg chol. ◆

by CHRISTINE WEBER HALE

NORMAN A. PLATE

Savory polenta gratin can be on the table in 25 minutes.

A hearty gratin with ready-made polenta

It's really no more than cooked cornmeal—grits if you're in the South. But take just one taste, and it's easy to understand why polenta is so admired. The nutty, slightly sweet corn flavor, luscious with melted cheese, is the perfect complement to hearty stews and ragouts.

The traditional method of cooking polenta calls for at least 45 minutes of simmering with constant stirring—a labor of love. But, if your heart isn't into that kind of commitment, and you still crave polenta, ready-made is the answer. Cooked polenta is sold plain or seasoned, usually in plastic-wrapped logs or blocks.

The sturdy texture makes it easy to slice. To make individual gratin casseroles, drench oven-heated polenta slices with a lightning-quick tomato–porcini mushroom sauce, then top with cheese and slip under the broiler. For other uses for ready-made polenta, check at right.

What's for dinner?

Polenta Gratin with
Tomato-Porcini Sauce

Spinach Salad
with Vinaigrette

Crisp Breadsticks

Honeydew Melon Wedges

Zinfandel or Pinot Noir

Polenta Gratin with Tomato-Porcini Sauce

Prep and cook time: About 25 minutes
Makes: 4 servings

¼ ounce (about 2 tablespoons) **dried porcini mushrooms**

1 or 2 packages (about 2 lb. total) **cooked polenta,** plain or seasoned

1 can (28 oz.) **crushed tomatoes with basil**

¼ cup **dry red wine** such as Zinfandel or Pinot Noir

1 tablespoon minced **fresh basil** leaves or 1 teaspoon dried basil

½ pound **jack cheese,** shredded

¼ cup shredded **parmesan cheese**

1. In a bowl, combine mushrooms and ½ cup boiling water and let stand until limp, about 5 minutes.

2. Meanwhile, cut the polenta crosswise into ½-inch-thick slices. Divide slices among 4 shallow 2-cup gratin dishes or ramekins. Bake in a 450° oven until hot, about 5 minutes.

3. As polenta bakes, rub mushrooms gently to release grit, then lift from water, squeeze dry, and finely chop. Reserve liquid.

4. Put mushrooms in a 10- to 12-inch frying pan. Pour in most of the soaking liquid, discarding the gritty remainder. Add tomatoes, wine, and basil. Bring to a boil over high heat and boil about 5 minutes, stirring often.

5. Remove polenta from oven and spoon sauce evenly over it. Sprinkle with jack and parmesan cheeses.

6. Broil 6 inches from heat until cheeses begin to brown, about 6 minutes.

Per serving: 453 cal., 38% (171 cal.) from fat; 22 g protein; 19 g fat (11 g sat.); 40 g carbo (6.1 g fiber); 1,159 mg sodium; 64 mg chol.

MORE QUICK TRICKS WITH COOKED POLENTA

•For a light supper, heat polenta slices in the oven, then top with a vegetable stir-fry. (Use cut stir-fry vegetables from the produce section or frozen stir-fry vegetables.)

•Tuck teleme, cheddar, or blue cheese between thin slices of cooked polenta and broil or pan-brown for a new take on grilled cheese sandwiches.

•Pan-brown cooked polenta slices in a little butter for breakfast. Serve with powdered sugar or maple syrup.

•For appetizers, cut ½-inch-thick polenta slices with cookie cutter to make one or two bite-size pieces. Top shapes with purchased pesto, tapenade, or roasted red pepper spread, then sprinkle with grated parmesan and broil until sizzling.

•Use thin slices of cooked polenta instead of pasta in lasagna.

•Serve your favorite stew or chili over oven-warmed cooked polenta slices. ◆

DARROW M. WATT

Mole verde surrounds pork tenderloin slices garnished with parsley and pepper.

Tap the rich, complex flavors of green mole

Liven up menus with two versatile Mexican sauces

Mexican cuisine is filled with many sauces called moles (*mo*-lays). They come in many colors and flavors. The common vein is texture (*mole* means soft—mashed or puréed—as in guacamole). The ones known as green moles are fresh chili-and-vegetable mixtures that are simmered. Two particularly delicious traditional examples are mole verde from Oaxaca (in southern Mexico) and pipián verde.

The Oaxacan mole uses epazote, an herb found dried at most Mexican-food markets. This mole gets its body from lima beans and masa. The pipián verde's base is peanuts, pumpkin seeds, and tomatillos.

Both sauces go well with pork, chicken, or fish—even over enchiladas.

Mole Verde

Prep and cook time: About 1 hour

Notes: Buy masa fresh from a Mexican-food market, or make it, using dehydrated masa (corn tortilla) flour.

Makes: 4 to 6 servings

- 1¾ pounds **tomatillos**, husked and rinsed
- 2 **onions** (¾ lb. total), quartered
- 1 cup **frozen lima beans**
- 8 cloves **garlic**, peeled
- 2 **fresh serrano chilies** (1 oz. total), stemmed
- ¼ cup **masa**
- ½ cup chopped **fresh fennel**
- ½ cup chopped **fresh cilantro**
- ½ cup chopped **parsley**

- 2 tablespoons crumbled **dried epazote** (optional)
- About ½ cup **beef broth**
- About 2 pounds **baked pork tenderloin**, thinly sliced
- **Parsley** or cilantro sprigs
- **Salt** and **pepper**

1. In a 5- to 6-quart pan, combine tomatillos, onions, lima beans, garlic, chilies, and 3½ cups water.

2. Bring to a boil over high heat; reduce heat, cover, and simmer until vegetables are tender when pierced, about 20 minutes. Drain, reserving cooking liquid.

3. Whirl vegetable mixture in a food processor or blender until smooth. (If desired, chill purée and liquid airtight up to 1 day.)

4. Return purée to pan. Cook, uncovered, over medium heat, stirring often, until purée is as thick as catsup, about 15 minutes.

5. With a fork, blend prepared masa with 1 cup reserved cooking liquid; add to purée.

6. Whirl fennel, cilantro, parsley, and epazote with broth in a food processor or blender; add mixture to cooked sauce. Heat just until hot.

7. Ladle ¾ cup sauce onto each dinner plate; lay pork slices in sauce and garnish with parsley. Season with salt and pepper to taste. Accompany with remaining sauce.

Per serving: 307 cal., 23% (71 cal.) from fat; 37 g protein; 7.9 g fat (2.5 g sat.); 21 g carbo (3.1 g fiber); 93 mg sodium; 90 mg chol.

Pipián Verde

Prep and cook time: About 1½ hours

Makes: 8 servings

- 1 **onion** (6 oz.), quartered
- ½ pound **tomatillos**, husked and rinsed
- 2 **fresh jalapeño chilies** (2 oz. total), stemmed
- 4 cloves **garlic**, peeled
- 2 **romaine lettuce** leaves
- 1 cup lightly packed **fresh cilantro**
- ¼ cup **radish** leaves
- 1⅔ cups (about ½ lb.) **hulled, salted, and roasted pumpkin seeds**

by **BETSY REYNOLDS BATESON**

6 cups **chicken broth**

¾ cup (about ¼ lb.) **unsalted, dry-roasted peanuts**

⅓ cup **Asian sesame seed**

4 to 6 warm **poached** or baked **boneless, skinless chicken breast halves** (1¾ to 2½ lb. total), sliced, or 2 pounds warm cooked firm-flesh fish, such as halibut or swordfish

Cilantro sprigs

Salt and **pepper**

1. In a 6- to 8-quart pan, combine onion, tomatillos, chilies, garlic, and 2½ cups water.

2. Bring to a boil over high heat; reduce heat, cover, and simmer until vegetables are tender when pierced, about 20 minutes. Drain.

3. In a food processor or blender, smoothly purée vegetable mixture with romaine, cilantro, and radish leaves.

4. Pour about half the purée into a bowl; set aside.

5. Add 1½ cups pumpkin seeds and ½ cup broth to purée in food processor; whirl until mixture is smooth. Pour into cooking pan.

6. Pour purée from bowl back into food processor. Add peanuts, sesame seed, and ½ cup broth and whirl until smooth. Add to pan.

7. Add 3 cups broth to pan. Bring to a simmer over medium heat. Cover and cook over low heat, stirring occasionally, until sauce thickens, about 30 minutes. Sauce will look curdled.

8. In a food processor or blender, whirl about half the sauce and 1 cup broth until smooth. Pour into a fine strainer over a bowl, pressing sauce through with the back of a spoon; discard residue.

9. Purée remaining sauce and 1 cup broth, and rub through strainer. (If making ahead, cover when cool and chill airtight up to 2 days.)

10. Return sauce to pan and stir over medium heat until hot.

11. Ladle about ¾ cup sauce onto each dinner plate; lay chicken in sauce and garnish with cilantro sprigs and remaining pumpkin seeds. Accompany with remaining sauce and salt and pepper to add to taste.

Per serving: 438 cal.; 41% (180 cal.) from fat; 42 g protein; 20 g fat (3.8 g sat.); 25 g carbo (4.1 g fiber); 310 mg sodium; 79 mg chol. ◆

NORMAN A. PLATE

Programs like "The Cook's Palate" help you turn recipes into cookbooks.

Cookbooks byte by byte

Recipe software makes the process easy and gives custom results

When Lisa Umezawa fled her home just before it was destroyed by the 1991 Oakland Hills fire, she grabbed an irreplaceable piece of family history—her mother's binder filled with family recipes.

Unlike Umezawa, most of us have this treasured data jotted in notebooks, clipped and crammed into boxes, or tucked away in memory. And converting this mass of material into a more usable form that can be duplicated—even as a family cookbook to share—is a daunting task. But computer recipe software eases the grind.

HOW RECIPE PROGRAMS WORK

The six popular recipe programs we tested share many features, but the programs we liked best were easier to use and did more. In all the programs, you input the recipe ingredients, techniques, and other information on a template so recipes can be stored and retrieved.

Some of the programs let you type each recipe continuously into a text box—like a word-processing program. Others need each entry (quantity, ingredient, preparation) put into a separate text box. Some programs quick-fill common words as you type them. Usually this feature, which some people find distracting, can be turned off.

Each program has a search system to locate recipes in several ways, such as by category (soup) or ingredient (chocolate). Every program also includes recipes (some as many as 10,000), but as with a cookbook, you won't know if you like them until you've tried them.

Beyond these basics, some programs also calculate nutritional content of recipes, send and receive recipes by e-mail, make automatic shopping lists, have printing options (page or recipe card size), scale servings up or down, and have graphics.

All of the programs we tested were capable of the most important tasks—inputting, storing, and viewing recipes. But special features in some

by **ANDREW BAKER**

programs were complicated to execute or didn't deliver as promised, and instructions were confusing.

OUR FAVORITES

The Cook's Palate. CD-ROM or diskette for Windows; $49.99. Better Lifestyles; (800) 278-5136. Using this software is like paging through an on-screen book. It's easy to customize your cookbook with color graphics, a cover page, a table of contents, divider pages, and an index. The program will generate shopping lists and menus, and schedule meals on a built-in calendar. The import-export feature lets you exchange recipes with other *Cook's Palate* users.

Mangia. Diskette for Macintosh or Windows; $49.95. Upstill Software; (800) 568-3696, (510) 526-0178, or http://www.mangia.com/mangia. *Mangia* prints in booklet and recipe card formats, which you can enhance with artwork in the program. It also creates shopping lists and menus. Using your inputted pantry inventory, the program will list recipes for ingredients on hand.

OTHER CHOICES

Digital Gourmet. CD-ROM for Macintosh or Windows; $69. Books-On-Disk; (800) 717-4478, or http://www.teletype.com.

MasterCook. CD-ROM for Macintosh or Windows; $39.95. Sierra On-Line; (800) 757-7707, (206) 649-9800, or http://www.sierra.com.

Micro Cookbook. CD-ROM for Windows; $19.98. Pinpoint Publishing; (800) 258-2088, (707) 523-0400, or http://www.cookworks.com.

Micro Kitchen Companion. CD-ROM for Windows; $39.95. Lifestyle Software Group; (800) 289-1157, or http://www.lifeware.com.

The Internet is also a resource for recipe software. We downloaded several programs, but it took patience to locate them—and new possibilities unfold daily. The upside is that the programs are relatively inexpensive. Start with sites on the World Wide Web that offer Shareware—software you can try before you buy. Search http://www.shareware.com using the word *recipe,* and be sure to specify whether you're looking for Macintosh or Windows programs. ◆

HOLLY STEWART

A perfect lemon meringue pie is easy with the right techniques.

Weep-no-more lemon meringue pie

"Why, oh why, does my lemon pie always weep?" writes Nadia Niles from Los Angeles. Or have a saggy meringue? Or fall apart when cut? These woes, and more, are frequently sung in chorus for this all-time favorite dessert.

And, after making this pie for days on end—to weed out fact from fiction—my sympathy bordered on self-pity. But persistence prevailed, and here are the secrets for success.

WHY DOES THE PIE FILLING GET WATERY?

For a lemon filling that's glossy and translucent, and firm enough to cut yet melts in your mouth, cornstarch is the thickener of choice. It's also a risky one because heat and acid (in the lemon juice) can destroy cornstarch's ability to thicken or stay thick.

Happily, the most foolproof way to make a perfect lemon filling is also the easiest. Just dump in the ingredients—in a specific order, with a combination of cold, then hot water—and cook them together. As the starch granules swell with the heating liquid and begin to form a thickening network, the sugar and egg yolk proteins join forces, like suits of armor, to coat and protect the starch at its vulnerable bonding points from the effects of heat and acid.

by LINDA LAU ANUSASANANAN

WHY SHOULD THE FILLING BE HOT WHEN YOU TOP IT WITH THE MERINGUE?

Steam billowing from a hot filling quickly passes through the baking meringue instead of lingering at the filling-meringue interface. However, some of the steam will collect near the surface of the meringue. As the meringue cools, it contracts (shrinks) slightly—just enough, after a few hours, to pop this moisture onto the surface in tiny golden brown droplets, or beads. The beads form faster if the weather is humid or if the pie is chilled. A tiny bit of cornstarch (such as in the recipe at right) whipped with the sugar into the meringue traps some of this moisture and reduces beading.

If the meringue is swirled onto a cool filling and baked, steam in the reheating filling just reaches the meringue. As the pie cools, the steam condenses to form the sweet weeping (sometimes a pool) under the meringue. And when the pie is cut, the meringue is inclined to slip off the wedges.

WHY DOES MERINGUE SHRINK?

As egg whites are beaten, they stretch and trap air bubbles. The size and strength of the bubbles determine the durability of the meringue. Small, even bubbles are more lasting than big, uneven ones.

An acid, such as cream of tartar, makes egg-white bubbles stronger. Add it before beating the whites into a coarse foam. To further strengthen the protein in the whites and force the bubbles to break into firmer, tiny ones, gradually beat in the sugar. When the foamy mass is glossy and holds distinct peaks, the bubbles are still flexible enough to swell when heating air expands in them as the meringue bakes. If sugar is added before a coarse foam is established, the whites get too stretchy to make a stiff foam. If you add the sugar too fast, the granules won't dissolve and the bubbles will be uneven. If you overbeat the whites, the meringue loses its gloss and the bubbles are stretched to their maximum; when heated, they pop and drain liquid. In underbeaten egg whites, the insufficiently developed bubbles break and drain.

However, even perfectly whipped meringues are relatively short-lived (unlike hard meringues, which are made with twice as much sugar and linger forever). Heat firms the pie meringue, and one that is baked longer at a lower temperature will hold up better than one baked briefly at a high temperature. As the meringue cools, the air in the bubbles contracts and causes slight shrinkage. Eventually, the bubbles sag, moisture drains from them, and the mixture gets gummy and chewy.

The following recipe solves all the problems of freshly made pies.

Foolproof Lemon Meringue Pie

Prep and cook time: About 1 hour, plus 3 hours cooling time

Notes: Flavor and texture are best if pie is served within 24 hours.

Makes: 8 servings

1¾ cups **sugar**

6 tablespoons plus 2 teaspoons **cornstarch**

⅛ teaspoon **salt**

1 tablespoon grated **lemon** peel

½ cup **lemon juice**

4 **large eggs,** separated

1 tablespoon **butter** or margarine

Baked 9-inch **pie crust**

¼ teaspoon **cream of tartar**

1. In a 2- to 3-quart pan, mix 1¼ cups sugar with 6 tablespoons cornstarch and salt. Whisk in ½ cup cold water, lemon peel, and lemon juice, blending thoroughly. Whisk in the egg yolks. Add the butter and whisk in 1½ cups boiling water.

2. Set pan over medium-high heat and stir with a flexible spatula until mixture boils, about 7 minutes. Reduce heat to medium and stir filling 1 minute more.

3. Pour filling into pie crust.

4. In a small bowl, mix the remaining ½ cup sugar with the remaining 2 teaspoons cornstarch.

5. In a deep bowl, beat egg whites and cream of tartar with a mixer on high speed (use whisk attachment if available) until very foamy and no liquid whites remain in bottom of bowl. Continue to beat at high speed and gradually add the sugar-starch mixture, 1 tablespoon at a time. Then beat until whites hold stiff, glossy peaks.

6. Spoon meringue onto hot pie filling. With a spatula, swirl meringue to cover filling completely, touching the rim of the pie shell.

7. Bake in a 325° oven until meringue is browned, about 25 minutes. Set pie on rack until cool, about 3 hours. Serve, or invert a large bowl over pie (take care not to touch meringue) and chill up to 1 day.

Per serving: 367 cal., 29% (108 cal.) from fat; 4.7 g protein; 12 g fat (3.6 g sat.); 62 g carbo (0.4 g fiber); 207 mg sodium; 110 mg chol. ◆

Sunset's Kitchen Cabinet

A lime-garlic sauce seasons butterflied shrimp. Serve with grilled zucchini.

"I love this recipe because it's quick, easy, and tastes great," says Cynthia Oei. Serve these large grilled shrimp with a vegetable that also cooks quickly on the grill, such as zucchini or corn, and a rice pilaf.

Butterflied Garlic Shrimp

Cynthia Oei, San Jose, California

Prep and cook time: About 20 minutes
Makes: 3 or 4 servings

- 1¼ pounds **shrimp** (12 to 15 per lb.), peeled
- ½ cup **lime** or lemon **juice**
- 6 to 8 cloves **garlic**, minced
- 2 tablespoons melted **butter** or margarine
- 4 teaspoons **hot sauce**
- **Salt**

1. Cut almost through each shrimp down its back, from neck to tail. Pull out and discard veins. Rinse shrimp and lay open, cut sides down, pressing to flatten. Lay butterflied shrimp in a container, about 9 by 13 inches.

2. Mix lime juice, garlic, butter, and hot sauce and pour half over the shrimp. If making ahead, cover and chill shrimp and reserved sauce up to 1 hour.

3. Lay shrimp, spread open, on a grill above a solid bed of hot coals or over high heat on a gas grill (you can hold your hand at grill level only 2 to 3 seconds). Close lid on gas grill. Cook, turning once, until shrimp are pink and opaque but still moist-looking in thickest part (cut to test), 5 to 7 minutes total. Transfer to a platter as cooked.

4. Combine shrimp marinade and reserved sauce and heat until boiling. Spoon sauce over grilled shrimp and add salt to taste.

Per serving: 186 cal., 38% (70 cal.) from fat; 24 g protein; 7.8 g fat (3.9 g sat.); 4.6 g carbo (0.1 g fiber); 365 mg sodium; 190 mg chol.

Spiced Napa Cabbage Salad

Theresa M. Liu, Alameda, California

"This salad is great for potlucks," says Theresa Liu. "It's a refreshing change from those mayonnaise-heavy potato and macaroni salads."

Prep and cook time: About 35 minutes
Makes: 8 servings

- 1 **English cucumber** (about ½ lb.)
- 6 cups finely shredded **napa cabbage**
- 2 cups shredded **carrots**
- ½ cup **rice vinegar**
- 1 tablespoon **Asian fish sauce** (*nuoc mam* or *nam pla*)
- 1 tablespoon **Asian (toasted) sesame oil**
- 1½ teaspoons **soy sauce**
- 1½ teaspoons **sugar**
- 1 **fresh jalapeño chili,** stemmed, seeded, and minced
- 1 clove **garlic,** minced
- ¾ cup **unsalted dry-roasted peanuts**

1. Slice cucumber in half lengthwise, trim off ends, and scoop out and discard seeds. Thinly slice cucumber.

2. In a wide bowl, combine cabbage, carrots, and cucumber.

3. Mix vinegar, fish sauce, sesame oil, soy sauce, sugar, chili, and garlic. Pour over salad and mix. Serve, or cover and chill up to 4 hours. Sprinkle with peanuts and mix.

Per serving: 131 cal., 61% (80 cal.) from fat; 4.7 g protein; 8.9 g fat (1.2 g sat.); 10 g carbo (2.8 g fiber); 155 mg sodium; 0 mg chol.

Kid-friendly Enchiladas

Shirley Bomgaars, Kingston, Washington

To warm her kids up to spicy foods, Shirley Bomgaars diluted salsa with tomato soup to use in quick and easy enchiladas.

Now, for fuller flavor, she's upped the salsa ratio and uses tomato sauce instead of soup. For a hearty variation, add cooked ground beef or turkey to the filling.

by L I N D A   L A U   A N U S A S A N A N A N

Prep and cook time: About 1 hour
Makes: 4 servings

- 1 package (4 oz.) **black bean and rice mix**
- 1½ cups **tomato salsa**
- 1 can (8 oz.) **tomato sauce**
- 8 **flour tortillas** (8 in. wide)
- 1½ cups **shredded reduced-fat** or regular **cheddar cheese**
- **Sour cream** or reduced-fat sour cream (optional)
- **Canned sliced ripe olives** (optional)

1. Cook bean and rice mix according to package directions.

2. Meanwhile, combine salsa and tomato sauce and pour 1 cup of the mixture into a 9- by 13-inch casserole.

3. In a microwave oven on full power (100 percent), warm 2 or 3 tortillas at a time between paper towels, 20 to 30 seconds.

4. As tortillas are heated, spoon ¼ cup bean mixture and 1 tablespoon cheese down center of each, roll to enclose, and place, seam down, in casserole.

5. Pour remaining salsa mixture over enchiladas; top with remaining cheese.

6. Bake in a 400° oven until enchiladas are hot in center, 20 to 25 minutes. Garnish the casserole with sour cream and olives.

Per serving: 494 cal., 24% (117 cal.) from fat; 24 g protein; 13 g fat (6 g sat.); 68 g carbo (6 g fiber); 2,392 mg sodium; 30 mg chol.

Not-Much-Guilt Chocolate-Mint Ice Milk

Jennifer A. Kirkgaard, Burbank, California

At the Kirkgaard homestead, this low-fat ice milk is the latest rage. Its intense dark-chocolate flavor and smooth, silky texture make chocolate lovers forget it's relatively lean. Dutch cocoa is another name for the alkaline-treated product.

Prep and cook time: About 45 minutes
Makes: About 3 cups, 4 to 6 servings

- 2½ cups **canned low-fat evaporated milk**
- ½ cup packed **fresh mint leaves**
- ½ cup **sugar**
- 2 tablespoons **cornstarch**
- 2 **large egg** yolks
- ⅔ cup **Dutch-process unsweetened cocoa**
- ½ cup **plain nonfat yogurt**
- ¼ cup chopped **bittersweet** or semisweet **chocolate**

1. In a 2- to 3-quart pan over high heat, bring milk and mint just to a boil. Remove from heat, cover, and let stand 20 minutes.

2. Meanwhile, in a bowl, mix sugar and cornstarch. Whisk in egg yolks.

3. Pour milk mixture through a fine strainer into another bowl; discard mint. Whisk about ¼ of the mint-milk into egg yolk mixture. Add cocoa and whisk until blended; pour back into pan. Add remaining milk to pan.

4. Return pan to medium heat and stir with a whisk until mixture begins to bubble, 2 to 4 minutes.

5. Remove cocoa mixture from heat and pour into a bowl. Stir in yogurt. Cover surface of mixture with plastic wrap and chill until cold, at least 2 hours or up to 1 day.

6. Pour cold mixture into an ice cream maker and freeze according to manufacturer's directions. Midway through freezing, add chopped chocolate; continue freezing until ice milk is firm enough to mound and dasher is hard to turn. Serve, or cover and freeze up to 3 days. If making ahead, let the dessert soften in refrigerator about 30 minutes before serving.

Per ½ cup: 249 cal., 28% (69 cal.) from fat; 11 g protein; 7.7 g fat (2.9 g sat.); 39 g carbo (0.2 g fiber); 203 mg sodium; 88 mg chol.

Low-fat Granola

Roger Kisner, Anacortes, Washington

"My friend's original recipe was full of nuts and seeds. I worked it over and used fruit to maintain the taste," says Roger Kisner. "It has less than half the fat of commercial granola at half the price. I eat it six days a week."

Prep and cook time: About 1 hour
Makes: About 4 quarts

- 2 quarts (2½ lb.) **regular rolled oats**
- ¾ cup firmly packed **brown sugar**
- ½ cup **unprocessed bran** (optional)
- ¼ cup **salad oil**
- ¼ cup **honey**
- 2 teaspoons **vanilla**
- 1 cup chopped **dried apples, apricots, peaches, pears, or prunes**
- ½ cup **dried cranberries** or raisins
- 2 tablespoons chopped **crystallized ginger**

1. Place half the oats, sugar, and bran in each of 2 baking pans, 10 by 15 inches. With your hands, crumble sugar and mix ingredients well.

2. In a 1- to 2-quart pan over medium heat, stir oil, honey, and vanilla until bubbly. Pour half the hot mixture into each baking pan and mix well.

3. Bake, uncovered, in a 350° oven. After 10 minutes, stir granola mixture. If using 1 oven, switch pan positions. Continue baking until oats are lightly toasted, about 10 minutes more.

4. Stir in dried fruit, cranberries, and crystallized ginger, breaking up any clumps. Bake until oats are crisp, 5 to 10 minutes longer. Stir. Let cool 5 minutes and stir again. When cool, serve or store in an airtight container up to 1 month.

Per ¾ cup: 297 cal., 18% (54 cal.) from fat; 8.7 g protein; 6 g fat (0.9 g sat.); 53 g carbo (5.7 g fiber); 9.9 mg sodium; 0 mg chol. ◆

Toasted nuts enrich flavor without adding fat to a lean granola.

Enjoy succulent Blenheim apricots (above) and other varieties at peak flavor this month. For recipe ideas, see page 118.

June

food guide

by **JERRY ANNE DI VECCHIO**

RICHARD JUNG

Just how many ways can you cook salmon? Don't ask a Northwesterner unless you have all day; generations' worth of great ideas pour out. Clearly, this fish is versatile—and no shrinking violet when it comes to seasonings. Case in point: smoked salmon, the best of which is cured with salt and sugar. This combination enables the fish to draw flavors to its very core while, simultaneously, it develops a velvety succulence.

Curing is a little bit of food chemistry that I like to utilize when currying salmon. Despite variables in the blends, curry powders have common denominators that enhance salmon. The orange color comes from turmeric, intensifying the salmon's rich color. Cumin, the most overt spice in curry blends, also sets well with salmon. In addition, there are sweet aromatics such as coriander and cardamom. And even if mustard is evident, I like to add more. All its heat, but none of its taste, dissipates in the curing (currying) process.

Grilling is the easiest and most effective way to cook curried salmon. And there is no finer companion than a crisp, mint-cooled relish of summer's sweet onions—Walla Wallas from the Northwest, Mauis from Hawaii, or Imperials from California.

A TASTE OF THE WEST

Summer naturals: salmon and onions

Curry-cured Salmon with Sweet Onion Relish

Prep and cook time: About 25 minutes, plus at least 1 hour to cure
Makes: 8 or 9 servings

- 1 **salmon fillet** with skin (2½ to 3 lb.)
- 2 tablespoons **sugar**
- 1 tablespoon **salt**
- 1 tablespoon **curry powder**
- 1 tablespoon **dry mustard**
- 2 **Walla Walla,** Maui, or other sweet **onions** (about ¾ lb. each)

seasonal note

Italian and Mexican cooks have taught me how to use squash blossoms well, in everything from risotto to soft tacos. But however fine, these preparations ignore the natural shape of the flower—which begs to be stuffed.

To prepare **squash blossoms**, gently reach into the center of each, pinch out the stamens or pistil, and discard. Rinse the flowers carefully and invert to drain. I cook all blossoms with the stems, but some cooks don't like the texture of the straight stems (on the male flowers) and break them off first.

The easiest stuffing is cheese. Choose one that melts or gets creamy: a tangy **chèvre** (goat) or blue, a velvety fontina or cheddar, or cream **cheese** with a dab of grated parmesan. Fill blossoms sparingly (1 to 2 teaspoons each), then loosely twist tips closed. Cook stuffed flowers in melted **butter** in a frying pan over medium heat until wilted and tinged with brown, 1½ to 2 minutes.

My Italian mother-in-law dipped her squash blossoms in all-purpose flour, then in beaten egg (*fritto misto*–style), and browned them in olive oil with a few cloves of unpeeled garlic—wonderful.

Per 2 stuffed (cooked in 1 teaspoon butter): 55 cal., 91% (50 cal.) from fat; 1.3 g protein; 5.5 g fat (3.6 g sat.); 0.5 g carbo (0 g fiber); 69 mg sodium; 15 mg chol.

GREAT PRODUCT

Fragrant rice

Forever tempted by the bulk bargains in warehouse stores, I purchased an 11-pound bag of basmati rice. This prompted me to use the fragrant grain for more than just the traditional element in a special Indonesian dinner. The rice has a distinctive, toasty aroma and taste, cooks up dry and fluffy, and keeps these qualities when it cools. It doesn't get gummy if juicy ingredients are added, and it's lovely with fruit—in short, ideal for salads, which can be refreshingly lean and light because the rice doesn't need an oil-rich dressing.

Mango and Basmati Rice Salad

Prep and cook time: About 35 minutes
Makes: About 10 cups; 7 or 8 servings

- 2 cups **white basmati rice**
- 1 cup **orange juice**
- ½ cup **lime juice**
- 4 teaspoons **sugar**
  About ¼ teaspoon fresh-grated or ground **nutmeg**
- 2 firm-ripe **mangoes** (about 1 lb. each)
  Salt
  Edible flowers (optional)

1. In a large bowl, stir rice in cool water; drain. Repeat several times until water is no longer cloudy. Drain rice.

2. In a 2- to 3-quart pan, combine rice and 3 cups water. Bring to a boil over high heat, cover, and turn heat to lowest setting. Cook until rice is tender to bite, about 15 minutes; do not stir.

3. Pour hot rice into a colander to drain; let stand until warm, about 15 minutes, or cool.

4. In a wide bowl, combine orange and lime juices, sugar, and ¼ teaspoon nutmeg. Cut peel from mangoes, then cut fruit in small pieces into bowl; discard the pits.

5. Pour rice into bowl, mix, and add salt to taste. Sprinkle salad with more nutmeg, then flowers.

Per serving: 232 cal., 4.3% (9.9 cal.) from fat; 5.5 g protein; 1.1 g fat (0.1 g sat.); 56 g carbo (1.4 g fiber); 25 mg sodium; 0 mg chol.

About ⅓ cup **fresh mint** leaves

½ cup **seasoned rice vinegar**

1 cup **ice cubes** (optional)

1. Rinse salmon fillet, pat dry, and lay skin down in a rimmed pan.

2. Mix sugar with salt, curry powder, and dry mustard. Pat mixture evenly over top of salmon. Cover and chill 1 to 3 hours. (Coating dissolves.)

3. Peel and thinly slice onions. Chop enough mint to make 2 tablespoons.

4. In a bowl, combine onions, chopped mint, and vinegar. To serve within an hour, add ice. If making ahead, cover and chill relish up to 3 hours; stir occasionally.

5. Rinse salmon under cool running water, rubbing gently to release salt. Set fish, skin down, on a sheet of heavy foil and trim foil to fit outline of fish.

6. Prepare grill for indirect heat.
To use charcoal briquets, ignite 60 briquets on fire grate. When dotted with gray ash, in 20 to 25 minutes, push half the coals to each side of grate. Position grill about 6 inches above grate.
To use a gas grill, turn heat to high, close lid, and heat for at least 10 minutes. Adjust heat for indirect grilling (no flame beneath food).

7. Set salmon in center of grill, not over hot coals or flame. Cover; open vents on charcoal grill. Cook until fish is opaque but still moist-looking in thickest part, 12 to 15 minutes.

8. Slide a large, rimless baking sheet under fish, then slide fish onto a platter. Sprinkle with remaining mint leaves. Lift portions of fish off skin. Serve with onion relish.

Per serving: 225 cal., 33% (74 cal.) from fat; 26 g protein; 8.2 g fat (1.2 g sat.); 11 g carbo (1.3 g fiber); 511 mg sodium; 69 mg chol.

RICHARD JUNG

COOK'S SECRET

Caesar salads wrapped to go

Nancy Frumkes and Gordon Drysdale of Modern Catering at the San Francisco Museum of Modern Art do lots of imaginative presentations for big parties. And one of their solutions for serving a leafy salad as an appetizer is *Caesar Salad Roll Ups.* These tidbits are easy and quick to make.

Start with small inner **romaine lettuce** leaves (no more than 7 in. long) mixed with a **Caesar dressing** (your own or purchased, which is basically anchovies and parmesan plus oil and vinegar).

Frumkes and Drysdale make their own thin bread wrappers, but flour tortillas work as well. Trim a 6-inch-wide strip from the center of a soft, fresh **flour tortilla** (about 8 in. wide). Then cut the strip in half lengthwise. (Freshness is important—old tortillas will crack.)

Lay 4 or 5 dressed leaves crosswise on a tortilla strip with tips pointing from alternate sides; roll strip snugly around leaves. Secure the roll at two points, about ½ inch from each end, with strips of blanched **green onion** tops or toothpicks. Then cut the roll in half and set each piece upright. Repeat to make more. Save extra lettuce for salad. Butter tortilla scraps, bake crisp, and serve with a salad or as a snack.

GREAT INGREDIENT

Cool tofu

Raves rarely accompany initial exposure to tofu. Frankly, I wasn't much of a fan until Mitsuko Shrem served it as the first course of a very Western lunch to show off wines she and her husband make at Clos Pegase Winery in Calistoga, California.

She drained silken tofu on towels, chilled it, cut it into big diamonds, set the pieces on plates drizzled with extra-virgin olive oil, and sprinkled the diamonds with salt. Then she squeezed fresh lemon juice onto the tofu and sprinkled it with fresh-ground pepper, more salt, and chopped chives. It was memorably refreshing.

And it was a lesson. To unveil the discreet charms of silken tofu (one of many tofu styles now in most grocery stores), pair subtle with subtle. A partner I especially like is avocado. For a salad, arrange chunks of chilled silken tofu with avocado slices and sprinkle with thinly sliced green onions or minced shallots. Dress them generously with lemon juice, drizzle with a little extra-virgin olive oil, season with salt and pepper, and, for color and mellow flavor, add strips of roasted red pepper.

Or, for *tofu bruschetta,* coarsely chop ½ cup **silken tofu** and season with about 2 tablespoons **lemon juice,** and **salt** and **pepper** to taste. Mound onto 6 slices toasted **French bread,** top with about ½ cup diced **avocado** and, if you like, chopped **roasted red pepper.** Drizzle with a total of 2 teaspoons **extra-virgin olive oil** and more lemon juice to taste.

Per piece: 113 cal., 38% (43 cal.) from fat; 3.4 g protein; 4.8 g fat (0.7 g sat.); 15 g carbo (0.9 g fiber); 156 mg sodium; 0 mg chol. ◆

SHORT CUT

A clean plate safely

Andrew Baker, a *Sunset* writer who assists me in producing the Food Guide, does a lot of recipe testing on the barbecue, so he can't help but come up with time-saving steps. When he carries meat, fish, or poultry out to the grill, he puts them on a serving platter covered with plastic wrap. When the food is cooked, he discards the wrap and returns the food to the still-clean platter. Any raw juices that might contain harmful bacteria are tossed out with the wrap.

by KAREN MACNEIL

Look again at Chenin Blanc

RICK MARIANI

Chenin Blanc has become the Cinderella of white wines. Until just 10 years ago, there was more of this grape growing in California than Chardonnay. Now it's neglected by most U.S. wineries and is unknown to many wine drinkers. What happened?

It's impossible to say why we become enchanted (or not) with certain kinds of wine. For me, Chenin's current obscurity is about as fathomable as Merlot's current fame.

But no matter. What counts is this: Chenin Blanc not only makes delicious wine but also is one of the world's most prestigious white grapes, considered as capable of greatness as Chardonnay, Riesling, or Sauvignon Blanc. Moreover, savvy wine drinkers know that what's good and what's popular are not necessarily the same thing. Best of all, when a wine falls out of fashion and into the camp of ugly ducklings, that's the time to snap it up. Chenin Blanc is a steal right now.

If Chenin Blanc wasn't Cinderella, it would be Meg Ryan. Charming, sincere, friendly, pretty, and easy to be around. It's exactly the wine you want (1) lying in a hammock, (2) watching an old movie on a Saturday afternoon, (3) after cleaning out the garage, (4) with chicken salad. In other words, Chenin is an effortless wine, welcome in just about any circumstance. I'm talking here about American Chenin Blancs, which come mainly from California, Washington, and Texas. The best of these are fresh wines with lots of appley flavor and, sometimes, a hint of ginger or cinnamon. Poor versions are simply chenin blands.

The world's ultimate Chenin Blancs, however, come from the Loire Valley of France, specifically from the district of Vouvray. These wines are known as Vouvrays, and compared with American Chenin Blancs, they are entirely different animals.

First of all, Vouvrays are highly complex, intriguing, and challenging—more Hillary Clinton than Meg Ryan. They are legendary among all the world's white wines for their flashing, stiletto-sharp acidity. This acidity, which acts like lightning striking right through the middle of the wine, makes Vouvray one of the longest-lived (if not *the* longest) white wines. It's not uncommon for a 20-year-old Vouvray to taste as lively as a wine a fraction of its age. At the same time, however, an aged Vouvray's flavors take on soaring elegance and a whole new dimension of gorgeous floral, peach, and flint flavors. A great aged Vouvray—10 years old or more—is an experience every wine drinker should have at least once.

Unfortunately, aged Vouvrays are not well understood (you can imagine the trials of an importer trying to sell a 15-year-old white wine to a retailer). Still, with a little luck, you can find some older Vouvrays around, especially in fine wine shops.

Vouvray is the most famous appellation for Chenin Blanc but not the only one. The neighboring districts of Savennières, Coteaux du Layon, and Quarts de Chaume also specialize in Chenin Blanc. In fact, one of the most famous wines in the world is Clos de la Coulée de Serrant from Savennières. This is Chenin Blanc from another galaxy. The wine is so suffused with apple and caramel flavors, you feel as though you're inside a tarte Tatin.

Finally, Chenin Blancs are made in an entire range of sweetnesses—from bone-dry to quite sweet. In the United States, most are dry or semi-dry. In France, every style is popular. You'll know the wine is sweet by the designation *moelleux* on the label.

Champalou Vouvray 1994, $14 (Vouvray, France). Outrageously alive. Crushed minerals, earth, and laser beams of tart acidity.

Chappellet Dry Chenin Blanc 1995, $10 (Napa Valley, California). Lovely and zesty. Begging for grilled fish.

Chappellet Old Vine Cuvée 1995, $12 (Napa Valley). Slightly more sophisticated than its little sister above. Wonderful spiced-apple flavors. A scrumptious aperitif.

Clos de la Coulée de Serrant 1992, $39 (Savennières, France). Considered the greatest Chenin in the world. Difficult to find, but worth the effort.

Girard Dry Chenin Blanc "Old Vines" 1995, $8.50 (Napa Valley). Simple, fresh, and very pleasing.

Husch Chenin Blanc 1996, $8.50 (Mendocino, California). Refreshing and gingery with a slight spritz.

Prince Poniatowski Clos Baudoin 1992, $18 (Vouvray). Philippe Poniatowski, a descendant of the last royal family of Poland, makes opulent, vivid Vouvrays that taste best when aged five years or more. ◆

WINE DICTIONARY | AGING

Intentionally keeping a wine for a period of time so that the components in it can coalesce and the wine can grow softer and possibly take on more integrated flavors and more complexity. Wine may be aged in barrel or bottle or both (the wine evolves differently in each vessel). Most of the wines in the world are not aged at all. — *K. M.*

THICK, SIZZLING & JUICY...
it's steak season

Make the most of it with the right cuts and the best sauces

by LINDA LAU ANUSASANANAN

photographs by RICK MARIANI

■ In the wild heart of the West, beef steak is still king. At the Big Texan Steak Ranch in Amarillo, Texas, the draw of a free steak continues to pull in customers who can stagger away without a check if they manage to down a 4½-pound platter-size slab of beef and side dishes in an hour. Even less hearty appetites confirm statistics showing that beef is the meat Westerners most like to toss onto the coals. But quantity is no longer the measure of pleasure. And in sensible portions, even die-hard health fanatics have a hard time blacklisting a juicy piece of beef. So baste your steak with favorite seasonings. Or give it a flavorful rub. Then savor steak from the grill, cooked just the way you like it, served plain or with sauces, light to lavish.

The Perfect Grilled Steak

1. Select a 1- to 3-inch-thick **beef steak** (from chart on page 115).

2. Choose direct or indirect heat and cooking time based on the thickness of meat and desired doneness, using the chart on page 114. If using direct heat, trim excess surface fat from steaks to minimize flare-ups.

3. For the most accurate doneness test, check thick lean cuts—such as top round—with a thermometer instead of touch. They may take a few minutes longer to cook than well-marbled pieces. Thick steaks cooked to rare also include medium to well-done portions around the edges.

4. Transfer steak to a platter; let rest about 5 minutes in a warm place for juices to settle in meat, then cut portions and accompany the beef with one of the following sauces or any favorite steak sauce, or just season to taste with salt and pepper.

5. For a serving, allow 4 ounces fat-trimmed boneless raw steak (about 3 oz. when cooked).

Steak thickness	Method/Heat	Minutes* (Rare/Medium)
1 inch	Direct/Hot	8 to 10/12 to 15
2 inches	Direct/Medium	20 to 25/27 to 30
3 inches	Indirect heat	40 to 45/50 to 65

* When using charcoal. Gas barbecues may take a little less or a little more time, depending on design.

Direct heat. Place steak on grill with heat directly under it. Cook, turning once, until meat is browned and desired doneness.

If using charcoal briquets, cover firegrate with a single solid layer of ignited coals.

If using a gas barbecue, turn all burners to high and close lid for at least 10 minutes. Then adjust to desired heat and cook with lid closed.

HOT: You can hold your hand at grill level only 2 to 3 seconds.

MEDIUM: You can hold your hand at grill level only 4 to 5 seconds.

Indirect heat. Heat is balanced on opposite sides of steak, but not directly under it. Place meat on grill with a pan directly beneath it to catch drippings.

Cover barbecue (open vents if using charcoal) and cook steak, without turning, until browned and desired doneness.

If using charcoal briquets, mound and ignite 80 coals on the firegrate of a barbecue with a lid (20 to 22 in. wide). When briquets are dotted with gray ash, in about 15 minutes, push equal amounts to opposite sides of firegrate. Place a drip pan between coals. Add 10 more briquets (20 total) to each mound of coals. Position grill 4 to 6 inches above firegrate.

If using a gas barbecue, cover and turn heat to high for about 10 minutes. Adjust burners for indirect cooking (no heat down center) and keep on high. Set a drip pan beneath grill between ignited burners. Put grill in place.

COOKED RARE. *Interior meat color:* Red to pinkish red, pale pink near surface. *Temperature:* A thermometer in thickest part registers about 125°. *Feel:* When pressed, meat has a lot of give (like the flesh between thumb and forefinger when your hand is relaxed). For best flavor and texture, cook very lean steaks only to rare.

COOKED MEDIUM. *Interior meat color:* Pink in center, gray near surface. *Temperature:* A thermometer in thickest part registers about 135°. *Feel:* When meat is pressed, it springs back (like the flesh between thumb and forefinger when you make a fist).

- 1 tablespoon **sesame seed**
- 1 teaspoon **Asian (toasted) sesame oil**
- ½ cup thinly sliced **green onion**
- 2 tablespoons minced **fresh ginger**
- 1 tablespoon minced **garlic**
- ½ cup **sake** or dry sherry
- 2 tablespoons **soy sauce**
- 2 teaspoons **sugar**

1. In a 6- to 8-inch frying pan over high heat, frequently shake sesame seed until lightly toasted, about 4 minutes.

2. Add oil, onion, ginger, and garlic. Stir until onion is limp, 2 to 3 minutes. Add sake, soy, and sugar. Bring to a boil. Serve hot, reheated (on grill), or at room temperature. If making ahead, cover and chill up to 5 days.

Per tablespoon: 46 cal., 22% (9.9 cal.) from fat; 0.6 g protein; 1.1 g fat (0.2 g sat.); 4.5 g carbo (0.3 g fiber); 260 mg sodium; 0 mg chol.

Red Wine Glaze

Prep and cook time: About 20 minutes

Notes: Make sauce ahead and reheat on grill. Pour juices from sliced steak into sauce, heat to simmering, and serve.

Makes: About ¾ cup; 3 or 4 servings

- 2 tablespoons **butter** or margarine
- ¾ cup minced **shallots**
- 1 cup **dry red wine**
- **Salt**

1. Place a 6- to 8-inch frying pan over high heat. Add butter and shallots, and stir often until shallots are limp, but not browned, 2 to 3 minutes.

2. Add wine and boil until reduced to about ¾ cup, about 5 minutes. Add salt to taste. Finish as directed in notes.

Per tablespoon: 26 cal., 65% (17 cal.) from fat; 0.3 g protein; 1.9 g fat (1.2 g sat.); 2 g carbo (0.1 g fiber); 22 mg sodium; 5.2 mg chol.

Spiced Chili Rub

Prep time: About 2 minutes

Notes: For a more distinct chili flavor, use mild California or New Mexico ground chilies instead of seasoned chili powder. Rub into meat; grill. Then squeeze juice from orange wedges onto sliced meat and season with salt. Make a single batch of the rub, or a larger quantity to store airtight indefinitely.

Green Peppercorn Béarnaise

Prep and cook time: About 20 minutes

Notes: Cook sauce ahead, then warm on barbecue grill. Stir juices from sliced steak into sauce and serve.

Makes: About 1¼ cups; 6 servings

- ⅔ cup minced **shallots**
- 2 tablespoons **white wine vinegar**
- 1½ teaspoons chopped **fresh tarragon** leaves or ¾ teaspoon dried tarragon
- 1 cup **whipping cream**
- 2 tablespoons drained **canned green peppercorns,** rinsed
- 2 tablespoons **Dijon mustard**
- ¼ cup **cognac** or brandy
- **Salt**

1. Combine shallots, vinegar, and tarragon in an 8- to 10-inch frying pan. Boil over high heat, stirring often, until all the liquid evaporates, about 2 minutes.

2. Add ½ cup cream, peppercorns, and mustard. Boil, stirring often, until cream turns a golden brown, about 8 minutes. Stir in cognac and remaining cream. (If making ahead, set aside up to 2 hours, or cover and chill up to 1 day.)

3. Heat sauce, stirring, until it boils. Add salt to taste.

Per tablespoon: 48 cal., 69% (33 cal.) from fat; 0.4 g protein; 3.7 g fat (2.3 g sat.); 1.3 g carbo (0 g fiber); 71 mg sodium; 13 mg chol.

Sesame-Ginger Sauce

Prep and cook time: About 10 minutes

Notes: Rub steak with soy sauce before grilling to enhance flavor impact of this sauce.

Makes: About ½ cup; 3 or 4 servings

The fresh snap of ginger, the tender crunch of sesame seed, a good rub of soy sauce—together they balance the rich succulence of rib eye steak.

Makes: About 1½ tablespoons, enough for 1 steak about 4 by 10 inches

   1 tablespoon **chili powder**

   1 teaspoon **ground cumin**

   1 teaspoon **ground coriander**

   ¼ teaspoon **cayenne**

Mix chili powder, cumin, coriander, and cayenne. Use or store airtight.

Per teaspoon: 6.4 cal., 42% (2.7 cal.) from fat; 0.3 g protein; 0.3 g fat (0 g sat.); 1 g carbo (0.5 g fiber); 15 mg sodium; 0 mg chol.

CUTTING STEAK | DOWN TO SIZE

If you succumb to a whole steak, you usually exceed the recommended 3-ounce cooked portion limit, and the only remedy is to ration fat intake for several meals before or after you indulge.

It helps to know how fat-trimmed, cooked steak measures up. These USDA numbers are based on an average of three beef grades (select, choice, and prime). So if you use select grade, the leanest of these three, the numbers will be lower; and if you use prime, with more marbling, the numbers will be higher. For perspective, an equal amount of boned and skinned chicken breast has 3 grams of fat and a boned and skinned chicken thigh has 9 grams.

Beef cut (3 oz. fat-trimmed cooked)	cal.	% fat	g fat (g sat.)	g protein	mg chol.
Rib eye (market, Delmonico, Spencer)	189	48	10 (4)	22	66
Top loin (New York, strip, club)	176	41	8 (3)	24	65
T-bone	182	45	9 (3)	24	68
Porterhouse	185	44	9 (3)	24	68
Tenderloin (filet mignon, filet, chateaubriand)	179	45	9 (3)	24	71
Top sirloin (chateaubriand)	165	33	6 (2)	26	76
Top round (London broil)	153	24	4 (1)	27	71

STRAWBERRY
dazzler

A dramatic, edible centerpiece to pair with six easy dipping sauces

■ Summer strawberries deserve special treatment, and it doesn't take much to turn them into the showstoppers of backyard entertaining. You can raise them to new heights with an easy-to-make pedestal and six simple, flavorful dips.

by DANIEL GREGORY

TIME: 30 minutes

COST: About $15 (not including strawberries)

DESIGN: Françoise Kirkman

WHAT YOU NEED
• Terra-cotta flowerpot
• Large plastic foam ball (from a craft store) to fit the top of the pot
• Roll of florist's tape (from a floral supply store)
• Grape, fig, or other nontoxic leaves to cover ball
• Box of toothpicks
• Crate of large strawberries, washed

DIRECTIONS
1. Before you begin, make sure the plastic foam ball fits snugly into the pot, with half of the ball protruding from the top of the pot.
2. Line the inside lip of the pot with a strip of florist's tape. Wedge the ball into the pot, pressing it into the florist's tape for a secure fit.
3. Starting at the edge of the pot, cover the ball with leaves, using toothpicks as pins. Do not push toothpicks all the way into the ball.
4. Press stem ends of strawberries onto the toothpicks until the entire ball is covered and firmly packed. You may need to add toothpicks and strawberries to fill in any holes. ◆

Dip into these (clockwise): chocolate-hazelnut cream, whipped cream-coconut-orange, orange-pepper, mint cream.

PEAK-EXPERIENCE BERRY DIPS
• *Chocolate-hazelnut cream:* Mix 1 part chocolate-hazelnut spread, 3 parts sour cream, and a dash of cinnamon.

• *Honey-balsamic:* Mix equal parts honey and balsamic vinegar; add minced fresh ginger to taste.

• *Maple-cardamom:* Add a dash of ground cardamom to maple syrup.

• *Mint cream:* In a blender, whirl 1 part chopped fresh mint leaves with 3 parts powdered sugar. Stir into 6 parts sour cream.

• *Orange-pepper:* Mix equal parts hot-pepper jelly and orange marmalade.

• *Whipped cream-coconut-orange:* Fold toasted shredded coconut and grated orange peel to taste into sweetened whipped cream.

— *Andrew Baker*

On the trail of the best apricot

For spectacular flavor, search out the Blenheim variety in farmers' markets and orchards. Or bring out the flavor of other apricots in memorable recipes

The more you learn about apricots, the more you admire growers like Stephen Brenkwitz, whose family has nurtured this prima donna fruit for almost 150 years. The fruit is so fragile that, even in these days of high-tech mechanization, it must be harvested tediously and expensively by hand.

Then, even if all goes well, the best-eating varieties are rarely available fresh.

These realities bombard me as I sit in the small packing plant office at Eden Garden in Tracy, California. So I ask, half-jokingly, why the family persists in this masochistic effort.

"Because *he* did," Brenkwitz says proudly, as he points to an aged black-and-white photograph of a serious-looking man in suit and tie. It's his grandfather. But the family's association with apricots goes back much further—to Brenkwitz's great-great-grandfather, who came from Germany in 1850 to farm in Hayward, California.

By 1920, fruit farming was big business in Northern California, particularly south of Hayward, in the Santa Clara Valley—the basin at the southern tip of San Francisco Bay. So many apricots, peaches, plums, and cherries were grown there that it was called the Valley of Heart's Delight.

After World War II, with encroaching housing developments and the birth of the computer industry, the northwestern part of the basin acquired yet another name—Silicon Valley. Land prices soared, squeezing agriculture out. And the apricot growers migrated eastward, across the hills into the San Joaquin Valley, where most of California's 400-plus apricot growers are to-

day. California produces 95 percent of this country's apricots.

Driving through the Diablo Range into this valley in June, you'd never guess you were in apricot country. The parched, golden brown fields look hardly able to support the cattle lumbering over them—and certainly not water-thirsty fruit trees. But barely a mile off the highway, you're suddenly surrounded by apricot trees, their branches bent by the weight of ripening fruit. And here, Brenkwitz leads me through his 200-acre orchard, which has close to 30 apricot varieties. As the truck zooms and lurches over irrigation ruts and dirt paths at breathtaking speeds, I hang on, abandoning the

by CHRISTINE WEBER HALE

Stephen Brenkwitz (left) touts great-eating Blenheims (above) and good-canning Tiltons (bottom right). Both apricots are hard to come by fresh.

Peak-season apricots are delicious poached in Orange Muscat wine or baked in an apricot kugen with sour cream topping (top right).

RICK SZCZECHOWSKI

GARY PARKER (3)

slightest hope of taking notes. Mental ones will have to do.

First, we visit the apricot that Brenkwitz and many other growers consider king, the Blenheim. One bite, and I know why he goes to the effort of growing them. Warmed by sunshine, the fruit has a velvety texture that melts on the tongue. The flavor is heady and sweet-tart. We stand in silence as the juice drips down our chins and over our hands. This is how apricots are *supposed* to taste.

But they certainly aren't what I've come to know as apricots. Why do markets ignore this winner?

Looks and long shelf life—the criteria for supermarkets and produce wholesalers—are the antithesis of quality for apricots. Blenheims and other

> *"In season, I probably*
>
> *eat 10 to 20 or more a*
>
> *day. You have to truly love*
>
> *something to put this*
>
> *much work into it."*

flavorful varieties are shunned because they aren't rugged and picture-perfect. What most of us see are less tasty varieties—Patterson, which accounts for about half the crop, and Castlebrite.

Both are big, shapely, and well colored, and survive in produce bins for a week or more. In their defense, they do cook well—heat intensifies their flavor and softens their texture.

Brenkwitz grudgingly grows Pattersons to make a living. But he refuses to call them apricots. He refers to them wryly as "apricot-like products."

And he hasn't given up on flavor as the measure of a good apricot. Like many growers, he's developing and testing a number of varieties, searching for fruit that will please both consumers and marketers.

One of them is Mary Anne, "named after my wife," he says enthusiastically. It's a large apricot with a beautiful crim-

Grilled apricots with a mustard-tarragon glaze are great with meats.

son blush splashed over its golden skin. The texture is firmer and crisper than the Blenheim's, but the flavor is sweet and strong.

Orchard tour at an end, Brenkwitz sets me down to a warm, gargantuan piece of his wife's apricot kugen. After sampling so much fruit, I worry I won't be able to do the dessert justice. But those juicy, sweet ripe apricot halves nestling in buttery shortcake with a thick sour cream topping just seem to disappear.

I can't resist asking Stephen Brenkwitz if he ever tires of apricots. "Never!" he says firmly. "In season, I probably eat 10 to 20 or more a day. You have to truly love something to put this much work into it."

Apricot Kugen

Prep and cook time: About 1 hour and 50 minutes, plus at least 30 minutes to cool

Notes: Mary Anne Brenkwitz got this recipe from her husband's grandmother.

Makes: 8 to 10 servings

    ½ cup (¼ lb.) **butter** or margarine

    2 cups **sugar**

    8 **large eggs**

    1½ cups **all-purpose flour**

    9 cups halved, pitted firm-ripe
       apricots

    1 teaspoon **ground cinnamon**

    2 tablespoons **lemon juice**

    ¼ cup **cornstarch**

    1¼ cups **sour cream**

    1 teaspoon **vanilla**

1. With a mixer, beat butter and ½ cup sugar until fluffy. Add 4 eggs, one at a time, beating well after each addition. Stir in flour.

2. Spread batter evenly in a 9- by 13-inch pan.

3. Mix apricots with ½ cup sugar, cinnamon, and lemon juice. Arrange fruit, cut side up, in batter.

4. In a bowl, mix remaining sugar with cornstarch. Add sour cream, remaining eggs, and vanilla; beat until blended. Pour over apricots.

5. Bake in a 350° oven until cake surrounding apricots in the center is firm when gently pressed, about 1 hour and 20 minutes. Let cool at least 30 minutes; serve warm or cool.

Per serving: 507 cal., 36% (180 cal.) from fat; 9.9 g protein; 20 g fat (11 g sat.); 75 g carbo (2.4 g fiber); 163 mg sodium; 208 mg chol.

Grilled Apricots with Mustard-Tarragon Glaze

Prep and cook time: About 20 minutes

Notes: Serve with grilled chicken, pork, or lamb.

Makes: 6 servings

    2 pounds firm-ripe **apricots,** halved
       and pitted

    3 tablespoons **honey**

    2 tablespoons **Dijon mustard**

    2 teaspoons minced **fresh tarragon**
       leaves

1. Thread apricot halves onto 2 parallel 6- to 12-inch-long slender metal skewers (you will need several pairs).

2. Mix honey, mustard, and tarragon. Brush half of this mixture onto one side of fruit.

3. Place fruit, basted side down, on a barbecue grill over a solid bed of very hot coals or very high heat on a gas grill (you can hold your hand at grill level only 1 to 2 seconds). Cook until lightly browned, about 2 minutes; baste with remaining honey mixture and carefully turn skewers over. Cook to brown other side, about 2 more minutes.

4. Push fruit from skewers onto a platter.

Per serving: 105 cal., 4.3% (4.5 cal.) from fat; 2 g protein; 0.5 g fat (0 g sat.); 24 g carbo (1.9 g fiber); 122 mg sodium; 0 mg chol.

Apricots Poached in Orange Muscat

Prep and cook time: About 30 minutes, plus about 15 minutes to cool

Notes: For a dramatic presentation, spoon fruit over vanilla ice cream in big wine goblets.

Makes: 6 servings

- 1½ cups **Orange Muscat wine**
- 1 cup **orange juice**
- ½ cup **sugar**
- 2 pounds firm-ripe **apricots,** halved and pitted
- 2 tablespoons minced **crystallized ginger**
- 1 tablespoon grated **orange** peel

1. In a 5- to 6-quart pan, combine wine, orange juice, and sugar. Bring to a boil over high heat, stirring often.

2. Add apricots, cover, and simmer gently until fruit is just tender when pierced, 3 to 5 minutes.

3. With a slotted spoon, transfer fruit to a bowl. Add ginger and orange peel to pan and return syrup to a boil. Boil, uncovered, until syrup is reduced to 1¼ cups, 10 to 12 minutes.

4. Let fruit and syrup cool until just slightly warm. If making ahead, combine syrup and apricots, cover, and chill up to 1 day.

5. Spoon fruit and syrup into bowls.

Per serving: 262 cal., 2.1% (5.4 cal.) from fat; 2.3 g protein; 0.6 g fat (0 g sat.); 49 g carbo (1.9 g fiber); 11 mg sodium; 0 mg chol.

Apricot-Spinach Salad

Prep and cook time: About 30 minutes

Makes: 6 appetizer or 4 main-dish servings

- 1 cup **walnut** or pecan **halves**
- ⅓ cup **seasoned rice vinegar**
- 1 tablespoon **olive oil** or salad oil
- 1 teaspoon grated **lemon** peel
- 1 pound firm-ripe **apricots,** pitted and sliced
- ¾ pound **baby spinach leaves,** rinsed and crisped
- ¼ pound **blue cheese,** crumbled

  Fresh-ground **pepper**

1. In an 8- to 10-inch frying pan over medium heat, shake the walnuts until they are lightly browned, about 5 minutes. Pour from pan.

2. In a wide salad bowl, mix vinegar, oil, and lemon peel. Add apricots and spinach leaves, and mix to coat fruit and greens with dressing. Sprinkle salad with the nuts and cheese. Season to taste with pepper.

Per appetizer serving: 251 cal., 65% (162 cal.) from fat; 9 g protein; 18 g fat (4.8 g sat.); 16 g carbo (3.2 g fiber); 572 mg sodium; 14 mg chol.

Apricot Salsa

Prep time: About 30 minutes

Notes: If making ahead, cover and chill up to 4 hours. Serve salsa cold, or heat in the microwave oven until steaming. It goes well with meat and poultry.

Makes: 3 cups

- 1 pound firm-ripe **apricots,** pitted and chopped
- 1 **red bell pepper** (about 7 oz.), stemmed, seeded, and chopped
- 2 **fresh jalapeño chilies,** stemmed, seeded, and chopped
- 2 tablespoons minced **fresh cilantro**
- 2 tablespoons **lime juice**

  Salt

Mix apricots with bell pepper, jalapeños, cilantro, and lime juice. Season to taste with salt.

Per ¼-cup serving: 22 cal., 8.2% (1.8 cal.) from fat; 0.7 g protein; 0.2 g fat (0 g sat.); 5.2 g carbo (0.7 g fiber); 1.2 mg sodium; 0 mg chol. ◆

GARY PARKER

Brenkwitz relaxes amid the harvest from his 200-acre orchard.

Where are the Blenheims?

Because of its spectacular flavor, the Blenheim was virtually the only variety grown during California's early days. And although Blenheims, in season from about mid-June to mid-July, still represent about a quarter of California's total annual 100,000- to 120,000-ton apricot crop, most are dried or processed as fruit concentrate. Fresh Blenheims are rare in supermarkets.

However, you do stand a chance of finding the variety fresh in California farmers' markets, orchard produce stands, and natural-food stores.

At wholesale produce markets near San Francisco and in L.A., you can buy apricots by the box. Check at Carcione's Fresh Produce (415/583-8989) in the Golden Gate Produce Terminal, South San Francisco, or Giumarra Bros. Fruit Company (213/ 627-2900) in the Los Angeles Wholesale Produce Market, 1601 E. Olympic Blvd., Building 400, Suite 408, Los Angeles.

You can mail-order Blenheims from Eden Garden, 3711 W. Kenner Rd., Tracy, CA 95376; (209) 832-5891. E-mail: edngrdn@ix.netcom.com. A box (24 lb.) costs about $15 to $20, plus shipping.

Salad for supper: Hot potstickers with hoisin dressing.

NORMAN A. PLATE

1 pound **frozen potstickers** (any filling)

2 tablespoons **salad oil**

1 jar (7¼ oz.) **peeled roasted red peppers**, drained

¼ cup **hoisin sauce**

¼ cup **lemon juice**

1 tablespoon **Asian (toasted) sesame oil**

2 teaspoons **sugar**

1 teaspoon minced **fresh ginger**

1 clove **garlic**, minced

8 cups (about 9 oz.) **tender salad mix**, rinsed and crisped

1. In a 10- to 12-inch frying pan, arrange frozen potstickers in a single layer. Add ⅔ cup water and salad oil. Cover and bring to a boil over high heat, then reduce heat and simmer until liquid cooks away and potstickers begin to brown, 12 to 17 minutes. (Or cook as package directs.)

2. Cut red peppers into thin strips.

3. In a large bowl, mix hoisin, lemon juice, toasted sesame oil, sugar, ginger, and garlic.

4. Add salad mix to bowl and mix with dressing.

5. Spoon salad onto dinner plates and top with equal portions of red peppers and hot potstickers.

Per serving: 377 cal., 45% (171 cal.) from fat; 10 g protein; 19 g fat (3.8 g sat.); 44 g carbo (2.3 g fiber); 981 mg sodium; 32 mg chol.

MORE SPEEDY IDEAS FOR FROZEN POTSTICKERS

•For soup, drop frozen potstickers into boiling broth seasoned with minced fresh ginger, sliced green onions, and chopped fresh cilantro.

•For an appetizer, cook potstickers as directed in salad recipe. Serve with this dipping sauce: ½ cup **reduced-fat mayonnaise** mixed with 3 tablespoons **mirin** or dry sherry and 2 teaspoons **Dijon mustard.**

•For a cold salad, cook potstickers as directed in salad recipe. Immerse in cold water to chill quickly; when cold, drain and mix with 1 thawed package (10 oz.) **frozen petite peas**, ¼ cup **seasoned rice vinegar**, 2 tablespoons grated **lemon** peel, 1 tablespoon **salad oil**, ¼ teaspoon **ground nutmeg**, and **salt** and **pepper** to taste. ◆

A step beyond frozen potstickers

My husband and I are warehouse-store junkies. We love wandering the huge aisles in search of bargains—especially food. More than once, when carried away by a good deal, we've found ourselves stuck with a 20-pound bag of the weekly special, and just two of us to eat it. But when the product can be doled out as needed, our inventive spirit is challenged.

One item we depend on for quick dinners and snacks is frozen potstickers. A 3½-pound bag is enough for at least three suppers. But by the end of the second meal, plain potstickers can grow a trifle tedious—and there are more still in the bag. How could we make the remaining potstickers more interesting?

While judging a salad contest last summer, I came across a refreshing solution. Casa Garden Restaurant in Sacramento presented these Asian dumplings, pan-browned, in a salad. Hot potstickers and roasted red peppers, served on a bed of crisp salad greens, are seasoned with a pungent hoisin-ginger dressing. The dish takes minutes to prepare, is perfect as a whole-meal lunch or dinner, and is now the reason we're buying more potstickers.

Potsticker and Roasted Pepper Salad

Prep and cook time: About 30 minutes

Makes: 4 servings

What's for dinner?

Potsticker and
Roasted Pepper Salad

Crusty French Rolls

Watermelon Wedges
and Sugar Cookies

Iced Tea with Lime

Warm goat cheese over berries, served with salad and a Cabernet, makes an appealing summer lunch.

Cheese, berries & wine

Herb-spiked chèvre mellows blackberries' bite

Just because a Cabernet Sauvignon smells like ripe blackberries doesn't mean the combination is a good match. But for chef Gary Danko, the similarities were tempting.

At one of the annual Cakebread Cellars American Harvest workshops, Danko used this fruit to emphasize the berry-rich character of the wine that was chosen to go with this lunch. The big challenge: taming the berry tartness.

In these petite casseroles, the herb-spiked cheese mellows the sour bite of the berries, and heat intensifies the berry essence, which in turn emphasizes this quality in the wine. Danko suggests serving these casseroles for an indulgent lunch or light supper.

Cheese and Blackberry Ramekins

Prep and cook time: About 40 minutes
Makes: 4 servings

- 1 tablespoon minced **shallots**
- ½ teaspoon minced **garlic**
- 1 sprig **fresh thyme**, about 3 inches
- ¼ cup **extra-virgin olive oil**
- 1 tablespoon **cider vinegar**
- 1 **baguette** (about ½ lb.)
- ¼ pound fresh **chèvre** (goat) **cheese**
- 2 tablespoons grated **parmesan cheese**
- 1 **large egg**
- 1 tablespoon **whipping cream**
- 1 tablespoon chopped **fresh basil leaves**
- 1 tablespoon chopped **fresh chives**
- ¾ teaspoon chopped **fresh rosemary leaves**

  Salt and **pepper**

  About 1 cup **blackberries**, rinsed and drained
- ⅓ cup **walnut halves** or pieces
- 2 quarts (8 to 10 oz.) **tender salad leaves**, rinsed and crisped

1. With a spoon, bruise shallots, garlic, and thyme; add oil and vinegar. Set aside 20 minutes or up to 4 hours.

2. Slice baguette ¼ inch thick on a sharp diagonal to make pieces 3 to 6 inches long. Reserve ends for another use. Toast until golden; set aside.

3. Mix goat cheese, parmesan, egg, and cream. Stir in basil, chives, rosemary, and salt and pepper to taste.

4. Divide berries among 4 shallow ramekins (each about 6 oz.). Cover fruit with cheese mixture. Set ramekins on a baking pan. Place nuts in a 9-inch pie pan.

5. Place ramekins and nuts in a 350° oven. Bake nuts until golden, about 10 minutes, and cheese mixture until set when shaken, about 15 minutes.

6. Meanwhile, pour the oil mixture through a fine strainer into a large bowl, pressing the aromatics. Discard residue. To oil mixture, add salad greens, and mix. Mound salad on 4 dinner plates. Set ramekins alongside and sprinkle cheese and salad with nuts. Serve with baguette slices. Season with salt and pepper.

Per serving: 470 cal., 57% (270 cal.) from fat; 15 g protein; 30 g fat (8.5 g sat.); 37 g carbo (4.1 g fiber); 498 mg sodium; 72 mg chol. ◆

FOOD & WINE *in Napa*

Cakebread Cellars, in the Napa Valley, is presenting the 1997 American Harvest Workshop on September 7, 8, and 9. The program includes food and wine seminars, tastings of selected vintages, an on-site farmers' market, and the Chef's Dinner. Call (707) 963-5221 for reservations and prices.

by L I N D A   L A U   A N U S A S A N A N A N

Crisply crusted shrimp anchored in pineapple are hot, inviting, and easy to make.

A Maui shrimp lunch

This is salad, Maui-style. It's designed to get attention. The chef team from the Westin Maui created these shrimp on sticks, which they call "tangled tigers," for the island's annual A Taste of Lahaina food festival.

This salad looks more complicated to make than it is. The piquant sauce for the shrimp also serves as a dressing for the pineapple and the greens.

Start the meal with purchased or homemade sushi. End with blazing mangoes in a hot cardamom syrup. The dessert is another island special, this time from Derek Liburd, formerly the pastry chef at Kapalua Bay Hotel.

Tangled Tiger Shrimp and Pineapple Salad

Prep and cook time: About 2 hours

Notes: Spring roll wrappers (also called lumpia) are crêpe-thin. Usually, egg roll wrappers are a bit thicker. Look for the refrigerated wrappers, hot red chili paste, and black sesame seed with ethnic foods in supermarkets and in Asian grocery stores.

Makes: 4 servings

- 1¼ cups **rice vinegar**
- 1 cup **sugar**
- 2 teaspoons **Asian red chili paste** or sauce
- 1 teaspoon chopped **fresh cilantro**
- 16 **shrimp** (12 to 15 per lb.), peeled and deveined
- 1 **large egg** white
- 8 **spring roll** or egg roll **wrappers** (6 to 8 in. square)
- 1 **pineapple** (3½ to 4 lb.)
  Salad oil
- 2 quarts (8 to 10 oz.) **tender salad mix,** rinsed and crisped
- ⅓ cup finely shredded **daikon**
- ⅓ cup finely shredded **carrot**
- 1 tablespoon finely chopped **roasted, salted macadamia nuts**
- 1 teaspoon **black sesame seed**

1. In a 1- to 2-quart pan, mix 1 cup vinegar, sugar, chili paste, and cilantro. Bring to a boil over high heat. Reduce heat to medium and simmer, uncovered, until reduced to 1 cup, 15 to 20 minutes. If making ahead, cool, cover, and let stand up to 2 days.

2. Run a thin wood skewer (6 to 8 in.) lengthwise through each shrimp, pushing shrimp to the blunt end. Put egg white in a rimmed plate.

3. Separate spring roll wrappers (to be sure they aren't stuck), and restack. Cut the stack into thin strips about ¼ inch wide, leaving them in place.

4. Keeping strips aligned, divide into 16 equal portions and cover snugly with plastic wrap until ready to use. Working with 1 portion at a time, spread strips (they can overlap) out in a band as wide as the length of 1 shrimp. Dip shrimp in egg white to coat. Set shrimp perpendicular to strips on 1 end (see below).

5. Guiding with your hand or a small spatula, tightly roll strands around shrimp as you rotate shrimp. Set coated shrimp on a flour-dusted baking sheet, and cover airtight with plastic wrap. Repeat to wrap remaining shrimp. If making ahead, chill wrapped shrimp up to 2 hours.

6. Quarter pineapple lengthwise through the crown. Cut each wedge of fruit in 1 piece from peel. Trim core from the edge of fruit and set each wedge back on pineapple peel. Cut fruit crosswise at 1-inch intervals down to, but not through, peel. Set each pineapple section on a plate. If making ahead, cover and let stand up to 2 hours.

7. Pour about 1 inch salad oil into a deep 5- to 6-quart pan and set over high heat. Heat oil until a thermometer registers 350°, then adjust heat as

by **LINDA LAU ANUSASANANAN**

needed to maintain temperature. Place 4 wrapped shrimp at a time in oil. Cook, turning once, until wrapped shrimp are golden brown, 2 to 3 minutes.

8. With tongs or a slotted spoon, transfer shrimp to a towel-lined pan; keep warm in a 200° oven. Repeat to cook remaining shrimp. (If frying ahead, let shrimp cool as cooked, then cover and chill up to 4 hours. Reheat, uncovered, in a single layer on a baking sheet in a 350° oven just until hot and crisp, 5 to 6 minutes.)

9. Combine ¼ cup of the cooked vinegar-chili sauce with the remaining ¼ cup vinegar, and mix with salad greens. Spoon salad mixture onto plates and sprinkle with daikon, carrot, nuts, and sesame seed.

10. Stick 4 hot skewered shrimp into each pineapple wedge, pushing the skewers through fruit and securely into pineapple peel. Drizzle shrimp with a little of the vinegar-chili sauce. Serve remaining sauce to add to taste.

Per serving: 648 cal., 17% (108 cal.) from fat; 27 g protein; 12 g fat (1.6 g sat.); 111 g carbo. (4.6 g fiber); 513 mg sodium; 153 mg chol.

Flaming Mangoes with Cardamom Syrup

Prep and cook time: About 35 minutes
Notes: Chef Liburd also uses this cardamom syrup on fried bananas. Flame mangoes tableside for maximum effect. You can shape and freeze scoops of frozen yogurt ahead.
Makes: 4 servings

    8   **cardamom pods,** hulled
    ½   teaspoon finely shredded **lemon** peel
    ½   cup firmly packed **brown sugar**
    2   firm-ripe **mangoes** (about 1½ lb. total)
    ¼   cup **rum**
    3   cups **vanilla low-fat frozen yogurt** or ice cream, in scoops

1. In a 10- to 12-inch frying pan, crush cardamom seed and lemon peel with back of a spoon. Add sugar and 1 cup water. Stir over high heat until sugar dissolves. Boil gently, uncovered, until syrup is reduced to ½ cup, 8 to 10 minutes.

2. Meanwhile, cut peel off mangoes, discard pits, and cut fruit into ½-inch-wide slices, about 3 inches long. If making ahead, cover fruit and syrup and set aside up to 4 hours.

3. Add mangoes to hot syrup and cook over high heat, turning once, until fruit is hot, 2 to 3 minutes.

4. In a small pan (about 1-qt. size), warm rum until hot. Ignite rum and add to mangoes (not beneath a vent, fan, or flammables). Spoon mangoes and flaming syrup over frozen yogurt in bowls.

Per serving: 349 cal., 6.6% (23 cal.) from fat; 5.1 g protein; 2.6 g fat (1.6 g sat.); 73 g carbo (1.3 g fiber); 103 mg sodium; 7.5 mg chol. ◆

Skinny dips

by **BETSY REYNOLDS BATESON**

It's gratifying to dip without guilt. These boldly seasoned combinations, which work equally well as spreads, give you rich flavor without fat calories.

South-of-the-Border Layered Dip

Prep and cook time: 35 to 40 minutes
Notes: You'll find mole paste at Latino markets or in the international section at supermarkets. Serve dip with assorted sliced raw vegetables.
Makes: About 4 cups

    2   teaspoons **olive** or salad **oil**
    1   cup finely chopped **onion**
    1   clove **garlic,** minced
    2   tablespoons **mole paste** or 1 tablespoon chili powder
        About ½ cup **chicken broth**
    2   cans (15 oz. each) **black beans,** rinsed and drained
    2   cups loosely packed **fresh cilantro** leaves
    1   can (4 oz.) **diced green chilies**
    ¼   cup **green salsa** or green taco sauce
    ⅓   cup (1¾ oz.) crumbled **feta cheese**

1. To a 10- to 12-inch nonstick frying pan over medium-high heat, add oil, onion, and garlic. Stir often until onion is tinged golden, about 4 minutes. Add mole and ½ cup broth. Stir to incorporate mole and cook until most of the liquid evaporates, about 4 minutes more; remove from heat.

2. Add beans, mashing about half of them to thicken the mixture. If mixture is too thick for dipping easily, stir in 1 tablespoon broth at a time until mixture is the desired consistency. Spread bean mixture ¾ inch thick on a serving platter; set aside. (If making ahead, cover and chill until next day.)

3. In a food processor or blender, combine cilantro, chilies, and salsa. Whirl or grind until mixture forms a paste as thick as pesto. Occasionally scrape paste from sides of container down into blade area. Spoon cilantro mixture over center of beans

4. Distribute cheese over the spread; surround with sliced vegetables.

Per tablespoon: 13 cal., 28% (3.6 cal.) from fat; 0.7 g protein; 0.4 g fat (0.1 g sat.); 0.7 g carbo (0.5 g fiber); 49 mg sodium; 0.7 mg chol.

Chipotle-Corn Cream Cheese Dip

Prep time: About 15 minutes
Notes: Chipotles in adobado sauce can be found at Latino markets or in the international section at supermarkets. Serve dip with baked tortilla chips, sliced toasted cocktail bagels, or raw vegetables.
Makes: 2½ cups

    8   ounces *each* **nonfat cream cheese** and **reduced-fat cream cheese**
    3   tablespoons **lime juice**
    1   to 2 tablespoons minced **chipotle chilies in adobado sauce**
    1   can (15¼ oz.) **corn kernels,** rinsed and drained

1. With a mixer, beat the cream cheeses together until smooth. Add lime juice and chipotles, and beat to mix well. Stir in corn, then spoon dip into a serving bowl.

2. Serve, or cover and chill up until the next day.

Per tablespoon: 27 cal., 30% (8.1 cal.) from fat; 1.6 g protein; 0.9 g fat (0.6 g sat.); 3 g carbo (0.2 g fiber); 88 mg sodium; 3.2 mg chol. ◆

Lunch lightly upon a rejuvenating honeydew smoothie, turkey sandwich with peach chutney, spicy pickled carrots, and fresh cucumber salad.

10 low-fat foods to get you through the summer

You've got the shades, the sunscreen, and the flip-flops. Now all you need are some refreshing, satisfying foods that won't alter your swimsuit line. Ten of my favorites follow; they're a mix of super-easy recipes and terrific new products.

Look for the chutneys, pickled carrots, salad dressings, and court bouillons in the gourmet-foods section of your supermarket, or mail-order them. Shipping costs are extra unless noted.

1. Honeydew smoothie. Shake 'em up with this pale green thirst-quencher. In a blender, whirl until smooth ½ cup **lemon juice** and fruit from a 4-pound **honeydew melon.** Add **sugar** to taste (about 3 tablespoons). Pour into tall glasses over ice. Makes 4 servings.
Per serving: 117 cal., 1.5% (1.8 cal.) from fat; 1.1 g protein; 0.2 g fat (0 g sat.); 31 g carbo (1.9 g fiber); 21 mg sodium; 0 mg chol.

2. Peach and nectarine chutneys. Three brands capture the essence of summer: *Indira Delights Peach Chutney* ($6.75 for 9 oz.; 415/346-9077); *Judy Brown's Nectarine Chutney* with a generous measure of raisins ($5 for 10 oz.; 415/594-9757); and *Narsai's Nectarine Chutney* ($10.50 for 16 oz.; 510/527-7900).

For an outstanding low-fat turkey sandwich, generously slather **peach** or nectarine **chutney** on slices of coarse **Italian bread** such as ciabatta. Top with thinly sliced **roast turkey** (regular or smoked) and crisp **arugula.**

3. Pickled carrots. The sweet spiciness of *Hogue Farms Pickled Crunchy Carrots* ($4.45 for 12 oz.; 509/786-4557) will perk up any antipasto plate. Or try the carrots in tuna sandwiches: mix **water-packed tuna, reduced-fat mayonnaise,** plenty of minced **pickled carrots,** and fresh-ground **pepper**; sandwich with **bread** and **watercress.**

4. Sweeter cucumbers. I look forward every year to the season's sweeter, more "cucumbery" cucumbers. Try pale green, ridged Armenian; stubby, light green Persian (or Sfran); slim, dark green Japanese; and oval Lemon (2 to 3 in. wide and pale yellow).

For an easy salad, combine 1¼ cups paper-thin **cucumber** slices, 2 tablespoons **seasoned rice vinegar,** 1 teaspoon **sugar,** and **cayenne** to taste. Spoon over **lettuce.** Makes 2 servings.
Per serving: 29 cal., 3.1% (0.9 cal.) from fat; 0.4 g protein; 0.1 g fat (0 g sat.); 7 g carbo (0.7 g fiber); 298 mg sodium; 0 mg chol.

5. Low-fat salad dressings. The choices continue to increase. Check out *Meadow Lakes California Mountain Pear Dressing* ($4 for 12 oz.; 209/855-3448); *Rising Sun Farms Oil Free Raspberry and Balsamic Salad Vinaigrette and Marinade* (12.5 oz.; $23.95 price includes choice of three products; 800/888-0795); and *The Silver Palate Low Fat Roasted Garlic Balsam-*

RICHARD JUNG

by ELAINE JOHNSON

ico Salad Splash ($3.99 for 12.5 oz.; 201/568-0110).

6. *Mango-coconut pops.* Whip up these sweet-tart tropical treats with peak-season fruit. Combine 1½ cups puréed ripe **mangoes** (about 1½ lb.), 1 can (14 oz.) **reduced-fat coconut milk**, ½ cup **light corn syrup**, and ¼ cup **lime juice**. Pour into 16 frozen juice bar molds (about ⅓ cup each) and freeze until firm, about 4 hours. Makes 16.

Per frozen dessert: 75 cal., 11% (8.1 cal.) from fat; 0.2 g protein; 0.9 g fat (0.9 g sat.); 15 g carbo (0.3 g fiber); 22 mg sodium; 0 mg chol.

7. *Thai iced coffee.* For a sweet, creamy java drink, drizzle **low-fat sweetened condensed milk** (per 2 tablespoons, 120 cal. and 1.5 g fat) into a tall glass of **double-strength coffee** over ice. Stir briskly.

8. *Court bouillons.* *Burton & Company* (510/652-0101) has bottled simmered blends of wine and herbs for poaching foods. With a bottle at hand ($5.50 for 750 ml.; two bottles minimum), a light dinner can be ready in minutes. I especially like the tarragon court bouillon for cooking scallops, and the thyme version for poaching skinned chicken breasts.

9. *Pacific halibut in red sauce.* This sweet-flavored, snow-white, and low-fat fish returns to the fresh market in summer. Here's a quick way to try it.

Combine ¾ cup **tomato salsa** or canned caponata and 3 tablespoons water in an 8- to 10-inch frying pan. Add a ½-pound **Pacific halibut steak** and spoon some salsa over it. Cover and simmer over medium heat until fish is opaque but still moist-looking in thickest part (cut to test), about 7 minutes for a 1-inch steak. Lift out fish and if salsa is thinner than you like, briefly boil sauce to concentrate. Makes 2 servings.

Per serving: 155 cal., 15% (23 cal.) from fat; 24 g protein; 2.6 g fat (0.4 g sat.); 6 g carbo (0.7 g fiber); 1,021 mg sodium; 36 mg chol.

10. *Honey-fig sundae.* For a treatment of sweet, plump figs that gilds the lily, drizzle 1 tablespoon **honey** over ½ cup **vanilla frozen yogurt** and 3 sliced ripe **figs** (½ lb. total) to make each serving.

Per serving: 322 cal., 6.2% (20 cal.) from fat; 4.8 g protein; 2.2 g fat (1.1 g sat.); 78 g carbo (6.1 g fiber); 63 mg sodium; 5 mg chol. ◆

A new role for dessert wine

Sweet wines, suited to desserts or served as dessert on their own, also have a practical application in the kitchen as flavorings. For memorable homemade ice cream, try Orange Muscat with chocolate, port with vanilla and cinnamon, and cream sherry with fresh and candied ginger.

The foundation for all these ice creams is a basic cooked custard; pick the wine from the choices that follow. The ice cream mixture can be ready to chill in less than half an hour. To speed cooling so you can freeze the ice cream right away, chill the cooked custard in ice water. The wine makes the ice cream creamier than typical. To emphasize the flavor, serve the ice cream splashed with more of the same wine.

Basic Dessert Wine Ice Cream

Prep and cook time: About 35 minutes, plus 30 minutes to 3 hours to chill and 20 minutes to freeze

Notes: Flavor variations follow.

Makes: 4 or 6 cups

  1½ cups **low-fat milk**

  1½ cups **half-and-half** (light cream)

  ¾ cup **sugar**

      Flavoring (choices follow)

  3 **large eggs**

      Wine (choices follow)

1. In a 2- to 3-quart pan, mix milk, half-and-half, and sugar. Stir often over medium heat until mixture just begins to steam and bubbles form at pan edge.

2. In a bowl, whisk about ⅓ of the hot milk mixture into eggs, then return mixture to pan. Cook, stirring, until custard is thick enough to coat a metal spoon with a smooth, velvety layer, about 20 minutes. Immediately, set pan in ice water and stir often until custard is slightly cool, about 10 minutes, or until cold, about 30 minutes. Or cover

and chill cool custard at least 3 or up to 24 hours.

3. Mix wine with custard and pour into a 1-quart or larger ice cream freezer container (self-refrigerated or frozen cylinder, or use 8 parts crushed ice to 1 part salt).

4. Freeze according to manufacturer's directions or until dasher is difficult to turn. Serve ice cream soft-frozen. Or, if making ahead, pack ice cream in a freezer container and freeze airtight up to 1 week.

FLAVORING AND WINE CHOICES

Orange Muscat ice cream with bittersweet chocolate. Add 2 teaspoons grated **orange** peel to milk mixture before heating. To chilled custard, add 1 cup **Orange Muscat wine**. When mixture is partially frozen, add 4 ounces finely chopped **bittersweet** or semisweet **chocolate**, then continue as directed. Makes about 6 cups.

Per ½-cup serving: 198 cal., 39% (77 cal.) from fat; 4.1 g protein; 8.6 g fat (4.6 g sat.); 23 g carbo (0.2 g fiber); 45 mg sodium; 67 mg chol.

Port ice cream with cinnamon and vanilla. Add ½ teaspoon **ground cinnamon** and 1 split **vanilla bean** (about 4 in. long) to milk mixture before heating. Remove vanilla bean from chilled custard; scrape seeds free and return them to custard along with 1 cup **port**. Freeze as directed. Makes 4 cups.

Per ½-cup serving: 230 cal., 31% (71 cal.,) from fat; 5.2 g protein; 7.9 g fat (4.3 g sat.); 27 g carbo (0 g fiber); 68 mg sodium; 100 mg chol.

Cream sherry ice cream with double ginger. Add 1 tablespoon minced **fresh ginger** to milk mixture before heating. Pour chilled custard through a fine strainer into a bowl; discard ginger. Stir in ½ cup **cream sherry** and ⅓ cup minced **crystallized ginger**. Freeze as directed. Makes 4 cups.

Per ½-cup serving: 241 cal., 29% (71 cal.) from fat; 5.2 g protein; 7.9 g fat (4.3 g sat.); 34 g carbo (0 g fiber); 73 mg sodium; 100 mg chol. ◆

by CHRISTINE WEBER HALE

Cooling red-wine sangria is topped off with citrus juice and slices.

CARRIE LLOYD

Sunset's Kitchen Cabinet

When whipping up sangria for a dinner party, Peggy Deen uses purchased flavored syrups—the kind that are popular bar ingredients for fancy coffees, sparkling waters, and smoothies. Not only do the syrups save prep time, but they also put a smooth finish on the wine punch. The two syrup flavors that Deen favors for sangria are vanilla and orange.

Shortcut Sangria
Peggy Deen, Beaverton, Oregon

Prep time: About 7 minutes

Makes: About 2½ quarts; 10 servings

- 1 cup **vanilla-flavor syrup**
- 2 **oranges** (about 6 oz. each), thinly sliced
- 1 **lime,** thinly sliced
- 1 cup **orange juice**

- 2 bottles (750 ml. each) **dry red wine**
  Ice cubes

1. In a pitcher (at least 3-qt. size), combine syrup, orange slices, lime slices, and orange juice.

2. Add wine to pitcher; mix, and pour into ice-filled glasses.

Per cup: 188 cal., 0.5% (0.9 cal.) from fat; 0.7 g protein; 0.1 g fat (0 g sat.); 23 g carbo (0.6 g fiber); 7.8 mg sodium; 0 mg chol.

Chilly Willy's Avocado Soup
Leslie Giffin, Winthrop, Washington

On a trip to Puerto Vallarta in the mid-'80s, Leslie Giffin discovered this delicious chicken and avocado soup at Chilly Willy's—a quaint restaurant by the river. The restaurant is no more, but because the soup is so quick and easy, Giffin often re-creates it for guests. Any tiny pasta can be used instead of the orzo.

Prep and cook time: 30 to 35 minutes

Makes: 4 main-dish servings

- 7 cups **chicken broth**
- ½ cup chopped **onion**
- ½ cup chopped **celery**
- 1 clove **garlic,** pressed or minced
- 1 teaspoon **pepper**
- ¾ cup **dried orzo pasta**
- 2 **boned, skinned chicken breast halves** (about ½ lb. total)
- 3 tablespoons **lemon juice**
- 1 tablespoon chopped **parsley**
- ¼ cup **fresh cilantro** leaves
- 1 firm-ripe **avocado** (about 6 oz.)

1. In a 4- to 5-quart pan over high heat, bring broth, onion, celery, garlic, and pepper to a boil. Add pasta and chicken; return to a boil.

2. Reduce heat to low, cover pan, and simmer until chicken is white in thickest part (cut to test), about 5 minutes. With tongs, lift out breasts and let stand. Continue simmering soup until pasta is tender to bite, about 2 minutes more. Reduce heat to very low and keep soup warm.

3. When chicken is just cool enough to handle, in about 5 minutes, tear into coarse shreds and return to pan.

4. Stir lemon juice, parsley, and cilantro into soup. Ladle into wide bowls.

by LINDA LAU ANUSASANANAN

5. Peel, pit, and thinly slice avocado; add to bowls.

Per serving: 299 cal., 26% (78 cal.) from fat; 24 g protein; 8.7 g fat (2.3 g sat.); 32 g carbo (2.2 g fiber); 243 mg sodium; 39 mg chol.

Cold Turkey Loaf
Rodney Garside, Tuolumne, California

"I love a dinner of cold meat loaf along with a variety of salads and a bottle of good Gewürztraminer," writes Rodney Garside. But since beef and pork are not on his diet, he uses ground turkey and plain or Italian-style turkey sausages.

Prep and cook time: 10 to 12 minutes to assemble, plus 1½ hours to bake

Makes: 6 to 8 servings

   4 to 5 slices **white bread**
   ½ pound **raw turkey sausages**
   1 pound **ground lean turkey**
   1 **large egg**, beaten to blend
   1½ cups **nonfat milk**
   2 tablespoons chopped **green onion**
   1 tablespoon finely chopped **fresh sage** leaves or 1 teaspoon dried rubbed sage
   ½ teaspoon **salt**
   ½ teaspoon **black pepper**
   ½ teaspoon **white pepper**
   ¼ teaspoon **cayenne**

1. Tear bread into chunks and whirl in a food processor to make fine crumbs.

Turkey is the lean secret of low-fat meat loaf—which makes great sandwiches.

Measure 2 cups crumbs and put in a large bowl.

2. Squeeze sausages from casings into bowl. Add ground turkey, egg, milk, onion, sage, salt, black and white pepper, and cayenne. Mix well.

3. Pat meat loaf mixture into an oiled or nonstick 5- by 9-inch loaf pan.

4. Bake in a 350° oven until meat loaf is firm to touch in center, about 1½ hours.

5. Serve hot, or let cool, then cover and chill until cold, at least 3 hours. Or store, chilled, up to 2 days. Run a knife between meat and pan rim. Invert meat loaf onto a platter and cut into thick slices.

Per serving: 193 cal., 42% (81 cal.) from fat; 18 g protein; 9 g fat (2.4 g sat.); 9.5 g carbo (0.3 g fiber); 475 mg sodium; 84 mg chol.

Spicy Corn Relish
Aulii Pila, Honolulu

While Aulii Pila and her husband were house-sitting, he challenged her to create a new dish using ingredients on hand. The result was this versatile corn relish. Add it to tacos, burritos, or fajitas, or spoon it onto lettuce for a salad. Alternatives for canned corn are 1½ cups of frozen corn kernels or grilled corn cut off the cob.

Prep time: About 10 minutes

Makes: About 3 cups

   1 can (15 oz.) **corn kernels**, drained
   ½ cup diced **red bell pepper**
   ½ cup diced **green bell pepper**
   ½ cup chopped **red onion**
   2 tablespoons **lime juice**
   ½ teaspoon **olive oil**
   ½ teaspoon **sugar**
   Hot sauce
   Salt and **pepper**

1. In a bowl, mix corn, red and green bell peppers, onion, lime juice, oil, and sugar. Add hot sauce, salt, and pepper to taste.

2. Serve, or cover and chill up to 8 hours.

Per ½ cup: 72 cal., 10% (7.2 cal.) from fat; 2.1 g protein; 0.8 g fat (0.1 g sat.); 17 g carbo (1.5 g fiber); 195 mg sodium; 0 mg chol.

Strawberry-Peach Pie
Jeanette Angeletti, Kuna, Idaho

Whole strawberries, glazed with a cooked strawberry sauce, conceal this pie's layer of fresh peaches on sweetened cream cheese. Jeanette Angeletti recommends using ripe fruit that is really sweet and fragrant. The pastry shell must be at least 1¼ inches deep; most purchased frozen ones are too shallow to hold all the filling. And for a less rich dessert, use neufchâtel (light cream) cheese instead of cream cheese.

Prep and cook time: 20 to 25 minutes, plus 1 hour to chill

Makes: 8 or 9 servings

   6 cups **strawberries**
   1 package (8 oz.) **cream cheese**
   1 cup **sugar**
   2 tablespoons **milk**
   ½ teaspoon **vanilla**
   1 baked 9-inch **pastry shell**
   3 tablespoons **cornstarch**
   2 tablespoons **lemon juice**
   1 ripe **peach** (about 8 oz.)

1. Hull berries; rinse and drain. Set aside 4 cups of the prettiest berries to drain dry on towels.

2. Beat cream cheese with ¼ cup sugar, milk, and vanilla until smooth. Spread cheese mixture evenly over bottom of pastry shell.

3. In a blender or food processor, smoothly purée remaining berries with ½ cup water.

4. In a 1- to 2-quart pan, mix cornstarch and remaining ¾ cup sugar. Add berry purée and stir over high heat until mixture boils and thickens, about 4 minutes. Remove from heat and stir in lemon juice.

5. Peel and thinly slice peach, arranging slices on cheese filling. Set whole strawberries, tips up, on peaches. Spoon hot berry glaze over fruit to cover completely.

6. Chill pie until glaze is cool and set, at least 1 hour. If making ahead, cover when cold and chill up to 1 day. Cut into wedges.

Per serving: 332 cal., 43% (144 cal.) from fat; 4 g protein; 16 g fat (7.3 g sat.); 44 g carbo (3.3 g fiber); 187 mg sodium; 28 mg chol. ◆

For light summer meals, choose from these great low-fat dishes from the Caribbean, Vietnam, and India (see page 143).

130

July

foodguide

by **JERRY ANNE DI VECCHIO**

RICHARD JUNG

Before California's Santa Clara Valley became a high-tech epicenter, it was a sea of fruit trees. And every summer, a postcard from one special orchard came to our house. The message was as brief as the season: White peaches and nectarines are ready. And off we would race to buy all we could eat fresh, plus enough for freezing to appease our passion for the rest of the year.

Even then, these fragile, incredibly perfumed stone fruit weren't that easy to find. Most growers eschewed their demanding care.

Finally, white nectarines just disappeared commercially, and the white peaches seemed to grow less tasty. That is, until a few years ago.

What happened? Growers in the San Joaquin Valley responded to a demand from the Asian market. The desire for flavorful white fruit prompted large plantings and the development of more varieties that ripen over a longer period. These orchards are just coming into full production, and now there are more white peaches and nectarines. The price is right, and it's time to indulge.

White Nectarine Sorbet

Prep time: **5** minutes to assemble, plus 15 to 20 minutes to freeze

Notes: Serve the sorbet freshly made, while it's soft and very smooth. If making ahead and freezing, thaw partially and beat to a slush to serve.

Makes: 2½ to 2¾ cups; 4 servings

About 1½ pounds ripe **white nectarines,** chilled

3 tablespoons **lemon juice**

2 to 3 tablespoons **sugar**

1 tablespoon **orange-flavor liqueur** (optional)

¼ teaspoon **vanilla**

¼ cup **sour cream** or crème fraîche

A TASTE OF THE WEST

A flavor not forgotten

tool

No other cooking utensil—that I can think of—comes in such a range of sizes as the paella pan—from tiny (4 in. wide) up to huge (4 ft. wide, big enough for 100 servings or to use as a wading pond). Most well-stocked cookware stores have paella pans in at least three or four widths, and in a variety of materials.

I happen to fancy the least expensive models, made of rolled steel ($10 to $28 for 10- to 15-in.-wide pans), because they are the lightest and easiest to handle. However, steel rusts unless dried well and rubbed lightly with salad oil after use. The exception: steel pans with enameled exteriors and nonstick interiors.

Naturally, making paella in one of these pans is a snap. There's plenty of room to sauté onions, brown chicken, and toast rice. And a really wide paella pan, which works over two burners on a kitchen stove, also makes a great griddle on barbecues (at home or in camp).

Can't find the pan size you're looking for? Contact the Spanish Table in Seattle, (206) 682-2827 (fax 682-2814), or Magic Pan in Miami, (305) 252-3337 (fax 256-1039). Also, inquire about fire stands and portable gas burners.

COOK'S SECRET

A lighter goat cheese

Constantly on the lookout for good ways to cut fat, I was all attention when Anne Kupper said she had found a great way to make low-fat goat cheese. And Anne knows. She and Chuck Williams, of Williams-Sonoma fame, worked closely together for years.

Anne mashes a little of her favorite soft chèvre (goat) cheese and mixes it with nonfat yogurt. Then she spoons the mixture into a yogurt drainer (or cheesecloth-lined strainer nested in a bowl), covers the drainer (or wraps the strainer and bowl completely in plastic wrap), and chills the yogurt as it drains—at least overnight. For thicker cheese, drain up to two days. Discard the whey (or blend it into smoothies—it's full of protein). Scoop the drained cheese into a container and serve, or cover and chill up to a total of seven days.

For maximum flavor, use an aged cheese, such as bûcheron. If you use ½ cup aged **chèvre cheese** and 4 cups **nonfat plain yogurt** (made without gelatin, or it won't drain), you'll get about 2½ cups cheese.

Per ¼ cup: 56 cal., 32% (18 cal.) from fat; 5 g protein; 2 g fat (1.4 g sat.); 3.6 g carbo (0 g fiber); 67 mg sodium; 5.3 mg chol.

---

1. Slice nectarines into a bowl. Add lemon juice and mix with fruit to keep slices from darkening.
2. Pour fruit and juice into a blender or food processor. Add 2 tablespoons sugar, liqueur, vanilla, and sour cream. Whirl until peel is finely ground (it turns the purée pink). Taste and add more sugar if desired.
3. Pour nectarine mixture into a 1-quart or larger ice cream maker (refrigerated or frozen-cylinder kind, or one that uses salt and ice) and follow manufacturer's directions. Churn until dasher is very hard to turn.
4. Scoop nectarine sorbet into bowls and serve.

Per serving: 134 cal., 25% (34 cal.) from fat; 2 g protein; 3.8 g fat (1.9 g sat.); 26 g carbo (2.5 g fiber); 10 mg sodium; 6.3 mg chol.

GREAT INGREDIENT

For neat fruit pies

Are you frustrated by fruit pies that are too soupy to cut and serve? One way to avoid this is to use quick-cooking tapioca as the thickener. But for even better results, try tapioca flour. Now that the flour is easy to find, I use it regularly. It's a staple in Chinese and Southeast Asian cuisines and readily found in those food markets. In fact, a *Sunset* reader called me from Santa Fe to say that he now buys tapioca flour in natural-food stores there.

Tapioca flour is crystal clear when it thickens. Quick-cooking tapioca turns into tiny transparent beads as it cooks. Both forms of tapioca are unaffected by fruit acids, which can cause wheat flour– and cornstarch-thickened fruit pies to break down and ooze. Tapioca, however, does have one curious characteristic that doesn't show up in a pie. If you stir a tapioca mixture as it cooks after it boils, it gets exceptionally stringy.

For recipes, replace quick-cooking tapioca with an equal measure of tapioca flour and mix it with the sugar before adding the fruit.

JAMES CARRIER

4 **squab** (1 lb. each)

6 tablespoons **balsamic vinegar**

2 tablespoons **honey**

2 teaspoons **fresh thyme** leaves or dried thyme

Salt

1. With poultry shears or kitchen scissors, cut each squab in half through center of breast and back. Pull off and discard fat lumps. Cut off necks and reserve with giblets for other uses. Rinse birds and pat dry.

2. In a bowl, mix vinegar, honey, and thyme. Add squab and mix to coat with seasonings. Let stand at least 20 minutes or chill, covered, up to 1 day, turning pieces over several times.

3. Prepare barbecue for indirect heat.

If using charcoal, mound and ignite 60 briquets on the firegrate of a barbecue with a lid (20 to 22 in. wide). When briquets are dotted with gray ash, in about 15 minutes, push equal portions to opposite sides of the firegrate. Place a drip pan between coals. Set the grill in place.

If using a gas barbecue, cover and turn heat to high for about 10 minutes. Adjust burners for indirect cooking (no heat down center) and keep on high. Set a drip pan beneath grill between ignited burners. Set grill in place.

4. Lift squab from marinade and lay, bones down, in center of grill, not directly over the heat. Cover barbecue and open the vents.

5. Cook until birds are richly browned, basting squab frequently with marinade, using it all. For rare, breasts are moist and red in center (cut to test); allow about 25 minutes. For medium, cook 6 to 10 minutes longer. Season to taste with salt.

No nutritional information is available for cooked squab.

GRILL SKILLS

A glazed squab

The beauty of squab is that it cooks so quickly. The meat, richly flavored and all dark, is at its succulent best when rare. To get good browning, this means the birds have to cook at high heat—which introduces a problem. The fatty layer under the skin drips and smokes in the oven or catches fire on the barbecue. The solution: grill over indirect heat.

Serve the hot birds on tender salad leaves mixed with other leaves that have a little bite, such as arugula, frisée, or slivered Belgian endive or radicchio. Dress the salad with an extra batch of the squab marinade; the juices of the birds mingle deliciously with it.

Squab, or young pigeons, are about 1 pound each—dressed weight. You may have to order them a couple of days ahead at the supermarket, but both fresh and frozen birds are usually easy to get.

Honey-Thyme Squab

Prep and cook time: 50 to 60 minutes

Notes: If parts of the squab get quite dark before birds are done, drape affected areas with foil.

Makes: 4 servings

VIDEO CLIPS

A deliciously wicked wit

In her many eloquent books, and in conversation, Mary Frances Kennedy Fisher was never at a loss for engaging words about life and food. However, more than once, I watched her play a favorite game—cat and mouse with an interviewer, be it writer Cyra McFadden or public television's Bill Moyers. All disarming charm and wit before the "action," once on stage or before a camera, she became the master of yes and no answers, with arched, coy glances and a barely controlled smile. To get more, the host was often in a real sweat.

So when I saw *MFK Fisher: Writer with a Bite,* a video produced and directed by Kathi Wheater, I was impressed by the candor and natural commentary captured during the last years of Fisher's life in Glen Ellen, California.

And now, on the fifth anniversary of her death, this award-winning 28-minute video, which has aired on PBS and internationally, is being released again. Order it from Kathi Wheater Productions, 442 Shotwell St., San Francisco, CA 94110. Or call (415) 647-1086. The video costs $19.95, plus $3 shipping and handling. ◆

Syrah nights

Martha Stewart undoubtedly drinks red wine in winter and white wine in summer. What could be more correct?

The problem, of course, is that proper behavior and pleasure can be two different things. And for its part, wine is far more allied with the latter than with the former.

Then, too, there's the issue of food. On a July night, with the helplessly alluring aroma of steaks cooking on the grill, does one really crave white wine?

As I build my case for red wine in summer, one more point must be made: Loving red wine is chronic, progressive, and cumulative. You start out enjoying a glass of Zinfandel every now and then, and before you know it, you're an incorrigible red wine chauvinist, a person for whom wine means red, period.

You guys know who you are.

For me, summertime and red wine intersect at Syrah. Darkly masculine, earthy, spicy, even gruff, Syrah is my favorite wine with almost anything grilled. In part, that's because Syrah (like grilled foods themselves) is robust and a little brazen. Syrah doesn't know about passivity; most examples (at least from California) are not what you'd call

elegant or even well mannered. But *mm-mm,* are they compelling. Syrah is a tuxedo-clad Clint Eastwood with a 5 o'clock shadow.

The other day, a winemaker friend said to me, "Just watch. Syrah is going to be the next Merlot in California." A call to the Wine Institute confirmed Syrah's increasing popularity. While it's got a long way to go to catch up with Merlot, Syrah acreage has increased nearly tenfold since 1988. A third of these acres aren't yet in production.

The world's most famous Syrah comes from the Rhône Valley of France. In the north end of the valley, the famous wines of Côte Rôtie and Hermitage are made from Syrah. In the southern Rhône, Syrah is one of the chief wines that make up the blend in Châteauneuf-du-Pape and Gigondas. In the Rhône, Syrah's potent and exuberant flavors lean toward leather, damp earth, wild blackberries, smoke, roasted meats, and—especially—pepper and spice. The best have a kinetic mouth-feel with flavors that detonate on the palate like tiny grenades. (Consult your wine merchant; there are numerous great producers, though the wines are very expensive.)

These were the Syrahs that, in the early 1980s, inspired a whole group of maverick California winemakers. The "Rhône Rangers," as the group came to be called, went on to make some full-bodied, deliciously earthy wines, forging a whole new direction for red wine–making in America in the process.

But well before we became enchanted with the grape, South Africans and Australians did. In the 17th century, French Huguenots brought Syrah from France to South Africa's Cape of Good Hope, where it was rechristened "Shiraz." From South Africa, the grape was brought to Australia, where it's also called Shiraz and now produces delicious wine.

Shiraz (Syrah) is, in fact, the leading red grape in Australia, and the big-bodied wines made from it can be positively hedonistic with their almost syrupy boysenberry-jam flavors. The most legendary Australian Shiraz is Grange (formerly called Grange Hermitage), considered one of the top red wines in the world. Grange is expensive, but Australia also makes the world's best inexpensive Syrahs. Try, for example, the lip-smacking Rosemount Estate Shiraz ($12), a big teddy bear of a Syrah.

A final note: Petite Sirah (also spelled Petite Syrah) is not exactly the same as Syrah. Grape DNA "fingerprinting" indicates that what is called Petite Sirah in California is actually four or more different varieties, possibly including the obscure French grapes Durif and Peloursin as well as true Syrah. Look for a future column on Petite Sirah.

So back to the critical question: What to have with that grilled steak? Why not try one of the many intriguing Syrahs made in California? Below are just a few of my favorites.

Alban Syrah "Reva" 1994, $18 (Edna Valley). Wild blackberries meet wild herbs; smoky and sophisticated.

Cline Syrah 1995, $18 (Carneros). Exuberant with rushes of ripe raspberries.

Eberle Syrah "Fralich Vineyard" 1995, $18 (Paso Robles). Rich boysenberry flavors laced with white pepper.

Edmunds St. John Syrah 1995, $15 (California). Fascinating chocolate, violet, and menthol flavors.

Joseph Phelps Vin du Mistral Syrah 1994, $24 (Napa Valley). Exotic lavender and chocolate flavors.

Qupé Syrah "Bien Nacido Reserve" 1995, $22.50 (Santa Barbara County). Dense, brooding, the Heathcliff of Syrahs.

Truchard Syrah 1995, $24 (Carneros/Napa Valley). A dense, gamy style very reminiscent of the Rhône. ◆

WINE DICTIONARY | BODY

The perceived weight of the wine in the mouth. The higher the wine's alcohol content, the more full-bodied it will seem on the palate. A good method when determining the body of a wine is to imagine the relative weights in the mouth of skim milk, whole milk, and half-and-half. Light-bodied wines feel like skim milk, medium-bodied like whole milk, and full-bodied like half-and-half. — *K. M.*

In search of the *real*

STEPHEN SIMPSON (3)

And now, a brief cultural history of the tastiest export
to come out of Baja since *cerveza.* Recipes begin on page 139

by **MATTHEW JAFFE**

On an elemental level, the fish taco can be reduced to a very simple equation: Fish + Tortilla = Fish Taco. ◆ From this perspective, there is little question that people have been eating fish tacos in the coastal areas of Mexico for an awfully long time. It probably goes back thousands of years to when indigenous North American peoples first wrapped the plentiful offshore catch into stone-ground-corn tortillas. ◆ More recently, somewhere in Baja California, sometime in the last 30 or 40 years, someone concocted what is generally considered to be the prototypical fish taco. According to aficionados—call them the codnoscenti—this humble delicacy consists of a lightly battered mild white fish that is deep-fried, then served in a corn tortilla (often two) with shredded cabbage, a thin sour-cream- or mayonnaise-based sauce, a bit of salsa, and a most vital spritzito of lime. ◆ On this everyone agrees. What everyone doesn't agree on is where in Baja the archetype originated. San Diego fish-taco mogul Ralph Rubio, whose chain of 35 stores makes him the great white shark of the fish-taco world, cites San Felipe as the source. But the señoras hustling and hawking virtually identical fish tacos at virtually identical stands at Ensenada's fish market won't stand for that. They say

The three faces of fish tacos: Above left and center, the classic Baja fried-fish taco as served by Ensenada's Tacos Alan. Above right, taco excess, California-style, at Loews Coronado Bay Resort. At right, Sunset's own variation on the theme, topped with papaya-mango salsa.

NOEL BARNHURST

fish taco

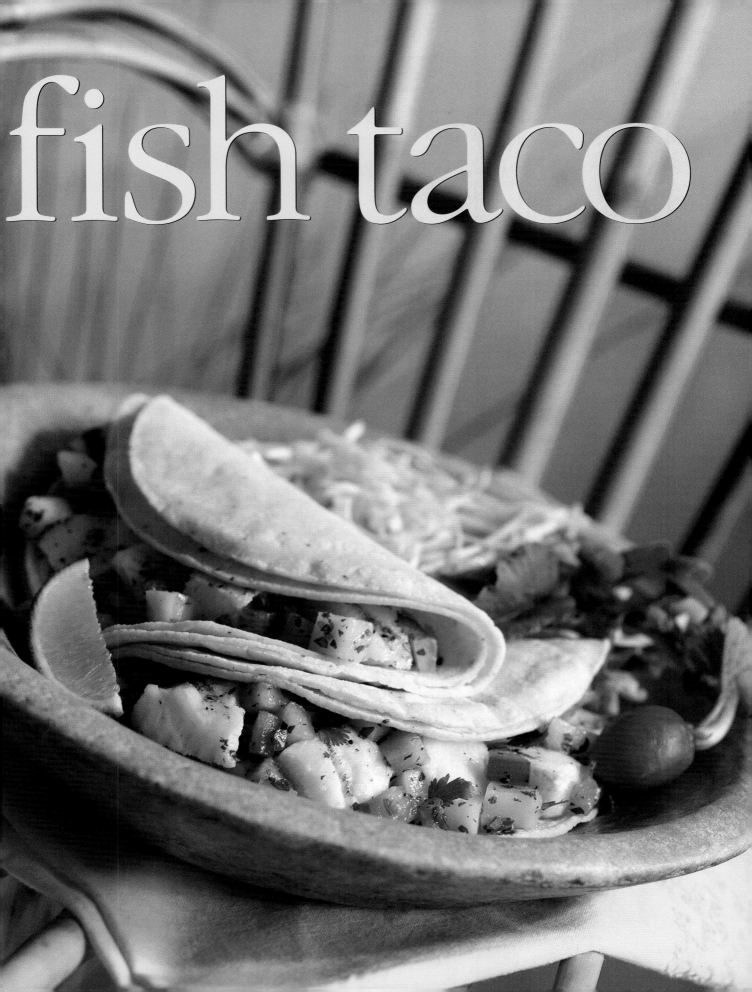

their port town is the fish taco's true home, dating at least from the opening of the Ensenada _mercado,_ in 1958.

Alicia Ramirez, owner of Señor Fish in Los Angeles since 1988, isn't sure who's right, but she is certain that fish tacos originated in Baja. "Baja is a place where the fish taco would have happened naturally," she says. "It probably just began with a fisherman bringing fish home to his wife."

The truth is out there—somewhere. In the meantime, this Baja export has become the border cuisine of the moment.

A FISH STORY

Though many Americans are only now learning about the simple virtues of fish tacos, surfers and seasoned Mexico travelers have long considered fish tacos an integral part of the Baja experience.

Take Irvine-based tour-company owner Len Daniello. Twenty years ago, he and his friends used to surf Baja's remote beaches. On the way to secret spots with nicknames like "181," Daniello and his pals would stop in Ensenada to fuel up on fish tacos. In those days you could pick up five or six for a dollar from pushcart vendors or the ladies at the market. The hood of a dusty car made a fine picnic table.

"Those were authentic fish tacos," muses Daniello. "When I see them on a menu up here, I always ask the waiter if they're _real_ fish tacos. He'll mumble something like 'Yeah, well, it's real fish,' and I'll know that they're probably not even worth ordering."

You see, as fish tacos reached El Norte, they went upscale—out of the fryer and onto the grill. These new heart-friendly tacos may be more healthful, but they tend to lose their soul along with the fat. Done right, however, grilled fish tacos can taste mighty good, authenticity issues notwithstanding.

Even so, the grill-or-fry debate is a mere subplot in the larger story of the rise of fish tacos to cultural icon in San Diego. Consider:

• They're now served at Jack Murphy Stadium during Padres games, making fish tacos, if not as American as apple pie, then at least as American as hot dogs. Or if you're a Dodgers fan, sushi.

• When the San Diego Chargers were trounced by the San Francisco 49ers in Super Bowl XXIX, Mayor Susan Golding paid off her bet with her norte counterpart in fish tacos.

Ralph Rubio, above, took an idle conversation with a San Felipe tacomonger and parlayed it into a $32-million business. At top, the stands in Ensenada are the fried-fish equivalent of Mecca.

• In 1996, Republicans had a Grand Old Party when fish tacos were chosen as the convention culinary standard-bearer.

All of which means that Ralph Rubio made the right call in 1974 when he decided not to stay home and study during spring break. That was the first year Rubio and friends at San Diego State went down to San Felipe on the Sea of Cortés. In addition to _cerveza,_ fish tacos at local stands proved to be their main sustenance, and became one of the prime reasons they would return to San Felipe each spring.

Rubio was particularly fond of the fresh fish tacos made by a vendor named Carlos. One night Rubio suggested that Carlos open up a stand in San Diego. Carlos, making a decision that he can only hope his wife never hears about, replied that he didn't want to leave Mexico. "I vividly remember the conversation," says Rubio today. "It was late at night, I'm drinking Coronas with my buddies, and the thought hit me: If he doesn't want to open a stand, why don't I just get the recipe?"

Carlos provided Rubio with a recipe, though he didn't specify exact amounts of ingredients. From there Rubio proceeded to experiment with various fish, batter mixes, and sauces—and not always successfully. Eventually he figured out a recipe that worked, and with the backing of his father, opened his first restaurant in 1983 in an old, failed hamburger stand near Mission Bay.

Not long after the opening, Rubio returned to San Felipe to see the legendary Carlos and give him some money as thanks. But Carlos had moved—some said to the rival fish-taco center of Ensenada. No one knew for sure.

Today Carlos's old San Felipe stand still operates, but under different ownership. Rubio's is a $32-million company.

"It was one of those rare moments of inspiration," says Rubio of that fateful night. "Besides, I wasn't the only gringo in San Felipe with a business major."

From classic to next wave

by ANDREW BAKER

Classic Baja Fried-Fish Tacos

Baja street vendors aren't big on written recipes, so we identified the key ingredients from the best fish-taco stands to create this recipe.

Prep and cook time: 25 minutes

Makes: 10 servings

- 1 cup **dark beer**
- 1 cup **all-purpose flour**
  About ½ teaspoon **salt**
- 1½ pounds **boned, skinned lingcod***
  Salad oil
- 20 warm **corn tortillas**
  About 5 cups shredded **cabbage**
  Mayonnaise thinned with a little water
  Tomato salsa
  Lime wedges

1. In a bowl, whisk beer, flour, and salt, blending well.

2. Rinse fish and pat dry. Cut into 10 equal pieces.

3. In a deep 5- to 6-quart pan, heat 1 inch salad oil to 360°. Using a fork, coat fish pieces with beer batter and lift out, draining briefly. Slide coated fish into oil, about 5 pieces at a time. Adjust heat to maintain oil temperature. When fritters are golden, in about 2 minutes, lift out with a slotted spoon and drain briefly on paper towels; keep warm. Repeat to fry remaining fish.

4. To assemble each taco, stack 2 tortillas; add a fish fritter, cabbage, mayonnaise, and salsa. Squeeze lime over filling, fold tortillas, and eat.

Loews Grilled-Fish Tacos

As fish tacos have moved north, they've gotten downright respectable, as Loews executive chef James Boyce's grilled variation proves.

Prep and cook time: 40 minutes

Makes: 6 servings

- 2 **whole striped bass** or rockfish (1½ to 2 lbs. each), cleaned and scaled
- 16 **thyme sprigs**
- 12 **dill sprigs**
- 2 **dried** or fresh **bay leaves**
- 8 cloves **garlic,** sliced
- 4 teaspoons **olive oil**
  Salt and **pepper**
- 12 warm **corn tortillas**
  Tomatillo salsa (recipe page 85)
  About 1 cup shredded **iceberg lettuce**
  About ½ cup chopped **Roma tomatoes**
  About ⅓ cup chopped **fresh cilantro**
  Lime wedges

1. Rinse fish and pat dry; stuff cavities with thyme, dill, bay leaves, and garlic. Rub outside of fish with olive oil and sprinkle with salt and pepper.

2. Place fish on a grill over a solid bed of medium-hot coals or on a gas grill set at medium-high (you can hold your hand at grill level only 3 to 4 seconds); close lid on gas grill.

3. Cook, turning once with a wide spatula, until fish is opaque but still moist-looking in thickest part (cut to test), 18 to 20 minutes total. Transfer to a serving platter.

4. To assemble each taco, stack 2 tortillas; top with chunks pulled from fish, salsa, lettuce, tomatoes, and cilantro.

Squeeze lime over filling, fold tortillas, and eat.

Sunset's Next Wave Fish Tacos

Here's an easy alternative for those who don't want to cook a whole fish or eat fried food.

Prep and cook time: 15 minutes

Makes: 6 servings

- 1½ pounds **boned, skinned Chilean seabass*** (½ in. thick), cut into 2 or 3 pieces
  Salt and **pepper**
- 12 warm **corn tortillas**
  Pickled cabbage relish (recipe page 84) or papaya-mango salsa (recipe page 85)
  About ½ cup **sour cream**
  Lime wedges

1. Rinse fish and pat dry.

2. Place on a grill over a solid bed of hot coals or on a gas grill set at high heat (you can hold your hand at grill level only 2 to 3 seconds); close lid on gas grill. Cook, turning once, until fish is opaque but still moist-looking in thickest part (cut to test), 12 to 14 minutes. Transfer fish to a platter. Season to taste with salt and pepper.

3. To assemble each taco, stack 2 tortillas; add chunks of fish, relish, and sour cream. Squeeze lime over filling, fold tortillas, and eat.

Per average taco: 250 cal., 26% (64 cal.) from fat; 20 g protein; 7.1 g fat (1.7 g sat.); 27 g carbo (3.1 g fiber); 226 mg sodium; 54 mg chol.

*Check fish for bones before cooking. Press surface with your fingers to locate; pull out with tweezers.

Classic Baja Fried-Fish Tacos

Loews Grilled-Fish Tacos

Sunset's Next Wave Fish Tacos

NOEL BARNHURST

Salsas, relishes, and guacamole

A compilation of condiments created by James Boyce, executive chef at the Loews Coronado Bay Resort, and Andrew Baker of *Sunset*

Cucumber Relish

Prep time: 15 minutes

Makes: 2 cups

- 1 cup diced peeled **English cucumber**
- ½ cup diced **red onion**
- ½ cup diced **Roma tomatoes**
- 1 tablespoon minced **fresh jalapeño chili**
- ¼ cup **red wine vinegar**
- 1 tablespoon chopped **fresh mint leaves**
- **Salt** and **pepper**

In a bowl, mix cucumber, onion, tomatoes, chili, vinegar, and mint. Add salt and pepper to taste.

Per tablespoon: 2.6 cal., 0% (0 cal.) from fat; 0.1 g protein; 0 g fat; 0.6 g carbo (0.1 g fiber); 0.8 mg sodium; 0 mg chol.

Spicy Cranberry Salsa

Prep and cook time: About 20 minutes

Makes: About 1¾ cups

- 1 teaspoon **olive oil**
- 1 **onion** (6 oz.), chopped
- 4 cloves **garlic**, minced
- 3 **fresh serrano chilies**, stemmed and chopped
- 1 cup (about 5 oz.) **dried cranberries**
- 2 firm-ripe **tomatoes** (about ½ lb. total), cored, seeded, and diced
- ½ cup **apple cider**
- 2 tablespoons chopped **parsley**
- **Salt** and **pepper**

1. In a 10- to 12-inch nonstick frying pan over medium heat, stir oil, onion, garlic, and chilies often until onion is lightly browned, about 5 minutes.

2. Add cranberries, tomatoes, and cider. Simmer, stirring often, until cranberries are soft when pressed, about 5 minutes.

3. Purée salsa mixture in a blender or food processor.

4. Add parsley, and season salsa with salt and pepper to taste. Serve at room temperature.

Per tablespoon: 23 cal., 7.8% (1.8 cal.) from fat; 0.1 g protein; 0.2 g fat (0 g sat.); 5.3 g carbo (0.5 g fiber); 1.2 mg sodium; 0 mg chol.

Citrus Guacamole

Prep time: About 15 minutes

Makes: 2 cups

- 1 **orange** (about ½ lb.)
- 1 firm-ripe **avocado** (about 10 oz.)
- 2 tablespoons **lime juice**
- ½ cup chopped **green onions**
- ½ cup chopped **fresh cilantro**
- **Hot chili flakes**
- **Salt**

1. Cut and discard peel and white membrane from orange. Cut between segments to release fruit. Cut fruit into ½-inch chunks and put in a bowl.

2. Peel and pit avocado. Cut into ½-inch chunks and mix with orange chunks. Stir in lime juice, onions, and cilantro. Add chili flakes and salt to taste.

Per tablespoon: 14 cal., 64% (9 cal.) from fat; 0.2 g protein; 1 g fat (0.2 g sat.); 1.3 g carbo (0.3 g fiber); 1.1 mg sodium; 0 mg chol.

Cucumber Relish

Chipotle Tartar Sauce

Prep time: About 10 minutes

Makes: About 1⅓ cups

- 2 tablespoons **canned chipotle chilies**
- 1 cup **mayonnaise**
- ¼ cup **sweet pickle relish**
- ¼ cup minced **onion**

1. Rinse chilies. Discard seeds and veins.

2. In a blender, purée chilies and mayonnaise. Stir in relish and onion.

Per tablespoon: 80 cal., 94% (75 cal.) from fat; 0.1 g protein; 8.3 g fat (1.2 g sat.); 1.5 g carbo (0 g fiber); 85 mg sodium; 6.2 mg chol.

Pickled Cabbage Relish

Prep time: About 12 minutes

Makes: About 2 cups (drained)

- 1 cup thinly sliced **red cabbage**
- ½ cup thinly sliced **green cabbage**
- ½ cup thinly sliced **onion**
- 2 tablespoons minced **fresh jalapeño chilies**
- ½ cup **distilled white vinegar**
- ½ teaspoon **salt**

In a bowl, mix cabbages, onion, chilies, vinegar, 1½ cups water, and salt. Let stand about 30 minutes. Lift out with a slotted spoon to serve.

Per tablespoon: 2.5 cal., 0% (0 cal.) from fat; 0.1 g protein; 0 g fat; 0.6 g carbo (0.1 g fiber); 35 mg sodium; 0 mg chol.

Fish finds

SAN DIEGO AREA

Brigantine, seven locations, including 1333 Orange Ave., Coronado; (619) 435-4166.

Cafe Pacifica, 2414 San Diego Ave., San Diego; 291-6666.

Cecil's Cafe, 5083 Santa Monica Ave., San Diego; 222-0501.

El Indio Shop, three locations, including the original store at 3695 India St., San Diego; 299-0333.

Las Brasas, 1890 San Diego Ave., San Diego; 291-6527.

Loews Coronado Bay Resort, 4000 Coronado Bay Rd., Coronado; 424-4000.

Rubio's Baja Grill, 35 Southern California locations, most in San Diego County. For the one nearest you, call (619) 452-1770.

ORANGE COUNTY

Wahoo's, 1862 Placentia Ave., Costa Mesa; (714) 631-3433. And 3000 Bristol St., Costa Mesa; 435-0130.

LOS ANGELES COUNTY

La Serenata de Gourmet, 10924 W. Pico Blvd., Los Angeles; (310) 441-9667. Also *La Serenata de Garibaldi,* 1842 E. First St., Los Angeles; (213) 265-2887.

Poquito Mas, in West Hollywood, North Hollywood, Studio City, and Burbank. For details, call (818) 766-0072.

> **EATING WITH THE FISHES**
> Even though fish tacos are primarily a Baja and Southern California phenomenon, they are becoming ubiquitous throughout the West. Got a favorite fish taco stand in your hometown? If so, send us its name and address so we can share it with readers.

Spicy Cranberry Salsa

Citrus Guacamole

Chipotle Tartar Sauce

Pickled Cabbage Relish

Papaya-Mango Salsa

NOEL BARNHURST

Papaya-Mango Salsa

Prep time: About 15 minutes

Makes: About 2 cups

- 1 cup diced **papaya**
- ½ cup diced **mango**
- ½ cup diced **red bell pepper**
- 1 tablespoon minced **fresh jalapeño chili**
- 1 tablespoon chopped **fresh cilantro**
- 2 tablespoons **lime juice**
  Salt

In a bowl, mix papaya, mango, bell pepper, chili, cilantro, and lime juice. Add salt to taste.

Per tablespoon: 4.1 cal., 0% (0 cal.) from fat; 0 g protein; 0 g fat; 1 g carbo (0.1 g fiber); 0.4 mg sodium; 0 mg chol.

Señor Fish, 424 E. First St., Los Angeles; (213) 625-0566. Also 618 Mission St., South Pasadena; (818) 403-0145. And 4803 Eagle Rock Blvd., Eagle Rock; (213) 257-7167.

BAJA CALIFORNIA

In Rosarito, try *Just for the Halibut* across Boulevard Benito Juárez from Festival Plaza, or *Taco de Paco* on the east side of Benito Juárez at the north end of town.

In Ensenada, the best tacos we had were from the *Tacos Alan* stand (also called Taco de Cali) on the alley that runs perpendicular to the main fish market and the lane of fish-taco stands that runs up from the waterfront.

In San Felipe, ask for Carlos …

Tomatillo Salsa

Prep and cook time: 18 minutes

Makes: 1½ cups

- ½ pound **tomatillos**
- 2 tablespoons finely chopped **red onion**
- 1 **fresh serrano chili**, stemmed and minced
- 1 tablespoon **lime juice**
- ½ cup chopped **fresh cilantro**
  Salt and **pepper**

1. In a 2- to 3-quart pan over high heat, bring 4 cups water to a boil. Husk and rinse tomatillos, then add to boiling water. Cook until barely soft when pressed, about 5 minutes.

2. Drain tomatillos and immerse in ice water. When cool, in about 3 minutes, purée in a blender or food processor. Pour purée into a bowl.

3. Add red onion, chili, lime juice, and cilantro and mix. Season to taste with salt and pepper.

Per tablespoon: 2.8 cal., 0% (0 cal.) from fat; 0.1 g protein; 0 g fat; 0.5 g carbo (0 g fiber); 0.3 mg sodium; 0 mg chol.

Salsa Borracho

Prep and cook time: About 25 minutes

Makes: About 2 cups

- ½ ounce (2 to 4) **dried New Mexico chilies**
- 1 **dried ancho chili**
- 3 firm-ripe **tomatoes** (¾ lb. total), cored
- ¼ cup chopped **onion**
- 2 cloves **garlic**, peeled
- 2 tablespoons **lime juice**
- 1 tablespoon chopped **fresh jalapeño chili**
- 1 to 2 tablespoons **tequila**
  Salt
- 3 tablespoons chopped **fresh cilantro**

1. Bake dried chilies in a rimmed pan in a 250° oven until fragrant, 4 to 5 minutes. Cool briefly, then break off and discard stems. Shake out and discard seeds. Place chilies in a bowl and pour 1 cup boiling water over them. Let stand until soft, about 10 minutes.

2. Meanwhile, broil tomatoes in a rimmed pan about 4 inches from heat, turning as needed, until charred, 5 to 8 minutes. Let cool.

3. With a slotted spoon, transfer soaked chilies to a blender or food processor. Purée until smooth, adding about 3 tablespoons of the soaking water to blend smoothly. Discard remaining water.

4. Add to blender the roasted tomatoes, onion, garlic, lime juice, and fresh chili. Whirl until coarsely puréed. Season to taste with tequila and salt, then stir in cilantro.

Per tablespoon: 6.5 cal., 14% (0.9 cal.) from fat; 0.2 g protein; 0.1 g fat (0 g sat.); 1 g carbo (0.3 g fiber); 1.4 mg sodium; 0 mg chol. ◆

TACO TOPPING

If you don't squeeze a bit of fresh lime on your fish taco, it isn't really a fish taco. In addition to lime, try these toppings:

- onions
- fresh or pickled jalapeño chilies
- radishes
- escabeche (pickled chilies, carrots, and onions)
- balsamic, malt, or cider vinegar
- red or green salsa
- hot sauce

Paella power in northern Baja

A summer food festival between Ensenada and Tecate draws families from both sides of the border. The outdoor cook-off climaxes a week-long wine festival

Imagine my distress. One night I'm swimming in the dark waters of the Sea of Cortés along with a few thousand other giant shrimp. The next day I'm flipping around in an open ice chest waiting to be part of a great Spanish cooking tradition.

I can see the chef who bought me, tending an almost-smoking lake of extra-virgin olive oil in a huge shallow pan over an open fire. Now he reaches down, avoiding my flailing claws.... Compadre! Don't you think you'd rather make an inland version of

paella? One with chicken and chorizo? Say, compadre, it's not too late to change your recipe! Aiyeee!

Pity the countless shrimp each summer who find themselves in the clutches of one of Baja California's best paella chefs at Concurso de Paellas, the Baja wine country's annual outdoor paella contest. This seafood, chicken, chorizo, and saffron-scented-rice extravaganza takes place in the agriculturally productive Guadalupe Valley between Ensenada and Tecate. The alfresco cook-off is the culmination of a week-long wine festival sponsored by seven Baja California vintners.

The paella fest, held in an ancient oak grove along a streambed, attracts cooking teams from all over northern Baja to a remote ranch 60 miles south of the U.S.–Mexican border. Restaurant chefs enter, of course, and they often work on a grand scale. Last year the Papas & Beer team's paella pan was so large and bursting that it developed a waterfall of broth off one edge. The team's paella master calmly caught the overflow in a bowl and sloshed it back into the bubbling golden sea.

Also here is Ensenada's Casa de España club, whose members and their paella-making children are adorned in bright garb. Other contestants are nonprofessionals—large families or groups of friends. All are following a tradition that dates back to the origins of paella on Spain's east coast, the Levante, which Spaniards call the Land of Rice. Many believe that a decent paella can't be made unless you do it outdoors over a roaring campfire. Here in Baja, cooks use oak cordwood or grapevine prunings. The heat, both from the summer sun and the fires, is ferocious.

Somehow the thousand or so peo-

ple attending the festival don't seem to mind. There's plenty of wine to taste, fresh trout-size sardines hot off a mesquite-charcoal grill, and shade for escape. The dance-around-the-pan, arrange-the-shrimp choreography of the paella makers is entertainment enough from about noon to 2. Then the winners are crowned and people start lining up next to their favorite contestants to fill their plates before retreating to the long tables beneath the trees.

Music provides a sound track to the afternoon. Last year the raucous Banda La Porteña from Ensenada brought its contingent of three snare drums, a tuba, a trumpet, a bass drum, a sax, and a clarinet, the results sounding like a collision between a cattle truck and polka night at a German beer hall.

During the lulls in the music, the afternoon takes on the languid rhythm of a painting by Renoir. Most of the handsome, well-dressed crowd is from Mexico, and the many well-behaved children are proof that this is truly a family affair.

Unless you are a giant shrimp.

PAELLA PLANNER

• *Where:* In Viñedo San Gabriel, a vineyard about 60 miles south of Tecate on Mexico Highway 3. Allow three hours to drive from San Diego. Parking attendants will be visible as you approach the valley festival site at Villa Juárez. Bring plenty of bottled water and your own picnic additions to the paella. (Salads are available for an additional charge.)

• *Cost:* $11.

• *When:* August 10.

• *Contact:* For tickets, directions, and a full schedule of the wine festival's many events, call Jorge or Gabriela Cuevas at Damiana Travel in Ensenada, 011-52-617-40170. ◆

Professional cooks enter this paella contest near Ensenada, as do families— who bring a multigenerational eye to the preparation of this traditional dish.

by **PETER JENSEN**

International *low-fat*

GEOFFREY NILSEN

Fifteen great dishes, three grand meals from the Caribbean, Vietnam, and India

Hot off the grill with Caribbean flair: mahimahi and a variety of vegetables, plus fresh mango salsa and coconut rice.

In other parts of the world, cooking light and lean often comes naturally. But do you have to go to the ends of the earth to find these specialties? Not at all. Many who are expert in their own native cuisines have settled in the West. And we followed three of these cooks into their kitchens to learn their secrets for light, refreshing summer meals. You'll find their recipes surprisingly easy, full of fresh ingredients, and adaptable enough to slip seamlessly into any menu.

Caribbean barbecue

"**I** like anything that reminds me of back home," says Yamilka Hayes. The Dominican Republic native now lives in Northern California, where she has no difficulty finding ingredients to reproduce the tropical tastes she enjoyed as a child. And, as a matter of habit, she keeps a close tab on fats and uses them sparingly.

Watermelon Rum Slush
(*Agua de Sandía*)

Fish with Mango Salsa
(*Pescado con Escabeche*)

Marinated Grilled Vegetables
(*Vegetales a la Parrilla*)

Rice with Coconut
(*Arroz con Coco*)

Grilled Pineapple with Lime
(*Piña a la Parrilla con Lima*)

Game plan: Days ahead, freeze melon for the slushes. Up to about 4 hours ahead, assemble ingredients and prep vegetables and fruit. Serve slushes while fish and vegetables grill and rice cooks. Yamilka Hayes turns pineapple slices on the grill to heighten their sweetness. Then she serves the fruit warm or at room temperature with a squeeze of lime. And adding a scoop of nonfat passion fruit or citrus sorbet does no harm.

Pineapple's sweetness, intensified by heat, makes fruit wedges with lime a tempting dessert.

FRANCE RUFFENACH

California freshness inspires Yamilka Hayes's Dominican Republic dishes.

Watermelon Rum Slush

Prep time: About 15 minutes, plus 1 hour to freeze fruit

Notes: Freeze the melon chunks up to 1 week.

Makes: About 6 cups; 6 to 8 servings

- 1 piece (3½ lb.) **seedless watermelon**
- ¾ cup **pineapple** or white grape **juice**
- ½ to ¾ cup **rum** or more fruit juice
- ⅓ cup **lemon juice**
- **Sugar**

1. Cut rind off watermelon and discard. Cut fruit into ½-inch chunks.

2. Line a 10- by 15-inch pan with plastic wrap. Arrange fruit on wrap in a single layer. Freeze until firm, 1 to 2 hours; if making ahead, transfer frozen chunks to a freezer bag.

3. In a blender, combine half the pineapple juice, rum, and lemon juice. Whirl, gradually dropping in half the frozen watermelon chunks, until smoothly puréed. Sweeten to taste with sugar and pour into a pitcher or directly into glasses. Repeat to make a second batch.

Per serving: 79 cal., 5.7% (4.5 cal.) from fat; 0.8 g protein; 0.5 g fat (0 g sat.); 11 g carbo (0.4 g fiber); 4.5 mg sodium; 0 mg chol.

Fish with Mango Salsa

Prep and cook time: About 20 minutes

Notes: A hinged wire grilling basket makes the fish easier to handle. Otherwise, cook fish on a lightly oiled grill.

Makes: 6 to 8 servings

- 2 tablespoons **soy sauce**
  About 5 tablespoons **lemon juice**
- 2 cloves **garlic**, minced
- 2 to 2½ pounds **skinned, boned mahimahi fillets**
- 1 teaspoon **olive oil**
- 1 **onion** (about 6 oz.), chopped
- ½ cup **refrigerated** or canned **mango nectar**
- 1 ripe **mango** (about 1 lb.), peeled, pitted, and coarsely chopped
- 3 tablespoons chopped **fresh cilantro**
- 1 teaspoon finely shredded **lemon peel**

1. Mix soy sauce, 2 tablespoons lemon juice, and half the garlic.

2. Cut fish into 6 or 8 equal pieces, then rinse and pat dry. Rub soy mixture all over fish. If making ahead, cover and chill up to 30 minutes.

3. In an 8- to 10-inch frying pan over high heat, combine oil, onion, and remaining garlic. Stir until onion begins to get limp, about 2 minutes. Add mango nectar and 3 tablespoons lemon juice; stir until boiling.

4. Remove onion mixture from heat. Stir in mango, cilantro, and lemon peel. Use hot or cool.

5. Arrange fish pieces, side by side, in a wire grilling basket. Close basket and lay it on a barbecue grill over a solid bed of hot coals or high heat on a gas grill (you can hold your hand at grill level only 2 to 3 seconds). Close lid on a gas grill.

6. Cook fish, turning once, until it is barely opaque and still moist-looking in thickest part (cut to test), 8 to 10 minutes total.

7. Serve with salsa and lemon juice.

Per serving: 150 cal., 9.3% (14 cal.) from fat; 22 g protein; 1.5 g fat (0.3 g sat.); 12 g carbo (0.8 g fiber); 362 mg sodium; 83 mg chol.

Marinated Grilled Vegetables

Prep and cook time: About 30 minutes, plus 10 minutes to marinate

GEOFFREY NILSEN

Notes: A wire grilling basket like the one used for the fish also makes the vegetables easier to manage.

Makes: 6 to 8 servings

- ⅓ cup **balsamic vinegar**
- 1 tablespoon **olive oil**
- ⅓ cup minced **shallots**
- 1 tablespoon minced **fresh oregano** leaves or 1 teaspoon dried oregano
- 1½ teaspoons **light molasses**
- 3 **onions** (6 oz. each)
- 2 **pattypan squash** (6 oz. each)
- 3 **yellow zucchini** (6 oz. each)
- 2 **red** or yellow **bell peppers** (½ lb. each)
- **Salt** and **pepper**

1. In a large bowl, mix vinegar, oil, shallots, oregano, and molasses.

2. Peel onions. Trim off and discard stem ends of pattypan squash and zucchini. Cut onions and pattypan into about 1½-inch-wide wedges. Cut zucchini into 1½-inch chunks.

3. Trim stems and seeds from peppers, then cut peppers into 1½-inch squares.

4. Put all the vegetables in bowl with vinegar mixture and stir to coat. Cover and let stand at least 10 minutes or up to 2 hours, stirring occasionally.

5. Lift vegetables from marinade and place in a wire grilling basket or thread vegetables onto thin metal skewers; leave marinade in bowl.

6. Lay vegetables on a barbecue grill over a solid bed of hot coals or high heat on a gas grill (you can hold your hand at grill level only 2 to 3 seconds). Close lid on gas grill. Turn vegetables as needed until browned, 8 to 10 minutes.

7. Put vegetables (push off skewers) back into marinade. Mix and serve vegetables warm or tepid; they can stand up to 2 hours. Add salt and pepper to taste.

Per serving: 78 cal., 23% (18 cal.) from fat; 2.6 g protein; 2 g fat (0.3 g sat.); 14 g carbo (2.6 g fiber); 7 mg sodium; 0 mg chol.

Rice with Coconut

Prep and cook time: About 45 minutes

Makes: 6 to 8 servings

- 1 tablespoon **olive oil**
- 1 **onion** (½ lb.), chopped
- 1 clove **garlic,** minced
- 1 **red bell pepper** (½ lb.), stemmed, seeded, and chopped
- 2 cups **long-grain white rice**
- ½ teaspoon **ground turmeric**
- 1 can (14 oz.) **reduced-fat coconut milk**
- 1½ cups **vegetable** or chicken **broth**
- 2 tablespoons shredded **fresh** or unsweetened shredded dried **coconut**
- **Salt** and **pepper**

1. In a 3- to 4-quart nonstick pan over high heat, stir oil and onion often until onion is limp, about 5 minutes. Add garlic and bell pepper; stir until pepper is limp, about 2½ minutes.

2. Add rice to pan and stir until grains begin to turn opaque, about 2 minutes. Add turmeric and stir about 30 seconds. Add coconut milk and broth. Bring to a boil, cover, and simmer on low heat until rice is tender to bite, 20 to 25 minutes.

3. Spoon the rice into a serving dish and sprinkle with coconut. Add salt and pepper to taste.

Per serving: 266 cal., 15% (39 cal.) from fat; 4 g protein; 4.3 g fat (2.4 g sat.); 46 g carbo (1.4 g fiber); 35 mg sodium; 0 mg chol.

Vietnamese supper

As a 12-year-old Vietnamese refugee, Lan Ngoc (Jenny) Tran dutifully cooked for her parents in the style of their homeland. All the while, she yearned to discover what American foods had to offer. And when she did, she quickly determined that her food could create a friendly bridge between the two worlds.

Many Vietnamese dishes are traditionally low in fat. Fresh vegetables and herbs grace the table in healthy abundance. No-fat fish sauce, lime, and chili are the backbone of refreshingly lean sauces and dressings. Well-trimmed meats, in modest portions, make effective additions to vegetable and noodle dishes.

Lan Ngoc Tran takes great pleasure in sharing food from her native Vietnam.

FRANCE RUFFENACH

Squash Soup
(Canh Bau)

Chicken Salad
(Goi Ga)

Sweet and Sour Fish Sauce
(Nuoc Mam Ngot)

Grilled Pork Noodles
(Bun Thit Nuong)

Vietnamese Iced Coffee
(Ca Phe Sua Da)

Game plan: A day ahead, season the pork, make the fish sauce, and toast sesame seed for salad. Up to 6 hours ahead, complete the chicken salad and prepare the ingredients for the soup.

Finish the soup and keep it warm while the skewered pork grills. Serve the soup first, or present it with the whole meal. Brew the dessert coffee during dinner.

Squash Soup

Prep and cook time: About 30 minutes

Notes: Upo is a long, smooth, light green squash that resembles a short baseball bat. Look for it in Asian markets.

Makes: 6 to 8 servings

⅓ pound **deveined shelled shrimp,** rinsed and chopped

1 **green onion,** ends trimmed, chopped

About 3 tablespoons **Asian fish sauce** (*nuoc mam* or *nam pla*)

¼ teaspoon **black pepper**

1 pound **upo** or zucchini

½ cup chopped **fresh cilantro**

White pepper

1. In a food processor or with a knife, mince shrimp with onion. Mix with 2 tablespoons fish sauce and black pepper.

2. Put shrimp mixture in a 5- to 6-quart pan. Stir over high heat until shrimp mixture is pink and crumbly, about 5 minutes.

3. Then add 1½ quarts of water to the shrimp mixture and bring to a boil over high heat.

4. Meanwhile, pare upo with a vegetable peeler (trim zucchini ends, but don't peel). Then cut squash into matchstick-size sticks.

5. Add squash to boiling shrimp broth. Cover and simmer gently until squash is tender to bite, 5 to 10 minutes.

6. Ladle soup into bowls, sprinkle with cilantro, and season to taste with more fish sauce and white pepper. Serve hot or cool.

Per serving: 43 cal., 21% (9 cal.) from fat; 5.4 g protein; 1 g fat (0.2 g sat.); 3.1 g carbo (0.4 g fiber); 253 mg sodium; 28 mg chol.

Chicken Salad

Prep and cook time: About 35 minutes

Notes: Store toasted sesame seed airtight up to 1 day. Look for Vietnamese mint in Southeast Asian markets, or use regular mint. To prepare ahead, make the salad up through step 7, cover, and chill up to 6 hours.

Makes: 6 to 8 servings

2 boned, skinned **chicken breast halves** (½ lb. total)

½ cup thinly sliced **white onion**

A *piquant, lean dressing turns chicken and cabbage into a refreshing salad.*

GEOFFREY NILSEN

3 tablespoons **cider vinegar**

2 tablespoons **sesame seed**

1 head (1½ lb.) **cabbage**

⅓ cup chopped **fresh cilantro**

⅓ cup chopped **fresh mint** leaves

⅓ cup chopped **fresh Vietnamese mint** leaves (*rau ram*) or more mint leaves

2 tablespoons **roasted, unsalted peanuts,** crushed or finely chopped

3 tablespoons **sweet and sour fish sauce** (recipe follows)

1. In a 4- to 5-quart pan, bring 2½ to 3 quarts water to a boil over high heat. Add chicken, and when water returns to a boil, cover pan and remove from heat. Let stand until chicken is white in thickest part (cut to test), 12 to 17 minutes. Remove from water and let cool 10 to 15 minutes.

2. Meanwhile, combine onion and vinegar. Let stand at least 15 minutes.

3. In a 6- to 8-inch frying pan, stir sesame seed over medium heat until golden, about 6 minutes. Pour from pan.

4. Pull the cool chicken breasts apart into fine shreds.

5. With a knife, finely shred enough cabbage to make 6 cups.

6. Drain onion.

7. In a large bowl, combine chicken pieces, cabbage, onion, cilantro, and both mints.

8. Add peanuts, sesame seed, and sweet and sour fish sauce to chicken salad and mix.

Per serving: 94 cal., 28% (26 cal.) from fat; 9 g protein; 2.9 g fat (0.4 g sat.); 9.1 g carbo (2.7 g fiber); 92 mg sodium; 16 mg chol.

Sweet and Sour Fish Sauce

Prep time: About 7 minutes

Notes: Use this versatile sauce to dress the chicken salad and to season the grilled pork noodles. Make the sauce up to 1 week ahead, storing airtight in refrigerator.

Makes: About 2 cups

½ cup **Asian fish sauce** (*nuoc mam* or *nam pla*)

¾ cup **sugar**

3 tablespoons **lime juice**

2 cloves **garlic,** minced

½ teaspoon **Asian red chili paste** or hot sauce

Stir fish sauce with sugar, lime juice, garlic, chili paste, and 1 cup water until sugar dissolves.

Per tablespoon: 28 cal., 13% (3.6 cal.) from fat; 0.6 g protein; 0.4 g fat (0.1 g sat.); 5.6 g carbo (0 g fiber); 151 mg sodium; 0 mg chol.

Effortlessly light: skewered pork with well-seasoned rice noodles and herbs, Vietnamese-style.

Grilled Pork Noodles

Prep and cook time: About 50 minutes

Notes: Up to 1 day ahead, thread marinated pork slices onto skewers; cover and chill.

Makes: 6 servings

- 2 stalks (about ¾ oz. total) **fresh lemon grass**
- 2 cloves **garlic**
- ½ cup sliced **onion**
- 2 tablespoons **oyster sauce**
- 2 tablespoons **hoisin sauce**
- 2 tablespoons **soy sauce**
- ¼ cup **honey**
- 1 teaspoon **pepper**
- 1½ pounds **boned center-cut pork loin**
- 1 pound **dried rice noodles** (*maifun,* rice sticks, or rice vermicelli)
- 6 ounces **red-leaf lettuce,** crisped and torn into bite-size pieces
- 4 cups (½ lb.) **bean sprouts,** rinsed and drained
- 12 **mint sprigs**
- 12 **cilantro sprigs**
- ½ cup crushed or finely chopped **roasted, salted peanuts**

    About 1 cup **sweet and sour fish sauce** (recipe precedes)

1. Soak 6 to 12 thin wood skewers (8 to 10 in. long) in water at least 15 minutes.

2. Meanwhile, trim off and discard tough tops and root ends of lemon grass. Remove and discard tough outer layers of stalks until you reach tender inner part. Cut tender part into ¼-inch pieces.

3. In a blender, combine lemon grass, garlic, onion, oyster sauce, hoisin, soy, honey, and pepper; whirl until finely ground and soupy.

4. Trim and discard fat from pork. Slice meat across grain as thin as possible, then slice into about 1-inch-wide strips. Coat pork slices with lemon grass mixture.

5. Weave wood skewers in and out of meat strips, down the center, at 1-inch intervals. Loosely push meat together so it bunches up, filling skewers equally.

6. In a 5- to 6-quart pan over high heat, bring about 3 quarts water to a boil. Add rice noodles and cook until they are barely tender to bite, 3 to 5 minutes. Drain, then immerse the hot noodles in cold water. Let stand until cool, then drain.

7. Divide lettuce, bean sprouts, and mint and cilantro sprigs among 6 wide soup bowls. Mound equal portions of noodles in the bowls.

8. Place pork on a barbecue grill over a solid bed of hot coals or high heat on a gas grill (you can hold your hand at grill level only 2 to 3 seconds); cover gas grill. Cook pork, turning to brown the meat on all sides, 6 to 8 minutes total.

9. Place skewers of meat on noodles in bowls. Sprinkle with peanuts. Push meat off skewers and eat with condiments in bowl, adding sweet and sour fish sauce to taste.

Per serving: 676 cal., 21% (144 cal.) from fat; 32 g protein; 16 g fat (4.2 g sat.); 103 g carbo (2.2 g fiber); 1,285 mg sodium; 68 mg chol.

Vietnamese Iced Coffee

Prep and cook time: About 15 minutes

Notes: Traditionally, this dessert coffee is brewed by the cup. A small metal coffee filter (found in many Asian markets) filled with fine-ground coffee is placed on a mug containing a generous spoonful of sweetened condensed milk. Water, poured into the filter and coffee, slowly drips into the milk. By dessert time, all the water has drained, and the coffee is poured into a glass filled with ice.

Makes: 6 servings

- ¾ to 1 cup **low-fat sweetened condensed milk**

- 1½ cups **fine-ground French roast** or espresso roast **coffee**

  Ice cubes

1. Pour ¾ cup condensed milk into a coffee pot or pitcher. Put the ground coffee into a filter cone and set it onto the pot.

2. Pour 3 cups boiling water, in batches, into filter until it all drips into the pot.

3. Mix coffee and milk. Taste, and if desired, add more milk. Pour into ice-filled glasses.

Per serving: 122 cal., 11% (14 cal.) from fat; 3.1 g protein; 1.5 g fat (1 g sat.); 23 g carbo (0 g fiber); 42 mg sodium; 5 mg chol.

Indian salad supper

Laxmi Hiremath, food columnist and author, arrived from India with no cooking experience. But she did bring a sensitive taste memory, an understanding of spices, and a clear vision of what she wanted to achieve in the kitchen.

As a vegetarian, she finds inspiration in the beautiful produce at local farmers' markets, and her imaginative touch turns foods into Indian classics with intriguing tweaks.

Hiremath doesn't hesitate to use modern tools to cut laborious steps. And although fried foods are popular in India, she offers fresher, lighter alternatives, keeping added fat to a vital minimum.

In this collection of salads—handsomely presented as a buffet—vegetables, grains, yogurt, legumes, and fruit provide sound, balanced nutrition. However, chances are you'll be so attracted to the bright colors, contrasting textures, and play of flavors, you'll never notice.

FRANCE RUFFENACH

A master of Indian spicing, Laxmi Hiremath creates provocative salads.

Asparagus and Beet Salad
(Anokhi Chaat)

Sweet Pea Salad with Coconut
(Nariyal Chaat)

Black-Eyed Pea Salad
(Lobhia Chaat)

Corn and Zucchini Raita
(Makai Aur Lauki Raita)

Bread Basket
(*Chapatis*, Whole-Wheat Tortillas, Baguettes, or Soft *Lavosh*)

Buttermilk Cooler
(Lassi)

Mangoes with Pistachios
(Shahi Aam)

Game plan: Ready-to-use ingredients and make-ahead steps will ease the cooking demands. Make the asparagus and beet salad and the raita up to a day ahead. The remaining salads and the dessert can be assembled at least 4 hours ahead. Whirl up the buttermilk cooler just before serving. It can be served as the beverage with the meal or as a refreshing aperitif.

Asparagus and Beet Salad

Prep and cook time: About 15 minutes

Notes: For variety, and if you have time, replace canned beets with 2 cups cooked and sliced fresh yellow beets. Up to 1 day ahead, cover chilled cooked asparagus and cooked fresh beets and refrigerate.

Makes: 6 servings

½   pound **asparagus**

1   teaspoon **ground cumin**

3   tablespoons **lemon juice**

1   can (15 oz.) **sliced beets**

1   can (15 oz.) **garbanzos**

1   cup thinly sliced **red onion,** rinsed and drained

¼   cup chopped **fresh cilantro**

3   tablespoons **roasted, salted pistachios**

Salt

1. Snap off tough ends of asparagus. Cut spears diagonally into 1-inch lengths.

2. In a 10- to 12-inch frying pan, bring about 1 inch water to a boil. Add asparagus and cook just until tender-crisp when pierced, about 3 minutes. Transfer asparagus with a slotted spoon to a large bowl of ice water. Lift out when cold.

3. Dry the frying pan and add cumin. Stir over low heat just until fragrant, about 30 seconds. Pour cumin into a wide bowl and add lemon juice.

4. Drain beets and garbanzos, rinse with cool water, and drain again. Add to bowl along with asparagus, onion, cilantro, and pistachios. Mix and add salt to taste.

Per serving: 106 cal., 28% (30 cal.) from fat; 5.2 g protein; 3.3 g fat (0.3 g sat.); 16 g carbo (3.5 g fiber); 210 mg sodium; 0 mg chol.

Sweet Pea Salad with Coconut

Prep and cook time: About 35 minutes

Notes: To use fresh instead of frozen peas, shell about 4 pounds in-the-pod peas to get 4 cups. The salad holds well up to 4 hours.

Makes: 6 servings

2   teaspoons **salad oil**

2   teaspoons **mustard seed**

2   teaspoons **cumin seed**

1½   to 2 teaspoons **hot chili flakes**

A salad buffet comes together, and tingling tastes are soothed by a buttermilk cooler.

4   cups **frozen petite peas,** thawed

1⅓   cups finely chopped **red bell pepper**

½   cup grated **fresh coconut** or unsweetened shredded dried coconut

4   cups (½ lb.) **bean sprouts,** rinsed and drained

⅓   cup **orange juice**

Salt

1. Pour oil into a 5- to 6-quart pan over medium heat. Add mustard seed and cumin seed. When seeds sizzle and pop, in about 30 seconds, add chilies and stir just until chilies begin to brown, about 1 minute.

2. Add peas, bell pepper, and coconut. Stir until peas are hot, 6 to 8 minutes.

3. Remove pan from heat and stir in bean sprouts. Pour salad mixture into a wide bowl.

4. Serve salad warm or cool; just before serving, stir in orange juice and add salt to taste.

Per serving: 144 cal., 30% (43 cal.) from fat; 7.1 g protein; 4.8 g fat (2.3 g sat.); 20 g carbo (5.4 g fiber); 113 mg sodium; 0 mg chol.

Black-Eyed Pea Salad

Prep time: About 30 minutes

Notes: Up to 4 hours ahead, prepare vegetables and dressing, then cover and chill separately.

Makes: 6 servings

1   firm-ripe **tomato** (½ lb.)

1   **cucumber** (½ lb.)

1   **red** or yellow **bell pepper** (½ lb.)

1   can (15 oz.) **black-eyed peas**

1   cup thinly sliced **green onions** (including tops)

1   cup lightly packed chopped **fresh dill**

⅔   cup **orange juice**

⅓   cup **wine vinegar**

1   teaspoon **ground cumin**

¼   teaspoon fresh-ground **pepper**

1   teaspoon minced **garlic**

Salt

Red-leaf lettuce leaves, rinsed and crisped

1. Rinse, core, and cut tomato into ½-inch cubes.

2. Peel, seed, and cut cucumber into ½-inch cubes.

3. Stem, seed, and cut bell pepper into ½-inch squares.

4. Drain peas, then rinse and drain again and put into a large bowl. Add tomato, cucumber, bell pepper, onions, and dill.

5. Mix orange juice, wine vinegar, cumin, ground pepper, and garlic; add dressing to bowl.

6. Mix dressing with vegetables. Add salt to taste.

7. Line a platter with lettuce and spoon salad onto it.

Per serving: 107 cal., 7.6% (8.1 cal.) from fat; 5.5 g protein; 0.9 g fat (0.1 g sat.); 22 g carbo (1.6 g fiber); 230 mg sodium; 0 mg chol.

Corn and Zucchini Raita

Prep and cook time: About 20 minutes

Notes: Make the yogurt mixture up to 1 day ahead. Garnish salad with seeds and chilies just before serving.

Makes: 6 servings

- 2 cups **fresh**, frozen, or canned **corn kernels**
- 2 **zucchini** (¾ lb. total), ends trimmed, cut into ½-inch cubes
- 2 **fresh serrano chilies**
- 1 teaspoon **salad oil**
- ¼ teaspoon **cumin seed**
- ¼ teaspoon **mustard seed**
- 1 cup **plain nonfat yogurt**
- 2 tablespoons **low-fat sour cream** (optional)
  Salt
- ¼ cup chopped **red bell pepper**
- 1 tablespoon minced **fresh cilantro**

1. Steam fresh corn and zucchini on a perforated rack over boiling water just until zucchini is tender when pierced, about 3 minutes. Let stand until cool.

2. Slit serrano chilies lengthwise into quarters, from tip to stem, leaving chili pieces attached at stem.

3. Pour oil into a 6- to 8-inch frying pan over medium-high heat. Add cumin seed and mustard seed. When seeds pop, in about 30 seconds, add chilies and stir 1 minute. Remove from heat. Cool.

4. In a bowl, mix corn, zucchini, yogurt, and sour cream. Season to taste with salt, then scrape yogurt raita into a salad bowl.

5. Spoon oil with seeds and chilies onto raita. Garnish with bell pepper and cilantro.

Per serving: 83 cal., 17% (14 cal.) from fat; 4.6 g protein; 1.5 g fat (0.2 g sat.); 15 g carbo (2 g fiber); 39 mg sodium; 0.8 mg chol.

Buttermilk Cooler

Prep time: About 10 minutes

Notes: Buy rosewater at Indian and Middle Eastern markets or at liquor stores.

Makes: 8 cups; 6 servings

- 6 cups **low-fat buttermilk**
- 4 **cardamom pods**, hulled
- 2 teaspoons **rosewater** (optional)
- 2 cups **ice cubes**
- 5 to 7 tablespoons **sugar**
  Salt
  Mint sprigs or thin lime slices

1. In a blender, combine 3 cups buttermilk, cardamom seed, rosewater, and ice. Whirl until ice is finely crushed; pour into a pitcher.

2. Stir in remaining buttermilk, 1⅓ cups water, and sugar and salt to taste.

3. Pour into glasses and garnish with mint sprigs.

Per serving: 139 cal., 14% (20 cal.) from fat; 8.1 g protein; 2.2 g fat (1.3 g sat.); 22 g carbo (0 g fiber); 257 mg sodium; 9.8 mg chol.

Mangoes with Pistachios

Prep time: About 15 minutes

Notes: The fruit can be cut and the nut topping prepared up to 6 hours ahead and wrapped separately. Keep these foods cool, but chilling isn't necessary.

Makes: 6 servings

- 3 **cardamom pods**, hulled
- 2 tablespoons **roasted, salted pistachios**
- 3 firm-ripe **mangoes** (about 2½ lb. total)
- 1 tablespoon **honey**
- ⅛ teaspoon fresh-grated or ground **nutmeg**

1. Crush cardamom seed in a mortar and pestle (or smash with flat bottom of a heavy glass).

2. Add pistachios and coarsely crush (or mince).

3. Cut or pull peel from mangoes and discard. Cut mangoes lengthwise, along each side of pit, to remove fleshy cheeks.

4. Slice fruit. Also slice remaining fruit from pit and discard pit. Arrange fruit on a platter.

5. Drizzle mangoes with honey, then sprinkle with cardamom mixture and nutmeg.

Per serving: 112 cal., 13% (15 cal.) from fat; 1.2 g protein; 1.7 g fat (0.3 g sat.); 26 g carbo (1.4 g fiber); 14 mg sodium; 0 mg chol. ◆

GEOFFREY NILSEN

Mangoes, perfumed by cardamom and pistachios, are sweetened with honey.

For an appetizer, offer warm wedges of flatbreads to dunk in olive oil. Or serve the breads at dinner along with a barbecued entrée.

NORMAN A. PLATE

Aromatic flatbreads from the grill

Onion-seasoned breads are topped with rosemary and parmesan

For your next barbecue party, wow guests with warm bread right off the grill—browned, puffed, and subtly smoky.

The yeast dough is enhanced with olive oil and onion. If time is tight, take a shortcut with frozen bread dough. You can roll out the flatbreads up to six hours before grilling. The Lark Creek Inn in Larkspur, California, shared the recipe with us.

Grilled Rosemary Flatbreads

Prep and cook time: About 55 minutes, plus 1 hour for rising

Notes: Have dough and fire ready at the same time. Roll out breads first, then heat grill. (For an easier version, use 1 pound thawed frozen bread dough; knead in 1½ tablespoons olive oil and the onion, then proceed from step 3.)

Makes: 6 flatbreads; 12 servings

1 package **active dry yeast**

2 teaspoons **salt**

⅓ cup finely diced **onion**

About 3 tablespoons **extra-virgin olive oil**

About 4 cups **all-purpose flour**

2 tablespoons minced **fresh rosemary**

⅔ cup finely shredded **parmesan cheese**

Fresh-ground **pepper**

1. In a bowl, sprinkle yeast over 1¼ cups warm (110°) water. Let stand until softened, about 5 minutes. Add salt, onion, 1½ tablespoons olive oil, and 2½ cups flour.

2. *If kneading by hand,* stir vigorously until dough is stretchy, about 5 minutes. Stir in 1¼ cups flour. Scrape dough onto a lightly floured board and knead until smooth, elastic, and no longer sticky, 10 to 12 minutes, adding flour as required to prevent sticking.

If kneading with a dough hook, beat on low speed until flour is incorporated. Add 1¼ cups flour. Beat on low speed to blend, then on high speed until dough no longer feels sticky, and pulls cleanly from bowl, 10 to 12 minutes. If dough is still sticky, beat in flour, 1 tablespoon at a time.

3. Place dough in an oiled bowl, turn over, cover airtight, and let rise in a warm place until doubled, about 1 hour.

4. On a lightly floured board or with a dough hook, briefly knead dough to expel air. Cut into 6 equal pieces and shape each into a smooth ball.

5. Flatten 1 ball by hand, then roll into an 8-inch round (or into a 7-in. round if using frozen bread dough), reflouring board and rolling pin as needed to prevent sticking. Brush round with about ¾ teaspoon olive oil and sprinkle with about 1 teaspoon rosemary, a scant 2 tablespoons parmesan, and pepper. Lightly press in seasonings. Cover a plate with plastic wrap. Place seasoned round on wrap, cover with plastic wrap, and chill. Repeat to shape remaining balls. As each round is finished, add to stack, cover with plastic wrap, and chill. (If making dough ahead, wrap stack airtight and chill up to 6 hours.)

6. Place a few dough rounds at a time, seasoned side up, on an oiled grill over a solid bed of medium-hot coals, or over medium-high heat on a gas grill (you can hold your hand at grill level only 3 to 4 seconds). Cover gas grill. With a wide spatula, occasionally lift and rotate breads for even browning. When bottoms are well browned, 2 to 3 minutes, turn breads over. Cook until seasoned sides are light brown, 1 to 2 more minutes.

7. Cut each flatbread into about 6 wedges. Dip into olive oil to eat.

Per serving: 206 cal., 23% (48 cal.) from fat; 6.4 g protein; 5.3 g fat (1.4 g sat.); 33 g carbo (1.4 g fiber); 451 mg sodium; 3.5 mg chol. ◆

by **E L A I N E   J O H N S O N**

By the bunch or by the sprig: Properly stored cilantro lasts up to two weeks.

NOEL BARNHURST

Keeping the fresh in herbs

Tender perishables last longer if you act like a florist

Fresh flavor is just a snip away if you keep a bouquet of tender green herbs in the kitchen. Basil, especially, thrives in a container of water on the kitchen counter, and the stems may even develop roots in several weeks.

But other delicate green-stemmed herbs, such as cilantro, parsley, and watercress, need more coddling. For their well-being, you need to control air, light, and temperature, says George K. York, extension food technologist at the University of California at Davis.

Oxygen in the air reacts with cut plants and creates brown or black spots on leaves. Spots first appear where the leaves are bruised.

Light breaks down the chlorophyll in herbs and makes yellow spots that often turn white. Chervil is quite sus-

ceptible to this damage because its leaves are so thin.

Temperature that's warm enough to keep us comfortable will release the volatile oils in tender herb leaves. The room gets the fragrance that the herbs lose—unless they begin to grow, as basil does. All tender herbs except basil keep their flavor best in the refrigerator (basil leaves are susceptible to cold and turn black).

How herbs are grown also affects how long they last. Commercially produced herbs and garden herbs may have different flavor and durability. Wendy Krupnick, former garden manager for Shepherd's Garden Seeds, explains that many commercially produced herbs are given high-nitrogen fertilizer to yield a quick crop. These herbs often contain more water, mak-

ing them more perishable, and are less flavorful because they have fewer essential oils.

How well commercially grown cut herbs will keep also depends on when they were cut and how they have been handled since then. Wilted leaves often perk up if you cut off the damaged part of the stem and put it in water.

Although rinsed herbs (except basil), wrapped in towels and enclosed in a plastic bag, keep well enough for a day or two, their life is greatly extended when you store as follows.

FOUR STEPS TO FRESHNESS

1. Untie herbs and immerse in cool water, shaking gently to dislodge any soil or insects. Discard decayed stalks and leaves. Snip off stems just above a break or a bruise. Gently shake excess water from leaves (don't use a lettuce spinner; it bruises leaves).

2. Place stems in a container of water (a vase or canning jar) that holds them snugly, leaves above the rim.

3. Cover leaves loosely with a plastic bag, such as a produce bag.

4. Refrigerate, changing water when it looks murky. Snip off any parts of stems that show signs of decay. If you're storing several jars, group them on a close-fitting rimmed tray to protect them from being knocked over. ◆

How to keep tender herbs fresh

Prepare herbs as described above, then use this chart as a storage guide. Their quality when stored affects how well they keep.

Herb	Storage	Days
Basil	countertop	up to 31
Chervil	refrigerator	up to 8
Chives	refrigerator	up to 9
Cilantro	refrigerator	up to 14
Dill	refrigerator	up to 9
Parsley	refrigerator	up to 21
Tarragon	refrigerator	up to 17
Watercress	refrigerator	up to 8

by **ANDREW BAKER**

Beautiful Bings

Dark, sweet, and
juicy on ice cream

by KAREN I. LIPMAN

Flavor is what makes Bing cherries exceptional. If they have a flaw, it would be the pit. And if pitting cherries has kept you from using them in desserts like this lavish sundae, take heart. With a little help, it's an easier, speedier task than you might suppose.

Gadgets for pitting cherries are available in cookware stores, starting at about $3. Just pop a cherry in the center of the tool and press down on the plunger—it pushes the pit out through the bottom of the cherry.

For prettier results, use a clean hairpin. Push the rounded end of the pin into the stem side of the cherry, slide the pin around the pit to release it, then pull it up and out.

Double Cherry Sundae

Prep and cook time: 15 to 20 minutes

Notes: If making sauce ahead, cool, cover, and chill up to a week. To use, stir over very low heat until smooth.

Makes: 8 servings

- ½ pound **semisweet chocolate,** coarsely chopped
- 2 tablespoons **sugar**
- ¼ cup **whipping cream**
- 1 tablespoon **kirsch** (cherry liqueur), optional
- 1 teaspoon **vanilla**
- 1 quart **vanilla ice cream**
- 2 cups pitted **Bing cherries**

1. In a 1½- to 2-quart pan over lowest heat, combine chocolate, sugar, cream, kirsch, and vanilla; stir until smooth. Serve warm or hot; makes 1 cup.

2. Scoop ice cream into bowls; top with cherries and pour sauce over fruit.

Per serving: 330 cal., 49% (162 cal.) from fat; 4.1 g protein; 18 g fat (11 g sat.); 43 g carbo (0.6 g fiber); 58 mg sodium; 37 mg chol. ◆

A shortcut to focaccia

Frozen bread dough is the key. Dress it up with cheese and herbs

Have you ever thought about making tender, fragrant focaccia like you find at restaurants and Italian bakeries, but been intimidated by visions of endless kneading and hours of rising dough? The following recipe puts all these concerns to rest.

Simply thaw two loaves of frozen bread dough, then stretch one in a shallow baking pan to give it the flatness of focaccia. Top with feta cheese, herbs, pepper, and another layer of dough, let it rise about 45 minutes, then bake to golden brown perfection. It's a versatile accompaniment to soups, salads, and entrées, or can stand on its own as a predinner nibble with a glass of wine.

ROBERT OLDING

Double-decker Focaccia

Prep and cook time: About 1 hour, plus thawing time and 45 minutes to rise

Notes: Thaw dough in the refrigerator overnight, or for 2 to 3 hours at room temperature. If making ahead, cool baked bread, cover airtight, and hold at room temperature up to 1 day. To reheat, cover lightly with foil and bake in a 350° oven until warm to touch, about 10 minutes.

Makes: One 2¼-pound loaf

- 2 loaves (1 lb. each) **frozen white bread dough,** thawed
- ½ pound **feta cheese**
- 1 tablespoon minced **fresh** or 1½ teaspoons dried **rosemary** leaves
- 1 tablespoon minced **fresh** or 1½ teaspoons dried **oregano** leaves
- **Cracked pepper** (optional)
- About 1 tablespoon **olive oil**

1. Place 1 loaf of thawed dough in a well-oiled 9- by 13-inch baking pan. Press and stretch dough to fill pan evenly. (If dough is too elastic, let rest a few minutes and stretch again; repeat as necessary.)

2. Crumble feta in chunks evenly over dough. Sprinkle with half the rosemary and oregano, and pepper to taste.

3. On a lightly floured board, roll or stretch and pat second loaf into a rectangle roughly the shape of the pan. Lay over feta and herb-covered dough. Stretch top layer to completely cover bottom layer. Cover pan lightly with plastic wrap; let dough rise in a warm place until about doubled, 45 to 60 minutes.

4. Brush dough with oil. With your fingers, gently press dough down all over, forming dimples in the surface. Sprinkle with remaining rosemary and oregano.

5. Bake in a 400° oven until dough is well browned on edges and bottom (lift with a spatula to check), about 45 minutes. (If top starts to brown too much, lay a sheet of foil lightly on top during baking.) Loosen edges from pan sides and bottom. Turn focaccia out onto a rack, then invert again so bread is upright. Cool slightly.

Per 1-ounce serving: 79 cal., 29% (23 cal.) from fat; 2.8 g protein; 2.5 g fat (1 g sat.); 11 g carbo (0.4 g. fiber); 217 mg sodium; 5.6 mg chol. ◆

by CHRISTINE WEBER HALE

Fast and fresh bow-tie pasta with shrimp has two kinds of tomatoes in its sauce.

CARRIE LLOYD

Sunset's Kitchen Cabinet

A chemistry education inspires Robin Grant to experiment in the kitchen—with one major difference. "Instead of using chemicals, I use food. It's hard to eat what you make in the lab."

Southwest Shrimp and Pasta

Robin Grant, Las Vegas

Prep and cook time: About 20 minutes

Makes: 3 or 4 servings

 1 pound **Roma tomatoes**

 6 **oil-packed dried tomatoes**, drained

 1 or 2 **fresh jalapeño chilies**, stemmed, seeded, and sliced

 ¼ cup chopped **fresh basil** leaves

 1 teaspoon **olive oil**

 3 tablespoons minced **shallot**

 4 to 6 cloves **garlic**, minced

 ¼ cup **dry sherry** or water

 ½ pound **dried bow-tie pasta**

 1 pound (22 to 24 per lb.) **fresh** or thawed frozen **shelled and deveined shrimp**

 2 tablespoons chopped **parsley**

   Salt and **pepper**

1. Core Roma tomatoes and coarsely chop. Put ⅔ of the chopped tomatoes into a food processor or blender. Add dried tomatoes, chilies, and basil; whirl until coarsely puréed.

2. In a 10- to 12-inch frying pan over medium-high heat, stir oil, shallot, and garlic until shallot is limp, about 2 minutes. Add remaining chopped tomatoes, puréed tomato mixture, and sherry. Simmer sauce over low heat, stirring occasionally, to blend flavors, 15 to 20 minutes. Add a little water if mixture begins to stick.

3. Meanwhile, cook pasta in about 3 quarts boiling water until barely tender to bite, 8 to 10 minutes. Drain and put in a wide serving bowl.

4. While pasta cooks, add shrimp to tomato sauce and stir often until shrimp are opaque but moist-looking in the center (cut to test), 3 to 5 minutes.

5. Mix sauce with pasta; sprinkle with parsley. Add salt and pepper to taste.

Per serving: 557 cal., 31% (171 cal.) from fat; 33 g protein; 19 g fat (2.7 g sat.); 59 g carbo (5.4 g fiber); 199 mg sodium; 173 mg chol.

Jordan's Apple Chicken

J. Thomas McLaughlin, Springfield, Oregon

A fortuitous combination of ingredients found in the refrigerator ended up in these richly browned and flavorful chicken thighs. The creator, J. Thomas McLaughlin, named the recipe after one of his sons.

Prep and cook time: About 40 minutes, plus at least 1 hour for marinating

Makes: 8 servings

 1 cup **apple juice**

 ½ cup **reduced-sodium soy sauce**

 ¼ cup chopped **fresh basil** leaves or 2 tablespoons dried basil

 1 teaspoon **fresh thyme** leaves or ½ teaspoon dried thyme

 ¼ teaspoon **white pepper**

 2 cloves **garlic**, pressed

 16 **chicken thighs** (about 4 lb. total)

1. In a large bowl, combine apple juice, soy sauce, basil, thyme, pepper, and garlic.

2. Pull off or trim and discard skin and excess fat from thighs. Add chicken to bowl and mix to coat pieces with the liquid. Cover and chill at least 1 hour or up to 24, stirring occasionally.

3. Lift chicken from marinade and lay on a grill over a solid bed of medium coals or medium heat on a gas grill (you can hold your hand at grill level only 4 to 5 seconds). Cover barbecue, open vents, and cook 15 minutes. Lift thighs from grill and dip in marinade to coat. Return chicken to grill, browned side up. Cover barbecue and cook until chicken is no longer pink at bone (cut to test), about 10 minutes.

Per serving: 218 cal., 45% (99 cal.) from fat; 26 g protein; 11 g fat (3 g sat.); 2.8 g carbo (0.1 g fiber); 387 mg sodium; 93 mg chol.

Garden Harvest Jambalaya

Jennifer Bauermeister, Connell, Washington

Motivated by her garden, teenager Jennifer Bauermeister assembled an all-vegetable jambalaya using a classic recipe as a guide. In lieu of the shellfish, she added more spices and a greater variety of vegetables.

Prep and cook time: About 1 hour

Makes: 6 to 8 servings

 2 firm-ripe **tomatoes** (about 10 oz. each)

 1 **red bell pepper** (about ½ lb.)

4 **kohlrabi** (about 1 lb. total)

2 **carrots** (about 10 oz. total)

1 **zucchini** (about ½ lb.)

1 cup **green beans**

1 **onion** (about ½ lb.)

1 tablespoon **olive oil**

3 cloves **garlic,** minced

½ teaspoon **cayenne**

½ teaspoon **pepper**

1⅓ cups **long-grain white rice**

2¼ cups **chicken** or vegetable **broth**

Salt

1. Core tomatoes. Chop 1 tomato and slice the other.

2. Stem, seed, and coarsely chop bell pepper.

3. Peel kohlrabi and cut into ½-inch chunks.

4. Trim ends from carrots, zucchini, and beans. Cut carrots in half lengthwise, then into 2-inch pieces. Quarter zucchini lengthwise, then cut into 2-inch pieces. Cut beans into 2-inch pieces. Chop onion.

5. In a 6- to 8-quart pan over medium heat, stir oil, onion, and garlic occasionally until onion is limp, about 4 minutes.

6. Stir in the chopped tomato, bell pepper, kohlrabi, carrots, cayenne, and pepper. Cover and simmer, stirring occasionally, until kohlrabi is barely tender when pierced, about 10 minutes.

7. Stir in rice and broth and bring mixture to a boil over high heat. Cover, reduce heat, and simmer until rice is almost tender to bite, about 20 minutes. Add zucchini and green beans; simmer, covered, just until beans are tender when pierced, 7 to 10 minutes longer.

8. Spoon onto a platter and top with sliced tomato. Add salt to taste.

Per serving: 202 cal., 12% (24 cal.) from fat; 5.7 g protein; 2.7 g fat (0.5 g sat.); 40 g carbo (3.9 g fiber); 60 mg sodium; 1.1 mg chol.

Rajas con Queso

Ludmila Dye, San Diego

In Tijuana, Ludmila Dye first tasted roasted chili strips and onions blanketed with melted cheese. It was an easy concept to duplicate, and she loves to serve it as a quick lunch or appetizer. The heart-shaped poblano chilies are sometimes labeled pasillas.

Prep and cook time: About 20 minutes

Makes: 4 appetizer servings

3 **fresh poblano chilies** (about 10 oz. total)

1 tablespoon **butter** or margarine

1 **onion** (about ½ lb.), sliced

¼ pound **sliced jack cheese**

4 to 6 warm **corn** or flour **tortillas** (6 to 7 in. wide)

1. Place chilies in a broiler pan and broil about 3 inches from heat, turning as needed to char and blister on all sides, about 8 minutes total. Let cool. Pull off and discard stems and seeds. Cut chilies into thin strips.

2. Meanwhile, in a 6- to 8-inch frying pan over medium-high heat, stir butter and onion often until onion is limp, 4 to 5 minutes.

3. Mix chilies with onions and lay cheese slices on the vegetables. Cover and cook over low heat until cheese melts, about 2 minutes.

4. Scoop hot cheese mixture into tortillas. Fold to enclose filling, and eat.

Per appetizer serving: 229 cal., 47% (108 cal.) from fat; 10 g protein; 12 g fat (6.9 g sat.); 22 g carbo (3 g fiber); 227 mg sodium; 38 mg chol.

Blueberry Buckwheat Pancakes

Mickey Strang, McKinleyville, California

"When we moved from the Mojave Desert to the coast, we went totally bananas over blueberries," says Mickey Strang. A local blueberry farm provides her with fruit for these light buckwheat cakes. A little cornmeal adds a pleasing crunch.

Prep and cook time: About 20 minutes

Makes: 12 pancakes; 4 servings

⅔ cup **blueberries** (or thawed frozen unsweetened berries)

⅓ cup **buckwheat flour**

⅓ cup **cornmeal**

⅓ cup **all-purpose flour**

2 tablespoons **sugar**

2 teaspoons **baking powder**

½ teaspoon **baking soda**

2 **large eggs,** separated

1 cup **buttermilk**

Butter or margarine

Blueberry or maple **syrup**

1. Rinse and drain fresh blueberries.

2. In a bowl, mix buckwheat flour with cornmeal, all-purpose flour, sugar, baking powder, and baking soda. Add egg yolks and buttermilk; stir just until batter is evenly moistened. Add blueberries.

3. In a deep bowl, whip egg whites with a mixer on high speed just until whites hold stiff peaks. Gently fold whites into batter.

4. Place a nonstick griddle or 11- to 12-inch nonstick frying pan over medium heat. When hot, pour batter, about ¼ cup for each cake, onto griddle. Cook until tops of pancakes are bubbly and edges appear dry, 1 to 1½ minutes. Turn over to brown other side.

5. Serve hot with butter and syrup.

Per serving: 213 cal., 15% (33 cal.) from fat; 8.6 g protein; 3.7 g fat (1.2 g sat.); 37 g carbo (2.7 g fiber); 499 mg sodium; 109 mg chol. ◆

Savor juicy blueberries in buckwheat pancakes with blueberry syrup.

CARRIE LLOYD

Celebrate the Northwest's bounty with farm-country drives, food and wine sampling, and a salmon feast (see page 184).

August

foodguide

by JERRY ANNE DI VECCHIO

gadgets

For the perfect latte or cappuccino, you need steamy, foamy milk. The marvelously effective, inexpensive bubble maker at left works much like an elegant French press or a filter coffeemaker. The fine mesh screen at the base of the plunger produces a dense milk froth in seconds. Just pour hot milk into the cylinder (or heat milk in it in a microwave oven) and gently agitate with a few strokes of the plunger. There are several brands, sizes, and styles (including some with microwave-safe handles). Shown is Caffé Froth by Bonjour, just under $20 in cookware stores. It can be ordered direct from Bonjour (800/226-6568) or Sur La Table (800/243-0852).

LEFT: CURTIS ANDERSON   BELOW: JAMES CARRIER   RIGHT: IAN REEVES

BACK TO BASICS

The perils of peaches

■ If you love a good peach half as much as I do, it's important to know that the fruit suffers sorely if put in the refrigerator before it's ready to eat.

It took Carlos Crisosto, a University of California at Davis pomologist, 30 years to find out why.

Peaches and nectarines harvested mature but hard, held at about 32° (recommended for commercial storage and shipping), then ripened at 51° to 77°, were bursting with juice and flavor. In the refrigerator or kept at a temperature up to 50°, the same kind of fruit, when "ripened," changed color and felt softer, but was mushy, cottony, and tasteless.

What to do? It's almost too easy. Pop underripe fruit (with hope that it hasn't been subjected to the danger zone) into a paper bag, fold the bag shut, and leave on the counter until the fruit gives slightly when gently squeezed, usually one to three days. If the temperature is over 80°, find a cooler spot or you'll run into other problems. You can keep ripe fruit in the refrigerator a few days more.

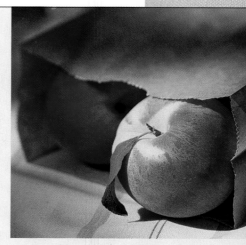

Fold bag to enclose peaches and retain natural ripening gases.

A TASTE OF THE WEST

Garlic and lamb

■ Washington rancher Jim Robison, who raises onions and shallots in Walla Walla, loves lamb, and he honors its tried-and-true relationship with garlic. However, he augments this pairing with the harmonious addition of some of his own shallots and a thick pack of aromatic herbs.

During the summer, Jim prefers to barbecue the lamb. And he turns to the garden for the rest of the menu. One household favorite starts with recently dug and well-scrubbed potatoes. The potatoes, unpeeled, are thinly sliced and placed in a single, slightly overlapping layer on a baking sheet. Then they're generously brushed with garlic-enriched butter, dusted with paprika, and baked in a hot oven until crisp. About the time the lamb is ready, just-picked spinach is wilted in sizzling butter full of softly cooked shallots and garlic.

Mint sauce? Jim makes his an old family way—with a generous portion of chopped fresh mint leaves stirred into boiling red wine vinegar. I like it with a touch of sugar to balance the bite.

Crushed-Herb Lamb

Prep and cook time: 1½ to 1¾ hours
Notes: For carving, select a leg of lamb with an exposed shank bone. It makes a great handle. Slice the meat parallel to the bone. Outside slices will be well done, and the center rare. The lamb shown here is served with oven-roasted potatoes.
Makes: 8 or 9 servings

    1 **leg of lamb** (5½ to 5¾ lb.)
    6 cloves **garlic**
    2 **shallots** (about 1 oz. each)
       About 2 teaspoons **rock salt** or kosher salt
    2 tablespoons **dried thyme**
    2 tablespoons **dried rosemary**
    2 tablespoons fresh-ground **pepper**
    ¼ cup **olive oil**

1. Trim and discard fat and any transparent membrane from surface of lamb.

2. Peel garlic and shallots and cut into ¼-inch-thick slivers. Pierce lamb all over with the tip of a small knife and insert garlic and shallots into cuts (lamb will look like a porcupine). Also tuck 2 teaspoons rock salt into cuts, spacing evenly over meat.

3. Mix thyme, rosemary, pepper, and olive oil. Pat mixture all over the lamb.

4. *If cooking over charcoal briquets,* ignite 60 briquets on firegrate of a barbecue with a lid. When coals are dotted with gray, about 25 minutes, push an equal number of coals to opposite sides of grate. Add 5 briquets to each mound of coals. Put a foil drip pan between coals. Set grill in place.

If using a gas barbecue, turn heat to high and close lid for at least 10 minutes. Adjust burners for indirect grilling (heat on parallel sides of grill but not in center). Set a drip pan between burners and put grill in place.

5. Put lamb on grill over drip pan, but not directly over heat. Cover barbecue; open all vents. (If cooking over charcoal, after 30 minutes add 5 more briquets to each mound of coals.) Cook until a meat thermometer inserted through thickest part of meat to bone registers 125° for rare (1 hour to 1 hour and 10 minutes), or 135° for medium-rare (about 1 hour and 10 to 30 minutes).

6. Transfer meat to a platter and let rest 10 minutes. Carve, and salt to taste.

Per serving: 324 cal., 47% (153 cal.) from fat; 38 g protein; 17 g fat (4.5 g sat.); 3.7 g carbo (0.5 g fiber); 421 mg sodium; 119 mg chol.

foodguide

SEASONAL NOTE

Beans, beans, and more beans

■ In summer, it's no challenge to have a different bean for supper every night of the week. Plump Blue Lakes, hot with a dab of sweet butter. Purple beans, bold with a tart-acid dressing to retain their color. Tiny haricots verts, Chinese long beans, fava beans, fresh cranberry beans. The list goes on. A salad I enjoy mixes young green beans and yellow wax beans. For more variety, I often use garlic chives or other specialty chives. If the chives have blossoms, I scatter these colorful edibles over the salad, too.

Green and Yellow Bean Salad with Chive Dressing

Prep and cook time: 15 to 20 minutes
Notes: If making ahead, wrap cold beans airtight and chill up to 1 day.
Makes: 6 servings

   ¾ pound **small, slender green beans**

   ¾ pound **small, slender yellow wax beans**
   1 tablespoon **Dijon mustard**
   2 tablespoons **white wine vinegar**
   2 tablespoons **extra-virgin olive oil**
   ⅓ cup chopped **fresh chives**
     Salt and **pepper**
     Whole **fresh chives**

1. In a covered 5- to 6-quart pan over high heat, bring about 3 quarts water to boiling.
2. Remove ends and any strings from green and yellow beans. Rinse beans and add to boiling water. Cook, uncovered, until beans are tender-crisp when pierced, 3 to 4 minutes. Drain, then immerse in ice water until cool, 3 to 4 minutes. Drain again.
3. In a wide salad bowl, stir together mustard, vinegar, olive oil, and chopped chives. Add beans and mix with dressing. Season to taste with salt and pepper. Garnish with whole chives.

Per serving: 79 cal., 54% (43 cal.) from fat; 2.1 g protein; 4.8 g fat (0.7 g sat.); 8.4 g carbo (2.1 g fiber); 67 mg sodium; 0 mg chol.

NEWS NOTES

Tortilla retro

■ Colored, flavored tortillas are taking hold, but not for the first time. Patricia Quintana, an author and cooking teacher in Mexico City, reports that the Aztecs served tortillas that were green, black, blue, yellow, purple, pink, and white. All were made from corn of various colors. The tortillas were also often flavored with other foods, such as beans, and herbs like epazote, and colored with chilies or the mild red annatto seed (the base of achiote pastes).

Of course, flavored *flour* tortillas are the real new-comers; you can spot them flavored with chilies, spinach, cilantro—there are even banana and cinnamon-apple versions. Use the savory ones as you would any tortilla, even wrapped around hot sausages off the grill. Try the fruit ones for breakfast, warmed and wrapped around more of the same fruit with some brown sugar and sour cream.

Tortillas with cilantro (top), chilies (center), and spinach (bottom).

GREAT INGREDIENT

Cactus fruit

■ Some applaud the first human who ate an oyster. But my hat is off to the first person who braved a prickly pear cactus. Prickly pears (cactus pear, Indian fig, and tuna are other names) are dethorned but still a trifle dangerous—wear heavy cotton gloves or use a thick towel to hold them when peeling.

LEFT: IAN REEVES FAR LEFT: JAMES CARRIER

The ruby color and cool, sweet floral taste come from the cactus.

Prickly Pear Lemonade

Prep time: 5 to 7 minutes
Notes: Garnish glasses with lemon slices.
Makes: About 2 cups, 2 or 3 servings

   2 **prickly pear fruit** (about 10 oz. total)
   ½ cup **lemon juice**
   2 tablespoons **sugar**
     Ice cubes

1. Cut ends from prickly pears. Cut a lengthwise slit through peel on each fruit. Pull back peel, scoop out fruit, and discard peel.

2. Put prickly pear pulp, lemon juice, sugar, and 1 cup water in a blender or food processor. Whirl until smooth.

3. Pour into ice-filled glasses.

Per serving: 70 cal., 6.4% (4.5 cal.) from fat; 0.7 g protein; 0.5 g fat (0 g sat.); 18 g carbo (0 g fiber); 12 mg sodium; 0 mg chol. ◆

The Wine Guide

by **KAREN MacNEIL**

British Columbia's boom times

■ If I had been asked five years ago to guess what grows well in British Columbia, I would have said bears.

Little did I know that, even then, British Columbia was on the cusp of becoming famous as one of North America's most exciting new wine regions. There are, in fact, about 40 wineries in the region today, and some of the wines show such promise that heads are beginning to turn.

British Columbia's recent emergence on the world wine scene belies the fact that vines grew here as early as the 1860s. But for more than a century, the industry barely hung on, as wave after wave of difficulties beset it. Today, thanks to political, economic, and social changes, the B.C. wine industry is strong enough to soar.

Most of British Columbia's wines come from the 150-mile-long Okanagan Valley, in the middle of which is pristine Okanagan Lake. Curiously, the southern end of the valley is the only classified desert in Canada. This fact is pivotal to the flavor of the wines. The combination of sunny, arid days and very cold nights (a viticulturist's dream scenario) means that the grapes ripen fully but are able to escape the kind of unrelenting heat that would make the wine taste flaccid and flabby.

But that's only part of the story. This part of British Columbia crosses the 50th parallel, making it one of the most northern wine regions in the world, commensurate with the Mosel region of Germany and the Champagne region of France. In northern climates like these, ripening generally happens more gently and slowly, resulting—in the best of cases—in wines with finely etched flavors.

And exactly what kinds of wine are we talking about? British Columbia is known mainly for its whites: Riesling, Chardonnay, Pinot Blanc, Pinot Gris, and Gewürztraminer, along with a handful of curious varieties that are almost impossible to find, say, in Califor-

RICK MARIANI

nia. These include Ehrenfelser and Bacchus (from Germany), Auxerrois (from France), and Chasselas (from Switzerland). A small amount of red wine is also made (notably Pinot Noir and Merlot), but the jury is still out on how well reds will eventually do here.

Then there's B.C.'s rarefied, scrumptious specialty: icewine. Icewine is so difficult to make, and requires such extraordinary circumstances, that only tiny amounts are made in the whole world, and the wines are expensive. Most icewine (or eiswein) is made in Germany and Canada, with small amounts coming from Austria and New York.

Icewine (often spelled as two words in the U.S.) is so called because it is made from frozen, very ripe grapes picked in the dead of winter. Often, the harvesters will wear gloves—not so much to keep their hands warm as to keep their hands from warming the frozen grapes. As the frozen grapes are pressed, the sweet, high-acid juice is separated from the ice (formerly, the water in the grape). The ice is thrown away, and the resulting wine is made solely from the super-intense juice. As a result, the greatest icewines are miraculously high in both sweetness and acidity, giving them mesmerizing finesse and making them an ethereal sensation to drink.

Whether you're looking for icewines or other B.C. wines, be patient. Although more and more B.C. wines are being imported to the United States, B.C.'s total production is tiny (there are a mere 2,600 acres of vines in all of British Columbia; by comparison, Napa Valley alone has 36,000 acres under vine). Moreover, Great Britain often beats us to the punch and snaps up B.C. wines first.

There is one foolproof way to experience the wines of British Columbia, however: go there. The region is exquisite, and virtually every winery encourages visitors to come for tastings. (Call the British Columbia Wine Institute at 800/811-9911 for a guide to the wineries and information about them.) Just remember that, as in all emerging wine regions, the wines themselves can differ vastly in style and quality (all prices below are in Canadian dollars). ◆

WINE LIST

■ *Gehringer Brothers Dry Riesling 1995,* $9.25 (Okanagan Valley). Like peach sorbet—scrumptious and lively.

■ *Inniskillin Okanagan Merlot "Inkameep Vineyard" 1995,* $17.95 (Okanagan Valley). Sleek, taut, and tarry.

■ *Mission Hill Grand Reserve Pinot Blanc 1994,* $12.95 (Okanagan Valley). Exotically perfumed; unusually spicy for a Pinot Blanc.

■ *Sumac Ridge "Stellar's Jay Cuvée" Brut 1993,* $19.95 (Okanagan Valley). A lean, refreshing bubbly with light, spicy flavors.

■ *Tinhorn Creek Kerner/Riesling Icewine 1995,* $39.50 (Okanagan Valley). Lip-smacking. A perfect balance of sweetness and acidity.

WINE DICTIONARY
Mouth-feel

The tactile impression of a wine in the mouth. Like cloth, wine can feel soft, rough, velvety, jagged, etc. — *K. M.*

Kelowna

B R I T I S H   C O L U M B I A

1

Vancouver

1   3

Sidney

97

17

Victoria

Okanogan River

Penticton

La Conner

Columbia River

W A S H I N G T O N

2

Quilcene

Seattle

Leavenworth

Spokane

Shelton

Puyallup

Wenatchee

90

THE PA

Grayland

Ellensburg

Pullman

Oysterville

5

Yakima

Snake River

Pacific Ocean

Astoria

82

Yakima River

Walla Walla

Tillamook

Vancouver

Columbia River

Hermiston

84

Portland

The Dalles

Pendleton

Canby

Newport

Woodburn

Salem

O R E G O N

Willamette River

Eugene

5

When it's in season…

Bringing Home the Harvest
(pp 162–169)

Dahlia fields
(Aug.–frost)

Heaven on a Half-Shell
(pp 170–175)

Bounty		**Season**	**Bounty**		**Season**
	Berries	June-Aug.		Onions	Sept.
	Cherries	July		Potatoes	Sept.
	Christmas trees	Nov.-Dec.		Salmon	Year-round
	Corn	Oct.		Shrimp	May-Aug.
	Crabs	Dec.-Aug.		Tulips	Mar.-Apr.
	Cranberries	Oct.		Wheat/grain	Sept.-Nov.
	Dairy	Year-round		Wine grapes	Sept.-Nov.
	Melons	Aug.-Oct.		Wool	Year-round

Coos Bay

Bandon

Dillard

Rogue River

Grants Pass

Medford

Ashland

ILLUSTRATION BY DEBRA LAMBERT

Coeur
d'Alene

BRINGING HOME
the harvest

*Our guide to the Northwest's bounty—from great
farm-country drives to conversations with tastemakers.
Plus where to find Washington's freshest oysters*

by JIM McCAUSLAND *with* JENA MacPHERSON

■ It's one thing to learn where apples come from in Miss Simpkins's fourth-grade class, and quite another to pick and eat a ripe Red Delicious on a hillside near Wenatchee, Washington. And while it's nice to get a box in the mail with "Rogue River Pears" stamped on its side, filling the box yourself is something else entirely. ■ All things considered, there's just no substitute for being there. ■ *There,* in this case, is the Pacific Northwest, a land of unparalleled plenty. In the following pages, we take you on a rich travel and food tour of the region's best farmland produce stands and hottest oyster bars. Along the way, you'll meet a few of the people who have made the Northwest the food mecca that it is—from restaurateurs to bakers to fishmongers. ■ So sit back and enjoy this vicarious visit to some of the best food regions of Oregon, Washington, and British Columbia. Or better yet, experience it for yourself.

*Smallwood's Harvest near Leavenworth,
Washington, one of six bountiful Northwest
regions described on pages 164–169.*

BRINGING HOME
THE HARVEST

Oregon

*Another day in paradise: The Goldbergs pick the last of
the Fortyniner peaches at their Valley View Orchard.*

ROGUE RIVER

■ You can't drive through Ashland and Medford without noticing the orchards that hug Interstate 5. A century ago, apples held sway here, but pears have been the money crop since World War I. Apples, however, are making a small comeback, and wine grapes may be the crop of the future.

At the valley's fruit stands, you'll also find apricots, nectarines, peaches, and a full range of vegetables.

If you like to pick your own fruit, start at **Valley View Orchard,** where the view is almost as good as the fruit and fresh cider. *1800 N. Valley View Rd., Ashland; (541) 488-2840.*

In Medford, the **Harry and David Country Village** retail store, in a shopping center just south of exit 27 off I-5, offers almost every kind of fruit you can imagine. If you plan to take fruit back to California, this is a good place to buy: show California agricultural inspectors a Harry and David receipt and they'll wave you through unless you have cherries, which are not allowed. *1314 Center Dr., Suite A, Medford; (541) 776-2277.*

From Medford, take Jacksonville Highway (State 238) west 2½ miles to **White's Country Farm,** where you can buy everything from local honey to White's own pies. They grow their own peaches and most of their sweet corn and salad crops, and import some scrumptiously sweet melons from Dillard and Hermiston. *4017 Jacksonville Hwy., Medford; (541) 773-8031.*

WHERE

To start at Valley View Orchard, take exit 19 from I-5 just north of Ashland,

Chris Knox and White's Country Farm stock everything from honey to pies.

head north up the hill about 1½ miles, and follow the signs to the orchard.

LODGING

In Ashland, try the **Peerless Hotel** *(800/460-8758)* in the railroad district, or find a bed-and-breakfast through the B & B Clearinghouse *(800/588-0338).* For a good hotel, try **Windmill's Ashland Hills Inn & Suites** *(800/547-4747)* in Ashland or the **Rogue Regency Inn** *(800/535-5805)* in Medford. For other Medford choices, call the Visitors and Convention Bureau *(800/469-6307).*

TRAVEL NOTES: "Dillard" melons are worth a word. Originally meaning grown at Dillard, near Roseburg, the appellation now applies to any melons grown in that part of the Umpqua River Valley. Because these melons are vine-ripened, they're extra-sweet but don't have a long shelf life. As a result, they're sold only in Oregon, chiefly at fruit stands where they can be marketed immediately after harvest. You can taste them at the source by stopping at Kruse Farms Produce Stand in Roseburg. Exit I-5 at Garden Valley Rd. (exit 125), and go west 2½ miles, then left on Melrose Rd. to the stand.

WILLAMETTE VALLEY

■ Wandering the Willamette Valley almost anywhere, you'll stumble over plenty of good fruit stands. The problem is in narrowing the field.

In the north-central valley, several stands cluster between Woodburn and Salem east of I-5. Start at **Bauman Farms,** where you'll find berries, nectarines, peaches, plums, and many kinds of vegetables. *12989 Howell Prairie Rd. N.E., Gervais; (503) 792-3524.*

While you're there, pick up an "Oregon Trail Farms Direct Market Association" guide, which leads you stand by stand south to Salem.

At the south end of the valley, in Junction City, **Thistledown Farms** and **Lone Pine Farms** grow most of the fruits, nuts, and vegetables they sell. Both replenish their stocks by harvesting daily, and offer free copies of the Lane County "Fresh Produce Buyer's Guide," which maps stands all over the county. *Thistledown Farms, 91455 River Rd., Junction City; (541) 689-2019. Lone Pine Farms, 91909 River Rd., Junction City; 688-4389.*

In the wine country around McMinnville, try one of the area's biggest fruit stands, **Laube Orchards** in Dayton, which sells its own fresh-picked produce and its neighbor's wines (Sokol Blosser Winery is right across the street). *18400 N. Hwy. 99W; (503) 864-2672.*

And just off U.S. 20 between Albany and Corvallis, stop by **Twedt's Willamettedale Farms.** For 36 years, Homer Twedt has been growing almost everything he sells. *2015 N.E. Seavy Ave., Corvallis; (541) 757-7814.*

WHERE

To start the more northern loop, exit I-5 at Woodburn (about 30 miles south of Portland), drive east about 2 miles on State 214 to State 99E, then go south 3 miles to Howell Prairie Rd. N.E., and left ½ mile to Bauman Farms.

To start the more southern route, take I-105 west 3 miles from I-5 to Eugene, exit at River Rd., and drive north to Junction City.

LODGING

In Eugene, try **Campbell House, A City Inn** *(800/264-2519),* which is a B & B in a restored 1892 building, or the **Valley River Inn** *(800/543-8266),* a hotel. To look further, try one of the valley's visitor associations: Lane County *(800/547-5445; http://www.cvalco.org),* Albany *(800/526-2256),* Corvallis *(800/334-8118),* or Salem *(800/874-7012; http://www.oregonlink.com/scva/).*

TRAVEL NOTES: The Willamette Valley also delights gardeners. Many of its specialized nurseries aren't far off the routes listed here. From August until the first frost, dahlias set growing fields ablaze with vibrant color.

Washington

The Wenatchee River accompanies U.S. Highway 2/97 out of Leavenworth, meandering through the region's rich farmlands.

LEAVENWORTH AND WENATCHEE

■ From the Seattle area, it's just over a two-hour drive to Leavenworth, whose Bavarian architecture, geranium-filled window boxes, and steep mountains really give it a European ambience.

As you roll into town on U.S. Highway 2, stop at **Alpine Coffees Northwest Gourmet** (just beyond the first traffic light) for a cup of fresh-roasted Valley Apple coffee. This blend of Colombian beans and Wenatchee apples should put you in the right frame of mind for cruising fruit stands. *Ninth St. and U.S. 2, Leavenworth; (800) 246-2761.*

South of Leavenworth, the valley opens into a quiltwork of orchards. After a little more than a mile, look on the right for **Prey's Fruit Barn,** which has built its reputation on tree fruit (30 kinds of apples, 15 of pears, for example). Prey's should have early apples and pears this month. Feel free to picnic under the trees beside the barn. *11007 Hwy. 2; (509) 548-5771.*

Just down the road, you'll come to **Smallwood's Harvest** and its trademark white farmhouse, windmill, and

flying flags. With llamas on the left, fruit trees on the right, and boxes of fruit and melons set artfully among the stand's antiques, this place could have been designed by Disney. Try fruit from the family's own orchards and vegetables from nearby farms; the Quincy-grown watermelons are especially good this month. *U.S. 2 at Stemm Rd., Peshastin; (509) 548-4196.*

From here, continue south toward Wenatchee and U.S. 97 north. **B & B Fruit Stand** is strong on local stone fruits and has great access. *3148 Hwy. 2/97, East Wenatchee; (509) 884-2522.*

Just 3 miles north of the U.S. 2/97 bridge across the Columbia River near Wenatchee is **Feil Fruit Stand,** which has been in Jack Feil's family for 70 years. They grow and tree-ripen almost

everything they sell. *13083 Hwy. 2/97, East Wenatchee; (509) 884-7570.*

WHERE

From I-5 in Everett, take U.S. 2 west 100 miles to Leavenworth to begin your journey. The stands listed are within 25 miles of Leavenworth on U.S. 2 and U.S. 2/97.

LODGING

Most of the best lodging choices are in Leavenworth. If you like the idea of being lodged in a perfect alpine chalet, try **Abendblume** (800/669-7634, or 509/ 548-4059 in Canada). For a beautiful riverside B & B, call **Run of the River** (800/288-6491). Or just call **Bedfinders** (800/323-2920), which can place you in almost any kind of lodging you want, from vacation house to hotel.

TRAVEL NOTES: Once you reach Wenatchee, orchards line the Columbia and Okanogan rivers all the way to Canada (more about the Okanagan Valley in Canada on page 168). It takes about 2½ hours to get to the border on U.S. 97. If you want less commitment but a stunning drive, follow the Columbia to Pateros, then go northwest up the Methow Valley and back to I-5 over U.S. 20.

■ The sere sagebrush-covered hills between Ellensburg and Yakima don't hint at the richness of the land that lies just beyond Yakima to the east. Explore it on a loop that follows the flat, rich bottomland southeast to Prosser, then returns along the Roza Canal—the base of the orchard- and vineyard-covered Rattlesnake Hills.

As you head down U.S. 97 from Yakima, you can choose from 70 varieties of peppers and other kinds of produce at **Kreuger Family Peppers** *(462 Knights Lane, Wapato; 509/877-3677),* or a broad range of vegetables at **Schell Farms** *(10 Harris Rd., Toppenish; 509/865-4511).*

For a treat, head southeast on State 22 to Prosser to visit the **Chukar Cherry Company** tasting room, where you can have your cherries or berries dried or chocolate-coated. *320 Wine Country Rd., Prosser; (509) 786-2055.*

To return to Yakima, take I-82 and stop in Sunnyside for a self-guided tour of **Darigold Dairy Fair.** You can see how cheese is made and pick up some extra-sharp cheddar or hand-dipped ice cream. *400 Alexander Rd., Sunnyside; (509) 837-4321.*

Wind up at **Donald Fruit and Mer-** *cantile* near Wapato, where fruits, vegetables, fresh peach sundaes, and tart cider are sold from a memorabilia-packed emporium. *Exit 44 off I-82; (509) 877-3115.*

WHERE

Start in Yakima at Washington's Fruit Place Visitor Center at 105 S. 18th St. (From the Yakima Ave. exit—33 or 33B—off I-82, go east on Yakima Ave. to 18th St., then right a block to the center.) While you're here, get the "Yakima Valley Farm Products Guide," which leads you to 26 farm-related stops. Also pick up "Yakima Valley Wine Tour" (or get a copy by calling 800/258-7270, or 509/786-1304 in Canada), which lists 26 wineries, as well as local lodging and dining suggestions. *9–5 Mon-Fri, 10–5 Sat, 12–4 Sun. (509) 576-3090.*

LODGING

For families, the **Doubletree Hotel Yakima Valley** *(509/248-7850)* in Yakima is a good choice (the kids will appreciate the pools). Its restaurant features local wines. In Prosser, the **Wine Country Inn** *(509/786-2855)* is a good place to stay or stop for a meal (lunch Mon-Sat, dinner Wed-Sat).

TRULY FRESH PRODUCE?

just ask

Many fruit stands started out like suburban lemonade stands: somebody's kids made a few dollars by the side of the road selling whatever the family farm produced.

Now the stands are permanent, and extras abound: you'll find petting zoos outside many stands, and everything from honey to bananas inside—and obviously those bananas came from Guayaquil, Ecuador, not Granger, Washington.

If you want only fresh, local, top-quality fruit, you'll need to taste some samples and ask some questions.

IS IT FRESH?
Most fruit varieties mature over a short season, but many have a remarkably long storage life. Make sure you're getting this year's harvest. An extra-low price can tip you off to fruit that's been in cold storage for months.

IS IT LOCAL?
Though imported and homegrown fruit can be identical varieties, the local crop is more likely to be field- or tree-ripened, since it can be sold immediately. Fruit destined for storage or export is picked earlier (greener) for longer shelf life.

IS IT TOP-QUALITY?
A few fruit stands sell mostly second-quality produce they buy from packing houses. Usually bruised, split on one end, misshapen, or off-size, this fruit may be fine for juicing, canning, or pies. But if you want quality, you're more likely to find it at a stand that sells from surrounding farms. Pay attention to grading—some stands sort and grade fruit and some sell orchard-run fruit: ungraded, it includes a random sampling of everything in the orchard.

Feil Fruit Stand near Wenatchee has been in business for more than 70 years— long enough to forgo the formalities.

TRAVEL NOTES: The site of the Yakama Nation Cultural Heritage Center (509/865-2800), Toppenish also preserves the Yakima Valley's colorful cowboy heritage in its historically accurate murals. All are done by Western artists; signs point the way. Check out the Toppenish Western Art Show (Aug. 22–24).

BRINGING HOME THE HARVEST

British Columbia

SAANICH PENINSULA

■ Think of Victoria, B.C., and flower gardens—like Butchart Gardens—come to mind. Yet minutes from Butchart, produce blankets the Saanich Peninsula on Vancouver Island. And farm stands dot the roads, marked by colorful "BCgrown" signs.

A mile east of Provincial Highway 17, you'll find **Michell Brothers,** with raspberries, vegetables, and great water and territorial views. *3047 Island View Rd.; (250) 652-2100.*

Nearby, **Firbank Farms** sells fresh eggs, cut flowers, and more. *2834 Island View; 652-0016.*

Go west and you'll find **Silver Rill Corn,** where more than 20 kinds of sweet corn are grown. Picked fresh daily, it is so sweet that, sampled raw, it tastes like candy. *7117 Central Saanich Rd., north of Island View; 652-3854.*

South of here, the cheery red-and-white-checked stands of **Oldfield Orchard and Market** are loaded with apples, peaches, strawberries, and plenty of vegetables. *6286 Oldfield Rd.; 652-1579.*

Across the road, **Stewart's Berry Patch** has blueberries, raspberries, strawberries, and tayberries, as well as other varieties. *6283 Oldfield; 652-6768.*

North of Sidney, **Hazelmere Farm Market** offers a wide variety of lettuces, fresh herbs, and apples, and does well with dried flowers. *11368 W. Saanich Rd.; 655-8887.*

WHERE

From Victoria, take Patricia Bay Hwy. (Hwy. 17) north and watch for Island View Rd., which lies to the east. This area—the midpeninsula—has dozens of producers and is a good place to start.

LODGING

To enrich your farm experience, stay at **Fairburn Farm Country Manor** *(250/*

Maureen and Robin Herlinveaux, owners of Hazelmere Farm Market on the Saanich Peninsula, specialize in apples, dried flowers, and herbs.

746-4637), a 130-acre working farm southwest of Duncan. For more lodging, call Tourism Victoria *(800/663-3883).*

OKANAGAN VALLEY

■ Because of Canada's climate, a huge part of its agriculture is represented along its southern border. From Osoyoos north through Penticton, Summer-land, Kelowna, and Vernon, determined farmers coax astounding quantities of tree fruits, vegetables, and wine grapes from every speck of arable land—and all of this in lake-filled valleys surrounded by high mountains, cliffs, and granite domes.

Orchards, wineries, and fruit stands pack the 105-mile (about 165 km.) stretch between the international bor-

TRAVEL NOTES: Pick up a farm guide from the Ministry of Agriculture office, from the concierge at the Empress Hotel in Victoria, or at your first farm stand stop. Extend your farm trails exploration by going north to the Cowichan Valley for a day trip or an overnight. You'll find wineries and a cidery, as well as more farms to explore. Do a circle by taking the Brentwood Bay–Mill Bay Ferry (25 minutes) to the valley, then making the one-hour drive on the Trans-Canada Highway back to Victoria. First Island Tours offers one-day wine tours of the valley. $125 Canadian. (250) 658-5367. For maps, a farm trail, and winery information, travelers can stop at any town's B.C. Visitor Information Centre, or at the Osoyoos Visitor Information Centre (250/495-7142, or 888/676-9667 in Canada) at the junction of Hwy. 97 and Hwy. 3 in Osoyoos.

der and Vernon along Provincial Highway 97. It's more helpful here to think in terms of fruit stand regions than of individual stands. For example, many of the biggest and best stands are grouped along fruit stand row in the Similkameen Valley (Hwy. 3) around Keremeos and Cawston. You can do the trip in a nice loop from Osoyoos up Highways 3 and 3A, then back to Highway 97 a few miles south of Penticton; the total diversion adds just 30 minutes to the drive from the border to Penticton.

WHERE

It's a four-hour drive from Vancouver to Kelowna via the Trans-Canada Hwy. (Hwy. 1) to Hope, the Coquihalla Hwy. (Hwy. 5; $10 toll) to Merritt, and the Okanagan Connector (Hwy. 97C) the rest of the way. If you take the southern route (Trans-Canada Hwy. and Hwy. 3), it's six hours. If you're coming from Seattle, add two hours to these times, or take the six-hour trip via Wenatchee and U.S. 97.

LODGING

Summer is the high season here, with numerous festivals and gatherings that can pack hotels. The Okanagan Similkameen Tourism Association *(250/860-5999)* can send you a list of accommodations and various festival dates. Or check the association's Web site: *http://travel.bc.ca/region/ok.* ◆

Suzanne Barton of Firbank Farms shows off two items the farm sells all year.

To market, to market …

… to buy a fat fig. Eight farmers' markets that offer the Northwest's fresh-picked bounty at its peak

It wasn't all that long ago that farmers' markets were somewhat scruffy affairs, relegated to the parking lots and side streets of Western towns and cities. But today's farmers' markets are upscale and ubiquitous—some even run year-round.

OREGON

Beaverton. The Beaverton Farmers' Market is strictly a horticultural and agricultural market. It features seafood, lamb, and fresh goat cheese.
- *Where:* On Hall Blvd. between Third and Fifth streets.
- *When:* 3–7 Wed, through September; 8–1:30 Sat, through October.
- *Contact:* (503) 643-5345.

Eugene. Seventy percent of the Lane County Farmers' Market's 40 booths sell organic or pesticide-free fruits and vegetables. This month two kinds of wild huckleberries are available; visit in the fall for boletes, chanterelles, and oyster mushrooms.
- *Where:* At Eighth Ave. and Oak St.
- *When:* 10–4 Tue, through mid-October; 9–5 Sat, through mid-November.
- *Contact:* (541) 686-8885.

Hood River. The Farmers in the Park market has 30 booths. Gravenstein Apple Days festival is August 23–24.
- *Where:* Jackson Park.
- *When:* 9–2 Sat, through October.
- *Contact:* (541) 354-2565.

Portland. About 50 farmers and vendors hawk wild mushrooms, huckleberries, and more than a dozen kinds of tomatoes. Tomato sampling is September 6 during the Harvest Festival.
- *Where:* 1200 N.W. Front Ave.
- *When:* 8–1 Sat, through October 25. Also at Pioneer Court House Square, 11–3 Wed, through September.
- *Contact:* (503) 705-2460.

WASHINGTON

Olympia. One of Washington's largest markets, the Olympia Farmers' Market boasts three bakery stalls as well as a wide array of seafood. Woodworkers, tile artisans, and silversmiths figure among the many craftspeople.
- *Where:* At the foot of Capitol Way, six blocks north of the capitol.
- *When:* 10–3 Thu-Sun, May-September; 10–3 Fri-Sun in October.
- *Contact:* (360) 352-9096.

Seattle. The University District Farmers Market is one of the youngest and most successful markets in the Seattle area, drawing students, urbanites, and anyone who appreciates the five different kinds of bok choy the market's Laotian farmers provide.
- *Where:* University Way at N.E. 50th St.
- *When:* 9–2 Sat, June-October.
- *Contact:* (206) 633-1024.

Spokane. The six-year-old Spokane MarketPlace has moved to a permanent shelter, where it operates year-round.
- *Where:* 1202 W. First Ave. (at Jefferson St.) near the Davenport Hotel.
- *When:* 9–5 Wed, Fri, Sat; 10–4 Sun.
- *Contact:* (509) 482-2627.

Vancouver. In summer the market swells with berries, corn, melons, tomatoes, and several kinds of peppers you can have roasted on the spot. The market celebrates its seventh anniversary August 16 with live music and games for children.
- *Where:* At Fifth St. and Broadway.
- *When:* 9–3 Sat, through October.
- *Contact:* (360) 737-8298.

FOR MORE INFORMATION

Roadside Stands and Farmers' Markets: A Travel Guide to Westcoast Produce, by Sandra Fuller and Annette McCormick Gierke (Creekside Publishing, Scotts Mills, OR, 1997; $14.95 plus $4.95 shipping), lists more than 350 farmers' markets in Washington, Oregon, and California. To order a copy, call (503) 873-2021. ◆

by **CHRISTINE COLASURDO**

heaven
ON A
half-shell

*An eater's guide to Washington's favorite oyster towns, oyster
bars, and oyster stew—plus an oyster tasting in Seattle*

■ For some of us, few things are more sublime than the
act of popping a raw, ice-cold oyster into the mouth, biting down once or twice, and then letting the partially
masticated creature slip down the throat. For others,
well … that sentence probably sent them fleeing. ■ Now
that we've cleared the room of nonbelievers, let's talk
oysters, by which we generally mean Pacific oysters, a
species native to Japan that now dominates the fishery.
Unlike Washington's native oyster, the Olympia, which
takes four years to reach the size of a quarter, Pacifics
grow fast and fat, and have the chameleon-like ability to
take on the character of the waters in which they're
raised. In recent years other species—Kumamotos from
Japan and European Flats—have become more plentiful. And perhaps most promising of all is the prolifera-
tion of nonspawning triploid Pacifics, which have
turned the food into a year-round pleasure. ■ So raise a
glass to the Washington oyster. But put away the champagne—this celebration calls for a beer.

CRAIG HARROLD

*Washington oysters, clockwise
from top in pairs: tiny native
Olympias, European Flats,
Kumamotos, and Pacifics.*

PHIL SCHOFIELD

Oysters are harvested when the tide is out, rain or shine, day or night, which is why Jeffrey Delia sometimes finds himself gathering oysters on his Dabob Bay beds by the light of a propane-fed flame.

oyster hangouts

From historic seaside spots
to upscale urban restaurants

COUNTRY OYSTER HOUSES

Oyster Bar. In the early '30s, it was just one more roadside oyster shack on Chuckanut Drive. Today entrées include crispy fried oysters with an herb-parmesan crust and a lightly tart apple aioli. Open daily for dinner; entrées $16–$29. *240 Chuckanut Dr. (exit 231 from I-5), Bow; (360) 766-6185.*

Oyster Creek Inn. North of the Oyster Bar sits this cozy cafe, which overlooks a wooded ravine above Oyster Creek. Bowls of oyster crackers and bottles of Tabasco sauce on the tables lend a casual air. Open 12–9 daily; entrées $10–$27. *190 Chuckanut, Bow; 766-6179.*

Longhorn Saloon & Oyster Bar. Don't let the pool tables fool you: chef Geoff Clark serves oysters on the half-shell with accents of ginger and lime; pesto, capers, and

The day's catch at the Brooklyn Seafood, Steak & Oyster House.

onion; or Thai sweet basil with raspberry vinaigrette. Open Tue-Sun for lunch and dinner; entrées $6–$15. *574 Cains Court, Edison; 766-6330.*

Xinh's Clam & Oyster House. This restaurant features the Pacific Rim–influenced creations of oyster-shucking champion Xinh Dwelley. The sautéed Pacifics with black-bean sauce and jasmine rice are heaven. Open Tue-Sat for dinner; entrées $8–$16. *221 W. Railroad Ave., Suite D, Shelton; 427-8709.*

Lonny's Restaurant. Though

Oysters grow on cultch, which is anything the oyster attaches itself to. Jeffrey Delia grows some of his oysters on lengths of plastic pipe.

LAND OF THE PE

Some folks swear by Quilcene ...

■ Pacific oysters are prolific throughout coastal Washington, but they really seem to thrive on Hood Canal, especially in Quilcene and Dabob bays at the canal's northern end.

This is not just my opinion. Two of the biggest shellfish companies in the world, Coast Seafoods and Taylor United, have oyster hatcheries here. They know that Dabob Bay is one of only three places on the West Coast where an oyster farmer can reliably collect wild oyster seed.

Jeffrey Delia and Kirk Lakenes know this, too. But unlike Coast and Taylor, which breed oyster larvae in a lab and farm thousands of acres of tidelands to produce millions of oysters per year, their companies, Delia's Broadspit Oyster Company and Lakenes's Hood Canal Seafood, cultivate mere handfuls of acres each.

"The waters here are clean and cold, producing a sweet-tasting oyster," says Delia. "To me, it's the last holdout," he adds, referring to both his home and his oysterman lifestyle.

The late Robert Canterbury Sr., the man most people credit with putting Quilcene oysters on the map, also liked to call what he did for a living a lifestyle. For decades, he harvested oysters on 50 acres of Quilcene Bay tidelands down at the end of Linger Longer Road.

From the beginning, the name was synonymous with an oyster of exceptional quality. Canterbury Quilcenes were served in the finest restaurants of the day, from Jake's in Portland (still going strong) to Rosellini's legendary Other Place in Seattle. Canterbury copyrighted the family name, and for a while some people thought a Canterbury was actually a species of oyster.

Like Canterbury, Delia has made his contribution to the oyster lexicon. Delia started farming oysters about 21 years ago; 16 years ago, he started selling his oysters as Quilcenes, even though his tidelands are actually on Dabob Bay. The name stuck.

"In reality, it's not true," says Canterbury's son, Ray, "but the bays are very similar. It would probably take a scientist to tell the difference between the oysters. The word Quilcene sells." Still.

Delia's Quilcene oysters are available from all fishmongers at Seattle's Pike Place Market. Lakenes's oysters can be bought at Hood Canal Seafood Marketplace in Quilcene, open 10–9 daily in summer. 294963 Highway 101; (360) 765-4880. — Ben Marks

Dan Driscoll displays a basket of Pacifics, which owe their flavor to the pristine waters—and mud—of Willapa Bay.

RFECT OYSTER?

...Others say it's Oysterville

■ My mom is wrong. She taught me how to eat raw oysters, but we disagree on technique. I say slurp them right out of the shell. She likes hers on a saltine. But we do agree on one thing—the best oysters come from Willapa Bay on Washington's Pacific Coast.

Oysters have been grown commercially in the bay's chilly, shallow waters for more than a century. Oysterville got wealthy on oysters. Many of its mansions were built with money made from Oysterville Gold, a reference to the oysters that were shipped to post–Gold Rush San Francisco to feed the newly rich and hungry.

Oyster farms are still sprinkled around Willapa Bay. Oysterville Sea Farms, housed in a rickety old shingled building that is listed on the National Register of Historic Places, has been in one family for three generations.

Dan Driscoll runs it now, and he's typical of local oyster farmers. He understands, respects, and loves his oysters. "Water quality is the pivotal factor," Driscoll says. "As far as I'm concerned, there is no such thing as a bad oyster. As long as it's grown in good water and it's fresh."

Clean water has kept the fishery alive. Mud, it turns out, has also helped. As businesses sprang up along the Columbia River and in Grays Harbor and Puget Sound, Willapa Bay was passed over because it was too shallow for industrial development. Instead, homesteaders settled here, fishing the bay and working the land. Later, well-to-do Oregonians from Portland and Astoria came here to build summer homes. As a result, the bay has stayed pretty much pollution-free.

The oysters from this clean, cold water have a complex flavor. Bite into a Willapa Bay oyster and the first thing you taste is salt (which is one reason I can do without the saltine), followed by a sweetness in the meat. Like a perfect summer watermelon, a Willapa Bay oyster can provoke one of the best food memories your synapses will ever transmit.

In fact, the taste is almost the easiest part. Says Driscoll, "The biggest battle of my business has been to keep the building standing."

Oysterville Sea Farms is on the Oysterville waterfront at the junction of First and Clark streets. It's open 10–5 daily June-September, weekends during the winter; (360) 665-6585 or http://www.leonardo.net/oysterville/oyseafarm.html. — Steven R. Lorton

not a true oyster house, it is the home of Lonny's Oyster Stew (see recipe on page 175) and has a rotating roster of oyster-based specials. Open Wed-Mon for dinner; entrées $8–$20. *2330 Washington St., Port Townsend; 385-0700.*

URBAN OYSTER BARS

Fish House in Stanley Park. Features fresh Royal Miyagis (Pacifics) from Pendrell Sound. *8901 Stanley Park Dr., Vancouver, B.C.; (604) 681-7275.*

Anthony's HomePort, Shilshole Bay. Home of the Oyster Olympics, held each spring. *6135 Seaview Ave. N.W., Seattle; (206) 783-0780.*

Brooklyn Seafood, Steak & Oyster House. Where the financial district goes for oysters on the half-shell. *1212 Second Ave. (at University St.), Seattle; 224-7000.*

Elliott's Oyster House and Seafood Restaurant. In summer, Elliott's imports oysters from South America. *At Pier 56, Seattle; 623-4340.*

F. X. McRory's Steak, Chop & Oyster House. Serving fresh-shucked oysters in the shadow of the Kingdome since 1977. *419 Occidental Ave. S., Seattle; 623-4800.*

Patrons at the Brooklyn's oyster bar.

Shuckers. Easily the most romantic oyster bar in town. In the Four Seasons Olympic Hotel. *411 University, Seattle; 621-1984.*

Dan & Louis' Oyster Bar. Its owners were once the biggest growers of Kumos on the West Coast; today this bar packs 'em in at lunch for its famous Yaquina Oyster Stew. *208 S.W. Ankeny St., Portland; (503) 227-5906.*

Jake's Famous Crawfish. A classic downtown fish house. *401 S.W. 12th Ave. (at S.W. Stark St.), Portland; 226-1419.* — Jena MacPherson

oyster tasting

■ So what's the best oyster in Washington? In a recent tasting at Anthony's Pier 66 in downtown Seattle, we posed that question to *Sunset* food editor Jerry Anne Di Vecchio, seafood marketer Jon Rowley, and four oyster shuckers from some of Seattle's best oyster bars—Chaz Johnson from the Brooklyn, Al Johnson from Anthony's Pier 66, Karen Matuschak from F. X. McRory's Steak, Chop & Oyster House, and Ethan Rossow from Elliott's. They tasted Pacific oysters from Discovery Bay, Dabob Bay, Hood Canal, Samish Bay, Totten Inlet, and Willapa Bay. Then for comparison, they tasted Olympias, Kumamotos, and European Flats.

CRAIG HARROLD (5)

Oyster shuckers and aficionados meet for a taste-test at Anthony's Pier 66.

THE RESULTS

■ Among the Pacifics there was no clear winner, though Delia's oysters from Dabob Bay and the Snow Creek oysters from Discovery Bay got two first-place votes each. Four tasters liked the oysters from Samish Bay least, though another rated them best for the same reason the others rated them the worst—pronounced salt flavor. To each his own oyster.

Pacific (Crassostrea gigas)

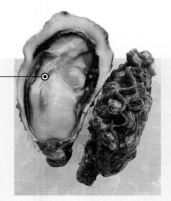

- *Description:* The large Pacific oyster, the most harvested and consumed oyster in the world, is a native of Japan, but has been harvested here since 1919. Like wine grapes, Pacifics have different characteristics depending on where they're grown. For example, Samish Bay oysters have wide, almost fan-shaped shells. Hood Canal oysters are smaller and straighter, with deep cups. And oysters raised in southern Puget Sound can get enormous, with an elongated shape that is greatly prized in Hong Kong and other Asian markets.
- *Availability:* Year-round. (Hatchery-bred triploid oysters are available from June through September, when Pacifics normally spawn.)
- *Taste:* Samish Bay oysters tend to be salty, Hood Canal oysters are sweet, and oysters raised in southern Puget Sound and Willapa Bay are pleasantly redolent of algae and mud.
- *Total 1996 production:* About 3,000,000 dozen.

Kumamoto (Crassostrea sikamea)

- *Description:* The medium-size Kumo, as it's called, is the hottest oyster on the market. Like the Pacific, it's a native of Japan; it wasn't cultivated in Washington until the '50s. Ironically, Kumos have disappeared entirely from the Kumamoto Prefecture in Japan, for which they are named.
- *Availability:* December-August.
- *Taste:* Sweet and buttery—the perfect oyster for beginners.
- *Total 1996 production:* About 400,000 dozen.

Olympia (Ostrea lurida)

- *Description:* The tiny Olympia oyster is the only oyster species native to the Pacific Coast. Overharvesting and pollution from pulp mills almost caused the Olympia to go extinct in the late '50s, but the past couple of decades have brought cleaner water and improvements in harvesting techniques, which in turn have enabled the fishery to make a significant recovery.
- *Availability:* December-May.
- *Taste:* Salty, slightly metallic.
- *Total 1996 production:* About 50,000 dozen.

European Flat (Ostrea edulis)

- *Description:* The European Flat oyster, sometimes referred to as a Belon, was introduced to the state during the '50s. It has a rounder shell than Pacifics and Kumos, and its medium size has made it popular with half-shell enthusiasts.
- *Availability:* October-June.
- *Taste:* Sweet and metallic.
- *Total 1996 production:* Less than 30,000 dozen.

getting sauced

■ When raw oysters are really fresh, why gild the lily? Well, it's all a matter of taste, and if you are ready to move beyond bottled cocktail sauce, try any of these potions.

•Asian balsamic

Combine equal parts **balsamic vinegar** and **soy sauce**, then stir in thinly sliced **green onions**.

•Gingered vinegar

Combine 4 parts **rice vinegar** and 1 part **Asian fish sauce** (*nuoc mam* or *nam pla*), ¼ teaspoon minced **fresh ginger** for each tablespoon of vinegar, and enough **sugar** to mellow the mixture's sharpness.

•Shallot and black pepper vinaigrette

Combine 4 parts **white wine vinegar,** 2 parts **water,** and 1 part minced **shallots**. Add a generous grinding of **black pepper.**

•Green chili–cucumber salsa

Combine 6 parts finely diced **cucumber,** 2 parts **seasoned rice vinegar,** and 1 part *each* minced **fresh cilantro** and minced **fresh jalapeño chilies.**

•Horseradish and chives

Combine 6 to 8 parts **lemon juice** and 1 part *each* **prepared horseradish** and finely chopped **chives** or green onion tops.

•Lime with red chilies

Combine 2 parts *each* **lime juice** and **Asian fish sauce,** 1 part minced **fresh ginger,** and ½ teaspoon **sugar** for each tablespoon lime juice. Then add **hot chili flakes** to taste.

— *Jerry Anne Di Vecchio*

NOEL BARNHURST

Some like it hot: Lonny's Oyster Stew is seasoned with pancetta, fennel, and anise-flavor liqueur.

Lonny's Oyster Stew

■ Lonny Ritter, owner of Lonny's Restaurant in Port Townsend, knows a can't-miss recipe when he sees it. As one *Sunset* recipe tester put it, "Pancetta, leeks, fennel, and oysters: What's not to like?"

Prep and cook time: 20 to 25 minutes

Makes: 6 servings

¼	pound **pancetta** or bacon
2	**leeks** (¾ in. thick), white parts only
2	heads (3 in. wide) **fennel**
1	teaspoon crushed **fennel seed**
6	cups **half-and-half** (light cream) or 2% milk
3	jars (10 oz. each) **shucked oysters** and their liquor (4 cups total)
¾	cup chopped **Italian parsley**
1	tablespoon **Pernod,** Sambuca, or other anise-flavor liqueur (not sweet)
	Fresh-ground **black pepper**
	Salt
1	to 2 tablespoons **butter** or margarine

1. Cut pancetta into ¼-inch dice. Put in a 5- to 6-quart pan.

2. Trim and discard root ends from leeks, then rinse well and chop.

3. Trim and discard tops, root ends, and bruised spots from fennel, then rinse and chop.

4. Add leeks, fennel, and fennel seed to pancetta and stir often over medium-high heat until limp but not browned, about 5 minutes.

5. Add cream and oysters and their liquor and turn heat to medium-high. Stir often just until soup is hot but not boiling, about 4 minutes.

6. Stir in ½ cup parsley, liqueur, and pepper and salt to taste.

7. Ladle into bowls and sprinkle equally with remaining parsley, then add a dot of butter to each.

Per serving: 539 cal., 65% (351 cal.) from fat; 21 g protein; 39 g fat (21 g sat.); 25 g carbo (1.5 g fiber); 556 mg sodium; 178 mg chol. ◆

O pioneers!

The Pacific Northwest just may have the best food in the nation.
Meet six of the tastemakers who shaped this
triumphant regional cuisine

by SCHUYLER INGLE

photographs by FRANCE RUFFENACH

■ Each year the Pacific Northwest's Native Americans celebrate the coming of First Salmon—chosen symbol of all the fat, hook-nosed chinook salmon that arrive at the mouth of the Columbia River. First Salmon's return is a signal that winter has ended and spring returned to shake off wet skies the color of cutlery. It has always been this way in the Pacific Northwest. Good food floods the region—stone fruits and berries, greens and root vegetables, new potatoes stolen from volcanic soil, game birds and venison, lamb and pork and beef, wild mushrooms, and the abundance of the sea—it's like a table set for a feast. ■ But it wasn't until relatively recently that creative cooks, restaurateurs, and growers and sellers of food came together to sing a culinary song distinct to the Northwest. Beginning in the late 1970s, these pioneers began to import food ideas from Asia and Europe and make them their own, using the region's bounty to speak with a common voice, saying, "Here in this place, this is the way it is, this is how it smells and tastes." It is a process that continues today and will continue well past tomorrow. ■ In the following pages are but six of the pioneers who have shaped the Pacific Northwest way with food. Master chefs, a baker, a seller of seafood, a brewer of coffee, and a maker of brandies—all have helped to create a regional cuisine unmatched by any in the country. ■ For the Pacific Northwest is an overflowing cornucopia. The magic happens where the cook and the bounteous food come together. When people in the Pacific Northwest gather, they make exciting food happen. It can be a simple meal among family and friends, or a feast celebrating the return of First Salmon. Whether feast or snack, there's no mistaking where you are.

GWENYTH BASSETTI
GRAND CENTRAL BAKERY

■

For two days this summer, Grand Central Bakery gave away silver dollar–size rolls for free. The bakery was celebrating its birth 25 years ago, when Gwenyth Bassetti and two partners opened a shop in Seattle's Pioneer Square. Called the Bakery, it was the '70s personified, featuring whole-grain pan breads that exemplified the era's love of hearty natural foods.

In 1988, after a hiatus that included breeding national champion sheep, Bassetti came back to refocus the Bakery, which had gotten a little dowdy. She changed its name to Grand Central Bakery. And, inspired by Carol Field's seminal cookbook, *The Italian Baker,* she handed Seattle a whole new world of Old World bread—slow-rising, hand-formed loaves that could have been baked in a wood-fired brick oven in a French or Italian village.

> **We were overwhelmed by requests for bread.**

"The minute we started, we were overwhelmed by requests for bread," Bassetti recalls. The scene at the bakery looked like a page out of the old Soviet Union, with customers lined up out the door. The limit in those early days was two loaves per customer.

Today, Grand Central Bakery has branched out to Portland, where it's called Grand Central Baking Company, and Bassetti's son Ben Davis runs the show. Together the bakeries put out 10,000 pounds of bread a day, for retail and restaurant customers alike. Each and every loaf is made with natural ingredients and formed by hand—and they still rise as slowly as possible for that incredible flavor.

Grand Central Bakery. *214 First Ave. S., Seattle; (206) 622-3644. 138 107th Ave. N.E., Bellevue; (425) 454-9661.*

Grand Central Baking Company. *2230 S.E. Hawthorne Blvd., Portland; (503) 232-0575. 3425 S.W. Multnomah Blvd., Portland; (503) 977-2024. 1444 N.E. Weidler St., Portland; (503) 288-1614.*

Flour power: Seattle's doyenne of dough, Gwenyth Bassetti, brought European-inspired breads to the shores of Puget Sound.

CORY SCHREIBER
WILDWOOD RESTAURANT

■

Somehow people born and raised in the Pacific Northwest always seem to come back home, no matter how far they might stray. Such is the case with Cory Schreiber of Wildwood Restaurant. Such is the luck of Portland.

Schreiber is a fifth-generation Oregonian who grew up in the food business. Until recently, his family owned the Oregon Oyster Company, a century-old oyster purveyor. At age 11, Schreiber began working at another long-time Portland institution, Dan & Louis' Oyster Bar. His culinary education continued at Portland's Benson Hotel, where he learned the workings of a big kitchen. "What I got in that initial apprenticeship," Schreiber explains, "was the discipline that comes from learning the basics of cooking, the French tradition. It's that discipline that underlies creativity in the kitchen."

Schreiber then left Portland to work in San Francisco, Boston, and Chicago before coming home with a reputation as one of America's great up-and-coming chefs. In the course of his continuing food education, he was able to work with and learn from Lydia Shire, Gordon Sinclair, and Bradley Ogden. He also found the kindred souls (Krista Anderson, chef de cuisine; Hal Finkelstein, general manager; Randy Goodman, director of service and wine program) who came back to Portland with him to open Wildwood in 1994. It's a sleek, unpretentious restaurant that states the case for a Pacific Northwest culinary identity, with dishes like Willamette Valley lamb shank with smoked bacon and white beans, and Hood River pear tart with apple brandy.

"I'm an American chef," Schreiber says with the intensity of a prizefighter, "and coming back home has given me the chance to turn inward and focus on that food tradition that reaches right down into my roots."

***Wildwood Restaurant**, 1221 N.W. 21st Ave., Portland; (503) 248-9663.*

> 66 Coming back home has given me the chance to turn inward and focus on that food tradition that reaches right down into my roots. 99

Return of the native: Cory Schreiber studied with America's finest chefs before opening Wildwood Restaurant in Portland.

TOM DOUGLAS
PALACE KITCHEN

Tom Douglas has lived in the Pacific Northwest for 20 years, which makes him a native. True, he did grow up in Delaware. But all he got there was a fondness for crab cakes. It was in the Pacific Northwest that he discovered what a glorious marriage a crab cake and a Dungeness crab could make. That and a good microbrew— we're talking a little bit of heaven.

When Douglas was the chef at Cafe Sport in Seattle's Pike Place Market in the 1980s, he began incorporating food ideas from all the local places he liked to eat at—which meant a lot of Asian influence. Nobody else was exploring and pushing the boundaries quite like Douglas. He had never been one to have a great meal out and then leave it at that. He was much too curious a soul, and too enthusiastic about getting his hands into the process. For Douglas, that great meal wasn't complete until he had brought the ideas home and tried a few things in his own kitchen. And then they would end up on the restaurant menu.

When he opened the Dahlia Lounge in 1989, Douglas brought in Shelley Lance and Steven Steinbock to share duties—not just on the cooking line, but in the development of those first few menus, which would take the flavors of the Pacific Northwest to another level. The three friends had worked together for years, giving each other permission to build wonderful, ephemeral palaces of flavor.

> **"** When you're eating a great meal ... passion and pleasure get all mixed up on the plate. **"**

Douglas's next endeavor was a seafood restaurant named Etta's (after his daughter, Loretta), which he opened in 1995 in the Pike Place space once occupied by Cafe Sport. Then in 1996 he opened the Palace Kitchen, named one of the top five new restaurants in the country by the James Beard Foundation.

With three restaurants, Douglas may have established his own small culinary empire. But he's after far more than profits. "You ever have that feeling when you're eating a great meal, where passion and pleasure get all mixed up on the plate?" he asks. "That's one of the great bottom lines."

Dahlia Lounge, *1904 Fourth Ave., Seattle; (206) 682-4143.*

Etta's, *2020 Western Ave., Seattle; (206) 443-6000.*

Palace Kitchen, *2030 Fifth Ave., Seattle; (206) 448-2001.*

The king in his palace: Tom Douglas blends Asian inspirations with the best of Northwest ingredients.

HARRY YOSHIMURA
MUTUAL FISH
MARKET

∎

As you might expect from its Puget Sound setting, there are a number of good fish markets in Seattle: Jack's Fish Spot in the Pike Place Market, which leans heavily toward salmon and shellfish; University Seafood & Poultry Co., which mixes high-quality seafood and poultry. But there's only one Mutual Fish—and it serves the most eclectic population in the city.

When Dick Yoshimura started the business in 1948, most of his customers were Japanese, though some Chinese, Filipinos, and African Americans bought their fish from him as well. A tight community. Supportive. "Back then," Dick's son, Harry, explains, "the Asian business community all worked together to help each other. A lot of the Asian restaurants came to my dad for fish."

Harry is the second generation, and the driving force of Mutual Fish today. His son, Kevin, could be the third generation of the Yoshimura fish dynasty, should he decide to stay in the family business. It's not the easiest act to follow. Dick set a standard for high-quality seafood. Harry has maintained that standard, and acted as a bridge between his culture and a much broader population in Seattle.

> **"** The more fearless among them would buy the strong-flavored, small, bony goatfish and kali kali favored by the older-generation Japanese. **"**

"Early on, only a couple of Caucasian chefs would try different things out," Harry recalls of his first years at Mutual Fish. "The more fearless among them would buy the strong-flavored, small, bony goatfish and kali kali favored by the older-generation Japanese, and put them on menus, boning them out in the kitchen."

That was then. Today, the Yoshimuras have brought the full riches of the sea to Seattle dinner tables. The best restaurants in the city call Mutual Fish in the morning to see what's fresh. Innovative chefs like Palace Kitchen's Tom Douglas have added kasu cod and ocean (seaweed) salad to their menus because Harry introduced them to these traditional seafood tastes. Teaching in his peculiar nonteaching way, Harry has shown the Pacific Northwest what quality, flavor, and tradition in seafood are all about.

Mutual Fish Market, 2335 Rainier Ave. S., Seattle; (206) 322-4368.

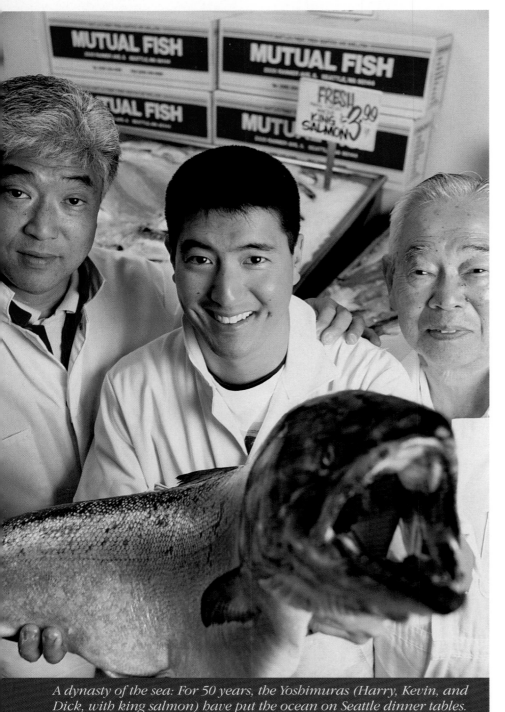

A dynasty of the sea: For 50 years, the Yoshimuras (Harry, Kevin, and Dick, with king salmon) have put the ocean on Seattle dinner tables.

CHUCK BEEK
MONORAIL ESPRESSO

■

When Chuck Beek bought his first espresso cart and started selling coffee to Seattle beneath the monorail (hence the name Monorail Espresso), there were only four basic drinks to choose from: espresso, cappuccino, latte, and mocha, in one size and with one kind of milk. He made them all strong, or in his words, "double restretto." It was 1980.

"The first time a customer asked me for a double-double," says Beek, "I thought I'd heard it all. But it was only the beginning."

Back then, there was one espresso cart on the streets of Seattle, and Beek owned it. He would own more carts over the next 15 years, and move them around to various locations in the city. He would see other carts spring up on the pavement, many of them owned and operated by people he had trained. He would see Seattle become to coffee what Bordeaux is to wine: the world capital, imitated but never duplicated. He would see new coffee drinks develop, flavorings added, different kinds of milk demanded. "There might be 1,000 different coffee drinks today," Beek says, "if you add up all the possible combinations."

His greatest business skill has been survival for all these years. "I just never knew it wasn't easy," Beek says of the street coffee business. "So I survived. I never quite saw how hard it was."

His wife, Susie, came into the business to help. They made many friends downtown, and a lot of those friends had occasion to help out through the years. Like when the Beeks were suddenly forced to move the cart and had no place to park it at night. A restaurant

> ❝ The first time a customer asked me for a double-double, I thought I'd heard it all. But it was only the beginning. ❞

Not any old cuppa joe: At Monorail Espresso, Chuck Beek helped brew a coffee revolution that spread from Seattle across the country.

owner came to the rescue and let them park the cart in his doorway at night—for a year. "That guy," Beek says, "gets free coffee for life."

No one taught Seattle more about what a good espresso drink should look, smell, and taste like than Chuck and Susie. No one ever lined up for a cup of coffee before the Beeks showed what a pleasure it could be. The city hasn't been the same since.

Chuck still has that original cart, in storage. And he still has Monorail Espresso, though it's now "off" the street. You'll find Susie across Puget Sound in Poulsbo (Chuck commutes to Seattle by ferry and bicycle), where she runs—that's right—a coffeehouse. It's called the Poulsbohemian.

Monorail Espresso, 510 Pike St., Seattle; (206) 625-0449.

Poulsbohemian Coffeehouse, 19003 Front St., Poulsbo; (360) 779-9199.

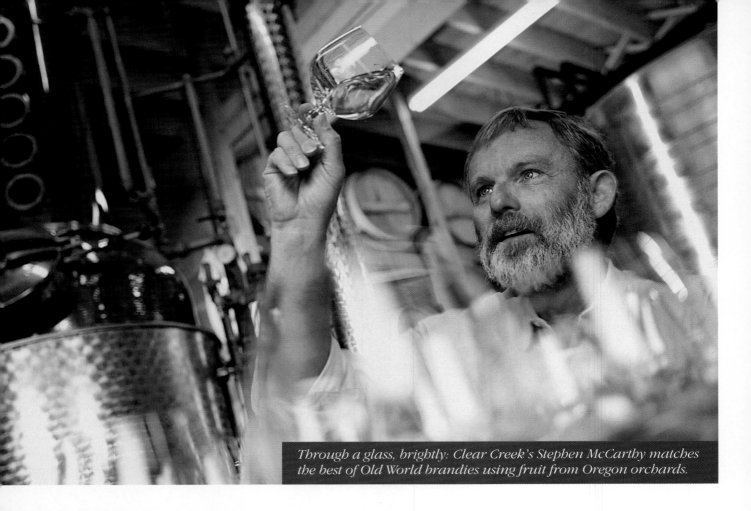

Through a glass, brightly: Clear Creek's Stephen McCarthy matches the best of Old World brandies using fruit from Oregon orchards.

STEPHEN McCARTHY
CLEAR CREEK DISTILLERY

Stephen McCarthy and his wife, Lucinda Parker, work in the same Portland building: she in her studio, he at his still. They are both Pacific Northwest artists of considerable merit—Parker known for her paintings, and McCarthy for his pear, apple, and plum brandies, his grappa and marc, his kirsch, and soon enough, his single-malt scotch.

From the time his grandfather came west from Yale, McCarthy's family has been in the fruit business in one way or another, mostly growing apples and pears in Oregon's rich orchard land. But to McCarthy, the vagaries of farming and getting fruit to market at an optimum time for an optimum price never quite made sense. Too many uncontrollable factors that could drop the price right through the grading room floor never let him rest easy.

Other Northwest pioneers had figured out ways of turning fruit into a value-added product—Harry and David and their holiday fruit baskets, the Aplets and Cotlets candy people. But there had to be something new, McCarthy figured. Something better. Something that showed the fruit the respect it truly deserved. Something that fit right in with the revolution in food and wine stirring around him.

He figured that if the French could make an industry out of distilling brandy from pears, why couldn't an Oregonian? Most people rolled their eyeballs when he posed the question. It had never been done before, people thought, so there must be a reason why. Even when he

> " We grow such wonderful fruit in Oregon. Just imagine pouring it into a bottle and sending it anywhere in the world. "

pointed out that the pears were the same—what the French call a Williams Bon-Chrétien, we call a Bartlett—he got little enthusiastic support.

So McCarthy simply plunged right in and tried. It took about two years of distilling fruit to figure out why it hadn't been done before. There were indeed many nuances to the art of making brandy, like selecting absolutely perfectly ripe fruit or risking shameful results. But learn the art he did, and the results are stunning.

Even today, all of Clear Creek's brandies are rooted in the Oregon soil. McCarthy still depends on apples and pears grown at the family orchard near Parkdale, in the Hood River Valley. The cherries for his kirsch come from nearby.

"We grow such wonderful fruit in Oregon," McCarthy says. "Just imagine pouring it into a bottle and sending it anywhere in the world."

Clear Creek Distillery, 1430 N.W. 23rd Ave., Portland; (503) 248-9470. Tours and tastings by appointment. Brandies are available for $20 to $30 at specialty liquor stores. ◆

The Low-Fat Cook
HEALTHY CHOICES FOR THE ACTIVE LIFESTYLE

by ELAINE JOHNSON

An ethereal dessert from a great berry

■ A low-fat lifestyle doesn't mean you have to skip dessert. Just ask Kaspar Donier, chef of Kaspar's Restaurant in Seattle. On Spa Wednesdays, the restaurant features a fixed-price, three-course dinner of light dishes, which during the summer is likely to include a delicious blackberry concoction.

Donier lets good sense guide the creation of these special dishes. Each contains a minimum of fat, cholesterol, calories, and sodium. He learned how to rethink recipes during a dietitian-directed training program he attended while working for Four Seasons Hotels. "Until then," he says, "I never thought about the calories I was adding to a meal with butter, sugar, and cream."

Working with a lighter hand, "I take out all the butter and cream, and most of the oil. I try to limit meat and fish portions to 3 ounces, and add a lot of vegetables and grains. We make a great no-oil vinaigrette based on chicken broth," says Donier.

But dishes like these aren't successful if they aren't every bit as flavorful as those on the regular menu, and Donier has no plans to change dishes that don't take well to a leaner design.

Capitalizing on local ingredients at their seasonal peak—when they need little embellishment—is one of Donier's lightening-up approaches that is especially easy to follow. And in August, this leads him to blackberries. Donier enhances the soft, plump fruit with sugar and yogurt beneath a cloud of warm meringue.

Blackberry Meringue Gratin

Prep and cook time: About 15 minutes

Makes: 4 servings

- 3½ cups **blackberries**
- ½ cup **sugar**
- ¾ cup **plain low-fat yogurt**
- ½ teaspoon grated **lemon** peel

Topping it off: Golden meringue floats on juicy blackberries in yogurt sauce.

RICHARD JUNG

- 3 **large egg** whites
- **Mint sprigs**

1. In a small bowl, combine ½ cup blackberries and 1 tablespoon sugar. Set aside.

2. In another bowl, combine 2 tablespoons sugar, yogurt, and lemon peel. Gently mix in remaining berries.

3. Spoon yogurt-berry mixture into 4 ovenproof ramekins or bowls, each 1½ to 2 inches deep and 4 to 5 inches wide.

4. In a deep bowl, whip egg whites with a mixer at high speed until foamy.

Continue to beat and gradually add remaining sugar (about 1 tablespoon every 15 seconds) until whites hold stiff peaks when beaters are lifted.

5. Swirl meringue equally over yogurt-berry mixture. Set dishes in a 10- by 15-inch rimmed pan. Broil about 4 inches from heat until meringue is browned, 30 to 60 seconds.

6. Spoon reserved sugared berries and their juice over meringues. Garnish with mint sprigs.

Per serving: 202 cal., 4.9% (9.9 cal.) from fat; 5.8 g protein; 1.1 g fat (0.4 g sat.); 44 g carbo (5.7 g fiber); 71 mg sodium; 2.6 mg chol. ◆

A summer salmon feast

How do you throw a memorable party in the spirit of the Northwest?
We give you three traditional ways to cook the fish

by LINDA LAU ANUSASANANAN

■ For a grand summer gathering, take your cue from Northwest natives. For centuries, salmon was the cornerstone of Indian potlatches—lavish celebrations with days of feasting and gift giving. Skillful Indian cooks took great pride in the dishes they served; some recipes were secret, others shared.

Ancestral traditions resonate in three very different salmon dishes that are the heart of this party menu. The Indian-style salmon bake is well known among Northwest cooks. Salmon cooked on a plank and salmon wrapped in leaves may be less familiar—but they're equally traditional and suited to the fish.

Seattle University alums and their families gather for a Northwest party. Center stage is a whole butterflied salmon cooked on a wood frame before a fire, in the style of coastal Native Americans.

photographs by
JON JENSEN

Northwest Salmon Party

**Field Greens with
Shallot and Herb Dressing**

•

Salmon Recipes:
#1 Indian-style Bake
or
#2 Leek-wrapped
or
#3 Pinot-plank

•

Grilled or Boiled Corn

•

Grilled or Boiled Red Potatoes

•

**Berry Bowl
(Blackberries, Blueberries,
Raspberries, and Strawberries)
with Honey and Cream**

•

Pinot Noir   Pinot Grigio

•

Lemonade

Indian-style salmon bake

#1 SALMON RECIPE

Prep and cook time: About 3 hours

Notes: Order salmon with head, tail, and back fin trimmed. Also have salmon butterflied from stomach side without separating fillets along the back, then boned (but not skinned). Any white membrane from belly area of fish should be trimmed. (All of this can be done at the market.) This shape is called a book fillet.

Makes: 12 to 16 servings

  1 **whole salmon** (6 to 8 lb.), book filleted (see notes)
  1 cup **rock salt**
  1 cup firmly packed **brown sugar**
  ¾ teaspoon **white pepper**
  Frame (see instructions below)
  2 tablespoons **butter** or margarine, melted
  2 tablespoons **lemon juice**
  Lemon wedges

1. Rinse salmon and pat dry. Mix rock salt, brown sugar, and white pepper. Spread half of the mixture over bottom of a 12- by 17-inch pan lined with plastic wrap. Lay fish, skin down, on salt mixture. Pat remaining mixture over salmon. Cover and chill 2 to 4 hours. Lift fish from pan, rinse thoroughly, and pat dry.

2. Meanwhile, select site (A, at right), work out frame support (B), and start fire (C).

3. Load salmon onto soaked frame (steps 1 through 7 below).

4. When fire is ready, secure salmon at proper angle over the glowing coals with flesh toward the fire and wide end of fish 1½ to 2 feet from heat (A). Check temperature by placing the back of your hand against the fish at the top and the bottom; you should be able to hold your hand in place for only 5 to 6 seconds. Adjust by pushing coals away from fish if too hot, closer if too cool.

(To use a gas grill, turn heat to high, tip lid open, position frame over heat, and use your hand to judge cooking temperature. Move fish closer for more heat; turn down gas for less.)

5. Mix butter with lemon juice. Baste fish several times with butter mixture as it cooks. Check heat often. If wood frame starts to smolder, squirt or brush with water.

6. Cook fish until surface turns evenly opaque, 20 to 30 minutes.

7. Handling frame gently (cooked fish breaks up easily), rotate salmon so skin side faces the heat. Secure frame and continue to cook just until fish feels firm to touch, 20 to 30 minutes more, basting several times.

8. Gently lay salmon in frame, skin down, on a large board or platter. Snip wires and gently pull wood frame from fish. Serve salmon hot or cool. Lift fish pieces off the skin and season with juice from lemon wedges.

Per serving: 177 cal., 43% (76 cal.) from fat; 22 g protein; 8.4 g fat (2 g sat.); 1.9 g carbo (0 g fiber); 476 mg sodium; 65 mg chol.

The tradition of the Indian salmon bake has deep roots in the Northwest. For centuries, Native Americans such as the Makah and S'Klallam have cooked salmon on a wood frame before an open fire. The practice is so widespread that no individual tribe lays claim to the technique, but typically, a straight, strong branch of cedar or ironwood is split lengthwise at one end, then the boned salmon is fitted into the split. To hold the fish flat so it will cook evenly, additional sticks are woven over and under the salmon at right angles to the branch.

Putting the salmon on the frame

Purchase frame parts: At a lumberyard, have wood cut to specific lengths. You will need two **pine 1-by-1s** (each 6 to 7 ft. long), five pieces of **¼- by ½-inch pine screen mold** (each 18 in. long), and 2 feet of **22-gauge** (or heavier) **wire**.

Fireproof wood: Soak frame pieces in water at least two hours. If you don't have a container long enough to immerse the wood, wrap the parts of the long stakes that will be exposed to fire in a thick layer of wet towels, seal with foil or plastic wrap, and saturate towels as needed.

To start, gather the soaked frame pieces, salad oil and a brush, wire, wire cutters, pliers, and fish.

Lightly brush salad oil onto a 24-inch section of one side of each of the long stakes, starting at one end. Lightly oil one side of each short wood piece.

Lay one long stake on a table, oiled side up. Starting about 5 inches from the end of the oiled part of the stake, lay three short pieces, oiled side up, about 5 inches apart across it.

The site, frame support, and the fire

A. Select a site that is protected from the wind. Set frame at a 45° to 60° angle over the fire, sticking stake ends into a hole to hold it (or lean frame against the barbecue). **B. Use rocks,** concrete building blocks, bricks, or bagged sand to brace frame base securely. **C. Build fire** in a portable barbecue (20 to 22 in. wide) with a firegrate, vents open: About 2½ hours before serving time, ignite four or five seasoned, split logs (each 4 to 5 in. wide, 12 to 14 in. long) on firegrate. Let wood burn down to medium glowing coals, 1 to 1½ hours; a few low flames are fine. Judge heat by holding your hand where fish will be. When you can barely hold your hand in this spot for five to six seconds, the fire's ready for cooking.

Center salmon, skin down, on frame, wide end pointed toward middle of stake. Adjust short wood pieces so fish overlaps frame by 2 to 3 inches on each end.

Lay the two remaining short wood pieces, oiled side down, across the salmon between the short pieces under it—in effect weaving the fish in place.

Place second long stake, oiled side down, directly over the one beneath the salmon. Wrap wire around top ends of stakes and twist tightly to secure.

Wrap wire around stakes at the other end of the fish. Twist wire tightly to secure.

SALMON RECIPE #2

Leek-wrapped Salmon

Prep and cook time: About 1½ hours

Notes: If leek strips aren't long enough to tie salmon packets, use cotton string. Moderately priced fresh salmon caviar, *ikura,* is sold at Japanese markets and fancy-food stores. Fernando Divina created this dish for his Portland restaurant, Fiddleheads, taking inspiration from traditional fern-wrapped salmon cooked in hot coals.

Makes: 4 servings

- 4 **leeks** (1½ in. wide and at least 12 in. long)
- 4 **red thin-skinned potatoes** (6 oz. each), scrubbed
- 4 **skinned and boned salmon fillets** (6 to 8 oz. each)
- 4 **dried juniper berries,** crushed

  Salt

  White pepper
- 4 **ears of corn** (¾ lb. each)

  About 2 tablespoons **hazelnut oil**
- ¼ cup **fresh** or canned **salmon caviar,** rinsed

1. Cut vertically through 1 whole outer layer of each leek and pull it off gently. Cut at least 7 inches off the top of each leek. Rinse outer layers and tops.

2. Trim off and discard leek root ends. Split white parts of leeks in half lengthwise and rinse thoroughly to remove dirt between layers. Tie each leek half in the center with a cotton string.

3. In a 5- to 6-quart pan over high heat, bring about 3 quarts water to boiling. Add leek outer layers and about ⅔ of the green tops (select the freshest-looking). Cook just until wilted, about 30 seconds; lift out with tongs and immerse in ice water. Discard remaining tops.

4. Add tied leek halves to water and simmer, uncovered, until tender when pierced, 5 to 7 minutes; lift out with a slotted spoon and immerse in ice water. When cool, drain well.

5. Add potatoes to boiling water, cover, and simmer just until tender when pierced, 20 to 25 minutes. Drain and cool. Cut into ½-inch-thick slices.

6. Rinse salmon and pat dry. Sprinkle each piece with a crushed juniper berry, salt, and pepper.

7. Tear leek outer layers lengthwise into strips about ¼ inch wide. Prepare wrappers and wrap salmon as shown below.

8. Pull back cornhusks; don't remove. Discard silk. Push husks back in place.

9. Prepare barbecue for indirect cooking (see facing page). Lay fish in center of grill, not over direct heat. Place potato slices and corn directly over heat. If space permits, also put leek halves directly over heat (otherwise, lay next to fish). Cover barbecue, open vents, and cook 8 minutes. Turn vegetables over and cook until they are hot and lightly browned, 4 to 6 minutes longer. Cook fish until a thermometer inserted in thickest part reaches 125°, about 16 minutes total. Transfer foods to a platter as they're cooked.

10. Open packets. Drizzle hazelnut oil over fish, potatoes, and corn. Spoon salmon caviar onto fish. Season to taste with salt and pepper.

Per serving: 676 cal., 31% (207 cal.) from fat; 47 g protein; 23 g fat (2.4 g sat.); 76 g carbo (8.6 g fiber); 377 mg sodium; 188 mg chol.

Unfold leaf packet and top hot salmon with salmon caviar and hazelnut oil.

Wrapping the salmon

1 **Cross** two leek strips. Unfold leek tops and lay flat, overlapping to make a rectangle.

2 **Center** a salmon fillet on a leek base slightly wider than the length of the fish.

3 **Fold** leek greens over fish to enclose.

4 **Tie** packet with leek strips to secure. Repeat to wrap remaining salmon.

Grilling with indirect heat

When you grill with indirect heat, the hot coals or flames are not under the food but on opposite sides of it. And the barbecue is covered.

If using charcoal briquets, mound and ignite 60 briquets on the firegrate of a barbecue (20 to 22 in. wide) with a lid; open vents. When briquets are dotted with gray ash, in 15 to 25 minutes, push equal amounts to opposite sides of the firegrate. Add 5 more briquets to each mound of coals (10 total).

If you use a gas barbecue, it must be equipped with a control to regulate heat in the center of the grill. To heat the barbecue, cover and turn on high for about 10 minutes. Turn off heat in center of barbecue, but leave heat on opposite sides on high.

Salmon and plank, soaked in Pinot Noir, develop rich aromatics as the fish cooks in a covered barbecue. Corn chars lightly over hot coals.

SALMON #3 RECIPE

Pinot-plank Salmon Fillet

Prep and cook time: About 30 minutes, plus 4 hours to soak corn

Notes: Select an untreated wood plank. Cedar is aromatic and historically correct, but it's expensive; clear fir works well. A 1-by-8 plank 18 to 19 inches long is big enough to hold the salmon and fits on a 20- to 22-inch-wide round barbecue.

Chef Emily Moore at Seattle's Theoz Restaurant and Bar soaks both the plank and fish in red wine, and the corn in white wine. You can use inexpensive wines for cooking. Serve small red potatoes, boiled and hot, and have butter for the potatoes and corn.

Makes: 6 servings

- 6 **ears of corn** (¾ lb. each)
- 1 bottle (750 ml.) **Gewürztraminer** or 3 cups water
- 2 to 4 cups **Pinot Noir**
  Wood plank (see notes)
- 1 **whole salmon fillet** (about 18 in. long, 2¼ to 2½ lb.)

- 2 cups **alder** or mesquite **wood chips**
- 3 to 6 **rosemary sprigs** (each 3 to 5 in. long)
- 3 to 6 **marjoram sprigs** (each 3 to 5 in. long)
- 3 to 6 **thyme sprigs** (each 3 to 5 in. long)
  Lemon wedges
  Salt and **pepper**

1. Pull back cornhusks but don't remove. Discard corn silk. Push husks back in place. In an 8- to 10-quart pan, combine Gewürztraminer and 1 gallon water. Add corn and set a plate on top of ears to keep immersed. Soak corn at least 4 hours at room temperature, or up to 1 day in the refrigerator.

2. In a container just wide and long enough to hold the plank (a sink, pan, or heavy plastic food bag), combine 2 parts water and 1 part Pinot Noir. Rinse plank; immerse in Pinot Noir mixture for at least 1 hour or up to 1 day.

3. About 30 minutes before cooking, immerse fish in the red wine mixture with the plank.

4. In another container, soak wood chips in 2 to 3 cups of the red wine mixture.

5. Prepare barbecue to cook with indirect heat (see above left). Drain

The salmon was succulent, the corn sweet, the company fun. And now it's time to wind down with a heart-of-summer dessert—blackberries, blueberries, raspberries, and strawberries. Nibblers munch them out of hand, but serious eaters douse bowls of fruit with rich cream and a touch of honey.

wood chips. Sprinkle them onto hot coals. Or, if using a gas barbecue, put chips in a smoke box or foil pan directly on heat in a corner as barbecue heats.

6. Lift fish and plank from liquid. Lay fish on plank, skin down, and top with 3 sprigs *each* of rosemary, marjoram, and thyme.

7. Put barbecue grill in place. Set plank and fish on grill between coals or gas heat. Cover barbecue, open vents, and cook 10 minutes. (If plank chars, squirt or mop dark areas with water.)

8. Drain corn and lay on grill directly over heat; cover barbecue. Turn corn as husks scorch, and cook fish until it is barely opaque but moist-looking in center of thickest part (cut to test), 15 to 20 minutes longer.

9. Transfer corn and plank with fish to the table. Replace scorched herbs with fresh ones and garnish fish with lemon. Cut fish in pieces and lift off with a spatula. Pull off cornhusks. Add salt, pepper, and lemon to taste.

Per serving: 348 cal., 31% (108 cal.) from fat; 38 g protein; 12 g fat (1.9 g sat.); 23 g carbo (3.9 g fiber); 95 mg sodium; 94 mg chol. ◆

Beyond burgers

Quick tips to help you eat well on the road

Traveling presents a serious challenge for anyone who cares about his or her diet. At home, or even at work, it's relatively easy to watch what you eat. But when you are on the road, you are at the mercy of the culinary elements. Fast-food establishments in particular, though undeniably convenient, offer fare that is typically high in fat and low in nutrition. Your basic deluxe cheeseburger, for example, contains all the fat and sodium a normal adult should consume in an entire day, and half of the caloric intake.

Travelers tend to eat more refined foods, which are generally low in fiber and vitamins. When you factor in the increased alcohol and caffeine consumption that typically accompanies travel, a vacation can be a nutritional nightmare.

Consider, then, the following strategies for eating well on the road.

1. Have a picnic. In addition to allowing you to get outside and explore the area you are visiting, a well-packed picnic is also a chance to eat more healthfully and cheaply than at most restaurants. For example, a picnic lunch of fresh fruit, juice, a peanut butter and jelly sandwich, and nuts can be every bit as filling as, and much better for you than, a burger, fries, and a soda. Just remember to keep hot things hot and cold things cold. Either prepare items when you intend to consume them, or pack them in an ice chest.

2. Snack smart. For in-betweens, keep fresh fruit handy (these days, you can even pick up apples and oranges at most airports). Or munch on carrot

and celery sticks. Even granola bars, popcorn, and baked pretzels are better than sugary soda or candy bars.

3. Manage menus. Most restaurant menus offer healthful items—look for dishes tagged with a heart or other symbol. Remember that frying equals fat-laden food—a grilled-chicken sandwich contains fewer calories and less fat than its breaded and deep-fried counterpart. As for french fries and onion rings, order these only if you're trying to up your intake of calories, salt, and fat.

4. Watch those salad bars. Don't be fooled into thinking that a trip to the salad bar is a safe, nutritious, and virtuous act. I've always been amazed by people who load up their plates with iceberg lettuce, bacon bits, eggs, and croutons, then smother the mess with ladlefuls of high-fat dressing. They would've been better off with a burger! Choose veggies like spinach leaves, carrots, and peppers, and limit dressing. ◆

by **STEVE SAINSBURY, M.D.**

The Quick Cook

MEALS IN 30-MINUTES-OR-LESS

by CHRISTINE WEBER HALE

Chicken express

■ If you think that purchased boned, skinned chicken breasts are the last word in time-savers, check out chicken breast nuggets and strips in the fresh poultry section of your supermarket.

Cut into bite-size chunks or slices usually no thicker than an inch, these petite breast pieces take advantage of an important principle of physics: smaller cooks faster. The payback—even if the product is priced a little higher—is time.

Chicken breast nuggets and strips are often available threaded on skewers, ready to broil or barbecue. Just baste with a favorite sauce.

The most important tip: Use high heat so meat cooks quickly—and don't overcook. Pieces are done as soon as they are no longer pink in the center. Even a few minutes more on the heat makes the meat dry and tough.

Thai Chicken Pasta

Prep and cook time: About 25 minutes
Makes: 4 servings

  1 pound **chicken breast nuggets** or strips

  7 cloves **garlic**

  ⅓ cup firmly packed **fresh cilantro**

  ⅓ cup firmly packed **fresh basil** leaves

  ⅓ cup firmly packed **fresh mint** leaves

  ½ cup **seasoned rice vinegar**

 12 ounces **fresh linguine**

  1 cup **prepared Asian-style peanut sauce**

     Mint sprigs

Herb-coated chicken tops linguine.

1. In a covered pan, bring 3 quarts water to a boil over high heat.

2. Meanwhile, rinse chicken, pat dry, and put in a bowl.

3. In a food processor, whirl garlic, cilantro, basil, and mint leaves until minced. Pour into a shallow bowl.

4. Mix vinegar with chicken, lift out pieces with a slotted spoon, and add to herb mixture. Mix and pour pieces into an oiled or nonstick 10- by 15-inch pan and spread out in a single layer.

5. Broil chicken about 4 inches from heat until no longer pink in center (cut to test), 4 to 5 minutes.

6. When chicken goes under the broiler, immediately add linguine to boiling water and cook until tender to bite, 3 to 5 minutes.

7. Drain pasta, return to pan, and add all but 2 tablespoons peanut sauce. Mix well and spoon onto plates. Top equally with chicken. Drizzle with remaining sauce; garnish with mint sprigs.

Per serving: 561 cal., 18% (99 cal.) from fat; 43 g protein; 11 g fat (1.8 g sat.); 70 g carbo (4.9 g fiber); 2,112 mg sodium; 128 mg chol. ◆

MORE IDEAS FOR NUGGETS AND STRIPS

■ Coat chicken pieces with blackberry jam thinned slightly with balsamic vinegar and a little chopped fresh rosemary. Broil as directed in recipe instructions.

■ Brush skewered chicken pieces with honey mustard. Broil or grill.

■ Mix chicken pieces with purchased jerk sauce. Stir-fry your choice of vegetables, then chicken. Spoon over rice cooked in reduced-fat coconut milk.

■ Flavor apricot jam with enough mustard to give it a bite, then thin slightly with lemon juice. Brush this glaze onto skewered chicken pieces. Broil or grill.

■ On skewers, alternate chicken pieces with vegetables such as cherry tomatoes and chunks of green onions and bell peppers. Broil or grill.

■ Use lively seasonings to enhance flavor. Dry rubs and liquid marinades soak instantly into these small pieces.

The real Pike Place

To get the most out of Seattle's legendary market,
rise at dawn and leave before noon—but not before lunch

Mongers at Pike Place Fish get ready for the day by setting out Dungeness crab and fresh salmon fillets on clean beds of ice. By 11, the fish begin to fly.

Seattle has a love-hate relationship with the Pike Place Market, or at least I do. The reasons to love this national historic site—a 9-acre jumble of late-19th- and early-20th-century buildings laid out like a jigsaw puzzle—are everywhere. Its iron-columned arcades, where the voices of vegetable vendors and fishmongers echo, are as cherished as the storefronts of Montmartre. Its smells are unduplicated. And its cracked walkways and stone-paved alleys are almost holy.

But between 11 A.M. and 6 P.M., June through mid-September, when the market is ablaze with light and crowds jam the aisles, most Seattleites don't go near the place. That's not the Pike Place Market we grew up with and love. Our mar-

ket is cozy, intimate, and unshaven—still in its bathrobe. Which is why, when friends from out of town ask me to show them the market, I say, "I'll pick you up at 6:30 tomorrow morning."

I park the car (no trouble at that hour), and we head to the **Athenian Inn.** Here we settle into a booth by the window to watch the morning traffic on Elliott Bay. With a cup of potent coffee in hand (no double-half-caf goat's-milk lattes here—just joe), we outline the day and eyeball the menu. Hmm … Chicken-liver omelet? Hangtown fry? Maybe one of the Farmer's Specials (there are six), more than you think you can eat for $3.95. I usually order one of those. And some pancakes, too. At that hour the place is quiet enough

to eavesdrop without even half trying ("… Bill Clinton, Madeleine Albright, or Paul Allen…"), and you find your attention divided between the arrival of the morning commuter ferries and the high-powered dish floating around this workingman's cafe.

An hour later, we head out of the Athenian and walk north. A few of the high stall vendors (year-round retailers) are setting up their fruit and produce displays. I herd my friends to the north end of the market and a little patch of grassy area, **Victor Steinbrueck Park.** It's still early, plenty of time to admire the two totem poles and the view of the Olympic Mountains.

Excellent restaurants,

most rich with atmosphere,

are the rule in the market.

From here we meander back south, dodging the delivery trucks as we walk cobblestoned Pike Place, drawn by whatever looks interesting. In the arcade, the low stalls are filling up with artisans, all of whom must make what they sell to qualify for the $9 to $25 daily rental fee. Plastic buckets sit filled with freshly cut flowers, and fruits and vegetables picked that morning are being put out for display. You often read the words "regional," "seasonal," and "fresh" on menus. Here it's for real.

Across Pike Place, the **Seattle Garden Center** calls out to the gardener in me, and selfishly I drag my group over to look at plants and pots, seeds and fertilizer, and assorted garden ornaments. I could live here, but I usually lose a friend or two to **Sur La Table** in the same building. Started by Shirley Collins in 1972, this is probably the most complete culinary store ever conceived. Now Sur La Table has expanded with a store in Kirkland, one in San Francisco, and another (Seattle grits its collective teeth) in Berkeley.

Anchoring the south end of the Market is **Read All About It Newsstand,**

by STEVEN R. LORTON *photographs by* CONNIE COLEMAN

which carries more than 1,500 magazines and 150 newspapers. Across the way is **DeLaurenti,** with its bins of colored farfalle and fusilli sold by the pound, and shelves of canned olives, tomatoes, pastes, and extracts. I always stop to look at the dozens of bottles of olive oil. Then we head over to **MarketSpice,** where Seattleites have been shopping for spices, spice blends, and teas since 1911.

By now the Farmer's Special is starting to wear off. No big deal. Excellent restaurants, most rich with atmosphere and full of good food, are the rule in the market. The tonier ones—**Campagne, Chez Shea, Il Bistro,** the **Pink Door**—are perfect for a long evening of merrymaking.

But for a late-morning lunch in summer, I steer my charges to one of two places. The **Copacabana** is a noisy Bolivian eatery on the second floor of a triangular brick building at about the market's midpoint. Typical dishes include *picante de pollo* (breast of chicken in a sauce of paprika, onions, and tomatoes) served with rice and a simple salad. Heaven. *Arroz con leche* (rice pudding) is a worthy and unpretentious finish.

Back at the south end of the market is **Maximilien-in-the-Market.** The menu is extensive, but I usually end up ordering sausage and new potatoes, and feel exceptionally lucky if owner François Kissel is in the kitchen.

Lunch on the deck of the Copacabana gives patrons one of the best market views.

If my friends are in a picnic mood (assuming the weather permits), we might stop at **Piroshky Piroshky,** which usually has more than a dozen kinds of the Russian staple in the window case, or at **Cucina Fresca** for torta di Melanzane, to go. And at **Le Panier** you can buy a sandwich, pain aux noix, pain de campagne, or baguette for the road, though I usually get a pain au chocolat and eat it there.

By 11 the musicians are playing away and the tourists are starting to swarm in like ants to spilled sugar. Up at **Pike Place Fish,** the hoarse voice of a clerk shouts, "8-pound king!" Then every workman and -woman shouts back, "8-pound king!" And like clockwork, an 8-pound king salmon flies over the heads of the crowd and is caught by a worker behind the counter, who wraps it up for the flight home to Kansas.

That's the signal: The minute the first fish flies, I'm outta there. ◆

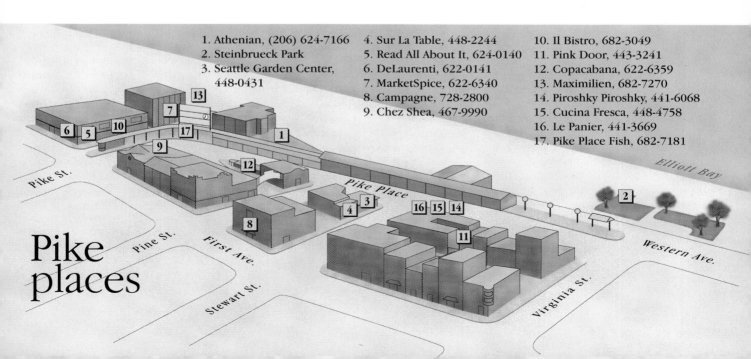

1. Athenian, (206) 624-7166
2. Steinbrueck Park
3. Seattle Garden Center, 448-0431
4. Sur La Table, 448-2244
5. Read All About It, 624-0140
6. DeLaurenti, 622-0141
7. MarketSpice, 622-6340
8. Campagne, 728-2800
9. Chez Shea, 467-9990
10. Il Bistro, 682-3049
11. Pink Door, 443-3241
12. Copacabana, 622-6359
13. Maximilien, 682-7270
14. Piroshky Piroshky, 441-6068
15. Cucina Fresca, 448-4758
16. Le Panier, 441-3669
17. Pike Place Fish, 682-7181

Pike places

A state of Beervana

What's brewing in Portland? A dozen of the city's best
brew pubs downtown and beyond provide the answer

*The Alameda Brewhouse (left) is a
hopping neighborhood pub near the
airport. Above, the stylish taps at the
Widmer Brothers Gasthaus. Right, a
copper brewing kettle dominates
Portland Brewing's Taproom & Grill.*

It's raining in Portland; the wipers on my car barely slap the water off the windshield as I head for a meeting with Mike McMenamin. Mike and his kid brother Brian (wags call them the Brews Brothers) run the largest chain of microbreweries and pubs in the Pacific Northwest—no small feat considering that their hometown boasts more craft brewers per capita than any other city in the United States.

We meet at the newest McMenamin brew pub, Ringlers, in the landmark Crystal Ballroom. I'm here to talk beer, but Mike wants to talk dance floors, specifically the one upstairs that's big enough to hold a thousand jumping, gyrating dancers. "Energy just builds out of this floor," he says. Ringlers brew pub is a fairly energetic place itself with Asian carvings, English antiques, and other assorted artifacts. If it weren't for the clicking of billiard balls on big slate tables accenting the noise of the growing lunch crowd, you'd think you had

walked into a garage sale for the British Empire.

Ringlers is just the latest of the McMenamins' 40 (and counting) properties, which include a historic roadhouse, two pub–movie theaters, and a bed-and-breakfast inn with a brewery and winery. Given Mike's penchant for the theatrical, it's tempting to credit his brew pub settings for the explosive growth of craft brewing in Portland.

"I think the main reason is because Oregonians still see themselves as part of the Wild West," Mike demurs. "There's a lot more individual thought going on here, and it's reflected in people's willingness to try different beers."

Fair enough, but can a region nicknamed "Beervana" actually take itself that seriously?

It's still raining as I work my way through the lunchtime traffic to Bridge-Port Brewing Co., Oregon's oldest microbrewery. Restaurant general manager Tim Bosworth insists that

Portland's dominance in per capita craft beer consumption is due to the wide range of beer styles available. For example, BridgePort is now touting its British-style beers. Naturally conditioned in small casks called firkins, these beers are hand-drawn into 20-ounce glasses. Less carbonated and served warmer than keg-conditioned-drafts, the porter has full, roast-coffee-tinged flavors that beg another sip.

Over at Portland Brewing Company's Taproom & Grill later that afternoon, cofounder Fred Bowman pulls a couple of frothy glasses of Scottish-style ale. Even in the gloomy light, the two huge copper brewing kettles showcased in the new brew pub's Bavarian decor gleam with a clean efficiency. Wiping the foam from his bushy mustache, Bowman discusses water purity and rhapsodizes about the quality of premium Oregon-grown hops and grains. I listen as fat raindrops pound the sidewalk outside, too afraid of be-

by **JEFF PHILLIPS**

C. BRUCE FORSTER

ing tossed out into the deluge to point out that Washington could make the same claims.

And so it goes, brew pub after brew pub, from the nonsmoking, dart-throwing warehouse bonhomie of the Lucky Labrador to the polished, hops farm–inspired wood-and-stainless-steel dining room of the Alameda Brewhouse. Winding through a seedy industrial district near the river in north Portland, I stop for a last beer at the new Gasthaus brew pub opened by Widmer Brothers Brewing Company in a restored brick building.

Ordering a pint of golden, cloudy *hefeweizen,* I bump into a stout, white-haired gentleman sipping the same. Fred Eckhardt, a local beer writer, has also stopped in for a quick pint. We chat, and as he gets ready to leave, I ask him the question that has been nagging me: why Portland?

Eckhardt doesn't miss a beat. Picking up his still-dripping umbrella, he shakes his head and chuckles, "Well, we certainly have the weather for it." ◆

A dozen of Portland's best

Alameda Brewhouse, 4765 N.E. Fremont St. (near the airport); (503) 460-9025.

B. Moloch Heathman Bakery and Pub, 901 S.W. Salmon St.; 227-5700.

BridgePort Brewing Co., 1313 N.W. Marshall St.; 241-7179.

Harborside Restaurant and Pilsner Room, 0309 S.W. Montgomery St.; 220-1865.

Hawthorne St. Ale House, 3632 S.E. Hawthorne Blvd.; 233-6540.

Lucky Labrador Brew Pub, 915 S.E. Hawthorne; 236-3555.

Nor'Wester Brewery and Public House, 66 S.E. Morrison St.; 232-9771.

Portland Brewing Company BrewHouse Taproom & Grill, 2730 N.W. 31st Ave.; 228-5269.

Portland Brewing Company

Flanders St. Brewpub, 1339 N.W. Flanders St.; 222-5910.

Ringlers, 1332 W. Burnside St.; 225-0543.

Rock Bottom Restaurant & Brewery, 210 S.W. Morrison St.; 796-2739.

Widmer Brothers Gasthaus, 955 N. Russell St.; 281-3333.

MORE BREW NEWS

Oregon Brewers Guild. For a virtually complete listing of Oregon brewers, call (800) 440-2537 or check out the Web site at http://www.oregonbeer.org/~beer.

Oregon Brewers Festival. At Portland's Waterfront Park, July 25–27. Call (503) 778-5917 or visit http://www.jhw.com/~jhw/brewfest.

Portland BrewBus. Take a guided bus tour of three or four different Portland breweries. Tours run 2–6 Sat, $29.95; (888) 244-2739.

Kitchen Cabinet

READERS' RECIPES TESTED IN SUNSET'S KITCHENS

by L I N D A   L A U   A N U S A S A N A N A N

Family favorites

■ Tanya Newgent says that Fresno, California, deserves the title of tri-tip city. When visiting there, she was struck by how easy it was to buy this bottom sirloin beef cut. And she noticed it because she likes to prepare tri-tip roasts the way her grandmother from the Dominican Republic does—by cutting slits in the meat and stuffing them with seasonings.

Grilled Tri-Tip Roast with Cilantro

Tanya Newgent, San Diego

Prep and cook time: About 50 minutes
Makes: 6 to 8 servings

- 1 **beef tri-tip roast** (2 to 2½ lb.)
- ¼ cup **reduced-sodium** or regular **soy sauce**
- ¼ cup chopped **fresh cilantro**
- 2 teaspoons **liquid smoke** (optional)
- 2 tablespoons chopped **fresh oregano** leaves or 2 teaspoons dried oregano
- 3 cloves **garlic,** minced
- ½ teaspoon **pepper**
- **Cilantro sprigs**

1. Trim and discard excess fat from beef. Cut 1-inch-long slits about ½ inch deep and about 1 inch apart over top and bottom of roast.

2. Mix soy sauce, chopped cilantro, liquid smoke, oregano, garlic, and pepper.

3. Set roast in a rimmed dish and spoon soy mixture into slits. Pour remaining mixture over meat.

4. Set roast on a grill above a solid bed of medium-hot coals or on a gas barbecue set on medium-high heat (you can hold your hand at grill level only 3 to 4 seconds). Cover gas grill. Cook roast, turning once, until a thermometer inserted in center of thickest part registers 125° for rare, 20 to 25 minutes total for a 1½- to 2-inch-thick piece.

5. Transfer meat to a board and let rest about 5 minutes. Cut across the grain in thin slices. Garnish with cilantro sprigs.

CARRIE LLOYD

Cool and crunchy soup: For a light lunch, enjoy gazpacho.

Per serving: 115 cal., 30% (34 cal.) from fat; 18 g protein; 3.8 g fat (1.3 g sat.); 0.7 g carbo (0 g fiber); 206 mg sodium; 52 mg chol.

Gazpacho

Nicole Perzik, Los Angeles

As a child in Toulouse, France, Nicole Perzik often crossed the nearby border to visit the home of her Spanish grandparents. There she ate this cool, refreshing soup.

Prep time: About 25 minutes

Makes: 6 to 8 servings

- 2 cans (28 oz. each) **tomatoes**
- 2 tablespoons chopped **fresh basil** leaves
- 1 tablespoon chopped **fresh cilantro**
- 1 tablespoon **balsamic vinegar**
- 2 teaspoons chopped **fresh marjoram** leaves
- 2 teaspoons chopped **fresh oregano** leaves
- 1 teaspoon **lemon juice**
- 1 cup **vegetable broth**
- 1 piece (about 6 oz.) **cucumber**
- 1 firm-ripe **tomato** (about 6 oz.)
- 1 **green bell pepper** (about 6 oz.)
- 1 **white onion** (about 6 oz.)
- **Salt** and **pepper**

1. In a blender or food processor, purée canned tomatoes and their juice, basil, cilantro, vinegar, marjoram, and oregano. Pour into a bowl and add lemon juice and broth. Cover and chill at least 1 hour or up to the next day.

2. Peel, seed, and cut cucumber into ½-inch cubes. Core tomato and cut into ½-inch cubes. Stem, seed, and cut bell pepper into ½-inch cubes. Finely chop onion, rinse, and drain well.

3. Stir cucumber, fresh tomato, green

pepper, and onion into chilled tomato soup. Season with salt and pepper to taste and ladle into bowls.

Per serving: 64 cal., 8.4% (5.4 cal.) from fat; 2.7 g protein; 0.6 g fat (0.1 g sat.); 14 g carbo (2.6 g fiber); 338 mg sodium; 0 mg chol.

Creamy Pesto Pasta

Wendy Nankeville, San Francisco

Thai and lemon were just two of the exotic basil varieties that Wendy Nankeville and a friend bought at the farmers' market one day. What to do with them? This creamy pasta sauce laced with the collection of basils was their solution.

Prep and cook time: About 20 minutes
Makes: 4 servings

- 8 ounces **dried rigatoni pasta**
- 1 **onion** (about 6 oz.), chopped
- 5 cloves **garlic**, minced
- 1 teaspoon **butter** or olive oil
- 1 package (8 oz.) **neufchâtel** (light cream) **cheese**
- ¾ cup **chicken broth**
- ¼ cup **dry white wine**
- 1 cup chopped **fresh basil** leaves (one or more varieties)

  Grated parmesan cheese

  Salt and fresh-ground **pepper**

1. Cook pasta in about 3 quarts boiling water until just barely tender to bite, 7 to 9 minutes. Drain.

2. Meanwhile, in a 10- to 12-inch non-stick frying pan, combine onion, garlic, and butter. Stir often over medium-high heat until onion is limp, about 5 minutes.

3. Add neufchâtel cheese and stir until melted, about 3 minutes. Stir broth and wine into pan and mix until blended. Add basil and stir until wilted, about 2 minutes.

4. Add pasta to sauce and stir until pasta is coated with sauce. If sauce gets too thick, stir in a little water to thin. Spoon onto plates. Add parmesan, salt, and pepper to taste.

Per serving: 409 cal., 35% (144 cal.) from fat; 15 g protein; 16 g fat (9.3 g sat.); 50 g carbo (2.9 g fiber); 263 mg sodium; 46 mg chol.

Mexican Zucchini and Eggs

Susan Mulvihill, Spokane

On her **5-acre** spread, Susan Mulvihill grows summer squash.

Last year she actually got ahead of the prolific zucchini by literally shrinking the squash. Shredded and cooked over high heat, zucchini loses moisture and drops in volume fast. Then, to make the mixture taste moist and creamy, Mulvihill scrambles in fresh eggs. Serve the dish with salsa and warm flour tortillas.

Prep and cook time: About 15 minutes
Makes: 3 or 4 servings

- 1 pound **zucchini**
- 1 teaspoon **olive oil**
- 1 cup coarsely chopped **onion**
- 2 teaspoons **dried oregano**

  Salt and **pepper**

- 6 **large eggs**
- ½ cup **shredded cheddar cheese**

  About ½ cup **tomato salsa**

1. Rinse zucchini, trim and discard ends, and shred.

2. In a 10- to 12-inch nonstick frying pan over high heat, stir oil, zucchini, onion, and oregano often until all the liquid has evaporated, about 6 minutes. Add salt and pepper to taste.

3. With a fork, beat eggs to blend with 1 tablespoon water.

4. Turn heat to low, pour egg mixture into pan and stir with a wide spatula, scraping pan bottom often, just until eggs are softly set, 2 to 3 minutes, or as firm as you like.

5. Spoon onto plates and sprinkle with cheese. Add tomato salsa, salt, and pepper to taste.

Per serving: 222 cal., 57% (126 cal.) from fat; 15 g protein; 14 g fat (5.5 g sat.); 10 g carbo (1.2 g fiber); 507 mg sodium; 334 mg chol.

Sweet Anise Pound Cake

Jalane Sclafani, Thousand Oaks, California

"People go nuts for it. No one's ever had cake this flavor before," says Jalane Sclafani about her pound cake. She invented the recipe by adding the seasonings she liked in her mother-in-law's anise-sesame cookies to a friend's recipe for pound cake.

Slice and eat the cake plain or top with coarsely chopped and sugared strawberries or peaches.

Prep and cook time: About 1½ hours
Makes: 10 to 12 servings

  About ¾ cup (⅜ lb.) **butter** or margarine

- ¾ cup **sugar**
- 3 **large eggs**
- 1 tablespoon grated **lemon** peel
- 1½ teaspoons **anise extract**

  About 1¼ cups **all-purpose flour**

- ½ teaspoon **baking powder**
- ¼ teaspoon **salt**

1. With a mixer, beat ¾ cup butter and sugar until well blended. Add eggs, 1 at a time, beating to blend well with each addition. Beat in lemon peel and anise extract.

2. Mix 1¼ cups flour with baking powder and salt. Add the flour mixture to batter, mixing slowly to incorporate dry ingredients, then beat at medium speed until well blended.

3. Scrape batter into a buttered and flour-dusted 4½- by 8-inch loaf pan. Spread level.

4. Bake in a 325° oven until cake is golden and just begins to pull from pan sides, about 1 hour and 10 minutes. Cool in pan on a rack about 15 minutes. Invert cake onto a plate and serve warm or cool, cut into thin slices.

Per serving: 226 cal., 52% (117 cal.) from fat; 3.1 g protein; 13 g fat (7.8 g sat.); 23 g carbo (0.4 g fiber); 203 mg sodium; 85 mg chol. ◆

Anise extract and lemon peel flavor tender slices of pound cake.

This classic salad is one quick and easy way to enjoy summer's ripe tomatoes. For more ideas and recipes, see page 220.

JAMES CARRIER

198

September

foodguide

by JERRY ANNE DI VECCHIO

tool

Of all the pans and tools for steaming foods, the one that I find most useful is a $1.49 rack I bought at a Vietnamese market. This rack (shown here with Le Creuset cookware) works best as a base for food in containers—a plate, pan, bowl, or mold. The racks come tall and short, wide and narrow, and with different tops. You'll find them in most large Asian food markets and in Asian hardware stores with cooking equipment.

LEFT: CURTIS ANDERSON BELOW: SUZANNE SMITH RIGHT: RICHARD JUNG

SEASONAL NOTE

Tackling pomegranates

■ Pomegranates are fun, if you know how to handle them. Two "tricks" make them a pleasure to keep in the kitchen.

The first is child's play. Gently roll a pomegranate to bruise and pop the seeds inside (without cracking the exterior), then cut a little hole through the skin. Poke a drinking straw into the fruit and start sipping.

The waxy white membrane inside tends to clog a straw, so blow it out now and then. Kids love this part.

As for cooks, they find pomegranates frustrating as well as intimidating. The juicy, edible seeds often pop when plucked out of the membrane maze, squirting bright red, staining juice on everything (including your hands). The solution: work underwater.

First, cut off the crown end of the fruit, then score the skin in segments like an orange. Immerse the pomegranate in a bowl of water and pull the fruit open. As you break the seeds free, they will tend to sink. Discard the skin and membrane and scatter the glossy seeds over fruit salads, spicy pilafs, or ice cream. Or just eat them.

Pasta with Mint and Peas

Prep and cook time: 20 to 25 minutes
Notes: Other pea options are Chinese pea pods and tender pea shoots.
Makes: 2 or 3 servings

- 2 cups (about ½ lb.) **sugar snap peas**
- ½ pound **dried capellini pasta**
- 1 clove **garlic**, minced
- 2 tablespoons **butter** or olive oil
- 1 tablespoon finely slivered **lemon** peel (yellow part only)
- 3 to 4 tablespoons **lemon juice**
- ⅓ cup slivered **fresh mint** leaves
- ½ cup **crème fraîche** or sour cream
- **Salt** and fresh-ground **pepper**

1. In a 4- to 5-quart pan, bring 2 to 3 quarts of water to boiling over high heat.

2. Meanwhile, pull off and discard stem ends and strings from peas. Rinse and drain.

3. When water boils, add pasta, pushing down into water. Cook until almost tender to bite, about 3 minutes. Add peas and cook until they turn bright green, about 2 minutes.

4. Drain peas and pasta well in a colander.

5. In the pan, combine garlic and butter over high heat, stirring until butter melts. Add peas and pasta and mix until pasta stops sizzling, about 1 minute.

6. Add about 2 teaspoons of the lemon peel, 2 tablespoons of the lemon juice, and about 1 tablespoon mint to pan. Mix.

7. Put pasta mixture in wide soup bowls, swirling to make a well in the center. Spoon crème fraîche into the center of bowls and sprinkle with remaining peel, mint, and lemon juice. Add salt and pepper to taste.

Per serving: 533 cal., 41% (216 cal.) from fat; 13 g protein; 24 g fat (14 g sat.); 65 g carbo (3.6 g fiber); 113 mg sodium; 54 mg chol.

A night for pasta

■ On pilgrimages to Santa Fe—what else can you call visits to this historically intense, graceful community—I'm always taken by the lack of contradiction between the old and the new. Buildings and houses conform to architectural guidelines, and interiors that would seem stark in more contemporary structures feel inviting. This was the environment at Cafe Escalera, which just recently closed. Few of the dishes I enjoyed there laid claim to traditional ties, but the natural, uncontrived presenta-

tions showed Santa Fe's freshest ingredients off to their advantage.

Last summer, I dined at Escalera several times with Sally, Gil, and David—longtime expedition partners. On one occasion, the pasta special created by chef Karla Helland caught our collective eye. It looked so light and appealing that warm evening. We usually chose a variety of dishes and shared tastes. But this time, the pasta got a unanimous vote.

It was a wise decision.

BACK TO BASICS

Relishing fresh plums

■ It's a curious thing, but plums with red or purple-blue skins always get tarter and livelier when they are cooked. In fact, the bluish-purple prune plums (the oval-shaped fruit also called French or Italian) are downright bland raw and, to my taste, good only when cooked. As to yellow and green plums, I can't vouch for their behavior because they never seem to capture my attention in such vivid company.

Tartness gives cooked plums versatility. When we expect a houseful of people, as when friends visit our Provence retreat in September, I keep a big bowl of plum relish in the refrigerator. It's a lively accent for simply cooked meat or poultry, splendid as a condiment for curry, and intriguing in a ham sandwich. It's even quite nice with yogurt for breakfast.

Red Wine Plum Relish

Prep and cook time: About 45 minutes
Notes: The relish thickens as it cools. Store in a covered jar in the refrigerator up to 10 days.
Makes: 3 cups

2 teaspoons grated **orange** peel
2 cups **orange juice**
2 cups **dry red wine**
   About ¾ cup **sugar**
¼ teaspoon **cardamom seed**
1 teaspoon **coriander seed**
1 tablespoon minced **fresh ginger**
2 pounds firm to ripe **prune plums**

1. In a 12- to 14-inch frying pan, combine orange peel, orange juice, wine, ¾ cup sugar, cardamom, coriander, and ginger. Boil over high heat until reduced to about 1 cup, about 20 minutes.

2. Meanwhile, rinse plums and cut into chunks; discard pits.

3. Add plums to reduced sauce. Simmer rapidly, stirring often, until fruit is very soft and mixture is reduced to about 3 cups, about 25 minutes. Taste and add additional sugar if desired, then simmer 2 to 3 minutes more.

4. Serve warm, cool, or cold.

Per ¼ cup: 125 cal., 1% (1.8 cal.) from fat; 0.9 g protein; 0.2 g fat (0 g sat.); 32 g carbo (0.1 g fiber); 3.3 mg sodium; 0 mg chol.

JAMES CARRIER (2)

BOOK NOTES

Fast food

■ Although a Reuben is the quintessence of deli sandwiches, its filling is equally at home in a toasty flour tortilla. *Sunset* food writer Andrew Baker, who often resorts to quesadillas for a quick supper, contributed his Reuben to the *Sunset 30 Minutes or Less Cookbook* ($29.95 hardbound, $19.95 paperback), available this month. The book's focus is fast main dishes (soups, salads, meat, poultry, seafood, pasta, and vegetarian). But the final chapter in this 240-page, 237-recipe volume is devoted to desserts, and they're fast, too. To order, call (800) 526-5111.

Also published this month are two additions to the Sunset Books Casual Cuisines of the World series. *Country Inn,* by George Mahaffey, presents recipes with hospitable histories. *Pizzeria,* by Evan Kleiman, has Italian roots with contemporary overtones. Both handsomely photographed books have 128 pages and cost $19.95. You'll find them in bookstores, too.

Reuben Quesadillas

Prep and cook time: About 15 minutes
Makes: 4 servings

½ cup **salsa**
½ cup **sour cream**
2 cups (½ lb.) shredded **Swiss cheese**
4 **flour tortillas** (10-in. size)
3 cups packaged **coleslaw mix**
½ pound thinly sliced **corned beef**

1. In a small bowl, mix salsa and sour cream.

2. Sprinkle ¼ cup of the cheese over half of 1 tortilla. Then place ¾ cup coleslaw mix on cheese. Drizzle about 3 tablespoons of the salsa mixture over coleslaw. Lay ¼ of the corned beef onto coleslaw; top with ¼ cup more cheese. Fold tortilla over to cover filling. Repeat to make 3 more quesadillas.

3. Place quesadillas slightly apart on baking sheets. Broil 4 to 6 inches below heat until crisp and lightly browned, 1 to 2 minutes (watch closely). Using a wide spatula, carefully turn each quesadilla over. Broil until crisp and lightly browned on other side, 1 to 2 minutes more.

4. Cut quesadillas into wedges. Serve with remaining salsa mixture.

Per serving: 640 cal., 52% (333 cal.) from fat; 34 g protein; 37 g fat (18 g sat.); 43 g carbo (2.1 g fiber); 1,414 mg sodium; 120 mg chol.

FOOD NEWS # Artisan cheeses

■ The Callahans at Bellwether Farms west of Petaluma are pioneers in sheep cheeses in the West, but now the family is making several cows' milk cheeses as well. I was especially pleased by three. Their fresh farmer's cheese is delicate and delicious, unlike the drier versions used by commercial bakers for pastries. I also liked the mellow, smooth semisoft Carmody and the custard-like and highly perishable Crescenza.

You can find these cheeses at many specialty and natural-food supermarkets. For more information, call Bellwether Farms at (707) 763-0993. ◆

The Wine Guide

by KAREN MacNEIL

A few good Merlots

■ One of the most perplexing things about Merlot is why so many people are so wild about it. I mean, Merlot can be sensational, but all too often this wine has about as much personality as a dish towel.

I'm probably making enemies by the minute, but let me explain.

For my money, Merlot is not, generally speaking, as rich and intense as Cabernet Sauvignon; it isn't as lively and lip-smacking as Zinfandel; it isn't as sensual as Pinot Noir. Moreover, as anyone who's ever tasted a lineup of California Merlots knows, the whole shtick about Merlot being "softer" than other reds is a bunch of malarkey. Merlot doesn't necessarily have more softness; what it has is good PR.

Let's consider some facts:

• The current restaurant craze for Merlot has sent vintners scurrying to buy whatever Merlot grapes they can find—no matter what quality. It's important to understand that when the mania started a few years ago, most vintners did not have substantial plantings of Merlot (many current Merlot makers had none at all).

• Much of the Merlot for sale, at least in California, is not from the top vineyards. In fact, huge amounts of Merlot come from vineyard areas that charitably could be called mediocre.

• As for the Merlot from top vineyard sites, many of those vines have been in the ground only a few years. Wine made from young vines lacks depth, richness, and complexity. The wine may have a simple, nice flavor. But without depth of flavor, there's a limit to how compelling such a wine can be.

• Winemakers, viticulturists, and scientists have spent years of research attempting to understand the nuances of Cabernet Sauvignon, Chardonnay, and

RICK MARIANI

Pinot Noir. The wisdom that now goes into the growing and making of these varietals is almost awesome. And you can taste the success in the wines. Does that mean we should drink only those varieties? Of course not. But it's important to know that in the United States, with the exception of a handful of vintners who have been making Merlot for a long time, relatively little research has been done on the varietal.

Where does all of this leave us? Needing to be cautious, because you can pay big bucks for these wines. And it helps to know what you are drinking.

Merlot (French for *little blackbird*) is the most widely planted grape in Bordeaux. Many people believe that Cabernet is Bordeaux's major grape. Not so. Merlot is, but it's almost always blended with Cabernet (and a few other grapes) to give it more focus, structure, flavor, and all-around oomph.

For more than a century, Merlot has also grown in northern Italy (though very little of this is exported). And, of course, it's produced in California and Washington (where it can be stellar).

WINE DICTIONARY

Aeration

The process of intentionally exposing wine to oxygen to "open up" the wine and soften it. Some varieties, such as Merlot and Cabernet Sauvignon, benefit greatly from aeration. Wine drinkers can aerate a wine simply by pouring it into a carafe or even just swirling the wine vigorously in a generous-size glass. — *K. M.*

BEST BETS

Among West Coast wineries, the Merlot standard-bearers have been Beringer, Duckhorn, and Markham in California, and Leonetti in Washington. All four make excellent wines. Here are other Merlots you may want to know about.

■ *Arrowood Merlot 1994,* $35 (Sonoma County, California). A grand, supple wine bursting with menthol.

■ *Chateau Souverain Merlot 1994,* $16.50 (Alexander Valley, California). Big and juicy. Begs for a grilled steak.

■ *Chateau Ste. Michelle Merlot, Cold Creek Vineyard, Indian Wells Vineyard, or Canoe Ridge Estate Vineyard, 1994,* $29–$31 (Columbia Valley, Washington). All three of these single-vineyard Merlots from Chateau Ste. Michelle are luscious blockbusters with big, ripe boysenberry fruit and textures like melted chocolate.

■ *Colour Volant Merlot 1995,* $9 (Vin de Pays d'Oc, Languedoc, France). Delicious mocha, berry, and coffee flavors.

■ *Estancia Merlot 1995,* $14 (Alexander Valley). Big, lively, and bright with terrific berry and coffee flavors.

■ *Robert Pecota Merlot, Steven Andre Vineyard, 1995,* $25 (Napa Valley, California). Loads of voluptuous chocolate with tinges of spice.

■ *Whitehall Lane Merlot Reserve, Leonardini Vineyard, 1995,* $36 (Napa Valley). Smoky and complex.

Lots of inexpensive Merlot is now coming from the Languedoc region of southern France and from Chile and Argentina. These inexpensive Merlots can actually be delightful, but as with all bargain hunting, you have to sift through a lot of passable stuff before you find a gem.

What are Merlot's flavors supposed to be like? I think of Merlot as Cabernet's understudy. However, Merlot can often have wonderful mocha, boysenberry, and chocolate flavors and a texture that reminds you of a flannel blanket. Cozy. Inviting. ◆

apple edens

A seasonal celebration of the West's best apple regions—plus a bushel of apple recipes and a grower's guide to the antique apples best suited to your garden

by

LINDA LAU ANUSASANANAN,

JIM McCAUSLAND,

and LAUREN BONAR SWEZEY

NO FRUIT IS MORE FUNDAMENTAL, more mythical, or more maligned than the apple. It is the source of all knowledge and the cause of our banishment from Eden. It has been credited with giving Isaac Newton the idea for gravity and Steve Jobs the idea for the home computer. And it is the obligatory staple of school lunch boxes the year round, usually in the form of a tasteless, mushy orb that children would rather deposit on their teacher's desk than munch. • But a fresh apple in season transcends all that. Bite into an impossibly sweet Golden Delicious or a mouth-puckering Newtown Pippin in September and you will never take apples for granted again. • If you are on the road this fall, consider a drive into Oregon's Hood River Valley and California's Apple Hill, two of the West's finest apple-growing regions, or any of 18 other apple countries. No time to make a trip? No problem: we bring the regions to you with apple-country recipes for pie, cake, butter, and chutney. And if all this talk about apples makes you long for an orchard in your backyard, turn to page 212 for advice on the antique apple varieties that grow best in your area.

Opposite page: Sierra Beauties at Sonoma Antique Apple Nursery (see pages 212 and 213). Above, left: Mutsus at Larsen Apple Barn in Apple Hill (story, page 208). Above, Mary's Apple Cake, a Hood River Valley tradition (recipe, page 206).

Hood River Valley, Oregon

■ Driving along Interstate 84 an hour east of Portland, you could zip right past the rich volcanic valley to the south and notice nothing more than a river tumbling out of the hills and into the Columbia. But about a mile up the Hood River Valley, the vista opens to reveal the vast orchards that make this Oregon's largest fruit-growing district.

Most of the trees in the valley produce winter pears, accounting for almost a third of the U.S. crop. But the Hood River area has been in the commercial apple business for 121 years, and its growers currently harvest about 33 million pounds of apples annually, including the best Newtown Pippins on the planet.

Much of the fruit from the Hood is destined for commercial markets at home and abroad, so most of the apples are picked on the green side (important for long-term cold storage). But a few stands harvest fruit a little closer to ripe since they know they'll sell it immediately. Ask when you buy, or better yet, try it. Fruit that's too green will taste a little starchy, but fruit that's been picked at its peak will make you glad you turned off the interstate.

OUTSTANDING STANDS

All the stands listed here let you sample different kinds of apples free—some sell cider and pie, too. To reach the area from Portland, take I-84 east to State Highway 35, turn south, and follow the directions on the map at right. For a free guide to the Hood River Valley's many farms, call (800) 366-3530. To preview the valley on-line, go to http://www.gorge.net/hrccc.

1. Wicklund Orchards. Pearl Wicklund has been selling Hood River Valley fruit since 1955, first in Portland, then direct from her orchard. Her packing shed, about 3 miles south of I-84, is loaded with bins of apples and pears, and is absolutely mouse-free—her many cats see to that. *1860 Highway 35; (541) 386-3888.*

2. Rasmussen Farms. U-pick pumpkins, a corn maze, and sunflowers supplement Dollie and Lynn Rasmussen's fruit business. They buy from neighbors in the valley, and offer a few special events through the season. Stop at their Pear Party September 20 and 21, and choose from more than 12 kinds of apples and 18 varieties of pears. *3020 Thomsen Rd.; (541) 386-4622.*

3. McCurdy Farms. Selling from a quaint, shake-roofed picker's cabin, Heather Blaine-McCurdy and Craig McCurdy, both of whom grew up in the Hood River apple business, raise 98 percent of what they sell. McCurdy's offers 25 varieties of apples, and its apple-cider slushies are the hottest ice-cold drink in the valley. *2080 Tucker Rd.; (541) 386-1628.*

4. River Bend Farm & Country Store. Part country store, part canning kitchen, part fruit stand, and part organic vegetable and flower farm, River Bend's weathered old store is named for its location on a bend in Hood River. Neighbors grow the apples, but River Bend makes its own 3-pound apple pies and preserves (everything from sweet huckleberry to tangy raspberry-rhubarb). Stop for a picnic under the trees. If you hurry, you might still catch Apple Days on August 23 and 24. *2363 Tucker; (541) 386-8766.*

5. Draper's Farm. When Roman Braun left his California aerospace job behind in 1962, he and his wife, Ann, decided to buy an orchard in Hood River Valley. That put them immediately into the fruit-stand business, and they've been there ever since. Now their daughter, Theresa, with her family, runs the operation, which is about a mile north of the town of Mount Hood. Because Draper's is 1,000 feet higher than the town of Hood River, its season starts September 1. (In general, varieties in the upper valley mature about two weeks later than those in the lower valley.) Draper's also does a booming business in homemade cider, honey from its own bees, and fall prunes, plums, peaches, and pears. *6200 Highway 35; (541) 352-6625.*

Mary's Apple Cake

Prep and cook time: About 1 hour

Notes: Using her great-grandmother's recipe, Cindy Davis sells this cake to River Bend Country Store customers.

Makes: 12 servings

About 2 cups **all-purpose flour**

1¼ cups **sugar**

2 teaspoons **baking powder**

½ teaspoon **salt**

¾ cup (⅜ lb.) plus 2 tablespoons **butter** or margarine

¼ cup **milk**

1 **large egg**

4 cups peeled, cored, and thinly sliced **apples** such as Golden Delicious, Granny Smith, or Newtown Pippin (about 1¼ lb. total)

1 teaspoon **ground cinnamon**

1. In a food processor or bowl, mix 2 cups flour, ¼ cup sugar, baking powder, and salt.

2. Cut the ¾ cup butter into small pieces and add to flour mixture. Whirl or cut in butter with a pastry

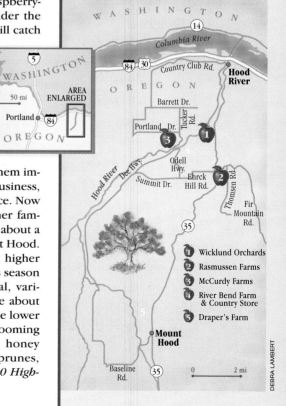

blender until mixture has texture of fine crumbs.

3. Beat milk and egg to blend. Pour into flour mixture and whirl or stir with a fork just to evenly moisten. On a lightly floured board, knead dough briefly until it holds together.

4. With floured hands, pat the dough evenly over bottom of a 9- by 13-inch pan and press edges up sides to form a slight ridge.

5. Place apple slices, overlapping slightly, in 3 rows down the length of the dough.

6. In a food processor or bowl, whirl or rub with your fingers the remaining 2 tablespoons butter, 1 cup sugar, and cinnamon until mixture has texture of fine crumbs. Sprinkle over apples.

7. Bake in the middle of a 350° oven until cake is browned, about 40 minutes. Cut into squares. Serve cake warm or cool.

Per serving: 318 cal., 40% (126 cal.) from fat; 3 g protein; 14 g fat (8.6 g sat.); 46 g carbo (1.3 g fiber); 318 mg sodium; 55 mg chol.

Columbia Gorge Hotel Apple Tart

Prep and cook time: About 1 hour

Notes: For a grand finale, serve wedges of this tart as the Columbia Gorge Hotel does, with both ice cream and vanilla crème anglaise (recipe follows), flaming the dessert with brandy at the table.

Makes: 6 to 8 servings

    About 2 pounds **tart apples** such as Granny Smith or Newtown Pippin

2   cups **sugar**

2   tablespoons **butter** or margarine

1   sheet **frozen puff pastry** (½ of a 17-oz. package), thawed

1   tablespoon beaten **egg**

1½ to 2 cups **vanilla ice cream**

½   cup **Calvados** or brandy

1. Peel, core, and cut apples into 1-inch-thick wedges to make about 6 cups.

2. Select a frying pan, with an ovenproof handle, that measures 10 inches across the top and holds 2½ to 2¾ quarts. In pan, mix sugar and ¾ cup water, then add apples and butter. Cook over high heat, shaking pan often, until sugar melts, then boil until apples begin to caramelize, 20 to 25 minutes.

3. On a lightly floured board, roll pastry into a 10-inch-wide round, trimming edges to make even. Lay pastry over apples in pan and brush lightly with beaten egg.

4. Bake apple tart in a 375° oven until crust is deep golden brown and juices bubble around the edge, 15 to 20 minutes.

5. Invert a rimmed serving plate over tart. Holding pan and plate together, turn dessert over. Lift off pan and fit any apples that are stuck to pan back onto dessert. Cut tart into wedges and transfer to dessert plates. Add ice cream.

6. Pour Calvados into frying pan over medium heat. When hot, ignite Calvados (away from flammable surfaces or vent) and spoon flaming brandy over servings.

Per serving: 532 cal., 30% (162 cal.) from fat; 3.6 g protein; 18 g fat (5.2 g sat.); 84 g carbo (2.3 g fiber); 127 mg sodium; 27 mg chol.

Vanilla Crème Anglaise

Prep and cook time: About 12 minutes

Notes: Make this custard sauce up to 1 day ahead. It's also delicious with plain baked apples.

Makes: About ¾ cup

½   cup **whipping cream**

⅓   cup **milk**

½   **vanilla bean** (3- to 4-in. piece), split lengthwise, or 1 teaspoon vanilla

2   **large egg** yolks

2   tablespoons **sugar**

1. In the top of a double boiler, combine whipping cream, milk, and vanilla bean. Set pan directly over medium heat and stir frequently until bubbles form at rim, about 2½ minutes. Lift out vanilla bean and, with a knife, scrape tiny black seeds free and add to hot cream mixture.

2. In a bowl, mix yolks with sugar to blend. Whisk about ⅓ of the hot cream mixture into bowl, then return egg mixture to pan.

3. Set pan over barely simmering water and stir until custard coats the back of a metal spoon in a velvety layer, 3 to 4 minutes. Remove sauce from heat and serve. Or nest pan in ice water, stir to cool custard quickly, about 3 minutes, and serve cold.

Per 2 tablespoons: 104 cal., 72% (75 cal.) from fat; 1.8 g protein; 8.3 g fat (4.6 g sat.); 5.5 g carbo (0 g fiber); 16 mg sodium; 95 mg chol.

Columbia Gorge Hotel Apple Tart

recipes

Apple Hill, California

■ Apples shouldn't grow here. That's your first impression as you turn off U.S. Highway 50 into Apple Hill. The soil is an almost Martian red, the sky feels too close, too blue. It's the sort of place where you'd expect to find prowling mountain lions—and people do—not tidy rows of fruit-laden trees.

But apples have grown in El Dorado County since the days of the forty-niners, who did not live by the lure of gold alone. Apple Hill was actually better known for its pears until about 30 years ago, when a blight all but wiped out the fruit, prompting growers to replant in apples, primarily Golden Delicious. Today more than 50 growers tend orchards on Apple Hill, farming anywhere from a couple of dozen to a couple of hundred acres.

And yes, the apples here *are* as golden and delicious as their name implies—in fall they are like nothing you've ever tasted. Some say it's that red, iron-rich soil. Others say it's the elevation—at 2,000 to 4,000 feet, Apple Hill gets cold enough for the trees to go dormant in the winter, which promotes a profusion of blossoms come

spring and high yields come fall. Summer heat makes the apples sweet, and cool evenings and mornings during harvesttime bring out the apples' natural acids. Whatever the reason, Apple Hill apples have a more complex, brighter flavor than apples grown down on the flats.

AN APPLE HILL ROMP

This month and next, Apple Hill apples are at their peak. Some growers also sell U-pick pumpkins in October. To reach the area from Sacramento (about 50 miles west of Apple Hill), take the Camino exit north off U.S. 50 and follow the directions on the map on page 87. To order a copy of the "Apple Hill Cider Press," a complete guide to the area, send $1 to Box 494, Camino, CA 95709, or call (916) 644-7692. Another good source of information is the growers' association Web site: http://www.applehill.com.

1. Larsen Apple Barn. The Larsen farm has been in the family since the Civil War; apples have been growing here since the turn of the century. It's got the oldest-producing apple tree in

El Dorado County, a modest museum, and a funny-looking, stuffed big-red-apple guy swinging over some picnic tables. But the main reason to visit Larsen's is the apples, specifically the Mutsus. Bite into one and you'll wonder why Larsen's doesn't devote its entire 150 acres of apple orchards to this sweet-and-sour gem. Also worth checking out is the packing shed, where most days you can watch fruit being sorted by size and boxed for seasonal delivery to Lucky grocery stores in the area. *2461 Larsen Dr.; (916) 644-1415.*

2. Denver Dan's. Just up the road from Larsen's, surrounding an old Quonset hut in a tight little canyon, are the orchards of Denver Dan's, one of the few places on Apple Hill where you can pick your own apples. This month you can fill your basket with Gravenstein, Red Delicious, Golden Delicious, Fuji, Winter Banana, McIntosh, and Jonathan apples. Next month Winesap, Granny Smith, Arkansas Black, two types of Romes, Pippins, and Rhode Island Greenings are ready. Inside the hut, a chart lists what's currently available. Denver Dan's also makes wonderful apple-cider vinegars—try the lemon sage variety. *4344 Bumble Bee Lane; (916) 644-6881.*

3. Bolster's Hilltop Ranch. Craftspeople fill the parking area on weekends, but the real craftsmanship is inside the apple shed, where the Bolsters produce an unparalleled hard cider. Among the apples on the ranch's 40 acres are varieties just for this blend—Hudson, Braeburn, and Pink Pearl among them. If you hurry, you may catch the last of the summer blueberries; pumpkins keep the place busy in October. *2000 Larsen; (916) 644-2230.*

4. Plubell's Family Orchard. The family's 12-acre orchard is a couple of hilltops away from its rustic retail outlet, but don't let that stop you from visiting this spot on the edge of the Eldorado National Forest. There's a petting zoo for the kids, a fine selection of dried fruits and nuts, and great barbecued chicken and ribs on many fall weekends. *1800 Larsen; (916) 647-0613.*

O'Halloran's Apple Trail Ranch

GARY PARKER

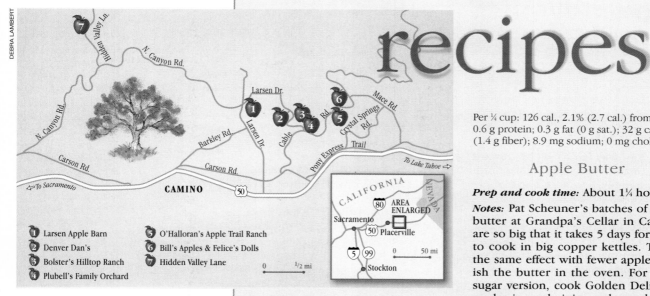

DEBRA LAMBERT

recipes

1 Larsen Apple Barn
2 Denver Dan's
3 Bolster's Hilltop Ranch
4 Plubell's Family Orchard
5 O'Halloran's Apple Trail Ranch
6 Bill's Apples & Felice's Dolls
7 Hidden Valley Lane

5. O'Halloran's Apple Trail Ranch. Drive around Apple Hill long enough, with the obligatory tastes of apple pie and the like, and you'll eventually want to stretch your legs. The short trail at O'Halloran's won't burn off all your collected calories (it takes just 10 or 15 minutes to make the walk), but it is a pleasant opportunity to wander a bit through a working apple orchard. Like most growers, O'Halloran's devotes most of its acres to Golden and Red Delicious, but you'll also find Fuji, Mutsu, Gala, Braeburn, and Winesap—all neatly displayed in wood crates inside the ranch's tasting shed. *2261 Cable Rd.; (916) 644-3389.*

6. Bill's Apples & Felice's Dolls. If you haven't sampled an apple by the time you reach Bill's, you will within minutes of walking through the doors because Bill himself hands just about everyone a peeled, cored, ribbon-sliced apple. Even if it's your third or fourth of the day, you'll be shocked by how fresh and sweet his Golden Delicious apples taste. Also on the grounds are all manner of knickknacks, which are sold in the gift shop. *2234 Cable; (916) 644-5283.*

7. Hidden Valley Lane. Most of the apple stands cited above are in the upper Apple Hill area. Hidden Valley Lane lies to the west. It's not as packed with places to visit as other parts of Apple Hill, but the road itself is lovely, running past rows and rows of green trees laden with yellow or red fruit. Early in the season, it's quite a sight.

Rose's Hot and Spicy Apple Chutney

Prep and cook time: About 2 hours
Notes: Rose Stuhlsatz, at the Big Apple stand in Camino, cans her chutney. But it can be refrigerated for up to 6 months.
Makes: About 6 cups

2¼ to 2½ pounds **apples** such as Granny Smith, Gravenstein, or Stayman Winesap

2 to 3 **fresh jalapeño chilies** (1½ to 2 oz. total)

1 cup **cider vinegar**

2 cups firmly packed **brown sugar**

1½ cups **raisins**

1 **onion** (½ lb.), chopped

⅓ cup minced **fresh ginger**

2 cloves **garlic,** minced

1 tablespoon **mustard seed**

1. Peel, core, and slice apples about ¼ inch thick to make about 8 cups. Put slices in a 6- to 8-quart pan.

2. Trim and discard chili stems. For less heat, discard chili seeds. Finely chop chilies; add to apples.

3. Also add vinegar, sugar, raisins, onion, ginger, garlic, and mustard seed. Bring to a boil over high heat. Reduce heat and simmer, stirring occasionally, until apples are very soft when pierced and juice is syrupy, about 1½ hours.

4. Serve warm or cool. Cover airtight and store in the refrigerator.

Per ¼ cup: 126 cal., 2.1% (2.7 cal.) from fat; 0.6 g protein; 0.3 g fat (0 g sat.); 32 g carbo (1.4 g fiber); 8.9 mg sodium; 0 mg chol.

Apple Butter

Prep and cook time: About 1¼ hours
Notes: Pat Scheuner's batches of apple butter at Grandpa's Cellar in Camino are so big that it takes 5 days for them to cook in big copper kettles. To get the same effect with fewer apples, finish the butter in the oven. For a no-sugar version, cook Golden Delicious apples in apple juice and use about 1 cup honey instead of the brown and granulated sugars.
Makes: 5 to 6 cups

5 pounds **apples** such as Gravenstein, Elstar, or McIntosh

1 cup **apple juice** or water

½ cup firmly packed **brown sugar**

1 to 1½ cups **granulated sugar**

1 tablespoon **ground cinnamon**

½ teaspoon **ground cloves**

¼ teaspoon **ground allspice**

1. Peel, quarter, and core apples.

2. In a 6- to 8-quart pan, combine apples and juice. Cover and bring to a boil over high heat. Reduce heat and simmer, stirring occasionally, until apples are very soft when pressed, 20 to 30 minutes.

3. In a blender or food processor, purée apple mixture, a portion at a time. Pour purée into a roasting pan about 12- by 17-inch size. Stir in brown sugar and granulated sugar to taste. Mix in the ground cinnamon, cloves, and allspice.

4. Bake, uncovered, in a 325° oven, stirring occasionally, until butter is thick enough to mound when spooned onto a plate, 30 to 45 minutes.

5. Serve warm or cool. To store, cover and chill airtight up to 1 month. Or spoon into freezer containers, leaving at least 1 inch headspace. Cover airtight and freeze up to 1 year.

Per ¼ cup: 121 cal., 2.2% (2.7 cal.) from fat; 0.2 g protein; 0.3 g fat (0 g sat.); 31 g carbo (1.8 g fiber); 2.8 mg sodium; 0 mg chol.

Other Western apple regions

ARIZONA

Willcox. Most of Arizona's commercial apple growing is done in the southeast part of the state. From Interstate 10 near Willcox, take exit 340 and head north on Fort Grant Road toward Bonita. Stands start about 8 miles north of the freeway. For more information, call (520) 384-2272.

BRITISH COLUMBIA

Cobble Hill. It's not an apple region per se, but this tiny town just south of the Cowichan Valley is home to one of the best places for apples, the Merridale Cidery. To get here from Victoria, take Trans-Canada Highway 1 north 40 kilometers and turn west on Shawnigan–Mill Bay Road, then turn north at Cameron-Taggart Road. (250) 743-4293.

CALIFORNIA

Sonoma County. State 116 between U.S. 101 and State 12 isn't called the Gravenstein Highway for nothing. For a guide to the county's bounty, send $2 to Sonoma County Farm Trails, Box 6032, Santa Rosa, CA 95406.

Tehachapi. The highest concentration of apple orchards and stands is off Highline Road, Casey Drive, and Robin Lane (from State 58, take Tehachapi Willow Springs Rd. south to Highline and turn right). Tehachapi hosts its Apple Harvest Fair in Railroad Park downtown on September 27 and 28.

See Canyon. Exit U.S. 101 south of San Luis Obispo at See Canyon/San Luis Bay Drive, go west a mile, then turn right on See Canyon Road; you'll find several apple ranches within 4 miles.

Oak Glen. From I-10 southeast of San Bernardino, take the Beaumont Avenue exit (State 79); drive north 9 miles to Oak Glen. For a recorded message of activities, call the Oak Glen Apple Growers Association at (909) 797-6833.

Julian. The best orchards to start with are Apple Lane, just east of town on State 78; Sun Mountain (for U-pick info, call 760/765-0808); and Meyer Orchards, between Julian and Santa Ysabel on State 78. In the town itself, practically every other store sells apple pie. To reach Julian from I-5 at Oceanside, take State 78 east 57 miles. For more information, call (619) 765-0707.

NEW MEXICO

For a free map of the state's apple-growing regions, call (505) 425-7015.

Española Valley. The biggest apple area in New Mexico lies along State 68 between Taos and Española.

Albuquerque area. Orchards and stands dot State 314 through Belen about 30 miles south of Albuquerque.

Mimbres Valley. You'll find orchards along State 152 between U.S. 180 and San Lorenzo. An apple festival is held over Labor Day weekend in Hillsboro, east of the Mimbres Mountains.

OREGON

Rogue River Valley. Apple orchards are making a comeback in this valley between Ashland and Medford, off I-5, although pears are still king.

UTAH

Box Elder County Fruitway. Orchards follow U.S. 89 just south of Brigham City almost to Ogden. For a list of growers, call (801) 734-3387.

Provo. Most apples grow south of town, but there are locations to the north and west of Utah Lake.

Hurricane. Apples abound southwest of Zion National Park off State 9.

WASHINGTON

Whatcom County. Apple growing is centered around Everson. Start at Cloud Mountain Farm (6906 Goodwin Rd; 360/966-5859) or Stoney Ridge Farm (2092 Van Dyk Rd.; 966-3919).

Green Bluff. From Spokane, go 7 miles east on I-90 to the Argonne Road exit, drive north 10 miles, turn right on Day–Mount Spokane Road, and follow the signs into Green Bluff.

Wenatchee River Valley. A mile or so south of Leavenworth on U.S. 2 is Prey's Fruit Barn, which grows 30 kinds of apples. Other stands are strung along U.S. 2 and U.S. 97.

Yakima. Washington's Fruit Place Visitor Center (105 S. 18th St.; 509/576-3090) is a good place to begin any exploration of this rich apple region.

Oak Glen Apple Pie with Cinnamon Sauce

Prep and cook time: About 1½ hours

Notes: In the Southern California community of Oak Glen, Theresa Law of Law's Oak Glen Coffee Shop and Steve Gillespie of Los Rios Rancho make similar apple pies. This recipe incorporates the best of both. Adjust sugar and lemon juice according to the sweetness of the apples you use.

Makes: 6 to 8 servings

- 9 cups peeled, cored, and thinly sliced **apples** such as Idared, Jonagold, Newtown Pippin, or Stayman Winesap (about 2½ lb. total)
- ½ to ¾ cup **granulated sugar**
- 4½ tablespoons **cornstarch**
- 1 to 2 tablespoons **lemon juice**
- 1 teaspoon **ground cinnamon**
- ½ teaspoon **ground nutmeg**
  Pastry for a double-crust 9-inch pie
- 1⅓ cups **apple juice**
- 1 **cinnamon stick** (3 in.)
- 1 strip **orange** peel (½ by 4 in., orange part only)
- ¾ cup firmly packed **brown sugar**
  Vanilla ice cream (optional)

1. Mix apple slices with ½ cup granulated sugar, 3 tablespoons cornstarch, 1 tablespoon lemon juice, and ground cinnamon and nutmeg. Taste and, if desired, add more granulated sugar and lemon juice.

2. On a lightly floured board, roll half the pastry into a round ⅛ inch thick. Line a 9-inch pie pan with pastry. Fill with apple mixture.

3. On a lightly floured board, roll remaining pastry into a ⅛-inch-thick round and lay over apple mixture. Fold edges of top pastry over edges of the bottom one and crimp to seal together. Cut decorative slits in top pastry and sprinkle with about 1 tablespoon granulated sugar.

4. Bake on the lowest rack in a 375° oven until juices bubble in center of pie, 1 to 1¼ hours. If pastry edges brown before pie is done, drape affected areas with foil. Cool pie on a rack at least 2 hours.

5. Meanwhile, in a 1½- to 2-quart pan, combine apple juice, cinnamon stick, and orange peel. Cover and simmer

recipes

NOEL BARNHURST

Which apple to cook?

Choose the market variety that suits the use. Remember, two apples, 3 inches wide, weigh about 1 pound. Peeled and sliced, they yield 3⅗ to 4 cups.

VARIETY	SAUCE	PIE
Akane	•	•
Cortland	•	•
Elstar	•	
Empire	•	•
Golden Delicious	•	•
Granny Smith	•	
Gravenstein	•	•
Idared	•	•
Jonagold		•
Jonathan	•	•
McIntosh	•	
Melrose	•	•
Newtown Pippin	•	•
Stayman Winesap	•	•

over low heat for 15 minutes. Stir in brown sugar until it dissolves. Mix remaining 1½ tablespoons cornstarch smoothly with 3 tablespoons water; stir into juice mixture over high heat until sauce boils. Discard cinnamon stick and orange peel.

6. Cut warm or cool pie into wedges; top each portion with vanilla ice cream and warm or cool cinnamon sauce.

Per serving: 476 cal., 28% (135 cal.) from fat; 3.2 g protein; 15 g fat (3.8 g sat.); 84 g carbo (3.2 g fiber); 244 mg sodium; 0 mg chol.

Los Rios Apple Crisp

Prep and cook time: About 1¼ hours

Notes: This crisp has become a classic at Los Rios Rancho's bakery.

Makes: 9 servings

8 cups peeled, cored, and thinly sliced **apples** such as Gravenstein, Granny Smith, or Stayman Winesap (about 2¼ lb. total)

½ cup **granulated sugar**

¾ cup plus 2 tablespoons **unbleached** or regular **all-purpose flour**

2 teaspoons **ground cinnamon**

1 cup **regular rolled oats**

¾ cup firmly packed **brown sugar**

½ cup (¼ lb.) **butter** or margarine, cut into ½-inch chunks

Top: Hot from the oven, Oak Glen Apple Pie. Above: Los Rios Apple Crisp.

¾ cup chopped **pecans**

Vanilla ice cream (optional)

1. In a 9-inch square baking dish or shallow 1½- to 2-quart casserole, mix apples with granulated sugar, 2 tablespoons flour, and cinnamon.

2. In a bowl, combine rolled oats, brown sugar, butter, and ¾ cup flour. Rub with your fingers until butter pieces are no longer distinguishable. Stir in chopped pecans. Sprinkle

topping evenly over apples.

3. Bake dessert in the middle of a 350° oven until apples are tender when pierced and topping is browned, 45 minutes to 1 hour. If topping browns first, drape with foil.

4. Spoon the apple crisp, warm or cool, into bowls. Top portions with vanilla ice cream.

Per serving: 404 cal., 38% (153 cal.) from fat; 3.8 g protein; 17 g fat (7 g sat.); 62 g carbo (3.7 g fiber); 112 mg sodium; 28 mg chol.

Growing your own antiques

■ Scattered throughout the West's apple country are growers who specialize in antique apples—varieties introduced before the turn of the century. Altogether, they sell nearly 100 varieties as nursery stock.

Which are the most flavorful antiques to grow? For recommendations, we turned to four growers—Carolyn and Terry Harrison, who offer 94 varieties, bare-root, by mail through *Sonoma Antique Apple Nursery* in the rolling hills of Healdsburg, California, and Catherine and Joe Brocard, who grow 189 apple varieties in the Sweet Home, Oregon, orchard they planted in 1979. After years in the business, all have well-honed apple-tasting skills—although, as in the case of 'Nonesuch', they don't always agree.

This month at the Brocards' *Antique Apple Orchard,* you can taste antique apples to help you decide which varieties to grow. It's at 28095 Santiam Highway in Sweet Home (541/367-4840) and open 10 to 5 Tuesdays through Saturdays. The mail-order suppliers listed at right (including the Harrisons' nursery) sell bare-root stock; place your orders this fall for delivery before spring.

NORMAN A. PLATE (16)

Carolyn Harrison

HARVEST TIPS

• "When you harvest an apple plays a big part in how it tastes," says Carolyn Harrison. To determine whether the crop is ripe enough to start picking, pluck an apple from the tree, cut it in half, and look at the seeds. If the seeds are dark, the apples should be ready to harvest (tasting always confirms it). If the weather is cool, you have a wider window for harvest—up to two weeks for optimum flavor (but just a matter of days for early apples). If it's hot, you should harvest right away.

• Early and midseason apples generally don't keep well. Late apples are good keepers.

BARE-ROOT SOURCES

• *In the Northwest*
Bear Creek Nursery, Box 411, Northport, WA 99157. Bear Creek has perhaps the best selection of antique bare-root in the state, and specializes in apples for cold climate zones. For a free catalog, send a fax to (509) 732-4417 or e-mail your request to BearCreekin@plix.com.

• *In California*
Sonoma Antique Apple Nursery, 4395 Westside Rd., Healdsburg, CA 95448; (707) 433-6420.

best for eating fresh

'Cox Orange Pippin' (1830). Small to medium-size green fruit has red-orange overlay. Crisp, sweet-tart flavor. Expect some apples to crack on the blossom end. Late midseason. *"It would be a good pie apple for flavor, but it's small. We put lots of these in our cider."* — Catherine Brocard

'Golden Russet' (1845). Medium-size, rust-colored fruit. Late midseason. *"I'd put its flavor just behind 'Ashmead's Kernel'. 'Golden Russet' is such a firm apple that it holds up too well in cooking, staying chunky even in pies. Eat it fresh."* — C. B.

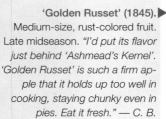

'Nonesuch', or 'Hubbardston' (1830). Large, with reddish skin. Moderately firm flesh. Crisp, rich, and sweet. Midseason to late. *"Not enough acid to cook with. A sweet, crisp apple that fills a gap between 'Gravenstein' and 'Spitzenburg'."* — Carolyn Harrison

'Seek-No-Further', or 'Westfield' (1796). Medium-large apple with yellow-green flesh and tough green skin. Late. *"When you eat this apple fresh, its aroma flavors the fruit in the same way that the 'McIntosh' fragrance affects the taste of the flesh."* — C. B.

'Ashmead's Kernel' (1700). ▶
A late, medium-size russet with golden-brown skin and crisp, aromatic flesh. Tart but sugary flavor. *"Good fresh, if you like a dense, chewy apple. Someone once told me this apple has too much taste. I'd call it a gutsy apple."* — C. H.

'Belle de Boskoop' (1856). ▶
Large, greenish-yellow fruit with a dark red blush and rough skin. Partial russet. Hard, dense flesh. Crisp, tangy, and aromatic. Harvest midseason. — C. H.

◀ **'McIntosh' (1870).** Red skin tinged with yellow; fragrant white flesh. Fruit is medium-size, and doesn't store well. Midseason. *"'McIntosh' cooks down fast into great, smooth applesauce that doesn't need a lot of sugar. But it also turns to sauce when you try to bake it into pies."* — C. B.

◀ **'Northern Spy' (1800).** Large, attractive red-and-yellow fruit with thin skin and firm, tender flesh. Fruity, juicy, and tart. Use in applesauce, cider, or pie, or eat it fresh. Similar to 'Gravenstein', but ripens later. Mid- to late season. *"Classic old-fashioned apple taste."* — C. H.

'Roxbury Russet' (before 1649). ▶
Medium-size apple, on the squat side. Dense, light-green fruit with a sweet, almost nutty flavor. Late midseason to late. *"Not as highly fruity as 'Ashmead's Kernel'. Bears an amazingly huge crop every year. Don't pick too early or sugars won't develop."* — C. H.

'Sierra Beauty' (about 1900). ▶
Large apples with green-and-yellow skin, striped or blushed red. Juicy and crisp, with a sweet-tart flavor. A great keeper. Late. *"It won't develop overlying sweetness until really ripe (it may not ripen in a cool climate)."* — C. H.

◀ **'Spitzenburg' (before 1800).** Medium to large, firm fruit with red-and-yellow skin and russet dots. A shy bearer. Late. *"The Gewürztraminer of apples. Its spiciness and fruitiness really come through. It's the flavor king of apples. My mother-in-law's childhood favorite."* — C. H.

◀ **'White Permain' (before 1858).** Medium to large, pale green fruit with one side blushed red. Firm, crisp flesh with sweet but slightly tart flavor; pear undertones when allowed to mellow after picking. Best keeper. Late. — C. H.

all-around favorites

'Bramley's Seedling' (1813). ▶
Large green apple, very high in vitamin C. Sharp, very acid. Early to midseason. *"Not for pies; it doesn't hold its shape."* — C. H.

'Calville Blanc d'Hiver' (1598). ▶
Medium to large green fruit tinged pink and yellow. Tart flavor. Late midseason. *"You'll pucker if you eat this fresh, but the fruit mellows in storage. Some overtones of pear or pineapple make it one of the best pie apples you can grow."* — C. B.

◀ **'Nonesuch', or 'Hubbardston' (1830).** This antique variety was selected as both a good eating and a good cooking apple. *"Not an especially pretty apple, but it cooks up well and makes fine cider."* — C. B.

◀ **'Pink Pearl' (about 1945).** A firm-fleshed, pearly-skinned apple that holds its shape. Sweet-tart flavor. Use in applesauce, cider, pies. Early. *"This apple has everything: good flavor and special color."* — C. H.

best for cooking

The Whole Tomato Story

A party for the season
page 215

Cooking up the classics
page 218

20 fast ideas,
from salads to sandwiches
page 220

The perfect harvest party

Gather your favorite tomatoes, invite friends who love good food, and celebrate the bounty of summer

by ELAINE JOHNSON

photographs by HOLLY STEWART

■ Gary Ibsen has been up since 3:30 A.M. on this September Sunday. That was when he strapped a lamp to his forehead and walked into his still-cool, dark fields to pluck a few more perfectly ripe tomatoes from his 1,000 plants. Now it's late afternoon and his annual TomatoFest in Carmel, California, is about to begin. "I've been waiting for this day all year," he says excitedly.

He's invited 260 guests, as passionate about tomatoes as he is, to wander the fields, taste the harvest, and share a dinner that celebrates this food. With wine glasses in hand, we tromp off to a comparative tasting inside a 175-foot-long tomato arbor. "Man, this one is like sex!" enthuses a taster. Flavors run the gamut from earthy and rich to intensely sweet. It's like sampling a 96-color box of crayons: lime green, sunny yellow, shocking orange, blood red.

Preparations began in December with Ibsen poring over garden catalogs. "Flavor totally drives what I select. Nearly all are heirlooms," he explains. Ibsen settled on 63 varieties this year, up from 35 last. "My friends are ready to have me committed."

Through the winter and spring, Ibsen nurtures seedlings, first in a spare bedroom, later in a makeshift greenhouse; finally they go into hand-dug, carefully amended holes. Then he waters, feeds, and trellises each vine as high as 10 feet.

As the tomatoes ripen, Ibsen survives on four hours' sleep a night, sandwiching his work in publishing between tending plants and carting tomatoes to local chefs and markets—"a feeble attempt to make my hobby pay for itself," he laments. "Racing sports cars would be cheaper." From his car filled with jewel boxes of tomatoes, Ibsen dispenses samples, tips, and stories to friends, chefs, and chance acquaintances, like the woman he met at the laundry and invited to the party.

Guests contribute to a tomato buffet, a veritable nirvana of the raw, the cooked, and the frozen. We sit down to overflowing plates and strolling musicians. Kids scamper through fragrant fields strung with red balloons and green streamers.

Was it all worth it? Ibsen replies with a big smile, "Today is the day where it all comes together."

Gary Ibsen (left) shares his obsession for tomatoes. Guests sample his work from a table under the arch of a 175-foot-long tomato arbor (above, right).

Roma–Goat Cheese Tarts

Prep and cook time: About 2½ hours, including chilling

Notes: Lisa Magadini, executive chef of Club XIX restaurant at Pebble Beach Resort in California, and Benjamin Brown, sous-chef, created this recipe.

Makes: 2 tarts; 12 servings total

- ¾ cup **pine nuts**
- 2 cups **whole-wheat flour**

  About 1 cup **all-purpose flour**
- 2 teaspoons minced **fresh thyme** leaves

  About 1½ teaspoons **salt**
- ⅔ cup (⅓ lb.) **butter** or margarine, cut into chunks
- ⅔ cup **solid shortening**
- 1¼ pounds **Roma tomatoes,** rinsed, cored, and cut into ⅛-inch slices
- 3 **large eggs**
- 3 tablespoons **pesto**

  About ½ cup (4 oz.) **fresh chèvre** (goat) **cheese**
- 1 cup **whipping cream**

1. In an 8- to 9-inch-wide pan, bake nuts in a 350° oven, stirring often, until golden, 5 to 7 minutes; let cool.

2. In a bowl, combine whole-wheat flour, 1 cup all-purpose flour, thyme, and 1 teaspoon salt. With a pastry blender or your fingers, cut or rub in butter and shortening until particles are pea-size. Stir in pine nuts. With a fork, gently stir in ½ cup ice-cold water, 1 tablespoon at a time.

3. Gather dough into a ball, divide in

A tomato bash for 12

Matching the scope of Gary Ibsen's project takes months of effort, but a party scaled for a dozen captures the essence in just hours.

• **The tomatoes.** If you don't have a garden or access to homegrown tomatoes, take advantage of the next best sources for a good selection: farmers' markets and produce stands. Buy tomatoes ripe, or allow time for them to ripen.

Five of Ibsen's favorites are *Brandywine* (a pink Amish slicer), *Paul Robeson* (an earthy, black, Russian variety), *Radiator Charlie's Mortgage Lifter* (huge, meaty, and flavorful), *Sungold* (exceptionally sweet, orange cherry), and *Wins All* (pink, mild, and sweet).

• **The tasting.** Like Ibsen, enlist friends to cut tomatoes and label plates for this event. And if you like, hand out printed descriptions of the tomatoes, as Ibsen does, for tasters to take home.

• **The buffet.** This selection of our favorite dishes from Ibsen's party will serve 12. Share recipes if you want to do a potluck. Grill sausages to round out the menu.

With tomato descriptions provided by Ibsen, tasters identify their favorites.

half, and flatten each portion into a 1-inch-thick disk. Wrap airtight and chill at least 45 minutes or up to 2 days.

4. On a board dusted with all-purpose flour, roll dough pieces, one at a time, into 11-inch rounds. Fit each round into a 9-inch tart pan with a removable rim; trim excess dough from rim.

5. Fit a piece of foil into each crust, with foil edges extending at least 2 inches above rim. Pour dried beans or pie weights into foil to half-fill crusts. Bake on the lowest rack in a 375° oven for 30 minutes. Remove foil and beans.

6. Overlap tomatoes in circles in hot crusts. Bake until tomatoes look dry at edges, about 15 minutes.

7. Meanwhile, in a bowl, whisk eggs, pesto, goat cheese, and ½ teaspoon salt to blend, then whisk in cream. Gently

Slices of Roma tomatoes bake like petals in pesto–goat cheese tarts.

pour mixture equally over tomatoes.

8. Bake until custard is set when gently shaken, about 25 minutes. Season to taste with salt. Serve hot or cold.

Per serving: 475 cal., 72% (342 cal.) from fat; 11 g protein; 38 g fat (16 g sat.); 27 g carbo (4.4 g fiber); 469 mg sodium; 108 mg chol.

Tomato-Eggplant Tortino

Prep and cook time: About 55 minutes

Notes: Silvano Merlo, executive chef of the Monterey Marriott in California, starts with eggplant, tomato, and cheese slices of the same size so they stack neatly. Use leftover pieces in other dishes.

Makes: 12 servings

⅔ cup **extra-virgin olive oil**

1 tablespoon minced **fresh thyme** leaves

1 tablespoon minced **fresh basil** leaves

1 tablespoon minced **parsley**

About 1 pound **eggplant** (2 to 2½ in. wide)

About 1½ pounds firm-ripe **yellow tomatoes** (2 to 2½ in. wide)

About ¾ pound firm-ripe **red tomatoes** (2 to 2½ in. wide)

About ¾ pound **fresh mozzarella** or fresh chèvre (goat) **cheese** (2 to 2½ in. wide)

Salt and **pepper**

¾ cup **balsamic vinegar**

Thyme, basil, or parsley **sprigs**

1. Combine oil and minced thyme, basil, and parsley.

2. Trim eggplant ends and discard. Rinse eggplant, cut into 24 equal rounds, and brush lightly with some of the herb oil.

3. Rinse and core tomatoes, then trim thin slices off tops and bottoms. Cut yellow tomatoes into 24 equal rounds; cut red tomatoes into 12 equal rounds.

4. Cut cheese into 12 equal rounds.

5. Lay tomato slices in a 10- by 15-inch pan. Drizzle with herb oil and sprinkle with salt and pepper.

6. Lightly oil a barbecue grill over a solid bed of medium-hot coals or medium-high heat on a gas grill (you can hold your hand at grill level only 3 to 4 seconds). Lay eggplant on grill; close lid on gas barbecue. Cook eggplant, turning once, until soft when pressed, 5 to 7 minutes total. Let cool.

7. For each tortino, stack 1 slice *each* yellow tomato, eggplant, mozzarella, and red tomato, then top with 1 more slice each eggplant and yellow tomato. Set stacks on a platter. Reserve 2 teaspoons of pan juices from tomatoes; use remainder in other salads.

8. In a 2- to 3-quart pan over high heat, boil vinegar until reduced to 2 tablespoons, 5 to 7 minutes, stirring as it nears the end of cooking.

9. Mix the reserved tomato juices with vinegar and drizzle over tortinos. Garnish with thyme sprigs.

Per serving: 217 cal., 79% (171 cal.) from fat; 6.1 g protein; 19 g fat (1.8 g sat.); 7.8 g carbo (1.7 g fiber); 30 mg sodium; 20 mg chol.

Tuscan Tomato Bread Salad

Prep and cook time: About 1¼ hours

Notes: Executive chef Brandon Miller of Stokes Adobe Restaurant in Monterey uses at least two colors of tomatoes in this salad.

Makes: 12 servings

- 1 quart lightly packed **baby spinach leaves**
- 1 quart lightly packed **fresh basil** leaves
- 1 pound **coarse-textured Italian bread** such as ciabatta or pugliese
- 3½ pounds soft-ripe **tomatoes**, peeled if desired (see page 219) and cored
- 4 cloves **garlic**, minced
- ½ cup **extra-virgin olive oil**
- ⅓ cup **red wine vinegar**
- 3 tablespoons minced **fresh jalapeño chilies**

    Salt and **pepper**

- 1 jar (12 oz.) **peeled roasted red peppers**, cut into wide strips
- 1 cup **oil-packed olives**, pitted
- ½ cup drained **capers**
- 2 cans (2 oz. each) **anchovy fillets**, drained

1. Rinse and drain spinach and basil; wrap in towels. Chill in a plastic bag.

2. Meanwhile, cut bread into 1-inch chunks and put in an 11- by 17-inch roasting pan. Bake in a 350° oven until chunks are light golden and soft parts of bread are crisp, about 30 minutes, stirring occasionally. Let cool.

3. Cut tomatoes into 1- to 2-inch chunks and place in a large bowl. Scoop juice from cutting board into bowl and add garlic, oil, vinegar, chilies, and salt and pepper to taste.

4. Gently mix tomatoes with bread, red peppers, and olives. Let stand at least 15 minutes, stirring occasionally, for bread to soften. Gently mix in spinach and basil. Scatter salad with capers and crisscross anchovies on top.

Per serving: 298 cal., 48% (144 cal.) from fat; 8.7 g protein; 16 g fat (2.4 g sat.); 32 g carbo (6.2 g fiber); 1,239 mg sodium; 4.1 mg chol.

Sweet Tomato Sorbet

Prep and cook time: About 55 minutes, plus 3 hours for freezing if a firmer texture is desired

Notes: For a handsome presentation, Shelly Schachter of Carmel Valley uses red Fantastic and yellow Chello tomatoes, making each into a half-batch of

Tomatoes for dessert? Basil-flecked sorbet uses two colors of tomatoes.

the sorbet. Freeze sorbet up to 2 weeks. To serve, let stand at room temperature until softened, about 15 minutes, then break into chunks and whirl in a food processor until slushy.

Makes: 8 cups; 16 servings

- 1 cup **sugar**

    About 3 pounds soft-ripe **tomatoes**, peeled (see page 219), cored, and cut into chunks

- 6 tablespoons minced **fresh basil** leaves

1. In a 1- to 2-quart pan over high heat, bring sugar and 1 cup water to a rolling boil. Nest pan in a bowl of ice and stir often until cold, 8 to 10 minutes.

2. In a food processor or blender, purée tomatoes, a portion at a time. Rub through a fine strainer into a bowl; discard any residue.

3. Combine syrup, tomato purée, and basil. Freeze in an ice cream maker according to manufacturer's directions or until dasher is hard to turn.

4. Serve sorbet softly frozen, or freeze airtight until firm, at least 3 hours.

Per serving: 67 cal., 4% (2.7 cal.) from fat; 0.8 g protein; 0.3 g fat (0 g sat.); 17 g carbo (1.2 g fiber); 7.9 mg sodium; 0 mg chol. ◆

Gary Ibsen's 1997 TomatoFest in Carmel is open to the public, by reservation only; attendance is limited to 500. The party begins at 12:30 P.M. September 28. Price is $38 ($12 ages 10–16) and includes tomato tasting, barbecue buffet, music, dancing, and wine. Call (408) 624-1581.

Multicolor tomato platter: Perfectly ripe tomatoes, in many colors and shapes on a bed of arugula leaves, make an easy salad. Scatter with crumbled feta cheese and calamata olives, then drizzle with pesto.

You can never have too many tomatoes!

Capture their perfectly ripe flavor in four great basic recipes to enjoy long after the season fades

For tomato lovers and avid gardeners, too many tomatoes isn't a complaint, it's a luxury. And as summer's heat brings tomatoes to perfect ripeness, it's time to freeze this moment of flavor for enjoyment later in the year.

You can use any color and any shape of tomato to make these culinary basics: pasta sauce, soup, salsa, or vegetable broth. All freeze beautifully and stand well on their own. But they can also easily be varied with a few extra ingredients to keep menus lively.

To help you figure out how many tomatoes you'll need, what to watch for when cooking them, and more, check the tips on the facing page.

Beefsteak-type Super Marmande tomatoes are flavorful and meaty.

Spaghetti Sauce

Prep and cook time: About 3 hours

Notes: Use sauce with any cooked pasta (allow about 1 cup sauce for each 1½ cups pasta). Or layer sauce into lasagna. For variety, simmer individual batches of the sauce briefly with Italian sausages, crumbled and browned ground meats, roasted vegetables, or additional herbs, such as basil or oregano.

Makes: About 12 cups

1 ounce (about 1 cup) **dried porcini mushrooms**

6 cloves **garlic,** minced

2 **onions** (1 lb. total), finely chopped

2 tablespoons **olive oil**

10 pounds **ripe tomatoes,** rinsed (or peeled, if desired), cored, and chopped

1 cup minced **parsley**

½ cup **dry red wine**

2 tablespoons minced **fresh thyme** leaves or 2 teaspoons crumbled dried thyme

1 tablespoon **sugar**

1 to 2 teaspoons **hot chili flakes**

Salt

1. In a small bowl, combine mushrooms and ⅔ cup boiling water. Let stand until soft, about 20 minutes. Rub mushrooms gently to release grit, then lift from water, squeeze dry, and finely chop. Reserve liquid.

2. Meanwhile, combine garlic, onions, and oil in an 8- to 10-quart pan over medium-high heat. Stir often until onions are lightly browned and taste sweet, about 10 minutes.

Yellow Ruffled tomatoes sport distinctive accordion pleats.

Sweet, mildly acidic Carmello tomatoes make good eating and cook well.

3. To pan, add mushrooms and most of the soaking liquid, discarding the gritty remainder. Also add tomatoes, parsley, wine, thyme, sugar, and chili flakes. Bring to a boil and simmer rapidly until reduced to 3 quarts, about 1¼ hours; stir often. Add salt to taste.

4. Use hot, or let sauce cool, then cover and chill up to 5 days. To store longer, freeze in easy-to-use portions.

Per cup: 133 cal., 24% (32 cal.) from fat; 4.5 g protein; 3.6 g fat (0.5 g sat.); 24 g carbo (6.4 g fiber); 38 mg sodium; 0 mg chol.

Roasted Tomato Soup

Prep and cook time: About 1½ hours

Notes: Serve this robust soup hot or chilled, allowing 1 to 1½ cups for a portion. Drizzle servings with sweet cream, sour cream, or yogurt; top with a tangy corn relish; or sprinkle with minced fresh basil and grated parmesan cheese.

Makes: About 20 cups

10 pounds **ripe tomatoes**

5 tablespoons **olive oil**

1 tablespoon **sugar**

6 cloves **garlic,** minced

2 **onions** (1 lb. total), chopped

6 cups **chicken broth**

Salt

1. Rinse, core, and cut tomatoes in half crosswise.

2. Fit tomatoes, cut sides up, in 10- by

by CHRISTINE WEBER HALE

15-inch pans (you'll need 3, or use 1 pan and refill). Brush the tops of the tomatoes in each pan with 1 tablespoon oil and sprinkle with 1 teaspoon sugar.

3. One pan at a time, broil tomatoes 3 to 4 inches from heat until tops are spotted black, about 20 minutes. Adjust pan position for even heat and remove tomatoes as they are charred.

4. Meanwhile, in an 8- to 10-quart pan over medium-high heat, combine remaining oil, garlic, and onions. Stir often until onions are lightly browned and taste sweet, 10 to 15 minutes.

5. In batches, smoothly purée tomatoes and onion mixture in a blender or food processor. To remove skins, if desired, rub tomato mixture through a fine strainer into a large bowl.

6. Return tomato mixture to pan and add broth; heat to simmering, stirring. Add salt to taste. To serve cold, cover and refrigerate until chilled. To store, cover airtight and chill up to 3 days, or put in freezer containers in easy-to-use portions and freeze up to 1 year.

Per cup: 99 cal., 41% (41 cal.) from fat; 3.1 g protein; 4.6 g fat (0.8 g sat.); 14 g carbo (3.3 g fiber); 53 mg sodium; 1.1 mg chol.

Freezer Salsa

Prep and cook time: About 1½ hours

Makes: 11 to 12 cups

- 1 pound **fresh poblano chilies** or green Anaheim (also called California or New Mexico) chilies
- ¼ pound **fresh jalapeño chilies**
- 5 pounds **ripe tomatoes,** rinsed (or peeled, if desired), cored, and chopped
- 2 **onions** (1 lb. total), chopped
- 1 cup minced **fresh cilantro**
- ½ cup **lime juice**
- **Salt**

Dona tomatoes, when ripe and red, have a fine sweet-acid balance.

Golden Mandarin Cross has more intense flavor than most yellow varieties.

1. Lay poblano and jalapeño chilies in a single layer in a 10- by 15-inch pan. Broil 3 to 4 inches from heat, turning occasionally, until skins are blackened and blistered, 15 to 20 minutes. Let cool. Wearing gloves, pull off and discard skin, stems, veins, and seeds. Rinse chilies and chop coarsely.

2. In a 6- to 8-quart pan, combine chilies, tomatoes, onions, cilantro, lime juice, and salt to taste. Bring to a boil over high heat, then simmer 10 minutes.

3. Let salsa cool, then serve, chill airtight up to 3 days, or pack in easy-to-use portions in freezer containers and freeze up to 1 year.

Per ¼ cup: 18 cal., 10% (1.8 cal.) from fat; 0.7 g protein; 0.2 g fat (0 g sat.); 4 g carbo (0.9 g fiber); 5.6 mg sodium; 0 mg chol.

Chipotle-Tomato Broth

Prep time: About 1½ hours

Notes: Strained, this seasoned tomato mixture makes a transparent broth with a little tomato sediment. Chilled, it makes a refreshing drink with a subtle tomato-chili taste. Or use it as a vegetable broth for cooking; its pale color and its flavor enrich but don't intrude, the way regular tomato juice does. Add the tomato residue to cooked tomato sauces.

Makes: About 2 quarts

- 5 pounds **ripe tomatoes**
- 1 or 2 **canned chipotle chilies**
- 2 cups chopped **celery**
- ⅓ cup **lemon juice**
- 2 tablespoons **Worcestershire**
- **Salt**

1. Rinse, core, and quarter tomatoes.

2. Rinse chilies; discard seeds and veins.

3. In batches, smoothly purée tomatoes, celery, and chilies to taste in a blender or food processor. As batches are puréed, rub mixture through a fine strainer into a bowl. Add lemon juice, Worcestershire, and salt to taste.

4. Line a large strainer with 1 layer of cheesecloth or a muslin towel. Set strainer over a large bowl and pour tomato mixture, a portion at a time, into cloth. Let drain, stirring occasionally. Transfer the juice to another container if it reaches the strainer bottom. Draw edges of cloth together and twist to extract as much moisture as possible.

5. Cover and chill liquid. Stir before serving. Refrigerate up to 3 days. To store longer, freeze in ice cube trays, then release cubes and store in a plastic freezer bag in the freezer up to 1 year.

Per cup: 71 cal., 13% (9 cal.) from fat; 2.9 g protein; 1 g fat (0.2 g sat.); 16 g carbo (4.2 g fiber); 150 mg sodium; 0 mg chol. ◆

Tomato tips

One pound of tomatoes equals:

- Two whole 3-inch tomatoes
- Three 2½-inch tomatoes
- Four or five 2-inch tomatoes
- About 2½ cups chopped
- About 3 cups quartered
- About 2 cups puréed

How to peel. Immerse tomatoes, a single layer at a time, in boiling water for 10 to 45 seconds (riper tomatoes take the least time; they're ready when skin begins to curl back when nicked with knife tip). Lift out, let cool briefly, then pull off and discard skin.

How long to cook. The amount of moisture in tomatoes differs with variety. To get the consistency you want in cooked tomato mixtures, such as sauces, you may need to simmer the mixture for a little more—or less—time than the recipe suggests.

How to can safely. For canning tomatoes in a hot water bath, the USDA recommends adding bottled lemon juice or a citric acid (found with canning supplies at supermarkets; also sold at pharmacies). To each quart of firm-ripe tomatoes, add 2 tablespoons bottled lemon juice or ½ teaspoon citric acid. To each pint, add 1 tablespoon bottled lemon juice or ¼ teaspoon citric acid. Then process tomatoes as canning instructions direct. — *Elaine Johnson*

For simple perfection, try a sandwich of really ripe tomatoes and basil leaves.

JAMES CARRIER

20 fresh and fast tomato ideas

Eaten ripe and sun-warm from the garden, a tomato is a flavorful, juicy, vitamin-packed orb of instant gratification. The simplest way to enjoy them is sliced, sprinkled with salt, pepper, olive oil, and balsamic vinegar, and garnished with basil (see cover).

STRAIGHTFORWARD AND SIMPLE

1. Vary a classic. Instead of mozzarella cheese, use the fresh Mexican cheese *panela,* and slice it to serve with tomatoes and fresh basil. Drizzle with extra-virgin olive oil, sprinkle with salt, and finish with fresh-ground pepper.

2. Get colorful. Select several colors of tomatoes, big or small. Slice and arrange on a platter. Drizzle with a flavored oil—garlic, cilantro, porcini,

chili, mustard, herb—then splash with rice vinegar. Season with coarse salt and Japanese *sansho* pepper (available in Japanese markets).

3. Substantial salad. Top thick tomato slices with thinly sliced sweet red onion rings, sprinkle with crumbled blue cheese, and season to taste with balsamic vinegar and olive oil. Serve with toast.

4. Quick appetizer. Cut pear-shaped yellow cherry tomatoes in half. Top cut sides with a dab of Rondelé or similar soft cheese (plain or seasoned) and grind fresh pepper over the cheese.

WHIRL THEM UP

5. Pour a cool soup. Purée equal amounts of ripe yellow and red toma-

toes separately. Pour each through a fine strainer into a separate bowl and season to taste with salt, pepper, and lemon juice or white wine vinegar. Pour purées simultaneously into opposite sides of shallow bowls, filling each with the two tomato mixtures. Sprinkle each serving with chopped fresh basil leaves or chives.

6. Purée a fish sauce. In a blender or food processor, purée about 2 parts ripe tomatoes, 1 part plain low-fat yogurt, and fresh dill, lemon juice, and salt to taste. Serve the sauce with hot or cold cooked salmon, sturgeon, or striped bass.

7. Dress a salad. Purée ripe tomatoes and flavor to taste with seasoned rice vinegar, olive oil, and chopped fresh mint. Mix with a salad of cooked sweet corn kernels, cooked black beans, and slivered romaine lettuce.

PASTA, PRESTO

8. Mix chopped ripe tomatoes, slivered fresh basil leaves, and capers with hot angel hair (capellini) pasta. Add enough hot chicken broth to make pasta moist and saucy.

9. Hollow firm-ripe beefsteak tomatoes; save the pulp for other uses. Fill tomatoes with a salad of cool cooked orzo or small shell-shape pasta, shelled cooked tiny shrimp, thawed petite peas, grated lemon peel, lemon juice, minced parsley, mayonnaise or nonfat yogurt, and salt to taste.

10. Season hot cooked tortellini with chopped ripe tomatoes mixed with a generous measure of chopped fresh basil leaves, a few crushed fennel seeds, and extra-virgin olive oil, salt, and pepper to taste.

BREAD AND TOMATOES

11. Redesign the BLT. Spread slices of toasted sourdough bread with mascarpone or cream cheese, then layer ripe tomato slices, crisp-cooked pancetta, and arugula between the sourdough slices.

12. Keep it simple. Lightly moisten slices of crusty, coarse-textured bread with extra-virgin olive oil. Pile ripe tomato slices and fresh basil leaves between the bread slices.

by **CHRISTINE WEBER HALE** *and* **ELAINE JOHNSON**

13. Add cheese. Start with *Keep it simple* (number 12), but instead of using olive oil, spread bread thickly with cambozola cheese and tuck fresh basil leaves among the tomato slices.

14. Use focaccia. Split a square of plain focaccia and toast cut sides. Spread with an herb-flavor soft cheese. Fill sandwich with ripe tomato slices and thinly sliced smoked salmon, adding capers and lemon juice to taste.

15. A Catalan specialty. Rub thick slices of crusty bread with a cut clove of garlic. Cut a ripe, juicy tomato in half. Rub cut sides of tomato over bread until slices are pink. Save tomato for other uses. Drizzle bread with extra-virgin olive oil and sprinkle with salt to taste.

HOT TOMATOES

16. Season cooked vegetables. Sauté chopped firm tomatoes with a few chopped shallots and ground cumin to taste in a little olive oil just until sizzling. Spoon over hot cooked asparagus, summer squash, or poached leeks and sprinkle with chopped roasted, salted pistachios.

17. Top off meat. Finely dice ripe red, yellow, and orange tomatoes; mix with an equal measure of slivered arugula and add shredded parmesan cheese to taste. Spoon over grilled chicken, beef, or lamb. Add salt to taste.

18. On the side. Cut firm-ripe tomatoes in half. Set cut side up in a shallow pan. Sprinkle generously with shredded parmesan cheese, lightly with dried bread crumbs, and sparingly with dried thyme, then drizzle with olive oil. Broil about 6 inches from heat until topping is browned and tomatoes are warm.

19. Make a nest. Sauté thinly sliced mushrooms in butter, stirring until limp and juices are gone. Add diced tomatoes and cook until soft. With the back of a large spoon, make impressions in vegetable mixture, 1 at a time, and break an egg into each nest. Cover pan, and cook over low heat until whites are firm and yolks are soft (or as firm as you like). Season with salt and pepper.

20. Fry 'em. Coat thick slices of unripe (green) tomatoes with cornmeal, then sizzle in salad oil (or part bacon drippings), turning once and browning well. Dust with salt and pepper or chili powder. ◆

Dining on a deck of the bay

Short cruises on San Francisco Bay for dinner, brunch, or hors d'oeuvres are tastier than ever

by **JEFF PHILLIPS**

Rule number one: The best views of San Francisco are from the water. Rule number two: The best dining in San Francisco is on the land.

For years it seemed those simple truths would remain irreconcilable, but a recent sampling of the bay's dining fleet convinced us that improved service and menus on several vessels have made brunch and dinner cruises not only pleasurable, but palatable. The timing couldn't be better: the perfect bay-cruising months are upon us. And this fall, boats ranging from square-rigged sailing ships to sleek yachts offer dining cruises, proving that some rules are made to be broken.

Blue & Gold Fleet. This summer's big news was Blue & Gold's acquisition of the Red & White fleet, whose boats have been repainted. Blue & Gold now offers informal evening buffet cruises serving barbecued ribs and chicken from MacArthur Park restaurants.
•*When:* Dinner and dancing 8–11 Fri-Sat through October.
•*Port:* Pier 39, San Francisco.
•*Cost:* $50.
•*Reservations:* (415) 705-5555.

Hawaiian Chieftain. The buffet of cheeses and fresh fruit is not especially surprising on either the Sunday brunch or the sunset cruises, but the presentation is artful, everything tastes great, and the wine flows freely.
•*When:* Dinner 6–9 Wed-Fri, brunch 9–1 Sat (since this is a hands-on working cruise, wine is not served) and 10–1 Sun (with live music).

What's not to smile about: Sunday brunch aboard the Hawaiian Chieftain, which sails from Sausalito.

•*Port:* Marina Plaza, Sausalito.
•*Cost:* $25–$45.
•*Reservations:* (415) 331-3214.

Hornblower Dining Yachts. When chef Derek Burns (Stars, Masa's, and Square One) came on board the bay's premier dinner-cruise line last winter as consulting executive chef, he improved both menu and presentation. The entrée 'choices of grilled filet mignon, roast chicken, or marinated mahimahi for the four-course, sit-down dinner aboard the *California Hornblower* are well executed if not adventuresome.
•*When:* Dinner and dancing 7:30–10:30 nightly.
•*Port:* Pier 33, San Francisco.
•*Cost:* $54.50–$74.50.
•*Reservations:* (415) 788-8866.

Pacific Marine Yachts. The elegant buffet aboard the sleek, 150-foot motor yacht *San Francisco Spirit* has everything from fruit and pastries to eggs Benedict and smoked salmon. There's plenty of time after your table is cleared to enjoy bay views from the upper deck.
•*When:* Brunch 11:30–1:30 Sun.
•*Port:* Pier 39, San Francisco.
•*Cost:* $50.
•*Reservations:* (415) 788-9100.

Rendezvous Charters. Except for the champagne, the menu doesn't rise above the standard continental breakfast found in a lot of hotels, but it seems good enough when you're cutting through bay waters under the 80-foot mast of the *Brigantine Rendezvous*, a classic 1930s schooner.
•*When:* Brunch 11–2 Sun.
•*Port:* Pier 40, San Francisco.
•*Cost:* $39.
•*Reservations:* (415) 543-7333. ◆

The Low-Fat Cook

HEALTHY CHOICES FOR THE ACTIVE LIFESTYLE

by ELAINE JOHNSON

Grilled seafood and corn get pizzazz from a lemon grass–flavor broth.

How to turn a light broth into a sauce

■ When you want to cook low-fat, take a look at how well it's done in Thailand and Vietnam. Cooks there are good at delivering satisfying flavor without fat.

Consider this grilled seafood dish, which is seasoned with a lean broth flavorful enough to work as a sauce. Southeast Asian touches of lime, chilies, lemon grass, and herbs give zip to clam juice. Add tomatoes and you have an Asian gazpacho that's good hot or chilled. While you're picking up the tomatoes, grab some corn for grilling. It will come off the barbecue with nuances of smoke, just like the seafood.

Seafood in Asian Broth

Prep and cook time: About 1 hour

Notes: If ripe tomatoes are not available, use canned ones.

Makes: 4 servings

- 3 ounces (3 to 6 stalks) **fresh lemon grass**
- 1 bottle (8 oz.) **clam juice**
- 1½ cups coarsely puréed soft, ripe **tomatoes**
- 1 teaspoon grated **lime** peel
- 2 tablespoons **lime juice**
- 1 tablespoon minced **fresh jalapeño chili**
- 12 (⅓ to ½ lb. total) **shelled, deveined shrimp**
- 6 (about ½ lb.) **sea scallops**, rinsed and halved crosswise
- 1 teaspoon **salad oil**
- 2 tablespoons minced **fresh mint** leaves
- 2 tablespoons minced **fresh basil** leaves
- 2 **ears of corn** (1 lb. total), husks and silk removed
- ¾ cup paper-thin slices **fennel**
- 1 tablespoon thinly sliced **fresh chives**

  Asian fish sauce (*nuoc mam* or *nam pla*)

1. Trim off root and pull coarse outer leaves from lemon grass and discard. Pound lemon grass to bruise slightly. Cut stalks in half lengthwise, then crosswise into about 3-inch pieces.

2. In a 2- to 3-quart pan over high heat, combine lemon grass and clam juice and bring to boiling. Reduce heat, cover, and simmer 10 minutes.

3. Pour clam broth through a fine strainer into a bowl. Return broth to pan and discard lemon grass.

4. Stir tomatoes, lime peel, lime juice, and jalapeño into clam juice; set aside.

5. Gently mix shrimp and scallops with oil, then mix with 1 tablespoon each of minced mint and basil. Thread seafood horizontally onto thin metal skewers.

6. Lightly oil a barbecue grill over a solid bed of hot coals or gas grill on high heat (you can hold your hand at grill level only 2 to 3 seconds); lay corn on grill. Close lid on gas grill. Turn corn often until it is speckled black, about 12 minutes.

7. About 5 minutes before corn is done, lay skewered seafood on grill. Cook, turning once with a wide spatula, until shrimp are opaque but still moist-looking in center of thickest part (cut to test), 3 to 4 minutes.

8. Cut kernels from corn, and pull seafood from skewers; keep warm.

9. Over high heat, bring broth mixture to simmering. Stir in remaining minced mint and basil. Ladle broth into wide bowls. Mound corn, seafood, and fennel in each bowl. Sprinkle with chives, and season to taste with fish sauce.

Per serving: 159 cal., 17% (27 cal.) from fat; 20 g protein; 3 g fat (0.4 g sat.); 14 g carbo (2.7 g fiber); 310 mg sodium; 76 mg chol. ◆

SUZANNE SMITH

The Quick Cook

MEALS IN 30 MINUTES OR LESS

by CHRISTINE WEBER HALE

Green curry paste, coconut milk, and basil add wonderful flavor to chicken and rice.

Quick starts with curry pastes

■ There's curry beyond curry powder. And it's not all Indian. You can create an interesting meal in a hurry with the help of prepared Thai curry pastes. The two most common types—green and red—share many of the same ingredients but have distinctive flavors. The green paste is most often used in poultry curries, the red paste with beef. Look for the pastes in well-stocked groceries and Asian markets.

Green Chicken Curry

Prep and cook time: About 25 minutes
Makes: 4 servings

- 2 tablespoons firmly packed **brown sugar**
- 1 tablespoon **cornstarch**
- 1 can (14 oz.) **reduced-fat coconut milk**
- ¾ cup **chicken broth**
- 3 tablespoons **soy sauce**
- 1½ tablespoons **prepared Thai green curry paste**
- 3 cups skinned and shredded cooked **chicken**
- 1 can (8 oz.) **bamboo shoots**, drained
- ½ cup slivered **fresh basil** leaves
- 3 cups hot cooked **rice**

1. In a 4- to 5-quart pan, mix sugar and cornstarch smoothly with coconut milk, broth, soy, and curry paste. Stir over medium-high heat until simmering.

2. Stir in chicken and bamboo shoots. When hot, add basil. Serve with rice.

Per serving: 606 cal., 21% (126 cal.) from fat; 37 g protein; 14 g fat (5.8 g sat.); 70 g carbo (1.6 g fiber); 1,035 mg sodium; 95 mg chol.

Red Curry Beef

Prep and cook time: About 30 minutes
Makes: 4 servings

- 2 tablespoons firmly packed **brown sugar**
- 1 tablespoon **cornstarch**
- 1 can (14 oz.) **reduced-fat coconut milk**
- ½ cup **beef broth**
- 2 tablespoons **soy sauce**
- 1½ tablespoons **prepared Thai red curry paste**
- 1 tablespoon grated **lemon** peel
- 1 pound **beef, cut for stir-frying**
- 5 cups hot cooked **linguine**
- 2 tablespoons minced **fresh cilantro**
- 1 tablespoon **Asian (toasted) sesame oil**

1. In a bowl, mix sugar and cornstarch. Whisk in coconut milk, broth, soy, curry paste, and lemon peel.

2. Place an 11- to 12-inch nonstick frying pan over high heat. When hot, add beef. Stir until beef is browned slightly, about 2 minutes. Remove beef from pan.

3. Add curry mixture to pan. Stir until boiling. Return beef to pan; stir just until hot, about 1 minute.

4. Mix pasta with cilantro and oil, then pour curry onto pasta.

Per serving: 600 cal., 24% (144 cal.) from fat; 36 g protein; 16 g fat (6.1 g sat.); 64 g carbo (2 g fiber); 761 mg sodium; 129 mg chol. ◆

Kitchen Cabinet

READERS' RECIPES TESTED IN SUNSET'S KITCHENS

by LINDA LAU ANUSASANANAN

Glossy pomegranate seeds add tang to a quick salad from Pakistan.

Salad with history

■ In her Pakistan homeland, Farah Ahmed ate this refreshing salad to break the fast of Ramadan, the ninth month of the Islamic year. With the cool crunch of pomegranates and cucumbers, it makes an appealing dish for a hot summer day.

Garbanzo Salad with Pomegranate Seed

Farah Ahmed, Sunnyvale, California

Prep and cook time: About 20 minutes
Makes: 6 servings

 1   teaspoon **ground cumin**
 ⅓   cup **lime** or lemon **juice**
 1   tablespoon **sugar**
 1   tablespoon chopped **fresh cilantro**
 ¼   teaspoon **cayenne**
 1   cup **pomegranate seeds**
 2   cans (15 oz. each) **garbanzos,** rinsed and drained
 1   cup peeled, diced (½-in. cubes) **cucumber**
 ½   cup chopped mild **onion**
     Salt and **pepper**

1. In a 6- to 8-inch frying pan over low heat, stir cumin until fragrant, 3 to 4 minutes. Scrape cumin into a large bowl and add lime juice, sugar, chopped cilantro, and cayenne.
2. Add pomegranate seeds, garbanzos,

cucumber, and onion to bowl. Mix and add salt and pepper to taste.

Per serving: 139 cal., 16% (22 cal.) from fat; 5.7 g protein; 2.4 g fat (0.1 g sat.); 25 g carbo (4.3 g fiber); 162 mg sodium; 0 mg chol.

Belize Burrito

Noel Maria Kelton, San Francisco

While in Belize seeking recipes with Caribbean flavors, Noel Maria Kelton discovered curried lobster burritos. She borrowed the idea, modified it to accommodate shrimp, and now serves the dish at her Primo Patio Cafe in San Francisco. Customers love the results.

Prep and cook time: About 35 minutes
Makes: 4 servings

 1   package (6 oz.) **curry rice mix**
 1   carton (8 oz.) **plain nonfat yogurt**
 1   or 2 cloves **garlic,** pressed or minced
     Salt and **pepper**
 1   teaspoon **salad oil**
 6   cups (6 oz.) **washed spinach leaves**
 ½   pound **shelled cooked tiny shrimp,** rinsed and drained
 4   **flour tortillas** (10 in. wide)
     About 1 cup **tomato salsa**

1. Cook rice mix according to package directions.
2. Meanwhile mix yogurt, garlic, and salt and pepper to taste.
3. When rice is almost done, place a 10- to 12-inch frying pan over high heat. When pan is hot, add oil and spinach. Stir until leaves wilt, about 2 minutes. Mix in shrimp, remove from heat, and drain liquid from pan.
4. Enclose tortillas in microwave-safe plastic wrap and heat in a microwave oven at full power (100%) until hot and steamy, 45 to 60 seconds.
5. Onto each warm tortilla, spoon ¼ of the rice, ¼ of the spinach mixture, 1 tablespoon yogurt sauce, and 2 tablespoons salsa. Fold one side of the tortilla over the filling, then fold the sides over and roll to enclose.

Accompany the burritos with remaining yogurt sauce and tomato salsa, to add to taste.

Per serving: 442 cal., 13% (57 cal.) from fat; 24 g protein; 6.3 g fat (1 g sat.); 71 g carbo (3.2 g fiber); 1,526 mg sodium; 112 mg chol.

Grilled Lamb Chops on Minted Tomatoes

Linda Tebben, Menlo Park, California

The memory of the lamb entrée that Linda Tebben enjoyed in Arizona lingered. Back home, she tried duplicating the dish she had been served at the Scottsdale Princess resort's La Hacienda. Her recipe may not be authentic, but the lamb tastes just as she remembered it. She serves the chops with grilled polenta.

Prep and cook time: About 25 minutes
Makes: 2 servings

    1   firm-ripe **tomato** (½ lb.), peeled
    3   tablespoons chopped **fresh mint** leaves
    1   tablespoon **balsamic vinegar**
    ½   teaspoon **extra-virgin olive oil**
    6   **lamb rib chops** (each about ¾ in. thick; about 1 lb. total)
    3   tablespoons **salted, roasted sunflower seed,** chopped
        Salt and **pepper**

1. Cut tomato in half crosswise; gently squeeze out seed. Trim out and discard core; cut tomato into ½-inch cubes.

2. Mix tomato, mint, vinegar, and oil; spoon onto a platter or plates.

3. Trim excess fat off lamb. Barbecue

In about 25 minutes, grilled lamb and minted tomatoes are ready for the table.

chops on a grill over solid bed of hot coals or high heat on a gas grill (you can hold your hand at grill level only 2 to 3 seconds). Cook, turning once, until lamb is browned and still pink in the center (cut to test), 7 to 9 minutes total. Set chops on tomato mixture.

4. Sprinkle meat with sunflower seed. Season with salt and pepper to taste.

Per serving: 274 cal., 56% (153 cal.) from fat; 23 g protein; 17 g fat (4.2 g sat.); 8.1 g carbo (2.9 g fiber); 165 mg sodium; 66 mg chol.

Pocket Bread Crisps

Susan Campbell, Kailua, Hawaii

A new mini–food processor and a garden loaded with fresh herbs inspired Susan Campbell. She put the two together and made herb butter to spread on split pocket bread rounds. Baked crisp, the bread is an ideal partner for salad or soup.

Prep and cook time: About 30 minutes
Makes: 10 to 12 rounds

    ½   cup (¼ lb.) **butter** or margarine, at room temperature
    3   tablespoons minced **fresh basil,** thyme, marjoram, or oregano leaves (one or a mixture)
        Salt and **pepper**
    5   or 6 **pocket breads** (6 in. wide)

1. Mix butter with basil and salt and pepper to taste.

2. Split pocket breads in half to make rounds. Spread butter mixture lightly over rough side of each round. Place, buttered side up, in a single layer on baking sheets.

3. Bake in a 425° oven until bread is crisp and golden, 8 to 10 minutes (switch pan positions after 4 minutes if using 1 oven). Serve warm or cool.

Per piece: 151 cal., 48% (72 cal.) from fat; 2.8 g protein; 8 g fat (4.8 g sat.); 17 g carbo (0.5 g fiber); 239 mg sodium; 21 mg chol.

Pad Thai

Revadee Crabbe, Phoenix

Fish sauce smells very bad if you're not used to it," says Thai immigrant Revadee Crabbe. So when she cooks this popular Thai noodle dish for her husband and friends, she adapts it to American tastes by using salt instead of fish sauce, and much less chili. Look for

rice noodles in the Asian section of the supermarket. Those ¼ inch wide hold their shape best.

Prep and cook time: About 35 minutes
Makes: 2 servings

    4   ounces **dried rice noodles** (rice sticks or *mai fun*)
    2   tablespoons **catsup**
    1½ tablespoons **sugar**
    ½   to 2 teaspoons **hot chili flakes**
        Salt or Asian fish sauce (*nuoc mam* or *nam pla*)
    2   teaspoons **salad oil**
    2   cloves **garlic,** pressed or minced
    1   **boned, skinned chicken breast half** (6 oz.), sliced into thin strips
    ⅓   pound (24 to 30 per lb.) **shrimp,** peeled and deveined
    2   **large eggs,** beaten to blend
    3   **green onions,** ends trimmed, cut into 1-inch lengths
    3   cups (½ lb.) **bean sprouts,** rinsed and drained
    2   tablespoons finely chopped **unsalted roasted peanuts**
        Cilantro sprigs
    1   cup finely shredded **cabbage**
    ½   cup shredded **carrot**
        Lime wedges

1. Soak noodles in hot (not boiling) water to cover until soft, 5 to 10 minutes; drain.

2. Mix catsup, sugar, ½ to 1 teaspoon chili flakes (to taste), and ¼ teaspoon salt or 1 tablespoon fish sauce.

3. Place a nonstick 12-inch frying pan or 14-inch wok over high heat. When pan is hot, add oil, garlic, chicken, and shrimp. Stir-fry until shrimp begins to turn pink, about 1½ minutes.

4. Reduce heat to medium-high. Add eggs and drained noodles; stir until mixed. Add catsup mixture and stir until noodles are tender to bite, about 2 minutes.

5. Add onions, 2 cups bean sprouts, and salt or fish sauce to taste. Mix.

6. Spoon onto plates. Sprinkle with peanuts and cilantro sprigs. Offer remaining bean sprouts, cabbage, carrot, lime, and chili to add to taste.

Per serving: 638 cal., 24% (153 cal.) from fat; 46 g protein; 17 g fat (3.3 g sat.); 78 g carbo (4.8 g fiber); 515 mg sodium; 355 mg chol. ◆

Perfect for a party, Tortellini Torta layers braised eggplant with fresh pasta and tomato-based pasta sauce (recipe on page 240).

IAN REEVES

October

foodguide

by JERRY ANNE DI VECCHIO

produce

Hollandia Produce in Carpinteria, California, has seen the future. Pete and Art Overgaag's company grows—and sells—hydroponic lettuce. Under the brand Live Gourmet, mature, greenhouse-raised butter lettuce heads (5- to 6-oz. size) are now being sold, root system and all, in special plastic containers. The outer leaves, untraumatized by weather or soil, are exceptionally tender and usable. And the whole head, refrigerated, stays fresh two to three weeks because it's alive—the roots are nurtured by a well of moisture in the closed container. You'll find Live Gourmet lettuce in some regular and many specialty supermarkets priced from 99 cents to $1.99. For a source near you, call (805) 684-8737.

LEFT: CURTIS ANDERSON BELOW AND RIGHT: JAMES CARRIER

GREAT INGREDIENT

Pumpkin seed oil

■ Toasting gives pumpkin seed a nutty punch. It also gives Pepo pumpkin seed oil its rich flavor and dark color.

Although I consider pumpkin seed an all-American treat, this oil, surprisingly, comes from Austria, where it's been produced for more than 130 years. The oil is intensely flavored, so a little goes a long way. I find it delicious lightly brushed onto hot ears of corn. It's also a natural with avocados and salads *with* avocados, and comple-ments the earthiness of cooked celery root. And for a dipping sauce for artichokes, I mix a little of the oil with melted butter or mayonnaise.

Pepo importer Linda Parker suggests mixing the pumpkin seed oil with raspberry vinegar to season sliced tomatoes with mozzarella cheese and basil.

Tightly covered, the oil keeps in the refrigerator for a year or more.

Pumpkin seed oil is sold in some specialty food markets and natural-food stores. A 250-ml. bottle costs $16 to $20. You can order it by calling (707) 255-1252; e-mail delectus1@aol.com for information.

Steak Diane

Prep and cook time: About 20 minutes

Makes: 6 servings

- 1½ pounds **fat-trimmed narrow end of beef tenderloin**
- 1 to 1½ tablespoons coarse-ground **pepper**
- ¾ cup finely chopped **shallots** or onion
- 2 tablespoons **butter** or margarine
- ¼ cup **dry white wine**
- ¼ cup **white wine vinegar**
- ½ cup **beef broth**
- 2 teaspoons **dry mustard**
- 1 tablespoon **Dijon mustard**
- ⅓ cup **whipping cream**
- 2 tablespoons **dry sherry**
- 2 tablespoons **brandy**
- **Salt**

1. Cut thickest part of beef across the grain into 1½-inch-long pieces. Cut thinnest end into 2-inch-long pieces. Turn each piece onto a cut side and press down firmly to flatten.

2. Sprinkle meat evenly on each side with pepper, pressing it onto the surface.

3. In an 11- to 12-inch nonstick frying pan, combine shallots and 1 tablespoon butter. Stir over high heat until shallots are limp, about 1½ minutes. Add white wine, vinegar, broth, dry mustard, Dijon mustard, and cream. Boil over high heat, stirring, until reduced by half (to ¾ cup), 5 to 7 minutes. Pour sauce into a small bowl and set aside. Rinse pan and wipe dry.

4. Return frying pan to high heat. When hot, add remaining butter and swirl until it melts, then add meat (pieces should all fit in pan without overlapping). Brown beef on one side, about 2½ minutes. Turn over and continue to cook until brown, about 2½ minutes more for rare.

5. Transfer beef to a warm plate. Add sherry, brandy, and sauce to pan. Stir until bubbling. Pour the sauce, and any juices drained from the meat, onto plates. Top with the beef. Add salt to taste.

Per serving: 298 cal., 51% (153 cal.) from fat; 25 g protein; 17 g fat (8.3 g sat.); 5.1 g carbo (0.4 g fiber); 174 mg sodium; 95 mg chol.

Gourmet daze

■ There was a time when gourmet really meant something in a restaurant. Waiters didn't swoop up with a big smile and say, "My name is Amy" or "Andy." Nor did they wear Nicole Miller ties or Ralph Lauren shirts. They wore tuxedos, even white gloves, and somber faces. You were served. The fuss, if properly done, was so intimidating you assumed you could never create dishes such as tournedos Rossini or steak Diane in your own kitchen.

As restaurants became more casual and menus as descriptive as cook-books, dishes were easier to duplicate at home. Unfortunately, some of the really wonderful classics, confusingly described in French terms, fell by the way-side. But they're coming back.

At the Ritz in Newport Beach, California, steak Diane and veal Oscar are often on the menu. But chef Lupé Camarena makes no mystery about how they're prepared, acknowledging that all those individual sauces simmering in her vast professional kitchen can be broken down into a few ingredients for a single recipe.

JAMES CARRIER

BACK TO BASICS

The magic of soufflés

■ In 1965, Jack and Jamie Davies bought Schramsberg Vineyards and brought the Napa Valley winery (founded in 1862) back to life with the production of sparkling wines. They tell their story in *Sparkling Harvest: The Seasons of the Vine,* due out in November (Harry N. Abrams, New York; $45).

A charming vignette happened early on, when Jack called Jamie late one afternoon, asking if he could bring a guest who was tasting their wines to dinner. It was James Beard, a grand figure in girth and in the food world. With three young sons and little time, Jamie decided to serve a cheese soufflé. It's a rare refrigerator that doesn't yield most of the ingredients.

The soufflé was a success, and the evening went well—except for one detail: the Windsor wing chairs at the Davieses' table wouldn't accommodate Jim Beard, who found the piano bench more to his comfort.

Cheese Soufflé

Prep and cook time: 45 minutes
Makes: 6 servings

  4 tablespoons **butter** or margarine
  2 tablespoons **shredded parmesan cheese**
  6 **large eggs**
  2 **large egg** whites
  ½ teaspoon **cream of tartar**
  4½ tablespoons **all-purpose flour**
  1½ cups **low-fat milk**
  ¼ teaspoon **salt**
  ¼ teaspoon **pepper**
  ¼ teaspoon **cayenne**
  ¼ teaspoon **ground nutmeg**
  1¼ cups (about 5 oz.) shredded **gruyère cheese**

1. Coat interior of a 10- to 11-cup soufflé dish with 1½ teaspoons butter. Add parmesan cheese; tilt dish to coat.

2. Separate eggs; put yolks in a small bowl and all whites in a large mixer bowl. Add cream of tartar to whites.

3. Melt remaining butter in a 10- to 12-inch frying pan over medium-high heat. Add flour and stir until bubbling.

4. Remove from heat. Whisk milk into the mixture. Add salt, pepper, cayenne, and ground nutmeg. Return to high heat and stir until mixture boils, about 2 minutes; sauce will be very thick. Set aside about 2 tablespoons gruyère cheese, then add remainder to sauce and stir until melted. Remove from heat. Dump in egg yolks and mix well.

5. With a mixer on high speed, beat egg whites just until they hold soft but distinct peaks. Put a big spoonful of whites into the sauce and mix well.

6. Scrape sauce into whites, and with a flexible spatula, fold ingredients together; the mixture can look streaky.

7. Scrape mixture into soufflé dish. With the tip of the spatula, draw a circle on top of the soufflé, then sprinkle with reserved gruyère cheese.

8. Set on the center rack of a 400° oven. Bake until browned and center jiggles slightly when dish is gently shaken (for a saucy soufflé), about 25 minutes, or for a drier soufflé, about 10 minutes more. Serve at once.

Per serving: 306 cal., 65% (198 cal.) from fat; 18 g protein; 22 g fat (12 g sat.); 8.5 g carbo (0.2 g fiber); 390 mg sodium; 265 mg chol.

GREAT TECHNIQUE

Poaching meatballs

■ In Phoenix, the plastic-topped tables and washable plastic booths of the Tee Pee Mexican Food restaurant are particularly popular among families with young children. The other draws are mild but authentic-tasting Mexican dishes and the fact that the only meats used are beef and chicken. The *albóndigas* (meatballs) soup took me right back to Mexico. The flavor is fresh and simple, and the meatballs are exceptionally moist and tender because they are poached in the soup, not pan-browned first.

Albóndigas Soup

Prep and cook time: 35 to 40 minutes
Notes: If making ahead, cool, cover, and chill up to 2 days. Heat to simmering to serve.
Makes: 12 cups; 6 servings

  1 **onion** (½ lb.), chopped
  1 **carrot** (¼ lb.), peeled and diced
  1 **can** (14 to 15 oz.) **chopped tomatoes**
  6 cups **beef broth**
  1 pound **ground lean beef**
  ¼ cup **white rice**
  ¼ cup **all-purpose flour**

PHILIP SALAVERRY

  1 **large egg**
     About ¼ teaspoon **salt**
  1 cup chopped **fresh cilantro**

1. In a 4- to 5-quart pan, combine onion, carrot, tomatoes and their juices, 5½ cups broth, and ½ cup water. Set pan over high heat and cover.

2. Meanwhile, in a bowl combine remaining ½ cup broth, beef, rice, flour, egg, ¼ teaspoon salt, and ½ cup cilantro. Mix with your hands to blend well.

3. Uncover broth and vegetables and drop meat in 1-tablespoon portions into pan. When soup boils, reduce heat to a gentle simmer, cover pan, and cook 20 minutes.

4. Stir remaining cilantro into soup and ladle into bowls. Add salt to taste.

Per serving: 315 cal., 49% (153 cal.) from fat; 22 g protein; 17 g fat (6.6 g sat.); 18 g carbo (2 g fiber); 339 mg sodium; 92 mg chol. ◆

The Wine Guide

by KAREN MacNEIL

Don't forget Cabernet Sauvignon

■ I once asked a well-known chef why she didn't serve roast chicken. Her roast chicken, it should be added, was extraordinary. She had, in fact, spent more than a decade perfecting it.

But just at her moment of mastery, diners in the restaurant decided that chicken was, well, uninteresting. Didn't she make quail or something?

Cabernet Sauvignon has suffered a similar paradoxical fate. The grape variety that put American wine on the international map has come of age. But now that there are dozens upon dozens of delicious Cabs out there, the stylish thing to sip is Syrah (more glamorous), Zinfandel (more homey), Sangiovese (more Euro chic), or Merlot (more Gen X).

What's fascinating about top Cabernets, however, is their seemingly oxymoronic ability to taste both powerful and elegant at the same time. In the 1970s, Warren Winiarski, owner-winemaker of Stag's Leap Wine Cellars, gave Cabernet Sauvignon the ultimate description: "an iron fist in a velvet glove."

Cabernet is produced everywhere from Texas to the Golan Heights, but its historic home is Bordeaux, a large wine region on France's Atlantic coast. In Bordeaux, however, Cabernet is almost always blended with up to four other red varieties: Merlot, Malbec, Petite Verdot, and Cabernet Franc.

Here in the West, the top Cabernets come from California and Washington. These are the James Bonds of red wine—sophisticated, worldly, highly focused, sexy but driven. In both states, a wine labeled Cabernet can be either 100 percent Cabernet or blended with

other Bordeaux varieties (these latter wines are sometimes called Bordeaux blends or meritage wines).

There are also a slew of tasty Cabernets on the market from numerous other countries, including Australia (big, teddy bear–esque Cabernets) and Chile (leaner, but good and juicy and bargain-priced).

If a dozen of the top makers were asked why Cabernet is so good these days, one answer would keep cropping up: ripeness. Cabernet is rather like a melon. If it's even slightly underripe, it tastes green and one-dimensional. If it's overripe, it tastes flat and one-dimensional.

But at perfect ripeness, the flavor of a melon is rich and nuanced. And so it is with Cabernet.

Only in the last 10 years or so have winemakers truly understood Cabernet ripeness. For decades Cabernet was harvested when the sugars in the grapes reached a certain numerical point on a small instrument not unlike a thermometer. What winemakers now know, however, is that the sugar in wine grapes

WINE DICTIONARY

Tannin

Tannins are compounds found in a grape's skin, seeds, and stem. Because red wines are fermented with their skins, they have far more tannin than white wines. Tannins act as preservatives (which is why certain red wines can last for a long time). Tannins also give red wines their firm structure. It's common for highly tannic wines to feel "tight" in the mouth when the wine is young. But the wine is considered poorly made if the tannins are extremely dry, harsh, and scratchy. — *K. M.*

can be ripe even though other components in the grape are still immature.

Ripe sugar aside, the critical issue with Cabernet is whether the grapes have ripe tannin. How can a winemaker tell? By using the instrument used since antiquity—the tongue. Only by tasting a zillion grapes and by years of practice can a smart winemaker learn to determine when grapes are fully ripe. Like chefs, Cabernet makers must rely on their sense of taste and texture to determine that magical moment.

Finally, Cabernets can't be discussed without a word on price. They range from $6 to several hundred dollars a bottle. Inexpensive Cabs can be delightful wines full of good blackberry and cassis flavors. More expensive Cabernets are generally lusher and more nuanced, and their flavors last longer in the mouth. And of course, the very greatest (usually very expensive) Cabernets can be gorgeously deep in flavor and packed with personality. In all cases, what you want is a full-flavored Cab that's generous in the mouth. If it tastes thin and remotely like canned green beans, you've got the wrong Cab. ◆

Sonoma County rambles

Three country drives that lead you to the region's best meals, produce, and wine

■ A red tractor chugs along the crest of tawny hills speckled with sheep and black-faced goats. Bins overflowing with red peppers and fat tomatoes line produce stands along the byways. Curving country roads descend into lush valleys.

Sonoma is often compared to its showier neighbor, the Napa Valley. Both areas produce outstanding wines. But where Napa is spotless Jeep Cherokees and tony shops, Sonoma is pickup trucks and country stores. Like Debbie Reynolds in *Tammy and the Bachelor,* Sonoma is wholesome, down-to-earth, and more than a little bit country.

As it has been for a long time. The state's first premium winery, Buena Vista, opened here in 1857. Jack London built his Beauty Ranch here in 1904, startling his neighbors by growing grapes as well as raising cattle. Today, Sonoma's 505,000 agricultural acres yield products so choice that well-known chefs from all over the San Francisco Bay Area flock here to select supplies: free-range poultry, unique cheeses, succulent greens, and baby vegetables.

One reason for this bounty is Sonoma's varied topography and microclimates, which range from a misty, redwood-shaded river basin to dry, oak-studded hills. Between the Coast Range and the Mayacmas Mountains lie the most productive valleys—Russian River, Dry Creek, Alexander, and Sonoma.

Three driving tours give you a good sense of them: from Sonoma into the Valley of the Moon (Sonoma Valley); from Santa Rosa into the Russian River Valley; and from Healdsburg into the Dry Creek Valley.

by **LORA J. FINNEGAN**

Sonoma in fall: bicyclists passing a vineyard (top); the Zinfandel harvest (above); and salmon and Chardonnay at Chateau Souverain.

TERRENCE McCARTHY

Out to the country

The best of Sonoma remains a secret to most casual visitors, despite the fact that the county lies less than 50 miles from downtown San Francisco and right next door to its famous cousin, the Napa Valley. If you love wine and food—and the rural countryside that produces them—Sonoma offers a profusion of pleasures, from country roads to excellent wines to wonderful restaurants.

DEBRA LAMBERT

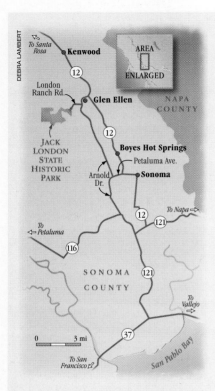

DEBRA LAMBERT

If you can manage only one Sonoma tour, this is the one to take; it encompasses the valley's history, from mission plantings to today's fresh-pressed olive oils.

From State Highway 121, head north on State 12 to the town of Sonoma to begin your tour, which is about a 20-mile drive.

Valley of the Moon

We start our tour at the Mexican-style plaza in the town of Sonoma. At the Sonoma Mission (part of Sonoma State Historic Park), plantings of agave, grape, and pomegranate hint at the food and medicinal plants the Spanish padres cultivated. Elbowing into the busy Sonoma Cheese Factory, we pick up picnic supplies.

Heading north on Arnold Drive and up the Valley of the Moon, we move through a tunnel of flame-colored maples and liquidambars before stopping at the Benziger Family Winery in Glen Ellen for a fascinating and comprehensive tour. Our guide, Michael, stands before a backdrop of rolling vineyards and the rock-candy peak of Sonoma Mountain. "Volcanic forces created the undulating landscape you see. And the different soils it gives us—red to black—is like having a spice rack for the grapes."

Jack London certainly would have agreed, having grown grapes on his own farm just up the road. Now a 1,500-acre state historic park has opened much of the author's Beauty Ranch to the public, including the tall concrete silos and the pig palace—an imposing brick structure.

As we roll down into Glen Ellen, the town appears little changed from London's era, with its Victorian homes and stone buildings. We prowl among the dusty volumes at the Jack London Bookstore, admire the elegant foodstuffs at Lesley B. Fay Fine Foods of Sonoma, and sip through the Glen Ellen Winery's tasting room and museum. But it's the massive old grinding wheel in front of a converted winery on Arnold Drive that captivates us.

"This is the way olives were pressed for centuries," says Ed Stolman, standing by the 3-ton granite pressing wheel in front of his shop, the Olive Press. A trip to France and Italy infused him with a passion for olive oil. Returning to Sonoma, he built a Tuscan-style villa, planted 2,400 olive trees, and opened this shop and oil-pressing facility.

As we wind along State 12 to Kenwood, then backtrack to return to Sonoma, we can't resist stopping at more tasting rooms—Kunde Estate Winery and Kenwood Vineyards are highlights—and stocking up at the produce stands.

DRIVE HIGHLIGHTS

Benziger Family Winery. 10–5 daily. 1883 London Ranch Rd., Glen Ellen; (707) 935-3000.

Glen Ellen Winery Tasting Room. 10–5 daily. 14301 Arnold Dr., Glen Ellen; 939-6277.

Jack London Bookstore. 10–5 Wed-Mon. 14300 Arnold, Glen Ellen; 996-2888.

Jack London State Historic Park. 9:30–7 daily through October 25, then 9:30–5. $6 per car. 2400 London Ranch, Glen Ellen; 938-5216.

Kenwood Vineyards. 10–4:30 daily. 9591 Sonoma Hwy. 12, Kenwood; 833-5891.

Kunde Estate Winery. 11–5 daily. 10155 Sonoma Hwy. 12, Kenwood; 833-5501.

Lesley B. Fay Fine Foods of Sonoma. 11–5 daily. 14301 Arnold, Glen Ellen; 996-2600.

Oak Hill Farm. Produce stand 10–4 Thu-Sat. 15101 Sonoma Hwy. 12, Glen Ellen; 996-6643.

Olive Press. 10–5:30 daily. 14301 Arnold, #15, Glen Ellen; 939-8900.

Sonoma Mission. 10–5 daily. At Spain and E. First streets, Sonoma; 938-1519.

Russian River loop

The drive from Santa Rosa begins on U.S. 101 north to River Road, which cuts inland onto a broad, flat plain.

Vineyards and produce stands beckon almost immediately. At the former hop barn that serves as Martinelli Winery's tasting room and store, we sample fruity Pinot Noir and stock up on local products: tapenades, mustards, jellies. Soon we hit the Russian River where it makes its sharp turn west through the Coast Range, cutting a meandering gorge.

BEN DAVIDSON

Tractors may share your road.

Fog pushes inland, fingering through the old-growth redwoods and cloaking the canoeists paddling the river below us. Its cooling influence is one reason grapes for sparkling wine do so well here. Three brothers from Bohemia figured that out long ago, and founded Korbel Champagne Cellars here in 1882. Today, over a million cases of sparkling wines pour from Korbel's imposing gabled brick building. We pause at the hillside rose garden (more than 250 antique varieties) before joining the tour to learn about the *méthode champenoise.*

A malty scent leads us to Korbel's latest development: the Russian River Brewing Company microbrewery, which uses its own hops. Its first four brews—wheat ale, pale ale, amber ale,

At Kitchen in Graton, enjoy dinner from the counter, at a table in the same art-filled room, or on the veranda, where you can watch people amble by.

neys, and salad dressings.

Down the road a bit, at Foxglove Farm, we're greeted by owners Mike and Joan Mortensson along with Rainey the dalmatian. Mike looks the part of a farmer in his red flannel shirt, jeans, boots, and elegant handlebar mustache. Their white farmhouse doubles as a produce stand: baskets of the farm's red, luscious tomatoes are piled next to bins of apples, beans, and squash. The farm is also visited by bluebirds in the fall, attracted by the birdhouses the Mortenssons put up. As we head back to the car, loaded down with bags of apples, we walk slowly, watching for the birds.

DRIVE HIGHLIGHTS

Burke's Canoe Trips. 10-mile self-guided day trips cost $30, including shuttle bus back to Burke's. 8600 River Rd. at Mirabel Rd., Forestville; (707) 887-1222 (call for reservations).

Foxglove Farm. 10–5 Thu–Tue through November 1. 5280 Gravenstein Hwy. N. (State 116), north of Sebastopol; 887-2759.

Korbel Champagne Cellars. Guided tours of the winery and cellar 10–3 daily. Deli and market 6–6 Mon-Fri, 9–6 Sat-Sun. Tasting room 9–4:30 daily. 13250 River Rd., Guerneville; 887-2294.

Kozlowski Farms. Bakery, deli, and espresso bar 9–5 daily. 5566 Gravenstein Hwy. N., Forestville; 887-1587.

Martinelli Winery. 10–5 daily. 3360 River, Windsor; 525-0570.

and porter—are sold in its deli and in a few local restaurants.

The road eases into Guerneville, which is bustling with repairs from last winter's floods. By fall, its seasonal riverside activity—canoe and boat rentals and swimming beaches—is winding down. We angle south on State 116, climbing slightly out of the river gorge and up into orchards and small

farms. Three decades ago, an abundance of raspberries here gave Carmen Kozlowski a new career. The homemaker began making red-raspberry jam in a big pot and selling it to a few friends. Now the Kozlowskis' store and produce stand are a local landmark where the family manufactures and sells 60 food products, from jams and apple butters to berry vinegars, chut-

This tour throws a wide loop north and west of Santa Rosa to meander alongside a lazy river, through old-growth redwoods, wine-grape and fruit-growing benchlands, and past small towns like Forestville and Guerneville. From U.S. 101, take the Mark West Springs Road/River Road exit west. The loop is about 29 miles. Here you'll learn how Korbel makes champagne, discover its new microbrewery, visit two charming farms, and sample some of Martinelli Winery's best offerings.

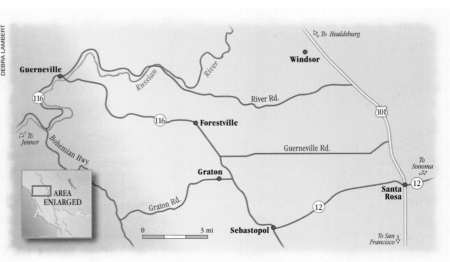

At the Healdsburg Farmers' Market on Saturday mornings, the early birds get the best of the basil, beets, and bell peppers.

ROBERTO SONCIN GEROMETTA

Dry Creek Valley

Healdsburg's Saturday morning farmers' market is our first stop on this loop. We stroll by umbrella-topped tables, tempted by arugulas (three varieties) and eggplants (green, white, and purple).

As we head west, then south, on Westside Road, it's quiet except for regular muffled "pops" as our tires crunch the walnuts littering the roadway. Fallen leaves of blue gum eucalyptus lace the brisk fall air with a slightly medicinal tang.

Moving down the steep-sided valley, we reach Middleton Farm, an organic concern whose centerpiece is a tidy white barn, where we greet co-owner Nancy Skall. "The Gish sisters really rule the roost here," says Skall, shooing two large, white Araucana chickens, who strut away on gray feet. Out in the field, Skall bends down to pick up a handful of dark brown earth. "I fell in love with this place when I heard it had 20 feet of topsoil and a neutral pH. We can grow anything here," she explains. Their pride and joy? "The strawberries—we sell them to Chez Panisse."

We have to move on, but the taste of berries lingers as we continue south on Westside, stopping for peppers, late tomatoes, and pumpkins at Westside Farms before returning north. Soon Westside becomes West Dry Creek

Road, and we pass turnoffs to tasting rooms—Dry Creek Vineyard, Ridge/Lytton Springs Winery, and Quivira Vineyards—and lowlands daubed peach and vermilion by the vineyards' turning leaves.

At the head of the valley, we reach barnlike Preston Vineyards. A neon sign in the tasting room proclaims owner Lou Preston's first love: Zinfandel. "I've been in the valley since 1973, when it was dominated by prune orchards. I figured since Zinfandel has been grown here since 1895, it might be the right wine for the area." Indeed, Zin has become a valley hallmark.

But these days Preston is branching out, producing olive oils and hearth-baked breads. "I guess you could say I'm an Italian wannabe," he laughs, pointing to the shaded bocce courts and "forno" bread oven.

We loop over Yoakim Bridge Road to Dry Creek Road to drink in the color at the outstanding Ferrari-Carano Vineyards and Winery gardens, where beds of red salvia, marigolds, and petunias border the paths that wander alongside a stream, waterfall, and water garden. The riot of blooms almost makes the Italian villa–style tasting room seem subdued. At last, the back seat of our car overflowing with baskets of tomatoes and strawberries, bread and wine, we roll contentedly back to Healdsburg.

DRIVE HIGHLIGHTS

Dry Creek Vineyard. 10:30–4:30 daily. 3770 Lambert Bridge Rd., Healdsburg; (707) 433-1000.

Ferrari-Carano Vineyards and Winery. 10–5 daily. 8761 Dry Creek Rd., Healdsburg; 433-6700.

Healdsburg Farmers' Market. 9–noon Sat, May-December. North and Vine streets; 431-1956.

Middleton Farm. 9–5 daily. 2651 Westside Rd., southwest of Healdsburg; 433-4755.

Preston Vineyards. 11–4:30 daily. 9282 West Dry Creek Rd., Healdsburg; 433-3372.

Quivira Vineyards. 10–4:30 daily. 4900 West Dry Creek, Healdsburg; 431-8333.

Ridge/Lytton Springs Winery. 11–4 daily through October. 650 Lytton Springs Rd., Healdsburg; 433-7721.

Westside Farms. 10–6 Wed-Sun, October 8–31. 7097 Westside, southwest of Healdsburg; 431-1432.

The Dry Creek Valley has impressive tasting rooms that are nearly empty, produce stands with heirloom vegetables, and one of the prettiest winery gardens anywhere. From U.S. 101, take the Central Healdsburg exit and go west on Westside Road. The loop, which involves a little backtracking, is about 30 miles.

Great eats and sleeps in Sonoma

DINING

From funky to French, a dozen restaurants stand out by focusing on fresh ingredients and local wines. Dishes constantly shift as seasonal ingredients change. Hours and days vary widely; call ahead for times and reservations.

Babette's. On the patio, sample a watercress sandwich and *pomme frites* at moderate prices. Inside, the restaurant is dark and expensive. The food is very French, but makes excellent use of local ingredients, including Sonoma foie gras. *464 First St. E., Sonoma; (707) 939-8921.*

Bear Flag Café. An off-the-wall setting is gentrified with white tablecloths; enjoy spinach salad, or flatiron steak with horseradish mashed potatoes. *18625 Hwy. 12, Boyes Hot Springs; 938-1927.*

Bistro Ralph. The large, trendy room suits stylish presentations, such as a whole artichoke with smoked salmon. *109 Plaza St., Healdsburg; 433-1380.*

Chateau Souverain. Savor a sweeping vista of the Alexander Valley; sit inside if it's windy. Food is predictable, but carefully executed. We enjoyed braised chicken over buckwheat polenta, and grilled lamb with lentils. *400 Souverain Rd., Geyserville; 433-3141.*

General's Daughter. Cornmeal onion rings with lemon aioli, risotto, and main-dish chicken salads are menu highlights, served in light, airy rooms hung with country paintings. *400 W. Spain St., Sonoma; 938-4004.*

John Ash & Co. Watch butterflies cavort in the herb garden against a backdrop of grapevines. Pizzas and crispy calamari are fortes, as are dishes with house-smoked ingredients. *4330 Barnes Rd., Santa Rosa; 527-7687.*

Kenwood Restaurant. Colorful decor. Try the braised rabbit or excellent lamb. Meals are heavy, prices relatively high. *9900 Hwy. 12, Kenwood; 833-6326.*

Kitchen. Sit on the veranda facing the sleepy main street and watch Graton ease by as the sun sets. Stuffed chilies, osso buco, and salads are noteworthy. *8989 Graton Rd., Graton; 824-0563.*

Mistral. Don't be misled by the generic mall setting; inside are treats such as salad with duck confit and many excellent vegetarian dishes. *1229 N. Dutton Ave., Santa Rosa; 578-4511.*

Mixx. Serves boldly seasoned foods, wonderful fresh-fruit sorbets, and other appealing heart-healthy choices, including cedar-planked roast salmon. *135 Fourth St., Santa Rosa; 573-1344.*

Ravenous. The freshest, most imaginative food of all in the tiniest setting. The portabella sandwich, potato and fennel soup, and fresh apricot galette are lunchtime showstoppers. *117 North St., Healdsburg; 431-1770.*

Willowside Cafe. In what feels like a country tavern, a brief, ever-changing menu's offerings might include king salmon and quail. *3535 Guerneville Rd., Santa Rosa; 523-4814. — Jerry Anne Di Vecchio and Andrew Baker*

PICNIC SHOPPING

On State 121: *Angelo's Country Deli.* Local favorite, famous fresh jerky. 23400 Hwy. 121; (707) 938-3688.

Viansa Italian Marketplace (at Viansa Winery). An upscale slice of Tuscan heaven. 25200 Hwy. 121; (800) 995-4740.

In Sonoma: *Vella Cheese.* Tangy aged jack is worth walking a block off the main drag. 315 Second St. E.; (707) 938-3232.

Sonoma Cheese Factory. Wide variety; jammed on weekends, so show up early. 2 Spain St.; 996-1931.

In Healdsburg: *Costeaux French Bakery.* French rolls, salads, and pastries. 421 Healdsburg Ave.; 433-1913.

Downtown Bakery. Focaccia and other breads. 308A Center St.; 431-2719.

Oakville Grocery. Everything you'd ever need for a picnic. 124 Matheson St.; 433-3200.

Russian River area: See *Kozlowski Farms* and *Korbel Champagne Cellars* in the Russian River loop listings.

LODGING

For complete lodging lists as well as other travel information, contact the Sonoma Valley Visitors Bureau (707/996-1090; http://www.SonomaValley.com) or the Sonoma County Convention & Visitors Bureau (800/326-7666). For the Healdsburg area, call the chamber of commerce (707/433-6935). In the Russian River region, call the visitor bureau (800/253-8800).

Applewood Inn. The rustic setting deep in the redwoods belies the comforts available: a pool and whirlpool bath, imposing rock fireplaces, and fluffy duvets on fanciful beds. Newer rooms are larger, with fireplaces and balconies or patios. All have private bath, telephone, and TV. Full breakfast included. *$125–$185; $200–$250 for new rooms. 13555 Hwy. 116, Guerneville; (707) 869-9093 or (800) 555-8509.*

Gaige House Inn. Roam the Italianate Victorian inn's lovely garden, or hang out by the swimming pool or small deck overlooking Calabazas Creek. Peet's coffee tops off a full breakfast. *$155–$255. 13540 Arnold Dr., Glen Ellen; (707) 935-0237 or (800) 935-0237.*

Honor Mansion. Set on a quiet backstreet in Healdsburg, the restored 1883 Italianate Victorian mansion has five rooms and a cottage, all with private baths and elaborately decorated with antiques. Sumptuous breakfast. *$120–$220. 14891 Grove St., Healdsburg; (800) 554-4667.*

Sonoma Mission Inn & Spa. This large inn (198 rooms and suites) has become a favorite of celebrities for its classic mission-style architecture, lavish spa, and privacy. Antique pine furniture, air-conditioning, telephone, private baths, and cable TV; some fireplaces and terraces. Ask about off-season packages (midweek after November 15). *Historic rooms, no fireplaces, $175–$325; more contemporary rooms with fireplaces, $265–$395; suites, $350–$780. On State 12 at Boyes Blvd., Boyes Hot Springs; (800) 862-4945.*

Vintners Inn. Set in Chardonnay and Sauvignon Blanc vineyards, the inn's 44 rooms are inspired by the French country style, with antique armoires and writing desks. Rooms have private bath, air-conditioning, TV, and telephone; some have a fireplace. Continental breakfast. *$148–$188, junior suites $185–$215. 4350 Barnes Rd., Santa Rosa; (800) 421-2584.* ◆

Reinventing the casserole

Labor-saving steps, ready-to-cook convenience, and contemporary foods can make your next party a breeze

■ A casserole for a party? If you still equate casseroles with canned tuna, potato chips, and unidentifiable ingredients, it's time to take a second look.

Today's casseroles have come a long way in appearance and taste. You start with more contemporary ingredients, such as portabella mushrooms, flavored tortillas, chipotle chilies, cooked polenta, and chicken breasts. Then use them in recipes that emphasize their best characteristics. Like their predecessors, these entertaining lifesavers can be made a day ahead.

To complete a casserole dinner, the party menu can be quite simple. Consider the suggestions on page 241.

A cool yogurt-mint sauce tops portabella mushroom, stuffed with lamb, that's served on curried bulgur.

Lamb-stuffed Portabellas

Prep and cook time: About 50 minutes to assemble, 35 minutes to bake (1 hour and 10 minutes if chilled)

Notes: If the casserole is chilled, the natural effects of the seasoning will keep the meat mixture pink in the center, even when it is cooked. Test doneness with a thermometer.

Makes: 8 servings

1	cup **dried apricots**
8	**portabella mushrooms** (4½-in.-wide caps), about 2½ lb. total
½	cup **pine nuts**
1	teaspoon **olive oil**
1	**onion** (½ lb.), finely chopped
¼	cup **curry powder**
2	cups **bulgur wheat**
5⅓	cups **chicken broth**
1½	pounds **ground lean lamb**
⅓	cup **fine dry bread crumbs**
3	cups **plain nonfat yogurt**
¾	cup chopped **fresh mint** leaves
	Salt

1. Cut apricots in half crosswise.

2. Rinse and drain mushrooms. Trim off stems flush with caps. Finely chop stems and set caps aside.

3. In a 4- to 5-quart nonstick pan over high heat, frequently shake pine nuts until lightly browned, about 2 minutes. Pour into a small bowl.

4. To pan, add chopped mushrooms, oil, onion, and curry powder. Stir over high heat until mushrooms and onion are limp and juices evaporate, about 3 minutes. Remove from heat and spoon half the mixture into a large bowl.

5. To mushroom mixture in the pan, add apricots, bulgur, and 5 cups broth. Bring to a boil, stir, cover, remove from heat, and let stand until bulgur is tender to bite, at least 8 minutes.

6. Meanwhile, combine reserved onion-mushroom mixture, ⅓ cup broth, lamb, and bread crumbs. Mix well. Pat an equal amount of lamb mixture onto the cup side of each mushroom cap, covering evenly. Scatter 1 tablespoon pine nuts onto each meat-filled mushroom and gently press nuts into meat.

7. Divide the curried bulgur mixture equally between 2 casseroles, each 3 quarts (about 9 by 13 in. and at least 2 in. deep).

8. Lay 4 mushrooms, meat side up, in each casserole (they can overlap slightly). If making ahead, cover and chill up to 1 day.

9. Bake, covered, in a 400° oven until lamb mixture is no longer pink in center (cut to test, or if chilled, it should register 150° on a thermometer; see notes), 35 to 40 minutes (about 1 hour and 10 minutes if chilled).

Streamlined techniques
Save hours of effort and cleanup

• *Stuff raw mushrooms with meat filling before baking.*

• *Replace time-consuming homemade pasta with egg roll wrappers to make cannelloni.*

• *Bake chicken breasts and asparagus together on purchased cooked polenta.*

• *Cook tortellini in a purchased enriched sauce instead of boiling in water.*

---

by **ANDREW BAKER**   *photographs by* **IAN REEVES**

10. Mix yogurt with mint. If making ahead, cover and chill up to 1 day.

11. Spoon portions onto plates and add yogurt sauce and salt to taste.

Per serving: 592 cal., 43% (252 cal.) from fat; 32 g protein; 28 g fat (10 g sat.); 60 g carbo (12 g fiber); 239 mg sodium; 66 mg chol.

Stacked Tortilla Pie with Carnitas

Prep and cook time: About 2 hours for sauce, 30 minutes to assemble, 50 minutes to bake (1 hour and 25 minutes if chilled)

Notes: Use red chili sauce (also labeled enchilada sauce), not a tomato-based chili sauce. Use tortillas flavored with red chili, spinach, tomato, or salsa. Packaged shredded Mexican cheese blends are available alongside other shredded cheese packs in supermarkets. Or use equal parts shredded cheddar cheese and shredded jack or Oaxaca cheese.

Makes: 8 servings

- 2 pounds **boned pork shoulder** or butt
- 1 **onion** (about ½ lb.), chopped
- 3 cloves **garlic,** pressed or minced
- 2 teaspoons **cumin seed**
- 1 cup **chicken broth** or water
- 2 cans (19 oz. each) **red chili sauce**
- 2 or 3 **canned chipotle chilies**
- 1 bag (1 lb.) frozen **corn kernels**
- 1 **red bell pepper** (¾ lb.), stemmed, seeded, and chopped
- ½ cup chopped **fresh cilantro**
  Salt
- 8 **flavored** or plain **flour tortillas** (10 in. wide)
- 2 cups **shredded Mexican cheese blend**
- 1 cup (about 5 oz.) crumbled **cotija** or feta **cheese**
- 1 firm-ripe **avocado** (about 6 oz.)
  Cilantro sprigs

1. Trim and discard excess fat from pork. Cut pork into ½-inch cubes.

2. In a 5- to 6-quart pan, combine pork, onion, garlic, cumin seed, and ½ cup broth. Cover, bring to a boil over high heat, and cook 10 minutes. Then boil, uncovered, stirring often as liquid evaporates and a brown film forms on pan bottom, 5 to 12 minutes. Add another ½ cup broth, stir browned bits

Succulent pork and mellow chili sauce separate flavored tortillas in this party pie.

free, and stir often until liquid evaporates again, 3 to 6 minutes. Add 1 can red chili sauce and stir browned bits free, then reduce the heat to simmering and cover.

3. Meanwhile, remove seeds and veins from chilies, then rinse and finely chop.

4. Add corn and red bell pepper to pork. Then stir in chilies to taste. Simmer until meat is tender enough to pull apart, about 1¼ hours total; stir often. Remove from heat and mix in chopped cilantro. Add salt to taste.

5. Pour remaining red chili sauce into a rimmed pan (at least 10 in. wide). Dip 1 tortilla in sauce, turning to coat each side, and lay in a round casserole or ovenproof platter, 12 to 14 inches wide. Cover tortilla with about ⅟₇ (about 1 cup) of the pork sauce. Sprinkle with ¼ cup Mexican cheese blend and 2 tablespoons cotija cheese. Repeat steps, ending with a tortilla on top. If making up to 1 day ahead, cover and chill pie, remaining chili sauce, and the cheeses separately.

6. Bake tortilla pie, covered, in a 350° oven for 25 minutes (1 hour if chilled). Uncover and continue to bake until hot in center (140° on a thermometer), about 20 minutes. Sprinkle with the remaining Mexican cheese blend and

bake until it melts, about 5 minutes longer.

7. Meanwhile, peel, pit, and slice avocado. Also heat remaining chili sauce. Drizzle about ¼ cup of the sauce over the tortilla pie. Garnish with avocado slices, remaining cotija cheese, and cilantro sprigs. Cut into wedges. Offer remaining chili sauce to spoon onto portions to taste.

Per serving: 745 cal., 35% (261 cal.) from fat; 42 g protein; 29 g fat (12 g sat.); 84 g carbo (4.4 g fiber); 2,570 mg sodium; 117 mg chol.

Cannelloni

Prep and cook time: About 1¼ hours to assemble, 10 minutes to bake

Makes: 8 servings

Filling:

- 1 tablespoon **butter** or olive oil
- 1 **onion** (½ lb.), chopped
- 1 clove **garlic**
- ¾ pound **boned, skinned chicken thighs,** fat-trimmed
- ½ pound **boned, fat-trimmed veal**
- ½ pound (2 cups) **part-skim ricotta cheese**
- ½ cup grated **parmesan cheese**

2 **large egg** yolks

⅛ teaspoon **ground nutmeg**

Salt

Sauce:

2 tablespoons **butter** or olive oil

2 tablespoons chopped **shallots**

1½ tablespoons **all-purpose flour**

1 cup **milk**

1½ cups **chicken broth**

2 cans (about 1 lb. each) **chopped tomatoes**

¼ cup chopped **fresh basil** leaves or 2 teaspoons dried basil

Pasta:

8 **egg roll wrappers** (6 in. square)

1 pound **teleme** or jack **cheese**

Basil sprigs

1. *Filling.* In a 10- to 12-inch ovenproof frying pan over high heat, stir butter, onion, and garlic frequently until limp but not browned, 5 to 7 minutes.

2. As onion cooks, cut chicken and veal into about 2-inch chunks. Stir into onion mixture. Bake in a 400° oven just until meat is no longer pink in center (cut to test), about 15 minutes.

3. Let mixture cool, then add ricotta. Coarsely purée mixture in a food processor (or grind through a food chopper). Add parmesan, egg yolks, nutmeg, and salt to taste, mixing well.

4. *Sauce.* In a 4- to 5-quart pan over

Velvety teleme cheese cloaks cannelloni filled with chicken and veal.

high heat, combine butter and shallots and stir often until shallots are limp, about 2 minutes. Add flour and stir until bubbling. Off the heat, whisk in milk and broth. Stir often over medium heat until reduced to 1⅓ cups, about 25 minutes. Remove from heat.

5. Drain tomatoes; save juice for other uses. Add tomatoes and the chopped basil to sauce.

6. *Pasta.* Mound ⅛ of the filling (about 6 tablespoons) evenly along 1 side of each egg roll wrapper. Roll each wrapper to enclose the filling. Set rolled cannelloni, seam down and slightly apart, in 2 lightly oiled 3-quart casseroles (about 9 by 13 in., and at least 2 in. deep).

7. Cut teleme cheese into thin pieces and lay pieces onto cannelloni so that each top is completely covered. Spoon the sauce around the cannelloni, adding an equal amount to each casserole. If making ahead, cover and chill up to 1 day.

8. Bake, uncovered, in a 425° oven until sauce bubbles and cannelloni are hot in the center, 10 to 15 minutes (the same time if chilled). Garnish casserole with basil sprigs. Use a wide spatula to transfer a cannelloni to each plate, spooning sauce around portions. Add salt to taste.

Per serving: 524 cal., 46% (243 cal.) from fat; 37 g protein; 27 g fat (7.2 g sat); 33 g carbo (2.2 g fiber); 960 mg sodium; 155 mg chol.

Tortellini Torta

Prep and cook time: About 40 minutes to assemble, 30 minutes to bake (1

hour if chilled), and 10 minutes standing time

Notes: If desired, heat additional pasta sauce to spoon onto individual servings.

Makes: 8 servings

3 **eggplant** (about 1 lb. each)

2 cloves **garlic,** minced or pressed

1 **onion** (about ½ lb.), chopped

2 cups **vegetable** or chicken **broth**

6 tablespoons chopped **fresh basil** leaves

3 cups **canned tomato-based pasta sauce**

3 packages (9 oz. each) **fresh cheese-filled tortellini**

2 cups (½ lb.) **shredded jack cheese**

½ cup grated **parmesan cheese**

Butter or margarine

2 tablespoons **fine dry bread crumbs**

1. Rinse eggplant; trim off and discard stems. Cut eggplant into ½-inch cubes.

2. In a 5- to 6-quart pan over high heat, combine eggplant, garlic, onion, 1 cup broth, and 4 tablespoons basil. Cover and bring to a boil. Boil, stirring often, until eggplant mashes very easily when pressed, 20 to 25 minutes.

3. Meanwhile, in a 4- to 5-quart pan over medium-high heat, bring pasta sauce and remaining broth to boiling, stirring often. Add tortellini and stir often until pasta is barely tender to bite, about 5 minutes. Remove from heat.

The party-size casserole

The cannelloni, the chicken with asparagus and morels, and the lamb-stuffed portabellas each can be baked in one large casserole. The container should be about 2½ inches deep and 11 to 12 by 16 to 17 inches (oval or rectangular). Cooking times will be about the same as in two smaller casseroles. However, if the casserole is made of heavy ceramic, which is slower to heat, you may need to allow a few minutes more in the oven.

If you use a metal roasting pan, tie a folded towel around the pan rim when you serve to conceal its utilitarian nature.

Stir in jack cheese and 6 tablespoons parmesan cheese.

4. Butter sides and bottom of a 9-inch cheesecake pan with removable rim. Dust pan with bread crumbs. Spoon ½ of the tortellini mixture into pan and spread level. Top tortellini with eggplant, spread level, then add remaining tortellini and spread level. If making ahead, cover and chill up to 1 day.

5. Bake, covered, in a 350° oven for 20 minutes (50 minutes if chilled). Uncover and bake until hot in center (about 130° on a thermometer), 10 to 15 minutes longer. Let stand 10 minutes.

6. Run a knife between pan rim and pasta; remove pan rim. Sprinkle pie with remaining parmesan cheese and basil. Cut into wedges.

Per serving: 546 cal., 33% (180 cal.) from fat; 26 g protein; 20 g fat (9.6 g sat.); 69 g carbo (6.6 g fiber); 983 mg sodium; 77 mg chol.

Chicken, Asparagus, and Morel Casserole

Prep and cook time: About 1¼ hours to assemble, 32 minutes to bake (37 minutes if chilled)

Makes: 8 servings

- 1 ounce (about 1½ cups) **dried morel mushrooms**
- 12 thin slices **prosciutto** (about 6 oz. total)
- 2 tablespoons **butter** or margarine
- ½ cup minced **shallots**
- 2 tablespoons **all-purpose flour**
- 1 cup **dry sherry**
- 1 cup **chicken broth**
- 1 cup **whipping cream**

Chicken breasts and asparagus wrapped in prosciutto are drenched with creamy morel sauce.

- 2 packages (1 lb. each) **prepared polenta**
- 8 **boned, skinned chicken breast halves** (3 to 4 oz. each)
- 16 **asparagus spears** (about ¾ in. thick), tough ends trimmed
- 1 cup shredded **gruyère cheese**
   Salt

1. Place morels in a bowl and add 2 cups boiling water. Let stand until soft, about 15 minutes. Gently squeeze mushrooms in water to release grit. Lift from water and squeeze out most of the liquid. Set mushrooms aside. Without disturbing grit, carefully pour reserved soaking liquid into another container. Discard grit.

2. Meanwhile, cut 4 slices of prosciutto into thin slivers. In a 5- to 6-quart pan, stir slivers over high heat until crisp and lightly browned, 5 to 8 minutes. Remove from pan; when cool, wrap airtight and chill up to 1 day.

3. Add butter and shallots to pan. Stir over high heat until shallots are limp, about 2 minutes. Add flour and stir until light golden brown, about 2 minutes. Remove from heat and whisk in mushroom liquid, sherry, broth, and cream, then add morels. Stir often over high heat until sauce is reduced to 2½ cups, 20 to 25 minutes.

4. Cut polenta into chunks, then mash with hands or a potato masher until it's fine crumbs. Divide polenta evenly between 2 casseroles, each 3 quarts (about 9 by 13 in. and at least 2 in. deep). Press polenta into an even layer.

5. Lay a chicken breast half and 2 asparagus spears on a prosciutto slice and wrap to enclose. Place chicken, asparagus side up, on polenta. Repeat to wrap remaining chicken and asparagus, and space pieces evenly apart in casseroles. With a slotted spoon, scatter morels around chicken. Pour sauce equally over chicken in each casserole. If making ahead, cover and chill up to 1 day.

6. Bake, covered, in a 400° oven until chicken breasts are no longer pink in center of thickest part (cut to test), 30 to 35 minutes (35 to 40 minutes if chilled). Uncover and sprinkle with cheese, then prosciutto shreds. Bake until cheese melts, 2 to 3 minutes more. Serve with salt to add to taste.

Per serving: 436 cal., 43% (189 cal.) from fat; 35 g protein; 21 g fat (11 g sat.); 24 g carbo (2.4 g fiber); 753 mg sodium; 124 mg chol. ◆

Putting together a casserole dinner

A knockout casserole with a salad and bread is all you need for a well-planned dinner party. And a memorable dessert—from a favorite bakery or sweet shop—is the ideal conclusion.

Lamb-stuffed Portabellas

Thinly Sliced Cucumber and Red Onion Salad

Dill and Lemon Juice Dressing

Split and Toasted Pocket Bread

Baklava with Lemon Ice

Stacked Tortilla Pie with Carnitas

Green Cabbage Slaw with Shredded Jicama

Lime and Orange Juice Dressing

Bolillos (Mexican Rolls)

Caramel Flan

Cannelloni

Romaine Lettuce Hearts

Dijon Mustard Dressing

Sourdough Baguettes

Lemon Curd Tart with Sliced Strawberries

Chicken, Asparagus, and Morel Casserole

Baby Spinach Leaves

Walnut Oil and Red Wine Vinegar Dressing

Ciabatta Loaf

Raspberries with Cassis (Currant Liqueur) and Raspberry Sorbet

Tortellini Torta

Arugula, Frisée, and Radicchio Salad

Balsamic Vinegar and Olive Oil Dressing

Warm Olive Bread

Coffee Ice Cream with Rum and Chocolate Sauce

Tear fragrant chunks from Oaxacan-style bread while it's still warm—and savor with a steaming cup of cinnamon-flavor Mexican chocolate.

A spirited loaf

Mexico's party for the dead includes this memorable bread

The gates between the dead and the living swing open in Mexico from October 31 through November 2. And the merrymaking of Día de los Muertos (the Day of the Dead) is noteworthy for its blend of whimsy and the macabre.

Paths of marigold petals lead to home altars. Cemeteries glow with candles. Skeletons are irreverently replicated in dangling sculptures and costumed characters; skulls are made of sugar. And special foods mark this occasion, particularly the lightly spiced, mildly sweet *pan de muertos* (bread of the dead). Each region treats the loaf differently. Some loaves are formed into fanciful likenesses of the deceased; others are crossed with leavened "bones." In Oaxaca, sesame seed coats a round loaf that's studded with a tiny

sugar or plastic skull or a brightly painted bread-dough face.

Symbolically adorned or plain, this sweet bread does very well at breakfast or for dessert.

Bread of the Dead

Prep and cook time: About 1 hour, plus 1½ to 2 hours for rising

Makes: 1 loaf, about 2 pounds

- 1 package **active dry yeast**
- ⅓ cup **milk**
- ⅓ cup (⅙ lb.) **butter** or margarine, cut into small pieces
- ½ cup **sugar**
- ½ teaspoon **salt**
- 3 **large eggs**
- 1 tablespoon **vanilla**

About 3¾ cups **all-purpose flour**

- ¾ teaspoon **ground nutmeg**
- ¾ teaspoon **ground cinnamon**
- 2 tablespoons **sesame seed**

1. In a large bowl, sprinkle yeast over ¼ cup warm (110°) water; let stand about 5 minutes.

2. Heat milk and butter to 110°. Add milk mixture, sugar, and salt to softened yeast.

3. Lightly beat eggs to blend. Spoon 1 tablespoon of the eggs into a small bowl, cover, and chill. Add remaining eggs and vanilla to yeast mixture; stir to blend. Add 2¼ cups flour, nutmeg, and cinnamon; stir to moisten, then beat with a mixer on high speed until dough is stretchy, 6 to 8 minutes. Stir in 1 cup flour to moisten.

4. Knead dough. *If using a dough hook,* beat on high speed until dough pulls cleanly from bowl and no longer feels sticky, about 5 minutes. If dough is still sticky, beat in more flour, 1 tablespoon at a time.

If kneading by hand, scrape dough onto a well-floured board. Knead until dough is smooth, elastic, and no longer sticky, about 12 minutes; add flour as required to prevent sticking. Return dough to bowl.

5. Cover bowl airtight and let dough rise in a warm, draft-free place until it doubles, about 1½ hours.

6. Punch dough down. Knead on a lightly floured board to expel air. Form into a 7-inch round and set on a buttered 12- by 15-inch baking sheet. Cover lightly with plastic wrap and let rise in a warm place until puffy, about 40 minutes.

7. Uncover dough and brush gently with reserved beaten egg. Sprinkle loaf with sesame seed. With a sharp, floured knife, make a slash about ½ inch deep across the middle of the loaf.

8. Bake loaf in a 350° oven until richly browned, 35 to 40 minutes. Serve warm or cool. If making ahead, wrap cool loaf airtight and let stand at room temperature up to 1 day; freeze to store longer.

9. If desired, cut a slit in the bread and insert a Day of the Dead decoration such as a miniature skull or skeleton.

Per ounce: 96 cal., 27% (26 cal.) from fat; 2.4 g protein; 2.9 g fat (1.4 g sat.); 15 g carbo (0.5 g fiber); 61 mg sodium; 25 mg chol. ◆

by **L I N D A   L A U   A N U S A S A N A N A N**

The Quick Cook

MEALS IN 30-MINUTES-OR-LESS

by CHRISTINE WEBER HALE

JAMES CARRIER

Precooked rice is the surprise ingredient in this fast and creamy risotto.

Take an instant for risotto

■ Most traditional Italian cooks are demandingly specific about risotto. Use only arborio rice. Toast it gently in butter. Add hot broth, one ladleful at a time, stirring until every drop is absorbed. The cheese, of course, must be freshly grated.

Chances are, by the time the dish reaches perfection, an intensive hour has been invested.

But if you have a risotto hankering and not much time, take the offensive.

FOUR MORE HIGH-SPEED RISOTTO RECIPES

Follow the recipe at right, omitting the nutmeg and pumpkin, and instead:

1. Cook asparagus slices and soaked porcini mushrooms with the onion until onion is limp, then add the grated lemon peel.

2. Stir in crumbled gorgonzola cheese instead of parmesan, along with thin slices of ripe pear. Sprinkle portions with chopped roasted, salted pistachios.

3. Add bite-size pieces of cooked chicken, pork, sausage, or small shrimp, blanched broccoli, and canned roasted red pepper strips along with the cheese.

4. Stir in shredded smoked mozzarella cheese instead of parmesan, along with chopped yellow tomatoes, pan-browned bits of prosciutto, and slivered basil leaves.

Use instant (precooked) rice. Just put it in the pan and add seasonings and broth blended with a little cornstarch to create the risotto creaminess, and bring it to a boil with a stir or two. You'll be ready to eat a good 45 minutes before the purist gets out of the kitchen.

15-Minute Pumpkin Risotto

Prep and cook time: About 15 minutes
Makes: 4 servings

  1 **onion** (about 8 oz.), chopped
  2 teaspoons **butter** or margarine
  ½ teaspoon **ground nutmeg**
  2 tablespoons **cornstarch**
  3½ cups **chicken broth**
  ½ cup **dry white wine**
  1 cup **canned pumpkin**
  3 cups **precooked dried white rice**
     About ¾ cup **grated parmesan cheese**
     Salt and fresh-ground **pepper**

1. In a 4- to 5-quart pan, combine onion, butter, and nutmeg. Stir often over high heat until onion is limp, 3 to 4 minutes.

2. Mix the cornstarch smoothly with a little of the chicken broth. Add to pan along with remaining broth, wine, pumpkin, and rice. Stir mixture over high heat until boiling, 3 to 4 minutes. Cover and remove from heat; let stand 5 minutes.

3. Stir in ¾ cup cheese. Sprinkle portions with additional cheese and add salt and pepper to taste.

Per serving: 461 cal., 16% (75 cal.) from fat; 16 g protein; 8.3 g fat (4.9 g sat.); 75 g carbo (3.2 g fiber); 402 mg sodium; 20 mg chol. ◆

Kitchen Cabinet

READERS' RECIPES TESTED IN SUNSET'S KITCHENS

by L I N D A   L A U   A N U S A S A N A N A N

Nonfat yogurt replaces fat in this light and tender cornbread.

Experiments that worked

■ This cornbread, once laden with fat and sugar, has been gradually redesigned over the past 20 years by Victoria Modarresi. Now the bread has a hearty corn flavor and a springy texture that holds up when it's dunked into soups and bean stews. For tender wedges, she bakes the bread in an 8-inch cast-iron frying pan. For browner, crunchier bread, she bakes the batter in cornstick pans for about 15 minutes, yielding 14 to 16 sticks.

Very Good Cornbread
Victoria Modarresi, Tucson

Prep and cook time: About 25 minutes
Makes: 8 or 9 servings

 1 cup **all-purpose flour**
 1 cup **yellow cornmeal**
 ¼ cup **sugar**
 1 teaspoon **baking soda**
 ¾ teaspoon **salt**
 1 cup **plain nonfat yogurt**
 2 **large eggs**

1. In a bowl, mix flour, cornmeal, sugar, soda, and salt. Add yogurt and eggs and mix just until blended. Pour into a buttered 8- to 9-inch square or round pan.

2. Bake in a 400° oven until bread springs back when gently pressed in center, 20 to 25 minutes. Cut in squares or wedges. Serve warm.

Per serving: 163 cal., 11% (18 cal.) from fat; 5.6 g protein; 2 g fat (0.5 g sat.); 30 g carbo (1.2 g fiber); 357 mg sodium; 48 mg chol.

Spiced Apple Quinoa Salad
Roxanne Chan, Albany, California

After trying and liking quinoa in another recipe, Roxanne Chan was prompted to experiment with this ancient Native American grain, which is still relatively unknown. She enhanced its mellow character with allspice and apples to create this refreshing salad.

Prep and cook time: About 15 minutes
Makes: 6 to 8 servings

 1 cup **quinoa**
 ⅓ cup **cider vinegar**
 3 tablespoons thawed **frozen apple juice concentrate**
 ¼ teaspoon **ground allspice**
 ¼ teaspoon **pepper**
 1 clove **garlic,** minced
 1 **Red** or Golden **Delicious apple** (½ lb.)
 ½ cup shredded **carrot**
 ⅓ cup chopped **red onion,** rinsed and drained
 ¼ cup chopped **fresh mint** leaves
   Butter lettuce leaves, rinsed and crisped (optional)
   Salt

1. Pour quinoa into a fine strainer and rinse well under cool running water.

2. In a 1½- to 2-quart pan, combine quinoa and 2 cups water. Bring to a boil on high heat, turn heat low, cover, and simmer until grain is tender to bite, 10 to 15 minutes. Let cool.

3. Meanwhile, combine vinegar, apple juice concentrate, allspice, pepper, and garlic. Mix with cool quinoa.

4. Core apple and cut in ¼-inch cubes. Mix apple, carrot, onion, and mint with quinoa.

5. Mound salad on a lettuce-lined platter. Add salt to taste.

Per serving: 114 cal., 11% (13 cal.) from fat; 3.1 g protein; 1.4 g fat (0.1 g sat.); 23 g carbo (3.8 g fiber); 18 mg sodium; 0 mg chol.

Mexican Pizza
Kathy Borst, Yorkville, California

A tradition was born when Kathy Borst first served this green-and-

(vertical, left of photo) JAMES CARRIER

red-splashed pizza at a Christmas Eve gathering. It was the hit of the party, and now it's requested at all family events.

Prep and cook time: About 35 minutes
Makes: 6 servings

1 cup lightly packed chopped **fresh cilantro**

¼ cup grated **parmesan**, romano, or dry jack **cheese**

2 tablespoons **olive oil**

1 teaspoon chopped **fresh ginger**

1 clove **garlic**

2 teaspoons **lemon juice**

Salt

1 **baked pizza crust** (16 oz., 12 in. wide)

½ cup **thick tomato salsa**

1 cup **shredded jack cheese**

1 can (2¼ oz.) **sliced ripe olives**, drained

¼ to ½ cup **canned sliced jalapeños**, drained

1 firm-ripe **avocado** (6 oz.), peeled, pitted, and sliced

1. In a blender or food processor, smoothly purée cilantro, parmesan cheese, oil, ginger, garlic, and lemon juice. Add salt to taste.

2. Set pizza crust in a 12-inch pizza pan (or on a 12- by 15-in. baking sheet). Spread salsa evenly over crust. Drop cilantro pesto by the spoonful evenly over the pizza. Sprinkle with jack cheese, olives, and jalapeños to taste.

3. Bake in a 425° oven until cheese is bubbly, about 20 minutes.

4. Peel, pit, and slice avocado. Lay avocado slices on hot pizza. Cut into wedges.

Per serving: 448 cal., 46% (207 cal.) from fat; 8.4 g protein; 23 g fat (7 g sat.); 48 g carbo (4.5 g fiber); 738 mg sodium; 23 mg chol.

Pork Tenderloin with Rum Chutney

Laura Yeager, Lacey, Washington

She likes fruit and pork. Her husband likes spicy food. Both like low-fat food. The result: a fast and delicious way to cook lean pork and make a chutney sauce.

Add zip to lean roast pork tenderloin with rum-flavor chutney.

Prep and cook time: About 25 minutes
Makes: 7 to 8 servings

2 **pork tenderloins** (about 1 lb. each)

About ½ teaspoon **salt**

About ½ teaspoon **pepper**

About ½ teaspoon **cayenne**

2 teaspoons **salad oil**

¼ cup **rum**

1 jar (12½ oz., 1 cup) **Major Grey mango chutney**

1. Trim and discard fat and any silvery membrane from pork. Sprinkle meat lightly with salt and pepper, and as much cayenne as you like.

2. Set a 10- to 12-inch frying pan over high heat. When hot, add oil and swirl to coat pan. Add pork and brown on all sides, turning as needed, about 4 minutes total.

3. Transfer meat to a 9- by 13-inch pan. Bake in a 400° oven until a thermometer inserted in center of thickest part of meat registers 155°, about 15 minutes. Put meat on a platter, and let stand for 5 minutes.

4. Meanwhile, add rum to the unwashed frying pan. Stir over medium heat to free browned bits, then pour these drippings into the roasting pan. Stir over low heat, mixing in chutney, until hot.

5. Cut pork on the diagonal into ½-inch-thick slices. Accompany with the chutney and salt and pepper to taste.

Per serving: 303 cal., 15% (45 cal.) from fat; 24 g protein; 5 g fat (1.5 g sat.); 33 g carbo (0.1 g fiber); 590 mg sodium; 74 mg chol.

White Chocolate Chip Mocha Torte

Lesley Cooper, Santa Rosa, California

For a football dessert buffet, Lesley Cooper gussied up her standby brownie recipe. Baked in a tart pan, cut into wedges, and served with whipped cream, the brownies turned into a mocha torte.

Prep and cook time: About 40 minutes
Makes: 8 servings

⅔ cup **all-purpose flour**

½ cup **unsweetened cocoa**

1 teaspoon **baking powder**

1 teaspoon **instant coffee espresso powder**

About ½ cup (¼ lb.) **butter** or margarine

1 cup **granulated sugar**

3 **large eggs**

1 teaspoon **vanilla**

⅓ cup **white chocolate chips**

½ cup coarsely chopped **walnuts**

¼ cup **raisins** (optional)

Powdered sugar

1. Mix flour, cocoa, baking powder, and espresso powder; set aside.

2. In a large bowl, beat ½ cup butter and granulated sugar with a mixer on high speed until fluffy. Add eggs and vanilla; beat until blended. Add flour mixture, about a third at a time, mixing on low speed until blended.

3. Stir in chocolate chips, nuts, and raisins.

4. Lightly butter a 9-inch tart pan with removable rim. Spread batter in pan.

5. Bake in a 325° oven just until cake begins to pull away from rim, 25 to 30 minutes. Set on rack to cool. To serve, warm or cool, remove pan rim, lightly dust torte with powdered sugar, and cut into wedges.

Per serving: 388 cal., 51% (198 cal.) from fat; 6.3 g protein; 22 g fat (11 g sat.); 45 g carbo (2.2 g fiber); 219 mg sodium; 112 mg chol. ◆

Enticing desserts for holiday feasts include (top to bottom) pecan pie, cranberry tart, and pumpkin pie (see page 266).

November

foodguide

by JERRY ANNE DI VECCHIO

tool

Once you're hooked on freshly ground coffee beans, the next step to a perfect cup is freshly roasted beans. The Coffee-Roasting Cone by Home Coffee Roaster does the job very well. You set the cone on a hot-air popcorn popper base, and in about six minutes you get enough richly roasted beans for a pot of coffee.

A starter kit with cone, including 2 pounds of green coffee beans and a list of beans to order, costs $29.95, plus shipping. A deluxe kit, $49.95, adds 1 pound of green decaffeinated beans and a book. Call (800) 589-8960 to order. The popcorn popper, about $16, is not included. It must take in air from the sides, not the bottom. (Be aware that using any appliance for other than its intended purpose invalidates its warranty.)

LEFT: CURTIS ANDERSON   BELOW, RIGHT, AND BOTTOM RIGHT: JAMES CARRIER

SEASONAL NOTE

Squash with bite

■ Chef Ben Davis at Gibson Restaurant in San Mateo, California, serves spiced kabocha squash with a venison salad. But the thin slices of kabocha, pickled in a sweet, mellow vinegar mixture, also go well with hot cooked meats, from beef to turkey. The squash is ready to eat as soon as it cools.

Spiced Kabocha Squash

Prep and cook time: 35 to 40 minutes

Notes: Pack the spiced squash with its liquid in small jars for gifts. The squash keeps well in the refrigerator for at least a month.

Makes: About 6 cups, drained

- 1 **kabocha squash** (about 2 lb.)
- 4 cups **seasoned rice vinegar**
- 1 cup **mirin** or dry sherry
- 8 slices **fresh ginger** (each the size of a quarter)
- 8 **whole star anise**

1. Cut squash in half; scoop out seeds.

2. With a vegetable peeler, pare green skin from squash; discard. Using a slicer or knife, cut squash into ⅛-inch-thick slices (makes about 6 cups); rinse slices.

3. In a 4- to 5-quart pan, combine vinegar, mirin, ginger, and anise. Bring to boiling over high heat, then reduce heat and simmer 5 minutes. Add squash and return to boiling over high heat.

4. Transfer spiced mixture to a jar. Let cool and serve, or cover and chill up to 4 weeks.

Per ¼ cup drained serving: 18 cal., 5% (0.9 cal.) from fat; 0.4 g protein; 0.1 g fat (0 g sat.); 4 g carbo (0.5 g fiber); 100 mg sodium; 0 mg chol.

Slices of golden kabocha squash absorb the flavors of spiced syrup.

Gift-wrapped baking

■ If you bake just once a year, you're probably ready to start right about now. And most likely, you're going to bake gifts.

I love to give—and serve—this orange-apricot bread, so tender and sweet it's just shy of being cake. It's oven-ready in 20 minutes or less, and I can double the recipe with no complications.

But this year, my production is speeding up because I'm baking right in the gift package. No more pans to empty, wash, or buy. I'm using paper baking molds.

Commercial bakers have long had access to paper molds, which come in many pan sizes and can be used at oven temperatures up to 450°. And now the molds are showing up in cookware stores and catalogs. Best of all, they're inexpensive (from 25 to 95 cents each).

If you order from a catalog, they're usually sold in sets. One mail-order source is Sur La Table; (800) 243-0852.

Orange-Apricot Sweet Bread

Prep and cook time: 55 minutes

Notes: If making ahead, package bread airtight when cool. Hold at room temperature up to 5 days; freeze to store longer. To reheat, unwrap bread (but leave it in its paper mold) and put in a 350° oven for 5 to 7 minutes.

Makes: A 4½- by 8½-inch loaf; 6 to 8 servings

> About ½ cup (¼ lb.) **butter** or margarine
>
> About ⅔ cup **sugar**
>
> ½ teaspoon hulled **cardamom seed,** crushed
>
> 1 tablespoon finely shredded **orange** peel
>
> 1 **large egg**
>
> 1 **large egg** yolk
>
> ½ cup **sour cream**
>
> ¼ teaspoon **baking soda**
>
> ¾ teaspoon **baking powder**
>
> About 1 cup **all-purpose flour**
>
> ½ cup diced **dried apricots**

1. In a bowl, beat ½ cup butter, ⅔ cup sugar, and cardamom with a mixer until fluffy. Add orange peel, egg, egg yolk, and sour cream. Beat to mix well.

2. Stir together soda, baking powder, 1 cup flour, and diced apricots. Add to butter mixture and stir until evenly blended.

3. Butter and flour-dust a 5- to 6-cup baking pan or paper baking mold (5 in. wide, 3 in. deep; 7 in. wide, 2½ in. deep; 4½- by 8½ -in. loaf pan; or 8-in. square or round cake pan).

4. Scrape batter into pan and spread level. If using smaller molds, fill no more than ⅓ full. (You'll have about 1½ cups batter.)

5. Sprinkle batter evenly (in one or more pans) with 1 tablespoon sugar.

6. Bake on rack slightly below center in a 350° oven until bread springs back when lightly pressed in center, and just begins to pull from pan sides, 35 to 40 minutes for the whole loaf, less for smaller portions.

7. Let cool on a rack. Serve warm or cool, inverted from pan, then turned top side up.

Per serving: 304 cal., 47% (144 cal.) from fat; 3.7 g protein; 16 g fat (9.8 g sat.); 37 g carbo (1.1 g fiber); 224 mg sodium; 92 mg chol.

Pocket bread topped with mushrooms, cheese, and chutney makes a speedy snack.

JAMES CARRIER

GREAT PRODUCT

Caramel confections

■ A jar of good caramel sauce—and there are many to choose from—doesn't have to justify its place in my kitchen. In fact, it's hard not to dip into it now and then for a spoonful. But I indulge sparingly so caramel is always available for emergencies.

Tarts. Whip until smooth 2 parts **cream cheese** and 1 part **caramel sauce**. Spoon into tiny tart shells and top with **strawberry** slices.

Faux bananas Foster. In a frying pan over medium heat, stir 2 parts **caramel sauce**, 1 part **rum**, and 1 part **butter** until bubbling. Drop in **banana** slices and turn to warm. Serve over **vanilla** or rum **ice cream**.

Rice pudding. Use **caramel sauce** in place of the sugar when making **rice pudding**.

Caramel pumpkin pie. Pour a thin layer of **caramel sauce** over **frozen pumpkin pie** and bake as directed; it sinks in. Serve with warm caramel sauce.

QUICK TRICK

Chutney pizzas

■ Use regular or whole-wheat pocket bread as the foundation for an appetizer or snack that's ready in less than 15 minutes.

1. In a food processor, mince ½ pound **mushrooms**.

2. In a 10- to 12-inch frying pan, combine mushrooms and 1 tablespoon **butter** or olive oil. Stir often over high heat until juices evaporate and mushrooms start to brown, 5 to 7 minutes.

3. Lay 4 **pocket bread** rounds (6 in. wide) cupped side up on a baking sheet and scatter the mushroom mixture equally on top of them. Sprinkle each with about 3 tablespoons (¾ cup total) **shredded Swiss** or fontina **cheese**.

4. Bake in a 400° oven until cheese melts and bread crisps, 5 to 7 minutes. Drizzle 2 to 3 teaspoons **chutney** (I prefer mango, but any will do) over each pizza and cut each round into quarters.

Per piece: 81 cal., 27% (22 cal.) from fat; 3.2 g protein; 2.4 g fat (1.4 g sat.); 12 g carbo (0.4 g fiber); 130 mg sodium; 6.8 mg chol.

FOOD NEWS

Fresh and frozen chestnuts

■ About 100 years ago, a blight destroyed most American chestnut trees, but now they're coming back. Small orchards in Washington, Oregon, and California have begun to harvest crops. The nuts go to farmers' markets or to retail stores, where they're sold alongside imported fresh chestnuts.

I love the fresh nuts, but peeling is a chore. A simple solution is to buy them peeled. More than ever before, I'm finding them frozen, from France and Italy, in fancy supermarkets. I've even found chestnuts on the shelf, vacuum-packed. The frozen have the freshest flavor, but both kinds taste better than chestnuts canned in water.

Fresh chestnuts are very perishable and should be refrigerated. They should feel heavy; if they're light and soft, don't buy them.

Fresh, frozen, or vacuum-packed, chestnuts cook delectably in this dish.

Chestnuts with Grapes

Prep and cook time: 40 to 50 minutes

Notes: If using fresh chestnuts, cut an X through shell on flat side. Immerse in boiling water and simmer 10 minutes. Drain, and while nuts are warm and wet, pull off shell and dark membrane with a small knife.
Serve with meats, the way you would potatoes.

Makes: 6 to 8 servings

- 4 cups (about 1⅓ lb.) **peeled chestnuts**
- 3 cups **seedless green grapes**
  About 3 cups fat-skimmed **chicken broth**
- ¼ pound **Italian sausage**
- 1 to 2 teaspoons **butter** or olive oil

1. In a 5- to 6-quart pan, combine the chestnuts, 1 cup grapes, and 2 cups chicken broth. Remove sausage from casing and crumble into pan.

2. Bring to a boil over high heat, cover, and simmer over medium heat until chestnuts are very soft and mash easily, about 30 minutes. Drain broth into a glass measure and add enough more broth to make 2 cups.

3. Whirl chestnut mixture in a food processor until smoothly puréed, then whirl in enough broth to give mixture the consistency of softly mashed potatoes. Or whirl mixture, a portion at a time, in a blender, adding enough broth to facilitate puréeing, then more for the desired consistency. Chestnuts continue to thicken as they stand.

4. Return purée to pan and stir over medium heat until steaming, 2 to 3 minutes; keep warm.

5. In 10- to 12-inch frying pan over high heat, melt butter and add remaining grapes. Swirl just until fruit is warm and brighter green, about 1½ minutes.

6. Scrape chestnut purée into a deep bowl and pour grapes on top.

Per serving: 257 cal., 22% (56 cal.) from fat; 6.6 g protein; 6.2 g fat (2.2 g sat.); 44 g carbo (1 g fiber); 139 mg sodium; 12 mg chol. ◆

The Wine Guide

by KAREN MacNEIL

The secret of sweet endings

■ For several years—until I knew better—I thought of dessert wine as overkill. From cake to crème brûlée, dessert was just fine all by itself. Who needed something sweet to drink besides?

Clearly, I didn't know what I was missing: one of the most indulgent pleasures on the planet.

Absolutely nothing compares to the deliciousness of a noble sweet wine. Today, if I had to make a choice between the two, I'd drink the dessert wine and skip the dessert.

Thankfully, though, the two are not mutually exclusive, for the marriage of a great dessert and a great dessert wine ranks as one of the most hedonistic experiences a wine drinker can have.

What makes a sweet wine great, ironically, is not the sweetness. There are dozens of sweet wines that are about as compelling as a lollipop. That's because sweetness alone can taste unpleasantly sugary and monodimensional.

As pastry chefs know, sweet things need a counterpoint. So although it seems counterintuitive, a dessert wine needs good acidity. Without it, the wine will seem like a big sugar bomb in your mouth.

Achieving that perfect tension between sweetness and acidity is anything but easy. In fact, great dessert wines are some of the most difficult wines to make. And despite the common misconception, none of the methods involves adding processed sugar. As it happens, the sweetness is simply the grapes' natural sugar.

So how does a dessert wine come to be? The grapes can be:
• picked after the regular harvest at a point where they are very full of natural sugar (these are usually called "late-harvest" wines).
• allowed to "raisin," thereby concentrating the sugars.

RICK MARIANI

• allowed to freeze (as in German icewine), so that when the grapes are pressed, the water remains as ice, leaving just the syrupy concentrated sugar.
• attacked by a fungus such as botrytis cinerea (the "noble rot" that makes French Sauternes), which sucks out the water, shriveling the grapes and concentrating the sugars.

All of these processes are difficult, and they carry with them countless risks: deer, birds, wild boars, and other animals love to eat sweet grapes; the grapes may be attacked by unfavorable molds or other diseases; weather may destroy the crop first; and so on. Dessert wines, as a result, are produced in small quantities and are almost universally expensive.

Almost every country that makes wine makes dessert wines, and some countries—such as France, Germany, Austria, and Italy—are treasure troves of luscious finds.

Theoretically, almost any grape variety could be made into a dessert wine. In practice, however, about a dozen varietals seem to possess just the right potential. Among the most popular of

WINE DICTIONARY

Cloying

Descriptive term for a wine with unbearable candylike sweetness. Dessert wines should not be cloying. — *K. M.*

BEST BETS

■ *Bonny Doon Muscat "Vin de Glacière" 1996,* $15 (California). Utter elegance. The essence of apricot coalesced with the essence of peach.

■ *Chateau St. Jean Special Select Late-Harvest Johannisberg Riesling 1992,* $25 (Alexander Valley). Voluptuously rich. Try with tarte Tatin.

■ *Joseph Phelps Late-Harvest Johannisberg Riesling 1995,* $20 (California). The liquid equivalent of a luscious pear-and-apricot tart.

■ *Madroña Select Harvest Riesling 1995,* $16.50 (El Dorado). A really zesty dessert wine evocative of pears drizzled with vanilla.

■ *Navarro Cluster Select Late-Harvest White Riesling 1994,* $19.50 (Mendocino). Made only in exceptional years. Pure spun honey.

■ *Quady Elysium 1996,* $8 (California). Complex litchi and rose flavors. Great with dark chocolate.

■ *Robert Pecota Moscato d'Andrea 1996,* $9 (Napa Valley). A fresh, lively Moscato (Italian for Muscat). Pour it over poached fruits and drink a glass alongside.

these are Riesling, Gewürztraminer, Semillon, and the whole family of Muscats, including Muscat Canelli, Muscat of Alexandria, Orange Muscat, and Muscat de Frontignan.

Finally, dessert wines range in intensity from light-bodied and almost sheer in their sweetness to rich, syrupy, and superconcentrated. In general, the Muscats are the lightest, while wines such as French Sauternes (made from botrytis-affected Semillon) and German beerenausleses and trockenbeerenausleses are the richest.

The latter are widely considered the most devastatingly delicious dessert wines in the world—and they are an experience every wine drinker should have more than once. For other fine choices, see our list above. (All are sold as 375-ml. half-bottles.) ◆

The Wente clan takes a Thanksgiving ride (above) in vineyards founded by Carl H. Wente (right, with mustache) more than 100 years ago. Jean Wente (below left) sips Cabernet Sauvignon, while son Philip (bottom right) gives his daughter Niki a relaxing swing. Then it's to the table for turkey with cornbread dressing (below center).

JAMES CARRIER

CONNIE COLEMAN (4)

A ranch Thanksgiving

On the Wente homestead, a winemaking family gives thanks with a relaxed feast

■ The afternoon before Thanksgiving, Carolyn Wente Layton, president of Wente Vineyards, steps into those vineyards and clips grape branches—ablaze with red, rust, and gold leaves—to decorate the dinner table in her brother Philip's home. In the kitchen, his wife, Julie, and daughters are rolling out pastry and peeling apples for pie. And Jean Wente, matriarch of this California winemaking clan, polishes silver. Collectively, they prepare all the elements for the holiday feast that can be made a day ahead.

On Thanksgiving morning, family and close friends gather at this year's designated host house. Some saddle up horses for a morning ride over the rolling green hills. Others head out for a round of golf or a game of hoops.

The roots for these festivities were put down more than a century ago. In 1883, Carl H. Wente planted grapes in California's Livermore Valley and founded Wente Brothers Winery. His property has grown into a 3,000-acre ranch that includes the vineyards and winery. It's also where Jean, who is the widow of Carl's grandson, and her three children—Eric, Philip, and Carolyn—have homes. And it's here that Jean manages the original 50 acres planted by Carl.

Around noon the crowd reunites for a cup of homemade chicken soup to contain appetites while the turkey roasts. Then, with just a little left to do, everyone helps bring forth a contemporary California dinner that blends the changing tastes of new generations with a German and Irish heritage (with a little of the South thrown in). The wine, of course, is made by Wente.

by **LINDA LAU ANUSASANANAN**

Spicy Herb Roasted Nuts

Prep and cook time: About 50 minutes

Notes: In lieu of fresh herbs, use dried ones (½ teaspoon of each). Store cool nuts airtight up to 3 days at room temperature or 1 month in the freezer.

Makes: 5 cups

1½ cups **almonds**

1½ cups **walnut halves**

1 cup **hazelnuts**

1 cup **pecan halves**

½ cup **maple syrup**

¼ teaspoon **cayenne**

1½ teaspoons chopped **fresh oregano** leaves

1½ teaspoons chopped **fresh sage** leaves

1½ teaspoons chopped **fresh thyme** leaves

1½ teaspoons chopped **fresh rosemary** leaves

1½ teaspoons chopped **fresh savory** leaves

1½ teaspoons chopped **fresh marjoram** leaves

3 tablespoons **olive oil**

About 1 teaspoon **kosher salt**

1. Mix almonds, walnuts, hazelnuts, pecans, maple syrup, cayenne, oregano, sage, thyme, rosemary, savory, marjoram, and oil in a 10- by 15-inch rimmed pan. Sprinkle nuts with 1 teaspoon salt.

2. Bake in a 300° oven, stirring occasionally, until all liquid evaporates and

Wente Ranch Thanksgiving dinner

Spicy Herb Roasted Nuts

Brut Reserve Sparkling Wine
Johannisberg Riesling

Romaine Salad
with Mandarins
and Asian Dressing

Roast Turkey

Chardonnay Gravy

Cornbread, Sausage, and
Dried Fruit Dressing

Trio of Peas
with Pearl Onions

Grandmother's Garlic
Mashed Potatoes

Julie's Brandied
Cranberry Sauce

Jean's Refrigerator Yeast Rolls

Reliz Creek Pinot Noir

Riva Ranch Chardonnay

Suggested dessert
Warm Apple Pie with
Vanilla Bean Ice Cream

Late-Harvest Riesling

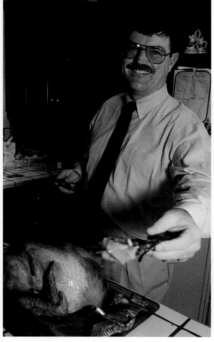

The menu (left) changes a little each year, but current repeat favorites include mashed potatoes from Grandmother Bess, Jean's yeast rolls, and Julie's cranberry sauce. Eric (above left) takes charge of the turkey. Pears marked with gold names (above right) decorate the table.

nuts are golden under the skin (break open to test), about 45 minutes.

3. Let cool. Taste and add more salt if desired.

Per ¼ cup: 217 cal., 79% (171 cal.) from fat; 4.2 g protein; 19 g fat (1.7 g sat.); 11 g carbo (2.3 g fiber); 77 mg sodium; 0 mg chol.

Romaine Salad with Mandarins and Asian Dressing

Prep and cook time: About 30 minutes

Notes: Up to a day ahead, toast nuts and make dressing; cover and let stand. Chill greens. Peel and segment mandarins up to 6 hours ahead; cover and chill. Or, instead of fresh fruit, use 1 or 2 cans (11 oz. each) mandarin sections, drained.

Makes: 12 servings

½ cup **slivered almonds**

⅓ cup **rice vinegar**

2 tablespoons **Asian (toasted) sesame oil**

1½ tablespoons **sugar**

1 tablespoon **soy sauce**

½ teaspoon **ground ginger**

½ teaspoon **dry mustard**

4 or 5 **mandarins** or small oranges (1½ lb. total)

2 firm-ripe **avocados** (¾ lb. total)

5 quarts **romaine lettuce** (about 2 heads) in bite-size pieces

Salt and **pepper**

1. In a 6- to 8-inch frying pan, shake almonds often over medium-high heat until lightly browned, about 7 minutes. Pour from pan.

2. In a large bowl, mix vinegar, oil, sugar, soy sauce, ginger, and mustard.

3. If peel is tight on mandarins, use a knife to cut it and white membrane from fruit, then cut between inner membranes to release fruit segments. Discard peel and membrane; reserve juice for another use. If peel is loose, pull off and discard, then separate segments. Pull off and discard any loose membrane. Add fruit to the bowl.

4. Peel and pit avocados; thinly slice into the bowl. Mix gently.

5. Add lettuce and almonds to bowl. Mix

Nibble nuts, roasted with maple syrup and herbs, with white wine before dinner.

Asian seasonings flavor salad with avocados, almonds, and mandarins.

cook 10 more minutes.

3. Pour broth through a fine strainer into a bowl. Discard vegetables. Pull meat off neck; finely chop neck meat and giblets. Measure broth and, if needed, add water to make 1 quart.

4. In the pan, smoothly blend cornstarch with $1/3$ cup water. Add broth and finely chopped giblets. Stir over high heat until boiling, about 5 minutes.

5. After turkey is done, skim and discard fat from pan juices. Add Chardonnay to roasting pan and, over low heat, scrape browned bits free. Add wine mixture to gravy and bring to a boil, stirring. Add salt to taste.

Per serving: 119 cal., 19% (23 cal.) from fat; 9.4 g protein; 2.5 g fat (0.9 g sat.); 7.8 g carbo (0.5 g fiber); 80 mg sodium; 77 mg chol.

Cornbread, Sausage, and Dried Fruit Dressing

Prep and cook time: About $1 1/4$ hours

Notes: If you use a mix for the cornbread, you'll need 1 box (13 oz.). The dressing can be made up to 1 day ahead; cover and chill. If stuffing turkey, just before roasting, fill neck and body cavities with dressing. Extra dressing can be heated, covered, in a microwave oven on full power (100%) for 5-minute intervals until steaming. Roast turkey according to chart on page 259. If desired, add fresh or dried herbs such as thyme to roasting juices and baste bird with them as it cooks.

Makes: About $3 3/4$ quarts (more than enough for a 16- to 20-lb. bird); 12 to 16 servings

  1 pound **bulk pork sausage**

  2 cups chopped **onions**

  2 cups chopped **celery**

  7 to 8 cups crumbled **cornbread**

  1 cup **dried apricots,** chopped

  1 cup **dried cranberries**

  2 **large eggs,** beaten to blend

  1 tablespoon chopped **fresh sage** leaves or $1/2$ teaspoon dried rubbed sage

  $1/2$ cup ($1/4$ lb.) **butter** or margarine, melted

   About $3/4$ cup **chicken broth**

   Salt and **pepper**

1. Crumble the sausage into a 10- to 12-inch frying pan over medium-high heat. Stir often until sausage is lightly

gently, adding salt and pepper to taste.

Per serving: 128 cal., 61% (78 cal.) from fat; 3.3 g protein; 8.7 g fat (1.1 g sat.); 11 g carbo (3.1 g fiber); 95 mg sodium; 0 mg chol.

Chardonnay Gravy

Prep and cook time: About $2 1/4$ hours

Notes: Up to 1 day ahead, make broth through step 4; cool, cover, and chill. After turkey roasts, add its pan drippings and the wine to broth and bring to a boil, stirring. For a more delicate flavor, replace 1 cup wine with equal amount of broth.

Makes: $1 1/2$ quarts; 10 to 12 servings

   Giblets and **neck** from a 16- to 20-pound turkey

  2 **onions** (about $3/4$ lb. total), quartered

  2 **carrots** (about $1/2$ lb. total), cut into chunks

  $3/4$ cup sliced **celery**

  1 quart **chicken broth**

  $1/2$ teaspoon **pepper**

  $1/2$ cup **cornstarch**

   Roast turkey (16 to 20 lb.; page 259)

  2 cups **Chardonnay**

   Salt

1. Rinse giblets and neck (chill liver airtight to add later, or save for other uses). Combine giblets, neck, onions, carrots, celery, and 1 cup broth in a 5- to 6-quart pan over medium heat; cover. Bring to a boil, then simmer for 15 minutes. Turn heat to high and boil, uncovered, stirring often as liquid evaporates. Then stir giblets and vegetables until browned and sticking to pan, 12 to 15 minutes.

2. Add remaining 3 cups broth and pepper, stirring to scrape browned bits free. Cover pan. Simmer gently until gizzard is tender when pierced, about $1 1/2$ hours. If desired, add liver and

JAMES CARRIER

browned, about 5 minutes. Using a slotted spoon, transfer sausage to a large bowl.

2. Discard all but 2 tablespoons fat in pan. Add onions to pan and stir often until limp, about 5 minutes. Add onions to sausage.

3. Add celery, cornbread, apricots, cranberries, eggs, sage, and butter and stir to mix well, adding just enough broth to lightly moisten dressing.

4. Spoon dressing into a shallow 2½- to 3-quart casserole and cover.

5. Bake in a 325° oven until hot, about 25 minutes (if chilled, 50 to 60 minutes). Then uncover and bake until top is lightly browned, 15 to 25 minutes more. Add salt and pepper to taste.

Per serving: 311 cal., 46% (144 cal.) from fat; 7.4 g protein; 16 g fat (6.8 g sat.); 34 g carbo (2.7 g fiber); 607 mg sodium; 81 mg chol.

Trio of Peas with Pearl Onions

Prep and cook time: About 45 minutes

Notes: Up to 1 day ahead, cook and peel fresh onions, shell fresh peas, and string pea pods. To save time, substitute 1 cup thawed frozen pearl onions and heat with peas.

Makes: 10 to 12 servings

- 2 cups (9 oz.) white and/or pink **pearl onions**
- 2 cups shelled **fresh** (about 2 lb. in shell) or frozen **peas**
- 2 cups (½ lb.) **sugar snap peas,** ends and strings removed
- 2 cups (½ lb.) **Chinese pea pods,** ends and strings removed
- 3 tablespoons **butter** or margarine
- 1 to 2 teaspoons finely chopped **fresh rosemary** leaves

  Salt and **pepper**

1. Place onions in a 5- to 6-quart pan; cover with water. Bring to a rolling boil over high heat. Drain in a colander.

2. When onions are cool enough to handle, trim off ends. To remove peel, pinch each onion with your index finger and thumb (the onion should squirt from the outside layer).

3. In the same pan, combine shelled peas and 1 cup water. Cover and bring to boiling over high heat. Cook, covered, over medium heat for 2 minutes. Stir in sugar snap peas and Chinese pea

Three kinds of peas—sugar snaps, Chinese, and shelled—go with tiny onions.

pods. Cover and cook until peas turn bright green and are tender-crisp to bite, 2 to 4 minutes. Drain in a colander.

4. Quickly melt butter in the 5- to 6-quart pan over high heat. Stir in rosemary and onions. Turn heat to low, add pea mixture, and mix gently until warm, 2 to 3 minutes. Add salt and pepper to taste.

Per serving: 68 cal., 40% (27 cal.) from fat; 2.5 g protein; 3 g fat (1.8 g sat.); 8.1 g carbo (1.9 g fiber); 33 mg sodium; 7.8 mg chol.

Grandmother's Garlic Mashed Potatoes

Prep and cook time: About 30 minutes

Notes: For a shortcut, buy refrigerated peeled garlic cloves.

Makes: 10 to 12 servings

- 5 pounds **russet potatoes**
- 1 cup **peeled garlic cloves**
- ¾ cup **whipping cream** or milk
- 3 tablespoons **butter** or margarine

  Salt and **white pepper**

1. Peel potatoes and cut into quarters. Place potatoes in a 5- to 6-quart pan and add enough water to cover. Cover pan and bring to a boil over high heat, then simmer until potatoes are tender when pierced, 15 to 20 minutes.

2. Meanwhile, in a 1- to 1½-quart pan

over low heat, combine garlic, cream, and butter. Cover and stir occasionally until garlic is tender when pierced, about 10 minutes.

3. In a blender or food processor, purée garlic mixture.

4. Drain potatoes, return to pan, and add garlic purée. Mash with a potato masher or mixer until smooth. Add salt and pepper to taste.

Per serving: 227 cal., 31% (71 cal.) from fat; 4.5 g protein; 7.9 g fat (4.7 g sat.); 35 g carbo (3.1 g fiber); 50 mg sodium; 24 mg chol.

Julie's Brandied Cranberry Sauce

Prep and cook time: About 1 hour

Notes: Sauce can be made up to 1 week ahead. To serve warm, reheat in a microwave oven.

Makes: About 2 cups; 10 to 12 servings

- 1 package (12 oz.) **fresh** or thawed frozen **cranberries**
- 1½ cups **sugar**
- ⅓ to ½ cup **brandy**
- 2 tablespoons finely shredded **orange** peel

1. Sort cranberries and discard any soft or spoiled ones. Rinse and drain berries.

2. Mix cranberries, sugar, brandy, and orange peel in an 8- or 9-inch square baking dish. Bake, uncovered, in a 325° oven until berries are tender when pierced and most of the liquid has evaporated, about 1 hour, stirring occasionally. Serve warm or cool.

Per serving: 112 cal., 0% (1 cal.) from fat; 0.1 g protein; 0.1 g fat (0 g sat.); 29 g carbo (1 g fiber); 0.6 mg sodium; 0 mg chol.

Philip's daughters have a hand in preparing apple pie for dessert.

CONNIE COLEMAN

Jean's Refrigerator Yeast Rolls

Prep and cook time: About 45 minutes, plus at least 4½ hours to rise

Notes: Dough can be made up to 2 days before baking. Rolls can be baked up to 1 day ahead. Store airtight. Reheat, uncovered, in a 350° oven just until warm, about 5 minutes.

Makes: About 2 dozen

- 1 cup plus 1 tablespoon **milk**
  About ½ cup (¼ lb.) **butter** or margarine, cut into chunks
- ¼ cup **sugar**
- ½ teaspoon **salt**
- 2 packages **active dry yeast**
- 3 **large eggs**
- 3½ to 4 cups **all-purpose flour**

- 2 tablespoons **sesame** or poppy **seed**

1. In a 1- to 1½-quart pan, warm 1 cup milk over high heat until small bubbles appear at edges. Add ½ cup butter, sugar, and salt. Remove from heat; cool to lukewarm (110°).

2. Soften yeast in ¼ cup warm water (110°) about 5 minutes.

3. In a bowl, combine milk mixture and yeast. Add 2 eggs and beat to blend. Add 2 cups flour. Beat at low speed to moisten. Then beat on high speed until dough is stretchy, 6 to 10 minutes.

4. On low speed (or with a spoon), mix in 1½ cups flour until well blended. Then gradually stir in as much of the remaining ½ cup flour as dough will absorb. Dough should still be soft and slightly sticky. Cover with plastic wrap

and place in the refrigerator for at least 4 hours or up to 48 hours.

5. Punch dough down and divide in half. Cover half the dough while shaping the remainder.

6. Butter muffin pans (with 2½-in.-wide cups). To make cloverleaf rolls, pinch off and shape dough into 1-inch-thick balls. Drop 3 balls into each cup. Cover lightly with plastic wrap.

7. Let rolls rise in a warm place until almost doubled, 30 to 45 minutes. With a fork, beat remaining egg to blend with 1 tablespoon milk. Brush rolls with egg mixture and sprinkle with sesame seed.

8. Bake rolls in 400° oven until golden, 8 to 10 minutes. Serve warm or cool.

Per roll: 137 cal., 40% (55 cal.) from fat; 3.4 g protein; 6.1 g fat (3 g sat.); 17 g carbo (0.7 g fiber); 99 mg sodium; 38 mg chol. ◆

Ranch Thanksgiving dinner countdown

These steps are based on the time it takes one person with one oven to prepare this meal

☐ **UP TO A WEEK AHEAD**
•*Bake* cranberry sauce.

☐ **AT LEAST 3 DAYS AHEAD**
•*Bake* spicy herb nuts.
•*Put* frozen turkey in the refrigerator to thaw.

☐ **UP TO 2 DAYS AHEAD**
•*Shop* for all other ingredients and turkey, if fresh.
•*Bake* cornbread for dressing.
•*Prepare* yeast dough for rolls.

☐ **UP TO 1 DAY AHEAD**
•*Assemble* dressing and chill if the turkey will be stuffed. Or put dressing in casserole and chill.
•*Make* salad dressing, toast nuts for salad, and crisp salad greens.
•*Cook* and peel onions; string and shell peas.

•*Make* and thicken broth for gravy.
•*Bake* rolls.
•*Bake* apple pie, purchased frozen or made from a favorite recipe. Or make a grand holiday dessert (see page 266).

THANKSGIVING DAY

☐ **UP TO 6 HOURS AHEAD**
•*Prepare* fruit for salad and chill.

☐ **3½ HOURS BEFORE SERVING**
•*Rinse* turkey. If stuffing, place dressing in bird. Put turkey in oven to roast (see facing page).

☐ **1 HOUR AHEAD**
•*Bake* casserole of dressing if chilled.

☐ **45 MINUTES AHEAD**
•*Peel* and cook potatoes; cook garlic.

☐ **20 MINUTES AHEAD**
•*Mash* potatoes; keep warm.

☐ **15 MINUTES AHEAD**
•*Remove* turkey from oven, put on platter, and keep warm.
•*Add* wine to roasting-pan drippings, then add drippings to gravy. Heat gravy and keep warm.

☐ **10 MINUTES AHEAD**
•*Heat* extra dressing (if bird was stuffed) in a microwave oven.
•*Cook* peas and onions.

☐ **5 MINUTES BEFORE SERVING**
•*Warm* rolls.
•*Warm* cranberry sauce, if desired.
•*Garnish* turkey platter.
•*Mix* salad with dressing.

☐ **15 MINUTES BEFORE DESSERT**
•*Warm* apple pie in a 350° oven.

Succulent secrets

How to cook the most delicious bird

Every year, we chant the same turkey mantra: Don't overcook. Buy a meat thermometer and use it. The objective—moist, juicy breast meat and succulent thighs.

Today's young, moist, tender turkeys take much less time to cook than tougher birds of yore. Almost without exception, if a bird is dry, it's been cooked too long—and the breast meat suffers most.

Through the years at *Sunset,* we literally have cooked a thousand turkeys or more, in ovens and on barbecues, charting their cooking temperatures and times. Here is the *Sunset* tried-and-true basic chart for cooking a turkey.

— *Elaine Johnson*

Best-ever Turkey, Roasted or Barbecued

Prep time: About 10 minutes, 20 if stuffing the bird. See chart below for cooking times

Notes: Thaw turkey, if frozen, at least 72 hours in the refrigerator. Reserve giblets, neck, and drippings for gravy, if desired. If stuffing the bird, do so just before cooking. Use the Cornbread, Sausage, and Dried-Fruit Dressing (page 256), Mushroom-Quinoa Dressing (page 263), or your favorite recipe.

Makes: For generous servings, allow ½ to ¾ pound uncooked turkey per person, more if you want leftovers

  1 **turkey** (10 to 30 lb.)

    Olive or salad **oil**

1. Remove and discard leg truss from turkey. Pull off and discard lumps of fat. Remove giblets and neck. Rinse the bird inside and out; pat dry with towels.

2. Rub turkey skin with oil. Insert a meat thermometer straight down through the thickest part of the breast to the bone. (If using an instant-read thermometer, insert when checking temperature.)

3. Cook the turkey until the meat thermometer registers 160°; see chart below for details. Baste with drippings, if desired.

To oven-roast, place turkey, breast up, on a V-shaped rack in a 12- by 17-inch roasting pan (or one that is at least 2 inches longer and wider than the bird). Roast in a 325° or 350° oven.

To barbecue with charcoal, use a barbecue (20 to 22 in. wide) with a lid. Mound and ignite 40 charcoal briquets on firegrate. When coals are spotted with gray ash, in about 20 minutes, push equal portions to opposite sides of firegrate. Place a metal drip pan between coals.

To each mound of coals, add 5 briquets now and every 30 minutes while cooking. Set grill 4 to 6 inches above coals. Set turkey, breast side up, on grill over drip pan.

To barbecue with gas, use a gas barbecue with indirect heat controls; heat should be parallel to each side of the bird. Turn heat to high, close lid, and heat for about 10 minutes. Adjust gas for indirect cooking (no heat down center) and set a metal drip pan in center. Set grill in place. Set turkey, breast side up, on grill over drip pan. Close the lid.

4. Transfer turkey to a platter; let stand 15 to 30 minutes (keep warm).

5. Carve bird. If thighs are still slightly pink at the joint, cook, uncovered, on a microwave-safe plate in a microwave oven at full power (100%) until pink disappears, 1 to 3 minutes.

Per ¼ pound boneless cooked turkey, based on percentages of white and dark meat found in average turkey (including skin): 229 cal., 39% (90 cal.) from fat; 32 g protein; 10 g fat (3 g sat.); 0 g carbo (0 g fiber); 82 mg sodium; 93 mg chol. ◆

TURKEY TASTE TEST

Should you pay extra for a fresh turkey? Or for a free-range bird? To put the issue to rest, we did a blind taste test of five turkeys that represent typical holiday choices.

Two contenders were supermarket house-brand birds—Safeway Manor House frozen (49 cents per lb. last holiday season) and Petrini frozen (99 cents per lb.). Two were brand-name turkeys—a frozen Butterball self-basting ($1.09 per lb.) and a fresh Norbest all-natural ($1.68 per lb.). The fifth turkey was an organically range-grown Diestel fresh ($1.79 per lb.). The birds were of similar size, 12 to 14 pounds each. And all were cooked simultaneously on separate, identical charcoal barbecues with identical amounts of heat to the same internal breast temperature.

The judges were *Sunset* staffers and members of a local television crew that filmed the tasting. Evaluations rated dark and light meat for flavor, tenderness, and juiciness.

The results: The Petrini, Safeway, Butterball, and Diestel birds were neck and neck, with close scores. Winner by a drumstick? The cheapest, Safeway's frozen turkey. Least favorite by an equally narrow margin—the Norbest bird. Its breast was the least juicy.

BIRD BASICS: *Oven-roasted or barbecued*

TURKEY WEIGHT with giblets	OVEN TEMP.	INTERNAL TEMP.	COOKING TIME
10 to 13 lb.	350°	160°	1½ to 2¼ hr.
14 to 23 lb.	325°	160°	2 to 3 hr.
24 to 27 lb.	325°	160°	3 to 3¾ hr.
28 to 30 lb.	325°	160°	3½ to 4½ hr.

Notes: See barbecuing instructions above and at right for charcoal and gas barbecue heat controls.

To measure the internal temperature of the turkey, insert a thermometer through the thickest part of the breast to the bone.

Times are for unstuffed birds. A stuffed bird may cook at the same rate as an unstuffed one; however, be prepared to allow 30 to 50 minutes more.

Thanksgiving, light and easy

A high-tech cook shares her low-tech secrets for a make-ahead meal that's bountiful and very low in fat

■ "My background is in the computer industry," says Kristene Fortier of San Carlos, California, as she describes her career change four years ago from high-tech Silicon Valley manager to food writer and culinary teacher.

"I've always loved food; I just didn't think it would be a practical career. But when Michelle was a baby and my son, Casey, was 3, I left the industry and be-

With two youngsters and a busy schedule, Kristene Fortier focuses her cooking on quick, easy, and wholesome.

gan teaching cooking classes that focused on healthy eating." Her classes included employees of high-tech companies, whose needs and Fortier's interest in make-ahead foods that are light, wholesome, and quickly prepared were a perfect fit.

Fortier's approach to a traditional Thanksgiving dinner follows in the same vein. Although a menu with 10 dishes takes longer than a typical sup-

per, you can prepare everything but the turkey, roasted potatoes, and gravy ahead. Even if you're alone in the kitchen, this meal is easily managed.

The reward is a feast that looks and tastes lavish. And a full portion adds up to 1,388 calories, 12% (162 cal., just 18 grams) from fat. Slightly indulgent, perhaps, but easily balanced if you go light on breakfast and lunch.

Low-fat Thanksgiving dinner for eight

Tomato-Caper Bruschetta*

Pumpkin Soup

Red and Green Salad with Cranberry Dressing

Rosemary Roast Turkey*

Turkey Gravy

Roasted Petite Yukon Gold Potatoes

Mushroom-Quinoa Dressing

Maple-Mustard Green Beans

Baby Leeks in Wine Sauce

Baked Cardamom Pears and Apricots*

*wine suggestions on p. 265

Tomato-Caper Bruschetta

Prep and cook time: About 25 minutes

Notes: Up to 2 days ahead, make tomato mixture, cover, and chill; bring to room temperature before serving. Up

to 1 day ahead, make toast and, when cool, seal airtight and hold at room temperature.

Makes: 24 pieces; 8 servings

  1   cup (about 2 oz.) firmly packed **dried tomato slices**

  1   **baguette** (½ lb.)

  1   **green onion** (including green top), ends trimmed, and coarsely chopped

  1   clove **garlic**

  1   tablespoon drained **capers**

  1   tablespoon **fresh oregano** leaves or 1 teaspoon dried oregano

  1½ tablespoons **lemon juice**

  1   tablespoon **balsamic vinegar**

      Salt

1. In a small bowl, combine tomatoes with 1 cup boiling water; let stand until soft and pliable, about 15 minutes. Drain tomatoes.

2. Meanwhile, cut baguette diagonally into 24 slices. Arrange on a 12- by 15-inch baking sheet. Broil 4 to 6 inches from heat until toasted on each side, about 2 minutes total.

3. In a food processor, finely mince tomatoes, onion, garlic, capers, and oregano with lemon juice and balsamic vinegar. (Or with a knife, mince tomatoes, onion, garlic, capers, and oregano, then add lemon juice and vinegar.) Add salt to taste.

4. Spoon tomato mixture into a small bowl and accompany with toast. Spread tomato mixture onto toast to eat.

Per piece: 34 cal., 7.9% (2.7 cal.) from fat; 1.3 g protein; 0.3 g fat (0.1 g sat.); 6.6 g carbo (0.7 g fiber); 76 mg sodium; 0 mg chol.

---

by **BARBARA GOLDMAN**   *food photographs by* **RICHARD JUNG**

Brimming with flavor but low in fat: turkey and gravy, green beans, mushroom-quinoa dressing, baby leeks, and tiny roasted potatoes.

Pumpkin Soup

Prep and cook time: About 25 minutes

Notes: If making ahead, cool, cover, and chill up to 1 day. Add sour cream after reheating.

Makes: 6 cups; 8 servings

- 1 **onion** (8 to 10 oz.), chopped
- 2 cloves **garlic,** minced
- 1 teaspoon **pumpkin pie spice**
- ⅛ teaspoon **cayenne**
- 3¾ cups **chicken** or vegetable **broth**
- 1 can (15 oz.) **pumpkin**
- 1 tablespoon **honey**
- 1 cup **nonfat milk**
- 4 teaspoons **cornstarch**
- 1 tablespoon **lemon juice**
  Salt
  About 2 tablespoons **nonfat sour cream** or plain nonfat yogurt

1. In a 4- to 5-quart pan, frequently stir onion, garlic, pumpkin pie spice, cayenne, and ¼ cup broth over high heat until pan is dry, about 3 minutes.

2. In a blender or food processor, smoothly purée onion mixture, adding a little more broth if needed to facilitate the process.

3. Return purée to pan; add remaining broth, pumpkin, and honey.

4. Smoothly mix milk with cornstarch and stir into soup. Stirring, bring to a boil over high heat. Add lemon juice and salt to taste.

5. Ladle soup into shallow bowls. Stir sour cream to soften, then drizzle a small amount into each bowl.

Per serving: 61 cal., 4.4% (2.7 cal.) from fat; 2.4 g protein; 0.3 g fat (0.1 g sat.); 13 g carbo (1.4 g fiber); 30 mg sodium; 1.2 mg chol.

Red and Green Salad with Cranberry Dressing

Prep time: About 25 minutes

Notes: Up to 1 day ahead, prepare dressing, cover, and chill. Also rinse and drain salad leaves, wrap in towels, put in a plastic bag, and chill.

Makes: 8 servings

- ¼ cup **fresh cilantro**
- 1 **shallot** (about 1 oz.), chopped
- ⅓ cup **seasoned rice vinegar**
- ⅓ cup **cranberry juice cocktail**
- 1 tablespoon **honey**
- 1 teaspoon **Dijon mustard**
- ¼ cup **dried cranberries**
- 10 cups **baby salad leaves,** rinsed and crisped
- 2 cups shredded **red cabbage** or radicchio
- ⅓ cup thinly sliced **red onion**
- 1 **red bell pepper** (7 or 8 oz.), stemmed, seeded, and thinly sliced
  Salt

1. In a food processor or blender, smoothly purée cilantro, shallot, vinegar, cranberry juice, honey, and mustard. Add dried cranberries to dressing.

2. In a large, shallow bowl, mix salad leaves, cabbage, red onion, bell pepper, and dressing. Add salt to taste.

Per serving: 70 cal., 1.3% (0.9 cal.) from fat; 1.4 g protein; 0.1 g fat (0 g sat.); 15 g carbo (1.9 g fiber); 232 mg sodium; 0 mg chol..

Rosemary Roast Turkey

Prep and cook time: About 1 hour and 50 minutes, plus 30 minutes to stand

Notes: Garnish turkey platter with more rosemary sprigs and Roasted Petite Yukon Gold Potatoes (recipe on facing page).

Makes: 10 to 13 servings, or 8 servings with leftovers

- 6 cloves **garlic**
- ¼ cup coarsely chopped **fresh rosemary** leaves
- 1 **turkey** (10 to 13 lb.)
- 1 tablespoon **olive** or salad **oil**
- 1 **lemon,** cut in half
- 5 to 8 **rosemary sprigs** (4 to 6 in. long)

1. Chop 3 garlic cloves. Mix chopped garlic with chopped rosemary.

2. Follow directions for getting turkey ready to roast (page 259).

3. Rub oil on skin. Squeeze juice from a

Make-ahead pumpkin soup cooks in less than half an hour.

Cranberry dressing, oil-free, anoints a salad of red and green leaves.

lemon half into body cavity, then add the peel. Rub juice of remaining lemon half onto turkey skin.

4. Slide your fingers under turkey skin to gently loosen it (but leave in place) on breast, around outside of thighs and legs, and over back (from the neck end).

5. Push the rosemary-garlic mixture under skin, distributing evenly. Place remaining garlic cloves and the rosemary sprigs inside the bird.

6. Roast turkey as directed on page 259, then put on a platter and let stand up to 30 minutes; keep warm.

7. Skim and discard fat from pan juices. Reserve pan with juices for gravy.

Per serving without skin: 193 cal., 25% (49 cal.) from fat; 33 g protein; 5.4 g fat (1.7 g sat.); 0.5 g carbo (0 g fiber); 84 mg sodium; 87 mg chol.

Turkey Gravy

Prep and cook time: About 15 minutes

Notes: Up to 2 days ahead, toast flour and store airtight.

Makes: 5 cups; 8 servings

- ½ cup **all-purpose flour**
  Rosemary Roast Turkey drippings (see preceding recipe)
- 4½ cups **chicken broth**
- ½ cup **dry white wine**
  Salt and **pepper**

1. In a 10- to 12-inch frying pan over high heat, stir flour until it's a medium-brown color, 6 to 7 minutes. If making ahead, pour into a jar and cover.

2. Add toasted flour to drippings in turkey roasting pan and smoothly whisk in the broth and wine. Set pan over high heat and stir, scraping drippings free, until gravy boils vigorously, then simmer and stir 4 to 5 more minutes. Add salt and pepper to taste.

Per serving: 64 cal., 22% (14 cal.) from fat; 3.3 g protein; 1.5 g fat (0.6 g sat.); 6.9 g carbo (0.2 g fiber); 60 mg sodium; 2.7 mg chol.

Roasted Petite Yukon Gold Potatoes

Prep and cook time: About 55 minutes

Notes: Add potatoes to oven with roasting turkey 20 minutes before bird is done, then continue to cook at a higher temperature along with the dressing while turkey rests.

Makes: 8 servings

- 4 pounds **Yukon Gold** or other thin-skinned **potatoes** (1 to 1½ in. wide)
- 2 to 3 teaspoons **olive oil** (optional)
  Salt and fresh-ground **pepper**

1. Scrub potatoes and put in a 10- by 15-inch pan. Add oil and roll potatoes to coat them.

2. Bake on the bottom rack of a 350° oven for 20 minutes, then turn temperature to 400°. Continue baking until potatoes are very tender when pierced, about 30 minutes longer.

3. Serve whole or cut in half. Season to taste with salt and pepper.

Per serving: 183 cal., 2% (3.6 cal.) from fat; 4.4 g protein; 0.4 g fat (0 g sat.); 41 g carbo (3.8 g fiber); 17 mg sodium; 0 mg chol.

Mushroom-Quinoa Dressing

Prep and cook time: About 1½ hours

Notes: Up to 2 days ahead, make dressing, wrap airtight, and chill. If desired, put in a microwave-safe casserole, cover, and cook in a microwave oven at full power (100%), stirring once or twice, until steaming, 5 to 10 minutes. Garnish dressing with thyme sprigs just before serving.

Makes: 10 cups; 8 servings

- ½ ounce (about ½ cup) **dried porcini mushrooms**
- 2 cups (13 oz.) **quinoa**
- 2½ cups **chicken** or vegetable **broth**
- 1 pound **common mushrooms**
- 1 cup finely chopped **shallots**
- 2 cloves **garlic,** minced
- 1 cup finely chopped **celery**

Tips for cooking lighter

When developing recipes, Kristene Fortier says, "I never try to remake higher-fat recipes into low-fat ones. Instead, I start with zero fat and add it only when it's needed." Techniques that work:

- **Instead of using water,** cook vegetables, chicken, and fish in compatibly flavored broth, wine, or fruit juice. Then boil down the cooking liquid to concentrate flavors for a fine sauce.
- **Toast flour** until golden brown (on the rangetop or in the oven) instead of browning it in fat to develop rich color and flavor for gravy. For liquid, use fat-free broth.
- **Use mild-tasting vinegars** such as balsamic or rice to season salads, or add a touch of sugar to soften the bite of other vinegars.
- **Thicken rice vinegar** for salad dressings by stirring in a compatibly flavored fruit purée.
- **Poach fruit in wine** or fruit juice for dessert. Boil down cooking liquid separately to concentrate flavor for a sauce.

1 tablespoon chopped **fresh rosemary** leaves

4 to 6 slices **whole-wheat bread,** torn into small pieces

2 tablespoons chopped **Italian** or curly **parsley**

1 tablespoon chopped **fresh thyme** leaves

Salt and fresh-ground **pepper**

1. In a large bowl, combine porcini and 1 cup boiling water. Let stand until mushrooms are limp, about 20 minutes. Squeeze mushrooms gently to remove grit, then lift from water, squeeze dry, and finely chop.

2. Without disturbing grit, pour most of soaking liquid into a glass measure; add water to make ²⁄₃ cup. Discard gritty liquid. Rinse and dry bowl.

3. Meanwhile, rinse quinoa in a fine strainer under cool running water.

4. Put quinoa in a 4- to 5-quart pan. Add the ²⁄₃ cup porcini soaking liquid and the broth. Bring to boiling over high heat, then reduce heat and simmer, covered, until quinoa is just tender to bite, 10 to 12 minutes. Drain and save liquid, adding enough water to make ½ cup. Put quinoa in the large bowl.

5. As quinoa cooks, rinse common mushrooms, trim off and discard discolored stem ends, and finely chop.

6. In a 10- to 12-inch nonstick frying pan over medium-high heat, stir shallots and garlic until shallots are limp and tinged brown, 3 to 4 minutes.

7. Add porcini, common mushrooms, celery, and rosemary. Stir often over high heat until mushrooms are limp and juices cook away, about 5 minutes.

8. Mix vegetables with quinoa, bread pieces, parsley, thyme, and salt and pepper to taste.

9. Pour quinoa dressing into a shallow 2½- to 3½-quart casserole and add reserved cooking liquid. Cover and bake in a 400° oven until hot, about 25 minutes (30 minutes if chilled).

Per serving: 252 cal., 13% (34 cal.) from fat; 10 g protein; 3.8 g fat (0.6 g sat.); 46 g carbo (8.1 g fiber); 135 mg sodium; 1.6 mg chol.

Maple-Mustard Green Beans

Prep and cook time: About 20 minutes

Notes: Up to 2 days ahead, make and chill maple-mustard sauce. One day

ahead, cook beans; drain and immerse at once in ice water until cold. Drain again, wrap airtight, and chill. To re-heat, dump beans in boiling water to cover, remove from heat and let stand about 1½ minutes, then drain. Or put beans in a microwave-safe bowl and heat, uncovered, in a microwave oven at full power (100%) until steaming, 2 to 4 minutes.

Makes: 8 servings

2 pounds **green beans,** ends trimmed

2 tablespoons **coarse-grain Dijon mustard**

3 tablespoons **balsamic vinegar**

1½ tablespoons **maple syrup**

2 teaspoons **extra-virgin olive oil**

2 tablespoons chopped **green onion** (including green tops)

Salt and fresh-ground **pepper**

1. In a 4- to 5-quart pan, bring 2 quarts water to a boil over high heat. Add beans and cook, uncovered, until tender-crisp, 5 to 8 minutes; drain and pour into a bowl.

2. Meanwhile, mix mustard with vinegar, maple syrup, and oil. Pour over hot beans and mix to coat well; sprinkle with onion. Season to taste with salt and pepper.

Per serving: 56 cal., 21% (12 cal.) from fat; 1.8 g protein; 1.3 g fat (0.2 g sat.); 9.9 g carbo (1.8 g fiber); 97 mg sodium; 0 mg chol.

For dessert, serve cardamom-scented pears baked with dried apricots.

Baby Leeks in Wine Sauce

Prep and cook time: About 35 minutes

Notes: If making up to 1 day ahead, cover leeks and sauce, chill, then bring to room temperature or reheat to serve.

Makes: 8 servings

24 **baby leeks** (about ½ in. wide)

¾ cup chopped **onion**

1 clove **garlic,** chopped

¾ cup **dry white wine**

¾ cup **chicken** or vegetable **broth**

½ **lemon,** thinly sliced

2 **Roma tomatoes** (about 6 oz. total), cored, seeded, and chopped

8 to 10 **parsley sprigs**

Thin strands of **lemon** peel

Salt and fresh-ground **pepper**

1. Trim off and discard leek roots and tops, making each leek 6 inches long. Rinse well.

2. In a 10- to 12-inch nonstick frying pan, combine onion and garlic. Stir over medium-high heat until onion is limp, 4 to 5 minutes.

3. Add wine, broth, lemon slices, toma-toes, and parsley to pan. Lay leeks in pan. Cover and bring to boiling over high heat. Turn heat to low and simmer until leeks are tender when pierced, about 10 minutes.

4. With a slotted spoon, transfer leeks to a shallow rimmed dish.

5. Discard lemon slices and parsley. Boil tomato mixture over high heat until reduced to about 1 cup, 3 to 5 minutes.

6. Pour sauce across center of leeks. Garnish with lemon peel and season to taste with salt and pepper. Serve warm or at room temperature.

Per serving: 64 cal., 5.6% (3.6 cal.) from fat; 1.5 g protein; 0.4 g fat (0.1 g sat.); 11 g carbo (1.2 g fiber); 25 mg sodium; 0.4 mg chol.

Baked Cardamom Pears and Apricots

Prep and cook time: About 1 hour and 10 minutes

Notes: Make up to 1 day ahead. Let baked fruit cool, then cover and chill. Pack cooled oat topping airtight and keep at room temperature.

To reheat fruit, add ¼ cup apple juice, cover, and bake in a 325° oven until hot, 30 to 35 minutes.

Makes: 8 servings

1½ tablespoons **butter** or margarine

⅓ cup **regular** or quick-cooking **rolled oats**

⅓ cup **toasted wheat germ**

⅓ cup firmly packed **brown sugar**

2 tablespoons **chopped almonds**

¼ cup **honey**

1½ tablespoons **lemon juice**

½ teaspoon **vanilla**

½ teaspoon **almond extract**

½ teaspoon **ground cardamom**

1 cup (about 6 oz.) **dried apricots**

4 firm-ripe **pears,** such as Bosc or Comice (2 to 2¼ lb. total)

1 quart **vanilla nonfat frozen yogurt**

1. Cut butter into small pieces. In an 8- or 9-inch square pan, mix butter with oats, wheat germ, brown sugar, and almonds.

2. Bake in a 350° oven until mixture is lightly browned and crisp, 10 to 15 minutes; stir several times. Let cool.

3. Meanwhile, in a 2- to 3-quart pan, combine honey, lemon juice, vanilla, almond extract, cardamom, apricots, and 2 tablespoons water. Bring to a boil and remove from heat.

4. Peel, halve, and core pears. Lay pears, cut side down, in a shallow 2- to 2½-quart casserole. Spoon honey-apricot mixture over pears and cover casserole tightly.

5. Bake until pears are tender when pierced, 35 to 40 minutes.

6. Spoon pears, apricots, and juices equally into wide bowls. Add scoops of frozen yogurt to each serving and sprinkle with topping.

Per serving: 343 cal., 12% (40 cal.) from fat; 5.5 g protein; 4.4 g fat (1.6 g sat.); 74 g carbo (5.5 g fiber); 74 mg sodium; 5.8 mg chol. ◆

Light and easy Thanksgiving dinner countdown

This schedule is based on the time it takes one person with one oven to prepare this meal

☐ **AT LEAST 3 DAYS AHEAD**

•*Put* frozen turkey in the refrigerator to thaw.

☐ **UP TO 2 DAYS AHEAD**

•*Shop* for all other ingredients and turkey, if fresh.

•*Make* tomato-caper spread for bruschetta.

•*Prepare,* but don't bake, mushroom-quinoa dressing.

•*Toast* flour for gravy.

•*Make* maple-mustard sauce for green beans.

☐ **UP TO 1 DAY AHEAD**

•*Make* toast for bruschetta.

•*Cook* green beans.

•*Prepare* pumpkin soup.

•*Make* salad dressing; *rinse* and *crisp* salad leaves.

•*Cook* leeks.

•*Bake* dessert.

THANKSGIVING DAY

☐ **2½ HOURS BEFORE SERVING**

•*Rinse* turkey. Prepare and season bird. *Put* turkey in oven to roast.

•*Let* tomato-caper spread and maple-mustard sauce come to room temperature.

•*Prepare* remaining salad ingredients and chill.

☐ **1 HOUR AHEAD**

•*Scrub* potatoes and *bake* with turkey.

☐ **30 MINUTES AHEAD**

•*Remove* turkey from oven, put on platter, keep warm.

•*Turn* oven to 400°.

•*Bake* mushroom-quinoa dressing along with potatoes.

•*Make* gravy and keep warm.

☐ **10 MINUTES AHEAD**

•*Heat* pumpkin soup; keep warm.

☐ **5 MINUTES AHEAD**

•*Mix* salad with dressing.

•*Heat* green beans and season.

•*Heat* leeks, if desired.

•*Add* potatoes and herb garnish to turkey platter.

•*Ladle* soup into bowls and garnish.

☐ **35 MINUTES BEFORE DESSERT**

•*Reheat* fruit.

WINE SUGGESTIONS

■ **Under $14**

With appetizer:
Husch Sauvignon Blanc 1995 (Mendocino), $9.50

With main course:
Zabaco Zinfandel 1994 (Sonoma), $9

With dessert:
Robert Pecota Moscato d'Andrea 1996 (Napa Valley), $9 for 375 ml.

■ **Over $14**

With appetizer:
Joseph Phelps Vin du Mistral Viognier 1995 (Napa Valley), $28

With main course:
Truchard Syrah 1995 (Carneros), $24

With dessert:
Bonny Doon Muscat "Vin de Glacière" 1996 (California), $15 for 375 ml.

— *Karen MacNeil*

Irresistible sweets

For dessert this holiday season, start with great Western ingredients

Fran's Cranberry Tart

■ The party is perfect. Dinner is progressing beautifully. But the pressure builds. Dessert must be too tempting to wave aside—even at Thanksgiving, when the turkey is carted off and groans of "I can't eat another bite" echo around the table.

For grand, enticing desserts, we turned to pastry masters who appreciate seasonal, regional ingredients. And they didn't disappoint, turning cranberries into a glistening tart, toasting pecans, filling a pie with fresh pumpkin, glazing macadamias for cheesecake, steaming persimmons in a pudding, and making a warm hazelnut caramel sauce for eggnog ice cream.

by **LINDA LAU ANUSASANANAN** *and* **ANDREW BAKER**

photographs by **PAUL FRANZ-MOORE**

Deer Valley Pecan Pie

The Bakeshop's Sugar Pumpkin Pie

Fran's Cranberry Tart

Prep and cook time: About 1 hour, plus 30 minutes for crust

Notes: Fran Bigelow, president of Fran's Chocolates in Seattle and Bellevue, Washington, also makes beautiful pastries. This one uses Northwest-grown cranberries, and she cautions that the berries must be cooked very briefly to hold their shape.

Makes: 10 to 12 servings

2 bags (12 oz. each, 6 to 8 cups total) **fresh** or frozen **cranberries**

2/3 cup **orange juice**

1 jar (10 oz.) **currant jelly**

1 1/2 cups **sugar**

Butter crust (recipe follows)

1 ounce **white chocolate**, chopped

1. Sort cranberries (thaw if frozen) and discard any that are soft or spoiled. Rinse and drain berries, then spread out on towels. Pat gently with more towels to dry quickly.

2. In a 5- to 6-quart pan over high heat, combine orange juice and jelly. Stir, mashing jelly until it melts, about 3 minutes.

3. Add sugar. Stir until syrup begins to smell slightly caramelized and drips slowly from a spoon, about 7 minutes. Immediately remove pan from heat. Add the cranberries and stir to coat with syrup.

4. Return pan to low heat and stir gently until cranberries are evenly warm and no longer taste raw, 3 to 4 minutes (a few berries may pop). Remove from heat and let stand until syrup is cool enough to coat berries evenly, about 20 minutes, stirring occasionally. Then scrape berry mixture into the baked crust, mounding fruit.

5. Seal chocolate in a small zip-lock plastic freezer bag (without pleats). Heat in a microwave oven at 50% power just until chocolate softens, about 2 minutes. Knead chocolate until smooth.

6. With a thin skewer, puncture a hole in 1 corner of the bag. Squeeze chocolate over tart in fine zigzag lines. Chill until chocolate and jelly glaze are firm, at least 30 minutes or up to 1 day. If making ahead, cover when jelly is set. To serve, remove cover and pan rim. Cut tart into wedges.

Per serving: 347 cal., 24% (82 cal.) from fat; 2.3 g protein; 9.1 g fat (5.3 g sat.); 67 g carbo (2.6 g fiber); 91 mg sodium; 38 mg chol.

Butter Crust

Prep and cook time: About 30 minutes

Notes: Use this crust for Fran's Cranberry Tart and the Deer Valley Pecan Pie, following.

Makes: A 10-inch crust

1 1/3 cups **all-purpose flour**

1/4 cup **sugar**

1/2 cup (1/4 lb.) **butter** or margarine

1 **large egg** yolk

1. In a food processor or a bowl, combine flour and sugar. Add butter, cut into small pieces; whirl (or rub with your fingers) until fine crumbs form. Add egg yolk; whirl (or mix with a fork) until dough holds together.

2. Firmly press the dough over bottom and sides of a 10-inch tart pan with removable rim.

3. Bake in a 300° oven until pale gold, 25 to 30 minutes; let cool. If making ahead, wrap airtight and let stand at room temperature up to 1 day, or freeze to store longer. Thaw unwrapped.

Per whole crust: 1,672 cal., 53% (891 cal.) from fat; 21 g protein; 99 g fat (59 g sat.); 177 g carbo (4.5 g fiber); 948 mg sodium; 461 mg chol.

Deer Valley Pecan Pie

Prep and cook time: About 50 minutes

Notes: Letty Flatt, pastry chef at the Deer Valley Resort in Park City, Utah, lightly toasts the pecans, browns the butter, and uses maple syrup in her recipe. Store cool pie airtight up to 3 days at room temperature.

Makes: 8 or 9 servings

1 3/4 cups **pecan halves**

6 tablespoons **butter** or margarine

3 **large eggs**

2 tablespoons **all-purpose flour**

1 cup firmly packed **brown sugar**

1/2 cup **maple syrup**

1 teaspoon **vanilla**

Butter crust (recipe precedes)

1. Spread pecans in a single layer in a 10- by 15-inch pan. Bake in a 350° oven until nuts are fragrant and just slightly darker, about 7 minutes.

2. In a 1- to 1 1/2-quart pan, cook butter over high heat just until it begins to brown and have a nutty aroma, 4 to 5 minutes; remove from heat.

3. In a blender or food processor, finely grind 1/4 cup pecans.

4. In a bowl, beat eggs to blend. Add ground pecans, pecan halves, browned butter, flour, brown sugar, maple syrup, and vanilla. Mix well. Pour nut mixture into the baked crust.

5. Bake in a 350° oven until center is set when pie is slightly shaken, about 25 minutes. Let pie stand at least 30 minutes or until cool.

6. Remove pan rim and cut pie into wedges.

Per serving: 564 cal., 56% (315 cal.) from fat; 6.3 g protein; 35 g fat (13 g sat.); 61 g carbo (1.9 g fiber); 216 mg sodium; 143 mg chol.

Macadamia Brittle Cheesecake

Prep and cook time: About 2 hours, plus at least 3 hours to chill

Notes: Retired chef Pat Allen of Pahoa, Hawaii, is a cheesecake genius who uses the Islands' macadamias in this lavish creation. If the nuts are salted, pour onto a cloth towel and rub briskly with the fabric before using.

Makes: 20 to 24 servings

1 cup **roasted macadamia nuts**

2 cups **sugar**

2 cups **graham cracker crumbs**

1/2 teaspoon **ground cinnamon**

1/4 cup (1/8 lb.) melted **butter** or margarine

4 packages (8 oz. each) **cream cheese**

4 **large eggs**

1 teaspoon grated **lemon** peel

1 teaspoon **lemon juice**

1/2 teaspoon grated **lime** peel

1 teaspoon **lime juice**

1 teaspoon **vanilla**

1/4 cup plus 1 tablespoon **macadamia nut–flavor liqueur** (optional)

2 cups **sour cream**

1. Coarsely chop nuts.

2. Pour 3/4 cup sugar into a 10- to 12-inch nonstick frying pan. Shake pan often over high heat until sugar melts and turns golden, 5 to 8 minutes; watch carefully. At once, stir in nuts, then immediately pour onto a 12- to 14-inch sheet of foil. With a spoon, press mixture to flatten slightly. Let cool, then break brittle into about ¼- to ½-inch chunks. If making ahead, store airtight up to 3 days.

3. In a 10-inch cheesecake pan with removable rim at least 2½ inches tall, mix cracker crumbs, ¼ cup sugar, cinnamon, and butter. Press crumb mixture evenly over the bottom and 1½ to 2 inches up sides of pan.

4. In a bowl, beat cream cheese and eggs with a mixer until smooth. Add ¾ cup sugar, lemon peel and juice, lime peel and juice, vanilla, and ¼ cup liqueur; beat until smooth. Stir in 1½ cups of the nut brittle. Pour into crust-lined pan.

5. Bake in a 325° oven until center barely jiggles when cake is gently shaken, about 1 hour.

6. Meanwhile, mix sour cream with ¼ cup sugar and 1 tablespoon liqueur. Spoon onto hot cheesecake and gently spread to cover top. Return to oven and bake until sour cream is set when gently shaken, 10 to 15 minutes longer.

Flaming rum sets steamed persimmon pudding aglow. When the blaze subsides, slice the pudding and serve.

7. Run a thin-bladed knife between cake and pan rim. Refrigerate cake until cool, at least 3 hours. Serve, or cover and chill up to 2 days.

8. Remove pan rim, sprinkle remaining nut brittle onto cake, and cut cake into wedges.

Per serving: 339 cal., 66% (225 cal.) from fat; 5.6 g protein; 25 g fat (13 g sat.); 25 g carbo (0.3 g fiber); 213 mg sodium; 91 mg chol.

The Bakeshop's Sugar Pumpkin Pie

Prep and cook time: About 2½ hours

Notes: Carolyn Weil of the Bakeshop in Berkeley makes her pumpkin pies from scratch, using Sugar Pie pumpkin. It has a dense, sweet consistency when cooked. Sugar Pie pumpkins are sold in farmers' markets, specialty produce stores, and some supermarkets, especially near Halloween. The squash keeps well for weeks if stored in a cool, dry place. Or you can freeze the cooked purée.

The crust must be at least 1½ inches deep. Most purchased pie crusts in pans are too shallow.

Makes: 2 pies, 8 or 9 servings each

1	**Sugar Pie pumpkin** (about 3 lb.)
4	**large eggs**
⅔	cup firmly packed **brown sugar**
1¼	teaspoons **ground cinnamon**
¾	teaspoon **salt**
¾	teaspoon **ground ginger**
¼	teaspoon **ground cloves**
1¼	cups **dark corn syrup**
1¾	cups **half-and-half** (light cream) or whipping cream
2	baked 9-inch **pie crusts**

1. Cut pumpkin in half crosswise and set cut side down in a 10- by 15-inch pan. Bake in a 350° oven until very soft when pressed, about 1 hour.

2. When cool enough to touch, scoop out and discard pumpkin seeds. Scoop pumpkin flesh from rind and discard rind. Smoothly purée flesh in a blender; you need 2 cups. Seal any extra purée in plastic freezer bags and freeze up to 6 months.

3. In a bowl, beat to blend the 2 cups pumpkin purée, eggs, sugar, cinnamon, salt, ginger, and cloves. Stir in corn syrup and cream.

4. Set pie crusts in pans on a foil-lined baking sheet. Set baking sheet on the bottom rack of a 350° oven. Pour half the pumpkin mixture into each crust.

5. Bake until pie centers barely jiggle when gently shaken, 50 to 55 minutes. If crust rims start to get too dark, drape affected areas with foil.

6. Cool pies on racks. Serve warm or cool. If making ahead, cover and chill up to 1 day.

Per serving: 262 cal., 38% (99 cal.) from fat; 3.9 g protein; 11 g fat (3.7 g sat.); 40 g carbo (0.3 g fiber); 263 mg sodium; 56 mg chol.

Persimmon Pudding

Prep and cook time: About 3½ hours (including steaming and cooling)

Notes: *Sunset* food editor Jerry Di Vecchio uses jelly-soft ripe Hachiya persimmons or firm-ripe Fuyus. Rinse persimmons, discard stems, and trim off any spoiled spots. You need 2 or 3 Hachiyas (each about 3 in. wide) or 4 or 5 Fuyus (each 2¾ in. wide). Chop Fuyus but leave Hachiyas whole, and purée fruit smoothly in a blender.

Serve hot pudding with whipped cream or vanilla or eggnog ice cream.

Makes: 10 to 12 servings

½	teaspoon **ground nutmeg**
¼	cup chopped **candied ginger**
¾	cup **golden raisins**
¾	cup **chopped pitted dates**
1	cup **roasted pistachios**
1½	cups **sugar**
1½	cups **all-purpose flour**
1	tablespoon **baking soda**
1½	cups puréed **ripe persimmon pulp** (see notes)
2	**large eggs**
	About ¾ cup **rum**
2	teaspoons **vanilla**
¾	cup (⅜ lb.) **butter** or margarine, melted and cooled

1. In a large bowl, stir together nutmeg, ginger, raisins, dates, nuts, sugar, and flour.

2. In another bowl, mix baking soda with 3 tablespoons hot water. Add persimmon pulp and whisk to mix well. At once add eggs, ⅓ cup rum, vanilla, and butter and whisk to blend.

3. Add persimmon mixture (it thickens) to dry ingredients and stir until

batter is thoroughly moistened.

4. Scrape batter into a buttered 9- to 10-cup pudding mold with a tube; cover tightly. Elevate a rack at least 1 inch in a pan deep enough to hold pudding mold (8 qt. or larger). Pour water up to top of rack. Set pudding on rack. Cover pan and bring water to boiling. Keep water at a rapid boil, adding more hot water as needed to maintain water level.

5. Steam pudding until it feels firm when pressed lightly in the center, about 2½ hours.

6. Uncover pudding and let stand until slightly cooled, 20 to 30 minutes. Invert onto a dish and lift off mold. Serve. Or let the pudding cool, then return to mold and cover, or seal in foil, and chill up to 4 days. To reheat, steam pudding in mold (or sealed in foil) on rack above simmering water until hot, at least 45 minutes.

7. To flame, warm remaining rum in a 2- to 4-cup pan until bubbling at edges. Carefully ignite with a match (not beneath or near a fan, vent, or flammables) and pour slowly over pudding. Slice and serve.

Per serving: 496 cal., 34% (171 cal.) from fat; 5.8 g protein; 19 g fat (8.6 g sat.); 73 g carbo (2.6 g fiber); 457 mg sodium; 69 mg chol.

Eggnog Ice Cream

Prep and cook time: About 40 minutes, plus 20 to 25 minutes to freeze

Notes: Jennifer Welshhons, pastry chef at Wildwood Restaurant in Portland, serves this rich ice cream topped with hot Hazelnut Caramel Sauce (recipe follows).

Makes: About 4½ cups; 8 or 9 servings

  ½ cup **bourbon** (optional)

  2 cups **milk**

  1¼ cups **sugar**

  8 **large egg** yolks

  2 cups **whipping cream**

  ¾ teaspoon **ground nutmeg**

1. In an 8- to 10-inch frying pan over high heat, bring bourbon to a simmer. Remove from heat, carefully ignite with a match (not beneath or near a fan, vent, or flammables), and shake pan gently until flame dies. Set aside.

2. In a 3- to 4-quart pan over high heat, stir milk with sugar until simmering. Remove from heat and whisk some of

Cascades of hazelnut caramel sauce flow over luscious eggnog ice cream.

the hot liquid into yolks; then return mixture to pan.

3. Stir over low heat until custard coats the back of a spoon in a smooth, velvety layer, 6 to 9 minutes.

4. Remove from heat and stir in whipping cream, bourbon, and nutmeg. Pour mixture through a fine strainer into a large metal bowl; discard residue. Nest bowl of custard in ice and stir often until the mixture is cold, about 15 minutes.

5. Pour custard into an ice cream maker and freeze, following manufacturer's directions or until dasher is hard to turn.

6. Serve or, for firmer ice cream, store airtight in freezer at least 3 hours (or up to 1 week).

Per serving: 349 cal., 59% (207 cal.) from fat; 5.4 g protein; 23 g fat (13 g sat.); 32 g carbo (0 g fiber); 51 mg sodium; 256 mg chol.

Hazelnut Caramel Sauce

Prep and cook time: About 30 minutes

Notes: Make sauce up to 1 week ahead; cover and chill. It thickens as it cools. Warm in a microwave oven or stir in a pan over medium heat.

Makes: 1½ cups; 8 or 9 servings

  ½ cup **hazelnuts**

  ¾ cup **sugar**

  3 tablespoons **butter** or margarine, cut into chunks

  ½ cup **whipping cream**

  ¼ cup **hazelnut-flavor liqueur**

1. Put hazelnuts in an 8- or 9-inch pan. Bake in a 350° oven until nuts are golden under skins, 15 to 20 minutes. Pour onto a clean towel and, when cool enough to touch, rub nuts with fabric to loosen skins. Lift nuts from towel; discard skins. Coarsely chop nuts.

2. In a 10- to 12-inch nonstick frying pan over high heat, combine sugar and butter. Shake pan frequently to mix until sugar and butter are melted and amber colored, about 5 minutes; watch carefully.

3. Off the heat, add whipping cream (mixture foams); stir until caramel is smoothly mixed with cream. Stir in chopped nuts and liqueur.

4. Return sauce to medium heat and stir until boiling vigorously. Use sauce hot or cool.

Per serving: 196 cal., 55% (108 cal.) from fat; 1.1 g protein; 12 g fat (5.2 g sat.); 20 g carbo (0.5 g fiber); 44 mg sodium; 25 mg chol. ◆

The Quick Cook

MEALS IN 30 MINUTES OR LESS

by CHRISTINE WEBER HALE

APPETIZER PARTY FOR 12

Gingered Shrimp with Belgian Endive

Baked Brie with Green Salsa

Smoked Salmon with Dill

Sausage Bites with Mustards

Sugar Snap Peas, Cherry Tomatoes, and Baby-cut Carrots

Savory Dips   Selection of Olives

Seasoned Nuts, Plain and Fancy

Ten appetizers in half an hour

■ So you'd love to have a party during the holidays but think you don't have enough time? Think again. This hearty appetizer menu relies on purchased, almost-ready foods. With a few tweaks, they look like specialties of the house.

In addition to the recipe ingredients, you'll need the following.

•**Sausages:** 1½ to 2 pounds ready-to-heat cooked sausages, such as chicken-apple, fennel, or Polish (kielbasa). Use mini-sausages or cut large ones into 1-inch chunks. Heat them in a frying pan,

PLAN OF ATTACK

■ **The night before:** Assemble serving containers, utensils, and ingredients. Measure any ingredients that can stand, covered, at room temperature or in the refrigerator.

■**30 minutes before guests arrive:**

☐ **Prepare and bake** brie.

☐ **Heat** sausages and keep warm (in chafing dish with hot-water bath or on electric warming tray).

☐ **Prepare** shrimp and Belgian endive.

☐ **Prepare** salmon.

☐ **Rinse** vegetables. Moisten peeled baby-cut carrots with seasoned rice vinegar to keep fresh-looking. Group vegetables and dips on trays.

☐ **Put** olives, nuts, breads, chips, mustards, and sour cream in serving dishes.

the oven, or a microwave oven. Accompany with two or three kinds of mustard and serve with miniature pocket bread (16 to 24 pieces, cut into halves).

•**Vegetables:** 2 to 3 pounds.

•**Savory dips:** 2 to 3 cups hummus, tapenade, guacamole, or other favorites.

•**Olives:** 2 to 4 cups, such as ascolano, kalamata, manzanillo, and niçoise.

•**Seasoned nuts:** 2 to 4 cups.

Gingered Shrimp with Belgian Endive. In a bowl, mix 1 pound rinsed and drained **shelled cooked tiny shrimp** with ¾ teaspoon **wasabi paste** or prepared **horseradish,** ¼ cup chopped **pickled ginger,** and ¼ cup **seasoned rice vinegar.** Sprinkle with 1 tablespoon chopped **green onion.** Place bowl on a tray. Rinse 1 pound **Belgian endive,** trim off root ends, and separate leaves; arrange on tray and sprinkle with **coarse-ground pepper.** Spoon shrimp onto leaves to eat.

Per serving: 57 cal., 6.3% (3.6 cal.) from fat; 8.3 g protein; 0.4 g fat (0.1 g sat.); 4.5 g carbo (0.8 g fiber); 208 mg sodium; 74 mg chol.

Baked Brie with Green Salsa. Place a **whole brie cheese** (½ to 1 lb.) in a

shallow ovenproof casserole or pan 2 inches wider than the cheese. Spoon **prepared green salsa** (with tomatillos) about ½ inch deep (¾ to 1½ cups) around cheese. Dust cheese with **ground New Mexico chili** or chili powder (use a stencil if desired).

Bake in a 400° oven until melted in center, 8 to 10 minutes. (Or heat in a microwave oven at full power, 100%, for 4 to 6 minutes.) Keep hot on an electric warming tray or over a candle warmer to serve. Offer **tortilla chips** (4 cups) to spoon cheese and salsa onto.

Per serving: 143 cal., 59% (84 cal.) from fat; 5 g protein; 9.3 g fat (0.8 g sat.); 11 g carbo (1 g fiber); 302 mg sodium; 19 mg chol.

Smoked Salmon with Dill. Arrange ¾ pound **sliced smoked salmon** on a platter. Mix 2 tablespoons *each* chopped **fresh dill** and chopped **green onion,** 2 tablespoons **lemon juice,** and 1 teaspoon **sugar.** Spoon over salmon. Serve with 1 cup **sour cream** and 1 pound **thin-sliced black bread**.

Per serving: 171 cal., 34% (58 cal.) from fat; 9.1 g protein; 6.4 g fat (2.9 g sat.); 19 g carbo (2.3 g fiber); 487 mg sodium; 15 mg chol. ◆

Kitchen Cabinet

READERS' RECIPES TESTED IN SUNSET'S KITCHENS

by LINDA LAU ANUSASANANAN

For fresh ideas, start with vegetables

■ When Gemma Sciabica's mom baked these onions, Gemma and her siblings would say, "Gee, they look like chrysanthemums."

The name stuck. Gemma makes them now with her family's Marsala Olive Fruit Oil because it adds a nice mellow flavor to the onions.

Onion Chrysanthemums

Gemma S. Sciabica, Modesto, California

Prep and cook time: About 1½ hours
Makes: 4 to 6 servings

- 4 to 6 **onions** (6 to 8 oz. each)
- ¼ cup **olive oil**
  Salt, pepper, and **cayenne**
- ¼ cup **white wine vinegar**
- ¼ cup **pine nuts,** whole, or pecans, chopped
- 1 teaspoon chopped **fresh chives** or fresh rosemary leaves

1. Peel onions; trim tops. If needed, trim root ends slightly so onions sit flat.

2. Set each onion on its root end. From top, cut through middle of each onion to within ½ inch from bottom. Repeat cuts ½ to ¾ inch apart to make 10 or 12 attached wedges on each onion.

3. Set onions, cuts up, in a 9- by 13-inch pan. Drizzle evenly with oil, then sprinkle lightly with salt, pepper, and cayenne.

4. Bake, covered, in a 400° oven until onions are very tender when pierced in center, about 1 hour.

5. Uncover. Sprinkle onions evenly with vinegar, nuts, and chives, and bake until onion tips are lightly browned, 10 to 15 minutes longer. Serve hot or warm, spooning pan juices over onions.

Per serving: 170 cal., 64% (108 cal.) from fat; 3.2 g protein; 12 g fat (1.7 g sat.); 14 g carbo (3.1 g fiber); 4.8 mg sodium; 0 mg chol.

As cut onions bake, they soften and open like flowers.

Crab-filled Portabella Mushrooms

Carolyn Murray and Cindy LeaVerenz, Aptos, California

Originally, Cindy LeaVerenz stuffed button mushrooms with this crab mixture to make appetizers. Later, when she planned a dinner with Carolyn Murray, they turned the ingredients into a main dish by switching to large, meaty portabella mushrooms.

Prep and cook time: About 35 minutes
Makes: 4 servings

- 4 **portabella mushrooms** (4-in.-wide caps)
- 6 ounces **shelled cooked crab**
- 2 cups (8 oz.) **shredded mozzarella cheese**
- ¾ cup thinly sliced **green onions**
- 2 teaspoons **Worcestershire**

1. Rinse mushrooms and pat dry. Remove and chop stems.

2. Mix chopped stems with crab, cheese, onions, and Worcestershire.

3. Place mushrooms, cup side up, in a buttered 9- by 13-inch pan. Spoon crab mixture equally onto mushrooms, then press lightly to fit within caps.

4. Bake in a 350° oven until cheese melts and browns lightly, 20 to 25 minutes. Serve hot.

Per serving: 240 cal., 49% (117 cal.) from fat; 22 g protein; 13 g fat (7.6 g sat.); 8.4 g carbo (1.9 g fiber); 365 mg sodium; 87 mg chol.

JAMES CARRIER (2)

Arabic Eggplant Stew

Kathren McIntyre, Roseburg, Oregon

Keep it easy. This is Kathren McIntyre's favorite approach to cooking, which she ably applies in this vegetarian stew. It is good as a main dish and as a pasta sauce. We like it cold, too.

Prep and cook time: About 1¼ hours
Makes: 6 to 8 servings

- 2 pounds **eggplant**
- 3 **onions** (6 oz. each), chopped
- 1 tablespoon **olive oil**
- 1 can (14 oz.) **garbanzos**
- 2 cans (14½ oz. each) **diced tomatoes**
- **Salt** and **pepper**

1. Rinse eggplant. Trim off and discard stems. Cut eggplant into 2-inch cubes.

2. In a 9- by 13-inch pan, mix eggplant, onions, and oil.

3. Bake in a 450° oven, stirring occasionally, until eggplant is very soft when pressed, about 45 minutes.

4. Drain and rinse garbanzos. Drain tomatoes and reserve juice. Measure juice and add water to make 1⅓ cups.

5. Add garbanzos, tomatoes, and juice mixture to eggplant.

6. Continue to bake, stirring occasionally, until vegetables are hot, about 20 minutes. Add salt and pepper to taste.

Per serving: 123 cal., 21% (26 cal.) from fat; 4.7 g protein; 2.9 g fat (0.3 g sat.); 22 g carbo (4.9 g fiber); 229 mg sodium; 0 mg chol.

Risotto with Bitter Greens

Paul Franson, St. Helena, California

In Italy, Paul Franson was intrigued by the popularity of vegetables with a bitter edge. Although he finds the taste a little strong on its own, he enjoys the flavor of broccoli rabe when it's subdued by a creamy risotto.

Prep and cook time: About 50 minutes
Makes: 4 servings

- 1 pound **broccoli rabe** or Chinese broccoli (*gai laan*)
- 3 tablespoons **olive oil**
- ½ cup finely chopped **onion**
- 2 cloves **garlic,** minced
- 1 cup **arborio** or short- to medium-grain white **rice**
- ½ cup **dry white wine**
- About 4 cups **chicken broth**
- ¼ cup crumbled **chèvre** (goat) **cheese**

1. In a 5- to 6-quart pan, bring 3 quarts water to a boil over high heat. Plunge broccoli rabe into water and cook until bright green, about 2 minutes. Drain and immerse in cold water. When cool, drain and coarsely chop.

2. In the same pan over medium-high heat, combine oil and onion. Stir often for 3 minutes. Add garlic and stir often until onion is limp, about 2 minutes. Add rice, stir, then add wine. Stir until wine evaporates, about 1 minute.

3. Add 4 cups broth and bring to a boil on high heat, stirring. Reduce heat to simmering and stir often until rice is tender to bite, about 15 minutes.

4. Stir in broccoli and, for a creamier risotto, a little more broth. Stir often until broccoli is warm, 2 to 3 minutes.

5. Stir cheese into risotto, then spoon into wide bowls.

Per serving: 359 cal., 35% (126 cal.) from fat; 11 g protein; 14 g fat (3.9 g sat.); 48 g carbo (0.9 g fiber); 171 mg sodium; 10.4 mg chol.

German Poppy Seed Cake

Joni Schaper, Lancaster, California

"When Mom pulled out the poppy seed cake recipe, we knew it was a special occasion," says Joni Schaper.

Prep and cook time: About 1¾ hours
Makes: 16 servings

- About 1 cup (½ lb.) **butter** or margarine, at room temperature
- About 2½ cups **all-purpose flour**
- ½ cup (about 2½ oz.) **poppy seed**
- 1 cup **buttermilk**
- 2 teaspoons **almond extract**
- 4 **large eggs,** separated
- 2 cups **sugar**
- 1 teaspoon **baking powder**
- 1 teaspoon **baking soda**
- ½ teaspoon **salt**
- 1 tablespoon **ground cinnamon**

1. Butter and flour-dust a 10-inch

Blanched broccoli rabe adds a pleasant nip to creamy risotto with goat cheese.

decorative tube pan.

2. In a small bowl, mix poppy seed, buttermilk, and almond extract.

3. In a deep bowl, beat egg whites with a mixer on high until foamy. Continue beating and gradually add ¼ cup sugar. Beat until whites hold stiff, shiny peaks.

4. In another bowl, using unwashed beaters, beat 1 cup butter and 1½ cups sugar on high speed until light and fluffy. Add egg yolks and beat until well blended. Stir in poppy seed mixture.

5. Mix 2½ cups flour, baking powder, baking soda, and salt.

6. Add dry ingredients to batter; beat slowly to blend. Mix at medium speed.

7. Fold in beaten whites until blended.

8. Mix ¼ cup sugar and cinnamon. Pour half the batter into pan. Sprinkle with half the cinnamon mixture. Add remaining batter and sprinkle with remaining cinnamon mixture. Holding a knife vertically, draw blade through batter around tube.

9. Bake in 350° oven just until cake springs back when lightly pressed in center, 1 to 1¼ hours.

10. Cool in pan 15 minutes. Invert cake onto a plate. Serve warm or cool.

Per serving: 327 cal., 44% (144 cal.) from fat; 5 g protein; 16 g fat (8 g sat.); 43 g carbo (1 g fiber); 328 mg sodium; 85 mg chol. ◆

JAMES CARRIER

Fragrant with anise and cinnamon, bizcochitos provide a sweet ending to a New Mexican holiday buffet (recipe on page 285).

KITTY LEAKEN

December

foodguide

by JERRY ANNE DI VECCHIO

sweet

I first met John Scharffenberger when he was starting a winery to produce sparkling wines. The wines still bear his name, but John has moved on.

Now, Scharffen Berger is a label on San Francisco–made chocolate—not chocolate confections, but pure chocolate made from cocoa beans. John is buying beans based on origin and quality—including the extremely promising cocoa beans from Hawaii—and then using boutique techniques to roast the beans even more precisely than fine coffee beans are roasted.

The Scharffen Berger product is just another bit of evidence that chocolate is in for a quality upgrade. Before long, you can expect chocolate packaging to note appellations of origin, with the same implications of character as for wines. Starting this month, John's chocolate can be ordered—to eat, for confections, or for cooking. A 1½-kilogram (3.3 lb.) bittersweet bar, gift wrapped, costs $38, plus shipping. Call (800) 930-4528.

LEFT: LEIGH BEISCH RIGHT: JAMES CARRIER

LIGHT & EASY

A grand deception

■ The dictionary says *gratinée* means "to have a covering or crust, such as buttered crumbs or cheese." When the French do potatoes gratin, they are generous with the topping—and make sure there's plenty of cream beneath.

Our lighter alternative tastes deceptively rich, is extremely easy, and offers a welcome addition to holiday meals. The potato slices bake in a well-seasoned, fat-free broth instead of cream. Only a smidgen of cheese is needed at the end for a traditional look.

Lean Potatoes Gratin

Prep and cook time: About 1½ hours
Notes: If potatoes are sliced thinner than suggested, they tend to get gummy. The baking liquid bubbles vigorously and will spill out if the container is too small.

Makes: 4 to 6 servings

- 3¼ to 3½ pounds **thin-skinned potatoes**
- 3 cups fat-skimmed **chicken** or vegetable **broth**
- ½ teaspoon **ground nutmeg**
- ½ teaspoon **pepper**
- ⅓ cup shredded **gruyère**, cheddar, or fontina **cheese**

1. Peel potatoes and cut into ⅛- to ¼-inch-thick slices. Put the slices in a casserole (11- to 12-cup size, about 10 in. wide and 2 in. deep) and shake to settle the potatoes down into the container.

2. Mix the broth, ground nutmeg, and pepper. Pour the mixture over potatoes.

3. Bake in a 425° oven until potatoes are very tender when pierced, 1 hour to 1 hour and 15 minutes. As potatoes get dry on top, tilt casserole and spoon up some of the broth to baste them.

4. Sprinkle potatoes evenly with cheese. Bake until it melts, about 3 minutes more.

5. Let casserole sit 5 to 10 minutes for most of the remaining juices to soak into potatoes, then serve.

Per serving: 155 cal., 14% (22 cal.) from fat; 8.5 g protein; 2.4 g fat (1.2 g sat.); 25 g carbo (2.3 g fiber); 69 mg sodium; 6.9 mg chol.

Southwest Eggs Benedict

Prep and cook time: 25 minutes

Notes: Cook the eggs as you like—poached, fried, scrambled. Serve with hot black beans and crisp bacon. If you make cornbread with a mix, use a 14- to 15-ounce package.

Makes: 4 servings

- ¼ cup minced **onion**
- ¼ cup **white vinegar** (wine or distilled)
- 7 tablespoons **butter** or margarine
- 2 tablespoons **ground New Mexico** or California **chili** (or chili powder)
- ¼ teaspoon **cumin seed**
- ½ cup **chicken broth**
- 4 pieces **cornbread** (about 4 in. square), split, buttered, and toasted
- 1 firm-ripe **avocado** (about ½ lb.), pitted, peeled, and thinly sliced
- 4 to 8 **large eggs**, cooked to taste

1. In an 8- to 10-inch frying pan, combine onion, white vinegar, 1 tablespoon of the butter, ground chili, and cumin seed. Stir often over high heat just until sizzling, 2 to 3 minutes.

2. Add broth and boil until reduced to about ½ cup, 3 to 4 minutes.

3. Scrape mixture into a blender. Whirl until very smooth, then whirl in remaining 6 tablespoons butter, in chunks.

4. Place cornbread, toasted side up, on plates and garnish equally with avocado slices. Put eggs on cornbread and spoon chili sauce over them.

Per serving: 643 cal., 63% (405 cal.) from fat; 14 g protein; 45 g fat (20 g sat.); 49 g carbo (4.3 g fiber); 1,025 mg sodium; 330 mg chol.

A TASTE OF THE WEST

Hollandaise with a nip

■ Low-fat cooking techniques nearly always produce delicious alternatives for calorie-laden dishes. But to my taste, butter is vital to hollandaise sauce, and there's just no satisfying substitute. This means that eggs Benedict are re-served for a rare indulgence, usually during the holidays.

To give this old classic a festive presentation, consider a Southwestern version. Chilies really wake up the hollandaise, cornbread replaces the English muffins, and bacon, avocado, and beans complete the plate.

This interpretation isn't any less excessive—just livelier and harder to resist, with onion and the ground chili replacing eggs as the sauce's foundation.

GREAT TOOLS

Designs on nutcrackers

■ If a tool does a job well, even if it's only one, it's a blessing to own and a joy to use. This is especially true when it comes to nutcrackers.

The Texan Nut Sheller nips pecan shells from the sides of the nut, releasing it in perfect halves. Also suitable for Brazil nuts, almonds, walnuts, and hazelnuts. $14.90, including shipping; check or money order only. The Texan Nut Sheller Co., Box 2900, San Angelo, TX 76902; (800) 844-2760.

Reed's Rocket Nut Cracker is recommended by the Hazelnut Marketing Board in Oregon. The manufacturer also suggests it for almonds, Brazil nuts, pecans, and walnuts. $16, including shipping; check or money order only. Reed's Machine Co., 900 Thayer St., Little Rock, AR 72202; (501) 372-3105.

The MacCrak guillotine twists down and neatly cuts right through tough shells—perfect for macadamias. It also does a tidy job of splitting walnut shells at the seam. $15, including shipping; check or money order only. Cooper's Nut House, 1378 Willow Glen Rd., Fallbrook, CA 92028; (760) 728-6407.

The MacBuster Nut Cracker, on the other hand, has the leverage to put enough pressure on a macadamia shell to pop it open. $29.95, plus shipping; credit cards okay. Bono Macs of Hawaii, 90 N. Lanikai Pl., Haiku, Maui, HI, 96708; (808) 572-1043. Or 11881 Arroyo St., Santa Ana, CA 92705; (714) 838-8539.

The Pistachio Nut Opener twists and splits shells apart. This sterling silver pick comes with a storage pouch. $25, plus shipping; Visa and MasterCard. JMB Imports; (800) 201-8382.

Shreds of parmesan cheese bake into crisp crackers.

QUICK TRICK

Crisp lace

■ All you need to make cheese crackers is one ingredient: a chunk of parmesan cheese. If you like that ingredient, you'll like this appetizer or salad accompaniment. And it's ready in 15 minutes or less.

Just lightly oil a nonstick baking sheet, or cover a regular baking sheet with silicone-finished parchment or a silicone liner. Mound thinly shredded **parmesan cheese** on the pan, using 2 tablespoons per cracker. Place the portions at least 6 inches apart, then spread each mound into a 5- to 6-inch round with your fingertips.

Bake in a 375° oven until cheese is pale golden brown and melded together, 3 to 4 minutes. Watch carefully—cheese tastes scorched if overbaked.

While crackers are hot and flexible, lift from pan 1 at a time with a wide spatula and drape over a rolling pin (or a room-temperature wine bottle) until cool and rigid. Then use or package airtight at once. (If making crackers ahead, refrigerate up to 6 days.)

Note: To get a lacy look, the cheese must be freshly shredded (the longer the shreds, the better) so it sticks together.

Per cracker: 58 cal., 60% (35 cal.) from fat; 5.1 g protein; 3.9 g fat (2.4 g sat.); 0.5 g carbo (0 g fiber); 227 mg sodium; 9.6 mg chol.

FLAVOR TRENDS

The tang of tamarind

■ Among the increasingly exotic soup mixes in the supermarket are Indian *sambar* and *rasam* and Thai lemon grass (*tom yum*). Look for ones with tamarind listed as an ingredient—it gives them an elusive, floral tartness. (If salt is listed first in a soup mix, you may want to dice a potato and add it to the soup as it simmers to tone down the saltiness.)

Tamarind is also an important element in many Indian chutneys, Thai curries, and other dishes. Tamarind is a curious, sticky brown fruit that looks like a big dried bean pod. The pods and pastes of the fruit are sold in some supermarkets and Mexican and Asian food markets. ◆

The Wine Guide

by KAREN MACNEIL

A toast for rosé

■ Like the intelligent, pretty child who gets more attention for looks than brains, rosé sparkling wine usually isn't taken seriously. It's pink, people say to themselves—how profound can it be?

In a word, very.

Rosé Champagne and rosé sparkling wine may well represent the most fascinating bubblies in the world. Far from being considered frivolous, these are the sparkling wines that well-studied wine drinkers crave.

Why? Well, first, because the great ones are scrumptious. Dry, crisp, and elegant, they often have irresistible creamy, wild berry flavors. But rosé bubblies are also treasured because they are rare and an enormous challenge to make (a rosé gone awry smells something like a bad permanent).

This leads us to the third, and perhaps most important, reason rosé sparklers are prized—they are usually made with a significant amount of Pinot Noir (all Champagnes and top sparkling wines are based on Chardonnay, Pinot Meunier, and Pinot Noir).

And Pinot Noir is anything but silly. In fact, it's Pinot that gives Champagne and sparkling wine much of their depth, body, and complexity. As a general rule, rosé Champagnes and sparklers often have more oomph and more moxie than many golden bubblies. This can be a real asset, especially when you're serving the wine with a flavorful food.

No discussion of Champagnes and sparkling wines is complete without an explanation of the difference between the two. In a nutshell: by France's definition, the wine called Champagne can technically come only from the region of Champagne, about 90 miles northeast of Paris. American sparkling wine comes mostly from California, though a little is made in Washington, Oregon, and

New York—there's even a sparkler made in New Mexico.

The place makes all the difference when it comes to wine. Different soils, different climates, different ways of picking, even different ideologies mean that Champagne and California sparklers have entirely different personalities.

We're talking here only about the top sparklers—those made by what is called the méthode Champenoise, or Champagne method. (This is almost always noted on the label.) The Champagne method is painstaking, complex, labor intensive, and expensive, but it's critical to the elegance and complexity of the wine. By comparison, cheap bubblies, which are made by injecting carbon dioxide gas into the wine, have all the nuance of a soft drink.

Producing the top rosé sparklers involves one of two procedures. The traditional approach is to let some of the wine sit in contact with Pinot Noir skins, picking up just enough color to tint the wine pink.

The other approach, more modern and more common, involves adding a

WINE DICTIONARY
Extra dry

A confusing designation, for the term actually refers to Champagne or sparkling wine that is slightly sweet, containing 1.2 to 2 percent residual sugar. — *K. M.*

small bit of still Pinot Noir wine to each bottle during the Champagne process. This technique is preferred for several reasons, among them the fact that such rosés seem to age better.

Both processes are complex, and achieving a certain coloration is difficult, as a lineup of rosé Champagnes will attest. The colors range from almost translucent pink to deep coppery salmon.

Most rosé sparklers from Champagne and the United States are made in a brut style—that is, dry. Some, in fact, are so dry they are positively racy on the palate.

This holiday season, why not think pink? Above are some of our favorites from California and France. ◆

FAVORITE FESTIVE ROSÉ SPARKLERS

■ *Codorniu Napa Brut Rosé*, $20 (Carneros, California). Very light and delicate with touches of boysenberry and hazelnuts.

■ *Deutz Cuvée Marie Damarisse Brut Rosé*, $35 (Champagne, France). Like drinking in a strawberry patch.

■ *Domaine Carneros Brut Rosé 1995*, $26 (Carneros). Sophisticated and elegant with creamy rushes of berry flavor.

■ *Roederer Estate Brut Rosé*, $22 (Anderson Valley, California). Very sleek and racy with hints of wild strawberry. A fabulous aperitif.

■ *Schramsberg Brut Rosé*, $23 (Napa Valley, California). Lush and creamy with biscuity berry flavors—liquid strawberry shortcake.

■ *Taittinger Comtes de Champagne Rosé 1991*, $150 (Champagne). Expensive, yes, but one of the great rosé experiences. Hauntingly deep, rich, and long.

■ *Veuve Clicquot Rosé 1988*, $65 (Champagne). Dramatic, elegant, and round with notes of spiced berries and roasted nuts.

Brimming with New Mexican favorites — tamales, posole, chili-corn muffins, and bizcochitos — this buffet table holds just half of the party menu.

CHRISTMAS EVE IN
Santa Fe

*Deck the halls with farolitos, fill the bowls with posole, and
invite friends to a holiday open-house buffet*

by LINDA LAU ANUSASANANAN

■ It's Christmas Eve on Santa Fe's well-known Canyon Road. Thousands of *farolitos,* twinkling like fallen stars, light the way for strollers who've come to enjoy this traditional procession. And as the neighborhood glows, parties flourish. ■ Michael McLaughlin and Christopher Hill, who have homes that share an adobe-walled courtyard, cohost a double open house. Farolitos, 500 in all, line their compound's walls. And a bonfire in the center keeps guests warm as they sing carols, then wander from one house to the other to enjoy New Mexican specialties from two buffets. ■ McLaughlin, a food writer and avid cook, prepares seven dishes ahead and then allocates each of them to one of the buffets, rounding out each menu with purchased items and edible gifts he and Hill receive. ■ This flexible menu grows or shrinks to fit large or small groups. You can make all these dishes and serve a grand buffet for 24, or cut the party in half—for 12 guests, select one appetizer, one soup, and one cookie, and offer either tamales or turkey for sandwiches. ■ Follow McLaughlin's design and serve a big party from two buffets, or to encourage guests to move and mingle, set up each self-serve course at a different location—coffee table, one end of a buffet, dining room table, even the patio if the weather is mild.

*Glowing farolitos illuminate the courtyard,
as a bonfire greets all comers.*

Open-House Buffet for 24
Sesame-Nut Crunch
Salsas, Dips, and Tortilla Chips
Christmas Posole
Black Bean Soup with Hot-Sauce Bar
Hickory-smoked Turkey
Apricot, Cherry, and Green Chili Chutney
Assorted Mustards and Mayonnaise
Sandwich Breads and Rolls
Tiny Chili and Corn Muffins
Steamed Tamales
Extra-Spicy Gingersnaps
Bizcochitos   House-Gift Desserts
Self-serve Beverage Bar
Chimayó Punch   Mexican Hot Chocolate

KITTY LEAKEN (2)

As guests flow through the neighboring homes, they enjoy savory posole and purchased tamales.

KITTY LEAKEN

Sesame-Nut Crunch

Prep and cook time: About 35 minutes

Notes: If desired, use salted butter and omit salt. If making up to 2 days in advance, store airtight.

Makes: 2½ pounds

    About ½ cup (¼ lb.) **unsalted butter**

1   cup firmly packed **brown sugar**

¼   cup **light corn syrup**

1¾ teaspoons **cayenne**

½   teaspoon **salt**

2½ cups (¾ lb.) **hulled salted roasted peanuts**

2½ cups (¾ lb.) **salted roasted cashews**

½   cup (2½ oz.) **hulled salted roasted sunflower seed**

3   tablespoons **sesame seed**

1. Butter a sheet of foil, about 12 by 17 inches.

2. In a nonstick 5- to 6-quart pan over medium heat, frequently stir ½ cup butter, brown sugar, corn syrup, cayenne, and salt until melted and smooth, about 5 minutes.

3. Add peanuts, cashews, sunflower seed, and sesame seed. Turn heat to high and stir until mixture is very thick and nuts begin to brown, 4 to 6 minutes.

4. Immediately pour mixture onto buttered foil, spreading as thinly as possible with back of a spoon. Cool until mixture is lukewarm, about 15 minutes.

5. With your hands, release brittle from foil, then pull or break it into bite-size pieces. When cool, immediately store airtight (otherwise, the coating absorbs moisture and gets sticky).

Per 2 ounces: 322 cal., 67% (216 cal.) from fat; 8.2 g protein; 24 g fat (6.1 g sat.); 23 g carbo (2.8 g fiber); 269 mg sodium; 13 mg chol.

Christmas Posole

Prep and cook time: About 3½ hours, plus 8 hours to soak posole

Notes: In lieu of posole (see below), use 3 to 4 cans (each about 14½ oz.) hominy, rinsed and drained. Add only 4 cups water to the soup, and add hominy after meat is tender. Make this dish up to 3 days ahead, cool, cover, and chill. It thickens, so thin with more broth or water when reheating.

Makes: 12 to 14 cups

¾ to 1 pound **dried posole** or 2 pounds soaked dried posole

1¼ pounds **boned, fat-trimmed pork shoulder** (butt) or shoulder end of pork loin

4   cups chopped **onions**

8   cloves **garlic,** minced

1   tablespoon **dried oregano**

1   can (49 oz.) or 6 cups **reduced-sodium chicken broth**

½   to 1¼ cups **canned red chili (enchilada) sauce**

    About ⅓ cup chopped **roasted poblano chilies** (directions follow) or canned green chilies

1   teaspoon **pepper**

    Salt

1. Rinse dried posole and let stand in 3 quarts water at room temperature at least 8 hours or up to 1 day. Drain.

2. Cut meat into ½-inch cubes.

3. In a 5- to 6-quart pan, combine pork, onions, garlic, oregano, and ½ cup broth. Cover and bring to a boil over high heat; reduce heat to medium and boil 20 minutes. Uncover and cook over high heat, stirring often, until juices evaporate and meat is sizzling in browned drippings, 15 to 20 minutes. Add ¾ cup broth, stir browned bits free, and boil until liquid evaporates, then stir pork until it's lightly browned, 10 to 15 minutes.

4. Add remaining broth, 5 cups water, and drained posole; stir drippings free. Bring to a boil, then cover and simmer until pork is almost tender to bite, about 1½ hours; stir occasionally.

5. Add ½ cup red chili sauce, ⅓ cup poblano chilies, and pepper. Simmer, covered, until pork and posole are very tender to bite, 15 to 30 minutes longer. Stew should be soupy; if needed, add more water to thin. Add salt and additional red chili sauce and poblano chilies to taste.

Per ½ cup: 82 cal., 22% (18 cal.) from fat; 5.5 g protein; 2 g fat (0.6 g sat.); 9.7 g carbo (1.6 g fiber); 203 mg sodium; 14 mg chol.

Roasted Poblano Chilies

Prep and cook time: About 20 minutes

Notes: Fresh poblano chilies, often mislabeled pasillas, are easy to identify because they are very dark green. If you can't find poblanos, use green New

---

Posole or *pozole,* corn or stew?

Ask for posole in New Mexico and you might get a bag of big, chewy corn kernels or a soupy, chili-spiked stew made with the corn.

Posole, the corn (in Mexico, it's spelled with a *z* instead of an *s*), is large, dried kernels of field corn boiled with water and hydrate lime. The lime mixture keeps the kernels firm and softens the hulls so they will slide off. The boiled posole is thoroughly washed and drained, but it still needs more cooking. Boiled posole is sold refrigerated or frozen in many Mexican supermarkets, particularly in New Mexico, Arizona, and Southern California.

The boiled posole can also be dried, in which case it needs to be soaked before it's ready to cook. You can order dried white- or blue-corn posole for $2.50 to $5 a pound, plus shipping. Canned hominy is an easy alternative.

    Bueno Foods, 2001 Fourth St. S.W., Albuquerque, NM 87102; (800) 952-4453. Minimum order, four packages (12-oz. size).

    Chile Shop, 109 E. Water St., Santa Fe, NM 87501; (505) 983-6080.

    Old Southwest Trading Company, Box 7545, Albuquerque, NM 87194; (505) 836-0168.

    Santa Fe School of Cooking, 116 W. San Francisco St., Santa Fe, NM 87501; (800) 982-4688.

Mexico chilies, which are also called California or Anaheim chilies. If making ahead, cover and refrigerate chilies up to 2 days; freeze to store longer.

Makes: About 1⅓ cups

1. Rinse about 1⅓ pounds **fresh poblano chilies** and pat dry. Lay in single layer on a 10- by 15-inch pan. Broil 3 to 4 inches from heat, turning as needed to char skin on all sides, about 10 minutes. Let stand until cool.

2. Pull off chili skins and discard. Remove and discard stems and seeds. Chop chilies.

Per ⅓ cup: 44 cal., 4.1% (1.8 cal.) from fat; 2.2 g protein; 0.2 g fat (0 g sat.); 10 g carbo (1.6 g fiber); 7.7 mg sodium; 0 mg chol.

Black Bean Soup

Prep and cook time: About 2 hours

Notes: If making soup up to 3 days ahead, cool, cover, and chill. Or make weeks ahead and freeze. The soup thickens, so thin with more broth or water when reheating. Offer sour cream and hot sauce as accompaniments.

Makes: 11 to 12 cups

2 tablespoons **olive oil**

3 cups chopped **onions**

1 **green bell pepper** (½ lb.), stemmed, seeded, and chopped

1 cup chopped **celery,** including leaves

4 cloves **garlic,** minced

1¼ teaspoons **dried thyme**

1 **dried bay leaf**

1 pound **dried black beans**

1 can (49 oz.) or 6 cups **reduced-sodium chicken broth**

1 **smoked ham hock** (about 1¼ lb.), cut in half lengthwise

⅓ cup **medium-dry madeira** or dry sherry

¾ teaspoon **pepper**

Salt

1. In a 6- to 8-quart pan over medium heat, combine oil, onions, green pepper, celery, garlic, thyme, and bay leaf. Cover and stir occasionally until vegetables are limp, about 10 minutes.

2. Sort through the beans and discard debris. Rinse and drain beans.

3. Add beans, broth, 3 cups water, and ham hock to pan. Bring to a boil over high heat.

4. Turn heat to low. Cover and simmer, stirring often, until ham hock is very tender when pierced, about 1½ hours.

5. With a slotted spoon, lift out hock. Let stand until cool enough to touch. If beans are soft when pressed, remove from heat. If not, cover and continue to simmer until they are. Pull meat off the hock, discarding bones and skin. Chop meat and return to soup.

6. Add madeira to soup and stir over medium heat until steaming. Discard bay leaf. Add pepper and salt to taste.

7. For a thicker soup, purée up to half of it in a blender or food processor, then return to pan and stir. Serve hot.

Per ½ cup: 109 cal., 18% (20 cal.) from fat; 6.1 g protein; 2.2 g fat (0.4 g sat.); 15 g carbo (3.1 g fiber); 340 mg sodium; 3.6 mg chol.

Apricot, Cherry, and Green Chili Chutney

Prep and cook time: About 1 hour

Notes: If making up to 1 month ahead, cool, cover, and chill.

Makes: About 4 cups

2½ cups **dried apricots,** coarsely chopped

1½ cups **cider vinegar**

1½ cups **sugar**

1 cup chopped **roasted poblano chilies** (directions precede) or canned green chilies

½ cup **dried sweet cherries,** chopped

½ cup chopped **red onion**

1 **cinnamon stick** (3 in.)

1½ teaspoons **mustard seed**

¾ teaspoon **salt**

1. In a 3- to 4-quart pan over high heat, combine apricots, vinegar, sugar, chilies, cherries, onion, cinnamon, mustard seed, and salt.

2. Bring to a boil. Turn heat to low. Cover and simmer, stirring occasionally, until apricots are soft when pierced, 20 to 25 minutes. Uncover and simmer until most of the liquid evaporates, about 5 minutes longer.

3. Let cool, discard cinnamon, and serve chutney, or cover and chill.

Per 2 tablespoons: 73 cal., 1.2% (0.9 cal.) from fat; 0.7 g protein; 0.1 g fat (0 g sat.); 19 g carbo (1 g fiber); 54 mg sodium; 0 mg chol.

Season black bean soup with liquid fire selected from the hot-sauce bar.

NOEL BARNHURST

Tiny Chili and Corn Muffins

Prep and cook time: About 50 minutes

Notes: Bake muffins 1 day ahead, cool, package airtight, and hold at room temperature. Or freeze to store longer; thaw wrapped. Reheat unwrapped muffins on a baking sheet in a 350° oven until warm, about 5 minutes.

Makes: 4 dozen

- ½ cup **pine nuts**
- About ½ cup (¼ lb.) **butter** or margarine, melted
- 1 cup **yellow cornmeal**
- 1 cup **all-purpose flour**
- ⅓ cup **sugar**
- 2½ teaspoons **baking powder**
- ¼ teaspoon **salt**
- ½ cup **canned cream-style corn**
- ½ cup **sour cream**
- ½ cup chopped **fresh jalapeño chilies**
- 1 **large egg**

1. Bake nuts in a 9-inch-wide pan in a 375° oven until golden, stirring occasionally, 4 to 6 minutes. Pour from pan into a large bowl.

2. Butter about 4 dozen muffin cups (1¼ in. across bottom). Bake in sequence if you don't have enough pans.

3. To nuts, add cornmeal, flour, sugar, baking powder, and salt. Mix.

4. In a small bowl, whisk corn with sour cream, chilies, egg, and ½ cup

One dessert choice: gingersnaps with frothy Mexican hot chocolate.

Easy apricot, cherry, and chili chutney zips up smoked-turkey sandwich.

NOEL BARNHURST (2)

melted butter until mixed. Add wet ingredients to dry and stir just until batter is moistened.

5. Fill muffin cups three-quarters full.

6. Bake in a 375° oven until lightly browned, 12 to 15 minutes. Cool in pans for 2 minutes. Tip out of pans into a cloth-lined basket or onto a rack to cool. Serve hot or warm.

Per muffin: 64 cal., 53% (34 cal.) from fat; 1.2 g protein; 3.8 g fat (1.9 g sat.); 6.6 g carbo (0.4 g fiber); 72 mg sodium; 12 mg chol.

Extra-Spicy Gingersnaps

Prep and cook time: About 40 minutes, plus 20 minutes to chill dough

Notes: Store airtight at room temperature up to 3 days or freeze for longer storage.

Makes: 5 dozen cookies

- 2 cups **all-purpose flour**
- 2 teaspoons **baking soda**
- 2 teaspoons **ground ginger**
- 1 teaspoon **ground cinnamon**
- ½ teaspoon **dry mustard**
- ½ teaspoon **white pepper**
- ½ teaspoon **ground cardamom**
- ¼ teaspoon **ground cloves**
- ¼ teaspoon **salt**
- About ¾ cup (⅜ lb.) **butter** or margarine
- 1 cup firmly packed **dark brown sugar**
- 1 **large egg**
- ¼ cup **molasses**
- 3 tablespoons **granulated sugar**

1. Mix flour, baking soda, ginger, cinnamon, mustard, pepper, cardamom, cloves, and salt.

2. In a large bowl, with a mixer on high speed, beat ¾ cup butter with brown sugar until well blended. Add egg and molasses; beat until fluffy.

3. Add flour mixture. Beat on low speed to blend, then on medium speed until well mixed.

4. Divide dough in half, shape each half into a ball, wrap in plastic wrap, and pat into a flat cake. Freeze about 20 minutes, or chill 1 to 2 hours until firm.

5. Shape dough into 1-inch balls. Roll to coat with granulated sugar, and set at least 2 inches apart on buttered baking sheets.

6. Bake cookies in a 350° oven until slightly darker brown on the bottom, about 10 minutes (if using 1 oven, switch pan positions after 5 min.).

7. Cool on pan about 5 minutes, then transfer cookies to racks to cool. Serve, or store airtight.

Per cookie: 58 cal., 40% (23 cal.) from fat; 0.6 g protein; 2.6 g fat (1.5 g sat.); 8.4 g carbo (0.1 g fiber); 79 mg sodium; 10 mg chol.

Bizcochitos

Prep and cook time: About 45 minutes

Notes: Butter can be used instead of lard, but the texture and flavor of the cookies will not be as authentic. Store cookies airtight up to 3 days; freeze to store longer.

Makes: 9 dozen, 1½ inches wide

About 3 cups **all-purpose flour**

1½ teaspoons **baking powder**

½ teaspoon **salt**

1 cup (½ lb.) **lard**

⅔ cup plus 2 tablespoons **sugar**

¾ to 1 teaspoon **anise seed**

1 **large egg**

¼ cup **medium-dry sherry**, brandy, or orange juice

1 tablespoon **Chinese five spice** or ground cinnamon

1. Mix 3 cups flour, baking powder, and salt.

KITTY LEAKEN

Without bizcochitos, it wouldn't be Christmas in New Mexico.

2. In a bowl, with a mixer on high speed, beat lard, ⅔ cup sugar, and anise seed until fluffy.

3. Beat in egg until blended.

4. On medium speed, mix in sherry.

5. Add dry ingredients. Stir to combine, then beat until well blended.

6. On a plate, mix remaining 2 tablespoons sugar and Chinese five spice.

7. Divide dough in half. Pat each half into a ball. On a well-floured board, roll dough, a portion at a time, ¼ inch thick. With a flour-dusted cookie cutter (plain or a simple design, about 1½ in.

wide), cut dough into shapes.

8. One at a time, dip top of each cookie in spiced sugar, pressing lightly so sugar sticks. Set cookies, sugar side up, about ½ inch apart on ungreased baking sheets. Gather dough scraps into a ball, roll out, and cut more cookies.

9. Bake cookies in a 325° oven until bottoms are golden, about 10 minutes (if using 1 oven, switch pan positions after 5 min.). Transfer to racks to cool. Serve, or let cool and package airtight.

Per cookie: 40 cal., 50% (20 cal.) from fat; 0.4 g protein; 2.2 g fat (0.8 g sat.); 4.3 g carbo (0.1 g fiber); 18 mg sodium; 4 mg chol. ◆

The party planner countdown

☐ **UP TO A MONTH AHEAD**
•***Make*** the chutney.

☐ **UP TO 3 DAYS AHEAD**
•***Make*** the posole, bean soup, gingersnaps, and bizcochitos.

☐ **UP TO 2 DAYS AHEAD**
•***Make*** the sesame-nut crunch.
•***Purchase*** a selection of tortilla chips, salsas, and dips, including refried beans, guacamole, and Latino creams such as crema Mexicana agria (salted sour cream) and crema Centroamericana (thick and tangy)—they're sold in Latino food markets.
•***Buy*** a cooked smoked turkey or two boned smoked turkey breasts.
•***Buy*** tamales from a Mexican restaurant or food market.
•***Buy*** hot sauces, mustards, mayon-

naise, ingredients for the Chimayó punch and Mexican hot chocolate, and supplies for the beverage bar, such as beer, wine, soft drinks, and ice.

☐ **UP TO 1 DAY AHEAD**
•***Make*** the muffins.
•***Buy*** sandwich breads and rolls.

☐ **PARTY DAY, IN THE MORNING**
•***Set out*** serving pieces and ***arrange*** buffets or small tables.
•***Put*** hot sauces where bean soup will be served.

☐ **ABOUT 2 HOURS AHEAD**
•***Arrange*** sesame-nut crunch; chips, salsas, and dips; and the beverage bar.

☐ **ABOUT 1 HOUR AHEAD**
•***Slowly warm*** posole and bean soup,

then keep warm in tureens for guests to ladle into mugs.
•***Steam*** tamales (or heat in batches in a microwave oven); keep warm in steamer until ready to serve.
•***Carve*** turkey, or present whole and let guests slice portions to make into sandwiches. Accompany with the chutney, mustards, mayonnaise, and breads.
•***Assemble*** Chimayó punch ingredients: Heat apple cider and keep warm. Guests ladle cider into mugs or glasses and enhance with tequila and a light touch of crème de cassis.
•***Make*** Mexican hot chocolate: chop chocolate flavored with cinnamon, almonds, and sugar (sold in many supermarkets and most Latino food markets), and heat with milk. Keep warm.
•***Reheat*** muffins and keep warm.
•***Set out*** cookies, and as guests arrive, add any sweet house gifts—fruitcake, chocolates, or cookies.

NATIVE AMERICAN
holiday feast

An Indian heritage and a love of good food inspire this special dinner

by LINDA LAU ANUSASANANAN
food photographs by RICHARD JUNG

■ "Sometimes I feel I'm at war with myself. I'm half Pilgrim and half Indian," says Loretta Barrett Oden. Her mother is a daughter of the Citizen Potawatomi Nation in Oklahoma. And her father is part Irish with *Mayflower* connections. The mix is complex. ■ Oden's riveting blue-green eyes and high cheekbones give evidence of her heritage, but her cooking is one-sided. As owner of Santa Fe's Corn Dance Cafe, Oden says, "I of-

fer a taste of Native America for today's palate."
■ And for this holiday dinner, she weaves together the rich bounty of foods native to the Americas—including some of the dishes she serves at the Corn Dance. The indigenous Plains and Southwest ingredients—buffalo, chilies, corn, juniper berries, pine nuts, sage, and squash—work with other New World foods like chocolate and quinoa. It all makes for a most memorable feast.

DOUGLAS MERRIAM

Loretta Oden's inspirations come from New World foods and Native American traditions.

Native American Christmas feast for 10 to 12

Potawatomi Popcorn

Chenin Blanc

**Field Greens
with Sage-Piñon Vinaigrette**

**Crusted Tenderloin
with Chipotle Onions**

Oven-roasted Roots

Quinoa and Wild Rice Stuffed Squash

Mushroom and Sunchoke Sauté

Cabernet Sauvignon

Simply A'Maize'ing Corn Ice Cream

Chocolate Sorbet • Raspberry Sauce

Sparkling Wine

The main course: juniper-crusted beef and vegetables served with stuffed squash and sautéed mushrooms.

Potawatomi Popcorn

Prep and cook time: About 6 minutes

Notes: Poultry seasoning may not sound native, but its principal ingredient is sage—which grows wild in the Southwest.

Makes: 10 to 12 servings

- 3 quarts popped **popcorn**
- 3 tablespoons melted **butter** or margarine
- 1½ teaspoons **poultry seasoning**
- ½ to ¾ teaspoon **cayenne**

  Salt

In a large bag or bowl, mix popcorn, melted butter, poultry seasoning, cayenne, and salt to taste.

Per serving: 57 cal., 51% (29 cal.) from fat; 1 g protein; 3.2 g fat (1.8 g sat.); 6.4 g carbo (1.2 g fiber); 30 mg sodium; 7.8 mg chol.

Field Greens with Sage-Piñon Vinaigrette

Prep and cook time: About 7 minutes

Notes: Up to 1 day ahead, toast nuts and store airtight. Make dressing and hold at room temperature. Also rinse salad leaves, wrap in towels, enclose in a plastic bag, and chill.

Makes: 10 to 12 servings

- ¼ cup **pine nuts**
- ¼ cup **olive oil**
- 2 tablespoons chopped **fresh sage** leaves or 1 teaspoon dried rubbed sage
- 2 tablespoons **balsamic vinegar**
- 1 clove **garlic,** minced
- 3 quarts (about 10 oz.) **mixed tender salad leaves,** rinsed and crisped

  Salt and **pepper**

1. In a 6- to 8-inch frying pan over medium heat, stir nuts until golden, about 4 minutes. Pour from pan and coarsely chop half the nuts.

2. In a blender, whirl chopped nuts, oil, sage, vinegar, and garlic until smooth.

3. In a large bowl, gently mix salad leaves with dressing to coat well, then add remaining nuts. Season to taste with salt and pepper.

Per serving: 61 cal., 90% (55 cal.) from fat; 1.1 g protein; 6.1 g fat (0.8 g sat.); 1.4 g carbo (0.6 g fiber); 5.7 mg sodium; 0 mg chol.

Crusted Tenderloin with Chipotle Onions

Prep and cook time: About 1 hour

Notes: Oden uses buffalo tenderloin, but it's costly (see box, facing page). Beef tenderloin is a good option. Both roasts take about the same time to cook. However, if buffalo is cooked beyond rare, the meat is dry.

Makes: 10 to 12 servings

- 1 tablespoon **juniper berries**
- 1 tablespoon **coriander seed**
- 1 tablespoon **dried oregano**
- 1½ teaspoons **black peppercorns**
- ½ teaspoon **kosher salt**
- 5 whole **allspice**
- 2 whole **cloves**
- 1½ tablespoons chopped **pecans**
- 4 cloves **garlic,** chopped
- 1 **beef** or buffalo **tenderloin** (4 to 5 lb.), fat trimmed, rolled, and tied
- 1 **canned chipotle chili**
- 1 **onion** (½ lb.), thinly sliced
- 1 tablespoon **salad oil**
- 2 cups **beef broth**

  Salt and **pepper**

1. In a blender, finely grind juniper berries, coriander, oregano, pepper, kosher salt, allspice, cloves, and pecans. Add the garlic and whirl to form a paste.

2. Rub seasoning paste all over tenderloin. Set meat on a rack in a 12- by 17-inch roasting pan. Roast in a 425° oven for 20 minutes.

3. Meanwhile, rinse the canned chipotle chili, discard seeds and veins, and mince chili.

4. Mix onion slices with oil and put in roasting pan around meat (not on rack). Continue to cook until a thermometer inserted in center of the thickest part of meat registers 130° for rare, 30 to 40 minutes longer.

5. Transfer roast to a platter and let rest in a warm place 10 to 15 minutes (to allow juices to settle and meat to firm slightly for neater slicing).

6. Skim and discard any fat from drippings in roasting pan. Add minced chipotle and broth to onions in pan. Set pan over high heat and scrape browned bits free, stirring until mixture boils vigorously. Pour into a bowl.

7. Slice meat and offer chipotle-onion

Root vegetables, seasoned with wine, balsamic vinegar, and herbs, are garnished with roasted garlic heads.

sauce to spoon over portions. Add salt and pepper to taste.

Per serving: 273 cal., 46% (126 cal.) from fat; 33 g protein; 14 g fat (4.6 g sat.); 2.8 g carbo (0.6 g fiber); 174 mg sodium; 94 mg chol.

Where to buy buffalo

Buffalo tenderloin is in limited supply and is at least twice as expensive (from about $23 a lb.) as beef tenderloin. You can order buffalo tenderloin several days to a week ahead from specialty meat markets. Or order from these overnight delivery sources (shipping costs extra).

Denver Buffalo Company, (800) 289-2833

Native Game Company, (800) 952-6321

Polarica Game USA, (800) 426-3872

Oven-roasted Roots

Prep and cook time: About 1¼ hours

Notes: Other root vegetables such as baby turnips, parsnips, and chunks of leeks can be used; total vegetable weight should be about 4½ pounds. Up to 4 hours ahead, roast vegetables and let stand at room temperature. To warm, set roasting pan over medium heat, add remaining ingredients, and stir until steaming. Garnish with rosemary sprigs or roasted garlic.

Makes: 10 to 12 servings

1½ pounds **blue,** Yukon Gold, or red **thin-skinned potatoes** (or a mixture of colors), 2 inches wide

1½ pounds short, slender **carrots** (½ in. thick), ends trimmed

1½ pounds **pearl onions** (¾ in. wide)

2 tablespoons **olive oil**

1 tablespoon **fresh thyme** leaves or 1 teaspoon dried thyme

1 tablespoon **fresh rosemary** leaves or 1 teaspoon dried rosemary

½ teaspoon fresh-ground **pepper**

⅓ cup **dry red wine**

⅓ cup **balsamic vinegar**

⅓ cup **chicken broth**

Salt

1. Scrub potatoes and carrots. Cut potatoes in half. Peel onions. In a 12- by 15-inch roasting pan, mix potatoes, carrots, onions, oil, thyme, rosemary, and pepper.

2. Roast vegetables in a 450° oven, stirring occasionally, until tender when pierced, 40 to 50 minutes.

3. Transfer pan from oven to rangetop and set over medium heat. Add red wine, balsamic vinegar, and chicken broth. Stir until brown drippings are scraped free and vegetables are coated, 2 to 4 minutes.

4. Spoon into a bowl. Add salt to taste.

Per serving: 117 cal., 20% (23 cal.) from fat; 2.3 g protein; 2.5 g fat (0.3 g sat.); 21 g carbo (2.8 g fiber); 33 mg sodium; 0.1 mg chol.

Quinoa and Wild Rice Stuffed Squash

Prep and cook time: About 1½ hours

Notes: Up to 1 day ahead, make grain stuffing and bake squash. Reheat grain mixture in a microwave oven at full power (100%) until steaming, 9 to 11 minutes; stir occasionally. Spoon hot filling into cold cooked squash and bake, covered, in a 350° oven until interior of the squash is hot, about 35 minutes.

Makes: 10 to 12 servings

    10 to 12 **Sweet Dumpling,**
         Carnival, or Delicata **squash**
         (about ¾ lb. each)

    ½ cup chopped **pecans**

    1 tablespoon **olive oil**

    2 **onions** (1 lb. total), chopped

    2 cups chopped **celery**

    5¼ cups **vegetable broth**

    1½ cups **wild rice,** rinsed and
         drained

    2 tablespoons chopped **fresh sage**
         leaves or 2 teaspoons dried
         rubbed sage

    1½ cups **quinoa,** rinsed and drained

    ⅔ cup chopped **dried apricots**

    ⅓ cup chopped **dried cherries**

    ⅓ cup chopped **dried cranberries**

       Salt

1. Rinse squash, pierce each with a fork several times, and set in a 10- by 15-inch pan. Add ¾ cup water to pan and cover tightly with foil.

2. Bake in a 350° oven until the squash are tender when pierced, 45 minutes to 1 hour.

Quinoa, tiny and tender, contrasts with chewier wild rice. The cooked mixture fills baked sweet squash.

3. Meanwhile, in a 4- to 5-quart pan, stir chopped pecans over medium heat until golden, about 5 minutes. Remove from pan.

4. Add olive oil, onions, and celery to pan; stir over medium-high heat until onions are limp, about 6 minutes. Add vegetable broth, wild rice, and sage. Bring to a boil over high heat. Cover, reduce heat, and simmer for 40 minutes. Stir in quinoa, cover, and simmer until both grains are tender to bite, 15 to 20 minutes longer.

5. Stir in apricots, cherries, cranberries, and pecans. Add salt to taste. Keep warm until squash are ready.

6. When the squash are cooked, hold with a thick towel to protect hands, and cut ½ to ¾ inch off tops (or sides of Delicata) to form lids. Scoop out and discard seeds. If needed, trim a little off squash bases so they sit steady and level.

7. Mound grain stuffing into squash cavities. Set squash lids on filling and serve, adding salt to taste.

Per serving: 334 cal., 17% (58 cal.) from fat; 10 g protein; 6.4 g fat (0.7 g sat.); 65 g carbo (9.5 g fiber); 73 mg sodium; 0 mg chol.

Mushroom and Sunchoke Sauté

Prep and cook time: About 45 minutes

Notes: Sunchokes are also called Jerusalem artichokes. If making up to 1 day ahead, cover and chill. To reheat, stir over medium heat until hot, about 5 minutes. Garnish with fresh rosemary or oregano sprigs.

Makes: 10 to 12 servings

2 pounds assorted **mushrooms** such as chanterelle, porcini, portabella, morel, shiitake, or common white and brown

½ pound **sunchokes**

2 tablespoons **olive oil**

2 tablespoons **butter** or margarine

1 cup thinly sliced **shallots**

2 cloves **garlic**, minced or pressed

1 tablespoon chopped **fresh rosemary** leaves or 1 teaspoon dried rosemary

2 teaspoons chopped **fresh oregano** leaves or ¾ teaspoon dried oregano

¼ cup **dry sherry**

Salt and **pepper**

1. Trim off any soil caked onto mushrooms. Trim and discard discolored stem ends and tough stems of shiitakes. Quickly immerse the mushrooms in water, swishing them around to release soil and insects, then lift from water and drain.

2. Cut large mushrooms into about 1-inch pieces; leave the small mushrooms whole.

3. Peel and coarsely chop sunchokes.

4. In a 5- to 6-quart pan over high heat, combine oil, butter, mushrooms, sunchokes, shallots, and garlic. Stir often until mushroom juices evaporate and the vegetables are browned, about 15 minutes.

5. Add rosemary, oregano, and sherry; stir until sherry evaporates, about 2 minutes.

6. Spoon vegetables into a serving dish. Add salt and pepper to taste.

Per serving: 87 cal., 47% (41 cal.) from fat; 2.3 g protein; 4.5 g fat (1.5 g sat.); 9.5 g carbo (1.1 g fiber); 25 mg sodium; 5.2 mg chol.

Simply A'Maize'ing Corn Ice Cream

Prep and cook time: About 1 hour

Notes: Use canned or thawed frozen corn kernels. If making ahead, store ice cream airtight in the freezer up to 1 week. To serve, soften at 5-second intervals in a microwave oven at full power (100%) before scooping into bowls. Serve with scoops of purchased chocolate sorbet or ice cream (buy 1 qt.), then top with raspberry sauce (recipe follows).

Makes: About 1 quart

1¼ cups **cooked corn kernels**

1½ cups **whipping cream**

1¼ cups **milk**

½ cup **raw sugar** or firmly packed light brown sugar

5 **large egg** yolks

1 teaspoon **vanilla**

1. In a blender, purée 1 cup corn and ¼ cup cream until very smooth.

2. Rub purée through a fine strainer into a 10- to 12-inch frying pan. Add remaining corn and the cream, milk, and sugar. Stir over high heat until bubbles form at pan rim.

3. In a small bowl, beat yolks to blend with about ½ cup of the hot corn mixture, then pour into the frying pan and stir over low heat until custard coats the back of a metal spoon thickly, about 9 minutes. Add vanilla.

4. Set the pan in ice water and stir often until mixture is cold, about 15 minutes. Cover and chill at least 3 hours or up to 1 day.

5. Pour cold mixture into an ice cream maker and freeze according to manufacturer's directions or until dasher is hard to turn.

Per ⅓ cup: 178 cal., 61% (108 cal.) from fat; 3.1 g protein; 12 g fat (7 g sat.); 15 g carbo (0.4 g fiber); 30 mg sodium; 125 mg chol.

Raspberry Sauce

Prep time: About 12 minutes

Notes: Spoon this sauce over the corn ice cream and chocolate sorbet. Make up to 1 day ahead, then cover and chill. If fresh raspberries aren't available, use thawed frozen unsweetened berries.

Makes: About 1 cup; 10 to 12 servings

2 cups **raspberries**

2 to 3 tablespoons **honey**

1. In a blender or food processor, purée berries. Rub through a fine strainer into a bowl.

2. Sweeten purée with honey to taste.

Per serving: 21 cal., 4.3% (0.9 cal.) from fat; 0.2 g protein; 0.1 g fat (0 g sat.); 5.3 g carbo (1 g fiber); 0.1 mg sodium; 0 mg chol. ◆

Indian sundae: Raspberry sauce, spooned over velvety corn ice cream, also complements chocolate sorbet that's on the bottom.

Cowboy Christmas

A chuckwagon chef shares his frontier menu for your holiday table

by **LINDA LAU ANUSASANANAN**   *photographs by* **DOUG MERRIAM**

In the pale lavender light of a New Mexico dusk, mugs of cowboy coffee bring this nostalgic Christmas dinner to a close on the Cox ranch. The meal was prepared from the chuckwagon—part of ranch life up until the '20s—and was cooked over an open fire.

■ East of the crags of the Organ Mountains in southern New Mexico lies the San Augustine Ranch, owned by Rob Cox's family. The ranch has been in the family since 1893, when Rob's grandfather W. W. Cox, fleeing Texas and a vindictive gunfighter, bought it and began running sheep.

History haunts this ranch in the water-scarce Tularosa Basin. The property's cluster of five crystal-clear springs attracted Indians, explorers, soldiers, settlers—and adventure: in wilder times, sheriff Pat Garrett gunned down one of the ranch hands right in the Cox kitchen. A short walk away are

the ruins (presumably) of an early Spanish mission. And a bit farther down the road, a plaque marks the site of the Civil War "battle" of San Augustine Springs (no shots were fired).

In those days the chuckwagon, a kitchen on wheels, was essential when the ranch crew took to the open range. On one end of the wagon, a box with compartments held utensils, staples, dishes, and medicines. Its hinged door flipped down to become a worktable. Food was cooked in heavy cast-iron pans over the campfire or right in the hot coals.

Today, that range is smaller—in 1945 the government took

Edson Way uses cast-iron pans to braise quail, butter-steam carrots with parsnips, and bake biscuits.

over a great deal of the Tularosa Basin, including much of the Cox land, and the ranch now abuts the White Sands Missile Range. But Rob, a cattle rancher, and his wife, Murnie, still live in the original ranch house. And they keep frontier traditions alive, occasionally sharing a real chuckwagon Christmas dinner with close friends Edson and Jenny Way of Las Cruces and Art and Wanda Evans of Chuchillo.

Ed Way provides the old-timer recipes, following the sage advice of cowboy cooks: use what you have, work with what you scrounge up. They may hunt for quail and gather watercress, but they always depend on long-lasting root vegetables, and use once-standard chuckwagon supplies—vinegar, sugar, shortening, and flour—for the makings of an ingenious pioneer dessert, vinegar cobbler (it mimics apple cobbler surprisingly well).

Cowboy coffee goes with the cobbler. When water in the big enamel coffeepot boils, ground coffee is added. Then the pot comes off the fire, and crushed eggshells are thrown in to settle the grounds.

Certainly this meal is easier to prepare in a contemporary kitchen (and ice cream from the freezer tastes great with the cobbler).

But Christmas was made for traditions—even chuckwagons. And as the shadows grow long and the air gets chillier, the Old West feels very real on the San Augustine Ranch.

Quail in Cranberry Sauce

Prep and cook time: About 1½ hours

Notes: Use cornstarch for a more transparent sauce. Buy or order quail at the supermarket, or use 3 Cornish hens (about 1¾ lb. each), cutting each in half through the back and breastbone with scissors.

Makes: 6 servings

- 12 **quail** (about 6½ oz. each)

  Salt and **pepper**

- 2 to 3 tablespoons **butter** or margarine

- 2 cups **fresh** or frozen **cranberries**

- ½ cup firmly packed **brown sugar**

- 2 tablespoons **cider vinegar**

- ½ teaspoon **ground cinnamon**

- ⅛ teaspoon **ground allspice**

- ⅛ teaspoon **ground cloves**

- 1 tablespoon **all-purpose flour** or 1½ teaspoons cornstarch

  About 2 cups **watercress sprigs**, rinsed and crisped

1. Remove giblets and trim necks from quail; save for another use. Rinse birds, pat dry, and lightly sprinkle with salt and pepper.

2. In a deep 11- to 12-inch frying pan over medium-high heat, melt 2 tablespoons butter. Add as many birds as will fit in pan and brown on all sides, 12 to 15 minutes. Lift out as browned, put in a bowl, and add remaining birds and more butter, if needed, to pan. When all the birds are out of pan, discard fat.

3. To pan, add cranberries, 1 cup water, brown sugar, vinegar, cinnamon, allspice, and cloves. Stir over high heat until simmering. Return birds and accumulated juices to pan.

4. Cover and simmer over low heat, turning birds over after 10 minutes, until thighs are tender when pierced, 20 to 30 minutes total.

5. With a slotted spoon, transfer birds to a warm platter.

6. Smoothly blend flour with 2 tablespoons water, then mix into pan. Stir over high heat until sauce comes to a rolling boil. Season with salt and pepper to taste, pour over birds, and garnish platter with watercress.

Per serving: 759 cal., 51% (387 cal.) from fat; 65 g protein; 43 g fat (13 g sat.); 24 g carbo (1.6 g fiber); 225 mg sodium; 260 mg chol.

Butter-steamed Carrots and Parsnips

Prep and cook time: About 20 minutes

Makes: 6 servings

- 6 **carrots** (about 1¼ lb. total)

- 6 **parsnips** (about 1¼ lb. total)

- 2 tablespoons **butter** or margarine

  Salt

1. Peel, then trim ends of carrots and parsnips. Cut the vegetables in half lengthwise.

2. In a 5- to 6-quart pan over medium-high heat, melt butter. Add carrot halves and ¾ cup water; cover and cook 3 minutes.

3. Add parsnip halves, cover, and continue cooking until vegetables are tender when pierced, 8 to 10 minutes longer.

4. Uncover pan and shake frequently until liquid evaporates. Pour vegetables into a bowl and add salt to taste.

Per serving: 130 cal., 29% (38 cal.) from fat; 1.9 g protein; 4.2 g fat (2.4 g sat.); 23 g carbo (6.3 g fiber); 76 mg sodium; 10 mg chol.

Vinegar Cobbler

Prep and cook time: About 50 minutes

Notes: Accompany cobbler with vanilla ice cream.

Makes: 6 to 8 servings

About 3 cups **all-purpose flour**

¹⁄₂ teaspoon **salt**

1 cup **solid shortening**

¹⁄₂ cup **cider vinegar**

2 cups **sugar**

2 teaspoons **vanilla**

1. Mix 3 cups flour with salt. With a pastry blender, cut in shortening until crumbly. With a fork, gradually mix in just enough water (about ¹⁄₂ cup) until dough holds together. Divide dough into 3 equal portions.

2. On a floured board, roll out each

Brooke Racki (above), Edson Way's niece, dips a drink from chuckwagon's water barrel. Vinegar cobbler dessert (left) typifies the inventiveness of range cooks.

portion into an oval ¹⁄₈ inch thick and 8 to 10 inches long. Cut lengthwise into 1-inch-wide strips.

3. In an ovenproof 5- to 6-quart pan that's about 10 inches wide, combine vinegar, sugar, vanilla, and 4 cups water. Bring to a boil over high heat.

4. Reserve 8 pastry strips, and tear the remainder into pieces about ¹⁄₂ inch long. Drop torn pieces into boiling liquid. Boil 5 minutes.

5. Remove pan from heat. Crisscross remaining 8 strips on top of the cooked dough pieces, making a lattice and trimming ends to fit. Push leftover trimmed dough scraps into syrup.

6. Bake in a 425° oven until lattice top is golden brown, 25 to 30 minutes. Serve hot or warm. Spoon into bowls.

Per serving: 599 cal., 39% (234 cal.) from fat; 4.9 g protein; 26 g fat (6.5 g sat.); 87 g carbo (1.3 g fiber); 138 mg sodium; 0 mg chol. ◆

Meanwhile, back at the ranch ...

Want to learn more about Old West ranching traditions? The New Mexico Farm & Ranch Heritage Museum, 4100 Dripping Springs Rd., Las Cruces, NM, officially opens in May 1998. But it is decorated for the holidays New Mexico–style and will offer free tours of its stunning new building on the hour from 9–3 (except 12) weekdays, December 6–23. From 9–6 December 6 and 11–5 December 7, there will be special events, with museums from southern New Mexico and west Texas participating. For details call (505) 522-4100.

DEBORAH JONES

Sautéed onion and bacon, parmesan, and spinach season a generous oyster omelet.

Ode to oysters and eggs

Local shellfish, spinach, and bacon fill classic omelets
at southern Washington's Shelburne Inn

For the grand breakfasts served at the Victorian-era Shelburne Inn, local ingredients are the byword. And here in Seaview, on southern Washington's Long Beach Peninsula, you can't get more local than oysters.

Oysters built the area's first towns during California's Gold Rush, when new wealth to the south fueled an appetite for Washington's native bivalves. Today, the peninsula's pristine waters nurture some of the country's most productive beds of cultured oysters.

David Campiche and Laurie Anderson, co-owners of the Shelburne, serve oysters dozens of ways, but their Hangtown Fry, prepared as either an omelet or a frittata, marks the area's historical connection with California's goldfields.

The story goes that a Hangtown Fry, a scramble of eggs, oysters, and bacon, was created in Placerville, California (then called Hangtown because of three famous hangings). Campiche's version has it that the miners who struck gold simply ordered the most expensive thing on the menu, the Hangtown Fry. In *Old San Francisco,* Doris Muscatine traces the fry to a condemned prisoner's last request, one whose rare ingredients would delay the proceedings.

Whatever the origin, this version of the Shelburne's recipe makes a simple but extravagant meal. For information on staying at the inn (rooms cost $99 to $169 per night), call (800) 466-1896.

by **ELAINE JOHNSON**

Shelburne Inn's Hangtown Omelets

Prep and cook time: About 35 minutes
Notes: To sliver an onion, halve lengthwise, then cut into thin lengthwise slices.
Makes: 2 servings

> 6 **large eggs**
> ¼ cup **half-and-half** or whipping cream
> 4 slices **bacon,** chopped
> 1 cup slivered **red onion**
> 1 jar (10 oz.) shucked small raw Pacific **oysters**
> ½ cup freshly shredded **parmesan cheese**
> 1½ cups shredded **spinach** leaves (¼- by 3-in. strips)
> **Salt** and **pepper**

1. In a bowl, beat eggs and half-and-half to blend; set aside. In an 8- to 10-inch nonstick frying pan over medium-high heat, stir bacon often until brown, 4 to 5 minutes. Spoon out all but 1 tablespoon fat and set aside. Add onion to pan and stir often until limp and brown, 7 to 8 minutes. Remove onion and bacon from pan and set aside. Measure reserved bacon fat; if needed, add salad oil to equal 1 tablespoon.

2. Meanwhile, in a 1- to 2-quart pan over high heat, bring oysters and their liquid to a boil. Remove pan from heat and let stand until oysters' edges curl, 2 to 3 minutes. Lift out the oysters with a slotted spoon (discard liquid), add to onion-bacon mixture, and keep warm.

3. Return half of bacon fat to frying pan over medium heat. Add half of egg mixture. As eggs begin to set, lift edges from pan bottom to let uncooked egg flow underneath. When eggs no longer flow when pan is tipped, scatter with half the parmesan; then on half of omelet, scatter half of oyster mixture and half of spinach leaves.

4. Tip pan; with a spatula, fold uncovered half of omelet over filling. Hold pan over a plate and shake omelet onto dish. Keep warm while making second omelet. Season with salt and pepper.

Per serving: 696 cal., 59% (414 cal.) from fat; 49 g protein; 46 g fat (18 g sat.); 20 g carbo. (2.4 g fiber); 1,114 mg sodium; 766 mg chol. ◆

The Quick Cook

MEALS IN 30-MINUTES-OR-LESS

Getting a feel for filo

■ In the rush of wrapping gifts, it's comforting to know that you can also wrap up a meal handsome enough for guests in about half an hour.

This savory filo strudel gets a head start with cooked ham and cooked rice (from a deli or Chinese take-out counter—or use instant rice). While the strudel bakes, stir together a simple

THREE MORE RECIPES FOR FILO MEALS

1. Spinach and cheese packets. Mix thawed frozen chopped spinach (squeezed dry) with shredded fontina cheese and nutmeg. Butter and layer filo as directed for strudel. Cut filo stack into 6- by 12-inch strips. Divide filling among strips; roll to enclose filling, tucking in the ends. Bake as directed for strudel, 13 to 15 minutes.

2. Filo-crusted potpie. Butter and layer filo as directed for strudel. Cut filo to the size of the top of a shallow casserole. Bake cut filo as directed for strudel until golden, 3 to 4 minutes. Heat chili or a stew, pour into casserole, and top with crust.

3. Filo napoleons. Butter and layer filo as directed for strudel. Cut into 5-inch squares. Bake as directed for strudel until golden, 3 to 4 minutes. Top half of the filo squares with one or more of the following: chicken or tuna salad, purchased hummus, tabbouleh, flavored cream cheese. Top with remaining filo squares. Serve with green salad.

mustard sauce and season watercress with rice vinegar to serve as salad and garnish.

Hungarian Ham Strudel with Watercress Salad

Prep and cook time: About 30 minutes

Notes: If filo is frozen, it handles best if thawed in the refrigerator at least 8 hours. If sheets tear, just piece them together. For a zippier flavor, use a hot paprika.

Makes: 4 servings

- 6 **green onions**
- 1½ cups **cooked rice**
- 1 cup (4 oz.) **shredded Swiss cheese**
- 2 tablespoons **paprika**
- 1 tablespoon **caraway seed**
- 2 tablespoons drained **capers**
- 6 sheets **filo dough** (about 12 by 18 in.)
- ⅓ cup **butter** or margarine, melted
- ½ pound **thin-sliced cooked ham**
- ⅓ cup **reduced-fat sour cream**
- 2 to 3 tablespoons **coarse-grain Dijon mustard**
- ½ pound **watercress**, rinsed and crisped
- 2 tablespoons **seasoned rice vinegar**

1. Trim and discard ends of green onions. Chop onions and mix with rice, cheese, paprika, caraway, and capers.

2. Lay 1 filo sheet flat (cover remaining filo with plastic wrap to prevent drying) and brush lightly with butter. Top with another filo sheet and brush lightly with more butter. Repeat to stack remaining filo.

3. About 1 inch from a narrow end, lay ham slices over filo (overlapping as needed) to cover about ⅓ of dough, leaving a 1- to 2-inch margin on the sides. Evenly pat rice mixture over ham. Roll filo from ham end to enclose filling. With seam down, gently transfer strudel roll to a buttered baking sheet (at least 11 by 14 in., without side rims). Lightly brush strudel with butter.

4. Bake in a 400° oven until golden brown all over, 15 to 17 minutes.

5. Meanwhile, mix sour cream with mustard in a small bowl. Mix watercress with vinegar.

6. Using 2 wide spatulas, slide strudel onto a platter, cut into thick slices, and accompany with watercress salad. Add sour cream sauce to taste.

Per serving: 606 cal., 49% (297 cal.) from fat; 29 g protein; 33 g fat (18 g sat.); 46 g carbo (2.7 g fiber); 1,821 mg sodium; 107 mg chol. ◆

Fresh from the streets of Morelia

Behind the scenes at a Mexican fruit gazpacho stand—plus the recipe that's made it so famous

Tinoco has run his Morelia gazpacho stand for 23 years. One secret of his success has been to chop his fruits (such as watermelon and pineapple) into very fine pieces.

Popular vendor Efrain Tinoco tops his gazpacho with chili and queso añejo.

A busy street corner in Mexico might not seem the likeliest place for fast food that's both nutritious and tasty, but in the colonial city of Morelia, in Michoacán, one vendor on one corner has proved that what's *rápido* can also be *saludable y sabroso.*

"We're called the Fruit City," says Marco Ruiz, a Morelia street vendor who works at the colorful streetside eatery owned by his uncle, Efrain Tinoco. "We have food traditions here that you can't find in other parts of Michoacán." Ruiz, a 19-year-old university student, is part of Tinoco's extended family, which for 23 years has earned its reputation as the premier fruit gazpacho vendor in a city with plenty of competition.

Tinoco's pristine gazpacho stand sits at the downtown intersection of four streets: Calle Andrés, Quintana Roo, Madero Poniente, and Avenida Francisco I. From early morning to early evening, every day of the week, giggling schoolkids, impatient taxi drivers, and cell phone–toting business types line up to taste the Tinoco handiwork.

"People like my uncle's gazpacho because the pieces are cut very small, and because he goes to the *mercado* each morning to buy only soft, perfect fruits," says Ruiz. "And we're always happy to make complicated mixtures of fruits, depending on what the customer wants."

What people find when they line up at the stand are workers in elbow-length sanitary gloves, wiping their razor-sharp knives and spotless cutting boards with purified water, and flailing away at fruits so fresh that the entire corner smells like a field of ripe strawberries. There's a Zen-like quality to the never ending *thwack, thwack, thwack* of knives against the boards.

Efrain Tinoco's basic fruit gazpacho consists of finely chopped pineapple, mango, and jicama, fresh-squeezed lime and orange juice, a splash of hot sauce, and spoonfuls of crumbled white queso añejo (also called añejado or cotija) sprinkled on top. Heaped until overflowing into 16-ounce plastic cups wrapped with sheets of waxed paper, the gazpacho costs only 8 pesos (a little more than $1) a cup.

Morelians are demanding customers, and about half of the orders that are shouted to the Tinocos from across their gazpacho stand are for substitutions—watermelon, papaya, and cantaloupe instead of pineapple and mango, or peeled, seeded cucumber instead of jicama. Unless customers

by **JOHN VILLANI**

specify otherwise, the Tinocos give their gazpacho a decidedly Mexican kick, but they will honor requests for gazpacho *poco chile* (not too hot). Other customers order extra chipotle chili powder, red chili sauce, or salt sprinkled between the layers of fruit.

And talk about delicious! These fabulous gazpachos (best eaten on the stone steps of the Parroquia de la Merced right across the street) are the quintessential Mexican urban experience. Dripping with fresh fruit juices, their combination of sweet tastes and medium-hot spices provides crunchy proof that south-of-the-border street foods can be elevated to surprisingly healthful heights.

Tinoco's Fruit Gazpacho

Prep time: About 30 minutes

Makes: 4 servings

- ⅓ cup **lime juice**
- ⅔ cup **orange juice**
- 2 cups ¼- to ½-inch diced **pineapple**
- 2 cups ¼- to ½-inch diced **jicama**
- 2 cups ¼- to ½-inch diced **mango**
- **Hot sauce**
- **Chili powder**
- ¼ cup crumbled **cotija** or feta **cheese**

1. Mix lime and orange juices.

2. In each of 4 tall glasses (12- to 14-oz. size), make a layer of ¼ cup pineapple. Add a layer of ¼ cup jicama, and top with ¼ cup mango.

3. In a bowl, combine the remaining pineapple, jicama, and mango, and spoon the mixture equally into each glass. Pour lime-orange mixture equally into each glass.

4. Top each serving with hot sauce and chili powder to taste, and sprinkle with 1 tablespoon cheese.

Per serving: 160 cal., 14% (23 cal.) from fat; 2.7 g protein; 2.5 g fat (1.3 g sat.); 35 g carbo (4.8 g fiber); 103 mg sodium; 7.5 mg chol.

— Recipe by Andrew Baker ◆

Mexico's bread pudding

Quick tricks for a traditional dessert

Old bread often ends up happily as a dessert pudding. In Mexico, bread pudding, called *capirotada,* usually includes cheese. The dish is traditional, but it doesn't require a lot of effort, especially if you start with purchased unseasoned dried bread cubes. And instead of making a flavored syrup to moisten the bread, as Mexican cooks do, just buy the kind served in coffee bars. These syrups are widely available in liquor stores, Italian delicatessens, and upscale supermarkets. For a delicious alternative to the apricot-flavor syrup we use, try a tamarind- or almond-flavor one. If desired, serve with vanilla ice cream or nonfat frozen yogurt.

Blueberry Mexican Bread Pudding

Prep and cook time: About 45 minutes

Notes: This recipe comes from Suzanne Carreiro, who teaches cooking in San Rafael, California.

If fresh blueberries aren't available, use frozen unsugared ones (don't thaw before adding). Instead of purchased bread cubes, toast 6 cups ½-inch cubes of French bread in a 10- by 15-inch pan in a 350° oven, stirring often, 10 to 15 minutes.

Makes: 8 servings

- 1½ cups **blueberries**
- ¼ cup (⅛ lb.) **butter** or margarine
- ½ teaspoon **ground cinnamon**
- ½ pound **jack cheese**
- 6 cups (1 package, about 7½ oz.) **unseasoned dried bread cubes**
- 1½ cups **apricot-flavor syrup**
- 2 teaspoons grated **lemon** peel
- 2 tablespoons **lemon juice**
- ¾ cup **chopped pecans**

1. Rinse and drain blueberries if fresh.

2. Put butter and cinnamon in a 9- by 13-inch casserole. Heat in a 350° oven until butter is melted, about 5 minutes.

3. Meanwhile, cut cheese into ½-inch cubes.

4. Add dried bread cubes to casserole and mix well.

5. Combine apricot-flavor syrup, lemon peel, lemon juice, and ¼ cup water. Pour over bread, mixing well.

6. Add pecans, cheese, and blueberries to casserole and gently mix to distribute evenly.

7. Cover casserole tightly with foil. Bake for 20 minutes in a 350° oven. Uncover casserole and bake until pudding top is crisp and golden brown, about 15 minutes longer.

Per serving: 498 cal., 42% (207 cal.) from fat; 11 g protein; 23 g fat (9.6 g sat.); 65 g carbo (2.4 g fiber); 445 mg sodium; 46 mg chol. ◆

by **BARBARA GOLDMAN**

Kitchen Cabinet

READERS' RECIPES TESTED IN SUNSET'S KITCHENS

by LINDA LAU ANUSASANANAN

Cookies for the holidays

■ For more than 50 years, Clarice Cox has made these decorative cookies for family, friends, cooking classes, and fund-raising events. And she often makes use of her collection of more than 60 cookie cutters to cut them out. The cookies are firm, so they stack neatly when packed for gifts.

Painted Cookies
Clarice Cox, Roseburg, Oregon

Prep and cook time: About 45 minutes
Makes: 2 dozen (3 in. wide)

1 cup (½ lb.) **butter** or margarine, at room temperature

1 cup **sugar**

1 **large egg**

1 teaspoon **vanilla** or almond extract

About 3 cups **all-purpose flour**

1 **large egg** yolk

Food coloring (4 choices)

1. Cut butter into chunks and put in a large bowl; add sugar. Beat with a mixer to blend, then beat on high speed until mixture is fluffy.

2. Add whole egg and vanilla and beat to mix thoroughly.

3. Add 3 cups flour and beat on low speed until dough is well mixed.

4. Divide dough in half, shape into balls, and flatten each into a round cake. If desired, wrap dough airtight and chill up to 1 day.

5. One portion at a time, roll out dough on a floured board to ¼ inch thick. With flour-dusted cookie cutters (2 to 3 in. wide), cut out cookies.

6. With a wide spatula, transfer cookies to baking sheets, spacing them at least 1 inch apart.

7. To make patterns on cookies, if desired, make impressions with a flour-dusted spoon tip or fork tines. Gently brush flour off cookies.

8. Mix egg yolk with ½ teaspoon water to blend. Divide mixture among 4 small bowls. Tint contents of each bowl with a different food coloring, mixing in a drop at a time to get desired intensity.

FRANCE RUFFENACH

Get the kids to paint the cookies, then bake and package for special gifts.

9. Using small brushes, paint surface of cookies with colored mixtures.

10. Bake in a 325° oven until cookies are golden on bottom, about 16 minutes (if using one oven, alternate pan positions after 8 minutes). Cool on pan about 5 minutes, then transfer with a wide spatula to racks to cool.

11. Serve, or store airtight at once for up to 5 days. Freeze to store longer.

Per cookie: 163 cal., 45% (74 cal.) from fat; 2 g protein; 8.2 g fat (4.9 g sat.); 20 g carbo (0.4 g fiber); 81 mg sodium; 38 mg chol.

Toffee Crisps
Ruby Roethler, Paradise, California

Years ago, when she was a high school student, Ruby Roethler (then Stratton) admired the baskets of assorted homemade cookies the principal's wife brought to meetings. Now Roethler has adopted this idea and brings a similar basket to potlucks for dessert. These toffee crisps are just one recipe from her delicious repertoire.

Prep and cook time: About 35 minutes
Makes: 5½ dozen

½ cup (¼ lb.) **butter** or margarine

1 cup **granulated sugar**

½ cup firmly packed **brown sugar**

2 **large eggs**

1½ teaspoons **vanilla**

2¼ cups **all-purpose flour**

1 teaspoon **baking powder**

½ teaspoon **baking soda**

½   teaspoon **salt**
1   bag (7.5 oz.) **almond brickle** or toffee **bits** or about 1 cup (6 oz.) chopped chocolate-covered toffee candy bars

1. Cut the butter into chunks and put in a large bowl; add granulated and brown sugars. Beat with a mixer to blend, then beat on high speed until the mixture is fluffy.

2. Add eggs and vanilla; beat to blend.

3. Add flour, baking powder, baking soda, and salt. Mix on slow speed to incorporate dry ingredients, then beat on medium speed until well blended.

4. Stir in almond brickle.

5. Drop cookie dough in rounded teaspoon portions about 2 inches apart on oiled or nonstick baking sheets.

6. Bake in a 375° oven until golden brown, 8 to 10 minutes (if using one oven, alternate pan positions after 4 to 5 minutes).

7. Cool about 2 minutes on pan. With a wide spatula, transfer cookies to racks to cool.

8. Serve, or store airtight at once for up to 3 days. Freeze to store longer.

Per cookie: 67 cal., 37% (25 cal.) from fat; 0.6 g protein; 2.8 g fat (1.2 g sat.); 9.8 g carbo (0.2 g fiber); 69 mg sodium; 11 mg chol.

Florentine Wedding Cakes
Lynne Tremble, Monarch Beach, California

The melt-in-your-mouth classic, Mexican wedding cakes, takes on an Italian veil as Lynne Tremble replaces the traditional walnuts with hazelnuts and adds a sprinkle of cocoa.

Prep and cook time: About 50 minutes
Makes: 5 dozen

¾   cup **hazelnuts**
1   cup (½ lb.) **butter** or margarine, at room temperature
    About 1¼ cups **powdered sugar**
1   teaspoon **vanilla**
2   cups **all-purpose flour**
¼   teaspoon **salt**
2   teaspoons **Dutch-process cocoa**

1. Put nuts in a 9-inch cake or pie pan. Bake in a 350° oven until pale gold under skin, 10 to 12 minutes. Pour nuts into a towel and rub briskly with the cloth to remove as much skin as

possible. Lift nuts from towel and finely chop. Wipe out pan.

2. Cut butter into chunks and put in a large bowl. Beat with a mixer on high speed until fluffy. Add ⅓ cup of the powdered sugar and the vanilla; beat on slow speed to incorporate, then beat on high speed until fluffy.

3. On low speed, mix in flour and salt, then beat until blended.

4. Stir in nuts.

5. Shape dough into 1-inch balls. Place about 2 inches apart on baking sheets.

6. Bake in a 300° oven until cookies no longer feel soft when gently touched but are not browned, about 18 minutes. (If using one oven, alternate pan positions after 8 to 10 minutes.) Cool on pans about 5 minutes.

7. Place remaining powdered sugar in cake pan. Gently roll hot cookies, a few at a time, in sugar to coat well. Set cookies slightly apart on piece of waxed paper (about 20 in. long) until almost cool, then roll in sugar again. Return cookies to paper in a single layer. Shake cocoa through fine strainer over cookies. Let cookies cool.

8. Serve, or store airtight at once for up to 3 days. Freeze to store longer.

Per cookie: 61 cal., 59% (36 cal.) from fat; 0.7 g protein; 4 g fat (2 g sat.); 5.9 g carbo (0.2 g fiber); 41 mg sodium; 8.3 mg chol.

J. J.'s Chewy Chews
Audrey Thibodeau, Mesa, Arizona

This recipe, a favorite with Audrey Thibodeau's family, had been made by many friends before she tried it and added her own innovation. She forms the chewy baked cookies into balls and wraps them individually in colored plastic wrap to tuck into food gift baskets.

Prep and cook time: About 50 minutes
Makes: 3 dozen

1   cup **granulated sugar**
¾   cup **all-purpose flour**
¼   teaspoon **salt**
1   cup **chopped pitted dates**
1   cup finely chopped **pecans**
2   **large eggs**
⅓   cup **powdered sugar**

1. In a bowl, stir together granulated sugar, flour, salt, dates, and pecans.

2. Beat eggs to blend, then add to sugar mixture and stir until well mixed.

3. Spread cookie dough level in an oiled 8- or 9-inch square pan.

4. Bake in a 350° oven just until very light brown on top, 16 to 18 minutes.

5. Cool on a rack for 5 minutes. Cut into 36 squares. With a wide spatula, remove squares from pan; roll each into a ball, then coat with powdered sugar.

6. Serve, or store airtight up to 1 day. Freeze to store longer.

Per cookie: 73 cal., 29% (21 cal.) from fat; 0.9 g protein; 2.3 g fat (0.2 g sat.); 13 g carbo (0.5 g fiber); 19 mg sodium; 12 mg chol.

Brown Sugar Petticoats
Anne Gripenstraw, San Francisco

As a child, Anne Gripenstraw loved this buttery shortbread as cutout cookies she could decorate with her friends. Now, as a busy mother to 10-month-old Henry, she bakes the dough as a single round, then quickly cuts the warm cookie into wedges—petticoats.

Prep and cook time: About 50 minutes
Makes: 12 to 16 cookies

1¼   cups **all-purpose flour**
⅔   cup firmly packed **brown sugar**
½   cup (¼ lb.) **butter** or margarine
2   teaspoons **granulated sugar**

1. In a bowl, mix flour and brown sugar. Cut butter into chunks and add to bowl.

2. With a pastry blender, cut butter until mixture is crumbly and no large particles remain.

3. Press dough with your hands to form a ball, then pat evenly in an 8- or 9-inch-wide cake or cheesecake pan with removable rim.

4. With the tines of a fork, make impressions around edge of dough. Then pierce surface of cookie all over.

5. Bake in a 300° oven until slightly darker golden brown, about 40 minutes.

6. While hot, remove pan rim and cut cookie into 12 to 16 wedges. Sprinkle with granulated sugar. Cool on a rack.

7. Serve, or store airtight up to 1 week. Freeze to store longer.

Per cookie: 123 cal., 42% (52 cal.) from fat; 1.1 g protein; 5.8 g fat (3.6 g sat.); 17 g carbo (0.3 g fiber); 62 mg sodium; 16 mg chol. ◆

The Low-Fat Cook

HEALTHY CHOICES FOR THE ACTIVE LIFESTYLE

by ZILLAH BAHAR

Crunchy onions and shredded cucumber go with moist pickled salmon on rye toast. Add sour cream for a cool touch.

For Hanukkah, serve light and easy appetizers

■ The Old World penchant for pickling to preserve fish, meat, and vegetables carried over into traditional Jewish homes on the East Coast. One staple was pickled salmon in a heavily salted marinade; another, cucumbers in a similar mixture.

But in the West, these Jewish preparations take a more healthful turn. Pickling is for flavor, not preservation, and salt is used sparingly. An assertive blend of spices, not salt, brings out this salmon's rich, mellow flavor. And other

vegetables team up with cucumbers for a Jewish version of salsa.

Pickled Salmon

Prep and cook time: 30 minutes, plus 2 hours to marinate and 3 hours to chill
Notes: Serve with toasted rye bread or pocket bread, shredded cucumber, and reduced-fat sour cream.
Makes: 4 appetizer servings

- ½ cup **kosher white wine vinegar** or distilled white vinegar
- ⅓ cup **lemon juice**
- 2 tablespoons **sugar**
- 10 **dried hot chilies** (each about 2 in. long)
- 4 **cardamom pods,** hulled
- 3 cloves **garlic,** peeled
- ¾ teaspoon **mustard seed**
- ½ teaspoon **black peppercorns**
- ½ teaspoon **fennel seed**
- ½ teaspoon **coriander seed**
- ½ pound **boned, skinned salmon,** 1 inch thick, cut into ½-inch slices
- 1½ cups very thin **white onion** slices
- 1½ cups very thin **red onion** slices

1. In a bowl, combine vinegar, lemon juice, ½ cup water, sugar, dried chilies, cardamom, garlic, mustard seed, peppercorns, fennel, and coriander.

2. Add the salmon and mix. Cover and chill at least 2 or up to 5 hours.

3. Place white and red onions in a nonstick 10- to 12-inch frying pan. Drain marinade from fish into pan. Bring to a boil over high heat.

4. Lay salmon on onions. Cover; simmer until fish is opaque but still moist-looking in center (cut to test), about 1 minute. Transfer fish and onion mixture to a jar or bowl. Let cool, then cover and chill at least 2 hours or up to 5 days.

Per serving: 171 cal., 25% (43 cal.) from fat; 14 g protein; 4.8 g fat (0.7 g sat.); 20 g carbo (2.9 g fiber); 40 mg sodium; 31 mg chol.

Cucumber Appetizer Salad

Prep time: About 15 minutes
Notes: Spoon onto bagel chips or lahvosh crackers.
Makes: 2½ cups

- 1 cup finely chopped **cucumber**
- ½ cup finely chopped **red radishes**
- ½ cup finely chopped **green onions**
- 1 can (14½ oz.) **diced tomatoes**
  About 3 tablespoons **distilled white vinegar**
  Salt and **pepper**

1. In a bowl, combine cucumber, radishes, and onions.

2. Drain tomatoes and reserve juice for other uses. Finely chop tomatoes and add to bowl. Mix ingredients and season to taste with vinegar, salt, and pepper.

Per ¼ cup: 13 cal., 7% (0.9 cal.) from fat; 0.6 g protein; 0.1 g fat (0 g sat.); 2.8 g carbo (0.7 g fiber); 69 mg sodium; 0 mg chol. ◆

Articles Index

Index of Recipe Titles

Low-Fat Recipes (30 percent or less calories from fat)

General Index

Risotto (*cont'd.*)
  quick, 243
Roasted fresh ham, 72
Roasted nuts, spicy herb, 254
Roasted petite Yukon Gold
  potatoes, 263
Roasted poblano chilies, 282
Roasted red peppers. *See* Red
  peppers, roasted
Roasted tomato soup, 218
Roast turkey, rosemary, 262
Rolls. *See* Breads and rolls
Roma–goat cheese tarts, 215
Romaine salad with mandarins
  and Asian dressing, 255
Roots, oven-roasted, 289
Rosemary flatbreads, grilled,
  151
Rosemary roast turkey, 262
Rose's hot and spicy apple
  chutney, 209
Rosé wines, 279
Rum chutney, pork tenderloin
  with, 245
Rum slush, watermelon, 144

Sage-piñon vinaigrette, field
  greens with, 288
Salad dressings, low-fat, 126
Salads
  apricot-spinach, 121
  asparagus and beet, 149
  black-eyed pea, 149
  Caesar salad roll-ups, 110
  chicken, 146
  citrus and bean, 56
  confetti coleslaw, 20
  cryin' cactus, 38
  cucumber, 126
  cucumber appetizer, 302
  field greens with sage-piñon
    vinaigrette, 288
  garbanzo, with pomegranate
    seed, 224
  grapefruit and avocado, 32
  green and yellow bean, with
    chive dressing, 160
  herbed filet mignon, bean,
    and arugula, 57
  Italian tossed, 85
  mango and basmati rice,
    109
  Mexican pasta, 19
  potsticker and roasted
    pepper, 122
  red and green, with cran-
    berry dressing, 262
  romaine, with mandarins
    and Asian dressing, 255
  Southwestern quinoa, 18
  spiced apple quinoa, 244
  spiced napa cabbage, 104
  sweet pea, with coconut,
    149
  tangled tiger shrimp and
    pineapple, 124
  Tuscan tomato bread, 217
  watercress, Hungarian ham
    strudel with, 297

Salmon
  bake, Indian-style, 186
  curry-cured, with sweet
    onion relish, 108
  fajitas, Larry's, 17
  fillet, Pinot-plank, 189
  leek-wrapped, 189
  pickled, 302
  poached in verjus, 23
  smoked, with dill, 271
Salsa
  apricot, 121
  borracho, 141
  chicken with linguine, 21
  cowboy, 66
  freezer, 219
  mango, fish with, 144
  papaya-mango, 141
  pork, 21
  pork chops, orange, 67
  spicy cranberry, 140
  tomatillo, 141
Sandwiches
  Greek pocket bread, with
    lamb, 82
  vegetarian hero, 65
Sangria, 81
Sangria, shortcut, 128
Sausage, dried fruit, and cornbread dressing, 256
Sausage, Thai turkey, 94
Sautéed soft-shell crabs, 90
Sauvignon Blanc, 53
Seafood. *See also* Fish; Shellfish
  in Asian broth, 222
  herb-poached, 98
Seattle restaurants, 42–44, 179,
  181, 192–193
Sesame
  -carrot muffins, 23
  -ginger sauce, 114
  -nut crunch, 282
Shallots, lamb rack with, 50
Shelburne Inn's Hangtown
  omelets, 296
Shellfish. *See also* specific Shell-
  fish
  Belize burrito, 224
  butterflied garlic shrimp,
    104
  crab-filled portabella mush-
    rooms, 272
  fish soup with potatoes and
    fennel, 70
  gingered shrimp with Bel-
    gian endive, 271
  sautéed soft-shell crabs, 90
  Southwest shrimp and pasta,
    154
  spaghetti with clams, tuna,
    and bacon, 63
  tangled tiger shrimp and
    pineapple salad, 124
Sherbet, Meyer lemon, 59
Shortcut sangria, 128
Short pastry for tarts, 72
Shrimp
  and pasta, Southwest, 154
  Belize burrito, 224

Shrimp (*cont'd.*)
  butterflied garlic, 104
  gingered, with Belgian en-
    dive, 271
  tangled tiger shrimp and
    pineapple salad, 124
Simply a'maize'ing corn ice
  cream, 291
Slush, watermelon rum, 144
Smashed potatoes, 98
Smoked salmon with dill, 271
Smoky black beans with grilled
  lamb, 56
Smoothie, honeydew, 126
S'mores, 95
Soft polenta with dry jack, 61
Soft-shell crabs, sautéed, 90
Soft tacos, turkey-chipotle, 17
Sonoma County, suggested
  trips through, 232–237
Sorbet
  apricot, 52
  sweet tomato, 217
  white nectarine, 132
Soufflé, cheese, 230
Soufflé, Meyer lemon, 59
Soups
  albóndigas, 230
  black bean, 283
  black bean and pumpkin, 14
  Chilly Willy's avocado, 128
  fish, with potatoes and fen-
    nel, 70
  gazpacho, 196
  pumpkin, 262
  red pepper bisque, 10
  red pepper–tomato, 47
  roasted tomato, 218
  squash, 146
  Tinoco's fruit gazpacho, 299
  tortilla, 14
  white and black, 55
South-of-the-border layered
  dip, 125
South-of-the-border potatoes,
  19
Southwest eggs Benedict, 277
Southwestern chicken pot pie,
  64
Southwestern quinoa salad, 18
Southwest shrimp and pasta,
  154
Spaghetti sauce, 218
Spaghetti with clams, tuna, and
  bacon, 63
Spiced apple quinoa salad, 244
Spiced chili rub, 114
Spiced kabocha squash, 248
Spiced napa cabbage salad, 104
Spicy aïoli, 98
Spicy corn relish, 129
Spicy cranberry salsa, 140
Spicy herb roasted nuts, 254
Spicy swordfish, 20
Spinach
  and cheese packets, 297
  pesto potato casserole, 83
  salad, apricot-, 121
Squab, honey-thyme, 134

Squash
  blossoms, stuffed, 109
  quinoa and wild rice stuffed,
    290
  soup, 146
  spiced kabocha, 248
Stacked tortilla pie with
  carnitas, 239
Steak
  Diane, 229
  perfect grilled, 112, 114
  sauces for, 114
Steaming rack, 200
Stews
  Arabic eggplant, 273
  early California, 94
  green chili, 15
  Lonny's oyster, 175
Stir-fried broccoli rabe, 71
Stir-fry beef pot pie, 64
Stir-fry, cabbage and radicchio,
  27
Strawberry
  centerpiece with dips, 117
  lemonade, 81
  -peach pie, 129
Strudel, Hungarian ham, with
  watercress salad, 297
Sunchoke sauté, mushroom
  and, 290
Sundae, double cherry, 153
Sundae, honey-fig, 127
Sunset's next wave fish tacos,
  139
Sweet and sour fish sauce, 146
Sweet anise pound cake, 197
Sweet onion relish, curry-cured
  salmon with, 108
Sweet pea salad with coconut,
  149
Sweet tomato sorbet, 217
Swordfish, spicy, 20
Swordfish with cilantro-lime
  cream, 46
Syrah, 135

Tacos
  chicken chili verde, 17
  fish, classic Baja fried-, 139
  fish, Loews grilled-, 139
  fish, Sunset's next wave, 139
  soft, turkey-chipotle, 17
Tamale casserole, vegetarian, 21
Tamale pie, turkey, 47
Tamarind, 278
Tangled tiger shrimp and
  pineapple salad, 124
Tapioca flour, 133
Tartar sauce, chipotle, 140
Tarts
  Columbia Gorge Hotel
    apple, 207
  Fran's cranberry, 268
  Roma–goat cheese, 215
  short pastry for, 72
Tea, Kashmir, 47
Thai chicken curry with
  coconut milk, 66
Thai chicken pasta, 191